Adobe®
Dreamweaver® CS4
Complete Concepts and Techniques

Gary B. Shelly
Dolores J. Wells

Shelly Cashman Series®

An imprint of Course Technology, Cengage Learning

COURSE TECHNOLOGY
CENGAGE Learning™

Australia • Brazil • Japan • Korea • Mexico • Singapore • Spain • United Kingdom • United States

COURSE TECHNOLOGY
CENGAGE Learning™

Adobe® Dreamweaver® CS4
Complete Concepts and Techniques,
Gary B. Shelly, Dolores J. Wells

Executive Editor: Kathleen McMahon

Senior Product Manager: Mali Jones

Associate Product Manager: Jon Farnham

Editorial Assistant: Lauren Brody

Director of Marketing: Cheryl Costantini

Marketing Manager: Tristen Kendall

Marketing Coordinator: Julie Schuster

Print Buyer: Julio Esperas

Director of Production: Patty Stephan

Content Project Manager: Matthew Hutchinson

Developmental Editor: Lisa Ruffolo

QA Manuscript Reviewers: John Freitas, Danielle Shaw, Marianne Snow, and Susan Whalen

Copyeditor: Harold Johnson

Proofreader: Kim Kosmatka

Indexer: Rich Carlson

Art Director: Marissa Falco

Cover and Text Design: Joel Sadagursky

Cover Photo: Jon Chomitz

Compositor: GEX Publishing Services

Printer: RRD Menasha

For product information and technology assistance, contact us at
Cengage Learning Customer & Sales Support, 1-800-354-9706

For permission to use material from this text or product, submit all requests online at **cengage.com/permissions**
Further permissions questions can be emailed to
permissionrequest@cengage.com

ISBN-13: 978-0-324-78832-7

ISBN-10: 0-324-78832-0

Course Technology
20 Channel Center Street
Boston, Massachusetts 02210
USA

Cengage Learning is a leading provider of customized learning solutions with office locations around the globe, including Singapore, the United Kingdom, Australia, Mexico, Brazil, and Japan. Locate your local office at:
international.cengage.com/region

Cengage Learning products are represented in Canada by Nelson Education, Ltd.

To learn more about Course Technology, visit **www.cengage.com/coursetechnology**
To learn more about Cengage Learning, visit **www.cengage.com**
Purchase any of our products at your local college bookstore or at our preferred online store **www.ichapters.com**

Printed in the United States of America
2 3 4 5 14 13 12 11 10

Adobe Dreamweaver CS4
Complete Concepts and Techniques

Contents

Appendices

Preface

The Shelly Cashman Series® offers the finest textbooks in computer education. We are proud of the fact that our previous Dreamweaver books have been so well received. With each new edition of our Dreamweaver books, we have made significant improvements based on the comments made by instructors and students. The Adobe Dreamweaver CS4 books continue with the innovation, quality, and reliability you have come to expect from the Shelly Cashman Series.

In 2006 and 2007, the Shelly Cashman Series development team carefully reviewed our pedagogy and analyzed its effectiveness in teaching today's student. An extensive customer survey produced results confirming what the series is best known for: its step-by-step, screen-by-screen instructions, its project-oriented approach, and the quality of its content.

We learned, though, that students entering computer courses today are different than students taking these classes just a few years ago. Students today read less, but need to retain more. They need not only to be able to perform skills, but to retain those skills and know how to apply them to different settings. Today's students need to be continually engaged and challenged to retain what they're learning.

As a result, we've renewed our commitment to focusing on the user and how they learn best. This commitment is reflected in every change we've made to our Dreamweaver book.

Objectives of This Textbook

Adobe Dreamweaver CS4: Complete Concepts and Techniques is intended for a course that offers an introduction to Dreamweaver CS4 and creation of Web sites. No experience with a computer is assumed, and no mathematics beyond the high school freshman level is required. The objectives of this book are:

- To teach the fundamentals and some more advanced features of Dreamweaver CS4
- To expose students to proper Web site design and management techniques
- To acquaint students with the proper procedures to create Web sites suitable for course-work, professional purposes, and personal use
- To develop an exercise-oriented approach that allows learning by doing
- To introduce students to new input technologies
- To encourage independent study and provide help for those who are working independently

Distinguishing Features

A Proven Pedagogy with an Emphasis on Project Planning Each chapter presents a practical problem to be solved, within a project planning framework. The project orientation is strengthened by the use of Plan Ahead boxes, that encourage critical thinking about how to proceed at various points in the project. Step-by-step instructions with supporting screens guide students through the steps. Instructional steps are supported by the Q&A, Experimental Step, and BTW features.

A Visually Engaging Book that Maintains Student Interest The step-by-step tasks, with supporting figures, provide a rich visual experience for the student. Call-outs on the screens that present both explanatory and navigational information provide students with information they need when they need to know it.

Supporting Reference Materials (Quick Reference, Appendices) The appendices provide additional information about the Application at hand, such as the Help Feature and customizing the application. With the Quick Reference, students can quickly look up information about a single task, such as keyboard shortcuts, and find page references of where in the book the task is illustrated.

Integration of the World Wide Web The World Wide Web is integrated into the Dreamweaver CS4 learning experience by (1) BTW annotations; (2) a Quick Reference Summary Web page; and (3) the Learn It Online section for each chapter.

End-of-Chapter Student Activities Extensive end of chapter activities provide a variety of reinforcement opportunities for students where they can apply and expand their skills through individual and group work.

Instructor Resources CD-ROM

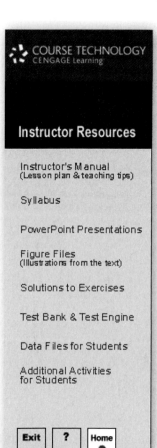

The Instructor Resources include both teaching and testing aids.

INSTRUCTOR'S MANUAL Includes lecture notes summarizing the chapter sections, figures and boxed elements found in every chapter, teacher tips, classroom activities, lab activities, and quick quizzes in Microsoft Word files.

SYLLABUS Easily customizable sample syllabi that cover policies, assignments, exams, and other course information.

FIGURE FILES Illustrations for every figure in the textbook in electronic form.

POWERPOINT PRESENTATIONS A multimedia lecture presentation system that provides slides for each chapter. Presentations are based on chapter objectives.

SOLUTIONS TO EXERCISES Includes solutions for all end-of-chapter and chapter reinforcement exercises.

TEST BANK & TEST ENGINE Test Banks include 112 questions for every chapter, featuring objective-based and critical thinking question types, and including page number references and figure references, when appropriate. Also included is the test engine, ExamView, the ultimate tool for your objective-based testing needs.

DATA FILES FOR STUDENTS Includes all the files that are required by students to complete the exercises.

ADDITIONAL ACTIVITIES FOR STUDENTS Consists of Chapter Reinforcement Exercises, which are true/false, multiple-choice, and short answer questions that help students gain confidence in the material learned.

Content for Online Learning

Course Technology has partnered with Blackboard, the leading distance learning solution provider and class-management platform today. The resources available for download with this title are the test banks in Blackboard- and WebCT-compatible formats. To access this material, simply visit our password-protected instructor resources available at www.cengage.com/coursetechnology. For additional information or for an instructor username and password, please contact your sales representative.

Blackboard

CourseCasts Learning on the Go. Always Available...Always Relevant.

Our fast-paced world is driven by technology. You know because you are an active participant — always on the go, always keeping up with technological trends, and always learning new ways to embrace technology to power your life. Let CourseCasts, hosted by Ken Baldauf of Florida State University, be your guide into weekly updates in this ever-changing space. These timely, relevant podcasts are produced weekly and are available for download at http://coursecasts.course.com or directly from iTunes (search by CourseCasts). CourseCasts are a perfect solution to getting students (and even instructors) to learn on the go!

CourseNotes

Course Technology's CourseNotes are six-panel quick reference cards that reinforce the most important and widely used features of a software application in a visual and user-friendly format. CourseNotes serve as a great reference tool during and after the student completes the course. CourseNotes for Microsoft Office 2007, Word 2007, Excel 2007, Access 2007, PowerPoint 2007, Windows Vista, and more are available now!

course|notes™
quick reference guide

Adobe Dreamweaver CS4 30-Day Trial Edition

A copy of the Dreamweaver CS4 30-Day trial edition can be downloaded from the Adobe Web site (www.adobe.com). Point to Downloads in the top navigation bar, click Trial Downloads, and then follow the on-screen instructions. When you activate the software, you will receive a license that allows you to use the software for 30 days. Course Technology and Adobe provide no product support for this trial edition. When the trial period ends, you can purchase a copy of Adobe Dreamweaver CS4, or uninstall the trial edition and reinstall your previous version. The minimum system requirements for the 30 day trial edition is a 1.8GHz or faster processor; Microsoft® Windows® XP with Service Pack 2 (Service Pack 3 recommended) or Windows Vista® Home Premium, Business, Ultimate, or Enterprise with Service Pack 1 (certified for 32-bit Windows XP and 32-bit and 64-bit Windows Vista); 512MB of RAM (1GB recommended); 1GB of available hard-disk space for installation; 1,024×768 display (1,280×800 recommended) with 16-bit video card; DVD-ROM drive; QuickTime 7.2 software required for multimedia features; and Broadband Internet connection required for online services.

Textbook Walk-Through

Plan Ahead boxes prepare students to create successful projects by encouraging them to think strategically about what they are trying to accomplish before they begin working.

Step-by-step instructions now provide a context beyond the point-and-click. Each step provides information on why students are performing each task, or what will occur as a result.

JPEG (.jpg) is an acronym for **Joint Photographic Experts Group**. JPEG files are the best format for photographic images because JPEG files can contain up to 16.7 million colors. **Progressive JPEG** is a new variation of the JPEG image format. This image format supports a gradually-built display similar to the interlaced GIFs. Older browsers do not support progressive JPEG files.

PNG (.png) stands for **Portable Network Graphics**. PNG, which is the native file format of Adobe Fireworks, is a GIF competitor, which is used for most Web site images. Some browsers do not support this format without a special plug-in. Generally, it is better to use GIF or JPEG images in your Web pages.

When developing a Web site that consists of many pages, you should maintain a consistent, professional layout and design throughout all of the pages. The pages in a single site, for example, should use similar features such as background colors or images, margins, and headings.

> **Plan Ahead**
>
> **Prepare images.**
> Nearly every Web site displays images such as photographs, drawings, and background textures. Before you add images to a Web site, prepare them using the following guidelines:
>
> - Acquire the images. To create your own images, you can take photos with a digital camera and store them in the JPG format, use a scanner to scan your drawings and photos, or use a graphics editor such as Adobe Photoshop to design images. You also can download images from public domain Web sites, use clip art, or purchase images from stock photo collections. Be sure you have permission to reproduce the images you acquire from Web sites, unless the images are clearly marked as in the public domain.
>
> - Choose the right format. Use JPG files for photographic images and complicated graphics that contain color gradients and shadowing. Use GIF files for basic graphics, especially when you want to take advantage of transparency. You also can use PNG for basic graphics, but not for photos.
>
> - Keep image file size small. Images with small file sizes appear in a browser faster than larger images. Use a graphics editor such as Adobe Photoshop to compress image files and reduce their file size without affecting quality. Background images in particular should have a small file size.
>
> - Check the dimensions. Determine the dimensions of an image file in pixels. You can reduce the dimensions on the Web page by changing the width and height or by cropping the image. Enlarging images generally produces poor results.

Background Colors and Background Images

Many Web pages are displayed with a default white or gray background. Generally, the browser used to display the Web page determines the default background. Recall that you can enhance your Web page by adding a background image or background color.

If you use a background color, be sure to use Web-safe colors. This means the colors will be displayed correctly on the computer screen when someone is viewing your Web page.

Background images add texture and interesting color to a Web page and set the overall appearance of the document. Most browsers support background images. A background image can be a large image, but more frequently it is a smaller image. The image tiles to fill the screen in the Dreamweaver Document window and in the browser window.

To Create a Relative Link Using Point to File

You will use the text Alaska National Preserves to create a link Preserves Sites to create a link to the historical_sites.htm page. The to-file method to create a relative link from the Alaska Parks home Web page.

1
- Drag to select the text Alaska National Preserves (Figure 2–60).

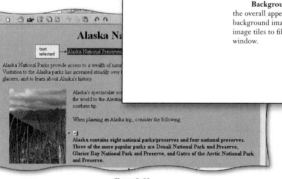

Figure 2–60

2
- Use the Point to File tool to point to the preserves.htm file in the Files panel.

- When the pointer is over the preserves.htm file in the Files panel, release the mouse button to display the linked text in the Property inspector Link box (Figure 2–61).

Q&A Why am I inserting a relative link?

You use **relative links** when the linked documents are in the same folder, such as those in your parks folder.

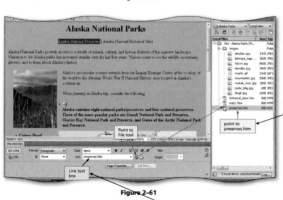

Figure 2–61

BTW **Screen Shots**
Callouts in screenshots give students information they need, when they need to know it. The Series has always used plenty of callouts to ensure that students don't get lost. Now, use color to distinguish the content in the callouts to make them more meaningful.

Navigational callouts in red show students where to click.

Explanatory callouts summarize what is happening on screen.

Textbook Walk-Through

Q&A boxes offer questions students may have when working through the steps and provide additional information about what they are doing right where they need it.

Experiment Steps within our step-by-step instructions, encourage students to explore, experiment, and take advantage of the features of Adobe Dreamweaver CS4. These steps are not necessary to complete the projects, but are designed to increase the confidence with the software and build problem-solving skills.

②
- Type the text of Part 2 as shown in Table 1–1 on the previous page, and then press the ENTER key to insert a blank line (Figure 1–44).

Q&A Why does my text wrap at different locations from those shown in Figure 1–44?

If your Dreamweaver window is maximized and the screen resolution is 1024 × 768, the text wraps in the same place. Otherwise, it might wrap at different places.

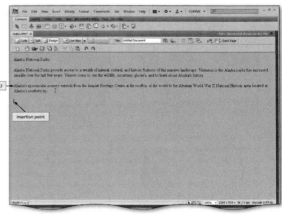

Figure 1–44

③
- Type the text of Part 3 as shown in Table 1–1, and then press the ENTER key to insert a blank line (Figure 1–45).

Figure 1–45

Images **DW 143**

Dreamweaver Chapter 2

④
- If necessary, click the Tlingit image to select it.
- Click the Brightness and Contrast tool to display the Brightness/Contrast dialog box. If a Dreamweaver caution dialog box appears, click the OK button (Figure 2–55).

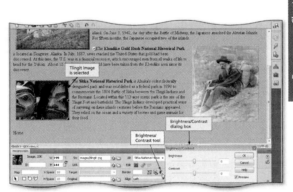

Figure 2–55

 Experiment
- Drag the Brightness slider and the Contrast slider so you can see how changing the value of each affects the Tlingit image.
- Drag the Brightness slider to the left and adjust the setting to –10 to change the brightness level.
- Drag the Contrast slider to the right and adjust the setting to 10 to change the contrast level (Figure 2–56).

Q&A What are the ranges for the Brightness and Contrast settings?

The values for the Brightness and Contrast settings range from –100 to 100.

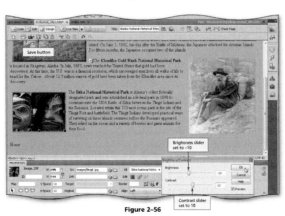

Figure 2–56

Textbook Walk-Through

Some steps ask students to personalize their assignments to help them better keep track of files and discourage academic dishonesty.

5
- Click the Create New Folder icon to create a folder and display the New Folder text box (Figure 1–17).

Q&A Why should I create a folder on the drive for my Web site?

Organizing your Web site folders now will save you time and prevent problems later. Create a main folder such as edwardsd for the sites in this book. (Substitute your name for "edwardsd.") Create a subfolder in that main folder for the Alaska Parks Web site. Finally, create a subfolder in the Alaska Parks Web site folder for images.

6
- Type your last name and first initial (with no spaces between your last name and initial) in the New Folder text box.

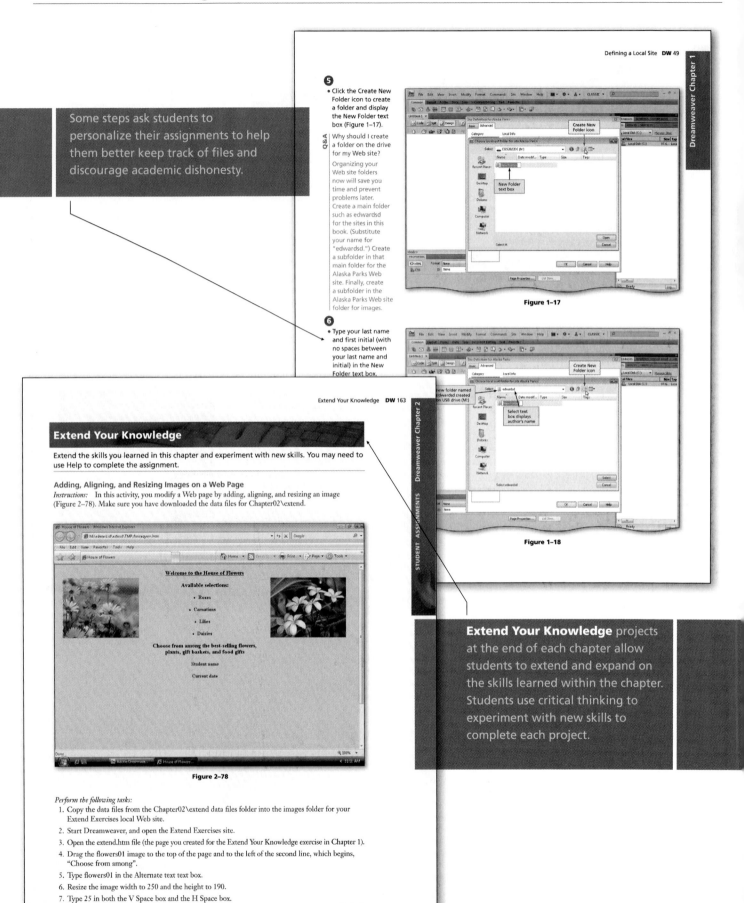

Figure 1–17

Figure 1–18

Extend Your Knowledge projects at the end of each chapter allow students to extend and expand on the skills learned within the chapter. Students use critical thinking to experiment with new skills to complete each project.

Extend Your Knowledge

Extend the skills you learned in this chapter and experiment with new skills. You may need to use Help to complete the assignment.

Adding, Aligning, and Resizing Images on a Web Page
Instructions: In this activity, you modify a Web page by adding, aligning, and resizing an image (Figure 2–78). Make sure you have downloaded the data files for Chapter02\extend.

Figure 2–78

Perform the following tasks:
1. Copy the data files from the Chapter02\extend data files folder into the images folder for your Extend Exercises local Web site.
2. Start Dreamweaver, and open the Extend Exercises site.
3. Open the extend.htm file (the page you created for the Extend Your Knowledge exercise in Chapter 1).
4. Drag the flowers01 image to the top of the page and to the left of the second line, which begins, "Choose from among".
5. Type flowers01 in the Alternate text text box.
6. Resize the image width to 250 and the height to 190.
7. Type 25 in both the V Space box and the H Space box.

Continued >

Textbook Walk-Through

Extend Your Knowledge *continued*

8. Align the image to the left.
9. Drag the flowers02 image to the right of the second line. Type flowers02 in the Alternate text text box.
10. Resize the image width to 250 and the height to 190.
11. Type 25 in both the V Space box and the H Space box.
12. Align the image to the right.
13. Move the sentence that begins with "Choose from among" after the bulleted list. Make sure the sentence remains centered and bold and does not have a bullet.
14. Save your document and then view it in your browser. Submit it in the format specified by your instructor.

Make It Right

> **Make It Right** projects call on students to analyze a file, discover errors in it, and fix them using the skills they learned in the chapter.

Analyze a document and then correct all errors and/or improve the design.

Adding an Image and E-mail Address to a Web Page

Instructions: In this activity, you modify an existing Web page by adding an image (Figure 2–79). Make sure you have downloaded the data files for Chapter02\right.

Figure 2–79

Cases and Places

Apply your creative thinking and problem solving skills to design and implement a solution.

• EASIER   •• MORE DIFFICULT

• 1: Create a Template for the Favorite Sports Web Site

Your sports Web site has become very popular. You have received many e-mails asking for statistics and other information. You decide to add a Web page that will contain statistics and will be updated on a weekly basis. Add a background image to the page and add a title to the page. Create a template using tables. Add descriptive prompts and then create editable regions. Add styles to the headings and text. Then create a page, apply the template, and save the page in your sports Web site. Create links to and from the home page.

• 2: Create a Template and New Web Page for the Hobby Web Site

You have decided to add a do-it-yourself section to your hobby Web site and want to use a consistent format and look for the page. You decide to use a template to create this new section. Create the template using a logo, tables, and links. Add descriptive prompts to the editable regions and apply styles to enhance the text and text size. Create the first do-it-yourself Web page and apply the template. Create links to and from the home page. Upload the pages to a remote server, if instructed to do so.

•• 3: Create a Template and Style Sheet for the Politics Web Site

Your campaign for political office is progressing well, and you are one of the top two candidates. You have decided to add a new section to your Web site featuring your campaign supporters. To provide consistency and control, you use a template for this site. After completing the template, attach styles. Next, create two new pages for the site and then apply the template. Create links to and from the home page. Upload the new pages to a remote server, if instructed to do so.

•• 4: Create a Template for the Favorite Music Web Site

Make It Personal

Create a template for your music hobby Web site and then add a background to the page. Insert logos, tables, and other appropriate elements. Add a background image to a table. Apply a border to the table. Use the CSS Styles panel and apply styles to the elements on the page. Create a new Web page featuring a new topic for your Web site and apply the template. Create links to and from the home page. Upload the page to a remote server, if instructed to do so.

•• 5: Create a Template and New Web Page for the Student Trips Web Site

Working Together

Each member of the group decides to create a template for the three vacation sites previously selected. Include on the templates headings, tables, links, and graphics. Present the three templates to the group and determine which one best meets the needs of the Web site. Next, add appropriate styles, including styles from the Type, Background, and Border categories. Include at least two images and a logo on the template. Create the three vacation site Web pages and apply the template. Then create links to and from the home page. Upload the new pages to a remote server, if instructed to do so.

> Found within the Cases & Places exercises, the **Make It Personal** call on students to create an open-ended project that relates to their personal lives.

About Our New Cover Look

Learning styles of students have changed, but the Shelly Cashman Series' dedication to their success has remained steadfast for over 30 years. We are committed to continually updating our approach and content to reflect the way today's students learn and experience new technology.

This focus on the user is refl ected in our bold new cover design, which features photographs of real students using the Shelly Cashman Series in their courses. Each book features a different user, refl ecting the many ages, experiences, and backgrounds of all of the students learning with our books. When you use the Shelly Cashman Series, you can be assured that you are learning computer skills using the most effective courseware available.

We would like to thank the administration and faculty at the participating schools for their help in making our vision a reality. Most of all, we'd like to thank the wonderful students from all over the world who learn from our texts and now appear on our covers.

Web Site Development and Adobe Dreamweaver CS4

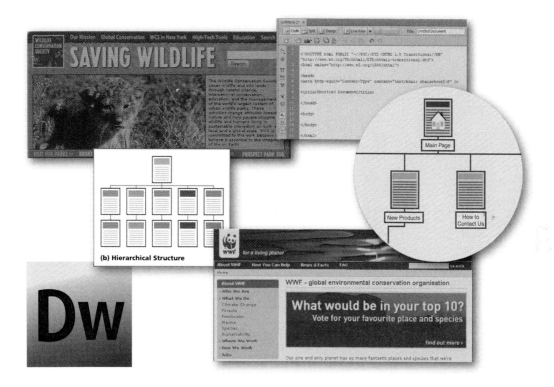

(b) Hierarchical Structure

Objectives

You will have mastered the material in this chapter when you can:

- Describe the Internet, the Web, and their associated terms

- Specify the difference between a Web page and a Web site

- Define Web browsers and identify their main features

- Identify the 12 types of Web sites

- Discuss how to plan, design, develop, test, publish, and maintain a Web site

- Identify the methods and tools for creating a Web page and Web site

- Recognize the basic elements within HTML/XHTML

- Discuss the advantages of using Web page authoring programs such as Dreamweaver

Web Site Development and Adobe Dreamweaver CS4

The Internet

The **Internet**, sometimes simply called the **Net**, is a global network connecting millions of computers. Within this network, a user who has permission at any one computer can access and obtain information from any other computer within the network. A **network** is a group of computers and associated devices that are connected by communications facilities. A network can span a global area and involve permanent connections, such as cables, or temporary connections made through telephone or other communications links. Local, regional, national, and international networks constitute a global network. Each of these networks provides communications, services, and access to information.

No one person or organization is responsible for the birth of the Internet. Its origin, however, can be traced to the early 1960s when the Advanced Research Projects Agency (ARPA), working under the U.S. Department of Defense, began a networking project. The purpose of the project was to create a network that would allow scientists at different locations to share military and scientific information. Today, the Internet is a public, cooperative, and self-sustaining facility that hundreds of millions of people worldwide access.

The World Wide Web and Web Browsers

The **World Wide Web (WWW)**, also called the **Web**, is one of the more popular services on the Internet. The Web consists of a system of global **network servers**, also known as **Web servers**, that support specially formatted documents and provide a means for sharing these resources with many people at the same time. A network server is known as the **host computer**, and your computer, from which you access the information, is called the **client**. **Hypertext Transfer Protocol** (**HTTP**) enables the transfer of data from the host computer to the client.

Accessing the Web

Users access Web resources, such as text, graphics, sound, video, and multimedia, through a **Web page**. A unique address, or Uniform Resource Locator (URL), identifies every Web page. The URL provides the global address of the location of the Web page. URLs are discussed later in this Introduction. Viewing data contained on a Web page requires a **Web browser**, a software program that requests a Web page, interprets the code contained within the page, and then displays the contents of the Web page on your computer display device.

Web Browsers

Web browsers contain special buttons and other features to help you navigate through Web sites. The more popular Web browser programs are **Microsoft Internet Explorer**, **Mozilla Firefox**, and **Netscape Navigator**. This book uses Internet Explorer as the primary browser. When you start Internet Explorer, it opens a Web page that has been set as the start, or home, page (Figure I–1). Using the browser's Tools menu, the user can designate any page on the Web as the home page or start with a blank page. Important features of Internet Explorer are summarized in Table I–1.

Figure I–1

Table I–1 Internet Explorer Features	
Feature	**Definition**
Title bar	Displays the name of the Web page you are viewing
Search box	Allows Web searches using your favorite search provider
Command bar	Contains buttons, boxes, and menus that allow you to perform tasks quickly
Address bar	Displays the Web site address, or URL, of the Web page you are viewing
Document window	Contains the Web page content
Web page tab	Provides the option to use tabs to switch from one site to another in a single browser window

Nearly all Web pages have unique characteristics, but almost every Web page contains the same basic elements. On most Web pages, you will find headings or titles, text, pictures or images, background enhancements, and hyperlinks. A **hyperlink**, or **link**, can connect to another place in the same Web page or site — or to an entirely different Web page on a server in another city or country. Normally, you click the hyperlink to follow the connected pathway. Figure I–2 contains a variety of link types. Clicking a link causes the Web page associated with the link to be displayed in a browser window. Linked pages can appear in the same browser window or in a separate browser window, depending on the HTML or XHTML code associated with the link. HTML and XHTML are discussed later in this Introduction.

Figure I–2

Most Web pages are part of a **Web site**, which is a group of related Web pages that are linked together. Most Web sites contain a home page, which generally is the first Web page visitors see when they enter the site. A **home page** (also called an **index page**) typically provides information about the Web site's purpose and content. Most Web sites also contain additional content and pages. An individual, company, or organization owns and manages each Web site.

Accessing the Web requires a connection through a regional or national Internet service provider (ISP), an online service provider (OSP), or a wireless service provider (WSP). Figure I–3 illustrates ways to access the Internet using these service providers. An **Internet service provider** (**ISP**) provides temporary connections to individuals, companies, or other organizations through its permanent Internet connection. Similar to an ISP, an **online service provider** (**OSP**) provides additional member-only services such as financial data and travel information. America Online and CompuServe are examples of OSPs. A **wireless service provider** (**WSP**) provides Internet access to users with Web-enabled devices or wireless modems. Generally, all of these providers charge a fee for their services.

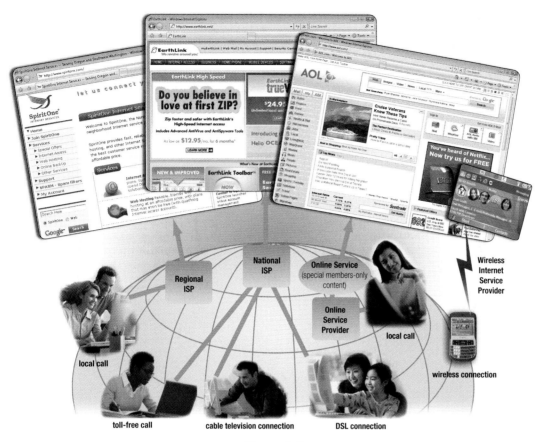

Figure I–3

Types of Web Sites

Web sites are classified as 12 basic types: portal, news, informational, business/marketing, educational, entertainment, advocacy, blog, wiki, social networks, content aggregator, and personal. A portal Web site (Figure I–4a) provides a variety of Internet services from a single, convenient location. Most portals offer free services such as search engines; local, national, and worldwide news; sports; weather; reference tools; maps; stock quotes; newsgroups; chat rooms; and calendars. A news Web site (Figure I–4b) contains news articles relating to current events. An informational Web site (Figure I–4c) contains factual information, such as research and statistics. Governmental agencies and nonprofit organizations are the primary providers of informational Web pages. A business/marketing Web site (Figure I–4d) contains content that promotes or sells products or services. An educational Web site (Figure I–4e) provides exciting, challenging avenues for formal and informal teaching and learning. An entertainment Web site (Figure I–4f) offers an interactive and engaging environment and contains music, video, sports, games, and other similar features. Within an advocacy Web site (Figure I–4g), you will find content that describes a cause, opinion, question, or idea. A blog (Figure I–4h), which is short for Weblog, uses a regularly updated journal format to reflect the interests, opinions, and personality of the author and sometimes of site visitors. A wiki (Figure I-4i) is a collaborative Web site that allows users to create, add to, modify, or delete the Web site content via their Web browser. Most wikis are open to modification by the general public. A social network (Figure I-4j) is an online community that encourages members to share their interests, stories, photos, music, and videos with other members. A content aggregator (Figure I–4k) is a business that gathers and organizes Web content and then distributes the content to subscribers free or for a fee. A personal Web site (Figure I–4l) is published by an individual or family and generally is not associated with any organization. As you progress through this book, you will have an opportunity to learn more about different types of Web pages.

Figure I–4

Planning a Web Site

Thousands of individuals create and publish Web pages every day, some using word processing software or markup languages, such as XHTML, to create their pages. Others use professional design and management editors such as Dreamweaver. Although publishing a Web page or a Web site is easy, advanced planning is paramount in ensuring a successful Web site. Publishing a Web site, which makes it available on the Internet, is discussed later in this Introduction.

Planning Basics — Purpose

Those who rush into the publishing process without proper planning tend to design Web sites that are unorganized and difficult to navigate. Visitors to this type of Web site often lose interest quickly and do not return. As you begin planning your Web site, consider the following guidelines to ensure that you set and attain realistic goals.

Purpose and Goal Determine the purpose and goal of your Web site. Create a focus by developing a purpose statement, which communicates the intention of the Web site. Consider the 12 basic types of Web sites mentioned previously. Will your Web site consist of just one basic type or a combination of two or more types?

Target Audience Identify your audience. The people who visit your Web site will determine the success of your site. Although you welcome all visitors, you need to know as much as possible about the primary group of people you wish to reach — your target audience. To learn more about the visitors to your Web site, determine whether you want to attract people with similar interests, and consider the gender, education, age range, income, profession/job field, and computer proficiency of your target audience.

Web Technologies Evaluate whether your potential visitors have access to high-speed broadband media or to baseband media, and use this information to determine what elements to include within your Web site. **Broadband** can transmit a large number of moving images or a vast quantity of data simultaneously at a high speed. Media and hardware such as **T1 lines**, **DSL (digital subscriber lines)**, **ISDN (Integrated Services Digital Network)**, **fiber optics**, and **cable modems** work with broadband. **Baseband** transmits one signal at a time over a telephone line and includes media and hardware such as 28K to 56K modems. Baseband works well with a Web site composed mostly of text and small images. Web sites that contain many images or multimedia, such as video and animations, generally require that visitors have a broadband connection.

Web Site Comparison Visit other Web sites that are similar to your proposed site. What do you like about these sites? What do you dislike? Look for inspirational ideas. How can you make your Web site better?

Planning Basics — Content

To ensure a successful Web experience for your visitors, consider the following guidelines to provide appropriate content and other valuable Web page elements.

Value-added Content Consider the different types of content you can include within your Web site. Use the following questions as guidelines:

- What topics do you want to cover?
- How much information will you present about each topic?
- What will attract your target audience to your Web site?

- What methods will you use to keep your audience returning to your site?
- What changes will you have to make to keep your site updated?

Text   Text accounts for the bulk of all content on most Web pages, so be brief and incorporate lists whenever possible. Statistical studies indicate that most people tend to scan the page, picking out individual words and sentences. Use common words and simple language, and check your spelling and grammar. Create your textual content to accomplish your goals effectively by highlighting key words, using bulleted lists, maintaining one idea per paragraph, and including meaningful subheadings.

Images   After text, images constitute the next most commonly included content. Ask yourself these questions with respect to your use of images:

- Will you have a common logo or theme on all of your Web pages?
- Are these images readily available?
- What images will you have to locate?
- What images will you have to create?
- How many images per page will you have?

Color Palette   The color palette you select for your Web site can enhance or detract from your message or goal. Do not think in terms of your favorite colors. Instead, consider how color can support your goal. Ask yourself the following questions:

- Do your selected colors work well with your goal?
- Are the colors part of the universal 216-color, browser-safe color palette?
- Did you limit the number of colors to a selected few?

Multimedia   Multimedia adds interactivity and action to your Web pages. Animation, audio, and video are types of **multimedia**. If you plan to add multimedia, determine whether the visitor will require plug-ins. A **plug-in** extends the capability of a Web browser. Some of the more commonly used plug-ins are Shockwave Player, Adobe Flash, and Windows Media Player. Most plug-ins are free and can be downloaded from the Web.

BTW

Web Site Development
To develop a Web site, start with and organize your content. Then create your navigation map.

Web Site Navigation

Predicting how a visitor will access a Web site or at what point the visitor will enter the Web site structure is not possible. Visitors can arrive at any page within a Web site by a variety of ways: a hyperlink, a search engine, a directory, typing a Web address directly, and so on. On every page of your Web site, you must provide clear answers to the three basic questions your visitors will ask: Where am I? Where do I go from here? How do I get to the home page? A well-organized Web site provides the answers to these questions. Once the visitor arrives at a Web site, **navigation**, the pathway through your site, must be obvious and intuitive. Individual Web pages cannot be isolated from the rest of the site if you want it to be successful. At all times and on all pages in your site, you must give the visitor a sense of place, of context within the site. Most Web designers use a navigation map to visualize the navigation pathway.

Design Basics — Navigation Map

A **navigation map**, or **site map**, outlines the structure of the entire Web site, showing all pages within the site and the connections from one page to the others. The navigation map acts as a road map through the Web site, but does not provide details of the content of the individual pages. Web site navigation should be consistent from page to page, so your visitors do not have to guess where they are within the site each time they encounter a new page. All pages in the site should contain a link to the home page. Consider the following for site navigation:

Structure   The goal and the type of Web site often determine the structure selected for a specific Web site. Create a navigation map to serve as a blueprint for your navigational structure. Consider the following navigational structures and determine which one best meets your needs:

- In a **linear structure** (Figure I–5a) the user navigates sequentially, moving from one page to the next. Information that flows as a narrative, as a timeline, or in logical order is ideal for sequential treatment. Simple sequential organization, however, usually works only for smaller sites. Many online tutorials use a linear structure.
- A **hierarchical structure** (Figure I–5b) is one of the better ways to organize complex bodies of information efficiently. Because many visitors are familiar with hierarchical charts, many Web sites employ this structure. Be aware that effective hierarchical structures require thorough organization of the content.
- A **Web structure** (Figure I–5c), which also is called a **random structure**, places few restrictions on organizational patterns. This type of structure is associated with the free flow of ideas and can be confusing to a user. A random structure is better suited for experienced users looking for further education or enrichment and is not recommended if your goal is to provide a basic understanding of a particular topic. If a Web site is relatively small, however, a random structure could work well.
- Use a **grid structure** if your Web site consists of a number of topics of equal importance (Figure I–5d). Procedural manuals, events, and item lists work well in a grid structure.

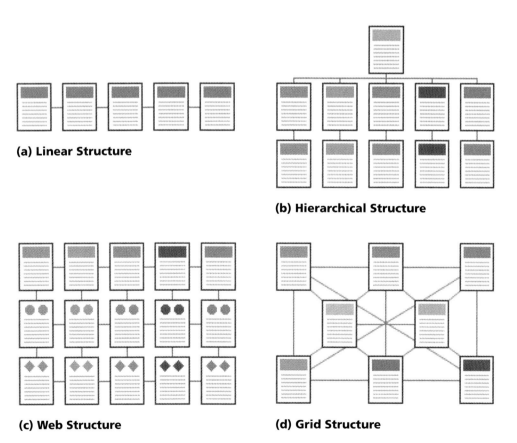

(a) Linear Structure

(b) Hierarchical Structure

(c) Web Structure

(d) Grid Structure

Figure I–5

• Large Web sites frequently use a **hybrid structure**, a combination of the previous listed structures, to organize information. See Figure I–6.

Figure I–6

Tools   Determine the tool necessary to create the navigation map (Figure I–7). For small Web sites, you might want to consider using the organizational chart included in the Microsoft PowerPoint application.

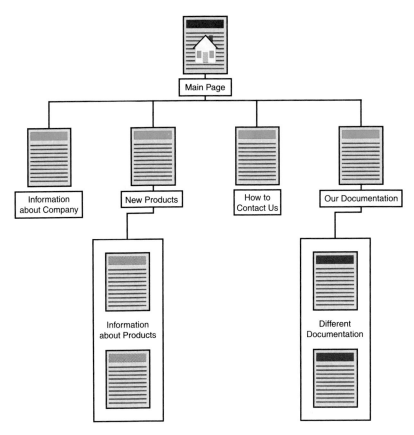

Figure I–7

For larger, more diverse Web sites, you can chart and organize your content using Visio Professional, Flow Charting PDQ, FlowCharter Professional, and SmartDraw.

Navigation Elements   The more common types of navigation elements include text, buttons, images, image maps, a site index, a menu, a search feature, navigation bars, and frames. Depending on the complexity of your Web site, you may want to include some or all of these elements.

Developing a Web Site

Once you have established a structure for your Web site, you can begin developing the site. Make text and images the main focus because they are the more common elements. Then consider page layout and color.

Development Basics — Typography, Images, Page Layout, and Color

Typography, images, page layout, and color are the key design elements that will make up your finished Web site. Correct use of these elements plays an important part in the development process. Consider the following guidelines:

Typography   As in all media, good **typography**, the appearance and arrangement of the characters that make up your text, is vital to the success of your Web page. A font consists of all the characters available in a particular style and weight for a specific design. Text should always be easy to read, whether in a book, magazine, Web page, or billboard. Keep readability in mind as you select fonts, especially when you consider that some of your visitors might only be viewing them on screen, and others might print them.

When selecting a font, determine its purpose on your Web page. Is it to be used for a title? For on-screen reading? Is it likely to be printed? Will the font fit in with the theme of the Web site? Is it a Web-safe font, such as Times New Roman, Courier, or Arial? **Web-safe fonts** are the more popular fonts and the ones that most visitors are likely to have installed on their computers. Also, while visitors to your Web page may never consciously notice the design of the text characters, or the **typeface**, it often subconsciously affects their reaction to the page.

Images   Images can enhance almost any Web page if used appropriately. Without the visual impact of shape, color, and contrast, Web pages can be visually uninteresting and will not motivate the visitor to investigate their contents. Consider the balance between the number of images and page performance as you develop your site. When adding images, consider your potential audience and the technology they have available. Remember that a background image or a graphical menu increases visitor download time. You may lose visitors who do not have broadband access if your Web page contains an excessive number of graphical items.

BTW

Keep the Page Simple
Some Web pages take a long time to download or view if they contain multiple elements and appear very "busy." Simple pages download faster and make an immediate impression on the reader.

Page Layout   The importance of proper page layout cannot be overemphasized. A suitable design draws visitors to your Web site. Although no single design system is appropriate for all Web pages, establish a consistent, logical layout that allows you to add text and images easily. The Web page layouts shown in Figure I–8 illustrate two different layouts. The layout on the left (Figure I–8a) shows a plain page with a heading and text. The page layout on the right (Figure I–8b) presents strong visual contrast by using a variety of layout elements.

(a)　　　　　　　　　　　**(b)**

Figure I–8

Maintaining consistency and updating changes throughout a site are two of the biggest challenges faced by Web designers. A **template,** a special type of document, can help with these challenges. Dreamweaver provides several page layout templates that can be modified easily. In laying out your Web pages, consider the following guidelines to ensure that visitors have the best viewing experience:

- Include only one topic per page.
- Control the vertical and horizontal size of the page.
- Start text on the left to match the way most people read text.
- Use concise statements and bulleted points to get your point across; studies indicate most people scan the text.

Color　When creating a Web page, use color to add interest and vitality to your site. Include color in tables, as backgrounds, and with fonts. Use the right combination of colors to decorate the layout and tie the Web site pages together.

Reviewing and Testing a Web Site

Some Web site developers argue that reviewing and testing should take place throughout the developmental process. While this may be true, it also is important to review and test the final product. This ongoing process ensures that you identify and correct any problems before publishing to the Web. When reviewing and testing your Web site, ask the following questions:

- Is the Web site free of spelling and grammatical errors?
- Is the page layout consistent, and does it generate a sense of balance and order?
- Are any links broken?
- Do multimedia interactivity and forms function correctly?
- Do the more widely used browsers display the Web site properly?
- Does the Web site function properly in different browsers, including older browser versions?
- Have you initiated a **group test**, in which you have asked other individuals to test your Web site and provide feedback?

Publishing a Web Site

After your Web site has been tested thoroughly, it can be published. **Publishing** a Web site, making it available to your visitors, involves the actual uploading of the Web site to a server. After you complete the uploading process, all pages within the Web site should be tested again.

Publishing Basics — Domain Name, Server Space, and Uploading

With your Web site thoroughly tested and any problems corrected, you must make the site available to your audience by obtaining a domain name, acquiring server space, and uploading the site. Consider the following to ensure site availability:

Obtain a Domain Name To allow visitors to access your Web site, you must obtain a domain name. Visitors access Web sites by an IP address or a domain name. An **IP address (Internet Protocol address)** is a number that uniquely identifies each computer or device connected to the Internet. A **domain name** is the text version of an IP address. The **Domain Name System (DNS)**, an Internet service, translates domain names into their corresponding IP addresses. The **Uniform Resource Locator (URL)**, also called a Web address, tells the browser on which server the Web page is located. A URL consists of a communications protocol, such as **Hypertext Transfer Protocol (HTTP)**, the domain name, and sometimes the path to a specific Web page (Figure I–9).

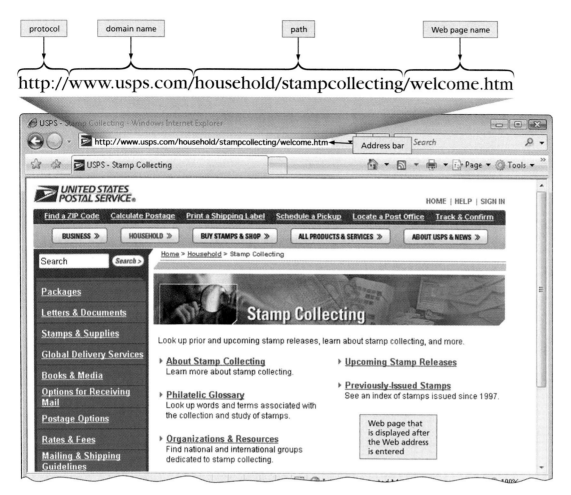

Figure I–9

Domain names are unique and must be registered. The **Accredited Registrar Directory** provides a listing of **Internet Corporation for Assigned Names and Numbers (ICANN)** accredited domain name registrars. Your most difficult task likely will be to find a name that is not registered. You can locate a name by using a specialized search engine at one of the many accredited domain name registrars listed on the ICANN Web site (icann.org/registrars/accredited-list.html). In addition to registering your business name as a domain name, you may want to register the names of your products, services, or other related names. Expect to pay approximately $10 to $35 per year for a domain name.

Consider the following guidelines when selecting a domain name:

• Select a name that is easy to pronounce, spell, and remember.

• Select a name that relates to the Web site content and suggests the nature of your product or service.

• If the Web site is a business, use the business name whenever possible.

• Select a name that is free and clear of trademark issues.

• Purchase variations and the .org, .net, and .mobi versions of your domain name.

• Some ISPs will obtain a domain name for you if you use their service to host your Web site.

Acquire Server Space   Locate an ISP that will host your Web site. Recall that an ISP is a business that has a permanent Internet connection. ISPs offer connections to individuals and companies free or for a fee.

If you select an ISP that provides free server space, most likely your visitors will be subjected to advertisements and pop-up windows. Other options to explore for free or inexpensive server space include the provider from which you obtain your Internet connection; online communities, such as Yahoo! GeoCities (geocities.yahoo.com), Tripod (tripod.lycos.com), and MSN Web Communities (members.freewebs.com/); and your educational institution's Web server. If the purpose of your Web site is to sell a product or service or to promote a professional organization, you should consider a fee-based ISP. Use a search engine such as Google (google.com) and search for Web site hosting, or visit the Web Site Host Directory (www.websitehostdirectory.com), where you will find thousands of Web hosting plans, as well as reviews and ratings of Web hosting providers. Selecting a reliable provider requires investigation on your part. Many providers offer multiple hosting plans. When selecting an ISP, consider the following questions and how they apply to your particular situation and Web site:

1. What is the monthly fee? Is a discount available for a year-long subscription? Are setup fees charged?

2. How much server space is provided for the monthly fee? Can you purchase additional space? If so, how much does it cost?

3. What is the average server uptime on a monthly basis? What is the average server downtime?

4. What are the server specifications? Can the server handle many users? Does it have battery backup power?

5. Are **server logs**, which keep track of the number of accesses, available?

6. What is the ISP's form of connectivity — that is, how does it connect to the Internet: OC3, T1, T3, or some other way?

7. Is a money-back guarantee offered?

8. What technical support does the ISP provide, and when is it available? Does it have an online knowledge base?

9. Does the server on which the Web site will reside have CGI capabilities and Active Server Page (ASP) support?

10. Does the server on which the Web site will reside support e-commerce, multimedia, and **Secure Sockets Layer (SSL)** for encrypting confidential data such as credit card numbers? Are additional fees required for these capabilities?

11. Does the ISP support Dreamweaver or other Web site development software programs?

12. Are mailboxes included in the package? If so, how many?

Publish the Web Site   You must publish, or upload, the files from your computer to a server where your Web site will then be accessible to anyone on the Internet. Publishing, or uploading, is the process of transmitting all the files that make up your Web site from your computer to the selected server or host computer. The files that make up your Web site can include Web pages, PDF documents, images, audio, video, animation, and others.

A variety of tools and methods exist to manage the upload task. Some of the more popular of these are FTP programs, Windows Web Publishing Wizard, Web Folders, and Web authoring programs such as Dreamweaver. These tools allow you to link to a remote server, enter a password, and then upload your files. Dreamweaver contains a built-in function similar to independent FTP programs. The Dreamweaver FTP function to upload your Web site is covered in Chapter 3 and in Appendix C.

Maintaining a Web Site

Most Web sites require maintenance and updating. Some types of ongoing Web maintenance include the following:

- Changing content, either by adding new text and images or by deleting obsolete material
- Checking for broken links and adding new links
- Documenting the last change date (even when no revisions have been made)

Use the information from the server logs provided by your ISP to determine what needs to be updated or changed. Statistics contained within these logs generally include the number of visitors trying to access your site at one time, what resources they request, how long they stay at the site, at what point they enter the site, what pages they view, and what errors they encounter. Learning to use and apply the information contained within the server log will help you to make your Web site successful.

After you make updates or changes to the site, notify your viewers with a What's New announcement.

Methods and Tools Used to Create Web Sites

Web developers have several options for creating Web pages: a text editor, an HTML or XHTML editor, software applications, or a WYSIWYG text editor (discussed in detail on page DW 20). Microsoft Notepad and WordPad are each examples of a **text editor**. These simple, easy-to-use programs allow the user to enter, edit, save, and print text. An **HTML** or **XHTML editor** is a more sophisticated version of a text editor. In addition to basic text-editing functions, these programs include more advanced features such as syntax highlighting, color coding, and spell checking. Software applications such as Microsoft Word, Excel, and Publisher provide a Save as Web Page command. This feature converts the application document into a file Web browsers are able to display. Examples of a WYSIWYG text editor are programs such as Microsoft Expression Web, and Adobe Dreamweaver. These programs provide an integrated text editor with a graphical user interface that allows the user to view both the code and the document as you create it.

A Web developer can use any of these options to create Web pages. Regardless of the option selected, however, it still is important to understand the specifics of HTML and XHTML.

Web Site Languages

Web pages are written in plain text and saved in the **American Standard Code for Information Interchange**, or **ASCII** (pronounced ASK-ee), format — the most widely used coding system to represent data. Using the ASCII format makes Web pages universally readable by different Web browsers regardless of the computer platform on which they reside.

The language of the Web is not static; it evolves just like most other languages. HTML (Hypertext Markup Language) has been the primary language of the Web and most likely will continue to be so for at least the near future. HTML is useful for creating headings, paragraphs, lists, and so on, but is limited to these general types of formatting. XHTML is a rewritten version of HTML using XML (Extensible Markup Language).

Unlike HTML, **Extensible Hypertext Markup Language (XHTML)** is an authoring language that defines the structure and layout of a document so that it displays as a Web page and is compatible with Web browsers such as Microsoft Internet Explorer,

BTW

W3C
The World Wide Web Consortium (W3C) develops and updates Web protocols. For example, they specified the most recent changes to XHTML, and are directing an effort to make it easier for people to browse the Web on mobile devices.

BTW

Test Web Pages
When considering which browsers you should use to test a Web page, be sure you use the most recent versions of the more popular browsers, such as Internet Explorer and Firefox.

Mozilla Firefox, or Netscape Navigator. Browser rules for interpreting HTML are flexible. XHTML, however, requires Web designers to adhere strictly to its markup language rules.

Two components constitute a Web page: source code and document content. The **source code**, which contains elements, acts as the program instructions. The **elements** within the source code control the appearance of the document content. Browsers display the **document content,** or the text and images. The browser interprets the elements contained within the code, and the code instructs the browser how to display the Web page. For instance, if you define a line of text on your Web page as a heading, the browser knows to display this line formatted as a heading.

All XHTML element formats and HTML tags start with a left angle bracket (< or less than symbol), are followed by the name of the element, and end with a right angle bracket (> or greater than symbol). Most elements have a start and an end element and are called **two-sided elements**. End elements are the same as start elements except they are preceded by a forward slash (/). Some XHTML elements, such as the one used to indicate a line break <br />, do not have an end element. Instead, the right angle bracket is preceded by a space and forward slash. These are known as **one-sided elements**, or **self-closing elements**. In some browsers, the end element can be omitted from certain elements, such as the end element for a new paragraph, </p>. Unlike HTML, however, XHTML standards require you to include both the start and end elements for all two-sided elements.

Some elements can contain an **attribute**, or **property**, which is additional information placed within the angle brackets. Attributes are not repeated or contained in the end element. Some attributes are used individually, while other attributes can include a value modifier. A **value modifier** specifies conditions within the element, and should always be enclosed in double quotation marks. For example, you can use a value modifier to specify the font type or size or the placement of text on the page. To create and display a centered heading, for instance, you would use the following code:

```
<h1 style="text-align:center">This is the largest header
element and the text will be centered</h1>
```

In this example, h1 is the XHTML element, align is the attribute, and center is the value modifier. Notice that the attribute does not appear as part of the end element, </h1>.

You can use the Dreamweaver Code window and Microsoft Notepad or WordPad (text editors) to create XHTML documents. Place each element in a pair around the text or section that you want to define (**mark up**) with that element. Use lowercase characters when typing XHTML elements.

XHTML elements also format the hyperlinks that connect information on the World Wide Web. While XHTML elements number in the hundreds, some are used more than others. All documents, however, require four basic elements. Figure I–10 illustrates the basic elements required for all XHTML documents. Table I–2 summarizes the more commonly used XHTML elements.

Dreamweaver Introduction

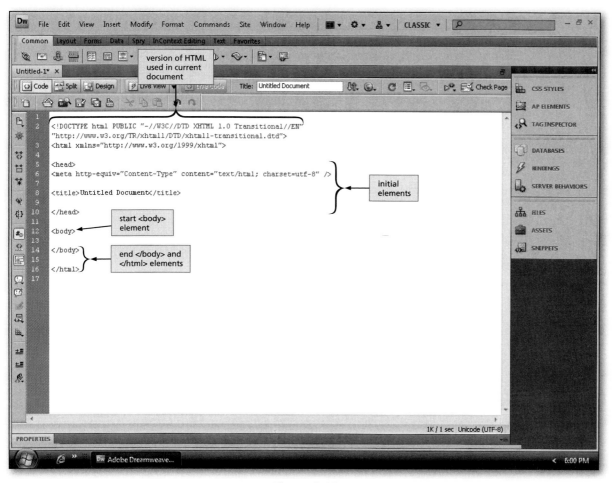

Figure I–10

Table I–2 Commonly Used XHTML Elements

Element (tags)	Structure
<html>...</html>	Encloses the entire XHTML document
<head>...</head>	Encloses the head of the XHTML document
<body>...</body>	Encloses the body of the XHTML document

Element (tags)	Title and Headings
<title>...</title>	Indicates the title of the document
<h1>...</h1>	Heading level 1
<h2>...</h2>	Heading level 2
<h3>...</h3>	Heading level 3
<h4>...</h4>	Heading level 4
<h5>...</h5>	Heading level 5
<h6>...</h6>	Heading level 6

Element (tags)	Paragraphs, Breaks, and Separators
<p>...</p>	Paragraph
 	Line break
<hr />	Horizontal rule
<ol>...</ol>	Ordered, numbered list
<ul>...</ul>	Unordered, bulleted list

Table I–2 Commonly Used XHTML Elements *(continued)*	
Element (tags)	**Paragraphs, Breaks, and Separators**
<li>...</li>	List item, used with <ol>, <ul>, <menu>, and <dir>
<dl>...</dl>	Definition of glossary list
<dt>...</dt>	Definition term; part of a definition list
<dd>...</dd>	Definition corresponding to a definition term
Element (tags)	**Character Formatting**
...	Bold text
<u>...</u>	Underlined text
<i>...</i>	Italic text
Element (tags)	**Links**
<a>...</a>	Combined with the href attribute, creates a link to another document or anchor
<a>...</a>	Combined with the name attribute, creates an anchor to which elements can be linked
Element (tags)	**Image**
<img />	Inserts an image into the document

Web Page Authoring Programs

Many of today's Web page authoring programs, including Dreamweaver, are What You See Is What You Get (WYSIWYG) text editors. As mentioned earlier, a **WYSIWYG text editor** allows a user to view a document as it will appear in the final product and to edit the text, images, or other elements directly within that view. Before programs such as Dreamweaver existed, Web page designers were required to type, or hand-code, Web pages. Educators and Web designers still debate the issue surrounding the necessity of knowing HTML and XHTML. Technically, you do not need to know either HTML or XHTML to create Web pages in Dreamweaver; however, an understanding of HTML and XHTML will help you if you need to alter Dreamweaver-generated code. If you know HTML and XHTML, then you can make changes to the code and Dreamweaver will accept the changes.

Adobe Dreamweaver CS4

The standard in visual authoring, Adobe Dreamweaver CS4 is part of the Adobe Creative Suite, which includes Adobe Flash, ColdFusion, Fireworks, and other programs depending on the particular suite. Dreamweaver provides features that access these separate products. Some of the new features of Dreamweaver CS4 include the following:

- New user interface
- New rendering mode that displays the design like a standard-based browser
- Related Files feature that displays all the documents associated with your current page
- Integration with Adobe PhotoShop CS4 and Adobe Contribute CS4
- The new code navigator element available in a pop-up window
- Code hinting available for Ajax and JavaScript objects
- User-created interface

Dreamweaver makes it easy to get started and provides you with helpful tools to enhance your Web design and development experience. Working in a single environment, you create, build, and manage Web sites and Internet applications. In Dreamweaver, you can customize the workspace environment to fit your particular needs.

Dreamweaver contains coding tools and features that include references for HTML, XHTML, XML, CSS, and JavaScript as well as code editors that allow you to edit the code directly. Using **Adobe Roundtrip technology**, Dreamweaver can import Microsoft Office or other software Web pages and delete the unused code. Downloadable extensions from the Adobe Web site make it easy to add functionality to any Web site. Examples of these extensions include shopping carts and online payment features.

Instead of writing individual files for every page, you can use a database to store content and then retrieve the content dynamically in response to a user's request. Implementing and using this feature, you can update the information once, in one place, instead of manually editing many pages. Another key feature is **Cascading Style Sheets styles (CSS styles)**. CSS styles are collections of formatting definitions that affect the appearance of Web page elements. You can use CSS styles to format text, images, headings, tables, and so forth. Implementing and applying this feature, you can update the formatting one time across many Web pages.

Dreamweaver provides the tools that help you author accessible content. These accessible pages comply with government guidelines and Section 508 of the Federal Rehabilitation Act. Accessibility is discussed in more detail as you progress through the book.

Dreamweaver allows you to publish Web sites with relative ease to a local area network, which connects computers in a limited geographical area, or to the Web, so that anyone with Internet access can see them. The concepts and techniques presented in this book provide the tools you need to plan, develop, and publish professional Web sites, such as those shown in Figure I–11 and Figure I–12 on the next page.

Figure I–11

Figure I–12

Chapter Summary

The Introduction to Web Site Development and Adobe Dreamweaver CS4 provided an overview of the Internet and the World Wide Web and the key terms associated with those technologies. An overview of the 12 basic types of Web pages also was presented. The Introduction furnished information on developing a Web site, including planning basics. The process of designing a Web site and each phase within this process were discussed. Information about testing, publishing, and maintaining a Web site also was presented, including an overview of obtaining a domain name, acquiring server space, and uploading a Web site. Methods and tools used to create Web pages were introduced. A short overview of HTML and XHTML and some of the more commonly used HTML tags and XHTML elements were presented. Finally, the advantages of using Dreamweaver in Web development were discussed. These advantages include a WYSIWYG text editor; a visual, customizable development environment; accessibility compliance; downloadable extensions; database access capabilities; and Cascading Style Sheets.

Learn It Online

Test your knowledge of chapter content and key terms.

Instructions: To complete the Learn It Online exercises, start your browser, click the Address bar, and then enter the Web address scsite.com/dwcs4/learn. When the Dreamweaver CS4 Learn It Online page is displayed, click the link for the exercise you want to complete and then read the instructions.

Chapter Reinforcement TF, MC, and SA
A series of true/false, multiple choice, and short answer questions that test your knowledge of the chapter content.

Flash Cards
An interactive learning environment where you identify chapter key terms associated with displayed definitions.

Practice Test
A series of multiple choice questions that test your knowledge of chapter content and key terms.

Who Wants To Be a Computer Genius?
An interactive game that challenges your knowledge of chapter content in the style of a television quiz show.

Wheel of Terms
An interactive game that challenges your knowledge of chapter key terms in the style of the television show *Wheel of Fortune.*

Crossword Puzzle Challenge
A crossword puzzle that challenges your knowledge of key terms presented in the chapter.

Apply Your Knowledge

Reinforce the skills and apply the concepts you learned in this chapter.

Creating a Web Site
Instructions: As discussed in this Introduction, creating a Web site involves planning, designing, developing, reviewing and testing, publishing, and maintaining the site. Open the document Apply I-1 Web Site Creation from the Data Files for Students. See the inside back cover of this book for instructions for downloading the Data Files for Students, or contact your instructor for information about accessing the required files.

As shown in Table I–3, the Apply I-1 Web Site Creation file contains information about the Web site creation process. Use the information contained in this table to develop a plan for creating a Web site.

Table I–3 Creating a Web Site

Planning	
Web site name	What is your Web site name?
Web site type	What is the Web site type: portal, news, informational, business/marketing, educational, entertainment, advocacy, blog, wiki, social network, content aggregator, or personal?
Web site purpose	What is the purpose of your Web site?
Target audience	How can you identify your target audience?
Web technologies to be used	Will you design for broadband, baseband, or mobile? Explain your selection.
Content	What topics will you cover? How much information will you present on each topic? How will you attract your audience? What will you do to entice your audience to return to your Web site? How will you keep the Web site updated?
Text, images, and multimedia	Will your site contain text only? What type of images will you include? Where will you obtain your images? Will you have a common logo? Will plug-ins be required?

Apply Your Knowledge *continued*

Table I–3 Creating a Web Site *(continued)*	
Designing	
Navigation map	What type of structure will you use? What tools will you use to design your navigation map?
Navigational elements	What navigational elements will you include?
Developing	
Typography	What font will you use? How many different fonts will you use on your site?
Images	How will you use images to enhance your site? Will you use a background image?
Page layout	What type of layout will you use? How many topics per page? How will text be presented: bulleted or paragraph style? Will the audience need to scroll the page?
Color	What color combinations will you use for your site? To what elements will you apply the color(s) — fonts, background, tables, other elements?
Reviewing and Testing	
Review	What elements will you review? Will you use a group review?
Testing	What elements will you test? Will you use self-testing? Will you use group testing?
Publishing	
Domain name	What is your domain name? Have you registered your domain name? What ISP will host your Web site? What criteria did you use to select the ISP?
Maintaining	
Ongoing maintenance	How often will you update your Web site? What elements will you update? Will you add additional features? Does your ISP provide server logs? Will you use the server logs for maintenance purposes?

Perform the following tasks:

1. With the Apply I-1 Web Site Creation file open in your word processing program, select a name for your Web site.

2. Use a specialized search engine at one of the many accredited domain name registrars to verify that your selected Web site name is available.

3. Answer each question in the Planning table. Use complete sentences to answer the questions. Type your answers in column 3.

4. Save the document with the file name Apply I-1_your initials. Submit the document in the format specified by your instructor.

Extend Your Knowledge

Extend the skills you learned in this chapter and experiment with new skills. You may need to use Help to complete the assignment.

Identifying Web Site Types

Instructions: As you learned in this Introduction, Web sites can be classified into 12 basic types. Use a browser such as Internet Explorer to identify Web site types.

Perform the following tasks:

Part 1: Web Site Types

1. Review the different types of Web sites described on pages DW 5–6.

2. Select three of the Web site types.

Part 2: Search for Web Sites

1. Start your word processing program.

2. Start your browser and search for each of your three selected Web site types. Locate at least two examples of each type.

3. Copy and paste the Web site address for each example, and then compose a short paragraph explaining how this Web site meets the selected criteria.

Make It Right

Analyze a Web site structure and suggest how to improve the organization or design.

Improving Navigation Structures

Instructions: Start your Web browser. Select and analyze a Web site and determine the navigation structure used within the Web site.

Figure I–5 (a) through (d) on page DW 9 contains examples of four types of navigation structures. This figure is reproduced as Figure I–13 on the next page. Select a Web site and review the structure of the Web site. Start your word processing program. Describe the structure used in your selected Web site. Include any suggestions you may have on how this structure could be improved. If you are using Microsoft Office Word 2007, click the Insert tab on the Ribbon. In the Illustrations group, use the Shapes or SmartArt options to create an image of the structure. Save your document and submit it in the format specified by your instructor.

Make It Right *continued*

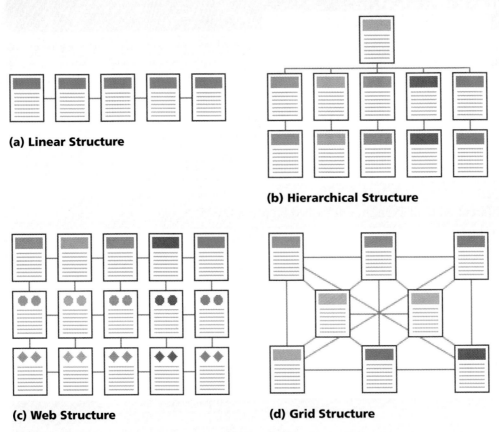

(a) Linear Structure

(b) Hierarchical Structure

(c) Web Structure

(d) Grid Structure

Figure I–13

In the Lab

Design and/or create a document using the guidelines, concepts, and skills presented in this chapter. Labs are listed in order of increasing difficulty.

Lab 1: Using Internet Explorer

Problem: Microsoft Internet Explorer (IE) has many features that can make your work on the Internet more efficient. Using the Media feature, for example, you can play music, video, or multimedia files; listen to your favorite Internet radio station; and enhance your browsing experience. You can customize the image toolbar that appears when you point to an image on a Web page. IE also includes other enhancements. Visit the Microsoft Internet Explorer: The Features Web page (Figure I–14) and select three articles concerning topics with which you are not familiar. Read the articles and then create a word processing document detailing what you learned.

Figure I-14

Perform the following tasks:

1. Start your browser. Open the Microsoft Internet Explorer: The Features Web page (microsoft. com/windows/products/winfamily/ie/features.mspx).

2. Scroll down the page.

3. Select three features with which you are not familiar.

4. Click the link for each article and read the article.

5. Start your word processing program.

6. List three important points that you learned from this Web site.

7. Write a summary of what you learned from each article. Include within your summary your opinion of the article and if you will apply what you learned or use it with your Web browser.

8. Save the document on a USB flash drive using the file name Lab I-1 IE Features.

9. Submit the document in the format specified by your instructor.

In the Lab

Lab 2: Identifying Types of Web Pages

Problem: A Web designer should be familiar with different types of Web pages and the sort of information displayed on these types of Web pages. The Introduction describes 12 types of Web pages. Search the Internet and locate at least one example of each type of Web page.

Perform the following tasks:

1. Start your browser. Open the Google (google.com) search engine Web page (Figure I–15) and search for an example of each of the following types of Web pages: portal, news, informational, business/marketing, educational, entertainment, advocacy, blog, wiki, online social networks, content aggregator, and personal.

Figure I–15

2. Start your word processing program.
3. Copy and paste the link for each of these Web page types into your word processing document.
4. Identify the type of Web page for each link.
5. Explain why you selected this Web page and how it fits the definition of the specific type.
6. Save the document with the file name Lab I-2 Web Page Types.
7. Submit the document in the format specified by your instructor.

In the Lab

Lab 3: Hosting a Web Site

Problem: Selecting the correct host or ISP for your Web site can be a confusing process. Many Web sites offer this service, but determining the best one for your particular needs can be somewhat complicated. Assume your Web site will sell a product. Compare several ISPs and select the one that will best meet your needs.

Perform the following tasks:

1. Review the information and questions on pages DW 14–16 discussing the guidelines for acquiring active server space to host your Web site.

2. Start your browser. Open the WebSite Hosting Directory Web page shown in Figure I–16 (websitehostdirectory.com).

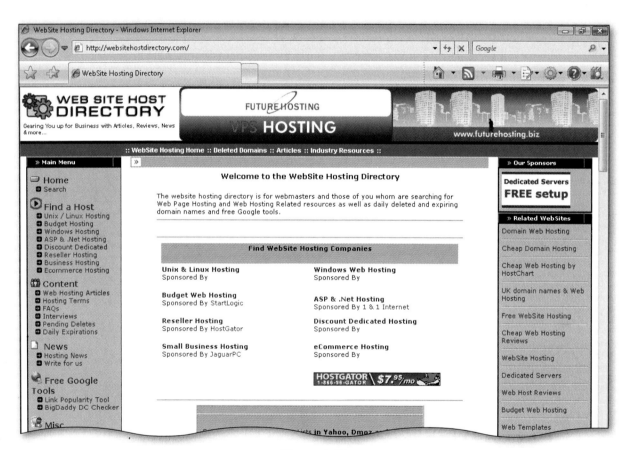

Figure I–16

3. In the Top Web Hosting Companies We Recommend list, click one of the host server links and review the information relating to the services offered by your selected ISP.

4. Start your word processing program.

5. Read and answer the questions on page DW 16. Use the information provided in the list of services offered by your selected ISP.

6. Use your word processing program to write a short summary explaining why you would or would not select this ISP to host your Web site.

7. Save the document with the file name Lab I-3 Web Site Hosting. Submit the document in the format specified by your instructor.

Cases and Places

Apply your creative thinking and problem solving skills to design and implement a solution.

• EASIER •• MORE DIFFICULT

• 1: Research Web Site Planning

You are working as an assistant to the marketing director of Renovation Workshop, a firm that specializes in kitchen and bath renovations. The marketing director is considering whether to create a Web site for Renovation Workshop, and asks you to conduct some research. Use a search engine such as Google (google.com) and research information about planning a Web site. Use your word processing program and write a two-page summary of what you learned. Save the document as Case I-1 Web Site Research. Check the spelling and grammar of the finished paper. Submit the document in the format specified by your instructor.

• 2: Explore Typography

Typography within a Web page is one of its more important elements. Start your browser and search for examples of Web sites that include what you consider appropriate typography and Web sites with inappropriate typography. Use your word processing program to write a short summary of why you consider these to be appropriate and inappropriate. Copy and paste the Web site addresses into your document. Check the spelling and grammar of the finished paper. Save the document as Case I-2 Typography. Submit the document in the format specified by your instructor.

•• 3: Research Web Site Plug-ins

You are working as an intern in an animal shelter, helping the director design a Web site. He wants to show a video of the animals at the shelter on the site, and has heard that viewers might need a plug-in to do so. He asks you to research the topic. Start your browser and search the Web for plug-ins. Prepare a list of and a short description of the plug-ins you found. Use your word processing program to create a summary statement describing how and why you could use each plug-in in a Web site. Include the link where you can download each of the plug-ins. Check the spelling and grammar of the finished paper. Save the document as Case I-3 Web Site Plug-ins. Submit the document in the format specified by your instructor.

•• 4: Create a Web Site Navigation Map

Make It Personal

In preparation for an upcoming reunion, your high school reunion committee is asking everyone in your class to create a personal Web site. As you get started, your goal is to create a personal Web site navigation map that contains three pages — a personal home page, a page about your favorite hobbies, and a page about places you like to visit. Use a software program of your choice to create a navigation map for your proposed Web site. Show the link(s) from the home page to the other two pages. Use your word processing program and write a sentence or two describing the type of structure you created and why you selected that structure. Check the spelling and grammar of the finished paper. Save the document as Case I-4 Navigation Map. Submit the document in the format specified by your instructor.

•• 5: Create Web Site Structures

Working Together

Each team member is to search the Internet for Web sites illustrating each of the Web site structures on pages DW 5–6. Each team member then will use word processing software to write a minimum of 100 words describing the Web sites and explaining why he or she thinks the structure used is appropriate or inappropriate for that particular Web site. Check the spelling and grammar of the finished paper. Save the document as Case I-5 Web Site Structures. Submit the document in the format specified by your instructor.

1 Creating a Dreamweaver Web Page and Local Site

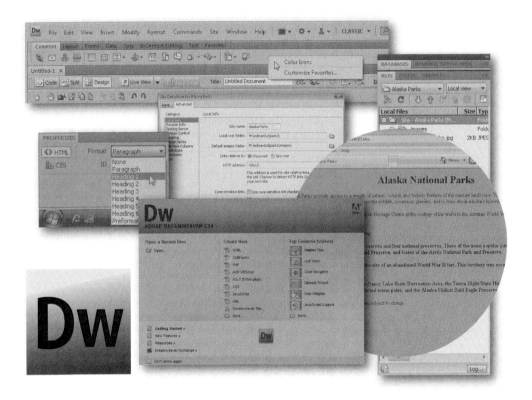

Objectives

You will have mastered the material in this chapter when you can:

- Describe Dreamweaver and identify its key features
- Start and quit Dreamweaver
- Describe the Dreamweaver window
- Define a local site
- Create and save a Web page
- Add a background image
- Open and close panels

- Display the Property inspector
- Format and modify text elements
- Define and insert a line break
- Change a Web page title and check spelling
- Preview and print a Web page
- Open a new Web page

1 | Creating a Dreamweaver Web Page and Local Site

What Is Adobe Dreamweaver CS4?

Adobe Dreamweaver CS4 is a powerful Web page authoring and Web site management software program with an HTML editor that is used to design, code, and create professional-looking Web pages, Web sites, and Web applications. The visual-editing features of Dreamweaver allow you to create pages without writing a line of code. Dreamweaver provides many tools and features, including the following:

- **Automatic Web page creation** — Dreamweaver provides tools you can use to develop Web pages without having to spend hours writing HTML code. Dreamweaver automatically generates the HTML code necessary to publish your Web pages.
- **Web site management** — Dreamweaver enables you to view a site, including all local and remote files associated with the selected site. You can perform standard maintenance operations such as viewing, opening, and moving files and transferring files between local and remote sites.
- **Standard Adobe Web authoring tools** — Dreamweaver includes a user interface that is consistent across all Adobe authoring tools. This consistency enables easy integration with other Adobe Web-related programs such as Adobe Flash, Director, Shockwave, and ColdFusion.

Other key features include the integrated user interface, the integrated file explorer, panel management, database integration, and standards and accessibility support. Dreamweaver CS4 is customizable and runs on many operating systems including Windows Vista, Windows XP, Mac OS X, and others.

When necessary, more specific details concerning the above guidelines are presented at appropriate points in the chapter. The chapter also will identify the actions performed and decisions made regarding these guidelines during the creation of a Web page.

Project Planning Guidelines

The process of developing a Web site that communicates specific information requires careful analysis and planning. As a starting point, determine the type of and purpose of the Web site. Once the type and purpose are determined, decide on the content to be included. Design basics and Web site navigation then should be considered. Finally, creating a navigation map or flowchart will help determine the design that will be most helpful in delivering the Web site content. With the structure in place, the Web site is ready to be developed. Details of these guidelines are provided in the Introduction. In addition, each project in this book provides practical applications of these planning considerations.

Project — Alaska Parks Web Site Home Page

To create documents similar to those you will encounter on the Web and in academic, business, and personal environments, you can use Dreamweaver to produce Web pages such as the Alaska National Parks Web page shown in Figure 1–1. This Web page is the index, or home, page for the Alaska National Parks Web site and provides interesting facts about three of Alaska's national parks. The page begins with a centered main heading, followed by two short informational paragraphs, and then an introductory sentence for a bulleted list. The list contains three bulleted items. A concluding sentence, the author's name, and current date end the page. A background image is applied to the page.

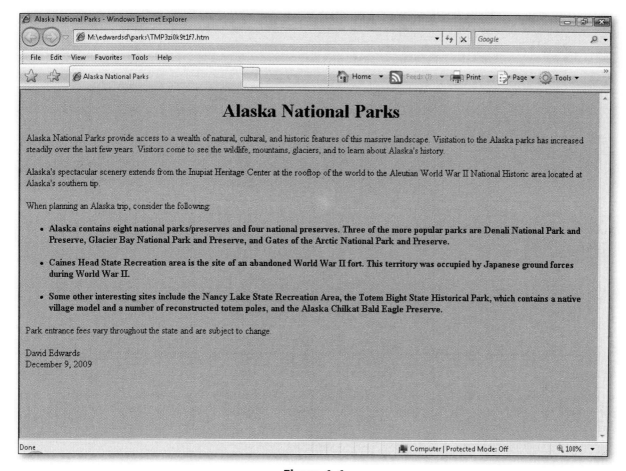

Figure 1–1

Overview

As you read this chapter, you will learn how to create the Web page shown in Figure 1–1 by performing these general tasks:

- Enter text in the document.
- Save the document.
- Add a background image.
- Format the text in the document.
- Insert a line break.
- Check spelling.
- Preview the Web page in a browser.
- Save and print the Web page.

General Project Guidelines

When creating a Dreamweaver Web site, the actions you perform and decisions you make will affect the appearance and characteristics of the entire Web site. As you create the home page, such as the page shown in Figure 1–1 on the previous page, you should follow these general guidelines:

1. **Review the Dreamweaver workspace window.** Become familiar with the various layouts and available panels.

2. **Determine the location for the local site.** Select the location and the storage media on which to save the site. Keep in mind that you will continue to add and modify pages to the site as you progress through the book. Storage media can be a hard disk, USB flash drive, or read/write CD. If you are using a flash drive and intend to complete all exercises, media storage capacity should be a minimum of 25 MB.

3. **Define the local site.** Create the local site using Dreamweaver's Site Definition Wizard.

4. **Add a background.** Adding a background color or background image adds interest and vitality to a Web site.

5. **Select the words and fonts for the text.** Text accounts for the bulk of the content on most Web pages, so it is best to be brief. Use lists whenever possible. Use common words and simple language. Use Web-safe serif fonts such as Times New Roman or sans-serif fonts such as Helvetica, Geneva, and Verdana.

6. **Identify how to format various elements of the text.** Determine the best font type, font color, and font size for each element on the Web page.

When necessary, more specific details concerning the above guidelines are presented at appropriate points in the chapter. The chapter also will identify the actions performed and decisions made regarding these guidelines during the creation of the Web site home page shown in Figure 1–1.

Starting Dreamweaver

If you are using a computer to step through the project in this chapter and you want your screen to match the figures in this book, you should change your screen's resolution to 1024 × 768. The browser used to display the Web page figures is Internet Explorer 7. The browser text size is set to Medium. For information about how to change a computer's resolution, see Appendix D.

Note: If you are using Windows XP, see Appendix E for alternate steps.

To Start Dreamweaver

Getting started in Dreamweaver is as easy as opening an existing HTML document or creating a new document. The steps on the following pages show how to start Dreamweaver based on a typical installation. You may need to ask your instructor how to start Dreamweaver for your computer.

- Click the Start button on the Windows Vista taskbar to display the Start menu.

- Point to Adobe Dreamweaver CS4 on the Start menu or point to All Programs on the Start menu and then point to Adobe Dreamweaver CS4 on the All Programs list (Figure 1–2).

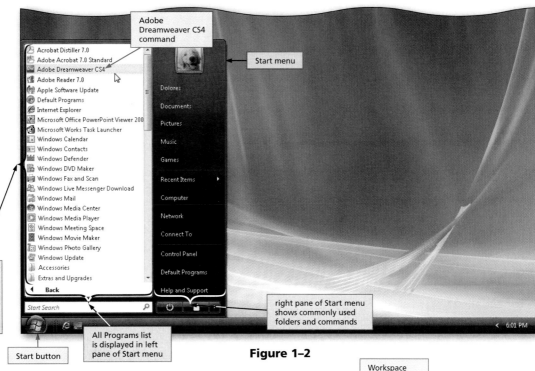

Figure 1–2

2

- Click Adobe Dreamweaver CS4 on the Start menu to start Dreamweaver and display the Welcome screen.

- If necessary, click the Workspace switcher arrow on the Application bar, and then click Classic to switch to the Classic workspace (Figure 1–3).

Q&A What is the Classic workspace?

The Classic workspace provides all the tools a beginning Web designer needs, and omits features for advanced designers and programmers.

Figure 1–3

③
- Click HTML in the Create New column to close the Welcome screen and display the Dreamweaver workspace.

- If necessary, click the Maximize button, and then click the Design button on the Document toolbar to switch to Design view.

- If the Insert bar is not displayed, click Window on the Application bar and then click Insert (Figure 1–4).

Q&A
What if a message is displayed regarding default file types?

If a message is displayed, click the Close button.

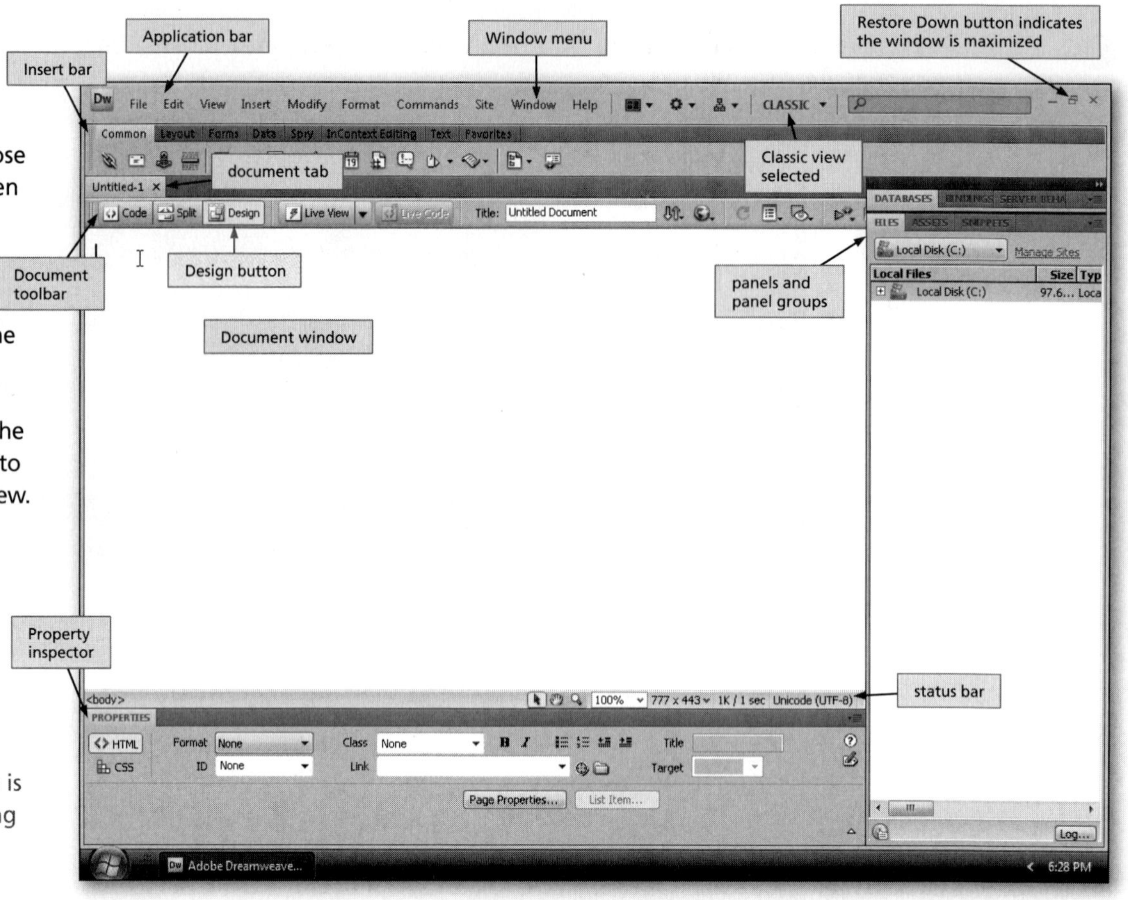

Other Ways
1. Double-click Dreamweaver icon on desktop

Figure 1–4

The Dreamweaver Environment and Workspace

The Dreamweaver environment consists of toolbars, windows, objects, panels, inspectors, and tools you use to create your Web pages and to manage your Web site. It is important to learn the basic concepts behind the Dreamweaver workspace and to understand how to choose options, use inspectors and panels, and set preferences that best fit your work style.

Dreamweaver provides the Web site developer with eight preset workspace layouts: App Developer, App Developer Plus, Classic, Coder, Coder Plus, Designer, Designer Compact, and Dual Screen. Programmers who work primarily with HTML and other languages generally select the Coder or App Developer workspace. The Dual Screen option requires two monitors. In this layout, the Document window and Property inspector are displayed on one monitor and the panels are displayed on a secondary monitor. The Classic workspace contains a visually integrated workspace and is ideal for beginners and nonprogrammers. The exercises in this book use the Classic workspace.

The settings on your computer determine what is displayed when the Dreamweaver CS4 program starts. By default, the Welcome screen is displayed each time you start Dreamweaver. The Welcome screen's visual representation is a good tool for beginners, but more proficient Dreamweaver users generally disable this feature. You will disable the Welcome screen at the end of this chapter. If you are opening Dreamweaver from a computer at your school or other location, most likely the program is set up and ready to use.

The screen in Figure 1–4 shows a typical Dreamweaver workspace, with some of the more commonly used components displayed. The **Dreamweaver workspace** is an

BTW
The Dreamweaver Window
The screen in Figure 1–4 shows how the Dreamweaver window looks the first time you start Dreamweaver after installation on most computers. Your screen might look different depending on your Dreamweaver and computer settings.

integrated environment in which the Document window and panels are incorporated into one larger application window. The panel groups are docked, or attached, on the right. The Insert bar is located at the top of the Document window, and the Property inspector is located at the bottom of the Document window. You can move, resize, close, and/or collapse the panels to accommodate your individual preferences.

This section discusses the following components of the Dreamweaver workspace: title bar, Document window, panels and panel groups, status bar, Application bar, and toolbars.

As you learn to use each of these tools, you will discover some redundancy. For example, to apply a Font tag, you can access the command through the CSS Property inspector, the Format menu, or the Text category on the Insert bar. The different options accommodate various user preferences. The chapters in this book present the more commonly used methods. The Other Ways boxes describe additional methods to accomplish a task when they are available. As you become proficient working in the Dreamweaver environment, you will develop techniques for using the tools that best suit your personal preferences.

Document Tab

The **Document tab** displays the Web page name and includes Untitled-1 as in Figure 1–4. (The "X" is the Close button for the document tab.) After you give a Web page a title and save the document, the Document tab reflects the changes by displaying the document name. When you make changes to the document, Dreamweaver includes an asterisk following the file name. The asterisk is removed after the document is saved, and the file path leading to the document's location is displayed to the right of the document tab.

Document Window

The **Document window** displays the current document, or Web page, including text, tables, graphics, and other items. In Figure 1–4, the Document window is blank. You work in the Document window in one of five views: **Design view**, the design environment where you assemble your Web page elements and design your page (Figure 1–4 displays Design view); **Code view**, which is a hand-coding environment for writing and editing code; **Split view**, which allows you to see both Code view and Design view for the same document in a single window; **Live View**, which shows the page such as it would appear in a browser; and **Live Code**, which displays any HTML code produced by JavaScript or server-side programming. When you open a new document in Dreamweaver, the default view is Design view. These views are discussed in detail in Chapter 2.

Panels and Panel Groups

Panel groups are sets of related panels docked together below one heading. Panels provide control over a wide range of Dreamweaver commands and functions. Each panel group can be expanded or collapsed, and can be undocked or docked with other panel groups. Panel groups also can be docked to the integrated Document window. This makes it easy to access the panels you need without cluttering your workspace. Panels within a panel group are displayed as tabs. Each panel is explained in detail as it is used in the chapters throughout the book. Some panels, such as the Insert bar and Property inspector, are stand-alone panels.

The **Insert bar** allows quick access to frequently used commands. It contains buttons for creating and inserting various types of objects — such as images, tables, links, dates, and

Change the Insert Bar to a Menu
Right-click any category name on the Insert bar and then click Show as Menu to change the horizontal tabs on the Insert bar to a vertical menu.

so on — into a document. As you insert each object, a dialog box allows you to set and manipulate various attributes. The buttons on the Insert bar are organized into several categories, such as Common and Layout, which you can access through tabs. Some categories also have buttons with pop-up menus. When you select an option from a pop-up menu, it becomes the default action for the button. When you start Dreamweaver, the category in which you last were working is displayed.

The **Property inspector** (Figure 1–4 on page 38) displays settings for the selected object's properties or attributes. This panel is context sensitive, meaning it changes based on the selected object, which can include text, tables, images, and other objects. When Dreamweaver starts, the Property inspector is positioned at the bottom of the Document window and displays text properties if a Document window is open. Otherwise, the Property inspector is blank.

Status Bar

The **status bar** located below the Document window (Figure 1–5) provides additional information about the document you are creating.

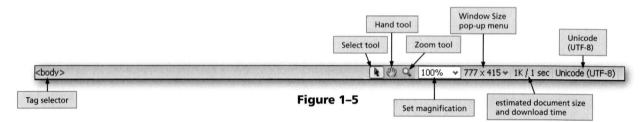

Figure 1–5

The status bar presents the following options:

- **Tag**: Click any tag in the hierarchy to select that tag and all its contents.
- **Select tool**: Use the Select tool to return to default editing after using the Zoom or Hand tool.
- **Hand tool**: To pan a page after zooming, use the Hand tool to drag the page.
- **Zoom tool**: Available only in Design view. Use the Zoom tool to zoom in and out from a document to check the pixel accuracy of graphics or to better view the page.
- **Set magnification**: Use the Set magnification pop-up menu to change the view from 6% to 6400%; default is 100%.
- **Window size**: Displays the Window size, which includes the window's current dimensions (in pixels) and the Window size pop-up menu.
- **Estimated document size and download time**: Displays the size and estimated download time of the current page. Dreamweaver CS4 calculates the size based on the entire contents of the page, including all linked objects such as images and plug-ins.
- **Unicode (UTF-8)**: An industry standard that allows computers to consistently represent and manipulate text expressed in most of the world's writing systems.

Vertical/Horizontal Bars

A vertical bar separates the panel groups, and a horizontal bar separates the Property inspector from the Document window. Clicking the Property inspector bar hides or displays the Property inspector. The panel groups contain a Collapse to Icons/Expand Panels button (Figure 1–6). If your screen resolution is set to 800 × 600, a portion of the Property inspector may not be displayed when the panel groups are expanded.

Application Bar

The **Application bar** displays the Dreamweaver menu names (Figure 1–6). Each menu contains a list of commands you can use to perform tasks such as opening, saving, modifying, previewing, and inserting data into your Web page. When you point to a menu name on the Application bar, the area of the Application bar containing the name is selected.

To display a menu, such as the Edit menu (Figure 1–6), click the menu name on the Application bar. If you point to a menu command that has an arrow at its right edge, a submenu displays another list of commands. Many menus display some commands that appear gray, or dimmed, instead of black, which indicates they are not available for the current selection.

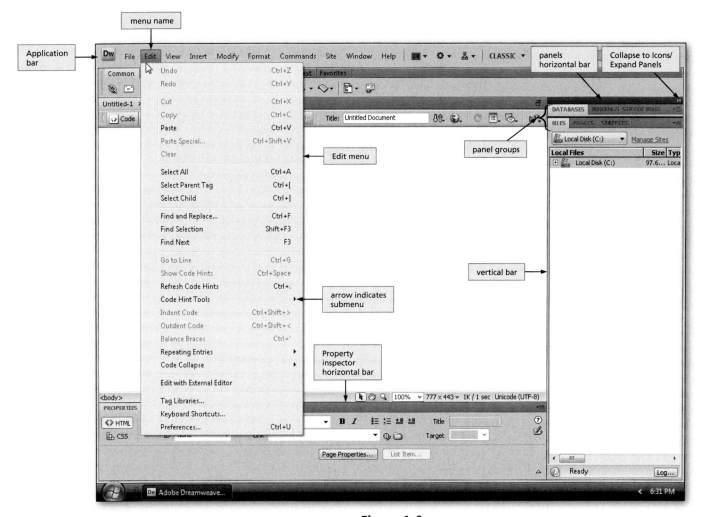

Figure 1–6

Toolbars

In the Classic workspace, or view, Dreamweaver can display three toolbars: Document, Standard, and Style Rendering. You can choose to display or hide the toolbars by clicking View on the Application bar and then pointing to Toolbars. If a toolbar name has a check mark next to it, it is displayed in the window. To hide the toolbar, click the name of the toolbar with the check mark, and it no longer is displayed. The Insert bar is considered a panel and was discussed previously in this chapter.

The **Document toolbar** (Figure 1–7) is the default toolbar displayed in the Document window. It contains buttons that provide different views of the Document window (e.g., Code, Split, and Design), the Document title, and some common operations, such as File Management, Preview/Debug in Browser, Refresh Design View, View Options, Visual Aids, Validate Markup, and Check Browser Compatibility.

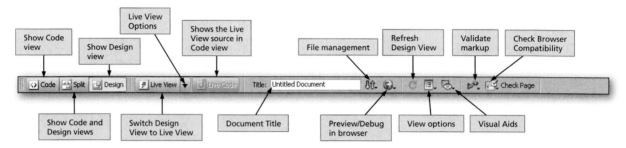

Figure 1–7

The **Standard toolbar** (Figure 1–8) contains buttons for common operations from the File and Edit menus: New, Open, Browse in Bridge, Save, Save All, Print Code, Cut, Copy, Paste, Undo, and Redo. The Standard toolbar is not displayed by default in the Dreamweaver Document window when you first start Dreamweaver. You can display the Standard toolbar through the Toolbars command on the View menu, or by right-clicking a blank area on the Document toolbar and then clicking Standard on the context menu. Similar to other toolbars and panels, you can dock or undock and move the Standard toolbar, so it might be displayed in a different location on your screen.

Figure 1–8

A recent addition to Dreamweaver is the **Style Rendering toolbar**, which provides options for designing for different media types, such as screen, print, handheld, projection, TTY (teletype), television, CSS Styles, and Style Sheets. The CSS (Cascading Style Sheets) Styles button works independently of the other seven buttons and provides the option to disable or enable the display of CSS styles.

Opening and Closing Panels

The Dreamweaver workspace accommodates different work styles and levels of expertise. Through the workspace, you can open and close the panel groups and display or hide other Dreamweaver features as needed. To open a panel group, select and then click the name of a panel on the Window menu. Closing unused panels provides an uncluttered workspace in the Document window. To close an individual panel group, click Close Tab Group on the context menu accessed through the panel group's title bar (Figure 1–9) or click the Window menu and then click the panel name. To expand/collapse a panel, click the Expand/Collapse button above the panel groups.

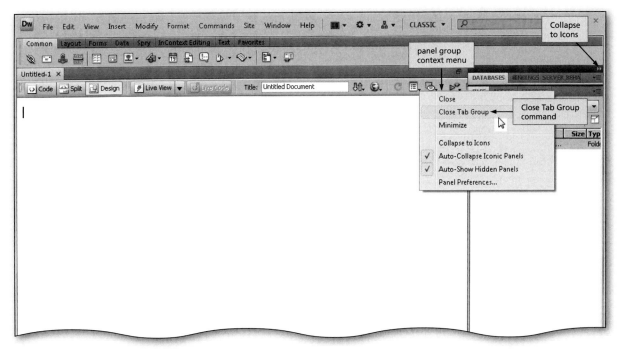

Figure 1–9

To Display the Standard Toolbar, Change the Icon Colors, and Close and Open Panels

The following steps illustrate how to display the Standard toolbar, change the icon colors, and close and open the panels.

- Click View on the Application bar to display the View menu.

- If necessary, click the down-pointing arrow at the bottom of the View menu to scroll the menu.

- Point to Toolbars, and then point to Standard on the Toolbars submenu to highlight Standard on the Toolbars submenu (Figure 1–10).

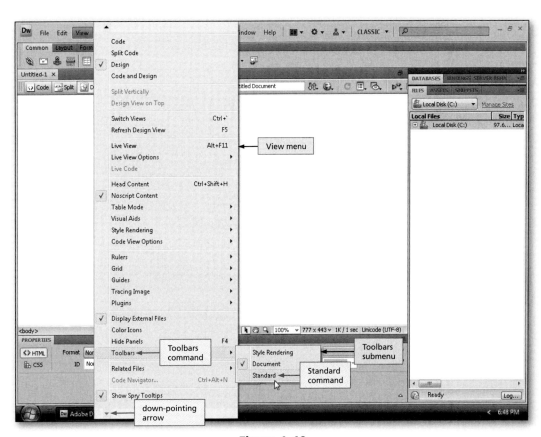

Figure 1–10

2

- Click Standard to display the Standard toolbar.

Q&A Can the location of the Standard toolbar change?

Yes. Previous settings determine the location of the Standard toolbar. It might be displayed below the Document toolbar or in another location in the Dreamweaver window.

- Right-click a blank spot on the Insert bar to display the context menu.

- Point to Color Icons (Figure 1–11).

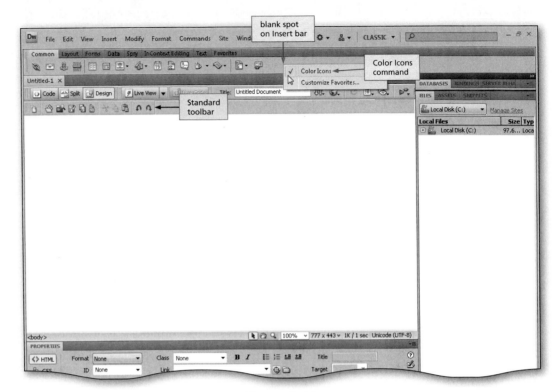

Figure 1–11

3

- If a check mark does not appear next to Color Icons, click Color Icons to add color to the icons.

- Press the F4 key to close all open panels and inspectors and to maximize the workspace available in the Document window.

- Press the F4 key again to redisplay the panels (Figure 1–12).

Q&A What is the fastest way to open and close panels?

The fastest way to open and close panels in Dreamweaver is to use the F4 key, which opens or closes all panels and inspectors at one time.

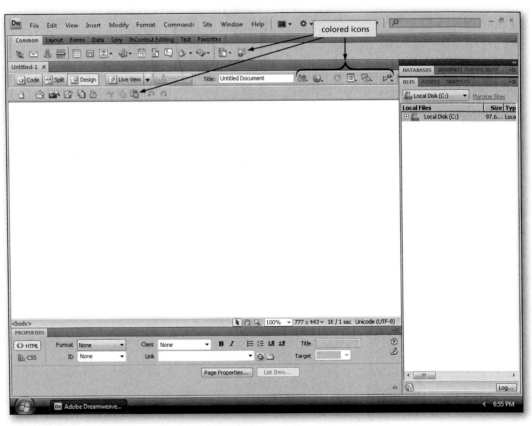

Figure 1–12

Defining a Local Site

Web design and Web site management are two important skills that a builder of Web sites must understand and apply. Dreamweaver CS4 is a site creation and management tool. To use Dreamweaver efficiently, you first must define the local site. After defining the local site, you then publish to a remote site. Publishing to a remote site is discussed in Chapter 3 and Appendix C.

The general definition of a **site**, or Web site, is a set of linked documents with shared attributes, such as related topics, a similar design, or a shared purpose. In Dreamweaver, however, the term site can refer to any of the following:

- **Web site**: A set of pages on a server that are viewed through a Web browser by a visitor to the site.
- **Remote site**: Files on the server that make up a Web site, from the author's point of view rather than a visitor's point of view.
- **Local site**: Files on your local disk that correspond to the files on the remote site. You edit the files on your local disk, and then upload them to the remote site.
- **Dreamweaver site definition**: Set of defining characteristics for a local site, plus information on how the local site corresponds to a remote site.

All Dreamweaver Web sites begin with a local root folder. As you become familiar with Dreamweaver and complete the chapters in this book, you will find references to a **local root folder**, **root folder**, and **root**. These terms are interchangeable. This folder is no different from any other folder on your computer's hard drive or other storage media, except for the way in which Dreamweaver views it. When Dreamweaver looks for Web pages, links, images, and other files, it looks in the designated root folder by default. Any media within the Web site that are outside of the root folder are not displayed when the Web site is previewed in a Web browser. Within the root folder, you can create additional folders or subfolders to organize images and other objects. A **subfolder** (also called a **nested folder**) is a folder inside another folder.

Dreamweaver provides two options to define a site and create the hierarchy: You can create the root folder and any subfolders, or create the pages and then create the folders when saving the files. In this book, you create the root folder and subfolders and then create the Web pages.

Plan Ahead

Managing Web Site Files

Before you create a Web site, you need to determine where you will save the site and its files.

- If you plan to work on your Web site in various locations or on more than one computer, you should create your site on removable media, such as a USB flash drive. The Web sites in this book use a USB flash drive because these drives are portable and can store a lot of data.

- If you always work on the same computer, you probably can create your site on the computer's hard drive. However, if you are working in a computer lab, your instructor or the lab supervisor might instruct you to save your site in a particular location on the hard drive or on removable media such as a USB flash drive.

Creating the Local Root Folder and Subfolders

Several options are available to create and manage your local root folder and subfolders: Dreamweaver's Files panel, Dreamweaver's Site Definition feature, or Windows file management. In this book, you use Dreamweaver's Site Definition feature to create the local root folder and subfolders, the Files panel to manage and edit your files and folders, and Windows file management to download the data files.

To organize and create a Web site and understand how you access Web documents, you need to understand paths and folders. The term, path, sometimes is confusing for new users of the Web. It is, however, a simple concept: A **path** is the succession of folders that must be navigated to get from one folder to another. In the DOS world, folders are referred to as **directories**. These two terms often are used interchangeably.

A typical path structure has a **master folder**, usually called the root and designated by the symbol "\". This root folder contains within it all of the other subfolders or nested folders. Further, each subfolder may contain additional subfolders or nested folders. These folders contain the Web site files. Most sites include a subfolder for images.

For this book, you first create a local root folder using your last name and first initial. Examples in this book use David Edwards as the Web site author. Thus, David's local root folder is edwardsd and is located on drive M (a USB drive). Next, for this chapter, you create a subfolder and name it parks. Finally, you create another subfolder within parks and name it images. All Alaska Parks-related files and subfolders are stored within the parks folder. When you navigate through this folder hierarchy, you are navigating along the path. The path to the Alaska Parks Web site is M:\edwardsd\parks\. The path to the images folder is M:\edwardsd\parks\images\. In all references to edwardsd, substitute your last name and first initial and your drive location.

Using Site Definition to Create a Local Site

You create a site definition using Dreamweaver's Site Definition dialog box. Two options are available: Basic or Advanced. The Basic method, or **Site Definition Wizard**, guides you through site setup step by step and takes you through a series of six screens. In the Advanced method, all options are contained on one screen. The Advanced method is more efficient. Using this view, you set all the same basic information that the Site Definition Wizard collects, plus additional options such as the following:

- **Case-sensitive links**: Provide for the use of case-sensitive link checking
- **Cache**: Allocates memory to store frequently used site data; checked by default
- **Default images folder**: An optional feature to specify the location of images in the site
- **HTTP address**: Used to define the URL of a Web site and to verify absolute links

The two main categories in a site definition are **Local Info** (Local Information) and **Remote Info** (Remote Information). In this chapter, you create the local site definition using the Advanced method. The site definition is stored in the Windows Registry and is not part of the site. If you use removable media to store your files and move to another computer, you must recreate the local site definition on that computer. Remote site definition is discussed in Chapter 3.

After you have completed the site definition, the hierarchy structure is displayed in the Dreamweaver **Local Files panel**. This hierarchy structure is similar to the Windows file organization. The Local Files panel provides a view of the devices and folders on your computer and shows how these devices and folders are organized.

To Use Site Definition to Create a Local Web Site

You define a local site by telling Dreamweaver where you plan to store local files. Use the Site Definition Advanced approach and the following steps to create a local Web site. A USB drive is used for all exercises in this book. If you are saving your sites at another location or on removable media, substitute that location for Removable Disk (M:).

- Click Site on the Application bar to display the Site menu, and then point to New Site (Figure 1–13).

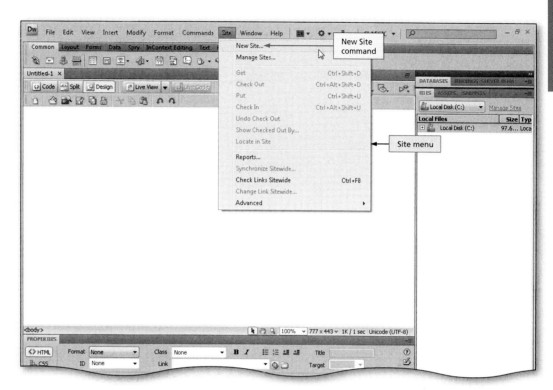

Figure 1–13

- Click New Site to display the Site Definition dialog box.

- If necessary, click the Advanced tab. Verify that Local Info is selected in the Category column (Figure 1–14).

Q&A

What is the difference between Local Info and Remote Info?

Local Info refers to information about a Web site that you create on your computer, which is the way you develop a site. Remote Info refers to information about settings on a remote computer, such as a Web server, which is where you publish a site.

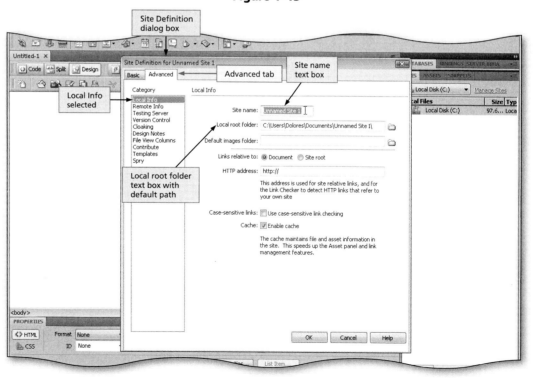

Figure 1–14

- Type `Alaska Parks` in the Site name text box to name the site (Figure 1–15).

Q&A Is the site name necessary?

This name is required, but it is for reference only. It is not part of the path and is not visible to viewers of your site.

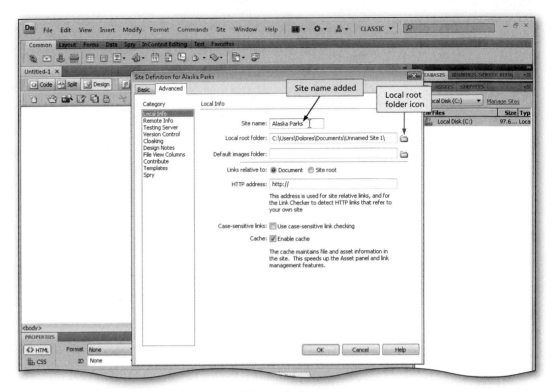

Figure 1–15

- Click the folder icon to the right of the Local root folder text box to display the Choose local root folder for site dialog box.

- Navigate to where you will store your Web site files (Figure 1–16).

Q&A On what drive should I store the Web site files?

Because most Web sites require many files, you should create the projects using a hard drive or removable drive with plenty of space — not the floppy drive (A:), if you have one. Steps in this

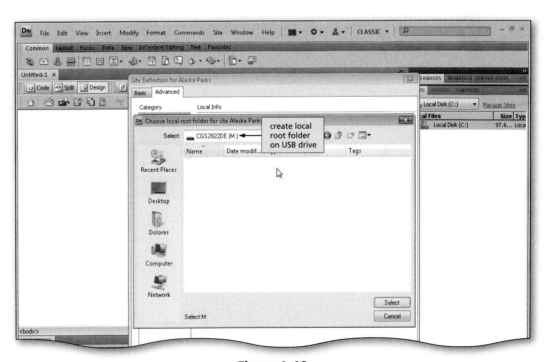

Figure 1–16

chapter assume you are creating the local site on a USB drive. Check with your instructor to verify the location and path you will use to create and save your local Web site. Other options may include a CD-RW disc or a network drive.

Q&A What if my USB flash drive has a different name or letter?

It is very likely that your USB flash drive will have a different name and drive letter from the one shown in Figure 1–16 and be connected to a different port. Verify that the device displayed in the Select text box is correct.

⑤

• Click the Create New Folder icon to create a folder and display the New Folder text box (Figure 1–17).

Q&A

Why should I create a folder on the drive for my Web site?

Organizing your Web site folders now will save you time and prevent problems later. Create a main folder such as edwardsd for the sites in this book. (Substitute your name for "edwardsd.") Create a subfolder in that main folder for the Alaska Parks Web site. Finally, create a subfolder in the Alaska Parks Web site folder for images.

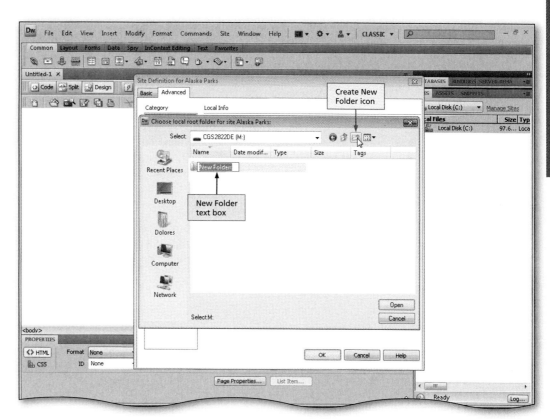

Figure 1–17

⑥

• Type your last name and first initial (with no spaces between your last name and initial) in the New Folder text box.

• Press the ENTER key to open the new folder.

• Click the Create New Folder icon to create a folder within the *your name* folder (Figure 1–18).

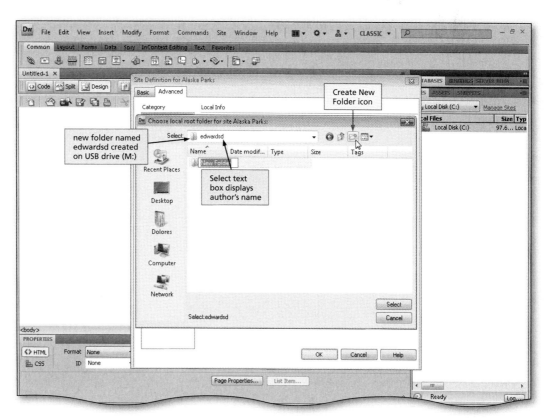

Figure 1–18

7

- Type `parks` as the name of the new folder and then press the ENTER key to create the parks subfolder (Figure 1–19).

 Q&A

Which files will I store in the parks folder?

The parks folder will contain all the files for the Alaska Parks Web site. In other words, the parks folder is the local root folder for the Alaska Parks Web site.

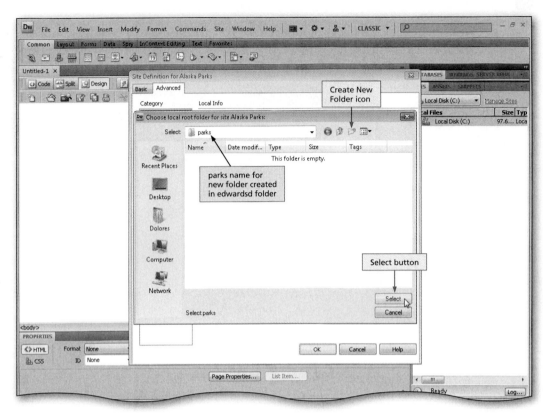

Figure 1–19

8

- Click the Select button to display the Site Definition dialog box and select parks as the local root folder (Figure 1–20).

Q&A

Am I finished defining the new Web site?

Not yet. Nearly every Web site displays graphics, photos, and other images, and you need to create a subfolder for these images.

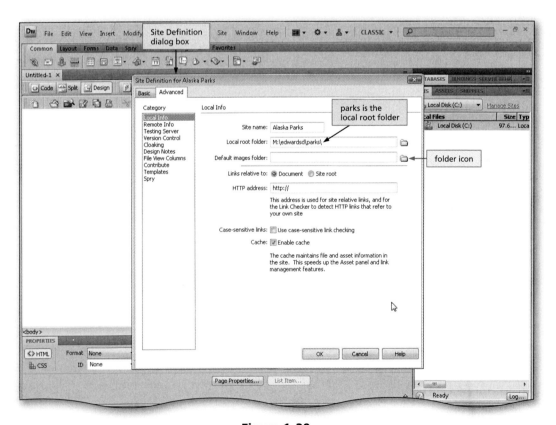

Figure 1–20

9

- Click the folder icon to the right of the Default images folder text box to specify the folder for the images.

- If necessary, navigate to the *your name* parks folder.

- Click the Create New Folder icon to create a subfolder in the parks folder.

- Type images as the name of the new folder and then press the ENTER key to create and open the folder (Figure 1–21).

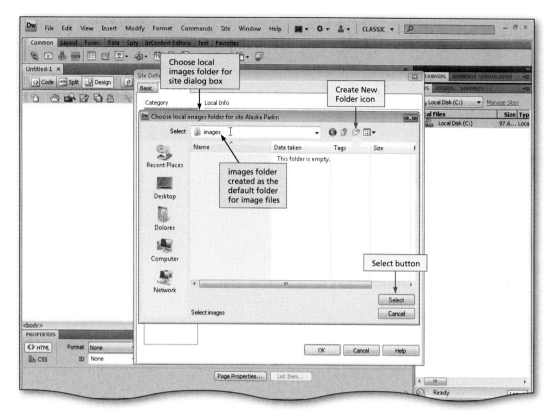

Figure 1–21

10

- Click the Select button to select the images folder as the default folder for images and to display the Site Definition dialog box.

- Verify that the Enable cache check box is selected in the Site Definition dialog box (Figure 1–22).

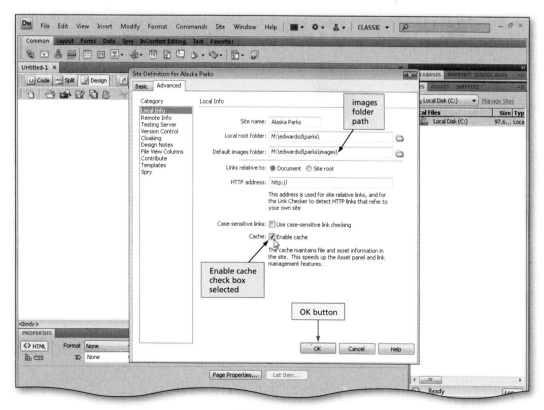

Figure 1–22

11
- Click the OK button to display the Dreamweaver workspace. The Alaska Parks Web site hierarchy is displayed in the Files panel (Figure 1–23).

Q&A What do the icons in the Files panel mean?

A small device icon or folder icon is displayed next to each object listed in the Files panel. The device icon represents a device such as the Desktop or a disk drive, and the folder icon represents a folder. Many of these icons have a plus or minus sign next to them, which indicates whether the device or folder contains additional folders. The plus and minus signs are controls that you can click to expand or collapse the view of the file hierarchy. In the Files panel, the site folders and files appear in a different color than non-site folders and files so that you easily can distinguish between the two.

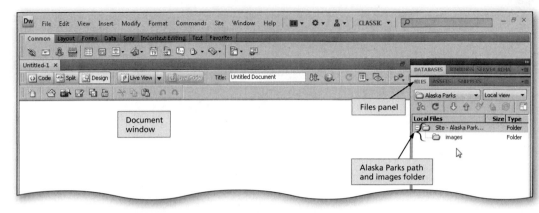

Figure 1–23

Q&A What else does the Local Files panel display?

The Local Files panel displays a site, including local, remote, and testing server files associated with a selected site. In this chapter, you view only the local site.

Other Ways

1. Click Site menu, click New Site, click Basic tab

To Copy Data Files to the Local Web Site

Your data files contain background images for the Chapter 1 project and exercises. You can copy the data files one by one through the Dreamweaver Files panel as you progress through this chapter. Alternatively, using the Windows Computer tool, you can establish the basic framework for the parks Web site by copying all the files and images at one time. The following steps illustrate how to copy data files to the local Web site.

Note: If you are using Windows XP, see Appendix E for alternate steps.

- Click the Start button on the Windows taskbar and then click Computer to display the Computer window. If necessary, click the Views button arrow on the toolbar and then click List.

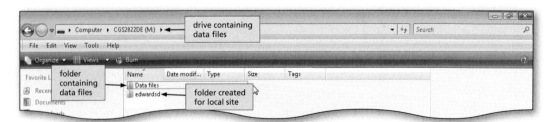

Figure 1–24

- Navigate to the location of the data files for Chapter 1 (Figure 1–24).

Q&A What if my data files are located on a different drive or folder?

In Figure 1–24, the location is CGS2822DE (M:), a USB drive. Most likely your data files are stored in a different location. Your data files might also be stored in a folder with a name other than "Data files."

2

- Double-click the folder containing your data files, and then double-click the Chapter01 folder to open it (Figure 1–25).

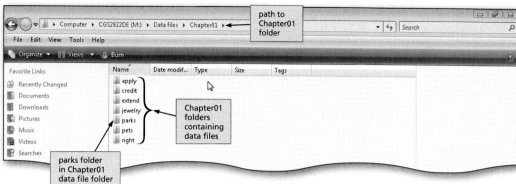

Figure 1–25

3

- Double-click the parks folder to open it (Figure 1–26).

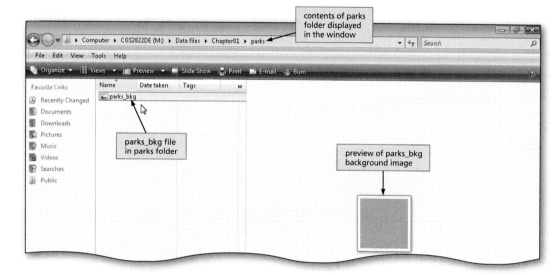

Figure 1–26

4

- Right-click the parks_bkg image file to display a context menu.

- Point to the Copy command on the context menu (Figure 1–27).

 My context menu contains different commands. Is that a problem?

No. A file's context menu often changes depending on the programs on your computer. The Copy command, however, always appears on this menu.

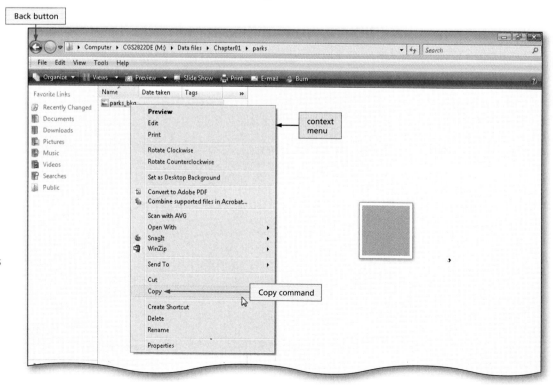

Figure 1–27

5

- Click Copy and then click the Back button the number of times necessary to navigate to the *your name* folder.

- Double-click the *your name* folder, double-click the parks folder, and then double-click the images folder to open the images folder for your Web site.

- Right-click anywhere in the open window to display the context menu.

- Point to the Paste command to highlight it (Figure 1–28).

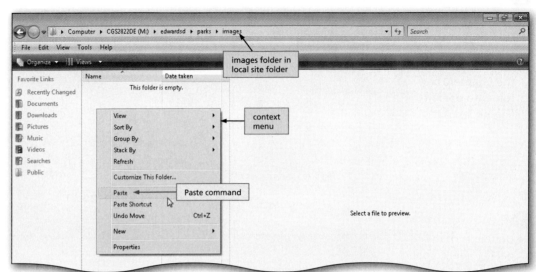

Figure 1–28

6

- Click the Paste command to paste the parks_bkg image into the Alaska Parks Web site images folder (Figure 1–29).

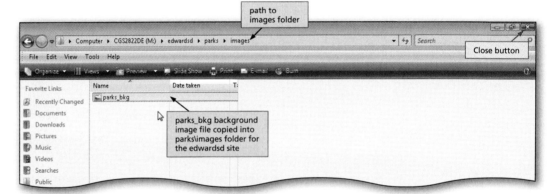

Figure 1–29

 7

- Click the images window's Close button to close the images folder window.

- Double-click the images folder in the Dreamweaver Files panel to open the images folder (Figure 1–30).

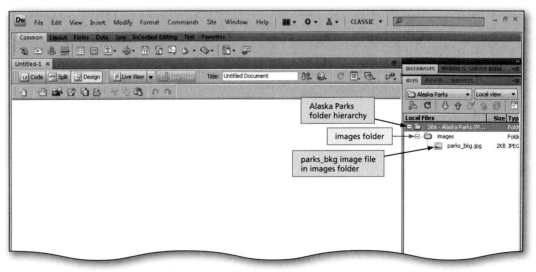

Figure 1–30

Removing or Editing a Web Site

On occasion, you may need to remove or edit a Web site. To remove or edit a Web site, click Site on the Application bar and then click the Manage Sites command. This displays the Manage Sites dialog box. Select the site name and then click the Remove button to remove the site. Dreamweaver displays a caution box providing you with an opportunity to cancel. Click the No button to cancel. Otherwise, click the Yes button, and Dreamweaver removes the site. Removing a site in Dreamweaver removes the settings for the site. The files and folders remain and must be deleted separately.

To edit a site, click the site name and then click the Edit button. Dreamweaver displays the Site Definition dialog box; from there, you can change any of the options you selected when you first created the site.

Preparing Your Workspace and Saving a Web Page

With the Alaska Parks site defined and the data file copied to the site, the next step is to save the untitled Dreamweaver document. When you defined the site, you designated a local root folder. You can copy and paste files into this folder using Windows Vista or XP, or use Dreamweaver's file management tools to copy and paste. You also can save a Dreamweaver document into this folder. Dreamweaver treats any item placed in the folder as part of the site.

When a document is saved as a Web page, the Web page also remains in the computer's memory and is displayed in the Document window. It is a good practice to save when you first open the document and then save regularly while you are working in Dreamweaver. By doing so, you protect yourself from losing all the work you have done since the last time you saved.

Rulers

Rulers help you measure, organize, and plan your layout. They are turned off by default in the Classic workspace. When rulers are turned on, they appear on the left and top borders of the page, marked in pixels, inches, or centimeters. They especially are helpful when working with tables or layers. Rulers, however, sometimes can be distracting when first learning how to use Dreamweaver, so you will make sure they are turned off shortly.

The Index Page

The **home page** is the starting point for the rest of your Web site. For most Web sites, the home page is named index. This name has special significance because most Web servers recognize index.htm (or index.html) as the default home page.

Dreamweaver comes with a number of default commands. These defaults are stored in 20 different categories in Dreamweaver's Preferences dialog box. Dreamweaver's default extension for new documents is .html. Although there is some debate about which extension to use — .htm or .html — most Web sites use .htm. You change the default through the Preferences dialog box. Therefore, when you save your document, Dreamweaver automatically appends the extension .htm to the file name. Documents with the .htm extension are displayed in Web browsers.

To Hide the Rulers, Change the .html Default, and Save a Document as a Web Page

The home page for your Alaska Parks Web site is named index.htm. The following steps show how to prepare your workspace by turning off the rulers, if necessary, and changing the .html default extension to .htm. You then save the untitled document as index.htm in the parks local root folder. If the Rulers are not displayed in your Document window, omit Steps 1 and 2.

Note: If you are using Windows XP, see Appendix E for alternate steps.

1

- If Rulers are turned on, click View on the Application bar, point to Rulers, and then point to Show on the Rulers submenu (Figure 1–31).

Q&A What should I do if rulers are not displayed in my Document window?

Skip Steps 1 and 2 and start with Step 3 to change the default file name extension.

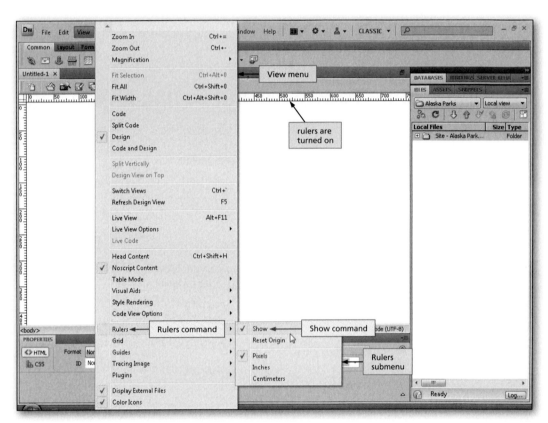

Figure 1–31

2

- Click Show to turn off the rulers (Figure 1–32).

Q&A How can I display the rulers again later?

Perform Steps 1 and 2 again: click View on the Application bar, point to Rulers, and then click Show.

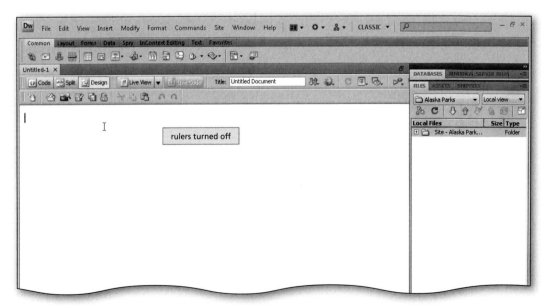

Figure 1–32

3

- Click Edit on the Application bar, and then click Preferences to display the Preferences dialog box (Figure 1–33).

What if the Preferences dialog box displays a category of options different from the one shown in Figure 1–33?

The Preferences dialog box displays the last category of options used on your computer. You'll select the category for changing the default extension in the next step.

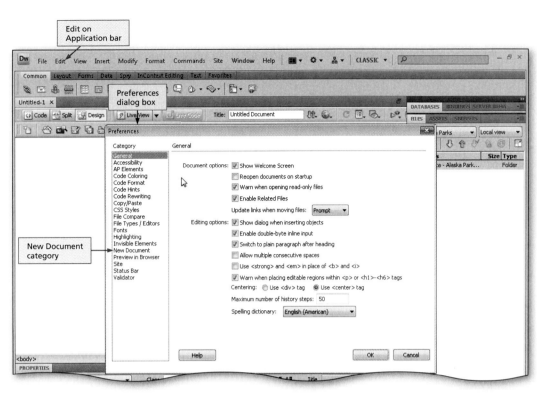

Figure 1–33

4

- Click the New Document category, if necessary, delete .html as the Default extension, and then type .htm as the default (Figure 1–34).

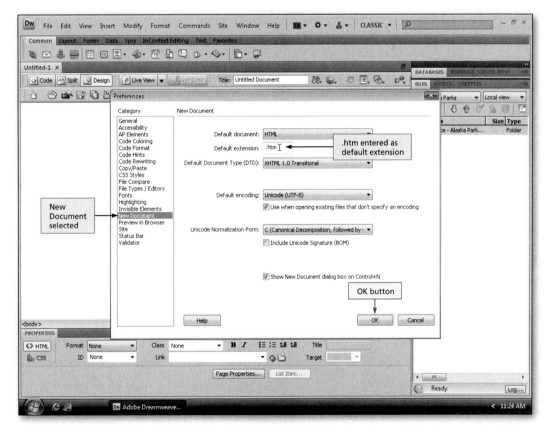

Figure 1–34

5

- Click the OK button to accept the setting and display the Document window.

- Click the Save button on the Standard toolbar to display the Save As dialog box (Figure 1–35).

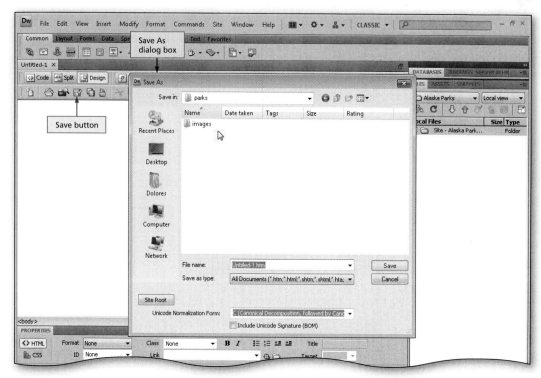

Figure 1–35

6

- Type index as the file name (Figure 1–36).

Why is the file name specified in all lowercase characters?

Some Web servers are case sensitive, which means that they consider a file named "index" different from one named "Index." It's common practice among Web designers to use only lowercase characters for the names of all Web site files, including documents and images.

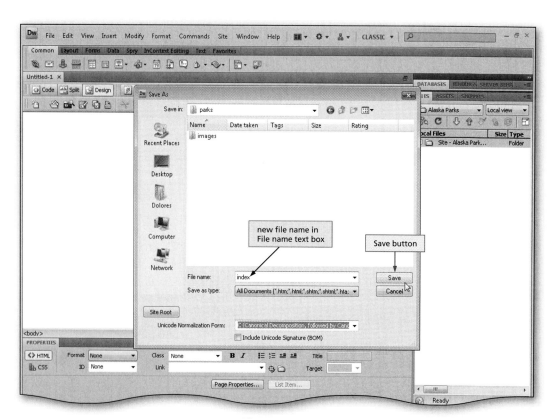

Figure 1–36

7

- Click the Save button to save the file in the Files panel under Local Files (Figure 1–37).

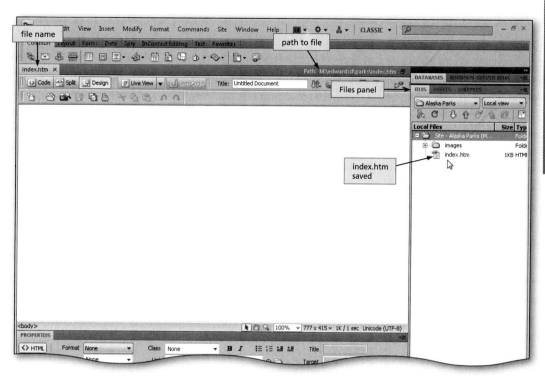

Figure 1–37

Web Page Backgrounds

Each new Web page you create is displayed with a default white or gray background and other default properties. You can modify these default properties using the **Page Properties** dialog box. The Page Properties dialog box lets you specify appearance, links, and many other aspects of page design. You can assign new page properties for each new page you create, and modify properties for existing pages. The page properties you select apply only to the active document.

Web Page Backgrounds

As you design and plan a Web page, consider the following guidelines for applying color and images to the background:

- You can change the default background and enhance your Web page by adding a background image or background color. If you use both a background image and a background color, the color appears while the image downloads, and then the image covers the color.

- Use a background image to add texture and interesting color to a Web page. You can find copyright-free background images on the Web or you can design them yourself.

- Be cautious when selecting or designing background images. Web page images displayed on top of a busy background image may not mix well, and text may be difficult to read. Images and image formats are discussed in more detail in Chapter 2.

Plan Ahead

To Add a Background Image to the Index Page

When you copied the data file earlier in this chapter, you copied an image file that will be the background for the Alaska Parks Web site pages. The following steps illustrate how to use the Page Properties dialog box to add that background image to the index page.

1

• Click Modify on the Application bar and then click Page Properties to display the Page Properties dialog box.

• Click the Appearance (HTML) category to display options for adding a background image to the page (Figure 1–38).

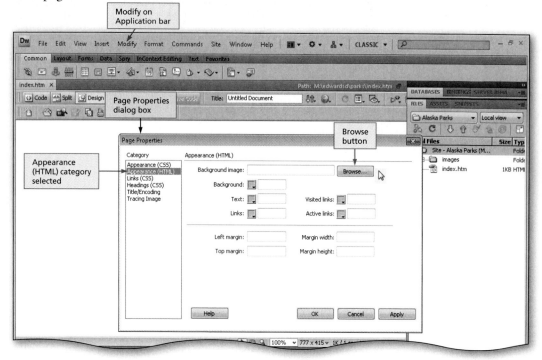

Figure 1–38

2

• Click the Background image Browse button to display the Select Image Source dialog box (Figure 1–39).

Q&A

Why should I use a background image on my Web pages?

Background images add texture and visual interest to your Web pages.

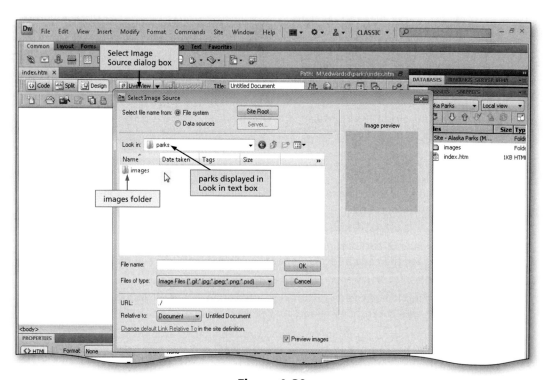

Figure 1–39

3

- Double-click the images folder to display the images file list and then click the parks_bkg file (Figure 1–40).

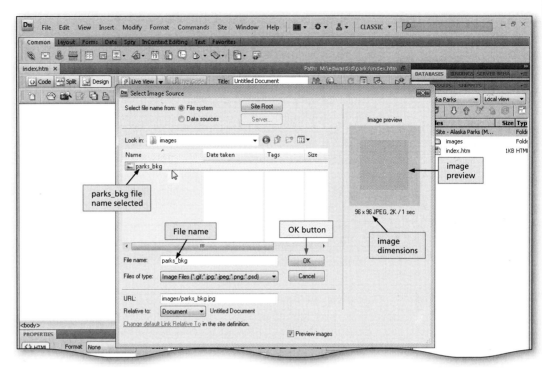

Figure 1–40

4

- Click the OK button to accept the background image, and then click OK to apply the image to the page.

- Click the Save button on the Standard toolbar to save the document (Figure 1–41).

How do I know the document is saved?

When the document is saved, the Save button on the Standard toolbar is dimmed.

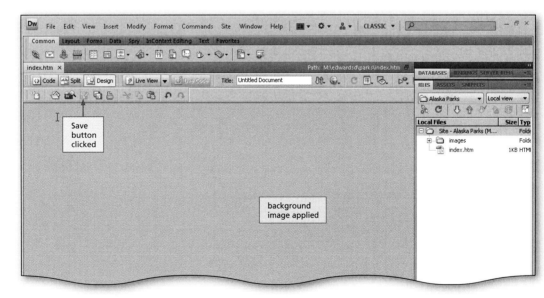

Figure 1–41

Other Ways

1. Right-click Document window, click Page Properties on shortcut menu
2. Click Page Properties button on Property inspector

Adding Text to a Web Page

In Dreamweaver, you can create a Web page in several ways: (1) you can add text to a new document; (2) you can open an existing HTML document, even if it was not created in Dreamweaver; (3) you can copy and paste text; and (4) you can import a Word document.

In this chapter, you create the index page for the Alaska Parks Web page by typing the text in the Document window. Entering text into a Dreamweaver document is similar to typing text in a word processing document. You can position the insertion point at the top left of the Document window or within another object, such as a table cell. Pressing the ENTER key creates a new paragraph and inserts a blank line. Web browsers automatically insert a blank line of space between paragraphs. To start a new single line without a blank line between lines of text requires a **line break**. You can insert a line break by holding down the SHIFT key and then pressing the ENTER key.

Plan
Ahead

Plan the Text

Most informational Web pages start with a heading, and then include paragraphs of text, one or more lists, and end with a closing line. Before you add text to a Web page, consider the following guidelines for organizing and formatting text:

- **Headings**: Start by identifying the headings you will use. Determine which headings are for main topics (Heading 1) and which are for subtopics (Heading 2 or 3).

- **Paragraphs**: For descriptions or other information, include short paragraphs of text. To emphasize important terms, format them as bold or italic.

- **Lists**: Use lists to organize key points, a sequence of steps, or other information you want to highlight. If amount or sequence matter, number each item in a list. Otherwise, use a bullet (a dot or other symbol that appears at the beginning of the paragraph).

- **Closing**: The closing is usually one sentence that provides information of interest to most Web page viewers or that indicates where people can find more information about your topic.

To Hide the Panel Groups

The following step shows how to provide more workspace by hiding the panel groups.

- Click Window on the Application bar and then click Hide Panels to close the Files panel and the Property inspector (Figure 1–42).

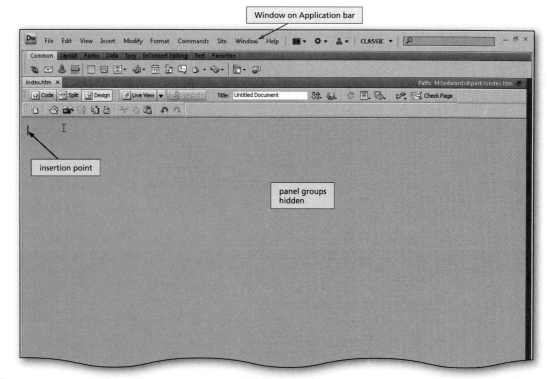

Figure 1–42

Adding Text

Table 1–1 includes the text for the Alaska National Parks Web page. After typing the sections of the document, you press the ENTER key to insert a blank line.

Table 1–1 Alaska National Parks Web Page Text			
Section	**Heading, Part 1, and Part 2 Text**	**Section**	**Part 3, Items for Bulleted List, and Closing Text**
Heading	Alaska National Parks	Part 3	When planning an Alaska trip, consider the following:
Part 1	Alaska National Parks provide access to a wealth of natural, cultural, and historic features of this massive landscape. Visitation to the Alaska parks has increased steadily over the last few years. Visitors come to see the wildlife, mountains, glaciers, and to learn about Alaska's history.	Items list	Alaska contains eight national parks/preserves and four national preserves. Three of the more popular parks are Denali National Park and Preserve, Glacier Bay National Park and Preserve, and Gates of the Arctic National Park and Preserve. <ENTER> Caines Head State Recreation area is the site of an abandoned World War II fort. This territory was occupied by Japanese ground forces during World War II. <ENTER> Some other interesting sites include the Nancy Lake State Recreation Area, the Totem Bight State Historical Park, which contains a native village model and a number of reconstructed totem poles, and the Alaska Chilkat Bald Eagle Preserve. <ENTER>
Part 2	Alaska's spectacular scenery extends from the Inupiat Heritage Center at the rooftop of the world to the Aleutian World War II National Historic area located at Alaska's southern tip.	Closing	Park entrance fees vary throughout the state and are subject to change.

To Add a Heading and Introductory Paragraph Text

The following steps show how to add text to the Document window and insert blank lines between sections of text.

1

- Type the heading Alaska National Parks as shown in Table 1–1, and then press the ENTER key.

- Type the text of Part 1 as shown in Table 1–1, and then press the ENTER key (Figure 1–43).

Q&A What should I do if I make a typing error?

Press the BACKSPACE key to delete text you typed, or select the text and then press the DELETE key. Correct your typing mistakes the way you would in a word processing program.

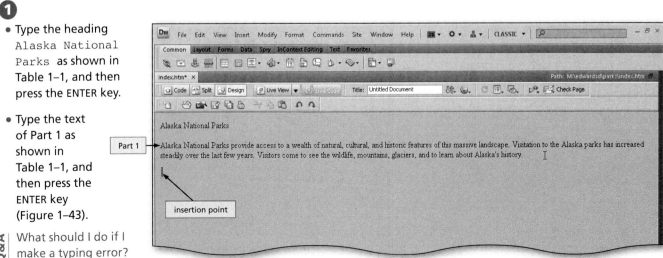

Figure 1–43

2

• Type the text of Part 2 as shown in Table 1–1 on the previous page, and then press the ENTER key to insert a blank line (Figure 1–44).

Q&A Why does my text wrap at different locations from those shown in Figure 1–44?

If your Dreamweaver window is maximized and the screen resolution is 1024 × 768, the text wraps in the same place. Otherwise, it might wrap at different places.

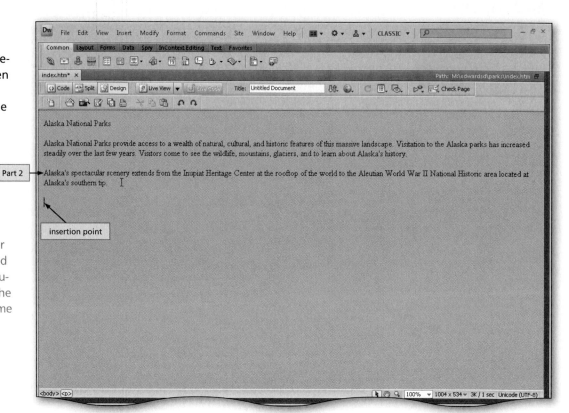

Figure 1–44

3

• Type the text of Part 3 as shown in Table 1–1, and then press the ENTER key to insert a blank line (Figure 1–45).

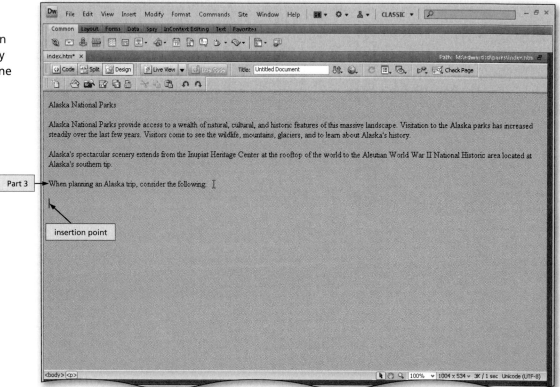

Figure 1–45

4

- Type the three items for the bulleted list as shown in Table 1–1. Press the ENTER key after each entry to insert space between the lines (Figure 1–46).

Q&A

When do I add bullets to the list?

You'll add bullets when you format the text in the next section of the chapter.

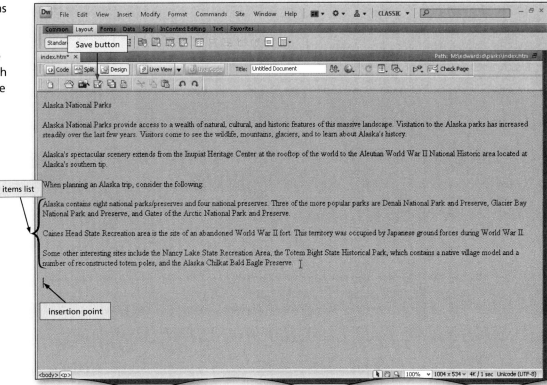

Figure 1–46

5

- Type the closing paragraph shown in Table 1–1, and then press the ENTER key to insert a blank line.

- Click the Save button on the Standard toolbar to save your work (Figure 1–47).

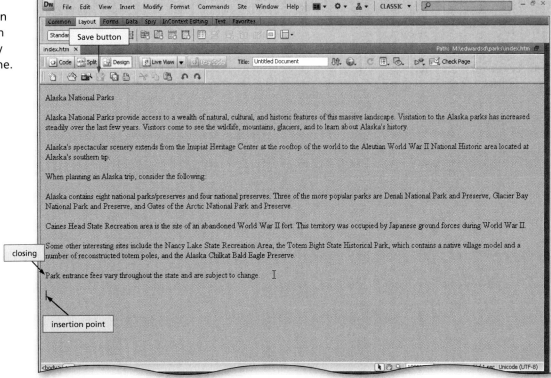

Figure 1–47

If you need to start over for any reason, Dreamweaver makes it easy to delete a Web page or other file. Save and close the page, display the panel groups by clicking the vertical bar expander arrow, click the name of the page you want to delete, right-click to display the context menu, point to Edit, and then point to and click Delete on the Edit submenu. Click the Yes button in the Dreamweaver caution dialog box to delete the page or the No button to cancel the action. You also can select a file and press the DELETE key. Dreamweaver will display a warning dialog box. If files are linked to other files, information will be displayed indicating how to update the links. To delete the file, click Yes in the dialog warning box or click No to cancel.

Formatting Features

The next step is to format the text on your Web page. **Formatting** means to change heading styles, insert special characters, and insert and/or modify other such elements that enhance the appearance of the Web page. Dreamweaver provides three options for formatting text: the Format menu on the Application bar, the Insert bar Text category, and the Property inspector. To format the text for the Alaska Parks index page, you use the text-related features of the Property inspector.

The Property inspector is one of the panels you will use most often when creating and formatting Web pages. The Property inspector initially displays the more commonly used attributes, or properties, of the selected object. The object can be a table, text, an image, or some other item. The Property inspector is context sensitive, so options within the Property inspector change relative to the selected object.

Property Inspector Features

Divided into two sections, the HTML Property inspector lets you see the current properties of the selected object and allows you to alter or edit them. You can click the expander arrow in the lower-right corner of the Property inspector to collapse the Property inspector to show only the more commonly used properties for the selected element or to expand the Property inspector to show more options (Figure 1–48).

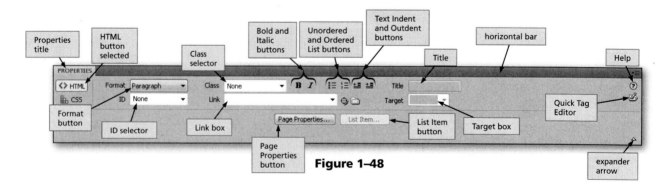

Figure 1–48

Collapsing/Hiding the Property Inspector

Having panels such as the Property inspector displayed in the Dreamweaver window requires considerable window space. If you are finished working with a panel, it generally is better to collapse it or close it. **Collapsing** it leaves the title bar in the window. Clicking the horizontal bar collapses and expands the Property inspector. Pressing CTRL+F3 also collapses/expands the Property inspector. **Closing** it removes the Property inspector from the Document window. To close the Property inspector, display the context menu by right-clicking the Properties title bar, and then selecting the Close Tab Group command. To open the Property inspector, click the Window menu and then click Properties.

The left side of the Property inspector contains two buttons: HTML and CSS. The majority of options for CSS are discussed in detail in Chapter 5. By default, the Property inspector displays the properties for text on a blank document. Most changes you make to properties are applied immediately in the Document window. For some properties, however, changes are not applied until you click outside the property-editing text fields, press the ENTER key, or press the TAB key to switch to another property. The following section describes the HTML-related features of the Property inspector (Figure 1–48).

Format   The **Format button** allows you to apply a Paragraph, Heading, or Preformatted style to the text. Clicking the Format button arrow displays a pop-up menu from which you can select a style.

The **Paragraph style** is the normal default style for text on a Web page. **Paragraph formatting** is the process of changing the appearance of text. **Heading styles** are used to create divisions and separate one segment of text from another. These formats are displayed based on how different browsers interpret the tags, offering little consistency and control over layout and appearance. When you apply a heading tag to text, Dreamweaver automatically adds the next line of text as a standard paragraph. You can use the **Preformatted style** when you do not want a Web browser to change the line of text in any way.

Class   Class displays the style that currently is applied to the selected text. If no styles have been applied to the selection, the pop-up menu shows None. If multiple styles have been applied to the selection, the menu is blank.

Bold and Italic   The **Bold button** and the **Italic button** allow you to format text using these two common font styles. Dreamweaver also supports a variety of other font styles, which are available through the Format menu Style command. To view these styles, click Format on the Application bar and then point to Style. The Style submenu contains a list of additional styles, such as Underline, Strikethrough, and Teletype.

Unordered List   Web developers often use a list to structure a page. An unordered list turns the selected paragraph or heading into an item in a bulleted list. If no text is selected before the **Unordered List button** is clicked, a new bulleted list is started. This command is also available through the HTML Property inspector and through the Application bar Format menu List command.

Ordered List   An ordered list is similar to an unordered list. This type of list, however, turns the selected paragraph or heading into an item in a numbered list. If no text is selected before the **Ordered List button** is clicked, a new numbered list is started. This command is also available through the HTML Property inspector and through the Application bar Format menu List command.

Definition List   A definition list is composed of items followed by an indented description, such as a glossary list. This command is available through the Application bar Format menu List command.

Indent and Outdent   To set off a block quote, you can use the Indent feature. The **Text Indent button** will indent a line or a paragraph from both margins. In XHTML and HTML, this is the blockquote tag. The **Text Outdent button** removes the indentation from the selected text by removing the blockquote tag. In a list, indenting creates a nested list, and removing the indentation removes the nesting from the list. A **nested list** is one list inside another list and is not the same as the block quote created by the Indent feature.

Title   Specifies the text ScreenTip for a hypertext link.

ID   Identifies the content of an element with a unique name; used to select an ID from any linked or external CSS style sheet. CSS style sheets are covered in Chapter 5.

Link   The **Link (Hyperlink) box** allows you to make selected text or other objects a hyperlink to a specified URL or Web page. To use the Property inspector to select the URL or Web page, you can (a) click the Point to File or Browse for File icon to the right of the Link box to browse to a page in your Web site and select the file name, (b) type the URL, or (c) drag a file from the Files panel into the Link box. Links are covered in detail in Chapter 2. The Insert menu on the Application bar also contains a Hyperlink option.

Target   In the **Target pop-up menu box**, you specify the frame or window in which the linked page should load. If you are using frames, the names of all the frames in the current document are displayed in the list. If the specified frame does not exist when the current document is opened in a browser, the linked page loads in a new window with the name you specified. Once this window exists, other files can be targeted to it.

Page Properties   Clicking the Page Properties button on the Property inspector or the Properties command on the Modify menu opens the Page Properties dialog box.

List Item   If the selected text is part of a list, click the List Item button to set list properties for the text, such as the type of bullet or the starting number.

Applying Text-Related Features

The text for your Web page is displayed in the Document window. The next step in creating your Web page is to format this text. You use commands from the Property inspector and the Format menu on the Application bar to format the text.

Within Dreamweaver, you can format text before you type, or you can apply new formats after you type. If you have used word processing software, you will find many of the Dreamweaver formatting commands similar to the commands within a word processing program. At this point, your Web page contains only text, so the Property inspector displays attributes related to text.

To set block formatting, such as formatting a heading or an unordered list, position the insertion point in the line or paragraph and then format the text.

Text Headings

Just as in a word processing document, designers use the heading structure in a Web page to set apart document or section titles. The six levels of HTML headings are Heading 1 through Heading 6. **Heading 1 <h1>** produces the largest text and **Heading 6 <h6>** the smallest. By default, browsers will display the six heading levels in the same font, with the point size decreasing as the importance of the heading decreases.

To Format Text with the Heading 1 Style

The following steps show how to format the heading.

1

• Click Window on the Application bar, and then click Properties to display the Property inspector.

• If necessary, scroll up and then position the insertion point anywhere in the heading text, Alaska National Parks (Figure 1–49).

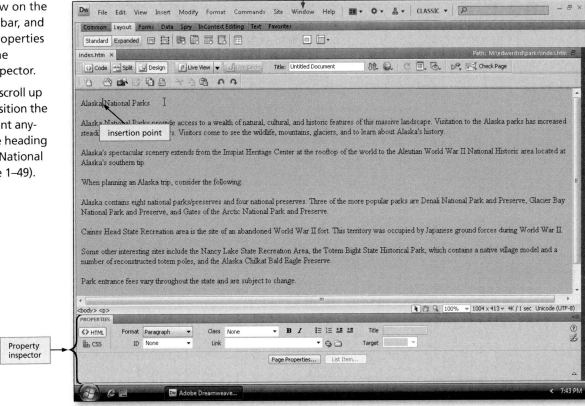

Figure 1–49

2

• Click the Format button arrow in the Property inspector, and then point to Heading 1 (Figure 1–50).

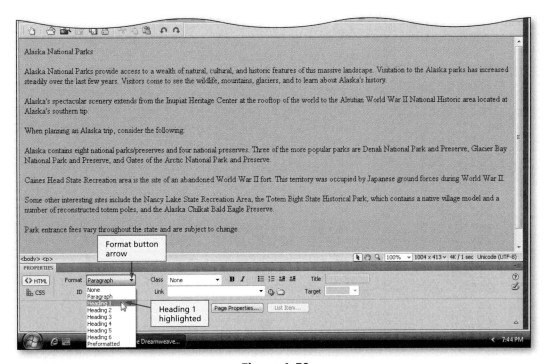

Figure 1–50

- Click Heading 1 to apply the Heading 1 style to the Alaska National Parks title text (Figure 1–51).

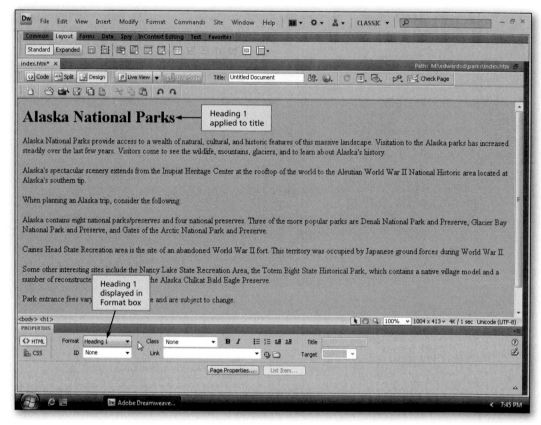

Figure 1–51

Centering Text

Using the Center command on the Align submenu on the Format menu allows you to center text. This command is very similar to the Center command or button in a word-processing program. To center a single line or a paragraph, position the mouse pointer anywhere in the line or paragraph, and then click the Format menu on the Application bar, point to Align, and then click Center to center the text. You do not need to select a single line or single paragraph to center it. To center more than one paragraph at a time, however, you must select all paragraphs.

To Center the Web Page Heading

The following steps illustrate how to center the heading.

1

- If necessary, click anywhere in the heading, Alaska National Parks.

- Click the Format menu on the Application bar, point to Align, and then point to Center (Figure 1–52).

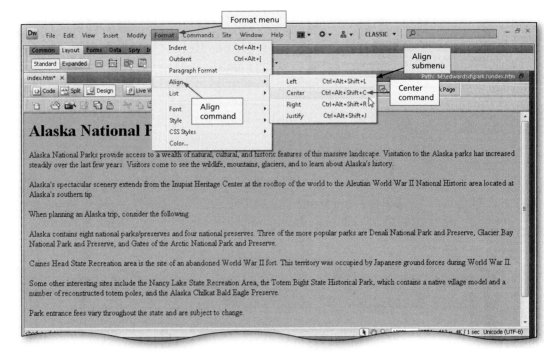

Figure 1–52

2

- Click Center on the Align submenu to center the heading. (Figure 1–53).

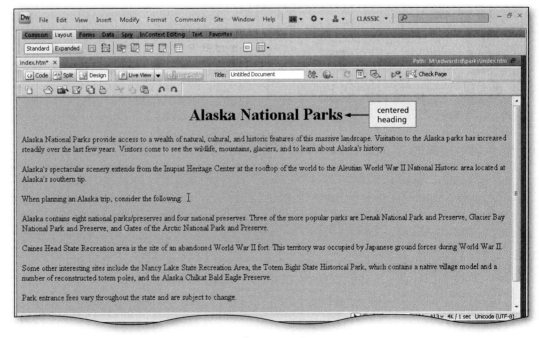

Figure 1–53

Other Ways

1. Right-click selected text, point to Align on context menu, click Center on Align submenu
2. Press CTRL+ALT+SHIFT+C

Types of Lists

Lists
You can remove the bullets or numbers from a formatted list just as easily as you added them. Select the formatted list, and then click the button in the Property inspector that you originally used to apply the formatting.

One way to group and organize information is by using lists. Web pages can have three types of lists: ordered (numbered), unordered (bulleted), and definition. Ordered **lists** contain text preceded by numbered steps. Unordered lists contain text preceded by bullets (dots or other symbols) or image bullets. You use an unordered list if the items need not be listed in any particular order. **Definition lists** do not use leading characters such as bullet points or numbers. Glossaries and descriptions often use this type of list.

The Unordered List and Ordered List buttons are available in the Property inspector. You can access the Definition List command through the Application bar List command submenu. Through the List Properties dialog box, you can set the number style, reset the count, or set the bullet style options for individual list items or for the entire list. To access the List Properties dialog box, click anywhere in the list, and then click the List Item button in the Property inspector.

You can create a new list or you can create a list using existing text. When you select existing text and add bullets, the blank lines between the list items are deleted. Later in this chapter, you add line breaks to reinsert a blank line between each list item.

To Create an Unordered List

The following steps show how to create an unordered list using existing text.

1

- Click to the left of the line, Alaska contains eight national parks/preserves and four national preserves.

- Drag to select the text, Alaska contains eight national parks/preserves and four national preserves. Three of the more popular parks are Denali National Park and Preserve, Glacier Bay National Park and Preserve, and Gates of the Arctic National Park and Preserve, and the next two paragraphs (Figure 1–54).

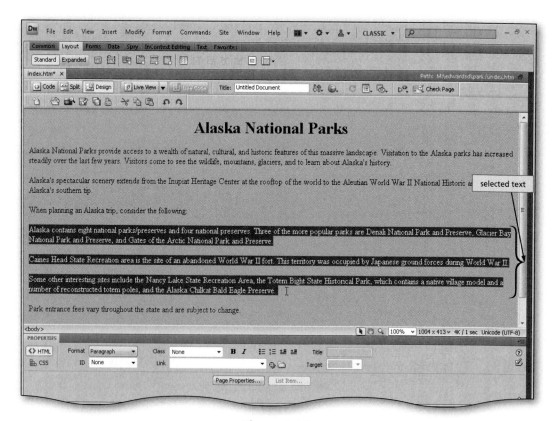

Figure 1–54

2

- Click the Unordered List button to indent and to add a bullet to each line (Figure 1–55).

Q&A How do I start a list with a different number or letter?

In the Document window, place the insertion point in the text of a list item you want to affect and then click the Format menu, point to List, and click Properties. In the List Properties dialog box, select the options you want to define.

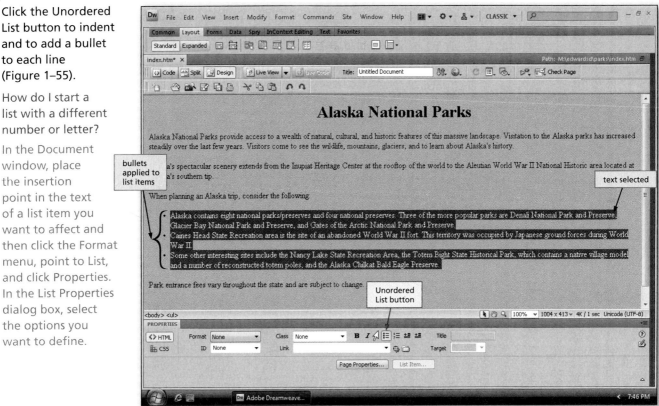

Figure 1–55

Other Ways

1. On Format menu point to List, click Unordered List on List submenu

2. Select text, right-click, point to List, click Unordered List on List submenu

Bold Formatting

Other text formatting options are applying bold or italic styles to text. **Bold** characters are displayed somewhat thicker and darker than those that are not bold. **Italic** characters slant to the right. The Property inspector contains buttons for both bold and italic font styles. To bold text within Dreamweaver is a simple procedure. If you have used word processing software, you are familiar with this process. You italicize text in a similar way.

To Bold Text

The following step illustrates how to emphasize the bulleted items by applying bold formatting.

1

- If necessary, drag to select all of the lines of the bulleted points.

- Click the Bold button in the Property inspector to bold the selected text, and then click anywhere in the Document window to deselect the text (Figure 1–56).

Q&A

What other types of formatting can I apply to text?

To select fonts, apply underlining, colors, and other attributes to text, you can use the commands and submenus on the Format menu. Chapter 5 also explains how to use CSS to format text.

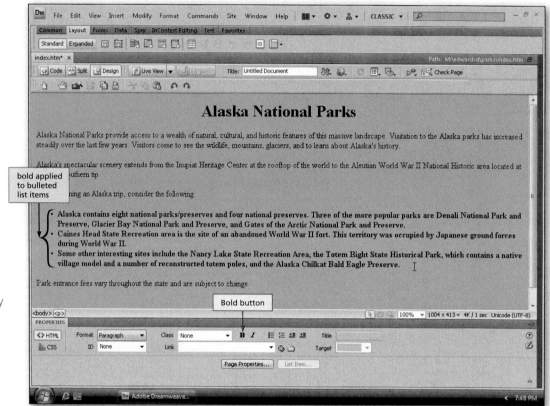

Figure 1–56

Understanding Line Breaks

When you added bullets to the items list earlier in this chapter, the blank line between each item was removed. Removing the blank line between items is a result of how Dreamweaver interprets the HTML code. A blank line between the bulleted items, however, will provide better spacing and readability when viewing the Web page in a browser. You can add blank lines in several ways. You might assume that pressing the ENTER key at the end of each line would be the quickest way to accomplish this. Pressing the ENTER key, however, adds another bullet. The easiest way to accomplish the task of adding blank lines is to insert line breaks. Recall that the line break starts a new single line without inserting a blank line between lines of text. Inserting two line breaks, however, adds a single blank line.

Dreamweaver provides a Line Break command through the Insert HTML Special Characters submenu. It is easier, however, to use the SHIFT+ENTER keyboard shortcut.

To Add a Line Break

The following steps show how to add a blank line between each of the bulleted items.

- Click at the end of the first bulleted item.

- Press SHIFT+ENTER two times to insert a blank line (Figure 1–57).

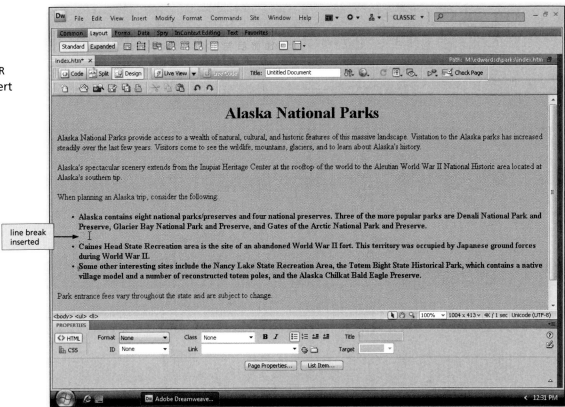

Figure 1–57

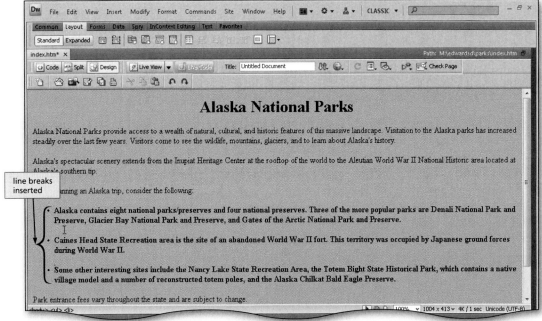

- Press SHIFT+ENTER two times at the end of the second bulleted item to insert a blank line between the second and third bulleted list items (Figure 1–58).

Figure 1–58

To Add Your Name and Date

When creating a Web document, it is a good idea to add your name and date to the document. Insert a single line break between your name and the date. The following steps show how to add this information to the page.

- If necessary, scroll down to display the closing paragraph. Click at the end of the closing paragraph.

- Press the ENTER key to move the insertion point to the next paragraph (Figure 1–59).

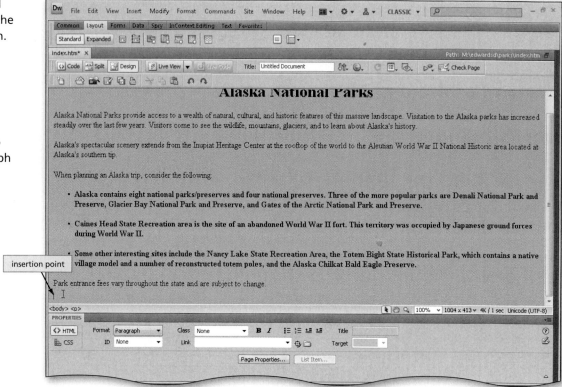

Figure 1–59

- Type your name and then press SHIFT+ENTER to move the insertion point to the next line.

- Type the current date and then press the ENTER key to add your name and the current date to the Web page (Figure 1–60).

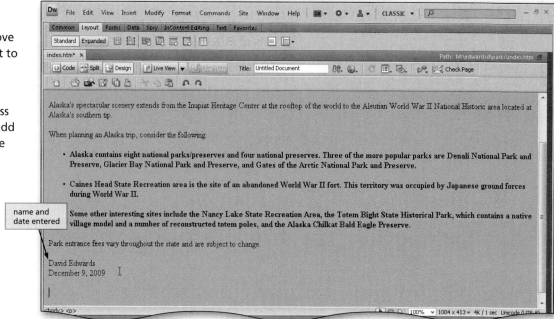

Figure 1–60

Final Tasks

Before completing a Web page, perform the following tasks to make sure it is ready for others to view:

- Give your Web page a title.

- Consider enhancements such as special characters to make the page look professional.

- Check the spelling and proofread the text.

- Preview the page in one or more browsers so you can see how it looks when others open it.

Plan
Ahead

Web Page Titles

A **Web page title** helps Web site visitors keep track of what they are viewing as they browse. It is important to give your Web page an appropriate title. When visitors to your Web page create bookmarks or add the Web page to their Favorites lists, the title is used for the reference. If you do not title a page, the page will be displayed in the browser window, Favorites lists, and history lists as Untitled Document. Because many search engines use the Web page title, it is important to use a creative and meaningful name. Giving the document a file name when saving it is not the same as giving the page a title.

BTW

Keep Data Confidential
Web pages reach a global audience. Therefore, to limit access to certain kinds of information, avoid including any confidential data on your Web pages. In particular, do not include your home address, telephone number, or other personal information.

To Change the Web Page Title

The following step shows how to change the name of the Web page to Alaska National Parks.

1

- Drag to select the text, Untitled Document, in the Title text box on the Document toolbar.

- Type Alaska National Parks in the Title text box and then press the ENTER key (Figure 1–61).

- Click the Save button on the Standard toolbar to save the document.

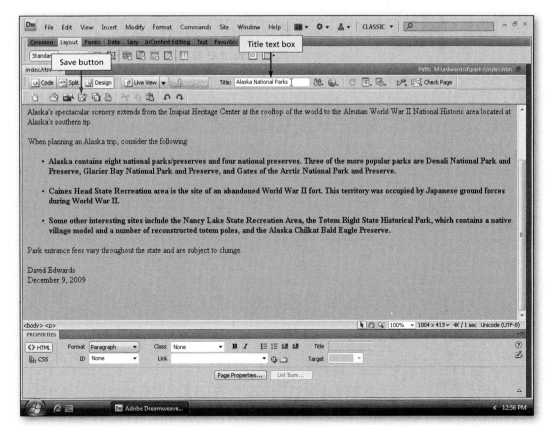

Figure 1–61

Other Web Page Enhancements

Dreamweaver includes many other features that you can use to enhance your Web page. Some of the more commonly used enhancements that you may want to apply to a Web page are special characters.

Special Characters

Sometimes it is necessary to enter non-alphanumeric characters such as quotation marks and ampersands as well as non-keyboard symbols like trademarks and registrations into a Web page. To have the browser display these special characters requires a character code. **Character entities**, another name for character codes, allow a browser to show special characters. HTML represents these codes by a name (named entity) or a number (numbered entity). Both types of entities begin with an ampersand (&) and end with a semicolon (;). HTML includes entity names for characters such as the copyright symbol (©), the ampersand (&), and the registered trademark symbol (®). Some entities, such as the left and right quotation marks, include a number sign (#) and a numeric equivalent (such as —). Table 1–2 contains a list of HTML entities supported by Dreamweaver. To add an entity to your Web page, you click Insert on the Application bar, point to HTML, point to Special Characters on the HTML submenu, and then click the entity name on the Special Characters submenu.

Table 1–2 Character Entities		
Name	**Description**	**HTML Tags and Character Entities**
Nonbreaking Space	Places a nonbreaking space at the insertion point	&#nbsp;
Left Quote	Places an opening, curved double quotation mark at the insertion point	&#147;
Right Quote	Places a closing, curved double quotation mark at the insertion point	&#148;
Em Dash	Places an em dash at the insertion point	&#151;
Pound	Places a pound (currency) symbol at the insertion point	&pound;
Euro	Places a euro (currency) symbol at the insertion point	&euro;
Yen	Places a yen (currency) symbol at the insertion point	&yen;
Copyright	Places a copyright symbol at the insertion point	&copy;
Registered Trademark	Places a registered trademark symbol at the insertion point	&reg;
Trademark	Places a trademark symbol at the insertion point	&#153;
Other Characters	Provides a set of special characters from which to select	Other ASCII characters select

Check Spelling

After you create a Web page, you should check it visually for spelling errors. In addition, you can use Dreamweaver's Check Spelling command to identify possible misspellings. The Check Spelling command ignores HTML tags and attributes. Recall from the Introduction that attributes are additional information contained within an HTML tag.

To Check Spelling

The following steps show how to use the Check Spelling command to spell check your entire document. Your Web page may contain different misspelled words depending on the accuracy of your typing.

1

- Click at the beginning of the document.

- Click Commands on the Application bar and then point to Check Spelling (Figure 1–62).

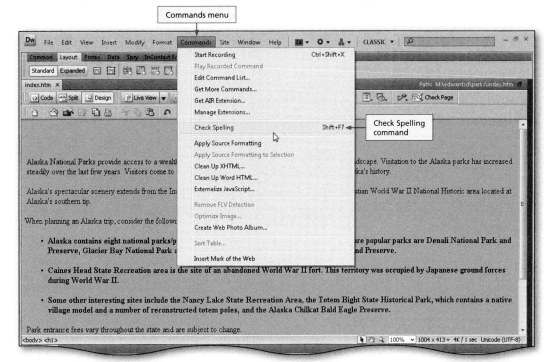

Figure 1–62

2

- Click Check Spelling to display the Check Spelling dialog box.

- The Dreamweaver spelling checker displays the word, Inupiat, in the Word not found in dictionary text box. Suggestions for the correct spelling are displayed in the Suggestions list (Figure 1–63).

Q&A

Does Dreamweaver contain a dictionary with American/ British spelling options?

Yes. Dreamweaver contains 15 different spelling option dictionaries, including English (British) and English (Canadian). Access the dictionaries by clicking the Preferences command on the Edit menu, selecting the General category, and then clicking the Spelling dictionary pop-up menu arrow.

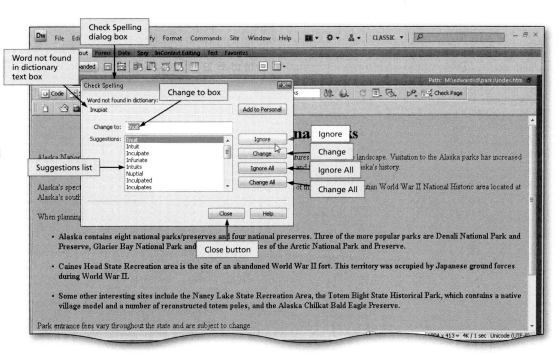

Figure 1–63

3

- The word is spelled correctly, so click the Ignore button to continue with the spell checking.

- Continue to check the spelling and, as necessary, correct any misspelled word by accepting the suggested replacement, by clicking the Change or Change All buttons, or by typing the correct word in the Change to text box. Click Ignore when proper names are displayed as errors.

- Click the OK button and then press CTRL+S to save any changes.

Before you can share your Web page with the world, you must select browsers to ensure your visitors can view the page properly. The two more popular browsers are Internet Explorer and Firefox.

Previewing a Web Page in a Browser

After you have created a Web page, it is a good practice to test your Web page by previewing it in Web browsers to ensure that it displays correctly. Using this strategy helps you catch errors so you will not copy or repeat them.

As you create your Web page, you should be aware of the variety of available Web browsers. More than 25 different Web browsers are in use, most of which have been released in more than one version. Most Web developers target recent versions of Microsoft Internet Explorer and Mozilla Firefox, which the majority of Web visitors use. You also should know that visitors viewing your Web page might have earlier versions of these browsers. You can define up to 20 browsers for previewing. In this book, browsers are defined for Internet Explorer and Firefox.

Selecting a Browser

The browser preferences are selected in the Preferences dialog box. This dialog box provides options to select and define the settings for a primary and a secondary browser. Additionally, a Preview using temporary file option is available. When the check box for this option is checked, you can preview a page without first having to save the page. Although it is a good practice to save before previewing in a browser, occasions will arise when you want to view a page before saving it.

To Select Primary and Secondary Target Browsers

The following steps show how to select your target browsers — Internet Explorer and Firefox. To complete these steps requires that you have both Internet Explorer and Firefox installed on your computer. Note, however, that it is not necessary to install a secondary browser. If your choice is to use just one browser, you can choose to install the one you would like to use. Or, you can choose to install additional browsers as well.

- Click Edit on the Application bar and then point to Preferences.

- Click Preferences and then, if necessary, click the Preview in Browser category in the Preferences dialog box (Figure 1–64).

Q&A What is the primary browser?

The primary browser was selected when Dreamweaver was installed on your computer. In this book, the primary browser is Internet Explorer. The browser name, IExplore, was selected automatically during the Dreamweaver installation. The browser name on your computer may be different.

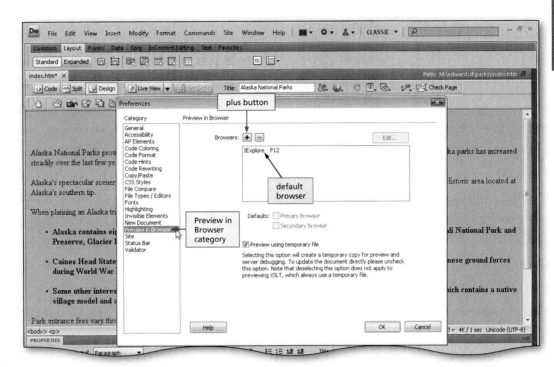

Figure 1–64

- Click the plus (+) button in the Preview in Browser area to display the Add Browser dialog box (Figure 1–65).

Q&A What should I do if the Preview in Browser dialog box already lists Firefox and IExplore?

Skip Steps 2 through 5. Click Firefox in the Preview in Browser dialog box, and then click the Secondary browser check box. Click the OK button to set Internet Explorer as the primary browser and Firefox as the secondary browser.

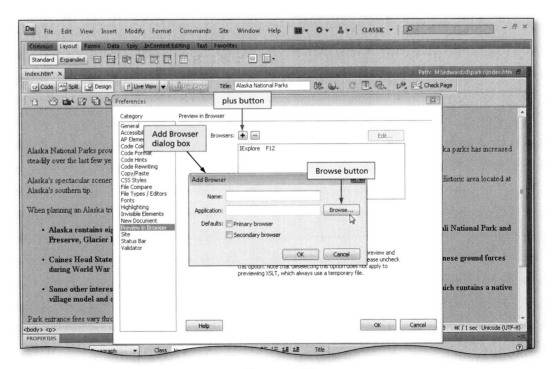

Figure 1–65

3

• Click the Browse button and then locate the Firefox file. Most likely this file is located on Local Drive (C:). Use the following path to locate the file: C:Program Files\Mozilla Firefox\firefox. The path and file name on your computer may be different.

• Click the Open button to add the browser name and path to the Add Browser dialog box (Figure 1–66).

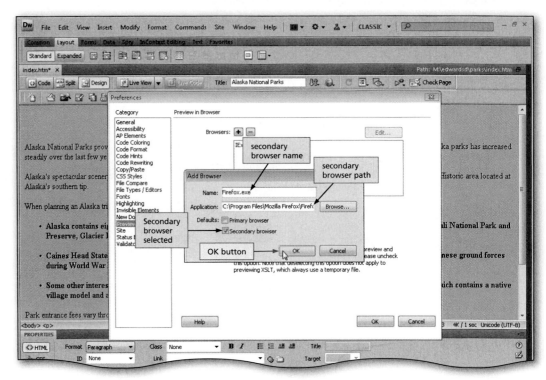

Figure 1–66

4

• If necessary, click the Secondary browser check box to select it. The Name text box displays Firefox. exe. The Application text box displays the path and file name. The path and spelling of Firefox on your computer may be different from those shown.

• Click the OK button to add Firefox as the secondary browser.

• If necessary, click the Preview using temporary file check box to select it (Figure 1–67).

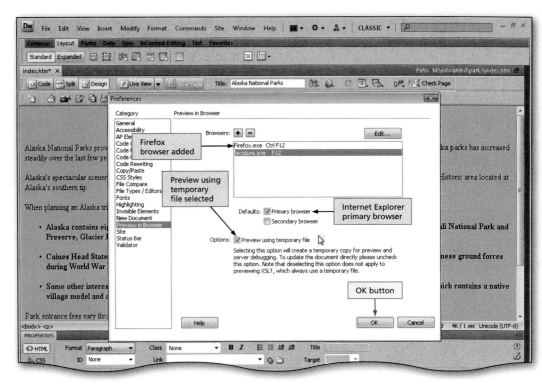

Figure 1–67

5

• Click the OK button. If a Dreamweaver CS4 dialog box appears, click the OK button.

Previewing a Web Page

With the target browsers set up, you can preview your Web pages in the browsers at any time. You do not have to save the document first.

To Preview the Web Page

The following steps illustrate how to preview a Web page.

- Click File on the Application bar, point to Preview in Browser, and then click to select IExplore or your selected browser name.

- If necessary, maximize your browser window (Figure 1–68).

- Click the Internet Explorer Close button.

- Click File on the Application bar and then point to Preview in Browser.

- Click Firefox.exe on the Preview in Browser submenu.

- Click the Firefox Close button.

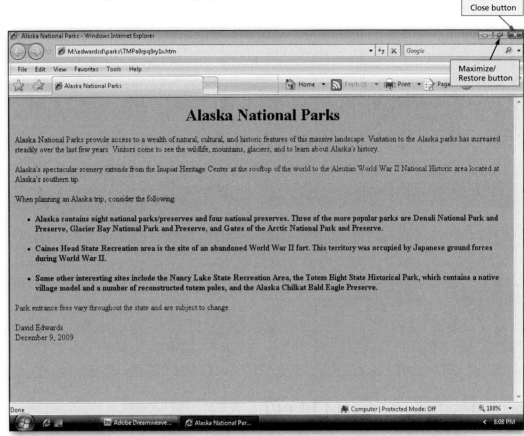

Figure 1–68

Other Ways

1. Press F12 to display primary browser

2. Press CTRL+F12 to display secondary browser

Printing a Web Page

You may want to print a Web page for a variety of reasons. Interestingly, Dreamweaver provides an option to print code, but does not provide an option to print Design view. To print a Web page, you first must preview it in a browser. Printing a page from your browser is similar to printing a word processing document.

To Print a Web Page

The following steps illustrate how to print the Web page in a browser.

- Press F12 to display the page in your primary browser.

- Point to the Print button on the Internet Explorer toolbar (Figure 1–69).

- Click the Print arrow on the Internet Explorer toolbar, and then click Print.

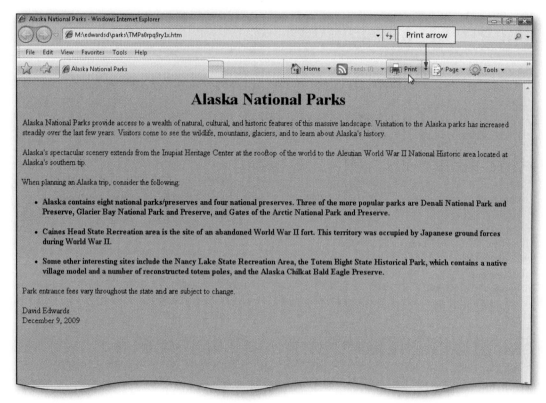

Figure 1–69

- The Print dialog box is displayed. Select an appropriate printer and click the Print button to send your Web page to the printer (Figure 1–70).

- Retrieve your printout.

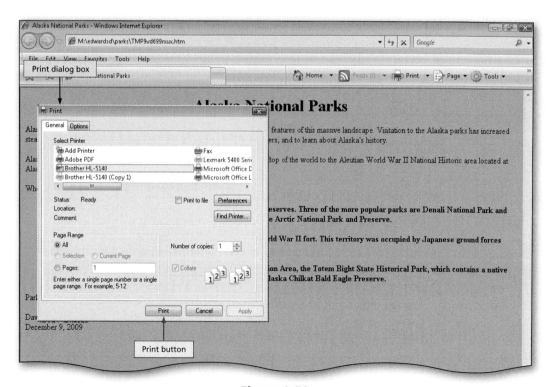

Figure 1–70

Dreamweaver Help System

Reference materials and other forms of assistance are available using the Dreamweaver Help system. You can display these documents, print them, or download them as a PDF file. All of the Dreamweaver CS4 Help is available online. Click Help on the Application bar, and then select one of the commands listed in Table 1–3, or press the F1 key. Your default Web browser starts and opens the main Help page on the Adobe Web site. Appendix A provides detailed instructions on using Dreamweaver Help.

Table 1–3 Dreamweaver Help System

Command	Description
Dreamweaver Help	Starts your default Web browser and displays the Dreamweaver online help system at the Adobe Web site. You can search for help or download a PDF file containing the program's documentation.
Reference	Opens the Reference panel, a searchable guide to HTML tags, Cascading Style Sheets, and JavaScript commands.
Dreamweaver Support Center	Opens the online Dreamweaver Support Center Web page in your browser. This page is part of the Adobe Web site and offers technical support for known bugs or common questions, downloadable updates to the program, and a link to online forums.

Disabling the Welcome Screen and Quitting Dreamweaver

After you create, save, preview, and print the Alaska Parks Web page and review how to use Help, your work in Chapter 1 is complete.

To Disable the Welcome Screen, Close the Web Site, and Quit Dreamweaver

The following steps show how to disable the Welcome screen, close the Web page, quit Dreamweaver CS4, and return control to Windows.

- Click Edit on the Application bar and then click Preferences.

- If necessary, click General in the Category column.

- Click the Show Welcome Screen check box under Document options to deselect it, and then click the OK button.

- Click the Close button in the upper-right corner of the Dreamweaver window to close Dreamweaver.

Other Ways
1. On File menu, click Exit
2. Press CTRL+Q

Starting Dreamweaver and Opening a Web Page

Opening an existing Web page in Dreamweaver is much the same as opening an existing document in most other software applications: that is, you use the File menu and Open command. In addition to this common method to open a Web page, Dreamweaver provides other options. The Dreamweaver File menu also contains the Open Recent command. Pointing to this command displays the Open Recent submenu, which contains a list of the 10 most recently opened files. Additionally, if you want to display the page on which you currently are working when you next open Dreamweaver, you can select the Reopen Documents on Startup command from the Open Recent submenu.

If the page you want to open is part of a Dreamweaver Web site, you can open the file from the Files panel. To open a Web page from the Files panel, you first must select the appropriate Web site. The Files pop-up menu in the Files panel lists sites you have defined. When you open the site, a list of the pages and subfolders within the site is displayed. To open the page you want, double-click the file name. After opening the page, you can modify text, images, tables, and any other elements.

Earlier in this chapter, you disabled the Welcome screen. The next time you open Dreamweaver, therefore, the Welcome screen will not be displayed. Instead, a blank window is displayed, requiring that you open an existing document or open a new document. Dreamweaver provides four options to open a new Document window:

- Click File on the Application bar, click New, and then select Blank Page
- Press CTRL+N and then select Blank Page
- Select the site's root folder, right-click, and then click New File on the context menu
- Click the Files panel Options menu, point to File on the pop-up menu, and then click the New File command

The first two options display the New Document dialog box. From this dialog box, you select the Blank Page category and the HTML page type and then click the Create button. When you select the third or fourth option, a default untitled file is created in the Files panel.

Chapter Summary

Chapter 1 introduced you to starting Dreamweaver, defining a Web site, and creating a Web page. You added an image background and used Dreamweaver's Property inspector to format text. You also learned how to use an unordered list to organize information. You added line breaks and learned about special characters. Once your Web page was completed, you learned how to save the Web page and preview it in a browser. You also learned how to print using the browser. To enhance your knowledge of Dreamweaver further, you learned the basics about the Dreamweaver Help system. The following tasks are all the new Dreamweaver skills you learned in this chapter, listed in the same order they were presented in the chapter. For a list of keyboard commands for topics introduced in this chapter, see the Quick Reference for Windows at the back of this book and refer to the Shortcut column.

1. Start Dreamweaver (DW 36)
2. Display the Standard Toolbar, Change the Icon Colors, and Close and Open Panels (DW 43)
3. Use Site Definition to Create a Local Web Site (DW 47)
4. Copy Data Files to the Local Web Site (DW 52)
5. Hide the Rulers, Change the .html Default, and Save a Document as a Web Page (DW 56)
6. Add a Background Image to the Index Page (DW 60)
7. Hide the Panel Groups (DW 62)
8. Add a Heading and Introductory Paragraph Text (DW 63)
9. Format Text with the Heading 1 Style (DW 69)
10. Center the Web Page Heading (DW 71)
11. Create an Unordered List (DW 72)
12. Bold Text (DW 74)
13. Add a Line Break (DW 75)
14. Add Your Name and Date (DW 76)
15. Change the Web Page Title (DW 77)
16. Check Spelling (DW 79)
17. Select Primary and Secondary Target Browsers (DW 81)
18. Preview the Web Page (DW 83)
19. Print a Web Page (DW 84)
20. Disable the Welcome Screen, Close the Web Site, and Quit Dreamweaver (DW 87)

Learn It Online

Test your knowledge of chapter content and key terms.

Instructions: To complete the Learn It Online exercises, start your browser, click the Address bar, and then enter the Web address `scsite.com/dwCS4/learn`. When the Dreamweaver CS4 Learn It Online page is displayed, click the link for the exercise you want to complete and then read the instructions.

Chapter Reinforcement TF, MC, and SA
A series of true/false, multiple choice, and short answer questions that test your knowledge of the chapter content.

Flash Cards
An interactive learning environment where you identify chapter key terms associated with displayed definitions.

Practice Test
A series of multiple choice questions that test your knowledge of chapter content and key terms.

Who Wants To Be a Computer Genius?
An interactive game that challenges your knowledge of chapter content in the style of a television quiz show.

Wheel of Terms
An interactive game that challenges your knowledge of chapter key terms in the style of the television show *Wheel of Fortune*.

Crossword Puzzle Challenge
A crossword puzzle that challenges your knowledge of key terms presented in the chapter.

Apply Your Knowledge

Reinforce the skills and apply the concepts you learned in this chapter.

Adding Text and Formatting a Web Page

Instructions: In this activity, you modify a Web page by adding a background image, changing the heading style, adding bullets, and centering text (Figure 1–71). To use Dreamweaver effectively, it is necessary to create a new site. Make sure you have downloaded the data files for Chapter01\apply.

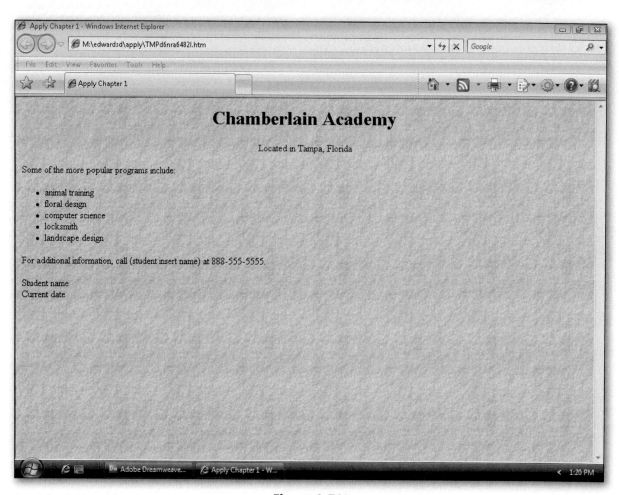

Figure 1–71

Perform the following tasks:

1. Start Dreamweaver. Use Site Definition to define a Local site under the *your name* folder. Name the site Apply Exercises.

2. In the Local root folder text box, create a new subfolder under the *your name* folder and name the subfolder apply. In the Default images folder, create a new subfolder and name the folder images.

3. Copy the apply.htm data file from the Chapter01\apply data files folder into your local Web site apply folder and the apply_bkg.jpg image into your apply\images folder.

4. Open the apply.htm page. If necessary, expand the Property inspector. Verify that the HTML button is selected on the left side of the Property inspector.

5. Click the Page Properties button and apply the background image to the Web page.

6. Apply the Heading 1 style to the first line of text.

7. Select the first two lines. Use the Format menu Align command to center the lines.

8. Select the list of items (beginning with animal training and ending with landscape design) and create an unordered list by applying bullets.

9. Click at the end of the last line and press Enter.

10. Add your name, insert a line break, and then add the current date. Title the document Apply Chapter 1.

11. Save your document and then view it in your browser. Submit it in the format specified by your instructor.

Extend Your Knowledge

Extend the skills you learned in this chapter and experiment with new skills. You may need to use Help to complete the assignment.

Adding Text and Formatting a Web Page

Instructions: In this activity, you modify a Web page by adding a background image, inserting line breaks, centering text, and checking spelling (Figure 1–72). To use Dreamweaver effectively, it is necessary to create a new site. Make sure you have downloaded the data files for Chapter01\extend.

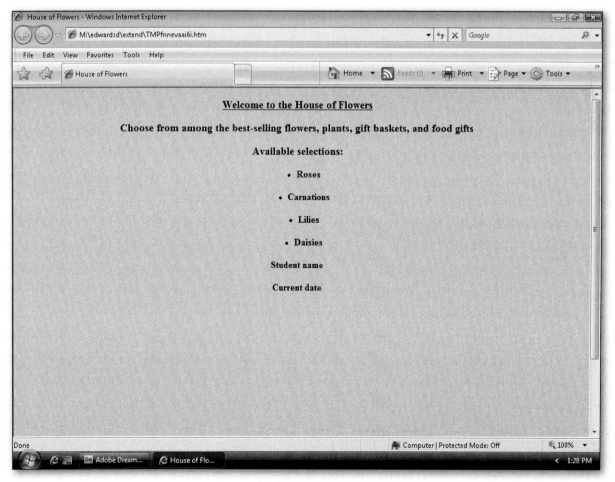

Figure 1–72

Continued >

Extend Your Knowledge *continued*

Perform the following tasks:

1. Start Dreamweaver. Use Site Definition to define a Local site under the *your name* folder. Name the site Extend Exercises.

2. In the Local root folder text box, create a new subfolder under the *your name* folder and name the subfolder extend. In the extend folder, create a subfolder named images. Copy the extend.htm data file from the Chapter01\extend folder into the Extend Exercises Web site extend folder and the extend_bkg.gif image into your extend\images folder.

3. Open the extend.htm page. If necessary, expand the Property inspector. Verify that the HTML button on the left side of the Property inspector is selected.

4. Click the Page Properties button and apply the background image to the Web page.

5. Type your name and the current date where indicated.

6. Apply the Heading 3 style to the first three lines.

7. On the Format menu, use the Underline command on the Style submenu to underline the first line.

8. Select the next four lines containing the names of flowers and bullet the text. Insert a blank line between each of the bulleted items.

9. Center all of the text. Bold the bulleted list, your name, and the date.

10. Title the document House of Flowers.

11. Click the Commands menu and then click Check Spelling. Correct all spelling errors.

12. Save your document and then view it in your browser. Submit it in the format specified by your instructor.

Make It Right

In this activity, you analyze a document, correct all errors, and/or improve the design.

Adding Text and Formatting a Web Page

Instructions: In this activity, you modify an existing Web page by formatting and adjusting text and adding data (Figure 1–73). To use Dreamweaver effectively, it is necessary to create a new site. Make sure you have downloaded the data files for Chapter01\right.

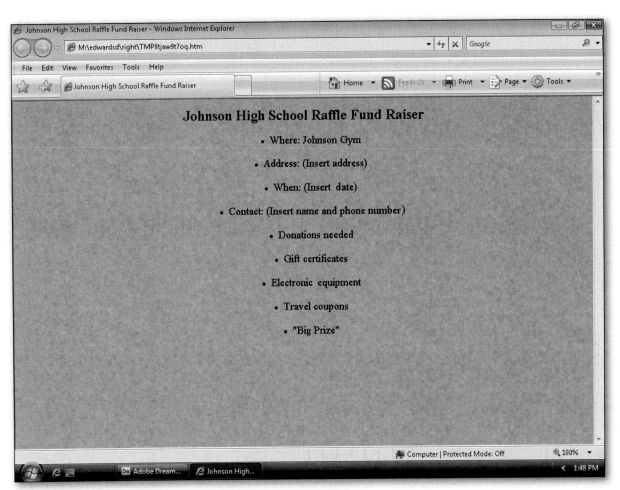

Figure 1–73

Perform the following tasks:

1. Start Dreamweaver. Use Site Definition to define a Local site under the *your name* folder. Name the site Right Exercises.

2. In the Local root folder text box, create a new subfolder under the *your name* folder and name the subfolder right. In the right folder, create a subfolder named images. Copy the right.htm data file for Chapter01\right into *your name* right folder and the right_bkg.jpg image into your right\ images folder.

3. Open the right.htm page. If necessary, expand the Property inspector. Verify that HTML is selected in the Property inspector.

4. Apply the background image to the Web page. Select and center the title. Apply the Heading 2 format.

5. Select the rest of the text and add bullets. Bold the bulleted text. Center the text and add a blank line between each item.

6. Insert an address, date, and your name and school phone number where indicated.

7. Add a title: Johnson High School Raffle Fund Raiser.

8. Save your document and then view it in your browser. Submit it in the format specified by your instructor.

In the Lab

Create a document using the guidelines, concepts, and skills presented in this chapter. Labs are listed in order of increasing difficulty.

Lab 1: Creating a Mobile Pet Services Web Site

Problem: After watching his mobile pet service grow, Bryan asks for your help creating a Web page describing his services. He asks you to assist him in preparing a Web site to list his activities and promote his mission statement.

Define a Web site and create and format a Web page for Bryan's Mobile Pet Service. The Web page as it is displayed in a browser is shown in Figure 1–74. The text for the Web site is shown in Table 1–4.

Software and hardware settings determine how a Web page is displayed in a browser. Your Web pages may display differently in your browser than the pages shown in the figure.

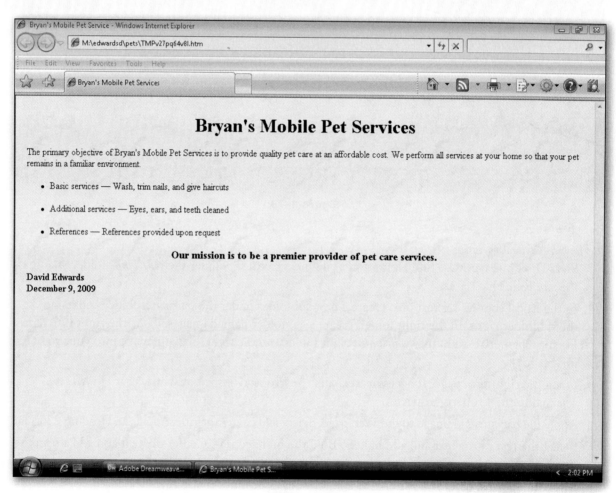

Figure 1–74

Table 1–4 Bryan's Mobile Pet Service

Section	Web Page Text
Heading	Bryan's Mobile Pet Services
Introductory paragraph	The primary objective of Bryan's Mobile Pet Services is to provide quality pet care at an affordable cost. We perform all services at your home so that your pet remains in a familiar environment.
List Item 1	Basic services — Wash, trim nails, and give haircuts
List Item 2	Additional services — Eyes, ears, and teeth cleaned
List Item 3	References — References provided upon request
Closing	Our mission is to be a premier provider of pet care services.

Perform the following tasks:

1. In Dreamweaver, click Site on the Application bar, click New Site, and use the Site Definition Advanced tab to create a local Web site under the *your name* folder. In the Site Definition Site name text box, name the site Pet Services. In the Local root folder text box, create a new subfolder under the *your name* folder, and name the new subfolder pets. The path will be M:*your name*\pets (substitute your name and the drive letter of the drive on which you are saving your files). In the Default images folder text box, create a new subfolder and name the folder images. The path will be M:*your name*\pets\images.

2. Copy the data file image (pets_bkg.jpg) to your pets\images folder.

3. Click File on the Application bar and then click New. Click Blank Page and HTML, verify that <none> is selected under Layout, and then click Create. Use the Save As command on the File menu to save the page with the name index.

4. Click the Modify menu and then click Page Properties. Apply the background image (located in the images folder) to the index page.

5. Type the Web page text shown in Table 1–4. Press the ENTER key after typing the text in each section and after each one of the list items in the table. The em dash, used in the three list items, is an HTML object. To insert the em dash, click the Insert menu, point to HTML, point to Special Characters, and then click Em-Dash.

6. Select the heading text and then apply the Heading 1 format. Use the Format menu to center the heading.

7. Select the three list items. Click the Unordered List button in the Property inspector to create a bulleted list with these three items.

8. Click at the end of the first bulleted item. Insert two line breaks between the first and second items and then insert two line breaks between the second and third items.

9. Select the closing paragraph. Center the sentence and then click the Bold button in the Property inspector. When this is complete, do not deselect the sentence.

10. Click the Format button in the Property inspector and apply Heading 3 to the sentence.

11. Title the Web page Bryan's Mobile Pet Services, using the Title text box on the Document toolbar.

12. Click at the end of the closing paragraph and then press the ENTER key. Point to Align on the Format menu and then click Left. Type your name, insert a line break, and then type the current date.

13. Select your name and the current date, and apply bold to the text.

14. Click the Commands menu and then click Check Spelling. Spell check your document and correct any errors.

15. Click File on the Application bar and then click Save.

Continued >

In the Lab continued

16. Press the F12 key to view the Web page in the primary browser. Submit the document in the format specified by your instructor.

In the Lab

Lab 2: Creating a Jewelry Sales Web Site

Problem: Making jewelry has long been a hobby of Eve Perry, a friend of yours. She enjoys the hobby so much that she has decided to start her own jewelry business. She has asked you to assist her in preparing a Web site to help her understand how to share her jewelry-making knowledge and her work with others and how to turn her hobby into a business (Figure 1–75). Software and hardware settings determine how a Web page is displayed in a browser. Your Web pages may be displayed differently in your browser than the one shown in the figure.

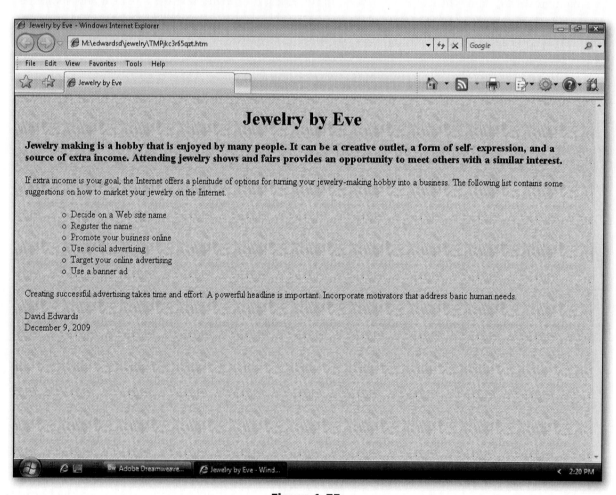

Figure 1–75

Define a Web site and create and format a Web page for Jewelry by Eve. The text for the Web page is shown in Table 1–5.

Table 1–5 Jewelry by Eve Web Page

Section	Web Page Text
Heading	Jewelry by Eve
Introductory Paragraph	Jewelry making is a hobby that is enjoyed by many people. It can be a creative outlet, a form of self-expression, and a source of extra income. Attending jewelry shows and fairs provides an opportunity to meet others with a similar interest.
Second Paragraph	If extra income is your goal, the Internet offers a plenitude of options for turning your jewelry-making hobby into a business. The following list contains some suggestions on how to market your jewelry on the Internet.
List Item 1	Decide on a Web site name
List Item 2	Register the name
List Item 3	Promote your business online
List Item 4	Use social advertising
List Item 5	Target your online advertising
List Item 6	Use a banner ad
Closing	Creating successful advertising takes time and effort. A powerful headline is important. Incorporate motivators that address basic human needs.

Perform the following tasks:

1. In Dreamweaver, click Site on the Application bar and then click New Site. Use the Site Definition Advanced tab to create a local Web site under the *your name* folder and name the site Jewelry Business. In the Local root folder text box, create a subfolder under the *your name* folder, and name the new subfolder jewelry. The path will be similar to M:*your name*\jewelry. (Most likely, your files will be stored on a different drive.) In the Default images folder text box, create a subfolder and name the folder images. The path will be similar to M:*your name*\jewelry\images.

2. Copy the data file image (jewelry_bkg.jpg) to your jewelry\images folder.

3. Click File on the Application bar, and then click New. Click Blank Page, verify that HTML and <none> are selected, and then click Create. Use the Save As command on the File menu to save the page with the name index.

4. Click the Modify menu and then click Page Properties. Apply the background image to the index page.

5. Click in the Document window and then type the Web page text shown in Table 1–5 on the previous page. Press the ENTER key after typing each section and after each list item in the table. Spell check your document.

6. Apply the Heading 1 format to the heading and then center the heading. Apply the Heading 3 format to the first paragraph.

7. Create an unordered list for the list items. With these items still selected, click the Text Indent button in the Property inspector.

8. Title the Web page Jewelry by Eve.

9. Click at the end of the closing line and then press the ENTER key. Type your name. Insert a line break and then type the current date.

10. Check the spelling of your document and correct any errors.

11. Save the file.

12. View the Web page in the primary browser. Submit the document in the format specified by your instructor.

In the Lab

Lab 3: Creating a Credit Protection Web Site

Problem: Identity theft increasingly has become a growing issue and one of the major concerns facing people today. Recently, you learned that two fellow employees became victims of identity theft and you have decided to create a Web site (Figure 1–76) that will provide some information on how to prevent becoming a victim.

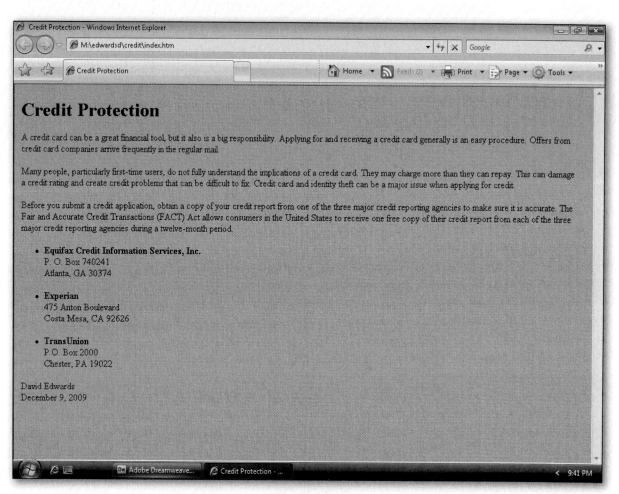

Figure 1–76

Table 1–6 Credit Protection Web Page

Section	Web Page Text
Heading	Credit Protection
Introductory Paragraph	A credit card can be a great financial tool, but it also is a big responsibility. Applying for and receiving a credit card generally is an easy procedure. Offers from credit card companies arrive frequently in the regular mail.
Second Paragraph	Many people, particularly first-time users, do not fully understand the implications of a credit card. They may charge more than they can repay. This can damage a credit rating and create credit problems that can be difficult to fix.
Third Paragraph	Before you submit a credit application, obtain a copy of your credit report from one of the three major credit reporting agencies to make sure it is accurate. The Fair and Accurate Credit Transactions (FACT) Act allows consumers in the United States to receive one free copy of their credit report from each of the three major credit reporting agencies during a twelve-month period.
List Item 1	Equifax Credit Information Services, Inc. P. O. Box 740241 Atlanta, GA 30374
List Item 2	Experian 475 Anton Boulevard Costa Mesa, CA 92626
List Item 3	TransUnion P.O. Box 2000 Chester, PA 19022

Perform the following tasks:

1. In Dreamweaver, define a local Web site under the *your name* folder. Name the site Credit Protection. Create a new subfolder under the *your name* folder and name the new subfolder credit. Create an images folder and copy the image data file (credit_bkg.jpg) into the images folder.

2. Open a new Document window and use the Save As command to save the page with the name index. Apply the background image to the index page.

3. Type the heading and first three paragraphs of the Web page text shown in Table 1–6. Press the ENTER key after typing each section of the text in the table. Insert line breaks where shown in Figure 1–76.

4. Type List Item 1 as shown in Table 1–6. Insert a line break after the company name and after the address. Press the ENTER key after the city, state, and zip code. Type List Items 2 and 3 in the same fashion.

5. Apply the Heading 1 style to the heading text. Align the heading to the left (to ensure it is displayed properly in the browser).

6. Select the three list items (companies and addresses) and create an unordered list. Insert two line breaks between item 1 and item 2, and between item 2 and item 3.

7. Bold the company name of the first item in the bulleted list (Equifax Credit Information Services, Inc.). Apply the bold attribute to the names of the other two companies.

8. Title the Web page Credit Protection.

9. Click at the end of the last line of text and then press the ENTER key. If a bullet is displayed, click the Unordered List button in the Property inspector to remove the bullet. Type your name, add a line break, and then type the current date.

10. Check the spelling of your document, correct any errors, and then save the page.

11. View the Web page in your browser. Submit the document in the format specified by your instructor.

Cases and Places

Apply your creative thinking and problem-solving skills to design and implement a solution.

• Easier   ••More Difficult

• 1: Create the Favorite Sports Web Site

Define a Web site named Favorite Sports with a subfolder named sports. Prepare a Web page listing your favorite sports and favorite teams. Include a title for your Web page. Bold and center the title, and then apply the Heading 1 style. Include a sentence or two explaining why you like the sport and why you like the teams. Bold and italicize the names of the teams and the sports. Give the Web page a meaningful title. Apply a background image to your Web page. Check the spelling in the document. Use the concepts and techniques presented in the chapter to format the text. Save the file in the sports folder. For a selection of images and backgrounds, visit the Dreamweaver CS4 Media Web page (scsite.com/dwCS4/media).

• 2: Create the Hobbies Web Site

Your instructor has asked you to create a Web page about one of your hobbies. Define the Web site using Hobbies for the site name and hobby for the subfolder name. Italicize and center the title, and then apply the Heading 2 style. Type a paragraph of three or four sentences explaining why you selected the subject. Select and center the paragraph. Add a list of three items and create an ordered list from the three items. Include line breaks between each numbered item. Title the Web page the name of the hobby you selected. Check the spelling in your document. Use the concepts and techniques presented in the chapter to format the text. For a selection of images and backgrounds, visit the Dreamweaver CS4 Media Web page (scsite.com/dwCS4/media).

•• 3: Create the Politics Web Site

Assume you are running for office in your city's local government. Define a Web site using the name of the city in which you live and a subfolder named government. Include the following information in your Web page: your name, centered, with Heading 1 and a font color of your choice; the name of the office for which you are running, bold and italicized; and a paragraph about the duties of the office. Create a bulleted list within your Web page. Change the title of the Web page from Untitled to your name. Use the concepts and techniques presented in the chapter to format the text. For a selection of images and backgrounds, visit the Dreamweaver CS4 Media Web page (scsite.com/dwCS4/media).

•• 4: Create the Favorite Music Web Site

Make It Personal

Define a Web site and create a Web page that gives a description and information about your favorite type of music. Name the Web site Favorite Music and the subfolder music. Apply a background image to the Web page. Include a left-aligned heading formatted with the Heading 1 style. Include a subheading formatted with Heading 2. List four facts about why you selected this type of music. Include the names of three of your favorite songs and the names of the artists. Bold and italicize the name of the songs and artists and apply a font color of your choice. Create an ordered list from the four facts. Title the Web page Favorite Music. Save the file as index in the music folder. Use the concepts and techniques presented in the chapter to format the text. For a selection of images and backgrounds, visit the Dreamweaver CS4 Media Web page (scsite.com/dwCS4/media).

• • 5: Create the Student Trips Web Site

Working Together

Your school has a budget for student trips. Your assignment and that of your teammates is to put together a Web site and Web page that lists locations and trips that students can select. Save the site in a subfolder named trips (stored in the *your name* folder). Apply an appropriate background image. Include a title, formatted with Heading 1, and a subtitle, formatted with Heading 2. Add a bullet to each location name. Include information about each location. Title the page Student Government. Use the concepts and techniques presented in the chapter to format the text. For a selection of images and backgrounds, visit the Dreamweaver CS4 Media Web page (scsite.com/dwCS4/media).

2 Adding Web Pages, Links, and Images

Dw

Objectives

You will have mastered the material in this chapter when you can:

- Add pages to a Web site
- Describe Dreamweaver's image accessibility features
- Describe image file formats
- Insert, resize, and align images within a Web page
- Describe the different types of links
- Create relative, absolute, and e-mail links

- Describe how to change the color of links
- Edit and delete links
- Check spelling
- Describe Code view, Split view, and Design view
- Display Code view
- Use Live view

2 | Adding Web Pages, Links, and Images

Introduction

The majority of Web sites consist of several pages with links between the pages. The pages in a site generally are linked and contain shared attributes, such as related topics, a similar design, or a shared purpose. Dreamweaver contains a site structure feature that provides a way to maintain and organize your files within a site. Most Web site developers also enhance a Web site by including images on their Web pages.

Project — Two New Pages, Links, and Images

When creating a Web site, you should follow a standard format or style for all pages contained within the site. The content, which is the information provided on the Web site, should be engaging, relevant, and appropriate to the audience. Accessibility issues should be addressed when developing the site. Experience level of the users, the types of tasks that will be performed on the site, and required connection speeds are important components.

In this chapter, you continue with the building of the Alaska Parks Web site. You create two additional Web pages, add image backgrounds to the two new pages, add images to the two new pages and to the index page, add links to and from the index page, and add absolute links to the national preserves and historic sites highlighted in the two new pages.

Each of the two new pages contains a link to the home (index) page, and the index page contains links to each of the new pages. This arrangement presents the information to the users in a logical order, making it easy to always return to the home page from any point within the Web site. The two new pages and the home page also follow Web site design guidelines that address accessibility principles (Figures 2–1a, 2–1b, and 2–1c).

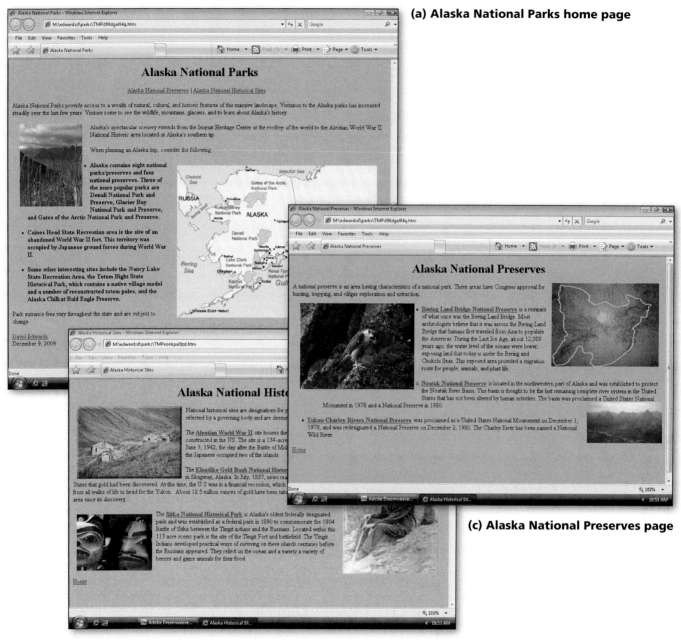

(a) Alaska National Parks home page

(c) Alaska National Preserves page

(b) Alaska National Historical Sites page

Figure 2–1

Overview

As you read this chapter, you will learn how to add pages to the Alaska Web site to create and modify the documents shown in Figure 2–1 and how to use Dreamweaver to perform the following tasks:

- Copy data files to the Web site folder
- Add pages to a Web site
- Use Dreamweaver's image accessibility features
- Insert, resize, and align images within a Web page

• Create relative, absolute, and e-mail links
• Edit, change color, and delete links
• Check spelling
• Use Live view
• Display a page in Code view

Plan
Ahead

General Project Guidelines

When creating a Web site, the organization of the site and how different users will approach the site is of paramount importance. Most Web sites have a home page or index page, but that does not necessarily mean that all visitors enter the Web site through the home page. Generally, with most Web sites, considering that the visitor has a Web page address, they can enter the site at any point. As you modify the home page and add the pages shown in Figures 2–1a, b, and c, you should follow these guidelines.

1. **Organize your content**. Create and organize the content for the two new pages.

2. **Link the new content**. Consider the content of each new page and how it will link to and from the home page.

3. **Organize images**. Organize your images within the Assets panel. Determine which one goes with which Web page.

4. **Consider image placement**. Consider where you will place the images on each of the pages. Determine how much vertical and horizontal space to designate around the image.

5. **Resize images as necessary**. Review each of the images regarding size and determine which ones, if any, need to be resized.

6. **Consider accessibility.** Consider accessibility issues, how they can be addressed, and which ones you need to address within the Web site.

7. **Verify browser viewing**. Use your browser to verify that the page is displayed appropriately and that the links work.

8. **Proofread and check spelling**. Proofread each page and check the spelling.

With a good understanding of the requirements, and an understanding of the necessary decisions and planning process, the next step is to copy the data files to the parks Web site.

Copying Data Files to the Local Web Site

Your data files contain images for Chapter 2. These images are in an images folder. You can use the Windows Computer tool to copy the Chapter 2 images to your parks\images folder. See the inside back cover of this book for instructions for downloading the data files, or see your instructor for information about accessing the files required for this book.

The folder containing the data files for this chapter is stored on Removable Disk (M:). The location on your computer may be different. If necessary, verify the location of the data files folder with your instructor.

To Copy Data Files to the Parks Web Site

The following step shows how to copy the files to the parks local root folder using the Windows Vista Computer tool. Before you start enhancing and adding to your Web site, you need to copy the data files into the site's folder hierarchy.

1

- Click the Start button on the Windows taskbar and then click Computer to display the Computer window.

- Navigate to the location of the downloaded data files for Chapter 2.

- Double-click the folder containing your data files, and then double-click the Chapter02 folder to open it.

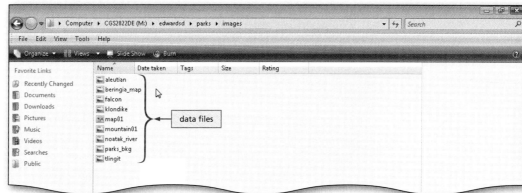

Figure 2–2

- Double-click the parks folder to display the data files.

- Click the aleutian image file, or the first file in the list.

- Hold down the SHIFT key and then click the tlingit image file, or the last file in the list.

- Right-click the selected files to display the context menu.

- Click the Copy command and then navigate to the *your name* folder, which contains the folders and files for the Alaska Parks Web site.

- Double-click the *your name* folder, double-click the parks folder, and then double-click the images folder.

- Right-click anywhere in the open window to display the context menu.

- Click the Paste command to copy the images into the Alaska Parks Web site images folder. Verify that the folder now contains nine images, including the parks_bkg image (Figure 2–2).

Q&A

Is it necessary to create a folder for images within the Web site?

The hierarchy of folders and files in a Web site is critical to Web development. Even for the simplest of sites, you should create a separate folder for the images. The folder name can be any name you choose, but it is best to use a descriptive, meaningful name.

Starting Dreamweaver and Opening a Web Site

Each time you start Dreamweaver, it opens to the last site displayed when you closed the program. You might therefore need to open the parks Web site. Clicking the **Files pop-up menu** in the Files panel lists the sites you have defined. When you open the site, a list of pages and subfolders within the site is displayed.

To Start Dreamweaver and Open the Alaska Parks Web Site

The following steps illustrate how to start Dreamweaver and open the Alaska Parks Web site.

1

- Click the Start button on the Windows taskbar.

- Point to Adobe Dreamweaver CS4 on the Start menu or point to All Programs on the Start menu, and then point to Adobe Dreamweaver CS4 on the All Programs list.

- Click Adobe Dreamweaver CS4 to start Dreamweaver.

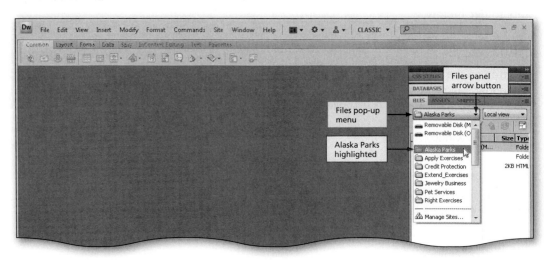

Figure 2–3

- If necessary, display the panel groups.

- If the Alaska Parks hierarchy is not displayed, click the Files panel arrow button and then click Alaska Parks on the Files pop-up menu to display the Alaska Parks Web site hierarchy in the Files panel (Figure 2–3).

2

- Click Alaska Parks to display the Alaska Parks Web site hierarchy (Figure 2–4).

Q&A What type of Web structure does this chapter use for the Alaska Parks Web pages?

The Introduction chapter illustrates four types of Web structures: linear, hierarchical, web (or random), and grid. This chapter uses a hierarchical structure. The index page is the home page, or entrance to the Web site. From this page, the visitor to this site can link to a page about Alaska National Preserves or to a page about Alaska Historical Sites.

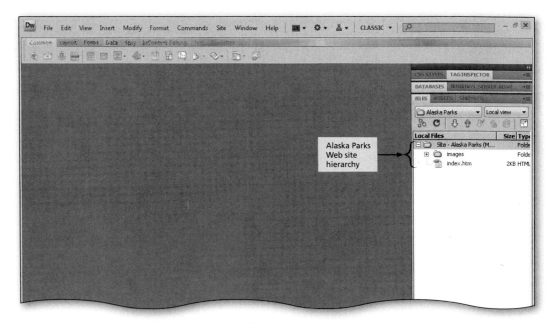

Figure 2–4

Q&A My Files panel is open, but the Alaska Parks files are not displayed. How can I display them?

Refresh the Files panel. To do so, click the Refresh button on the Files panel toolbar or press the F5 key.

Managing a Web Site

Organization is a key element of Web design. Dreamweaver works best with entire sites rather than individual Web pages and has many built-in tools, such as checking links and organizing files, to make site creation easy. You defined the parks Web site in Chapter 1 and created the index page. You can add pages to your site by creating a new page and saving it as part of the site, or by opening an existing page from another source and saving it as part of the site. In this chapter, you will create two new pages.

Almost all Web sites have a home page. Compare the home page to your front door. Generally, the front door is the first thing guests see when they visit you. The same applies to a Web site's home page. When someone visits a Web site, he or she usually enters through the home page.

The home page normally is named **index.htm** or **index.html**. Recall that this file name has special significance. Most Web servers recognize index.htm (or index.html) as the default home page and automatically display this page without requiring that the user type the full Uniform Resource Locator (URL), or Web address. For example, if you type *microsoft.com* into a Web browser address box to access the Web site, what you see is http://www.microsoft.com/en/us/default.aspx — the actual file name of the site's home page — even though you did not type it that way.

Organizing your Web site and using Dreamweaver's site management features can assure you that the media within your Web page will be displayed correctly. Bringing all of these elements together will start you on your way to becoming a successful Web site developer.

The Files Panel

Organization is one of the keys to a successful Web site. Creating documents without considering where they belong in the folder hierarchy generally creates a difficult-to-manage Web site. The Dreamweaver **Files panel** provides a view of the devices and folders on your computer and shows how these devices and folders are organized. You can create new folders and files for your site through the Files panel, which is similar to the Windows file organization method. You also can use the Files panel to drag or copy and paste files from one folder to another on your computer or from one Web site to another. You cannot, however, copy a file from a Windows folder and paste it into a site in the Dreamweaver Files panel.

In Windows, the main directory of a disk is called the **root directory** or the **top-level directory**. A small device icon or folder icon is displayed next to each object in the list. The **device icon** represents a device such as the desktop or a disk drive, and the **folder icon** represents a folder. Many of these icons have a plus or minus sign next to them, which indicates whether the device or folder contains additional folders or files. Windows arranges all of these objects — root directory, folders, subfolders, and files — in a hierarchy. The plus and minus signs are controls that you can click to expand or collapse the view of the file hierarchy. In the Files panel, Dreamweaver uses the same hierarchy arrangement, but site folders and other file icons appear in a different color than non-site folders and files so that you easily can distinguish between the two.

The Home Page

Most Web sites have a starting point, called a home page. In a personal home page within a Web site, for example, you probably would list your name, your e-mail address, some personal information, and links to other information on your Web site. The index page you created in Chapter 1 is the home page for the parks Web site.

Adding Pages to a Web Site

You copied the data files necessary and pasted them in the parks local root folder in the Files panel. It is time to start building and enhancing your site. You will create two additional pages for the Web site: Alaska National Preserves and Alaska National Historical Parks. You will add links and Web page images to the index (or home) page and add links, a background image, and Web page images to the two new pages.

To Open a New Document Window

The first task is to open a new document window. This will become the Alaska National Preserves Web page. The following steps illustrate how to open a new document window and save the page as preserves.htm.

- Click File on the Application bar and then point to New (Figure 2–5).

Q&A What are other ways to add a Web page to a site?

If you have already created a document that you can use as a Web page, store it in the root folder for your site, and then use the Open command on the File menu (or the Open button on the Standard toolbar). You can then edit the page in Dreamweaver. You also can insert the contents of a document such as a Microsoft Word or Excel file into a new or existing Web page. To do this, use the Import command on the File menu.

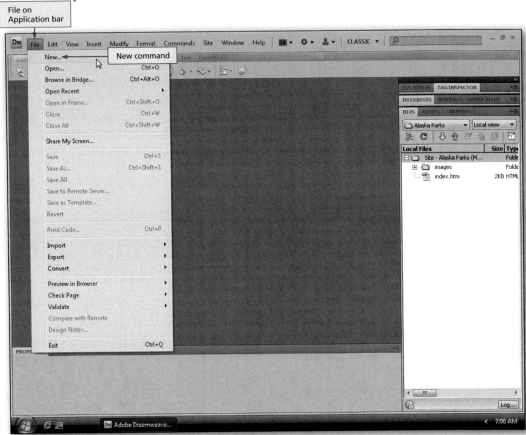

Figure 2–5

2

- Click New to display the New Document dialog box. If necessary, click Blank Page.

- Click HTML in the Page Type column to specify the type of Web page you are creating. Verify that XHTML 1.0 Transitional is selected in the DocType pop-up menu (Figure 2–6).

Q&A What is XHTML and why is it important?

XHTML is an authoring language that defines the structure and layout of a document so that it is displayed as a Web page and is compatible with most Web browsers.

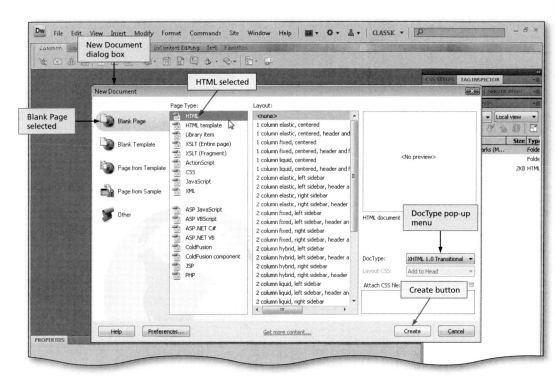

Figure 2–6

3

- Click the Create button to create and display a new Untitled-1 document.

- If necessary, display the Standard toolbar (Figure 2–7).

Q&A Is it a problem if my new Web page is named Untitled-2?

No. Dreamweaver increments the number for untitled Web pages. You save the page with a more descriptive name in the next step.

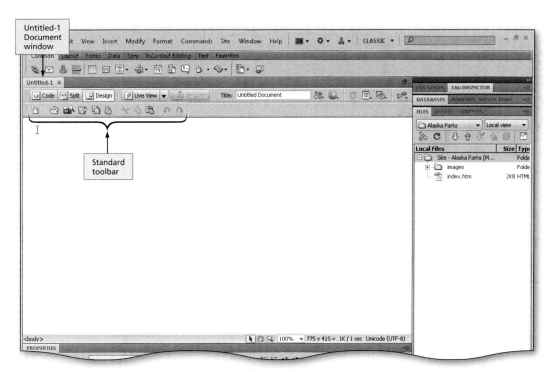

Figure 2–7

4

- Click the Save button on the Standard toolbar to display the Save As dialog box.

- Type preserves.htm in the File name text box to provide a descriptive name for the Web page (Figure 2–8).

Q&A

Do I need to specify the path or folder for the new Web page?

No. Dreamweaver assumes you want to save the new Web page in the root local folder, which is parks for the preserves page.

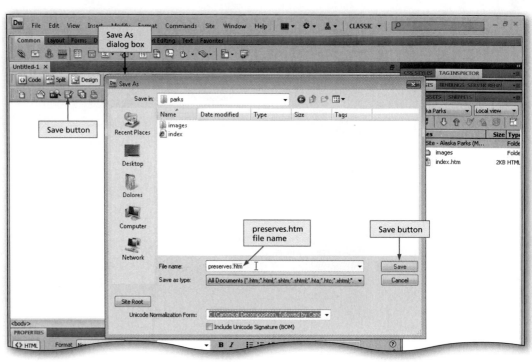

Figure 2–8

5

- Click the Save button to save the preserves page in the parks local folder (Figure 2–9).

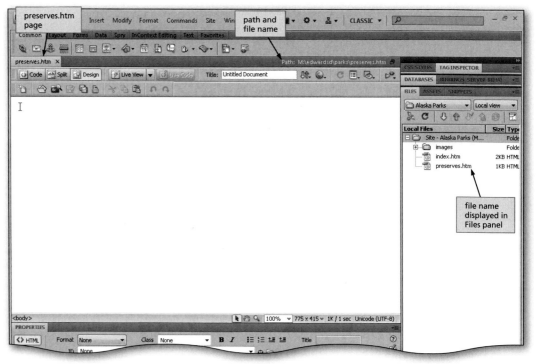

Figure 2–9

Other Ways

1. Click the New button on the Standard toolbar

Creating the Alaska National Preserves Web Page

To create the Alaska National Preserves Web page, you type the text in the Document window. Table 2–1 includes the text for the Alaska Preserves Web page. Press the ENTER key after typing each section as indicated in Table 2–1.

Table 2–1 Alaska National Preserves Web Page Text	
Section	**Text to Add**
Main Heading	Alaska National Preserves <ENTER>
Introduction	A national preserve is an area having characteristics of a national park. These areas have Congress' approval for hunting, trapping, and oil/gas exploration and extraction. <ENTER>
Part 1	Bering Land Bridge National Preserve is a remnant of what once was the Bering Land Bridge. Most archeologists believe that it was across the Bering Land Bridge that humans first traveled from Asia to populate the Americas. During the Last Ice Age, about 12,000 years ago, the water level of the oceans was lower, exposing land that today is under the Bering and Chukchi Seas. This exposed area provided a migration route for people, animals, and plant life. <ENTER>
Part 2	Noatak National Preserve is located in the northwestern part of Alaska and was established to protect the Noatak River Basin. This basin is thought to be the last remaining complete river system in the United States that has not been altered by human activities. The basin was proclaimed a United States National Monument in 1978 and a National Preserve in 1980. <ENTER>
Part 3	Yukon-Charley Rivers National Preserve was proclaimed as a United States National Monument on December 1, 1978, and was redesignated a National Preserve on December 2, 1980. The Charley River has been named a National Wild River. <ENTER>
Closing	Home <ENTER>

To Create the Alaska National Preserves Web Page

The following step shows how to create the Web page.

1

- Type the heading for the Alaska National Preserves Web page as shown in Table 2–1. Press the ENTER key to create a new paragraph.

- Type the rest of the text as shown in Table 2–1. Press the ENTER key as indicated in the table to add blank lines between the paragraphs (Figure 2–10).

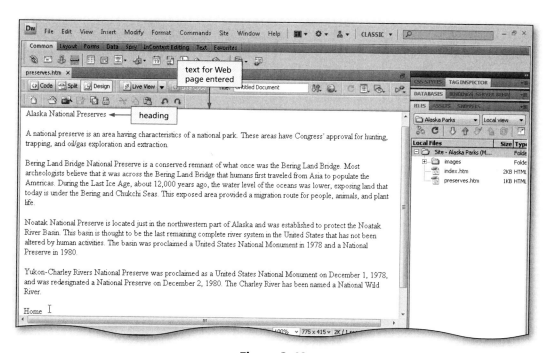

Figure 2–10

To Format the Alaska National Preserves Web Page

In Chapter 1, you formatted the index page by adding headings and bullets and by centering and bolding text. The following steps show how to apply similar formatting to the Alaska National Preserves page.

- If necessary, scroll up to the top of the Web page, and then apply Heading 1 to the heading text.

- Center the heading.

- Add bullets to the following three paragraphs that begin: Bering Land Bridge National Preserve, Noatak National Preserve, and Yukon-Charley Rivers National Preserve (Figure 2–11).

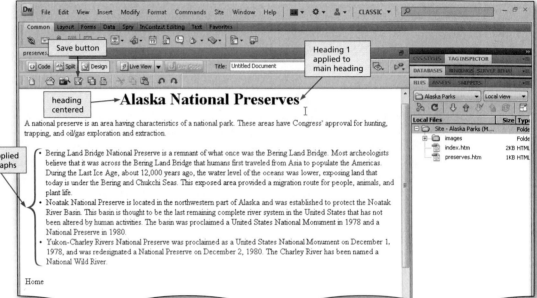

Figure 2–11

- Bold the names of the preserves at the beginning of each of the three paragraphs: Bering Land Bridge National Preserve, Noatak National Preserve, and Yukon-Charley Rivers National Preserve.

- Add two line breaks after the bullet paragraphs describing the Bering Land Bridge National Preserve, and the Noatak National Preserve.

- On the Document toolbar, type Alaska National Preserves in the Title text box and then press ENTER.

- Click the Save button to save your changes to the preserves.htm Web page (Figure 2–12).

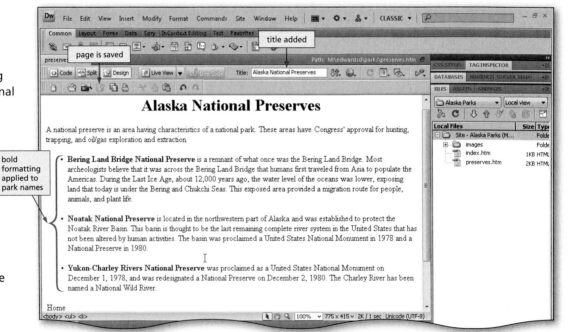

Figure 2–12

Creating the Alaska Historical Sites Web Page

You create the Alaska Historical Sites Web page by entering text the same way you entered the text for the Alaska National Preserves page. Start by opening a new document window, add the text, and then format it.

To Open a New Document Window

The following step shows how to open a new document window for the third Web page for the Alaska Parks Web site — the Alaska National Historical Sites page.

- Click File on the Application bar, click New, and then, if necessary, click Blank Page.

- Click HTML in the Page Type column to select the page type for the Web page.

- Click the Create button to create and display the new blank document Web page.

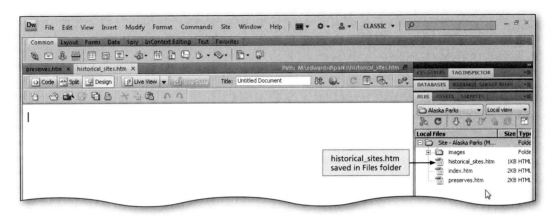

Figure 2–13

- Save the Web page as historical_sites.htm in the parks folder (Figure 2–13).

Entering Text for the Alaska National Historical Sites Web Page

Type the text for the Alaska National Historical Sites Web page using Table 2–2 and the following steps on the next page. Press the ENTER key as indicated in the table.

Table 2–2 Alaska National Historical Sites Web Page Text	
Section	**Text to Add**
Main Heading	Alaska National Historical Sites <ENTER>
Introduction	National historical sites are designations for protected areas of national historical interest. Generally, these areas are selected by a governing body and are deemed to contain important sites or resources of national historical interest. <ENTER>
Part 1	The Aleutian World War II site houses the military ruins of Fort Schwatka, the highest coastal battery ever constructed in the U.S. The site is a 134-acre tract of land located in Unalaska, Alaska on Amaknak Island. On June 3, 1942, the day after the Battle of Midway, the Japanese attacked the Aleutian Islands. For fifteen months, the Japanese occupied two of the islands. <ENTER>
Part 2	The Klondike Gold Rush National Historical Park is located in Skagway, Alaska. In July, 1887, news reached the United States that gold had been discovered. At this time, the U.S. was in a financial recession, which encouraged men from all walks of life to head for the Yukon. About 12.5 million ounces of gold have been taken from the Klondike area since its discovery. <ENTER>
Part 3	The Sitka National Historical Park is Alaska's oldest federally designated park and was established as a federal park in 1890 to commemorate the 1804 Battle of Sitka between the Tlingit Indians and the Russians. Located within this 113-acre scenic park is the site of the Tlingit Fort and battlefield. The Tlingit Indians developed practical ways of surviving on these islands centuries before the Russians appeared. They relied on the ocean and a variety of berries and game animals for their food. <ENTER><ENTER>
Closing	Home

To Create the Alaska National Historical Sites Web Page

The next step is to add text to the Web page and then format it.

1

• Type the text of the Web page as shown in Table 2–2 on the previous page, and then click the Save button to save your changes (Figure 2–14).

Q&A

If I have already entered text in another document, how can I add it to a new Web page?

You can copy and paste the text just as you do in a word processing document. Copy text from another application, switch to Dreamweaver, position the insertion point in the Design view of the Document window, and then press CTRL+V to paste the text.

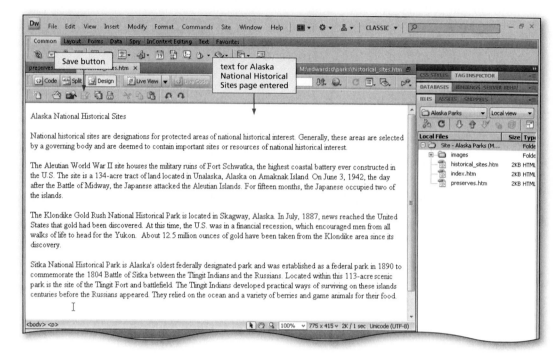

Figure 2–14

2

• If necessary, scroll to the top of the Web page and then apply Heading 1 to the title.

• Center the title.

• Bold the names of each of the three historical sites where they are used as subtitles to make them stand out on the page.

• Type Alaska National Historical Sites as the Web page title.

• Click the Save button on the Standard toolbar to save your work (Figure 2–15).

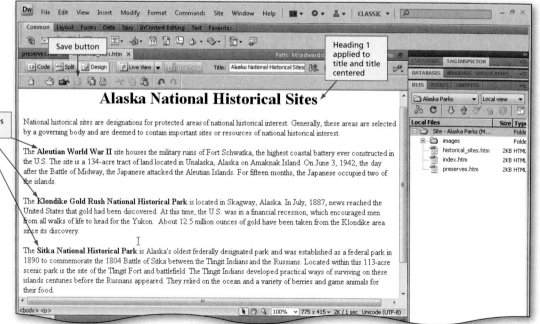

Figure 2–15

Images

You have finished entering and formatting the text for the two new pages and copied the images to the parks local root folder in the Files panel. It is time to add other enhancements to your site. In Chapter 1, you added a background image to the index page. In this chapter, you learn more about images. You will add the same background image to the two new pages, and then add images and links to all three pages.

If used correctly and with an understanding of the Web site audience, images add excitement and interest to a Web page. When you are selecting images for a Web site, you should understand that the size and type of image or images used within a Web page affect how fast the Web page downloads and is displayed in the viewer's Web browser. A Web page that downloads too slowly will turn away visitors.

Image File Formats

Graphical images used on the Web are in one of two broad categories: vector and bitmap. **Vector images** are composed of key points and paths, which define shapes and coloring instructions, such as line and fill colors. The vector file contains a description of the image expressed mathematically. The file describes the image to the computer, and the computer draws it. This type of image generally is associated with Adobe Flash or LiveMotion animation programs. One of the benefits of vector images is the small file size, particularly relative to the larger file size of bitmap images.

Bitmap images are the more common type of image file. A bitmap file maps out or plots an image on a pixel-by-pixel basis. A **pixel**, or **picture element**, is the smallest point in a graphical image. Graphic monitors display images by dividing the display screen into thousands (or millions) of pixels, arranged in a **grid** of rows and columns. The pixels appear connected because they are so close together. This grid of pixels is a **bitmap**. The **bit-resolution** of an image is described by the number of bits used to represent each pixel. There are 8-bit images as well as 24- or 32-bit images, where each bit represents a pixel. An 8-bit image supports up to 256 colors, and a 24- or 32-bit image supports up to 16.7 million colors.

Web browsers currently support three bitmap image file types: GIF, JPEG, and PNG.

GIF (.gif) is an acronym for **Graphics Interchange Format**. The GIF format uses 8-bit resolution, supports up to a maximum of 256 colors, and uses combinations of these 256 colors to simulate colors beyond that range. The GIF format is best for displaying images such as logos, icons, buttons, and other images with even colors and tones. GIF images come in two different versions: GIF87 format and GIF89a format. The GIF89a format contains three features not available in the GIF87 or JPEG formats: transparency, interlacing, and animation. The **transparency** feature allows you to specify a transparency color, which allows the background color or image to display. The **interlacing** feature lets the browser begin to build a low-resolution version of the full-sized GIF picture on the screen while the file is still downloading, so there is something visible to the visitor as the Web page downloads. The **animation** feature allows you to include moving images. Animated GIF images are simply a number of GIF images saved into a single file and looped, or repeated, over and over. A number of shareware GIF editors are available to create animated GIFs. If you do not want to create your own animations, you can find thousands of free animated GIFs on the Internet available for downloading.

JPEG (.jpg) is an acronym for **Joint Photographic Experts Group**. JPEG files are the best format for photographic images because JPEG files can contain up to 16.7 million colors. **Progressive JPEG** is a new variation of the JPEG image format. This image format supports a gradually-built display similar to the interlaced GIFs. Older browsers do not support progressive JPEG files.

PNG (.png) stands for **Portable Network Graphics**. PNG, which is the native file format of Adobe Fireworks, is a GIF competitor, which is used for most Web site images. Some browsers do not support this format without a special plug-in. Generally, it is better to use GIF or JPEG images in your Web pages.

When developing a Web site that consists of many pages, you should maintain a consistent, professional layout and design throughout all of the pages. The pages in a single site, for example, should use similar features such as background colors or images, margins, and headings.

Plan Ahead

Prepare images.
Nearly every Web site displays images such as photographs, drawings, and background textures. Before you add images to a Web site, prepare them using the following guidelines:

- Acquire the images. To create your own images, you can take photos with a digital camera and store them in the JPG format, use a scanner to scan your drawings and photos, or use a graphics editor such as Adobe Photoshop to design images. You also can download images from public domain Web sites, use clip art, or purchase images from stock photo collections. Be sure you have permission to reproduce the images you acquire from Web sites, unless the images are clearly marked as in the public domain.

- Choose the right format. Use JPG files for photographic images and complicated graphics that contain color gradients and shadowing. Use GIF files for basic graphics, especially when you want to take advantage of transparency. You also can use PNG for basic graphics, but not for photos.

- Keep image file size small. Images with small file sizes appear in a browser faster than larger images. Use a graphics editor such as Adobe Photoshop to compress image files and reduce their file size without affecting quality. Background images in particular should have a small file size.

- Check the dimensions. Determine the dimensions of an image file in pixels. You can reduce the dimensions on the Web page by changing the width and height or by cropping the image. Enlarging images generally produces poor results.

Background Colors and Background Images

Many Web pages are displayed with a default white or gray background. Generally, the browser used to display the Web page determines the default background. Recall that you can enhance your Web page by adding a background image or background color.

If you use a background color, be sure to use Web-safe colors. This means the colors will be displayed correctly on the computer screen when someone is viewing your Web page.

Background images add texture and interesting color to a Web page and set the overall appearance of the document. Most browsers support background images. A background image can be a large image, but more frequently it is a smaller image. The image tiles to fill the screen in the Dreamweaver Document window and in the browser window.

To Add a Background Image to the Alaska National Historical Sites Web Page

In Chapter 1, you added a background image to the index page. Now you use the Page Properties dialog box to add the same image to the National Historical Sites Web page and the National Preserves page. The following step shows how to add a background image to the Alaska National Historical Sites page.

1

- If necessary, click the historical_sites.htm tab.

- Click Modify on the Application bar and then click Page Properties to open the Page Properties dialog box.

- Click Appearance (HTML) in the Category column.

- Click the Browse button to the right of the Background image text box to navigate to the images folder.

- If necessary, navigate to and then open the images folder.

- Click parks_bkg.jpg and then click the OK button in the Select Image Source dialog box to select the image.

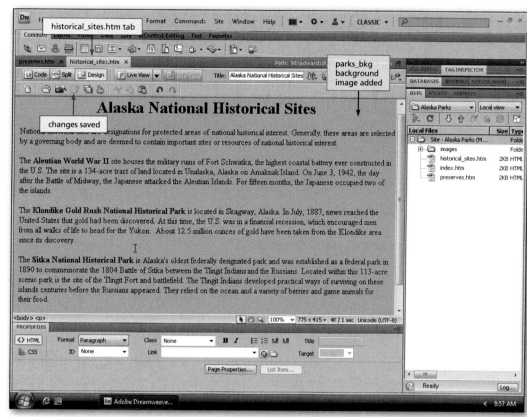

Figure 2–16

- Click the OK button in the Page Properties dialog box to apply the background image.

- Click the Save button on the Standard toolbar (Figure 2–16).

Q&A Is it necessary to add a background image to a Web page?

No, you do not need to add a background image. If you do add a background image to your Web page, however, select an image that does not clash with the text and other content. The background image should not overwhelm the Web page.

Q&A How can I apply a background color instead of a background image?

To apply a background color to a Web page, you can click the Page Properties button in the Property inspector, click the Appearance (HTML) category, and then click the Background icon to display a color picker, which provides a palette of Web-safe colors. Click a color in the palette, and then click the OK button to apply the color to the Web page background.

Other Ways

1. Right-click document window, click Page Properties on context menu
2. Expand the Property inspector, click Page Properties button

To Add a Background Image to the Alaska National Preserves Web Page

The following step illustrates how to add a background image to the Alaska National Preserves page.

- Click the preserves. htm tab.

- Click Modify on the Application bar and then click Page Properties to open the Page Properties dialog box.

- Click Appearance (HTML) in the Category column.

- Click the Browse button to the right of the Background image box to navigate to the images folder.

- Click parks_bkg.jpg and then click the OK button in the Select Image Source dialog box.

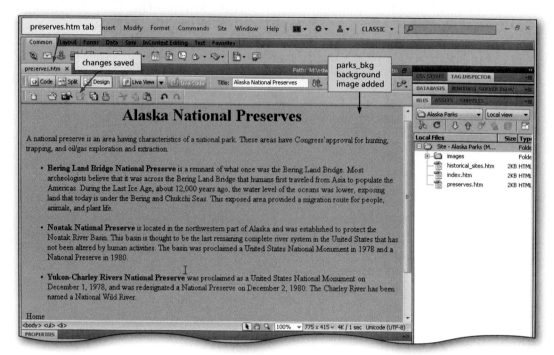

Figure 2–17

- Click the OK button in the Page Properties dialog box to apply the background image.

- Click the Save button on the Standard toolbar (Figure 2–17).

Assets Panel

Besides adding background images, you also can add images to your Web pages. To enhance your index.htm Web page further, you will add two images. One of the images will be displayed in the upper-left part of the page, and the second image will be displayed to the right of the bulleted list. Dreamweaver has features to assist with placement and enhancement of images. The Assets panel provides visual cues for your images, the invisible element feature provides placement control for the images, and the accessibility feature provides information for individuals with disabilities.

Assets are elements, such as images or Flash files, that you use in building a page or a site. The **Assets panel**, which is grouped with the Files panel, helps you manage and organize your Web site's assets (Figure 2–18). This panel contains a list of all the asset types (images, colors, URLs, Flash and Shockwave files, movies, scripts, templates, and library items) within the selected local root folder. The Site option shows the assets in your site. The Favorites list shows only the assets you have selected and added to the list. The Assets panel in Figure 2–18 on the next page is resized to show all options.

You can insert most asset types into a document by dragging them into the Document window, using the Insert button at the bottom of the Assets panel, or using the Media command on the Insert menu. Also, you can either insert colors and URLs or apply them to selected text in Design view. Additionally, you can apply URLs to other elements in Design view, such as images. When an image file name is selected, a thumbnail of the image is displayed at the top of the Assets panel. You will use the Assets panel to insert the images into the Alaska Parks Web pages.

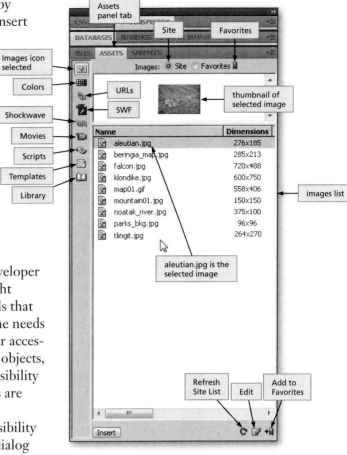

Figure 2–18

Accessibility

When developing a Web page, the Web page developer needs to consider the full spectrum of visitors who might access the site. Dreamweaver provides accessibility tools that allow the Web site developer to create pages to meet the needs of all visitors, including those with disabilities. The four accessibility object tools included in Dreamweaver are form objects, frames, media, and images. This chapter includes accessibility information relative to images. The three other objects are covered in later chapters.

When you insert an image, the Image Tag Accessibility Attributes dialog box is displayed (Figure 2–19). This dialog box contains two text boxes — one for Alternate text and one for Long description. Screen readers translate and recite the information you enter in both text boxes. The information you enter for Alternate text is displayed when a Web site visitor moves the mouse pointer over the image. You should limit your Alternate text entry to 50 characters or less. For a more detailed description of the image, create and save a text file and then add it as a link to the file. When the link is activated, the screen reader recites the text for visually impaired visitors. Clicking Cancel removes the dialog box and inserts the image. The Accessibility feature is turned on by default when you install Dreamweaver. To turn off the Accessibility feature, click Edit on the Application bar and then click Preferences. Click Accessibility in the Category column and then deselect the check boxes for the four attributes. Appendix B contains a full overview of Dreamweaver's accessibility features.

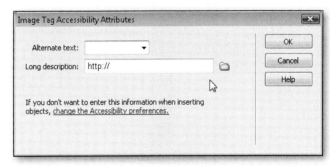

Figure 2–19

Invisible Elements

Dreamweaver's Document window displays basically what you see in a Web browser window. It sometimes is helpful, however, when designing a Web page to see the placement of certain code elements. For example, viewing the Line Break code <br/> provides a visual cue regarding the layout. Dreamweaver lets you control the visibility of 13 different codes, including those for image placement, through the Preferences dialog box.

When you insert and then align an image in a Document window, Dreamweaver can display an **invisible element marker** that shows the location of the inserted image within the HTML code. This visual aid is displayed as a small yellow icon. When you select the icon, it turns blue, and you can use it to cut and paste or drag and drop the image. When using invisible elements with images, however, the invisible element marker is not displayed if the image is aligned to the left. Dreamweaver provides the invisible element marker for 12 other elements, including tables, ActiveX objects, plug-ins, and applets. To hide all invisible elements temporarily, select Hide All on the View menu Visual Aids submenu or use CTRL+SHIFT+I.

To Set Invisible Element Preferences and Turn on Visual Aids

The following steps illustrate how to display the invisible element marker for aligned elements such as images and how to turn on invisible elements through the Visual Aids submenu command. After you turn on the invisible marker, note that no visible changes are displayed in the Document window.

- Click Edit on the Application bar and then click Preferences to display the Preferences dialog box (Figure 2–20).

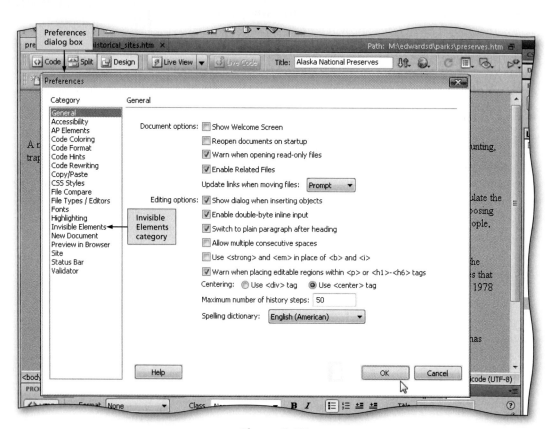

Figure 2–20

2

• Click Invisible Elements in the Category list to display the Invisible Elements options in the Preferences dialog box (Figure 2–21).

Q&A Is it necessary for me to display the invisible element markers when working with images?

No. You can work with images without displaying the invisible element markers. However, the markers help you locate and work with images on a Web page in Design view.

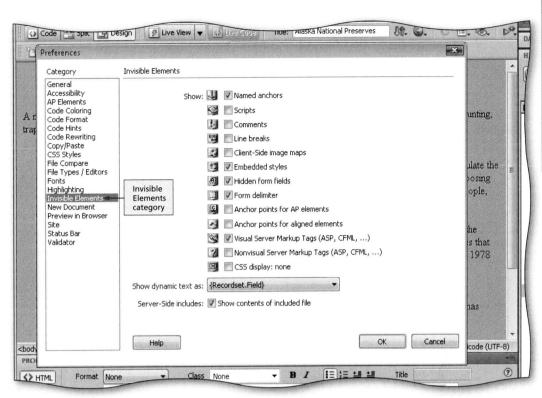

Figure 2–21

3

• Click the Anchor points for aligned elements check box to make it easier to align elements (Figure 2–22).

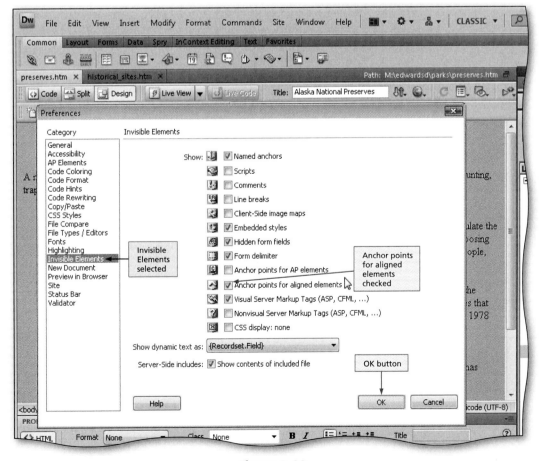

Figure 2–22

4

- Click the OK button to redisplay the Document window.

- Click View on the Application bar, point to Visual Aids, and then point to and highlight Invisible Elements on the Visual Aids submenu (Figure 2–23).

BTW

Invisible Elements and Precision Layout
Displaying invisible elements can change the layout of a page slightly, so for precision layout, when moving elements by a few pixels might change the entire page, hide the invisible elements.

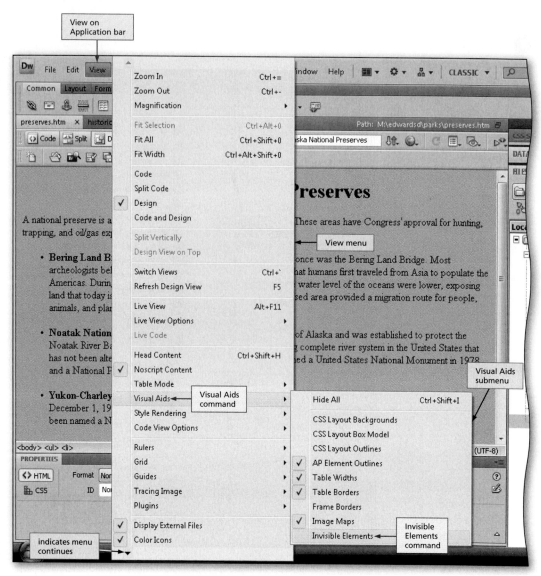

Figure 2–23

5

- If necessary, click Invisible Elements to add a check mark to the Invisible Elements command (Figure 2–24).

Q&A

What if a check mark already appears to the left of the Invisible Elements command?

Do not complete Step 5 — the Invisible Elements command already is selected.

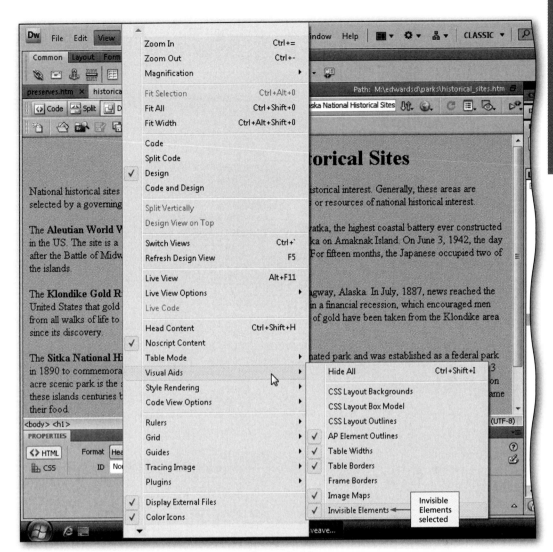

Figure 2–24

Other Ways

1. Click Visual Aids button on Document toolbar, click Invisible Elements

Opening a Web Page

Once you have created and saved a Web page or copied a Web page to a Web site, you often need to retrieve it from a disk. Opening an existing Web page in Dreamweaver is much the same as opening an existing document in most other software applications; that is, you use the File menu and Open command or Open Recent command, or you can click the Open button on the Standard toolbar. If, however, the page is part of a Web site created with Dreamweaver, you also can open the file from the Files panel. After opening the page, you can modify text, images, tables, and any other elements.

To Open a Web Page from a Local Web Site

The following step illustrates how to open a Web page from a local site in the Files panel.

- Double-click index.
htm in the Files
panel to open the
index page. If neces-
sary, double-click
images to expand
the images folder.

- If the Standard
toolbar is not dis-
played, click View on
the Application bar,
point to Toolbars,
and then click
Standard to display
the Standard toolbar
(Figure 2–25).

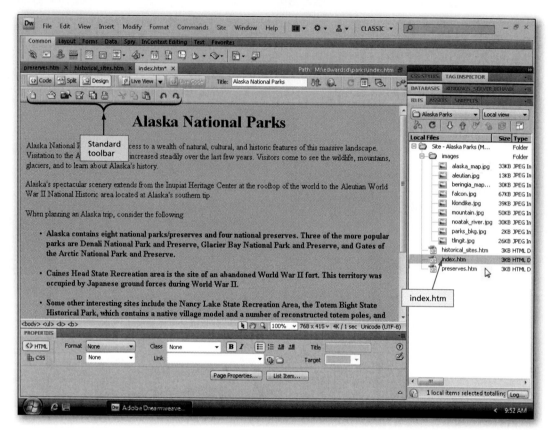

Figure 2–25

Other Ways

1. On File menu, click
   Open, select file

Inserting an Image into a Web Page

Inserting images into your Web page is easy and quick with Dreamweaver — you
drag and drop the image from the Files panel or the Assets panel. Image placement, however, can be more complex. When you view the Web page in a browser, the image might
be displayed differently than in the Document window. If the images are not displayed correctly, you can select and modify the placement of the images in the Document window by
dragging the invisible element marker to move the image.

To Insert an Image into the Index Page

In the following steps, you add an image of a map of Alaska to the index.htm Web page.

1

- If necessary, scroll to the top of the page.

- Click the Assets panel tab to display the panel. Verify that the Images icon is selected.

- Click map01.gif in the Assets panel to select the image file (Figure 2–26).

Q&A How do I resize the Assets panel?

You resize panels by pointing to the panel's vertical bar until it changes to a two-headed arrow, and then you hold down the mouse button and drag.

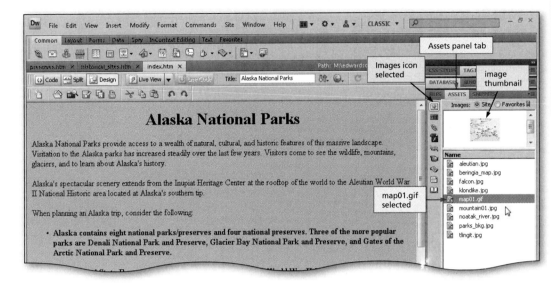

Figure 2–26

Q&A How do I add an asset to the Favorites list?

To add an asset to the Favorites list, select the item in the Site list and then click the Add to Favorites button. Remove an item from the list by selecting the Favorites option button, selecting the item, and then clicking the Remove from Favorites button.

2

- Drag map01.gif from the Assets panel to the left of the first bulleted line. The Image Tag Accessibility Attributes dialog box is displayed (Figure 2–27).

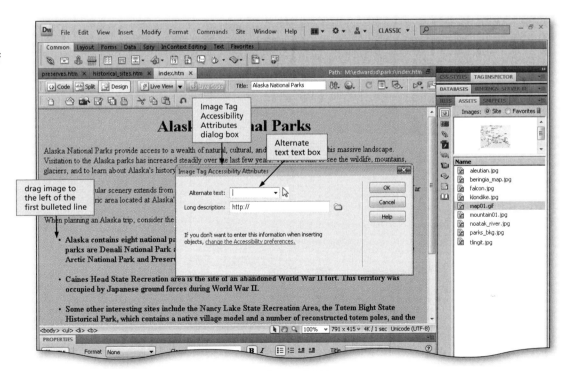

Figure 2–27

- Type Alaska Map in the Alternate text text box to provide alternate text for the map01 image (Figure 2–28).

Q&A Am I required to enter text in the Alternate text or Long description text box?

No. It is not required that you enter text in either text box. For images in this chapter and other chapters, however, instructions are included to add alternate text.

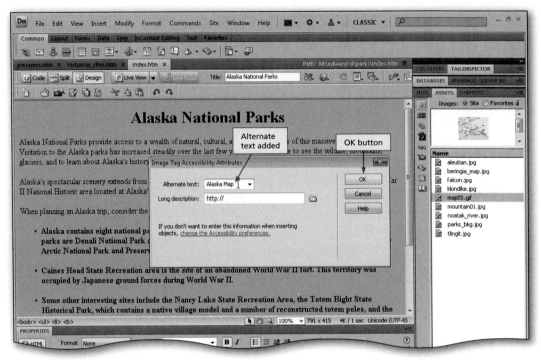

Figure 2–28

- Click the OK button to display the selected image in the Document window and to view the attribute changes in the Property inspector (Figure 2–29).

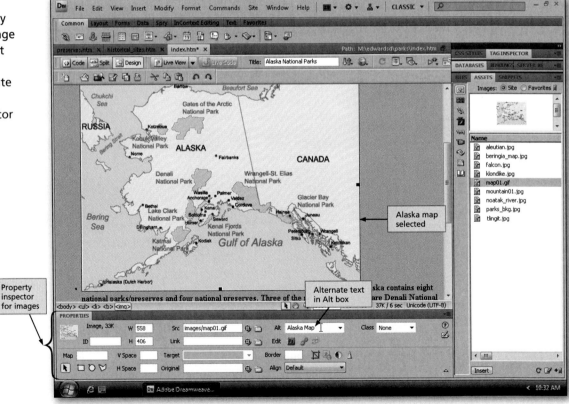

Figure 2–29

Property Inspector Image Tools

In addition to the visual aid feature, you can use the Property inspector to help with image placement and to add other attributes. When you select an image within the Document window, the Property inspector displays properties specific to that image. The Property inspector is divided into two sections. Clicking the expander arrow in the lower-right corner of the Property inspector expands or collapses the Property inspector. When it is collapsed, it shows only the more commonly used properties for the selected element. The expanded Property inspector shows more advanced options. The Property inspector for images contains several image-related features in the top and lower sections.

The following section describes the image-related features of the Property inspector (Figure 2–30).

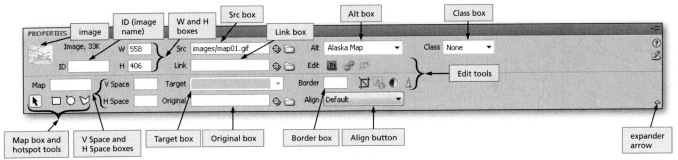

Figure 2–30

Align Set the alignment of an image in relation to other elements in the same paragraph, table, or line with **Align**. This property option is discussed in more detail later in this chapter.

Alt Use Alt to specify alternate text that appears in place of the image for text-only browsers or for browsers that have been set to download images manually. For visually impaired users who use speech synthesizers with text-only browsers, the text is spoken aloud. In most browsers, this text also appears when the mouse pointer is over the image.

Border The **Border** is the width, in pixels, of the image's border. The default is no border.

Edit Use **Edit** to select from editing option tools: (a) **Edit** opens the computer's default image editor, which is PhotoShop; (b) **Edit Image Settings** opens the Image Preview dialog box, which contains options to remove colors, add smoothing to the edges, modify colors, and other image formatting choices; (c) crop (reduce the area of the image), update from original, modify the brightness and contrast of pixels in an image, resample (add or subtract pixels from a resized JPEG or GIF image file to match the appearance of the original image as closely as possible), and sharpen (adjust the focus of an image by increasing the contrast of edges found within the image).

ID Specifies the image name that is contained in the source code.

Link The **Link** box allows you to make the selected image a hyperlink to a specified URL or Web page. To create a relative link, you can click the Point to File or Browse for File icons to the right of the Link box to browse to a page in your Web site, or you can drag a file from the Files panel into the Link box. For an external link, you can type the URL directly into the Link box or use copy and paste.

Map and Hotspot Tools Use the **Map** box and the **Hotspot tools** to label and create an image map.

Reset Size If you change an image size, the **Reset Size** tool is displayed after an image size has been changed. Use this tool to reset the W and H values to the original size of the image.

Target Use **Target** to specify the frame or window in which the linked page should load. This option is not available when the image is linked to another file.

V Space and H Space Use V Space and H Space to add space, in pixels, along the sides of the image. **V Space** adds space along the top and bottom of an image. **H Space** adds space along the left and right of an image.

W and H The W and H boxes indicate the width and height of the image, in pixels. Dreamweaver automatically displays the dimensions when an image is inserted into a page. You can specify the image size in the following units: pc (picas), pt (points), in (inches), mm (millimeters), cm (centimeters), and combinations, such as 2in+5mm. Dreamweaver converts the values to pixels in the source code.

Aligning the Image and Adjusting the Image Size

After you insert the image into the Web page and then select it, the Property inspector displays features specific to the image. As discussed earlier, alignment is one of these features. **Alignment** determines where on the page the image is displayed and if and how text wraps around the image.

You also can adjust the image size easily through the W and H text boxes in the Property inspector or manually adjust the size by using the handles surrounding the image. Additionally, when you insert an image into a Web page that contains text, by default, the text around the image aligns to the right and bottom of the image. The image alignment options on the Align pop-up menu in the Property inspector let you set the alignment for the image in relation to other page content. Dreamweaver provides 10 alignment options for images. Table 2–3 describes these image alignment options.

Table 2–3 Image Alignment Options

Alignment Option	Description
Default	Aligns the image with the baseline of the text in most browser default settings
Baseline	Aligns the image with the baseline of the text regardless of the browser setting
Top	Aligns the image with the top of the item; an item can be text or another object
Middle	Aligns the image with the baseline of the text or object at the vertical middle of the image
Bottom	Aligns the image with the baseline of the text or the bottom of another image regardless of the browser setting
TextTop	Aligns the image with the top of the tallest character in a line of text
Absolute Middle	Aligns the image with the middle of the current line of text
Absolute Bottom	Aligns the image with the bottom of the current line of text or another object
Left	Aligns the image at the left margin
Right	Aligns the image at the right margin

To Align an Image

The following steps show how to align the Alaska map image to the right and wrap text to the left of the image. To have a better overview of how the page will display in a browser, you start by collapsing the panel groups.

1

- Click the panel groups Collapse to Icons arrow to collapse the panel groups.

- If necessary, click the map01 image to select it.

- Click the Align button arrow in the Property inspector.

- Point to Right on the pop-up menu (Figure 2–31).

Q&A What are the most widely used Align options?

The most widely used options are Left and Right.

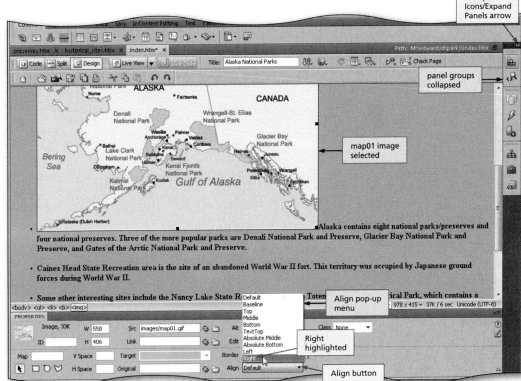

Figure 2–31

2

- Click Right to move the selected image to the right side of the window and to display the element marker (Figure 2–32).

Q&A What should I do if the element marker is not displayed?

First, open the Preferences dialog box, click the Invisible Elements category, and then make sure the Anchor points for aligned elements box is checked. Next, click View on the Application bar, point to Visual Aids, and make sure the Invisible Elements command is checked.

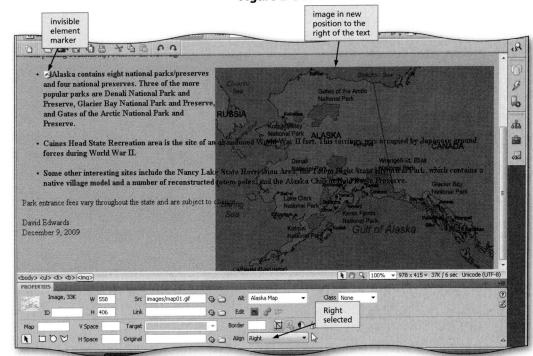

Figure 2–32

Adjusting Space Around Images

When aligning an image, by default, only about three pixels of space are inserted between the image and adjacent text. You can adjust the amount of vertical and horizontal space between the image and text by using the V Space and H Space settings in the Property inspector. The V Space setting controls the vertical space above or below an image. The H Space setting controls the horizontal space to the left or right side of the image.

To Adjust the Image Size and the Horizontal and Vertical Space

The following steps show how to resize an image and add vertical and horizontal space around an image.

1

- If necessary, click to select the image.

- Click the W text box in the Property inspector and type 525 to adjust the width of the image.

- Press the TAB key and type 390 in the H text box to adjust the height of the image.

- Press the ENTER key.

- Click the V Space text box and type 10 to adjust the vertical space between the image and the text.

- Press the TAB key and type 25 in the H Space text box to adjust the horizontal space between the image and the text.

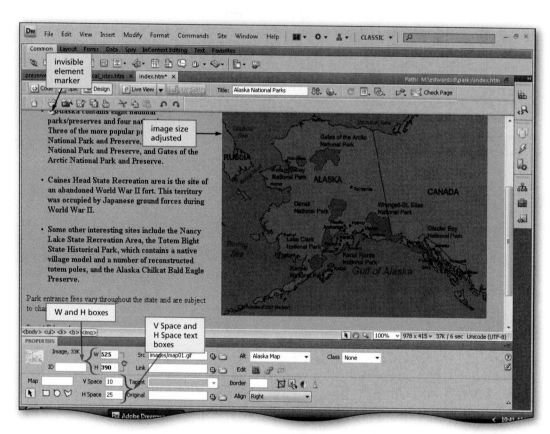

Figure 2–33

- Press the TAB key (Figure 2–33).

Q&A Why do I need to adjust the width and height of the image?

In many instances, adjusting the image size creates a better balance on the page.

Q&A How do the V Space and H Space settings change the placement of the image?

V Space adds space along the top and bottom of an image. H Space adds space along the left and right of an image.

2

• Click the image to remove the high-lighting and to view the added space and the reduced size (Figure 2–34).

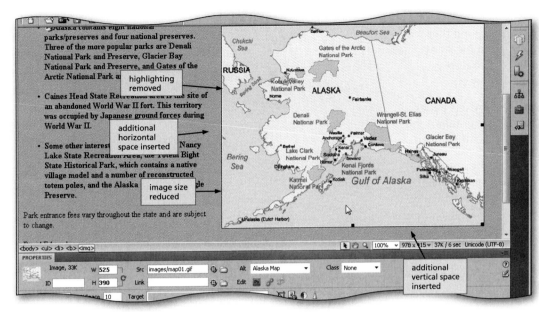

Figure 2–34

To Insert the Second Image

To enhance your index Web page further, you will add a second image. This image will appear on the left side of the page, below the first paragraph.

1

• If necessary, scroll up and position the insertion point to the left of the second paragraph (Figure 2–35).

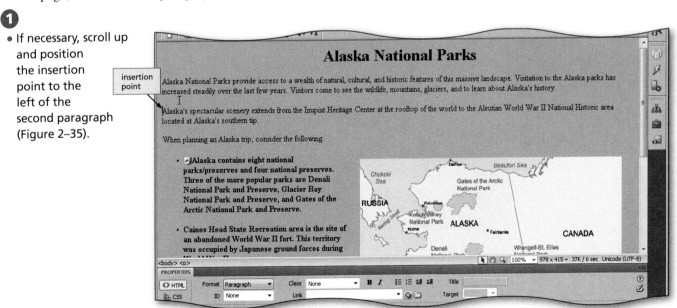

Figure 2–35

2

- Expand the panel groups, and then expand the Assets panel to display the images.

- In the Assets panel, click mountain01.jpg to select the image.

- Drag the image to the insertion point to add the image to the Web page.

- Type Alaska Mountains in the Alternate text text box, and then click the OK button to insert the mountain01 image into the Web page (Figure 2–36).

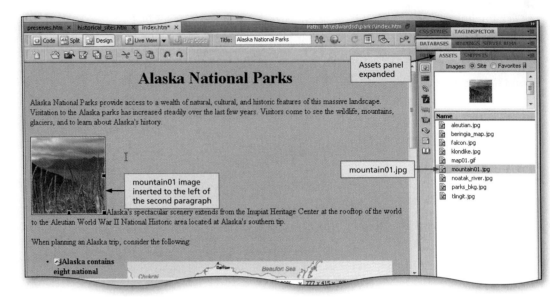

Figure 2–36

Q&A How does the Alternate text help make my Web page more accessible?

The Alternate text appears in place of the image for text-only browsers or for browsers that have been set to download images manually. For visually impaired users who use speech synthesizers with text-only browsers, the text is spoken aloud.

3

- In the Property inspector, click the Align button arrow.

- Click Left in the Align pop-up menu to move the image to the left side of the window and to adjust the text to the right. The bullets and part of the text are hidden by the image, indicating the horizontal and vertical spacing needs to be adjusted (Figure 2–37).

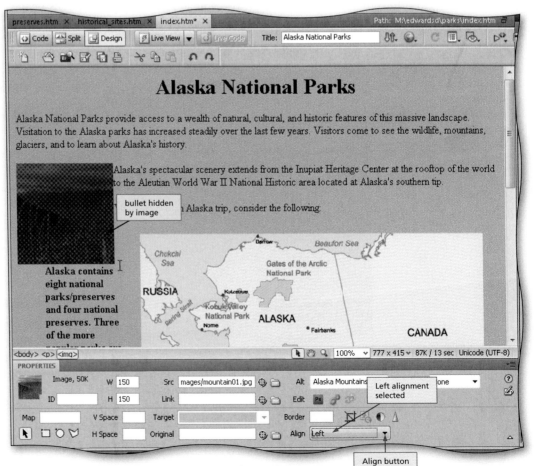

Figure 2–37

4

- In the Property inspector, adjust the W to 165 and the H to 210.

- Click the H Space box and type 20 as the horizontal space.

- Press the TAB key.

- Click anywhere in the Document window to deselect the image and view the additional vertical and horizontal space added between the text and images (Figure 2–38).

Figure 2–38

5

- Click the Save button on the Standard toolbar.

- Press the F12 key to view the Web page in your browser.

- Move the mouse pointer over the mountain01 and map01 images to display the Alt text (Figure 2–39).

6

- Close the browser to return to Dreamweaver.

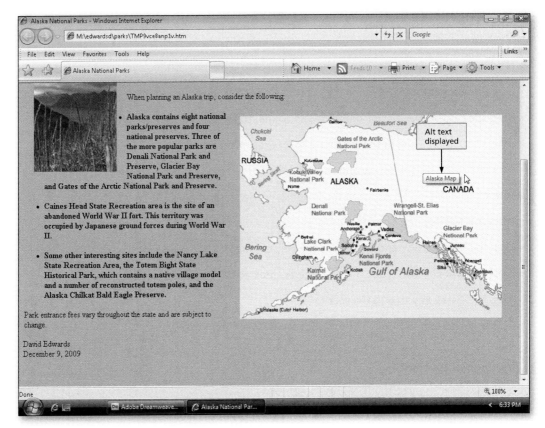

Figure 2–39

To Insert and Align Images in the Alaska National Preserves Web Page

The next page in your Web site is the Alaska National Preserves page. The following steps show how to further develop this Web page by adding three images to it.

1

- Click the preserves. htm document tab. If necessary, display the panel groups and click the Assets tab.

- Position the insertion point to the left of the first sentence after the heading.

- Drag the beringia_ map image file from the Assets panel to the insertion point.

- Type `Beringia Map` in the Alternate text text box and then click the OK button to display the map (Figure 2–40).

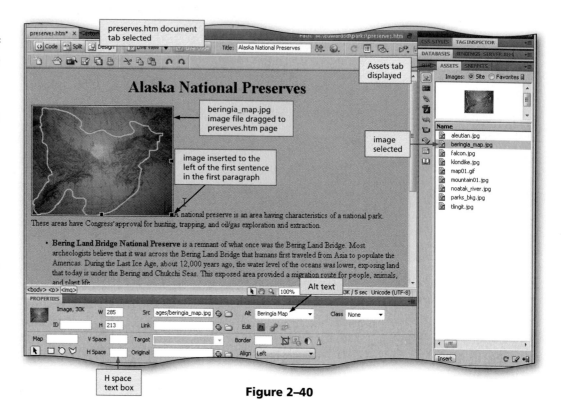

Figure 2–40

2

- Type `10` in the H Space box to add horizontal space. Press the ENTER key.

- Click the Align button arrow and then click Right to align the image to the right side of the window.

- Drag the falcon image file from the Assets panel to the end of the first sentence.

- Type `Alaska Falcon` in the Alternate text text box and then click the OK button.

- Click the Align button arrow and then click Left to align the image to the left.

- Select the value in the W box in the Property inspector and type `300`.

- Press the TAB key and type `220` in the H box.

- Click the V Space box and type `15` as the vertical space.

- Press the TAB key and type `20` in the H Space box as the horizontal space.

- Press the ENTER key to add the space.

- Click anywhere in the Document window to deselect the image.

BTW

Resizing Images Visually
Besides using the W and H boxes in the Property inspector, you can click an image and then drag a selection handle to visually resize the image. Whether you resize by dragging or by using the Property inspector, you are not changing the size of the original image file, only the appearance of the image on the Web page.

- Click the Save button on the Standard toolbar (Figure 2–41).

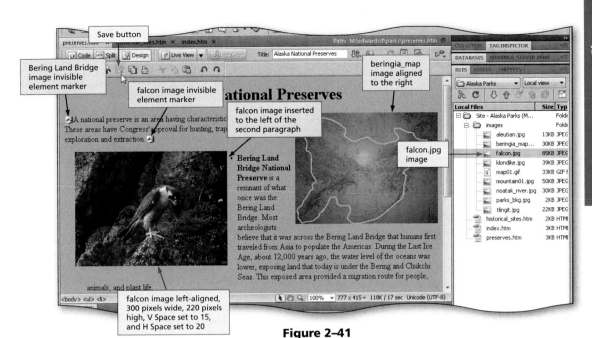

Figure 2–41

3

- Drag the noatak_ river image to the right of the last sentence in the third paragraph.

- Type Noatak River in the Alternate text text box and then click the OK button.

- Click the Align button arrow and then click Right to align the image to the right.

- Select the value in the W box in the Property inspector and type 200 to set the image width.

- Press the TAB key and type 105 in the H box to set the image height, and then press ENTER.

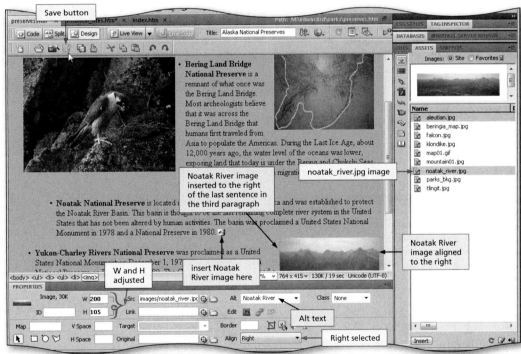

Figure 2–42

- Click anywhere in the Document window to deselect the image.

- Click the Save button (Figure 2–42).

- Press the F12 key to display the Alaska National Preserves page in the browser (Figure 2–43).

- Close the browser to return to Dreamweaver.

Figure 2–43

To Insert and Align Images in the Alaska National Historical Parks Web Page

The third page in your Web site is the Alaska National Historical Parks page. To add interest to this page, you will add three images. You will align two of the images to the left and one to the right. When you added images to the index.htm and preserves.htm pages, you expanded and collapsed the panel groups. In the following steps, you leave the panel groups expanded. This enables you to experience both methods and determine the one which works best for you. The following steps illustrate how to add the images to the Alaska Historical Sites Web page.

- Click the historical_sites.htm Web page tab. Display the panel groups and click the Assets tab, if necessary.

- Click the aleutian.jpg file in the Assets panel.

- Position the insertion point to the left of the first sentence (Figure 2–44).

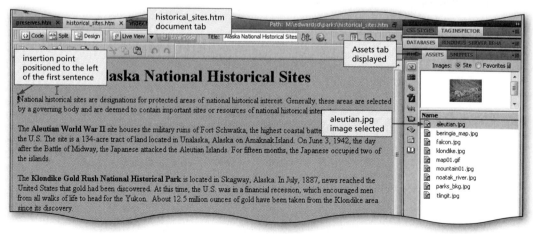

Figure 2–44

2

- Drag the aleutian. jpg file from the Assets panel to the insertion point.

- Type Aleutian World War II Historical Site in the Alternate text text box and then click the OK button.

- Click the Align button arrow in the Property inspector and then click Left on the Align pop-up menu to align the image to the left side of the page (Figure 2–45).

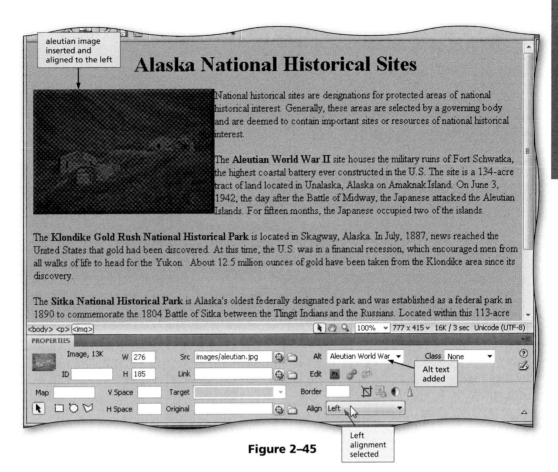

Figure 2–45

3

- Click the H Space box, type 10 as the horizontal space, and then press the ENTER key to add the space (Figure 2–46).

 When I add horizontal and vertical space, what are the measurement units?

The measurement units are in pixels, so when you enter 10 in the H Space box, you are specifying 10 pixels of horizontal space around the image.

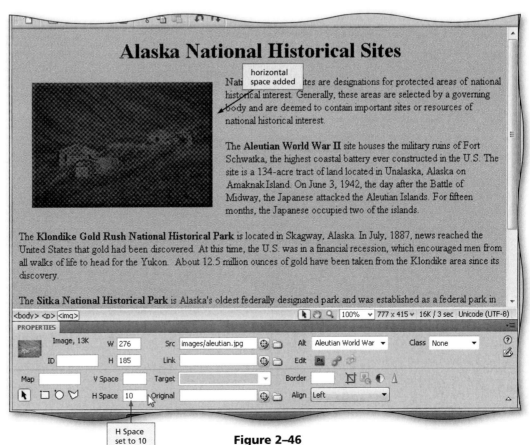

Figure 2–46

• If necessary, scroll down and then position the insertion point to the left of the paragraph describing the Klondike Gold Rush National Historical Park (Figure 2–47).

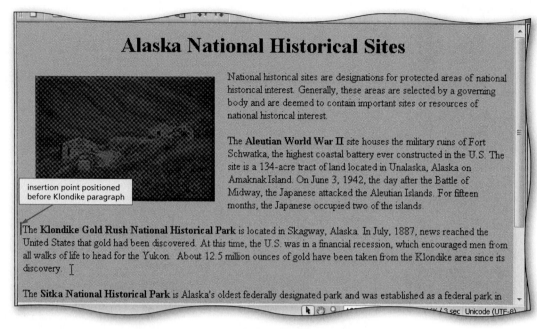

Figure 2–47

• Drag the klondike.jpg image to the insertion point.

• Type Klondike Gold Rush Prospector in the Alt text box and then press ENTER. If necessary, scroll down to view the image.

• Click the Align button arrow and then click Right on the Align pop-up menu.

• Double-click the W text box and then type 250 for the width.

Figure 2–48

• Press the TAB key and then type 275 for the height in the H text box.

• Click the H Space box and then type 20 as the horizontal space.

• Press the ENTER key to position the image (Figure 2–48).

5

- Position the insertion point to the left of the Sitka National Historical Park paragraph.

- Drag the tlingit.jpg image from the Assets panel to the insertion point.

- Type Sitka National Historical Park in the Alt text box and then press the ENTER key. If necessary, scroll down to view the image (Figure 2–49).

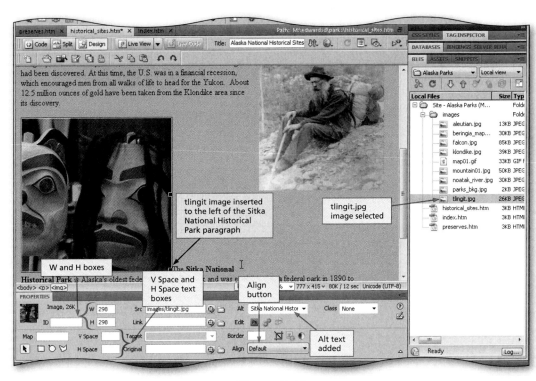

Figure 2–49

6

- Click the Align button arrow and then click Left on the Align pop-up menu.

- Double-click the W box and then type 225 for the width.

- Press the TAB key and then type 160 for the height in the H box.

- Click the V Space box and then type 10 as the vertical space.

- Click the H Space box and then type 10 as the horizontal space.

- Press the ENTER key to resize and position the image.

- Click anywhere on the page to deselect the image.

- Click the Save button on the Standard toolbar (Figure 2–50).

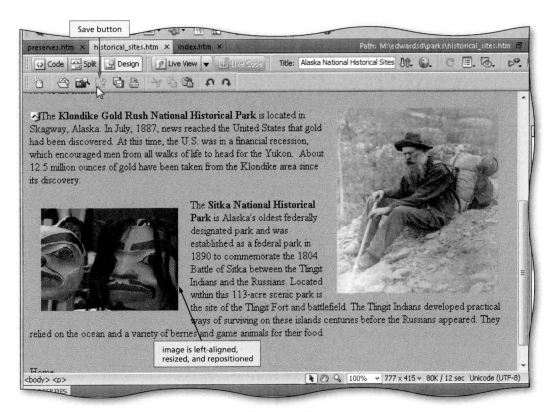

Figure 2–50

- Press the F12 key to view the Alaska National Historical Sites page in your browser (Figure 2–51).

- Close the browser.

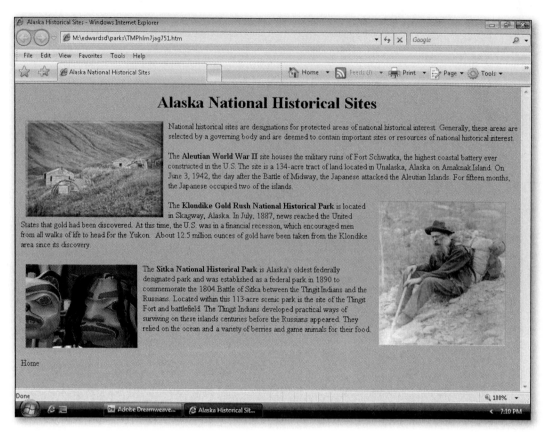

Figure 2–51

Image Editing Tools

Dreamweaver makes available several basic image editing tools to modify and enhance an image. You access these functions through the Property inspector.

- Use an external image editor: Adobe PhotoShop is the default image editor, but you can specify which external editor should start for a specified file type. To select an external editor, click Edit on the Application bar and display the Preferences dialog box. Select File Types/Editors from the Category list to display the Preferences File Types/Editors dialog box. Select the image extension and then browse for the External Code Editor executable file.

- Crop an image: **Cropping** lets you edit an image by reducing the area of the image and allows you to eliminate unwanted or distracting portions of the image. When you crop an image and then save the page, the source image file is changed on the disk. Prior to saving, make a backup copy of the image file in case you need to revert to the original image.

- Resampling: The process of **resampling** adds or subtracts pixels from a resized JPEG or GIF image file to match the appearance of the original image as closely as possible. Resampling an image also reduces an image's file size, resulting in improved download performance. When you resize an image in Dreamweaver, you can resample it to accommodate its new dimensions. To resample a resized image, resize the image as previously described and then click the Resample button in the Property inspector.

• Brightness and Contrast: The **Brightness and Contrast** tool modifies the contrast or brightness of the pixels in an image. Recall that a pixel is the smallest point in a graphical image. Brightness makes the pixels in the image lighter or darker overall, while Contrast either emphasizes or de-emphasizes the difference between lighter and darker regions. This affects the highlights, shadows, and midtones of an image.

• Sharpening: **Sharpening** adjusts the focus of an image by increasing the contrast of edges found within the image.

To Crop and Modify the Brightness/Contrast of an Image

The Tlingit image in the Alaska National Historic Sites page extends below the last line of the text. Cropping the image and emphasizing a better view of the masks in the image will enhance the page. The following steps show how to crop the image, and then modify the brightness and contrast.

1

• If necessary, open the historical_sites.htm page.

• Select the tlingit.jpg image.

• Click the Crop tool icon in the Property inspector to apply the bounding box. If a Dreamweaver caution dialog box is displayed, click the OK button (Figure 2–52).

Q&A

When is cropping an image effective?

Cropping can be very effective for improving the appearance of a photo by highlighting the main point of interest in an image.

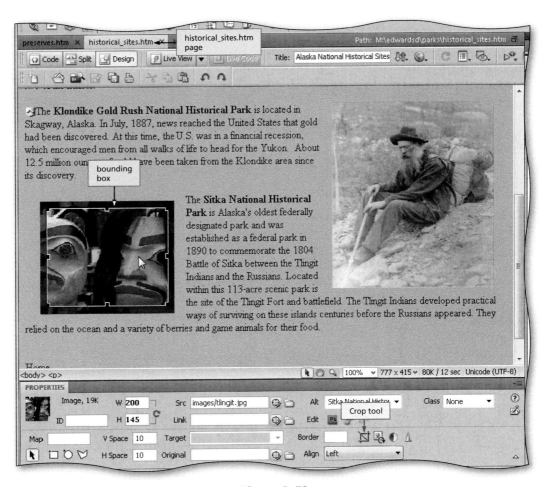

Figure 2–52

- Collapse the panel groups so you have more room to work.

- Click the crop handle in the lower-right corner and adjust the handles until the bounding box surrounds the area of the image similar to that shown in Figure 2–53.

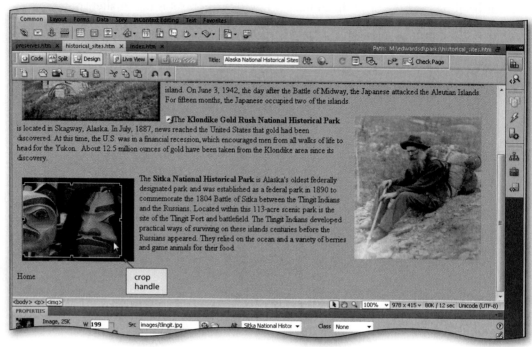

Figure 2–53

- Double-click inside the bounding box.

- Click the image to apply the cropping (Figure 2–54).

Q&A

How can I make changes after I apply the cropping?

If you need to make changes, click the Undo button on the Standard toolbar and repeat the preceding steps.

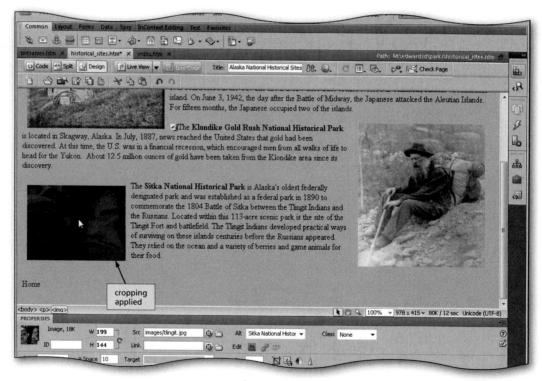

Figure 2–54

4

- If necessary, click the Tlingit image to select it.

- Click the Brightness and Contrast tool to display the Brightness/Contrast dialog box. If a Dreamweaver caution dialog box appears, click the OK button (Figure 2–55).

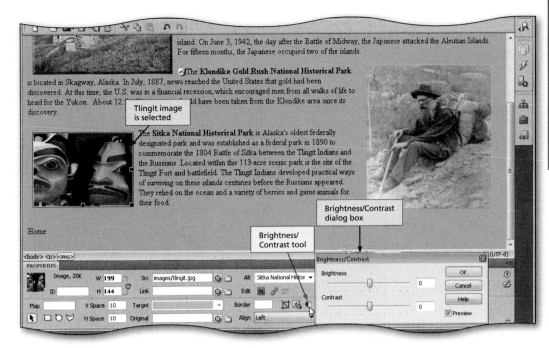

Figure 2–55

5

🔍 **Experiment**

- Drag the Brightness slider and the Contrast slider so you can see how changing the value of each affects the Tlingit image.

- Drag the Brightness slider to the left and adjust the setting to −10 to change the brightness level.

- Drag the Contrast slider to the right and adjust the setting to 10 to change the contrast level (Figure 2–56).

Q&A

What are the ranges for the Brightness and Contrast settings?

The values for the Brightness and Contrast settings range from −100 to 100.

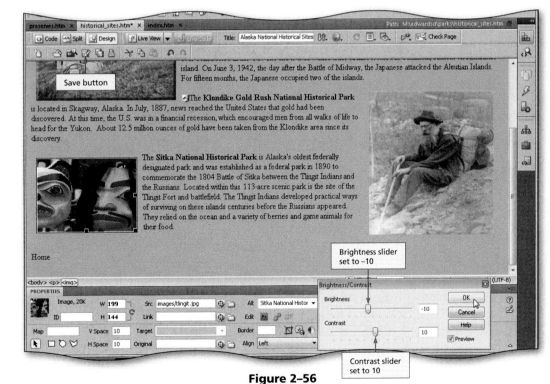

Figure 2–56

- Click the OK button to accept the Brightness and Contrast settings.

- Click the Save button on the Standard toolbar.

- Press the F12 key to view the historical_sites.htm page in your browser (Figure 2–57).

- Close the browser to return to the Dreamweaver window.

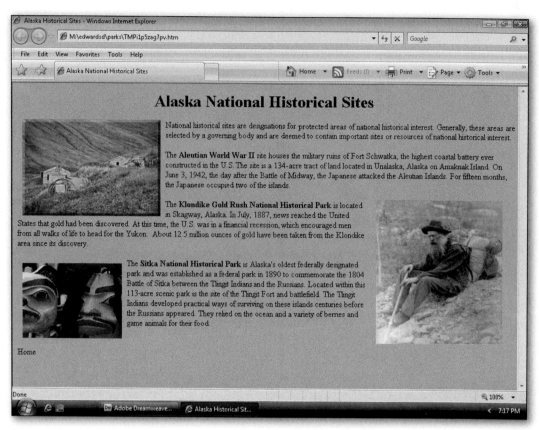

Figure 2–57

Understanding Different Types of Links

To connect the pages within the Web site, you create links. Links are the distinguishing feature of the World Wide Web. A link, also referred to as a hyperlink, is the path to another document, to another part of the same document, or to other media such as an image or a movie. Most links are displayed as colored and/or underlined text, although you also can link from an image or other object. Clicking a link accesses the corresponding document, other media, or another place within the same document. If you place the mouse pointer over the link, the Web address of the link, or path, usually appears at the bottom of the window, on the status bar.

Three types of link paths are available: absolute, relative, and root-relative. An **absolute link** provides the complete URL of the document. This type of link also is referred to as an **external link**. Absolute links generally contain a protocol (such as http://) and primarily are used to link to documents on other servers.

You use **relative links** for local links. This type of link also is referred to as a **document-relative link**, or an **internal link**. If the linked documents are in the same folder, such as those in your parks folder, this is the best type of link to use. You also can use a relative link to link to a document in another folder, such as the images folder. All the files you see in the Files panel in the Local Files list are internal files and are referenced as relative links. You accomplish this by specifying the path through the folder hierarchy from the current document to the linked document. Consider the following examples.

- To link to another file in the same folder, specify the file name. Example: preserves.htm.
- To link to a file in a subfolder of the current Web site folder (such as the images folder), the link path would consist of the name of the subfolder, a forward slash (/), and then the file name. Example: images/falcon.jpg.

You use the **root-relative link** primarily when working with a large Web site that requires several servers. Web developers generally use this type of link when they must move HTML files from one folder or server to another folder or server. Root-relative links are beyond the scope of this book.

Two other types of links are named anchor and e-mail. A **named anchor** lets you link to a specific location within a document. To create a named anchor, click the Named Anchor command on the Insert menu. An **e-mail link** creates a blank e-mail message containing the recipient's address. Another type of link is a **null**, or **script**, **link**. This type of link provides for attaching behaviors to an object or executes JavaScript code.

Relative Links

Dreamweaver offers a variety of ways in which to create a relative link. Three common methods are point to file, drag-and-drop, and browse for file. The point to file and drag-and-drop methods require that the Property inspector and the Files or Assets panels be open. To use the **point to file method**, you drag the Point to File icon to the file or image in the Files or Assets panel. In the **drag-and-drop method**, you drag the file from the Files or Assets panel to the Link text box in the Property inspector. The **browse for file method** is accomplished through the Select File dialog box, which is accessed through the Make Link command on the Modify menu. A fourth method is to use the context menu. To do this, you select the text for the link, right-click to display the context menu, and then select the Make Link command.

Identify Links

Before you use links to create connections from one document to another on your Web site or within a document, keep the following guidelines in mind:

- Prepare for links. Some Web designers create links first, before creating the associated page. Others prefer to create all the files and pages first, and then create links. Choose a method that suits your work style, but be sure to test all your links before publishing your Web site.

- Link to text or images. You can select any text or image on a page to create a link. When you do, visitors to your Web site can click the text or image to open another document or move to another place on the page.

- Know the path or address. To create relative links, the files need to be stored in the same root folder or a subfolder in the root folder. To create absolute links, you need to know the URL to the Web page. To create e-mail links, you need to know the e-mail address.

- Test the links. Test all the links on a Web page when you preview the page in a browser. Fix any broken links before publishing the page.

Plan Ahead

To Add Text for Relative Links

To create relative links from the index page, you add text to the index page and use the text to create the links to the other two Web pages in your Web site. You will center the text directly below the Alaska National Parks heading. The following steps show how to add the text for the links.

- Expand the panel groups, and then click the Files panel tab to display the Files panel.

- Click the index.htm tab in the Document window. If necessary, scroll to the top of the page and then position the insertion point at the end of the title, Alaska National Parks.

- Press the ENTER key to move the insertion point to the next line. If necessary, click the Align command on the Format menu and select Center to center the insertion point (Figure 2–58).

Figure 2–58

- Type Alaska National Preserves and then press the SPACEBAR.

- Hold down the SHIFT key and then press the vertical line key (|).

- Press the SPACEBAR and then type Alaska National Historical Sites to add the text for the links (Figure 2–59).

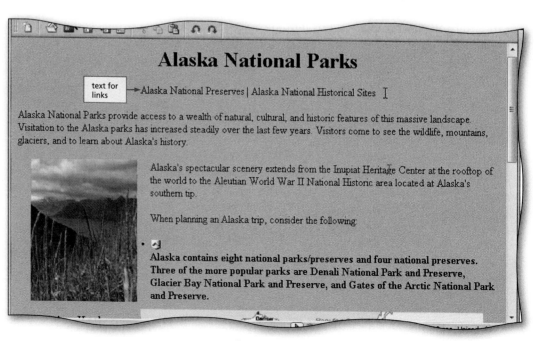

Figure 2–59

To Create a Relative Link Using Point to File

You will use the text Alaska National Preserves to create a link to the preserves.htm page and the text Alaska Preserves Sites to create a link to the historical_sites.htm page. The following steps illustrate how to use the point-to-file method to create a relative link from the Alaska Parks home page to the Alaska National Preserves Web page.

1
- Drag to select the text Alaska National Preserves (Figure 2–60).

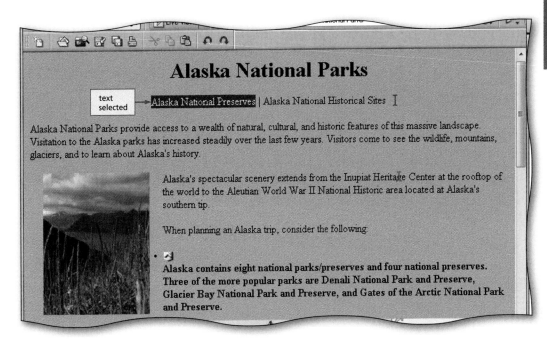

Figure 2–60

2
- Use the Point to File tool to point to the preserves.htm file in the Files panel.

- When the pointer is over the preserves. htm file in the Files panel, release the mouse button to display the linked text in the Property inspector Link box (Figure 2–61).

 Why am I inserting a relative link?

You use **relative links** when the linked documents are in the same folder, such as those in your parks folder.

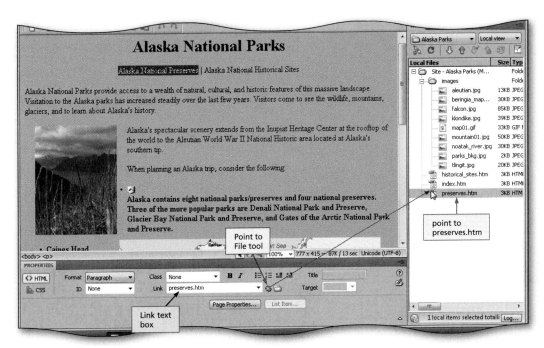

Figure 2–61

To Create a Relative Link Using the Context Menu

The context menu is a second way to create a link. Using this method, you select the file name in the Select File dialog box. The following steps illustrate how to use the context menu to create a link to the Alaska National Historical Sites page.

- Drag to select the text Alaska National Historical Sites, and then right-click the selected text to display the context menu.

- Point to Make Link (Figure 2–62).

Q&A How can I create a link from an image?

Use the same techniques as you do for creating a link from text. Select the image, and then use the context menu to select the Web page file. You can also type or drag the file name into the Property inspector Link box.

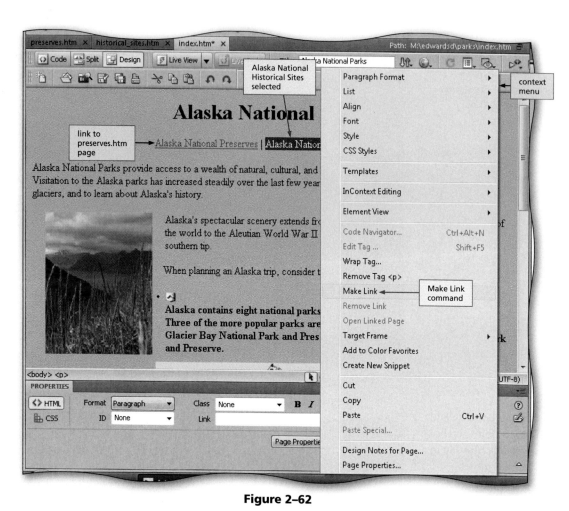

Figure 2–62

Q&A Can I create links on a new page that doesn't contain any text or images yet?

No. You must select something on a page that becomes the link to another location, so you need to add text or images before creating links. If you want to create links on a new page, it's a good idea to save the page before making the links.

2

• Click the Make Link command and then click historical_sites in the Select File dialog box to indicate you want to link to the Alaska National Historical Sites page (Figure 2–63).

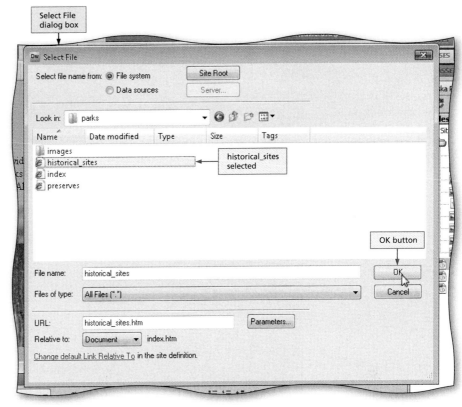

Figure 2–63

3

• Click the OK button and then click the selected text, Alaska National Historical Sites, to display the underlined link (Figure 2–64).

 Q&A Can I link to any of the files listed in the Files panel?

Yes. All the files you see in the Files panel in the Local Files list are internal files and are referenced as relative links.

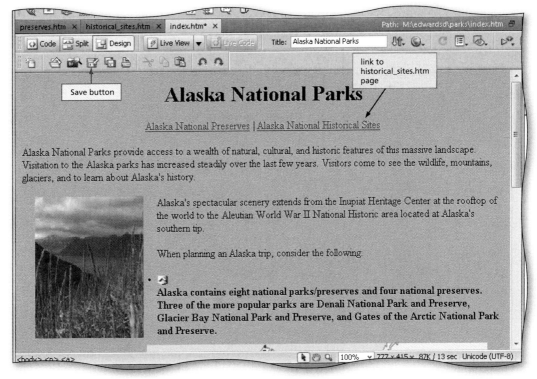

Figure 2–64

- Click the Save button on the Standard toolbar.

- Press the F12 key to view the index page in your browser (Figure 2–65).

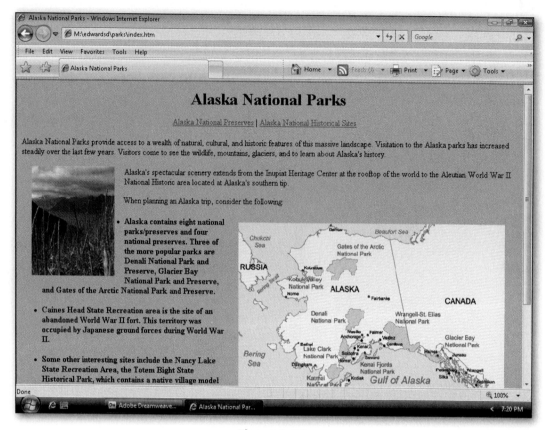

Figure 2–65

- Click the Alaska National Preserves link to verify that the link works and then click the browser Back button to return to the index page.

- Click the Alaska National Historical Sites link to verify that the link works.

- Close the browser.

Other Ways

1. Click Link box, type file name

Plan Ahead

Standard Links

Visitors to your Web site will use links to navigate the site, and expect to find the following types of links:

- **Links to the home page**. If your site is organized around a home page, include a link to the home page on every page in your site so visitors can easily return to it.

- **Links to main topics**. For each Web that discusses a main topic, include links to other main-topic Web pages.

- **Descriptive links**. For text links, make sure the text is descriptive so that visitors know what kind of information will appear when they click the link.

- **E-mail links**. If visitors have problems with your Web site, they expect to be able to contact someone who can help them. Include an e-mail link to the appropriate person.

To Create a Relative Link to the Home Page

Visitors can enter a Web site at any point, so you should always include a link from each page within the site to the index page. To accomplish this for the Alaska Parks Web site, you create a relative link to the index page from the Alaska National Historical Sites page and from the Alaska National Preserves page, as shown in the following steps.

1

- Click the preserves. htm tab and then scroll to the bottom of the page. Drag to select the text, Home.

- Drag the index. htm file name from the Files panel to the Link box, and then click in the Document window to deselect the text.

- Click the Save button on the Standard toolbar.

- Press the F12 key to view the Alaska National Preserves page in your browser (Figure 2–66).

Figure 2–66

Q&A Do I need to specify the complete path to the index.htm page?

No. When you link to another file in the same folder, you only need to specify the file name.

Q&A Can I make a linked Web page open in a new browser window?

Yes. By default, when you click a link, the linked Web page opens in the current browser window. However, you can specify that a linked Web page opens in a new browser window. To do this, first select the item and create the link. Next, in the Property inspector, click the Target box arrow and then click _blank on the Target pop-up menu. When you view the page in a browser and click the link, it is displayed in a new window.

● Click the Home link
to display the index
page (Figure 2–67).

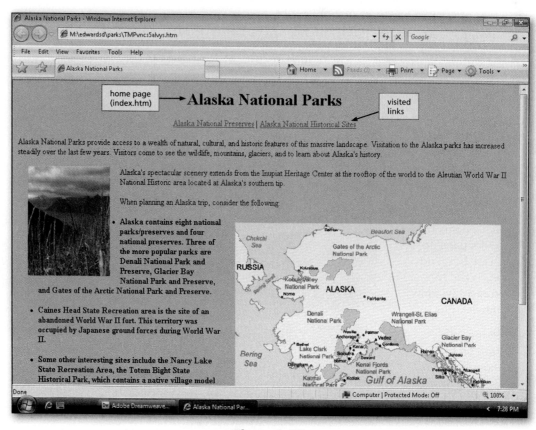

Figure 2–67

● Close the browser
to redisplay
Dreamweaver.

● Click the historical_
sites.htm tab. If nec-
essary, scroll to the
end of the document
and then drag to
select the text, Home.

● Drag the index.htm
file name from the
Files panel to the
Link box to create
the link, and then
click anywhere in the
Document window
to deselect the text.

● Click the Save
button on the
Standard toolbar.

● Press the F12 key
to view the Alaska
National Historical
Sites page in your
browser (Figure 2–68).

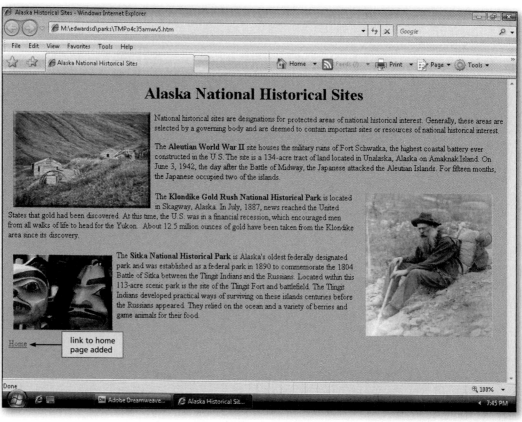

Figure 2–68

- Click the Home link to verify that it works.

- Close the browser.

Creating an Absolute Link

Recall that an absolute link (also called an external link) contains the complete Web site address of a document. You create absolute links the same way you create relative links — select the text and paste or type the Web site address.

To Create Absolute Links

You now will create three absolute links in the Alaska National Preserves page and three absolute links in the Alaska National Historical Sites page. These links are from the name of each of the three preserves to a Web page about the selected preserve and to the three historical sites listed in the Alaska National Historical Sites page. The following steps show how to create the six absolute links. Keep in mind that Web site addresses change. If the absolute links do not work, check the Dreamweaver CS4 companion site at *www.scsite.com/dwCS4/* for updates.

1

- Collapse the panel groups.

- Select the Alaska National Preserves page (preserves.htm). Drag to select the text Bering Land Bridge National Preserve.

- Click the Link box in the Property inspector and then type http://www.nps.gov/bela/index.htm as the link. Press the ENTER key.

- Drag to select the text Noatak National Preserve. Click the Link box and then type http://www.nps.gov/noat/index.htm as the link. Press the ENTER key.

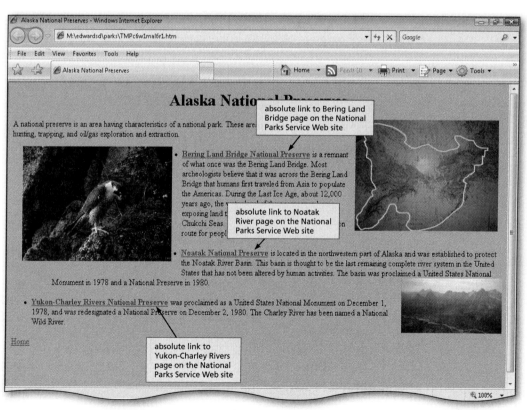

Figure 2–69

- Drag to select the text Yukon-Charley Rivers National Preserve. Click the Link box and then type http://www.nps.gov/yuch/index.htm as the link. Press the ENTER key.

- Save the Web page.

- Press the F12 key and then click each link to verify that they work (Figure 2–69).

- Close the browser.

- Select the historical_ sites.htm page. If necessary, scroll down and then drag to select the text Aleutian World War II. Click the Link box and then type `http://www.nps.gov/aleu/` as the link. Press the ENTER key.

- Drag to select the text Klondike Gold Rush National Historical Park. Click the Link box and then type `http://www.nps.gov/klgo/index.htm` as the link. Press the ENTER key.

- Drag to select the text Sitka National Historical Park. Click

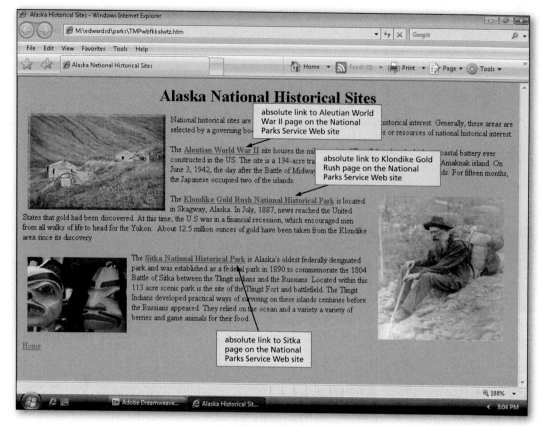

Figure 2–70

the Link box and then type `http://www.nps.gov/sitk/index.htm` as the link. Press the ENTER key, and then deselect the linked text, if necessary.

- Click the Save button on the Standard toolbar.

- Press the F12 key and then click each link to verify that they work (Figure 2–70).

- Close the browser.

Other Ways

1. Start browser, open Web page, select URL, copy URL, close browser, paste in Link box

---

E-Mail Links

An **e-mail link** is one of the foundation elements of any successful Web site. Visitors must be able to contact you for additional information or to comment on the Web page or Web site. When visitors click an e-mail link, their default e-mail program opens a new e-mail message. The e-mail address you specify is inserted automatically in the To box of the e-mail message header.

To Add an E-Mail Link

The following steps show how to create an e-mail link for your home page using your name as the linked text. You do this through the Insert menu.

- Click the index.htm tab, scroll down to the end of the page, and then drag to select your name. Click Insert on the Application bar and then point to Email Link (Figure 2–71).

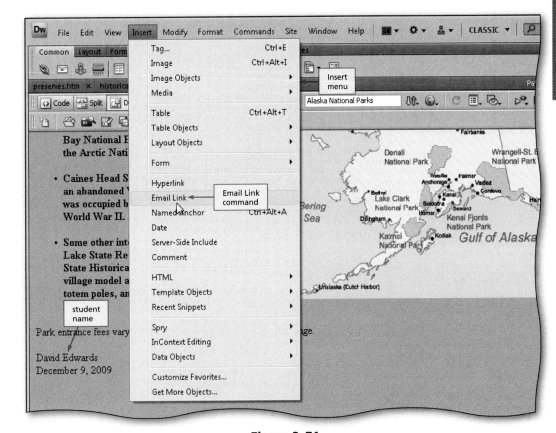

Figure 2–71

- Click Email Link to display the Email Link dialog box (Figure 2–72).

Q&A

What happens if I change the name in the Text box?

The text that you selected to create the e-mail link is also changed.

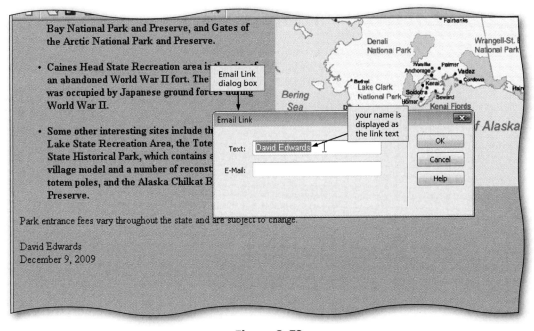

Figure 2–72

- Click the E-Mail text box and then type your e-mail address (Figure 2–73).

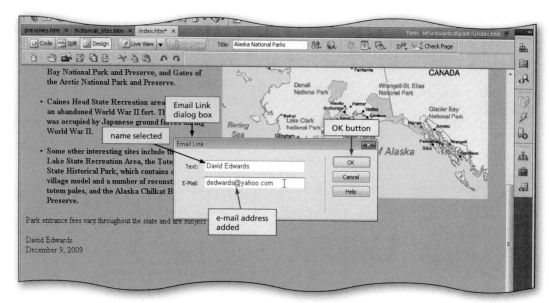

Figure 2–73

- Click the OK button.

- Click anywhere in the selected text of your name to view your e-mail address in the Property inspector Link box (Figure 2–74).

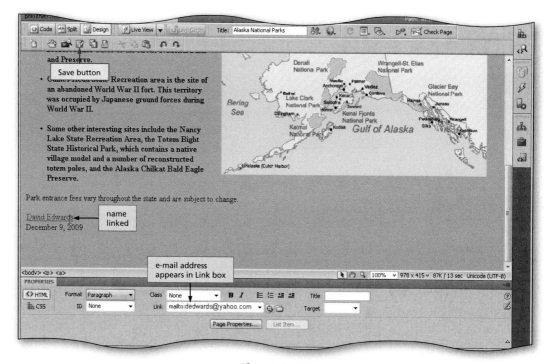

Figure 2–74

- Click the Save button on the Standard toolbar.

- Press the F12 key to view the page in your browser. Click your name to open your e-mail program. Send a message to yourself and one of your classmates.

- Close your e-mail program and then close the browser.

Changing the Color of Links

The Page Properties HTML dialog box provides three options for link colors: Link (the link has not been clicked), Active Link (the link changes color when the user clicks it), and Visited Link (the link has been visited). The default color for a link is blue and a visited link is purple. You easily can make changes to these default settings and select colors that complement the background and other colors you are using on your Web pages. This is accomplished through the Page Properties dialog box. You display the Page Properties dialog box by clicking Modify on the Application bar or by clicking the Page Properties button in the Property inspector and then selecting the Appearance (HTML) option. You then can click the box that corresponds to one of the three types of links (Links, Visited links, and Active links) and select a color to match your color scheme.

Editing and Deleting Links

Web development is a never-ending process. At some point, it will be necessary to edit or delete a link. For instance, an e-mail address may change, a URL to an external link may change, or an existing link may contain an error.

Dreamweaver makes it easy to edit or delete a link. First, select the link or click the link you want to change. The linked document name is displayed in the Link box in the Property inspector. To delete the link without deleting the text on the Web page, delete the text from the Link box in the Property inspector. To edit the link, make the change in the Link box.

A second method to edit or delete a link is to use the context menu. Right-click the link you want to change, and then click Remove Link on the context menu to eliminate the link or click Change Link on the context menu to edit the link. Clicking the URLs icon in the Assets panel displays a list of all absolute and e-mail links within the Web site.

Dreamweaver Views

Dreamweaver provides several ways to look at a document: **Design view**, **Code view**, **Split view**, and **Live View**. Thus far, you have been working in Design view. As you create and work with documents, Dreamweaver automatically generates the underlying source code. Recall that the source code defines the structure and layout of a Web document by using a variety of tags and attributes. Even though Dreamweaver generates the code, occasions occur that necessitate the tweaking or modifying of code.

Dreamweaver provides several options for viewing and working with source code. You can use Split view to split the Document window so that it displays both Code view and Design view. You can display only Code view in the Document window, or you can open the Code inspector.

Using Code View and Design View

In Split view, you work in a split-screen environment. You can see the design and the code at the same time. When you make a change in Design view, the HTML code also is changed but is not visible in the Document window. You can set word wrapping, display line numbers for the code, highlight invalid HTML code, set syntax coloring for code elements, and set indenting through the View menu's Code View Options submenu. Viewing the code at this early stage may not seem important, but the more code you learn, the more productive you will become.

BTW

Using the Quick Tag Editor
If you are familiar with HTML, you can use the Dreamweaver Quick Tag Editor to quickly review, insert, and edit HTML tags without leaving Design view. To use the Quick Tag Editor, select the text or image associated with the code you want to view, and then press CTRL+T. The Quick Tag Editor window opens displaying the HTML code, if appropriate, so you can examine or edit the code. If you type invalid HTML in the Quick Tag Editor, Dreamweaver attempts to correct it by inserting quotation marks or angle brackets where needed.

Within HTML source code, tags can be entered in uppercase, lowercase, or a combination of upper- and lowercase. The case of the tags has no effect on how the browser displays the output.

If the code is XHTML compliant, however, all tags are lowercase. In this book, if you use the instructions provided in Chapter 1 to create a new Web page, then your page is XHTML compliant. XHTML was discussed in the Introduction chapter. Therefore, when describing source code tags, this book uses lowercase letters for tags and attributes to make it easier to differentiate them from the other text and to coordinate with the XHTML standard.

To Use Design View and Code View Simultaneously

The following steps show how to use the Split button to display Code view and Design view at the same time and examine the code for the
 (line break) and <p> (paragraph) tags. The paragraph tag has an opening tag, <p>, and a closing tag, </p>. The
 (line break) tag does not have a closing tag.

1

- Click the preserves.htm tab.

- Collapse the Files panel and hide the Property inspector, if necessary.

- Position the insertion point to the left of the heading, Alaska National Preserves.

- Click the Split button to display Code view in the upper window and Design view in the lower window. If line numbers do not appear, click the Line Numbers button (Figure 2–75).

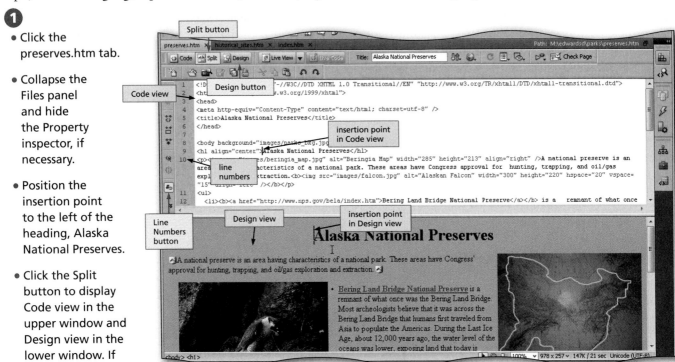

Figure 2–75

Q&A What is the advantage of working in Split view?

Splitting the Document window to view the code makes it easier to view the visual design while you make changes in the source code.

2

- Click the Design button to return to Design view.

Modifying Source Code

One of the more common problems within Dreamweaver and the source code relates to line breaks and paragraphs. Occasionally, you inadvertently press the ENTER key or insert a line break and need to remove the tag. Or, you may copy and paste or open a text file that contains unneeded paragraphs or line breaks.

Pressing the BACKSPACE key or DELETE key may return you to the previous line, but does not always delete the line break or paragraph tag within the source code. The deletion of these tags is determined by the position of the insertion point when you press the BACKSPACE or DELETE keys. If the insertion point is still inside the source code, pressing the BACKSPACE key will not delete these tags and your page will not display correctly. When this occurs, the best solution is to delete the tag through Code view.

Live View

Generally, to view a Web page in a browser such as Internet Explorer or Firefox requires that you leave Dreamweaver and open the browser in another window. If the Web designer wants to view the source code, an additional window also needs to be opened. Dreamweaver's **Live View** feature, however, allows you to preview how the page will look in a browser without leaving Dreamweaver. If you want to view and modify code, you can do so through a split screen; and the changes to the code are reflected instantly in the rendered display.

To Use Live View

In the following steps, you switch to Live View.

- Click Live View on the Document toolbar to view the page as it would appear in the browser and to verify that the line spacing is correct and that the document is properly formatted (Figure 2–76).

Q&A What should I do if an Information bar appears explaining a Flash Plug-in was not found?

Click the Close link in the Information bar, and then install the Flash plug-in from the Adobe Web site at *www. adobe.com*.

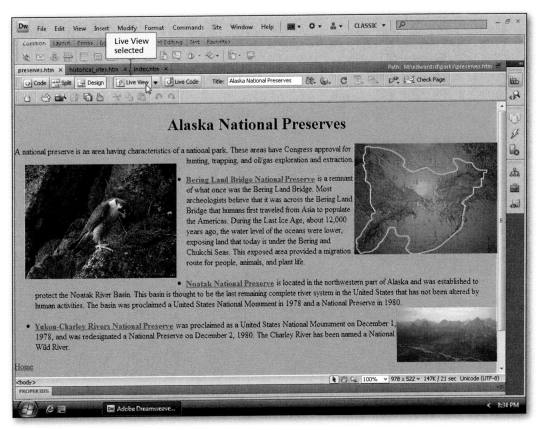

Figure 2–76

- Click the Live View button to return to Design view and make any necessary corrections. If necessary, click the Save button.

BTW

Quick Reference
For a table that lists how to complete tasks covered in this book using the keyboard, see the Quick Reference at the end of this book.

Quitting Dreamweaver

After you add pages to your Web site, including images and links, and then view your pages in a browser, Chapter 2 is complete.

To Close the Web Site and Quit Dreamweaver

The following step shows how to close the Web site, quit Dreamweaver, and return control to Windows.

- Click the Close button on the right corner of the Dreamweaver title bar to close the Dreamweaver window, the Document window, and the Alaska Parks Web site.

- Click the Yes button if a prompt is displayed indicating that you need to save changes.

Chapter Summary

Chapter 2 introduced you to images and links, and discussed how to view source code and use Live View. You began the chapter by copying data files to the local site. You added two new pages, one for Alaska National Historical Sites and one for Alaska National Preserves, to the Web site you started in Chapter 1. Next, you added images to the index page. Following that, you added a background image and page images to the two new pages. Then, you added relative links to all three pages. You added an e-mail link to the index page and absolute links to the Alaska National Preserves and Alaska National Historical Sites pages. Finally, you learned how to view source code. The items listed below include all the new Dreamweaver skills you have learned in this chapter.

1. Create the Alaska National Preserves Web Page (DW 111)
2. Create the Alaska National Historical Sites Web Page (DW 114)
3. Set Invisible Element Preferences and Turn on Visual Aids (DW 120)
4. Open a Web Page from a Local Web Site (DW 124)
5. Insert an Image into the Index Page (DW 125)
6. Align an Image (DW 129)
7. Adjust the Image Size and the Horizontal and Vertical Space (DW 130)
8. Insert and Align Images in the Alaska National Preserves Web Page (DW 134)
9. Insert and Align Images in the Alaska National Historical Parks Web Page (DW 136)
10. Crop and Modify the Brightness/Contrast of an Image (DW 141)
11. Add Text for Relative Links (DW 146)
12. Create a Relative Link Using Point to File (DW 147)
13. Create a Relative Link Using the Context Menu (DW 148)
14. Create a Relative Link to the Home Page (DW 151)
15. Create Absolute Links (DW 153)
16. Add an E-Mail Link (DW 155)
17. Use Design View and Code View Simultaneously (DW 158)
18. Use Live View (DW 159)

Learn It Online

Test your knowledge of chapter content and key terms.

Instructions: To complete the Learn It Online exercises, start your browser, click the Address bar, and then enter the Web address `scsite.com/dwCS4/learn`. When the Dreamweaver CS4 Learn It Online page is displayed, click the link for the exercise you want to complete and then read the instructions.

Chapter Reinforcement TF, MC, and SA
A series of true/false, multiple choice, and short answer questions that test your knowledge of the chapter content.

Flash Cards
An interactive learning environment where you identify chapter key terms associated with displayed definitions.

Practice Test
A series of multiple choice questions that test your knowledge of chapter content and key terms.

Who Wants to Be a Computer Genius?
An interactive game that challenges your knowledge of chapter content in the style of a television quiz show.

Wheel of Terms
An interactive game that challenges your knowledge of chapter key terms in the style of the television show *Wheel of Fortune*.

Crossword Puzzle Challenge
A crossword puzzle that challenges your knowledge of key terms presented in the chapter.

Apply Your Knowledge

Reinforce the skills and apply the concepts you learned in this chapter.

Adding, Aligning, and Resizing an Image on a Web Page

Instructions: In this activity, you modify a Web page by adding, aligning, and resizing an image (Figure 2–77). Make sure you have downloaded the data file for Chapter02\apply.

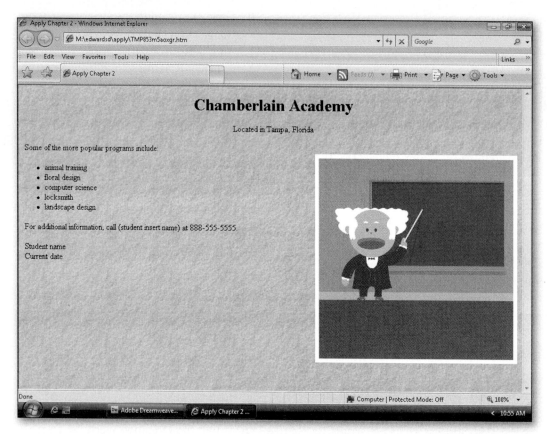

Figure 2–77

Perform the following tasks:

1. Use the Windows Computer tool to copy the teacher.jpg image from the Chapter02\apply data files folder into the images folder for your Apply Exercises local Web site.

2. Start Dreamweaver.

3. Open the Apply Exercises site.

4. Open the apply.htm file (the page you created for the Apply Your Knowledge exercise in Chapter 1).

5. Select the teacher.jpg image and drag it to the right of the colon at the end of the first sentence.

6. Type the following text in the Image Tag Accessibility Attributes text box: teacher. Click the OK button.

7. If necessary, select the image. Double-click the W text box and type 400. Double-click the H text box and type 400.

8. Click the Align button arrow and align the image to the right.

9. Title the document Apply Chapter 2.

10. Save your document and then view it in your browser. Submit it in the format specified by your instructor.

Extend Your Knowledge

Extend the skills you learned in this chapter and experiment with new skills. You may need to use Help to complete the assignment.

Adding, Aligning, and Resizing Images on a Web Page

Instructions: In this activity, you modify a Web page by adding, aligning, and resizing an image (Figure 2–78). Make sure you have downloaded the data files for Chapter02\extend.

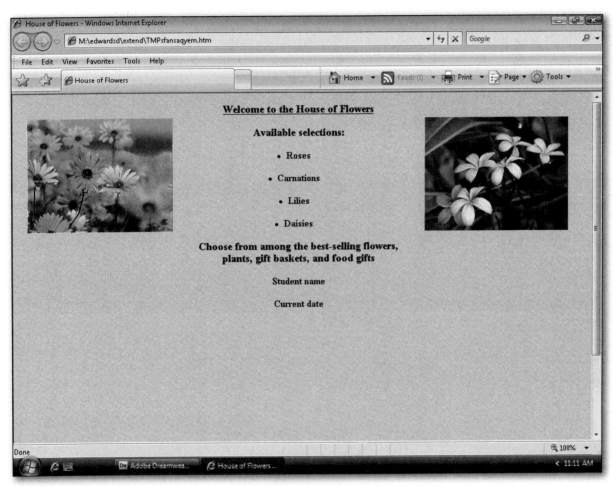

Figure 2–78

Perform the following tasks:

1. Copy the data files from the Chapter02\extend data files folder into the images folder for your Extend Exercises local Web site.

2. Start Dreamweaver, and open the Extend Exercises site.

3. Open the extend.htm file (the page you created for the Extend Your Knowledge exercise in Chapter 1).

4. Drag the flowers01 image to the top of the page and to the left of the second line, which begins, "Choose from among".

5. Type flowers01 in the Alternate text text box.

6. Resize the image width to 250 and the height to 190.

7. Type 25 in both the V Space box and the H Space box.

Continued >

Extend Your Knowledge *continued*

8. Align the image to the left.

9. Drag the flowers02 image to the right of the second line. Type flowers02 in the Alternate text text box.

10. Resize the image width to 250 and the height to 190.

11. Type 25 in both the V Space box and the H Space box.

12. Align the image to the right.

13. Move the sentence that begins with "Choose from among" after the bulleted list. Make sure the sentence remains centered and bold and does not have a bullet.

14. Save your document and then view it in your browser. Submit it in the format specified by your instructor.

Make It Right

Analyze a document and then correct all errors and/or improve the design.

Adding an Image and E-mail Address to a Web Page

Instructions: In this activity, you modify an existing Web page by adding an image (Figure 2–79). Make sure you have downloaded the data files for Chapter02\right.

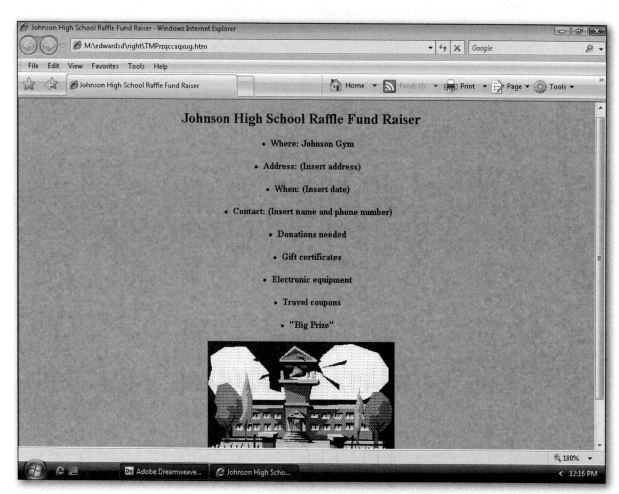

Figure 2–79

Perform the following tasks:

1. Copy the data file from the Chapter02\right data files folder into the images folder for your Right Exercises local Web site.

2. Start Dreamweaver, open the Right Exercises site, and then open the right.htm page. If necessary, expand the Local Files panel and the Property inspector. Verify that HTML is selected.

3. Click below the last item in the list. If a bullet is displayed, click the Unordered List button in the Property inspector. Center the line, if necessary.

4. Drag the school image to the center of the page below the last line of text. Type school for the alternative text.

5. Adjust the image width to 325 and the height to 215.

6. Make any other adjustments as necessary to make your Web page match the one shown in Figure 2–79 on the previous page.

7. Save your document and then view it in your browser.

8. Submit your Web page in the format specified by your instructor.

In the Lab

Create a document using the guidelines, concepts, and skills presented in this chapter. Labs are listed in order of increasing difficulty.

Lab 1: Modifying the Mobile Pet Services Web Site

Problem: Now that Bryan has a basic Web page for his Mobile Pet Services Web site, he wants to make the page more appealing to visitors. He asks you to help him add images of pets to his Web page.

Image files for the Bryan's Mobile Pet Service Web site are included with the data files. See the inside back cover of this book for instructions for downloading the data files or see your instructor for information on accessing the files in this book.

You need to add two new pages to the Bryan's Mobile Pet Service Web site: a services page and a references page. In this exercise, you will add relative and absolute links to each page. You also will add a background image to the new pages. Next, you will insert images on all three pages and use the settings in Table 2–4 on page DW 168 to align the images and enter the alternate text. You then will add an e-mail link to the home page and relative links from the two new pages to the home page. The pages for the Web site are shown in Figures 2–80a, 2–80b, and 2–80c on the following page. (Software and hardware settings determine how a Web page is displayed in a browser. Your Web pages may be displayed differently in your browser from the pages shown in the figures.)

In the Lab *continued*

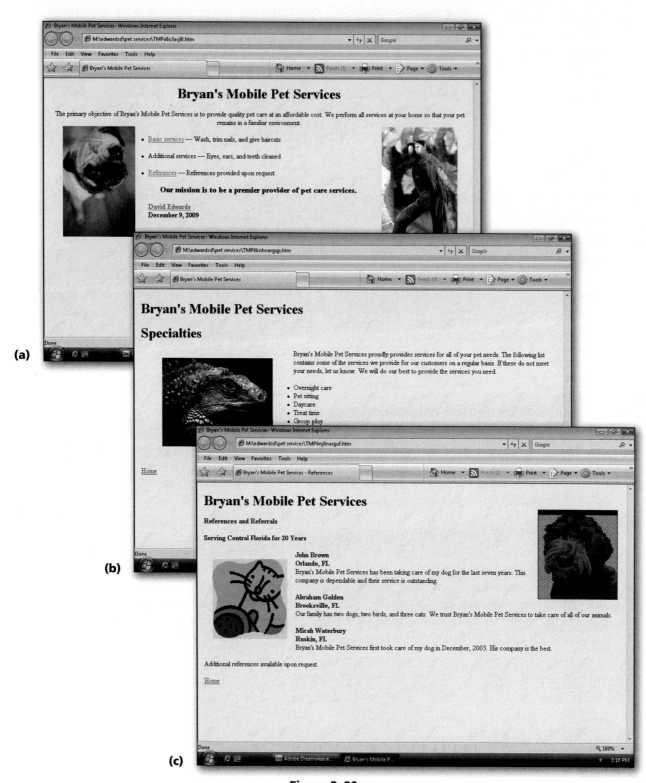

(a)

(b)

(c)

Figure 2–80

Table 2–4 Image Property Settings for the Bryan's Mobile Pet Services Web Site						
Image Name	W	H	V Space	H Space	Align	Alt
dog01	170	250	0	30	left	dog
bird01	175	250	0	30	right	birds
iguana	260	200	20	50	left	iguana
cat	175	180	20	20	left	cat
dog02	-	-	-	-	right	dog

Perform the following tasks:

1. Copy the data files to your pets folder and the pets\images folder as appropriate.

2. Start Dreamweaver and display the panel groups. Open the Pet Services site, and then open the index.htm file.

3. If necessary, click the expander arrow to expand the Property inspector and display the Standard toolbar.

4. If necessary, click the Expand/Collapse button to the left of the images folder in the Files panel to display the contents of the images folder. Position the insertion point at the end of the first sentence (which ends "…so that your pet remains in a familiar environment.") Drag the dog01 image to the insertion point, add the alternate text as indicated in Table 2–4, and then apply the settings shown in Table 2–4 to resize and align the image. Position the insertion point at the end of the first sentence again. Drag the bird01 image to the insertion point and then apply the settings shown in Table 2–4.

5. Select the text Basic services in the first bulleted item. Use the drag-and-drop file method to create a link to the services page. Repeat this process to add a link from the References text to the references page. Select your name. Use the Insert menu to create an e-mail link using your name. Center the first sentence, if necessary. Save the index page (Figure 2–80a on the previous page).

6. Open the services page. Click Modify on the Application bar and then click Page Properties. Apply the background image (located in the images folder) to the services page.

7. Position the insertion point to the left of the first sentence. Drag the iguana image to the insertion point, and then apply the settings shown in Table 2–4.

8. If necessary, scroll down. Select Home and then create a relative link to the index page. Save the services page (Figure 2–80b on the previous page).

9. Open the references page. Apply the background image (located in the images folder) as you did in Step 6 for the services page.

10. Position the insertion point to the right of the heading and then drag the dog02 image to the insertion point. Position the insertion point to the left of the first reference in the list (John Brown). Drag the cat01 image to the insertion point. Apply the settings shown in Table 2–4 to both images.

11. Scroll to the bottom of the page. Select Home and then create a relative link to the index page. Save the references page (Figure 2–80c on the previous page).

12. View the Web site in your browser. Check each link to verify that it works. Submit the documents in the format specified by your instructor.

In the Lab

Lab 2: Modifying a Jewelry Sales Web Site

Problem: Eve Perry, for whom you created the Jewelry by Eve Web site and Web page, is very pleased with the response she has received. She asks you to add two images to the index page and to create a second page with links and images. Eve wants the new page to include information about her company's history.

Add a second Web page to the Jewelry by Eve Web site. The revised Web site is shown in Figures 2–81a and 2–81b. Table 2–5 on the next page includes the settings and alternate text for the images. Software and hardware settings determine how a Web page displays in a browser. Your Web pages may be displayed differently in your browser from those in the figures.

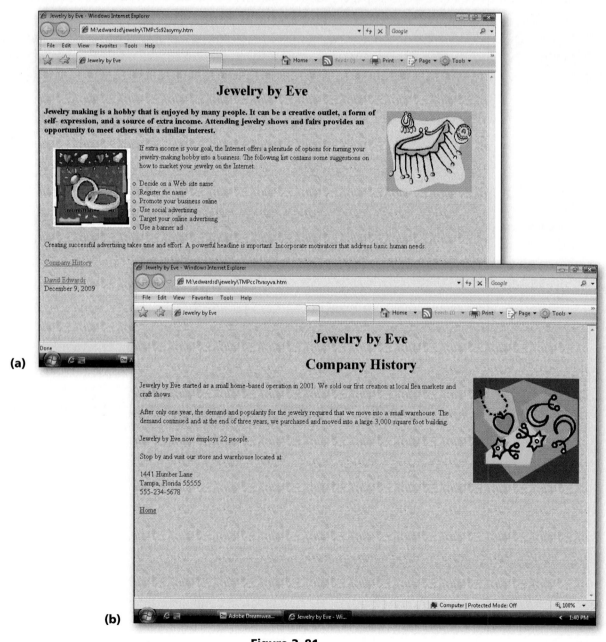

(a)

(b)

Figure 2–81

Table 2–5 Image Property Settings for the Jewelry by Eve Web Site

Image Name	W	H	V Space	H Space	Align	Alt
Necklace1	190	174	25	25	right	necklace
Rings	174	170	10	20	left	rings
Necklace2	234	224	10	10	right	necklace

Perform the following tasks:

1. Copy the data files to your jewelry folder and jewelry\images folder as appropriate.
2. Start Dreamweaver and display the panel groups. Open the Jewelry Business site, and then open the index.htm file.
3. If necessary, click the expander arrow to expand the Property inspector and display the Standard toolbar.
4. Position the insertion point to the right of the heading and then drag the necklace1.jpg image to the insertion point. Enter the Alt text, and then apply the settings shown in Table 2–5 to align the image.
5. Position the insertion point to the left of the paragraph that begins, "If extra income is your goal", and then drag the rings image to the insertion point. Apply the settings shown in Table 2–5.
6. Position the insertion point to the right of the last sentence and then press ENTER.
7. Type the following text: Company History. Select the Company History text and use the drag-and-drop method to create a link to the history page. Select your name. Use the Insert menu to create an e-mail link using your e-mail address. Save the index page.
8. Open the history page. Open the Page Properties dialog box. Click the Background image Browse button, and then add the background image (jewelry_bkg.jpg) to the history page.
9. Position the insertion point at the end of subhead, Company History, and then drag the necklace2.jpg image to the insertion point. Apply the settings shown in Table 2–5.
10. Select Home and then create a relative link to the index page. Save the history page.
11. Check the spelling of your document and correct any errors.
12. Save the file.
13. View the Web site in your browser. Check each link to verify that it works. Submit the documents in the format specified by your instructor.

In the Lab

Lab 3: Modifying the Credit Protection Web Site

Problem: Linda Reyes has received favorable comments about the Web page and site you created on credit information. Her bank wants to use the Web site to provide additional information to its customers. Linda has asked you and another intern at the bank to work with her to create two more Web pages to add to the site. They want one of the pages to discuss credit protection and the other page to contain information about identity theft.

Revise the Credit Protection Web site. The revised pages for the Web site are shown in Figures 2–82a, 2–82b, and 2–82c on the following pages. Table 2–6 on page DW 171 includes the settings and Alt text for the images. Software and hardware settings determine how a Web page displays in a browser. Your Web pages may be displayed differently in your browser from those in the figures.

Continued >

In the Lab *continued*

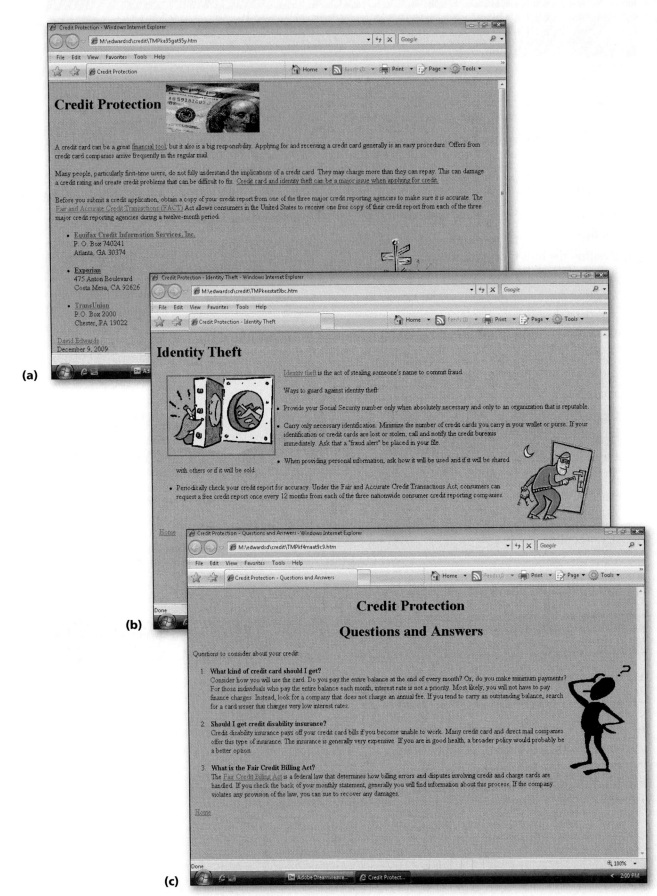

(a)

(b)

(c)

Figure 2–82

Table 2–6 Image Property Settings for the Credit Protection Web Site						
Image Name	W	H	V Space	H Space	Align	Alt
answer	172	204	None	100	Right	Reporting options
money	211	107	None	10	Middle	Money
protection	240	170	14	20	Left	Identity theft
question	140	238	None	15	Right	Questions?
theft	179	183	20	None	Right	Protect personal information

Perform the following tasks:

1. Copy the data files to your credit folder and credit\images folder as appropriate.

2. Start Dreamweaver and display the panel groups. Open the Credit Protection site, and then open index.htm.

3. If necessary, display the Property inspector and the Standard toolbar. Expand the Property inspector.

4. Position the insertion point to the right of the heading and then drag the money image to the insertion point. Apply the settings shown in Table 2–6. Position the insertion point to the right of the text, Equifax Credit Information Services, Inc. Drag the answer image to the insertion point. Apply the settings shown in Table 2–6.

5. Select the text, financial tool, located in the first sentence of the first paragraph. Create a relative link from the selected text to the questions page. Select the text, Fair and Accurate Credit Transactions (FACT), located in the second sentence of the third paragraph. Create an absolute link to http://www.annualcreditreport.com. Select the name of the company in the first bulleted list item (Equifax Credit Information Services, Inc.) and create an absolute link using http://www.equifax.com. Create absolute links from the other two company names, using http://www.experian.com and http://www.transunion.com, respectively.

6. Position the insertion point at the end of the second paragraph (after the word fix). Press the SPACEBAR. Type the following text: Credit card and identity theft can be a major issue when applying for credit. Select the text you just typed and then create a relative link to the theft page. Add an e-mail link to your name. Save the index page (Figure 2–82a on the previous page).

7. Open the theft page and apply the background image (credit_bkg) to the page.

8. Position the insertion point to the left of the second line and then drag the protection image to the insertion point. Apply the settings shown in Table 2–6. Position the insertion point after the second sentence in the second bulleted point and then drag the theft image to the insertion point. Apply the settings shown in Table 2–6.

9. Drag to select the text, Identity theft, at the beginning of the first sentence and then create an absolute link using http://www.consumer.gov/idtheft/ as the URL. Create an absolute link from the protection image using the same URL. Select the image and then type the URL in the Link box. Select Home and then create a relative link to the index.htm page. Save the theft page (Figure 2–82b on the previous page).

10. Open the questions page. Apply the background image that you added to the theft page in Step 7. Use the text, Home, at the bottom of the page to create a relative link to the index page.

11. Position the insertion point to the right of the first line of text, Questions to consider about your credit:, and then drag the question image to the insertion point. Apply the settings in Table 2–6.

Continued >

In the Lab *continued*

12. Create an absolute link from the Fair Credit Billing Act text in the answer to question 3. In this link, use the following as the URL: http://www.ftc.gov/bcp/edu/pubs/consumer/credit/cre16.shtm. Title the page Credit Protection – Questions and Answers. Save the questions page (Figure 2–82c on page DW 170).

13. View the Web site in your browser and verify that your external and relative links work. *Hint*: Remember to check the link for the image on the theft.htm page. Submit the documents in the format specified by your instructor.

Cases and Places

Apply your creative thinking and problem solving skills to design and implement a solution.

• Easier   ••More Difficult

• 1: Modify the Favorite Sports Web Site

In Chapter 1, you created a Web site named Favorite Sports with a Web page listing your favorite sports and teams. Now, you want to add another page to the site. Create and format the new page, which should include general information about a selected sport. Create a relative link from the home page to the new page and from the new page to the home page. Add a background image to the new page and insert an image on one of the pages. Include an appropriate title for the page. Save the page in the sports subfolder. For a selection of images and backgrounds, visit the Dreamweaver CS4 Media Web page (scsite.com/dwCS4/media).

• 2: Modify the Hobbies Web Site

Several of your friends were impressed with the Web page and Web site you created about your favorite hobby in Chapter 1. They have given you some topics they think you should include on the site. You decide to create an additional page that will consist of details about your hobby and the topics your friends suggested. Format the page. Add an absolute link to a related Web site and a relative link from the home page to the new page and from the new page to the home page. Add a background image to the new page. Create an e-mail link on the index page. Title the page with the name of the selected hobby. Save the page in the hobby subfolder. For a selection of images and backgrounds, visit the Dreamweaver CS4 Media Web page (scsite.com/dwCS4/media).

•• 3: Modify the Politics Web Site

In Chapter 1, you created a Web site and a Web page to publicize your campaign for public office. Develop two additional pages to add to the site. Apply a background image to the new pages. Apply appropriate formatting to the two new pages. Scan a picture of yourself or take a picture with a digital camera and include the picture on the index page. Add a second image illustrating one of your campaign promises. Include at least two images on one of the new pages and one image on the other new page. Add alternative text for all images, and then add appropriate H Space and V Space property features to position the images. Create e-mail links on all three pages and create relative links from the home page to both pages and from each of the pages to the home page. Create an absolute link to a related site on one of the pages. Give each page a meaningful title and then save the pages in the government subfolder. For a selection of images and backgrounds, visit the Dreamweaver CS4 Media Web page (scsite.com/dwCS4/media).

•• 4: Modify the Favorite Music Web Site

Make It Personal

Modify the music Web site you created in Chapter 1 by creating a new page. Format the page. Discuss your favorite artist or band on the new page. Add a background image to the new page. On the index page, add an image and align the image to the right, and on the new page, add a different image and align the image to the left. Add appropriate alternative text for each image. Position each image appropriately on the page by using the H Space and V Space property features. Add an e-mail link on the index page, and add text and a relative link from the new page to the index page. View your Web pages in your browser. Give the page a meaningful title and then save the page in your music subfolder. For a selection of images and backgrounds, visit the Dreamweaver CS4 Media Web page (scsite.com/dwCS4/media).

Continued >

Cases and Places *continued*

• • 5: Create the Student Trips Web Site

Working Together

The student trips Web site you and your classmates created in Chapter 1 is a success. Everyone loves it. The dean is so impressed that she asks the group to continue with the project. Your team creates and formats three additional Web pages, one for each of three possible locations for the trip. Add a background image to all new pages. Add two images to each of the pages, including the index page. Resize one of the images. Add the Alt text for each image, and then position each image appropriately using the H Space and V Space property features. Create a link from the index page to each of the three new pages and a link from each page to the index page. Create an absolute link to a related informational Web site on each of the three new pages. Add an appropriate title to each page. Preview in a browser to verify the links. Save the pages in your trips subfolder. For a selection of images and backgrounds, visit the Dreamweaver CS4 Media Web page (scsite.com/dwCS4/media).

3 | Tables and Page Layout

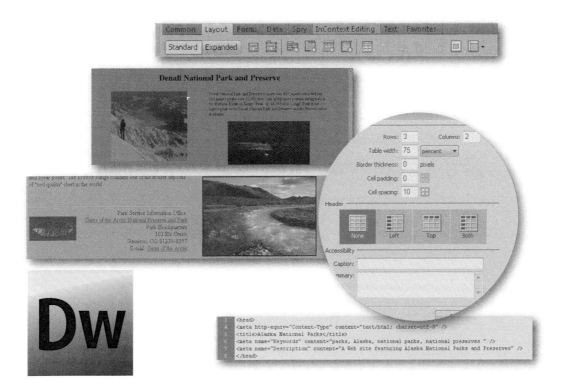

Objectives

You will have mastered the material in this chapter when you can:

- Understand page layout
- Design a Web page using tables
- Create a table structure
- Modify a table structure
- Describe HTML table tags
- Add content to a table
- Add a border to a table
- Format table content
- Format a table
- Add borders to images
- Create head content

3 | Tables and Page Layout

Introduction

Chapter 3 introduces you to using tables for page layout and adding head content elements. Page layout is an important part of Web design because it determines the way your page will be displayed in a browser, which is one of the major challenges for any Web designer.

Dreamweaver's table feature is a great tool for designing a Web page. One reason is that it is very similar to the table feature in word processing programs such as Microsoft Office Word. A table allows you to add vertical and horizontal structure to a Web page. Using a table, you can put just about anything on your page and have it be displayed in a specific location. Using tables in Dreamweaver, you can create columns of text or navigation bars and lay out tabular data. You can delete, split, and merge rows and columns; modify table, row, or cell properties to add color and adjust alignment; and copy, paste, and delete cells in the table structure.

Project — Formatted Tables with Images

In this chapter, you continue creating the Alaska Parks Web site. You use tables to create two new Web pages focusing on two of Alaska's more popular parks — Denali National Park and Preserve and Gates of the Arctic National Park and Preserve. You then add these new pages to the park's Web site and link to them from the index.htm Web page (Figures 3–1a and 3–1b on pages DW 177 through 178). When you complete your Web page additions, you add keywords and a description as the head content. Figures 3–1a and 3–1b show the two final pages.

In the second part of this chapter, you learn the value of head content and how to add it to a Web page. When you create a Web page, the underlying source code is organized into two main sections: the head section and the body section. In Chapters 1 and 2, you created Web pages in the body section, which contains the page content that is displayed in the browser. The head section contains a variety of information, including keywords search engines use. With the exception of the page title, all head content is invisible when viewed in the Dreamweaver document window or in a browser. Some head content is accessed by other programs, such as search engines, and some content is accessed by the browser. This chapter discusses the head content options and the importance of adding this content to all Web pages.

(a) Denali National Park and Preserve page

Figure 3–1

(b) Gates of the Arctic National Park and Preserve page

Figure 3–1 (*continued*)

Overview

As you read this chapter, you learn how to add to your Web site the pages shown in Figures 3-1a and 3-1b by performing these general tasks:

- Insert a table into a Dreamweaver Web page
- Center the table
- Change vertical alignment within the table
- Specify column width
- Merge cells
- Add accessibility attributes
- Add text and images to a table
- Add links
- Add borders to tables and images

Plan
Ahead

General Project Guidelines

When adding pages to a Web site, consider the appearance and characteristics of the completed site. As you create and add the two Web pages to the Alaska Parks Web site shown in Figure 3–1a and Figure 3–1b, you should follow these general guidelines:

1. **Plan the Web pages.** Determine how the pages will fit into the Web site.

2. **Organize your content.** Create and organize the content for the two new pages. The images should be copied and pasted into the images folder.

3. **Link the new content.** Consider the content of each new page and how it will link to and from the other pages in the Web site.

4. **Organize images.** Organize your images within the Assets panel. Determine which image belongs on which Web page. Determine the text content to designate for the accessibility attributes.

5. **Place images.** Consider where you will place the images within the tables. Determine the vertical and horizontal space that you need to better place the image. Determine which images need to be resized and how much resizing needs to be done.

6. **Determine when to add borders.** Consider when and where to add borders to tables and images. Determine the number of pixels that should be added for these elements.

7. **Identify cells to merge.** Determine whether cells within the table need to be merged to provide a better layout. If so, determine which cells need to be merged to provide a more attractive Web page.

When necessary, more specific details concerning the above guidelines are presented at appropriate points in the chapter. The chapter also will identify the actions performed and decisions made regarding these guidelines during the creation of the Web pages shown in Figures 3–1a and 3–1b on pages DW 177–178.

Starting Dreamweaver and Opening a Web Site

Each time you start Dreamweaver, it opens to the last site displayed when you closed the program. It therefore may be necessary for you to open the parks Web site.

To Start Dreamweaver and Open the Alaska Parks Web Site

With a good understanding of the requirements, the necessary decisions, and the planning process, the next step is to start Dreamweaver and open the Alaska Parks Web site.

- Click the Start button on the Windows taskbar.

- Point to Adobe Dreamweaver CS4 on the Start menu or point to All Programs on the Start menu, and then point to Adobe Dreamweaver CS4 on the All Programs list.

- Click Adobe Dreamweaver CS4 to start Dreamweaver.

- If necessary, display the panel groups.

- If the Alaska Parks hierarchy is not displayed, click the Files panel button and point to Alaska Parks on the Files pop-up menu to highlight it (Figure 3–2).

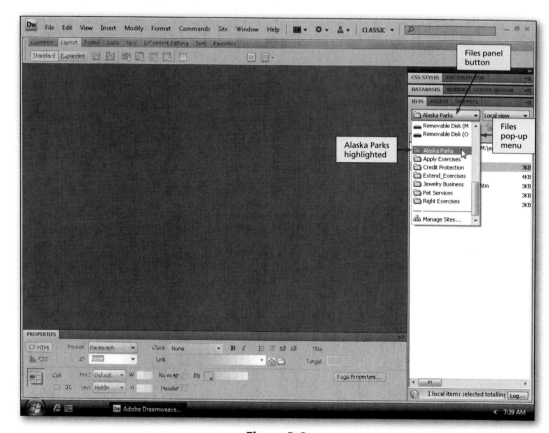

Figure 3–2

Q&A

How can I see a list of the sites I have defined in Dreamweaver?

Clicking the **Files pop-up menu** in the Files panel lists the sites you have defined. When you open the site, a list of pages and subfolders within the site is displayed.

- If necessary, click Alaska Parks to display the Alaska Parks Web site hierarchy in the Files panel.

Copying Data Files to the Local Web Site

In the following steps, the data files for this chapter are stored on drive M:. The location on your computer may be different. If necessary, verify the location of the data files with your instructor.

To Copy Data Files to the Parks Web Site

Your data files contain images for Chapter 3. In Chapters 1 and 2, you copied the data files using the Windows Computer tool. Now that you are more familiar with the Files panel, you can use it to copy the data files for Chapter 3 into the images folder for your Alaska Parks Web site. In the following steps, you copy the data files for Chapter 3 from the Chapter03 folder on a USB drive to the parks\images folder stored in the *your name* folder on the same USB drive.

1

- Click the Files panel button, and then click the name of the drive containing your data files, such as Removable Disk (M:).

- If necessary, click the plus sign (+) next to the folder containing your data files to expand that folder, and then click the plus sign (+) next to the Chapter03 folder to expand it.

- Expand the parks folder to display the data files.

- Click the first file in the list, which is denali_bear image file, to select the file.

- Hold down the SHIFT key and then click the last file in the list, which is the gates_plane image, to select all the data files.

- Press CTRL+C to copy the files.

- If necessary, click the Files panel button, and then click the drive containing the Alaska Parks Web site. Expand the *your name* folder and the parks folder, and then click the images folder to select it (Figure 3–3).

Q&A What if my Files panel doesn't match the one in Figure 3–3?

In Figure 3–3, the Files panel displays the contents of the USB drive, Removable Disk (M:), which includes both the data files for Chapter 3 and the *your name* folder for the Web sites you create in this book. If your Alaska Parks Web site is stored on a drive other than Removable Disk (M:), the name of the drive appears in the Files panel button, and the data files for Chapter 3 are listed on your designated drive.

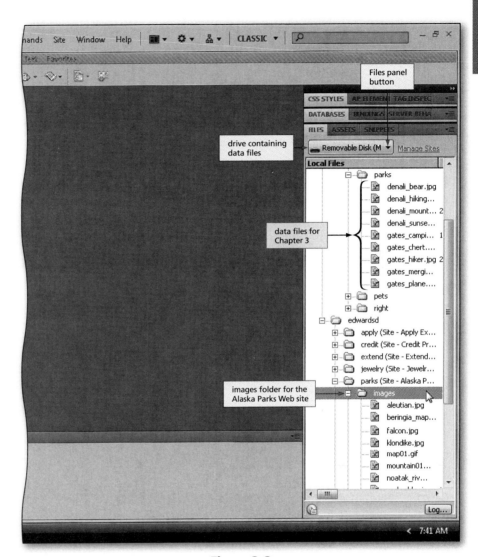

Figure 3–3

2

- Press CTRL+V to paste the files in the images folder.

Q&A Is there another method for copying data files into the Web site folder?

Yes, you can copy the files using the Windows Computer tool.

Adding Pages to a Web Site

You copied the images necessary to begin creating your new Web pages in the Alaska Parks local root folder in the Files panel. You will add two pages to the Web site: a page for the Denali National Park and Preserve and a page for the Gates of the Arctic National Park and Preserve. You first create the Denali National Park and Preserve Web page. You add the background image and a heading to each new page. Next, you use Dreamweaver's Standard and Expanded modes to insert tables and add text, images, and links into the cells within the table.

To Open a New Document Window

The following step illustrates how to open a new document window, which will become the Denali National Park and Preserve page, and then save the page as denali.htm.

1

- Click File on the Application bar and then click New to display the New Document dialog box.

- If necessary, click Blank Page to indicate you are creating a new page.

- If necessary, click HTML in the Page Type list to indicate the page is a standard HTML page.

- Click the Create button to create the page.

- Click the Save button on the Standard toolbar to open the Save As dialog box.

- Type denali as the File name. If necessary, select the parks folder, and then click the Save button to save the denali.htm page in the Alaska Parks local folder and to display the path and file name on the document tab (Figure 3–4).

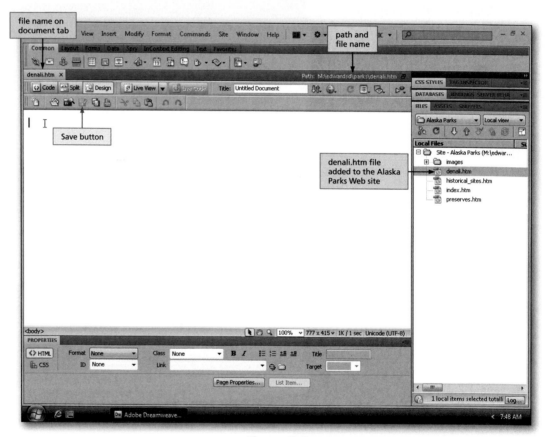

Figure 3–4

Creating the Denali National Park and Preserve Web Page

You start creating the Denali National Park and Preserve page by applying a background image. This is the same background image you used for the Alaska Parks Web site pages in Chapters 1 and 2.

To Add a Background Image to the Denali National Park and Preserve Web Page

To provide additional space in the document window and to create a better overview of the layout, collapse the panel groups. Next, expand the Property inspector to display the additional table options. The following step also illustrates how to apply the background image.

- Click the panel groups expander arrow to collapse the panel groups.

- If necessary, click the Property inspector expander arrow to display both the upper and lower sections.

- Click the Page Properties button in the Property inspector to open the Page Properties dialog box.

- If necessary, click Appearance (HTML) in the Category column.

- Click the Browse button to the right of the Background image box to open the Select Image Source dialog box.

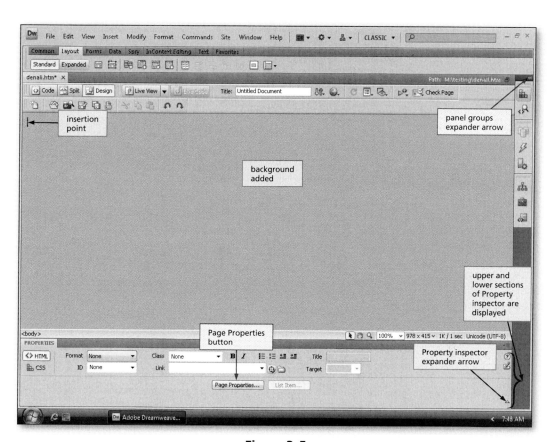

Figure 3–5

- If necessary, navigate to and open the parks\images folder.

- Click parks_bkg.jpg and then click the OK button to select the background image.

- Click the OK button in the Page Properties dialog box to apply the background to the page. If necessary, click the Document window to display the insertion point aligned at the left (Figure 3–5).

To Insert and Format the Heading

Next, you insert and format the heading. You apply the same heading format you applied to the heading in the index page. The following step shows how to add the heading and apply the Heading 1 format.

- Type Denali National Park and Preserve as the page heading.

- Click the Format button in the Property inspector, and then click Heading 1 to apply Heading 1 to the text.

- Click Format on the Application bar, point to Align, and then click Center to center the heading.

- Click anywhere on the page to deselect the heading.

- Select the text in the Title box on the Document toolbar, and then type Denali National Park and Preserve as the page title.

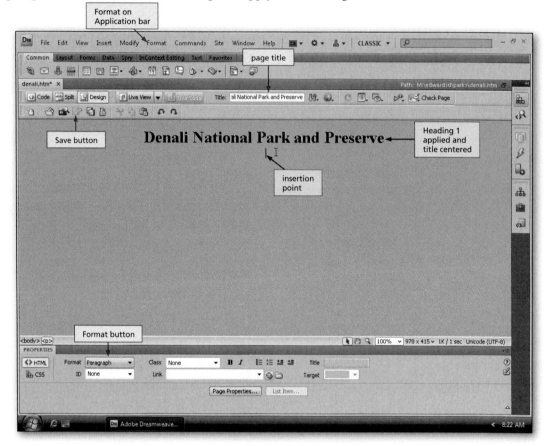

Figure 3–6

- Press the ENTER key to move the insertion point to the next line.

- Click the Save button on the Standard toolbar to save the page with the centered and formatted heading (Figure 3–6).

Understanding Tables and Page Layout

Tables have many uses in HTML design. The most obvious is a table of data; but, as already mentioned, tables also are used for page layout, such as placing text and graphics on a page at just the right location. **Tables** also provide Web designers with a method to add vertical and horizontal structure to a page. A table consists of three basic components: rows, columns, and cells. A **row** is a horizontal collection of cells, and a **column** is a vertical collection of cells. A **cell** is the container created when the row and column intersect. Each cell within the table can contain any standard element you use on a Web page. This includes text, images, and other objects.

Page layout is the process of arranging the text, images, and other elements on the page. The basic rules of page layout are that your site should be easy to navigate, easy to read, and quick to download. Studies indicate that visitors lose interest in your Web site if the majority of a page does not download within 15 seconds. One popular design element that downloads quickly is tables.

Tables download quickly because they are created with HTML code. They can be used anywhere — for the home page, menus, images, navigation bars, frames, and so on. Tables originally were intended for presenting data arranged by rows and columns, such as tabular data within a spreadsheet. Web designers, however, quickly seized upon the use of tables to produce specific layout effects. You can produce good designs by using tables creatively. Tables allow you to position elements on a Web page with much greater accuracy. Using tables for layout provides the Web page author with endless design possibilities.

Plan Ahead

Determine when to insert tables.
A typical Web page is composed of three sections: the header, the body, and the footer.

- The **header**, generally located at the top of the page, can contain logos, images, or text that identifies the Web site. The header also can contain hyperlinks to other pages within the Web site.

- The **body** of the Web page contains information about your site. This content may be in the form of text, graphics, animation, video, and audio, or a combination of any of these elements.

- The **footer** provides hyperlinks for contact information and navigational controls.

  The controls in the footer might be in addition to the navigation controls in the header. Other common items contained in a footer are the name and e-mail address of the author or the Webmaster. Sometimes, hyperlinks to other resources or to Help information are part of the footer.

  Tables make it easy to create this header/body/footer structure or to create any other layout structure that meets your specific Web page needs. The entire structure can be contained within one table or a combination of multiple and nested tables. A nested table is a table inside another table. You will use tables to create the two new pages for the Alaska Parks Web site.

Inserting a Table into the Denali National Park and Preserve Page

You will add two tables to the Denali National Park and Preserve page and then add text and images to the cells within the tables. The first table will consist of three rows and two columns, with a cell padding of 5 and cell spacing of 10. **Cell padding** is the amount of space between the edge of a cell and its contents, whereas **cell spacing** is the amount of space between cells. The border will be set to 0, which is the default. When the table is displayed in Dreamweaver, a border outline appears around the table. When the table's border is set to 0 and the table is viewed in a browser, however, this outline is not displayed.

The table width is 90 percent. When specifying the width, you can select percent or pixels. A table with the width specified as a **percent** expands with the width of the window and the monitor size in which it is being viewed. A table with the width specified as **pixels** will remain the same size regardless of the window and monitor size. If you select percent and an image is larger than the selected percent, the cell and table will expand to accommodate the image. Likewise, if the **No Wrap** property is enabled and the text will not fit within the cell, the cell and table will expand to accommodate the text. It is not necessary to declare a table width. When no value is specified, the table is displayed as small as possible and then expands as content is added. If modifications are necessary to the original specified table values, you can change these values in the Property inspector.

The second table for the Denali National Park and Preserve page is a one-cell table, consisting of one row and one column. This table will contain links to the Home page and to other pages in the Web site. You use the Layout category on the Insert bar and the Property inspector to control and format the tables.

BTW

Getting Help
Press the F1 key for comprehensive information about all Dreamweaver features.

The Insert Bar

The Insert bar appears at the top of the window below the Application bar. This toolbar contains several categories, or tabs, and is fully customizable through the Favorites tab. The Insert bar contains buttons for creating and inserting objects such as tables and advanced elements such as div tags, frames, the Spry Menu Bar, and other Spry options.

The Insert bar generally is displayed when you start Dreamweaver. You can, however, hide, customize, or display the Insert bar as necessary. All selections within the categories also are available through the Application bar and many of the selections also are available through the Property inspectors. The Table button command also can be accessed through the Insert menu on the Application bar.

To Display the Insert Bar and Select the Layout Tab

You use the Table buttons on the Layout tab of the Insert bar to assist with page design. The following steps illustrate how to display the Insert bar if necessary and select the Layout tab.

1

- If necessary, click Window on the Application bar and then click Insert to display the Insert bar.

Q&A | What should I do if the Insert bar is already displayed on my computer?

If the Insert bar already is displayed on your computer, skip the first action in Step 1.

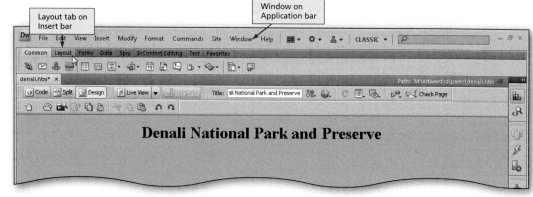

Figure 3–7

- Point to the Layout tab on the Insert bar (Figure 3–7).

2

- Click the Layout tab to display the Insert bar Layout category (Figure 3–8).

Q&A | What kinds of options are available on the Layout tab of the Insert bar?

The Layout tab contains options for working with tables and table features.

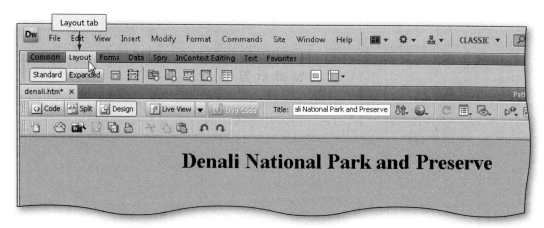

Figure 3–8

Q&A | What are the dimmed buttons to the right of the Table button?

When any part of a table is selected, the four dimmed buttons are displayed so you can format the table.

Layout Tab

You use the Layout tab (Figure 3–9) to work with tables and table features. Dreamweaver provides two modes, or ways, to use the table feature: Standard mode and Expanded Tables mode. Standard mode uses the Table dialog box. When you create a table, the Table dialog box opens in Standard mode by default so you can set the basic structure of the table. It then is displayed as a grid and expands as you add text and images.

You use the Expanded button on the Layout tab to switch to Expanded Tables mode. This mode temporarily enlarges your view of the cells so you can select items easily and place the insertion point precisely. Use this mode as a temporary visual aid for selection and insertion point placement. After placing the insertion point, return to Standard mode to make your edits and to provide a better visualization of your changes. Other buttons on the Layout tab are for working with Spry objects, which don't apply to tables.

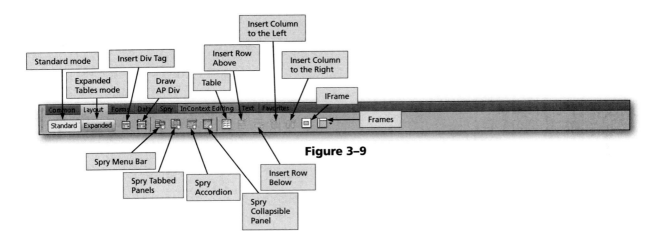

Figure 3–9

Table 3–1 lists the button names and descriptions available in the Insert bar Layout category.

Table 3–1 Buttons on the Layout tab of the Insert Bar	
Button Name	**Description**
Standard mode	Displays a table as a grid of lines
Expanded Tables mode	Temporarily adds cell padding and spacing
Insert Div Tag	Inserts a <div> tag
Draw AP Div	A fixed absolute point within a Web document
Spry Menu Bar	An AJAX predefined control
Spry Tabbed Panels	Inserts a tabbed panel widget directly into the Web page
Spry Accordion	Creates horizontal regions on a Web page that can be expanded or collapsed
Spry Collapsible Panel	Displays collapsible panels that have a clickable tab and a content area that displays/hides when a tab is clicked
Table	Places a table at the insertion point
Insert Row Above	Inserts a row above the selected row
Insert Row Below	Inserts a row below the selected row
Insert Column to the Left	Inserts a column to the left of the selected column
Insert Column to the Right	Inserts a column to the right of the selected column
IFrame	Displays data (text and image) that is stored in a separate page
Frames	Displays Frames pop-up menu

Table Defaults and Accessibility

When you insert a table, the Table dialog box is displayed and contains default settings for each of the table attributes (Figure 3–10). After you create a table and change these defaults, the settings that are displayed remain until you change them for the next table. Table 3–2 lists and describes the defaults for each table attribute.

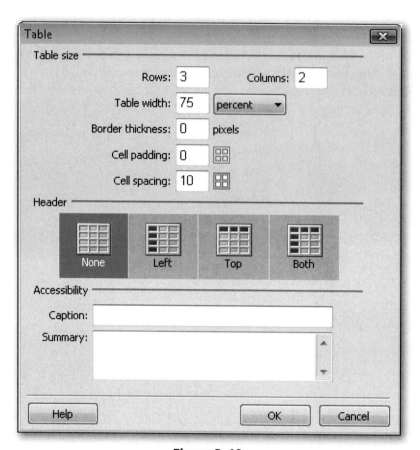

Figure 3–10

Table 3–2 Table Dialog Box Default Values

Attribute	Default	Description
Rows	3	Determines the number of rows in the table
Columns	2	Determines the number of columns in the table
Table width	75 percent	Specifies the width of the table in pixels or as a percentage of the browser window's width
Border thickness	0	Specifies the border width in pixels
Cell padding	0	Specifies the number of pixels between a cell's border and its contents
Cell spacing	10	Specifies the number of pixels between adjacent table cells
Header	None	Specifies whether the top row and/or column is designated as a header cell
Caption	None	Provides a table heading
Summary	None	Provides a table description; used by screen readers

It is advisable to use headers for tables when the table presents tabular information. Screen readers scan table headings and help screen-reader users keep track of table information. Additionally, the Caption option provides a table title that is displayed outside of the table, the Align Caption option specifies where the table caption appears in relation to the table, and the Summary option provides a table description. Summary text is similar to the Alt text you added for images in Chapter 2. You add Summary text to the tables you create in this chapter. Screen readers read the summary text, but the text does not appear in the user's browser.

Table Layout

As indicated previously, the Header and Caption options are important when a table displays tabular data. When using a table for layout, however, other options apply. Structurally and graphically, the elements in a table used for layout should be invisible in the browser. For instance, when using a table for layout, use the None option for Headers. The None option prevents the header tags <th> and </th> from being added to the table. Because the table does not contain tabular data, a header would be of no benefit to the screen-reader user. Screen readers, however, read table content from left to right and top to bottom. Therefore, it is important to structure the table content in a linear arrangement.

To Insert a Table

The following steps illustrate how to insert a table with three rows and two columns into the Denali National Park and Preserve Web page.

1

• Click the Table button on the Layout tab to display the Table dialog box (Figure 3–11).

Q&A

Should the settings in my Table dialog box match those in the figure?

The settings displayed are the settings from the last table created, so your dialog box might contain different values.

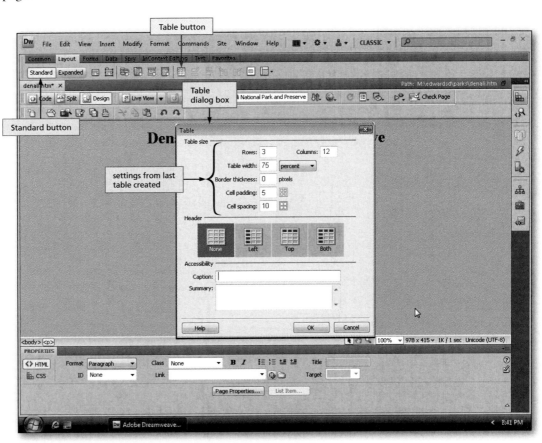

Figure 3–11

- If necessary, type 3 in the Rows box to create a table with three rows, and then press the TAB key to move to the Columns box.

- Type 2 to create a table with two columns, and then press the TAB key to move to the Table width box.

- Type 90 to set the table width, and then click the Table width button arrow to display the Table width options.

- Click percent to specify the table width as a percentage, and then press the TAB key to move to the Border thickness box.

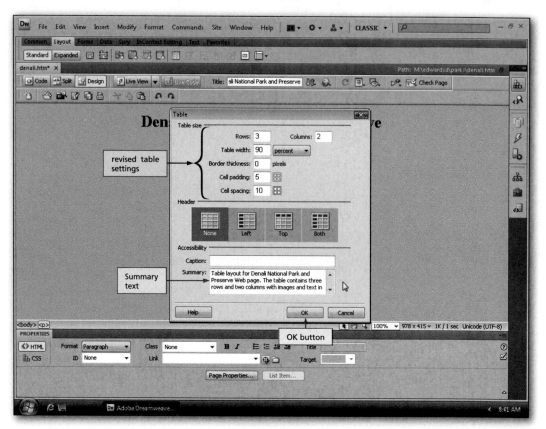

Figure 3–12

- If necessary, type 0 to set the border thickness, and then press the TAB key to move to the Cell padding box.

- Type 5 to add five pixels of cell padding, and then press the TAB key to move to the Cell spacing box.

- Type 10 to add ten pixels between adjacent table cells.

- Click the Summary text box and type `Table layout for Denali National Park and Preserve Web page. The table contains three rows and two columns with images and text in the table cells.` (Figure 3–12).

3

• Click the OK button to insert the table into the document window (Figure 3–13).

Q&A Why does a border appear around the table if the Border thickness is set to 0?

Although the border thickness is set to 0, it appears as an outline in the Document window. The border will not appear when displayed in the browser.

Q&A Can I add rows after I create a table?

Yes. Right-click a row to display the context menu, point to Table, and then click Insert row to add a row after the current one.

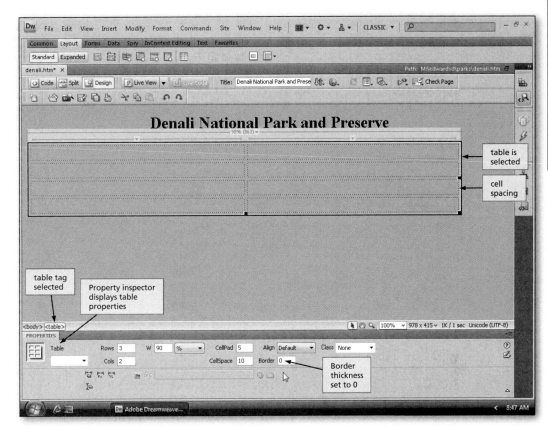

Figure 3–13

Other Ways

1. On Insert menu, click Table, select table properties, click OK button
2. Press CTRL+ALT+T

Property Inspector Table Features

As you have seen, the Property inspector options change depending on the selected object. You use the Property inspector to modify and add table attributes. When a table is selected, the Property inspector displays table properties in both panels. When another table element — a row, column, or cell — is selected, the displayed properties change and are determined by the selected element. The following section describes the table-related features of the Property inspector shown in Figure 3–14.

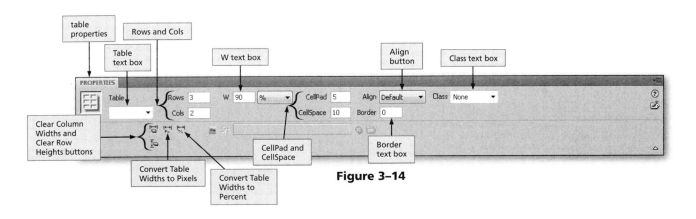

Figure 3–14

Table   Specifies the table ID, an identifier used for Cascading Style Sheets, scripting, and accessibility. A table ID is not required; however, it is a good idea always to add this identifier.

Rows and Cols   The number of rows and columns in the table.

W   Specifies the minimum width of the table in either pixels or percent. If a size is not specified, the size can vary depending on the monitor and browser settings. A table width specified in pixels is displayed as the same size in all browsers. A table width specified in percent is altered in appearance based on the user's monitor resolution and browser window size.

Cellpad   The number of pixels between the cell border and the cell content.

Cellspace   The number of pixels between adjacent table cells.

Align   Determines where the table appears, relative to other elements in the same paragraph such as text or images. The default alignment is to the left.

Class   An attribute used with Cascading Style Sheets.

Border   Specifies the border width in pixels.

Clear Column Widths and Clear Row Heights   Deletes all specified row height or column width values from the table.

Convert Table Widths to Pixels   Sets the width of each column in the table to its current width expressed as pixels.

Convert Table Widths to Percent   Sets the width of each column in the table to its current width expressed as a percentage of the Document window's width and also sets the width of the whole table to its current width as a percentage of the Document window's width.

Cell, Row, and Column Properties

When a cell, row, or column is selected, the properties in the upper pane of the Property inspector are the same as the standard properties for text. You can use these properties to incorporate standard HTML formatting tags within a cell, row, or column. The part of the table selected determines which properties are displayed in the lower pane of the Property inspector. The properties for all three features (cell, row, and column) are the same, except for one element — the icon displayed in the lower-left pane of the Property inspector. The following section describes the row-related features (Figure 3–15), cell-related features (Figure 3–16), and column-related features (Figure 3–17) of the Property inspector.

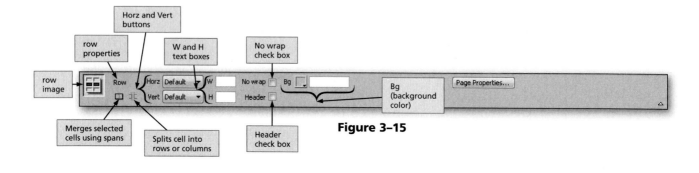

Figure 3–15

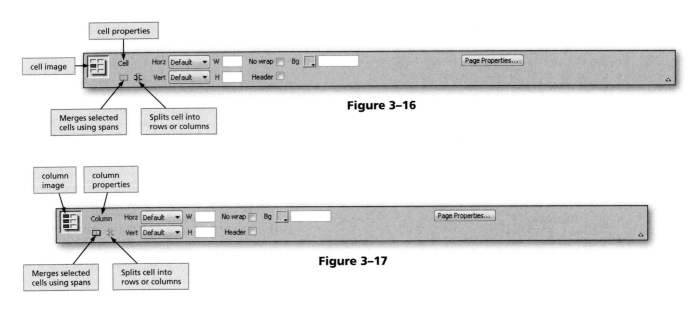

Figure 3–16

Figure 3–17

Horz   Specifies the horizontal alignment of the contents of a cell, row, or column. The contents can be aligned to the left, right, or center of the cells.

Vert   Specifies the vertical alignment of the contents of a cell, row, or column. The contents can be aligned to the top, middle, bottom, or baseline of the cells.

W and H   Specifies the width and height of selected cells in pixels or as a percentage of the entire table's width or height.

Bg (background color)   Sets the background color of a cell, row, or column selected from the color picker (use the Bg icon) or specified as a hexadecimal number (use the Bg text box).

No Wrap   Prevents line wrapping, keeping all text in a given cell on a single line. If No Wrap is enabled, cells widen to accommodate all data as it is typed or pasted into a cell.

Header   Formats the selected cells as table header cells. The contents of table header cells are bold and centered by default.

Merge Cells   Combines selected cells, rows, or columns into one cell (available when two or more cells, rows, or columns are selected).

Split Cells   Divides a cell, creating two or more cells (available when a single cell is selected).

Table Formatting Conflicts

When formatting tables in Standard mode, you can set properties for the entire table or for selected rows, columns, or cells in the table. Applying these properties, however, introduces a potential for conflict. To prevent conflicts, HTML assigns levels of precedence. The order of precedence for table formatting is cells, rows, and table. When a property, such as background color or alignment, is set to one value for the whole table and another value for individual cells, cell formatting takes precedence over row formatting, which in turn takes precedence over table formatting.

For example, if you set the background color for a single cell to green, and then set the background color of the entire table to red, the green cell does not change to red, because cell formatting takes precedence over table formatting. Dreamweaver, however, does not always follow the precedence. The program will override the settings for a cell if you change the settings for the row that contains the cell. To eliminate this problem, you should change the cell settings last.

Understanding HTML Structure in a Table

As you work with and become more familiar with tables, it is helpful to have a basic understanding of the HTML structure within a table. Suppose, for example, you have a table with two rows and two columns, displaying a total of four cells, such as the following:

First cell	Second cell
Third cell	Fourth cell

The general syntax of the table is:

```
<table>
<tr>
  <td> First cell </td>
  <td> Second cell </td>
</tr>
<tr>
  <td> Third cell </td>
  <td> Fourth cell </td>
</tr>
</table>
```

In Dreamweaver, the tag selector displays the <table>, <td>, and <tr> tags. The <table> tag indicates the whole table. Clicking the <table> tag in the tag selector selects the whole table. The <td> tag indicates table data. Clicking the <td> tag in the tag selector selects the cell containing the insertion point. The <tr> tag indicates table row. Clicking the <tr> tag in the tag selector selects the row containing the insertion point.

Selecting the Table and Selecting Cells

The Property inspector displays table attributes only if the entire table is selected. To select the entire table, click the upper-left corner of the table, click anywhere on the top or bottom edge of the table, or click in a cell and then click <table> in the tag selector. When selected, the table is displayed with a dark border and selection handles on the table's lower and right edges (Figure 3–18).

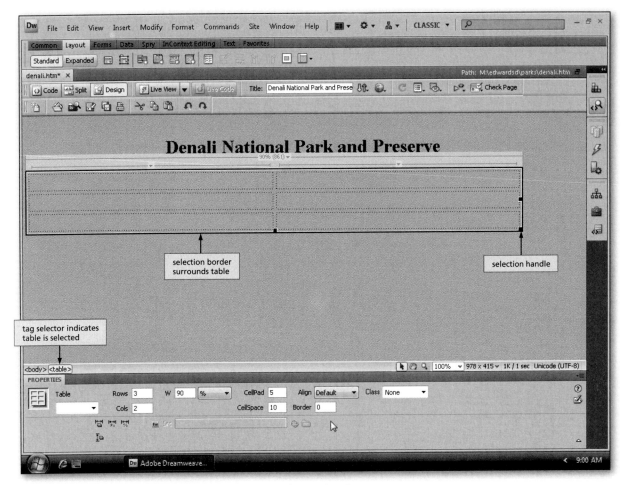

Figure 3–18

Selecting a cell, row, or column is easier than selecting the entire table. When a cell, row, or column is selected, the selected item has a dark border. To select a cell, click inside the cell. When you click inside the cell, the <td> tag is displayed as selected on the status bar. To select a row or column, click inside one of the cells in the row or column and drag to select the other cells. When you select a row, the <tr> tag is displayed on the status bar. In Figure 3–19 (on the next page), a row is selected.

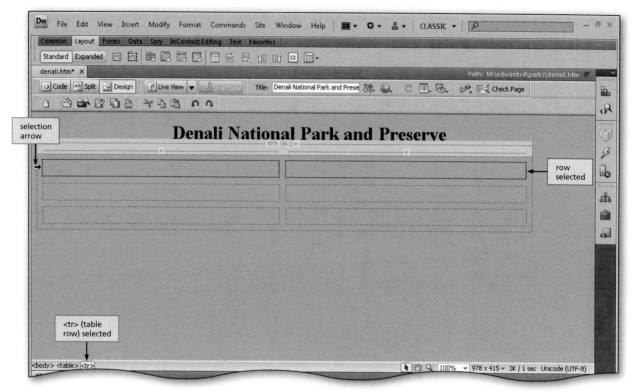

Figure 3–19

A second method for selecting a row or column is to point to the left edge of a row or the top edge of a column. When the pointer changes to a selection arrow (Figure 3–19 and 3–20), click to select the row or column.

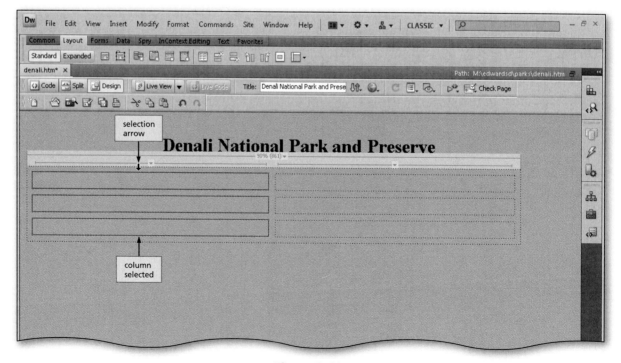

Figure 3–20

In Figure 3–20, a column is selected.

Centering a Table

When a table is inserted into the document window with a specified width, it aligns to the left by default. Using the Property inspector, you can center the table by selecting it and then applying the Center command.

To Select and Center a Table

The following steps illustrate how to select and center the table using the Property inspector.

- Click in row 1, column 1 to place the insertion point in the first cell of the table (Figure 3–21).

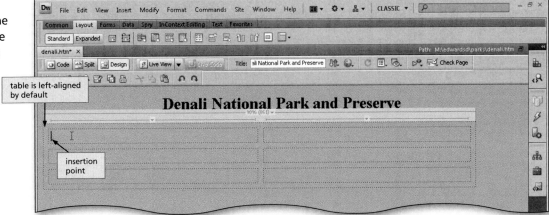

Figure 3–21

- Click <table> in the tag selector to select the table and to display handles on the lower and right borders of the table.

- Click the Align button arrow in the Property inspector and then point to Center (Figure 3–22).

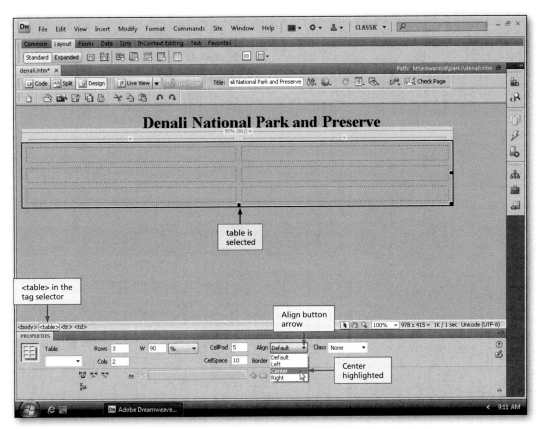

Figure 3–22

• Click Center to center the table (Figure 3–23).

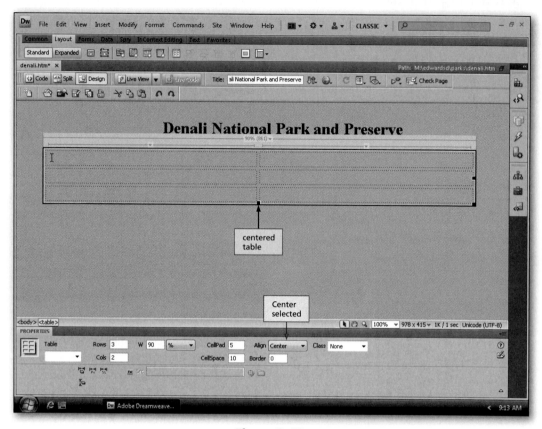

Figure 3–23

Changing the Default Cell Alignment for Text

The default horizontal cell alignment for text is left. When you enter text in a cell, it defaults to the left margin of the cell. You can change the horizontal alignment through the Property inspector Align pop-up menu by clicking the cell and then changing the default to Center or Right. The default vertical cell alignment is Middle, which aligns the cell content in the middle of the cell. Table 3–3 describes the cell alignment options.

Table 3–3 Cell Alignment Options	
Alignment	**Description**
Default	Specifies a baseline alignment; default may vary depending on the user's browser
Baseline	Aligns the cell content at the bottom of the cell (same as Bottom)
Top	Aligns the cell content at the top of the cell
Bottom	Aligns the cell content at the bottom of the cell
TextTop	Aligns the top of the image with the top of the tallest character in the text line
Absolute Middle	Aligns the middle of the image with the middle of the text in the current line
Absolute Bottom	Aligns the bottom of the image with the bottom of the line of text
Left	Places the selected image on the left margin, wrapping text around it to the right; if left-aligned text precedes the object on the line, it generally forces left-aligned objects to wrap to a new line

Table 3–3 Cell Alignment Options (*continued*)	
Alignment	**Description**
Middle	Aligns the middle of the image with the baseline of the current line
Right	Places the image on the right margin, wrapping text around the object to the left; if right-aligned text precedes the object on the line, it generally forces right-aligned objects to wrap to a new line

You can change the alignment through the Align pop-up menu on the Property inspector by clicking the cell and then selecting another alignment option. These properties can be applied to a single cell, to multiple cells, or to the entire table.

To Change Vertical Alignment from Middle to Top

The following steps show how to select all of the cells and change the default alignment from middle to top.

1

- Click in row 1, column 1 and then drag to the right and down to select the three rows and two columns in the table.

- Click the Vert button to display the Vert pop-up menu and then point to Top (Figure 3–24).

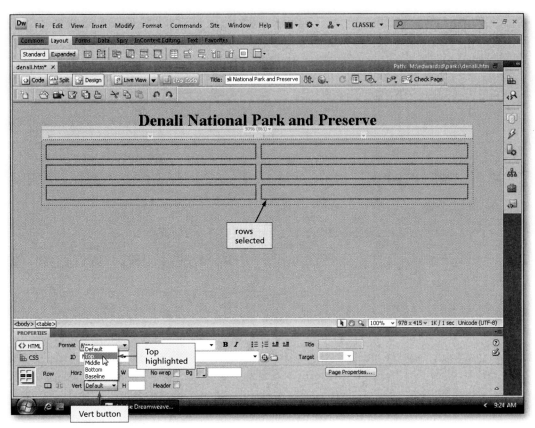

Figure 3–24

②

- Click Top to change the vertical alignment from Middle to Top (Figure 3–25).

Q&A

Should the appearance of the table change after applying a new vertical alignment?

The change is not visible in the Document window yet — the new alignment is noticeable when the cells contain text or images.

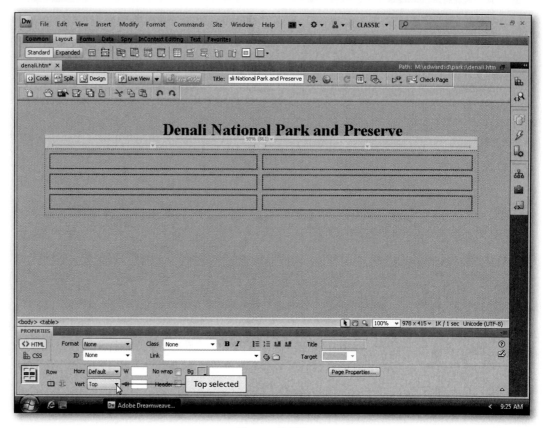

Figure 3–25

Specifying Column Width

When a table width is specified as a percentage, each column's width expands to accommodate the text or image. When you add content to the table, this expansion can distort the table appearance and make it difficult to visualize how the final page will be displayed. You can control this expansion by setting the column width.

BTW

Column Width
In addition to using the Property inspector to change the width or height of a column, you can drag the right border of a column to resize it. To change a column width without affecting other columns in the table, hold down the SHIFT key as you drag. If you are familiar with HTML, you can change cell widths and heights directly in the HTML code.

BTW

Clear Column Widths and Row Heights
To clear all the column widths you set in a table, select the table, and then click the Clear All Column Widths button in the Property inspector. To clear all the row heights you set, select the table, and then click the Clear All Row Heights button.

To Specify Column Width

The objective for the Denali National Park and Preserve page is to display the page in two columns — column 1 at 40% and column 2 at 50%. The following steps show how to specify column width.

1

- Click the cell in row 1, column 1 and then drag to select all cells in column 1.

- Click the W box in the Property inspector, type 40% and then press the ENTER key to set the width for column 1 at 40%.

- Click the cell in row 1, column 2, and then drag to select all cells in column 2.

- Click the W box in the Property inspector, type 50%, then press the ENTER key to set the width for column 2 at 50% (Figure 3–26).

2

- Click anywhere in the table to deselect the column.

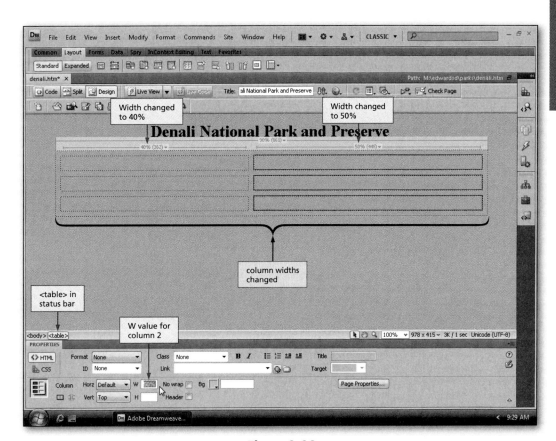

Figure 3–26

Adding an ID

Tables, images, and other Web site elements can be assigned a name through the Table field located in the Property inspector. This ID identifies the content of an object within the HTML code. Spaces and characters cannot be used except for the dash or underscore.

To Add a Table ID to the Denali National Park and Preserve Table

The following step illustrates how to select the table and add a table ID to the Denali National Park and Preserve feature table.

- Click <table> in the status bar to select the table.

- Click the Table text box and then type denali as the ID text.

- Press the ENTER key to add the table ID (Figure 3–27).

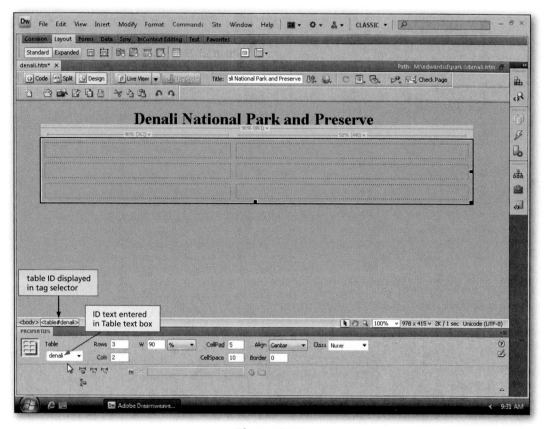

Figure 3–27

Plan
Ahead

Laying out Web pages with tables.

Tables help you lay out Web pages that contain text and images. After creating a Web page and setting its properties, add tables, text, and images in the following order:

1. **Table:** Insert a table before entering any text other than the page heading. Set table properties such as size, cell padding, and cell spacing.

2. **Text:** Add text to the table cells. You can apply formats to the text such as Heading 1 and bold text to emphasize it, for example.

3. **Images:** Insert images after you enter text to balance the images and the rest of the table content. Then you can resize each image, align it, and set other image properties.

Importing Table Text

If you saved tabular data in a delimited text format using another program such as Microsoft Office Excel, you can import the tabular data into Dreamweaver. When you import table data, you can set cell padding, cell spacing, and border values, and specify how to format the top row, such as in bold.

Adding Text to the Denali National Park and Preserve Web Page

Next, you enter and format the text for the Denali National Park and Preserve Web page. Table 3–4 includes the text for the first table. The text is entered into the table cells. If you have not set the width and height of a cell, when you begin to enter text into a table cell, the cell expands to accommodate the text. The other cells may appear to shrink, but they also will expand when you type in the cells or add an image to the cells.

Table 3–4 Denali National Park and Preserve Web Page Text

Section	Text
Part 1	Denali National Park and Preserve is more than 415 square miles and has 114 named peaks over 10,000 feet. One of the more popular hiking trails is the Keyhole Route on Longs' Peak. At 14,255 feet, Longs' Peak is the highest peak in the Denali National Park and Preserve and the fifteenth tallest in Alaska. <ENTER>
	The park contains three distinct ecosystems which correspond to elevation: the montane, which is 7,000 to 9,000 feet above sea level; the subalpine ecosystem, which is 9,000 to 11,500 feet and spans the tree line; and the alpine tundra, at the top, which is over 11,500 feet.
	Birds and animals add color and interest to the landscape. The park contains 65 species of mammals, 260 species of birds, and 900 species of plants. Black bears, mountain lions, and bobcats live in the park, but seldom are seen. Moose and mule deer are more visible. In autumn, herds of American elk roam the park and frequently are visible, even at the lower elevations. <ENTER>
Part 2	Interesting facts: a) In the summer of 2005, a dinosaur footprint was found. The print was identified as belonging to a three-toed foot of a Cretaceous Theropod. b) The park contains over 650 species of flowering plants as well as many species of mosses, lichens, fungi, algae, and other plant life.
Part 3	The park is open 24 hours a day year round< br /> Park Service Information Office: Denali National Park and Preserve 1000 Highway 36 Estes Park, CO 80517-8397 <ENTER>
	E-mail: Denali National Park and Preserve

To Add Text to the Denali National Park and Preserve Web Page

The following steps show how to add text to the Denali National Park and Preserve page. Press the ENTER key or press SHIFT+ENTER to insert a line break, <br />, as indicated in Table 3–4. Press the TAB key to move from cell to cell.

- Type the first two paragraphs of Part 1 in Table 3–4 in row 1, column 2 of the table in the document window. Press the ENTER key as indicated in the table (Figure 3–28).

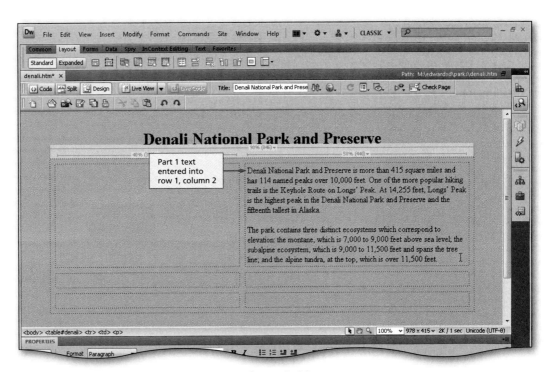

Figure 3–28

2

- Type the third paragraph of Part 1, as shown in Table 3–4 on the previous page, into row 2, column 2 of the table.

- If necessary, scroll down to display the rest of the table. Type the paragraph of Part 2, as shown in Table 3–4, into row 3, column 2 of the table.

- Type the paragraph of Part 3, as shown in Table 3–4, into row 3, column 1 of the document window. Use SHIFT+ENTER to insert

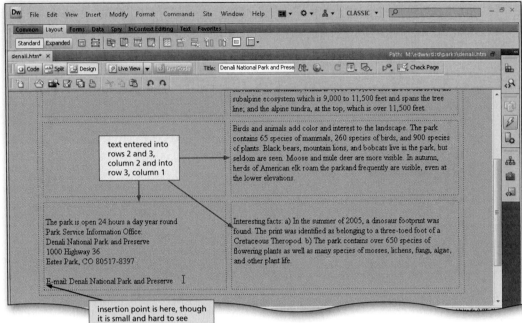

the line breaks. The insertion point is within the cell below the last line and may not be visible because a line break was added (Figure 3–29).

Figure 3–29

3

- Select the text in row 3, column 1 to prepare for aligning the text.

- Click the Horz button in the Property inspector, and then click Right to align the text to the right.

- Click anywhere on the page to deselect the text (Figure 3–30).

4

- Click the Save button to save the page.

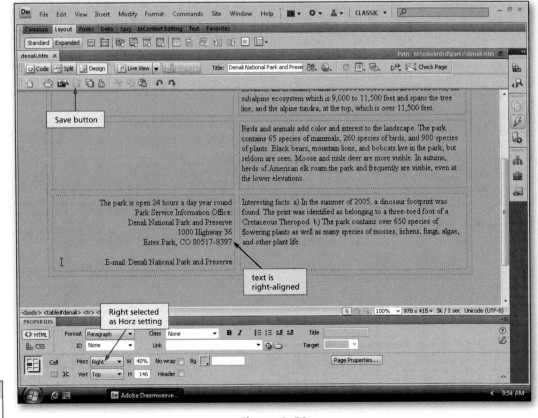

Figure 3–30

Other Ways

1. Right-click selected text, point to Align on context menu, click Right on Align submenu

Adding a Second Table to the Denali National Park and Preserve Web Page

Next, you add a second table to the Denali National Park and Preserve Web page. This table will contain one row and one column and will serve as the footer for your Web page.

To Add a Second Table to the Denali National Park and Preserve Web Page

The text for the footer should be centered in the cell and contain links to the home page and to the other pages within the Web site. When you create the page for the Gates of the Arctic park, you can copy and paste these links into that page. The following steps show how to add the second table and text.

- Click outside the right border of the existing table to position the insertion point outside the table (Figure 3–31).

Q&A
Where is the insertion point after completing this step?

The insertion point, a long dark line, is located and blinking to the right of the table border.

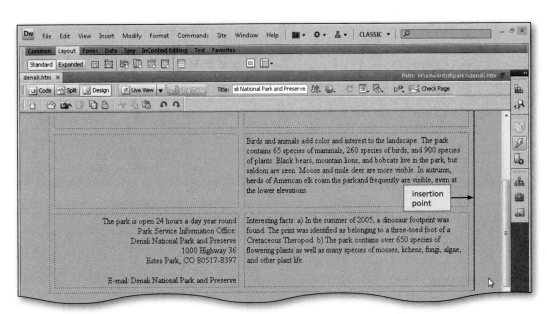

Figure 3–31

- Press the ENTER key to move the insertion point below the table.

- Click the Table button on the Layout tab on the Insert bar to display the Table dialog box (Figure 3–32).

Q&A
Should the settings in my Table dialog box match those in Figure 3–32?

Not necessarily. The dialog box on your computer may show different settings.

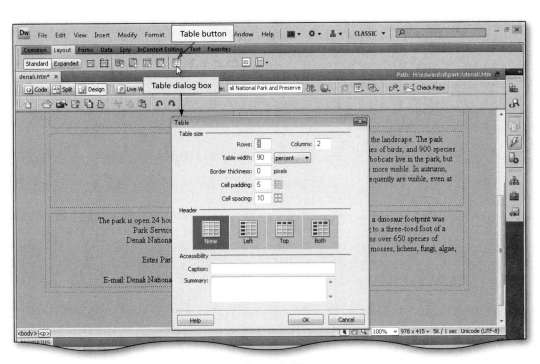

Figure 3–32

3
- Change the number of rows to 1, the number of columns to 1, the width to 75 percent, the cell padding to 0, and the cell spacing to 10 to set the properties for the table.

- Type Footer table for links in the Summary text box to add the table description.

- If necessary, change other settings to match the settings shown in Figure 3–33.

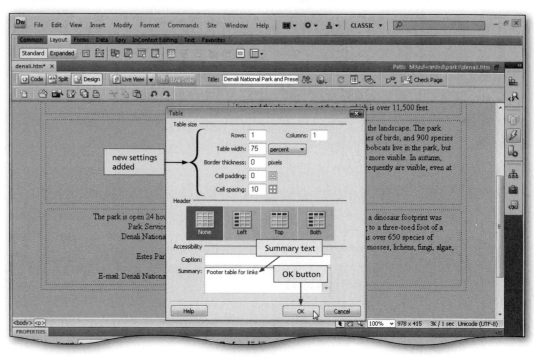

Figure 3–33

 4
- Click the OK button to insert the one-cell table.

- Click the Align button and then click Center to center the one-cell table. The dark border and handles indicate that the table is selected (Figure 3–34).

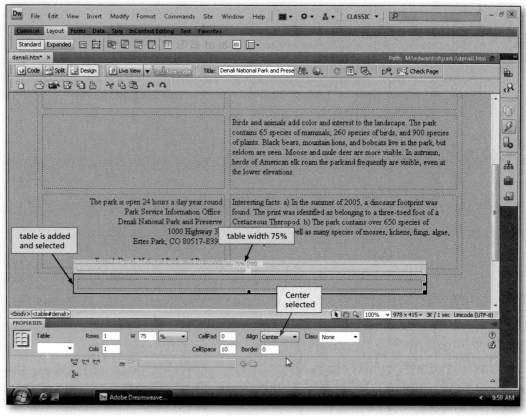

Figure 3–34

⑤

- Click the cell in the table. Type Home and then press the SPACEBAR to enter the first link. Press SHIFT+| (vertical bar) and then press the SPACEBAR to separate the links.

- Type Denali National Park and then press the SPACEBAR to enter the next link.

- Press SHIFT+| and then press the SPACEBAR to separate the links.

- Type Gates of the Arctic to enter the last link (Figure 3–35).

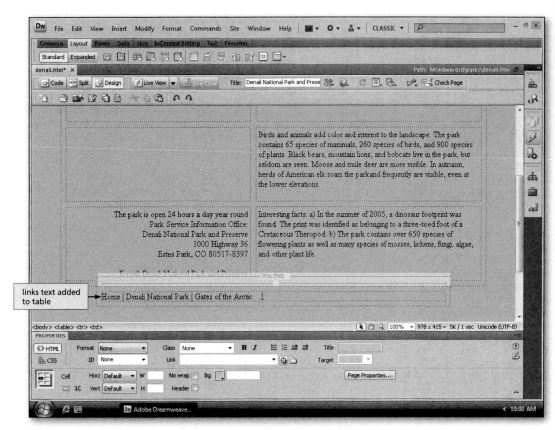

Figure 3–35

Adjusting the Table Width

Determining table width is a matter of judgment. You may overestimate or underestimate the table width when first inserting a table into the Document window. When this happens, it is easy to make adjustments to the table width through the Property inspector.

Sorting Table Data

If a table contains data you want to sort, you can perform a simple table sort based on the contents of a single column, or you can perform a more complicated sort based on the contents of two columns. Click Commands on the menu bar and then click Sort Table.

Hiding the Table Width Bar

You can hide the bar that shows the column and table widths by clicking the down-pointing arrow next to the table width indicator and then clicking Hide Table Widths.

To Adjust the Table Width, Center the Text, and Add the Table ID

The links table is too wide for the text it contains and needs to be adjusted. You adjust the table width by selecting the table and then changing the width in the Property inspector. The following steps illustrate how to adjust the width and add the table ID.

- If necessary, click in the cell in table 2 to make table 2 the active table.

- Click <table> in the tag selector to select the table.

- Double-click the W box in the Property inspector to select the width value.

- Type 60 and then press the ENTER key to decrease the table width. If necessary, click the W button arrow and select % (the percent sign) (Figure 3–36).

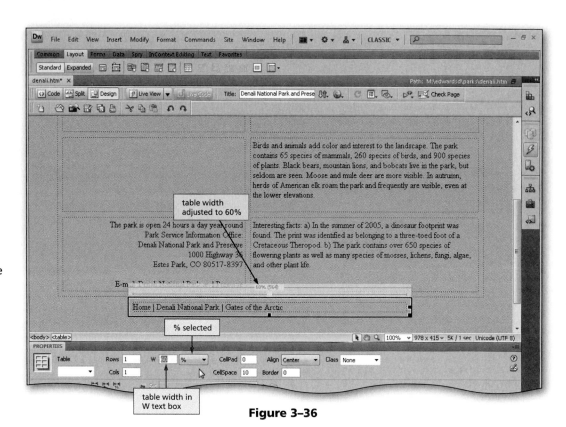

Figure 3–36

- Click the cell in the table to select the cell.

- Click the Horz button, then click Center to center the text.

- Click <table> in the tag selector to select the table.

- Click the Table text box, type alaska_ parks_links, and then press the ENTER key to name the table (Figure 3–37).

- Click anywhere in the document window to deselect the table.

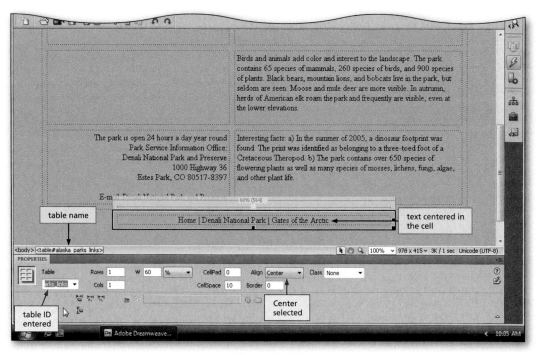

Figure 3–37

To Add Links to the Denali National Park and Preserve Web Page

Next, you add absolute, e-mail, and relative links to the Denali National Park and Preserve page. The following steps show how to add the links. The relative link you add for the Gates of the Arctic page is not active at this point. You will add a page for the Gates of the Arctic later in this chapter.

- Select the first instance of Denali National Park and Preserve located in the first table in row 3, column 1.

- In the Link box, type `http://www.nps.gov/dena/` and then press ENTER to create an absolute link.

- Select the second instance of Denali National Park and Preserve located in the first table in row 3, column 1.

- Click Insert on the Application bar and then click Email Link. When the Email Link dialog box is displayed, select any text in the Email Link Text text box, type `dena@parks.gov` as the e-mail address, and then click the OK button to enter an e-mail link.

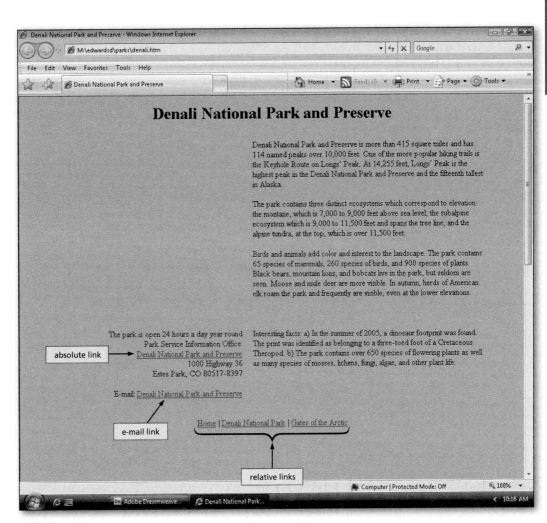

Figure 3–38

- Select Home in the second table, click the Link box, type `index.htm` and then press ENTER to create the relative link to the home page.

- Select Denali National Park in the second table, click the Link box, type `denali.htm` and then press ENTER to create the relative link.

Q&A

Why are we creating a link to the current page?

The links table serves as the footer, and will be repeated on each page in the site.

- Select Gates of the Arctic in the second table, click the Link box, type `gates.htm` and then press ENTER to create the relative link to a page named gates.htm, which you haven't created yet.

- Click the Save button on the Standard toolbar.

- Press the F12 key to view the Web page. Scroll down to view the links, as shown in Figure 3–38.

❷

- Click the Home link to display the index.htm page, and then click the browser Back button and test each of the links.

Why doesn't the Gates of the Arctic link work?

Recall that the Gates of the Arctic link will not work until the page is added later in this chapter.

- Test the e-mail link.

- Close the browser and return to the Dreamweaver window.

Editing and Modifying Table Structure

Thus far, you have created two tables and made adjustments in Dreamweaver for the Denali National Park and Preserve Web page. For various reasons, as you create and develop Web sites, you will need to edit and modify a table, change the dimensions of a table, add rows and columns, or delete the table and start over. The following section describes how to edit, modify, and delete table elements within the structure. Several options are available to accomplish the same task.

BTW

Deleting Cells
If you delete a cell, the content also is deleted. Dreamweaver does not caution you that this will occur. If you accidentally remove content, click the Undo button on the Standard toolbar, or, on the Edit menu, click the Undo command.

Delete a Row or Column Select a row or column and then press the DELETE key. You also can delete a row or column by clicking a cell within the row or column, clicking Modify on the Application bar, pointing to Table, and then clicking Delete Row or Delete Column on the submenu. Or click a cell within a row or column, right-click to display the context menu, point to Table, and then click Delete Row or Delete Column.

Insert a Row or Column Click in a cell. Right-click to display the context menu, point to Table, and then click Insert Row or Insert Column on the Table submenu. To add a row automatically, press the TAB key in the last cell of a table. Click Modify on the Application bar, point to Table, and then click Insert Row or Insert Column on the submenu. To insert more than one row or column and to control the row or column insertion point, click in a cell, right-click to display the context menu, point to Table, and then click Insert Rows or Columns on the Table submenu to display the Insert Rows or Columns dialog box (Figure 3–39). Make your selection and then click the OK button. To add a row automatically, press the TAB key in the last cell of a table.

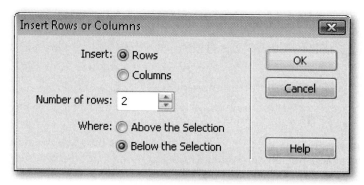

Figure 3–39

Merge and Split Cells   By merging and splitting cells, you can set alignments that are more complex than straight rows and columns. To merge two or more cells, select the cells and then click Merge Cells in the Property inspector. The selected cells must be contiguous and in the shape of a line or a rectangle. You can merge any number of adjacent cells as long as the entire selection is a line or a rectangle. To split a cell, click the cell and then click Split Cells in the Property inspector to display the Split Cell dialog box (Figure 3–40). In the Split Cell dialog box, specify how to split the cell and then click the OK button. You can split a cell into any number of rows or columns, regardless of whether it was merged previously. When you split a cell into two rows, the other cells in the same row as the split cell are not split. The same is true if a cell is split into two or more columns — the other cells in the same column are not split. To select a cell quickly, click in the cell and then click the <td> tag on the tag selector.

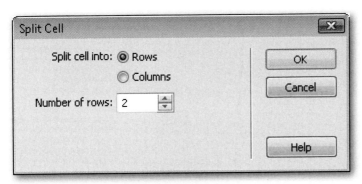

Figure 3–40

Resize a Table, Columns, and Rows   You can resize an entire table or resize individual rows and columns. To resize the table, select the table and change the W (width) in the Property inspector. A second method is to select the table and then drag one of the table selection handles. When you resize an entire table, all of the cells in the table change size proportionately. If you have assigned explicit widths or heights to a cell or cells within the table, resizing the table changes the visual size of the cells in the Document window but does not change the specified widths and heights of the cells. To resize a column or row, select the column or row and change the W or H numbers in the Property inspector. A second method to resize a column is to click the column border and then drag the border right or left. A second method to resize a row is to click the row border and then drag up or down.

Delete a Table   You easily can delete a table. Select the table tag in the tag selector and then press the DELETE key. All table content is deleted along with the table.

Merging Cells and Adding Images

The concept of merging cells most likely is familiar to you if you have worked with spreadsheets or word processing tables. In HTML, merging cells is a more complicated process. Dreamweaver, however, makes this easy by hiding some complex HTML table restructuring code behind an easy-to-use interface in the Property inspector. Dreamweaver also makes it easy to add images to a table. When you add and then select an image in a table cell, the Property inspector displays the same properties as were displayed when you added and selected an image in the Document window in Chapter 2. When the image in the cell is not selected, the Property inspector displays the same properties as it does for any cell. These properties were described earlier in this chapter.

BTW

Resizing a Table
Before resizing a table, first clear any cell widths or row heights you set. Select the table and click the Clear Row Heights button or the Clear Column Widths button in the Property inspector.

BTW

Splitting and Merging Cells
An alternative approach to merging and splitting cells is to increase or decrease the number of rows or columns spanned by a cell.

To Merge Two Cells in a Table

You will merge two cells (rows 1 and 2, column 1) and add four images to the Denali National Park and Preserve page. The first and second images go into the merged cells, the third image goes in row 1, column 2 between the two blocks of text, and the fourth image goes into row 2, column 2, below the text. The following steps show how to merge two cells.

1

- If necessary, scroll up and then click in row 1, column 1 in the first table.

- Drag to select the cells in rows 1 and 2 in column 1 (Figure 3–41).

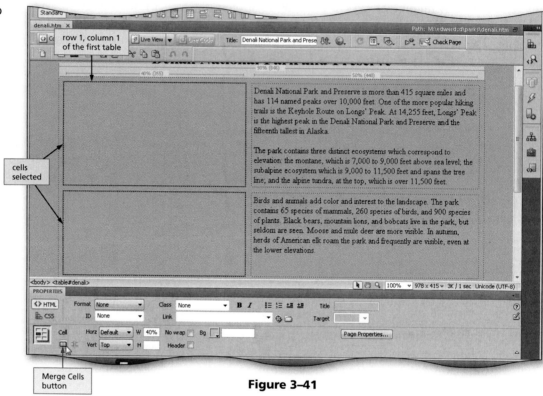

Figure 3–41

2

- Click the Merge Cells button to merge the cells (Figure 3–42).

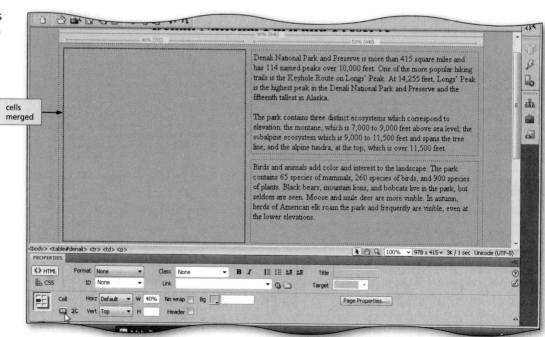

Figure 3–42

Recall from Chapter 2 that when you inserted an image, the default Image Tag Accessibility Attributes dialog box was displayed. In this box, you can add Alternate text or create a link to a text file with a long description. For images in this chapter and the other chapters in this book, instructions are to add alternate text. The Property inspector for images contains an Alternate text option. Therefore, you will disable the Image Tag Accessibility Attributes dialog box and add the Alternate text through the Property inspector.

To Disable the Image Tag Accessibility Attributes Dialog Box

The following steps show how to disable the Image Tag Accessibility Attributes dialog box.

- Click Edit on the Application bar and then click Preferences to display the Preferences dialog box.

- Click Accessibility in the Category list to display the accessibility options.

Q&A

Where can I find more information on accessibility?

For additional information on making Web content accessible for people with disabilities, search for *Accessibility* in the Dreamweaver CS4 help.

- If necessary, click the check boxes to deselect Form objects, Frames, Media, and Images to disable the Image Tab Accessibility Attributes dialog box (Figure 3–43).

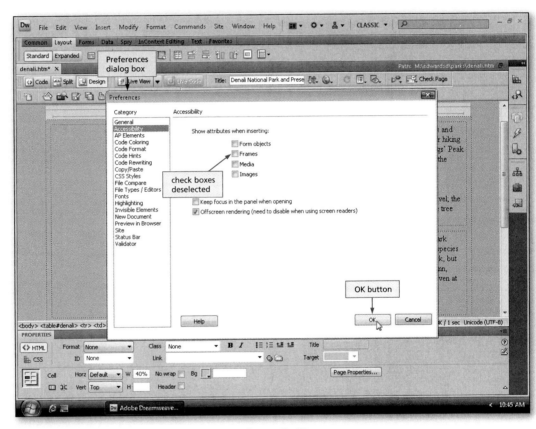

Figure 3–43

- Click the OK button.

To Add Images to a Table

Next, you add four images to the table. You then align the four images and modify the size of the images. The following steps illustrate how to display the images in the Assets panel and then add, align, and modify images in a table using Standard and Expanded modes.

1

- Expand the panel groups and then click the Assets tab in the panel groups to display the assets for this Web site.

- If necessary, click the Images button and the Site option button in the Assets panel to display the images for this Web site.

Q&A

What should I do if the Assets panel does not display all my images?

Click the Refresh Site List button to view the images.

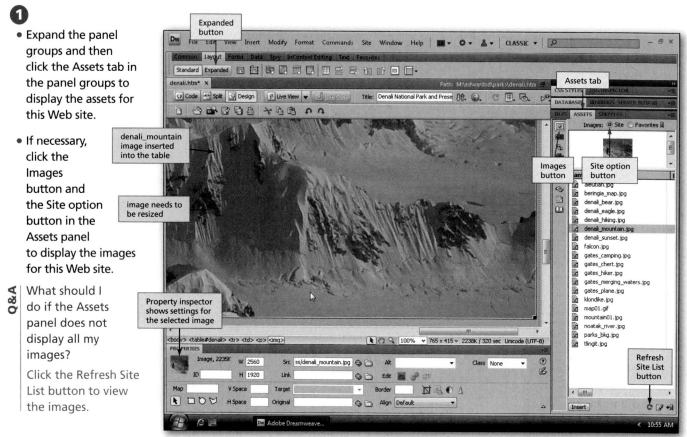

Figure 3–44

- Scroll to the top of the table and then click row 1, column 1 to select this cell.

- Press the ENTER key to insert a blank line.

- Drag the denali_mountain image from the Assets panel to the insertion point in the merged cell (Figure 3–44).

2

- Click the Expanded button on the Layout tab to switch to Expanded Tables mode, and then click to the right of the denali_mountain image to deselect the image.

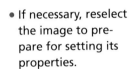

Q&A

The Getting Started in Expanded Tables mode dialog box is displayed when I complete this step. What should I do?

Read the information in the dialog box, and then click the OK button. The dialog box may not appear if the Don't show me this message again check box was checked previously.

Figure 3–45

- If necessary, reselect the image to prepare for setting its properties.

- Click the ID text box in the Property inspector and type mt_mckinley as the image ID.

- Press the TAB key and then type 300 in the W box to set the image width. Press the TAB key and then type 265 in the H box to set the image height.

- Click the Alt box, type Mt. McKinley as the Alt text, and then press the ENTER key to apply the specified properties. Scroll as necessary to see the completed image (Figure 3–45).

Q&A

The left column of the table is still widened, even after resizing the image. What should I do?

If the table column isn't resized when you resize the image, move the insertion point above the column, and then click to select the column, or click anywhere outside the cell containing the image.

- If necessary, scroll up. Click to the right of the image to deselect the image (Figure 3–46).

Figure 3–46

④

- Press the ENTER key to insert a blank line after the image (Figure 3–47).

Figure 3–47

5

- Drag the denali_bear image from the Assets panel to the insertion point to insert the image in the table.

- Verify that the denali_bear image is selected, click the ID box in the Property inspector, and then type alaskan_bear to name the image.

- Press the TAB key and then type 315 in the W box to set the image width.

- Press the TAB key and then type 395 in the H box to set the image height.

- Click the Alt box, type Alaskan bear as the Alt text, and then press the ENTER key.

Figure 3–48

- Click the Align button arrow and select Absolute Bottom to align the bottom of the image at the bottom of the cell.

- Click Format on the Application bar, point to Align, and then click Left to move the resized image to the left margin. Scroll as necessary to display the bear image (Figure 3–48).

Q&A

How are the alignment options in the Property inspector different from those on the Format menu?

When you are working with images, you use the options on the Align pop-up menu in the Property inspector to align the image in relation to other objects, such as the current line or table cell. You use the options on the Align submenu on the Format menu to align text or objects in relation to the page. However, when you're working in a table, the options in the Align submenu align text or objects with a column.

6

- Click to the right of the first paragraph in row 1, column 2, and then press ENTER to insert a blank line.

- Drag the denali_ sunset image to the insertion point to insert the image in the table.

- Click the ID text box in the Property inspector and then type denali_sunset as the image ID.

- Press the TAB key and then type 320 in the W box as the image width.

- Press the TAB key to move to the H box and then type 240 as the image height.

- Click the Alt box, type Denali Park Sunset as the Alt text, and then press ENTER.

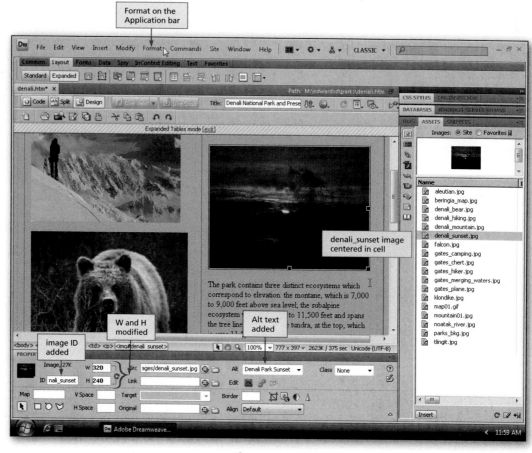

Format on the Application bar

denali_sunset image centered in cell

W and H modified

Alt text added

image ID added

Figure 3–49

- Click Format on the Application bar, point to Align, and then click Center to center the resized image. Scroll as necessary to display the sunset image (Figure 3–49).

7

- Click to the right of the last line of the first paragraph cell in row 2, column 2, and then press the ENTER key to insert a blank line (Figure 3–50).

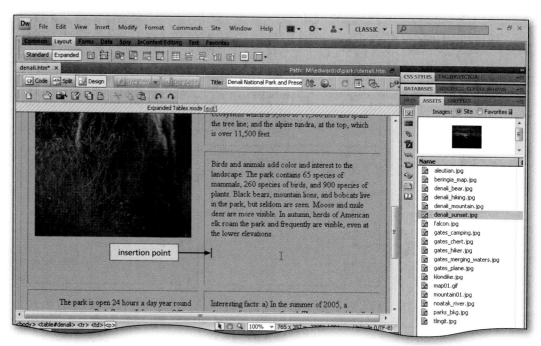

insertion point

Figure 3–50

- Drag the
denali_hiking
image to the
insertion point
(Figure 3–51).

Figure 3–51

- Click the ID text
box and then type
denali_hiking to
name the image.

- Press the TAB key
and type 450 in the
W box to set the
image width.

- Press the TAB key
and type 175 in the
H box to set the
image height.

- Click the Alt box,
type Hiking
Denali as the Alt
text, and then press
the ENTER key.

- Click Format on the
Application bar,
point to Align, and
then click Center to
center the resized
image. Scroll as
necessary to display
the hiking image
(Figure 3–52).

Figure 3–52

- Select the text in row 3, column 1, and left-align the text to balance the text with the images.

- Click the exit link next to Expanded Tables mode to return to Standard mode.

- Click the Save button on the Standard toolbar to save your work.

- Press the F12 key to view the page in your browser (Figure 3–53).

- Close the browser window to redisplay Dreamweaver.

Figure 3–53

Creating the Gates of the Arctic National Park and Preserve Web Page

To create the Gates of the Arctic National Park and Preserve Web page, you open a new document window. You start by applying the background image.

To Open a New Document Window and Add a Background Image to the Gates of the Arctic National Park and Preserve Web Page

The following step illustrates how to open a new document window and apply a background image.

1

• Click File on the Application bar and then click New to begin creating a new Web page. If necessary, click Blank Page and then click HTML in the Page Type list.

• Click the Create button to create the page.

• Click the Save button on the Standard toolbar to name the file, and then type gates as the file name. Save the Web page in the parks folder.

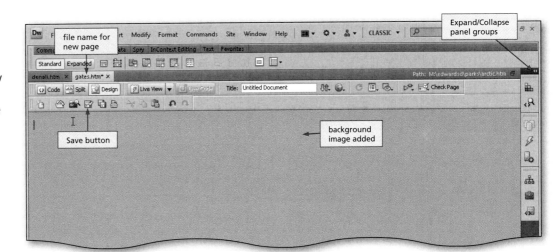

Figure 3–54

• If necessary, display the Property inspector and then click Page Properties to prepare for applying the background image.

• Click Appearance (HTML) in the category list to display the Appearance options.

• Click the Browse button to the right of the Background image box to find the background image.

• If necessary, navigate to and open the parks\images folder. Click parks_bkg.jpg and then click the OK button to select the background image.

• Click the OK button in the Page Properties dialog box to apply the background image. If a warning dialog box is displayed, click OK.

• Collapse the Panel groups to provide more work space in the window (Figure 3–54).

Next, you enter a title, and then insert and center a four-row, two-column table. You use the table to create the Gates of the Arctic National Parks and Preserve page by adding text and five images. You modify image placement and image size. You also add an absolute link and e-mail addresses for the park. Then you copy and paste the Links table from the Denali National Park and Preserve page to the Gates of the Arctic National Park and Preserve page.

To Insert and Center a Table

The next steps involve adding a page title, inserting and centering a table, and then adding a table ID to the table.

1

- Select the text in the Title box on the Document toolbar, and then type Gates of the Arctic National Park as the page title.

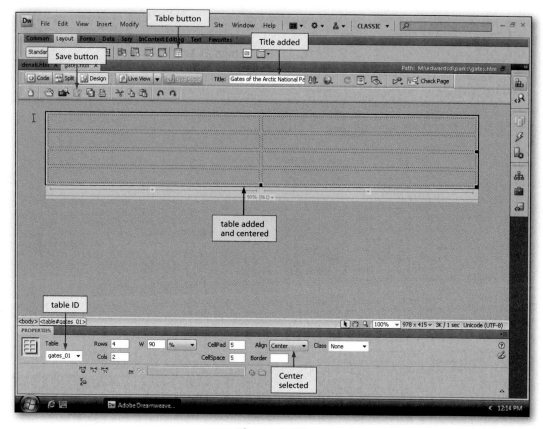

Figure 3–55

2

- Click the Table button on the Layout tab on the Insert bar to begin inserting a new table.

- In the Table dialog box, change the settings as follows: Rows 4, Columns 2, Table width 90 Percent, Cell padding 5, and Cell spacing 5.

- Click the Summary text box and then type Gates of the Arctic National Park and Preserve feature page as the Summary text.

- Click the OK button to insert the table.

- Click the Table text box in the Property inspector, type gates_01 as the table ID, and then press the ENTER key to accept the new ID.

- Click the Align button arrow and then click Center to center the table.

- Click the Save button on the Standard toolbar to save the table (Figure 3–55).

An understanding of HTML and how it relates to a table and to parts of a table provides you with the ability to use code to select a table and table components and to modify a table. Merging and varying the span of columns (as you did in the Denali National Park and Preserve page) and merging and varying the span of rows is helpful for grouping information, adding emphasis, or deleting empty cells. When you merge two cells in a row, you are spanning a column. Continuing with the <table> example on page DW 194 and spanning the two cells in row 1, the HTML tags would be <td colspan="2">First cellSecond cell</td>. When you merge two cells in a column, you are spanning a row. The attribute rowspan would replace colspan in the above example. Understanding colspan and rowspan will help you determine when and if two columns or two rows have been merged.

BTW

Displaying a Grid
You can display a grid as a visual guide that allows for precise positioning. The grid does not appear in the browser window. To turn on the grid, click View on the Application bar, point to Grid, and then click Show Grid on the Grid submenu.

To Adjust the Cell Alignment and Column Width

In the following steps, you will adjust the width for columns 1 and 2 in the Gates of the Arctic National Park and Preserve page, and then change the vertical alignment to Top within both columns.

- Click in row 1, column 1, and then drag to select all the cells in the table.

- Click the Vert button in the Property inspector, and then click Top to top-align the cells.

- Click table#gates_01 in the tag selector to select the table.

- Click row 2, column 1 to adjust the width of column 1.

- Click the W box in the Property inspector, type 60%, and then press the ENTER key to set the width of column 1.

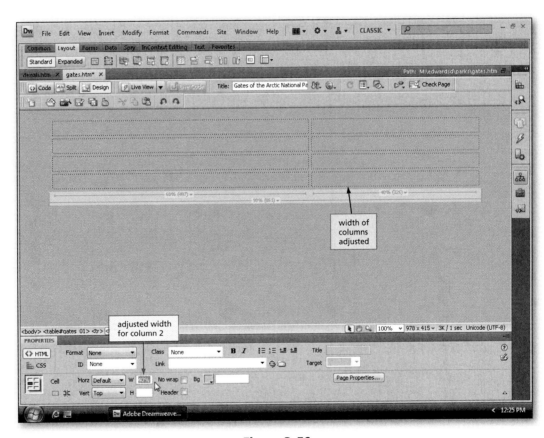

Figure 3–56

❷

- Click row 2, column 2 to adjust the width of column 2.

- Click the W box in the Property inspector, type 40%, and then press the ENTER key to set the width of column 2 (Figure 3–56).

To Merge Cells in Row 1

For the Denali National Park and Preserve page, you entered a heading outside the table and links to the other pages in a second table. For the Gates of the Arctic National Park and Preserve page, you merge the cells in row 1 of the table and enter a heading. Then you merge rows 2 and 3 in column 1. The following step illustrates how to merge the cells.

1

- Click row 1, column 1 and then drag to select all of row 1.

- Click the Merge Cells button in the Property inspector to merge the selected cells into one row.

- Click row 2, column 2 and then drag to select row 3, column 2.

- Click the Merge Cells button in the Property inspector to merge the selected cells into one column (Figure 3–57).

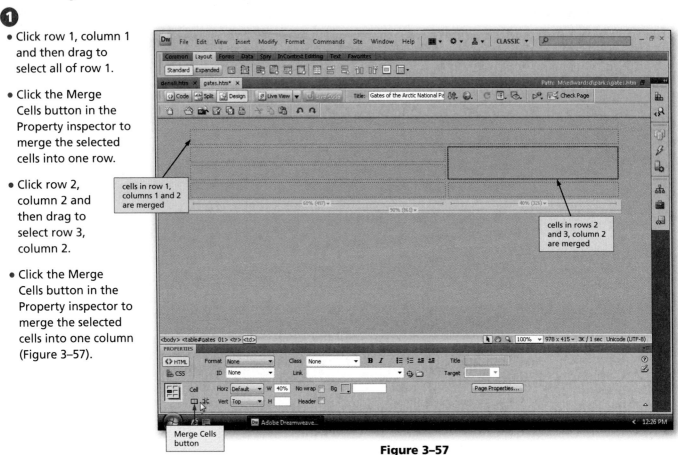

Figure 3–57

Adding Text to the Table

Now you add text to the table. Table 3–5 contains the text for the Gates of the Arctic National Park and Preserve Web page.

Table 3–5 Text for the Gates of the Arctic National Park and Preserve Page	
Section	**Text**
Part 1	Gates of the Arctic National Park and Preserve
Part 2	The Gates of the Arctic National Park and Preserve resides in Alaska's Brooks Range. This vast area of natural beauty contains rugged mountains, wild rivers, glaciated valleys, boreal forests, and arctic tundra vegetation. The area is inhabited by wolves, caribou, Dall sheep, and both grizzly and black bears. <ENTER> In 1978, President Jimmy Carter designated this area as a national monument. In 1980, Congress passed the Land Claims Act, creating 106 million acres of new protected lands in Alaska. The final boundaries for Gates of the Arctic National Park and Preserve encompass eight million contiguous acres.

Table 3–5 Text for the Gates of the Arctic National Park and Preserve Page (*continued*)

Section	Text
Part 3	The entirety of the park lies north of the Arctic Circle and is the northernmost national park in the United States. There are no established roads, trails, visitor facilities, or campgrounds in the park. Access into the park is by charter plane from Bettles or other locations. <ENTER>
Part 4	Ten small communities are within the resident zone for the park and are home to approximately 1,500 people. Many of these residents depend on resources within the park to sustain their livelihood and to maintain cultural traditions. <ENTER> **Interesting fact:** Chert is a fine-grained rock used by the prehistoric inhabitants of the Brooks Range to create tools such as scrapers, knives, and spear points. The Brooks Range contains one of the richest deposits of "tool quality" chert in the world.
Part 5	Park Service Information Office: Gates of the Arctic National Park and Preserve Park Headquarters 102 Elk Creek Gunnison, CO 81230-8397 <ENTER> E-mail: Gates of the Arctic

To Add and Format Text for the Gates of the Arctic National Park and Preserve Web Page

Now you are ready to add text to the table. The following steps illustrate how to add and format text for the Gates of the Arctic National Park and Preserve Web page.

- Click row 1, and then type the text of Part 1 as shown in Table 3–5 on page 224.

- Click the Format button arrow in the Property inspector and apply Heading 1 to the title.

- Click the Horz button arrow and select Center to center the heading (Figure 3–58).

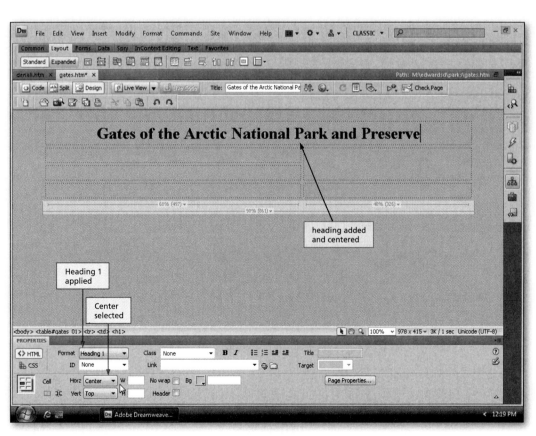

Figure 3–58

2

- Click row 2, column 2, and then type the text of Part 2 as shown in Table 3–5 on page 224, pressing the ENTER key as indicated in Table 3–5 (Figure 3–59).

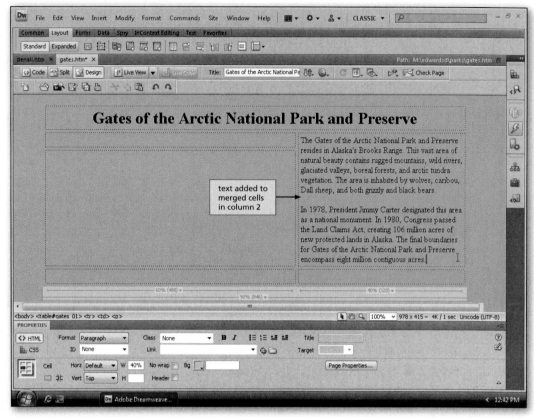

Figure 3–59

3

- Click the last row in column 2, and then type the text of Part 3 as shown in Table 3–5, pressing the ENTER key as indicated in Table 3–5 (Figure 3–60).

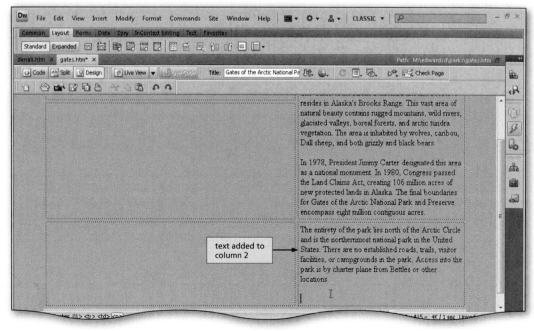

Figure 3–60

4

- Click row 3, column 1, and then type the text of Part 4 as shown in Table 3–5, pressing the ENTER key and inserting a line break as indicated in Table 3–5 (Figure 3–61).

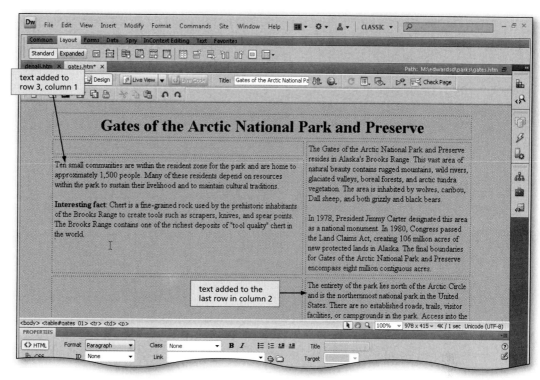

Figure 3–61

5

- Click row 4, column 1, and then type the text of Part 5 as shown in Table 3–5, pressing the ENTER key and insert line breaks as indicated in Table 3–5 (Figure 3–62).

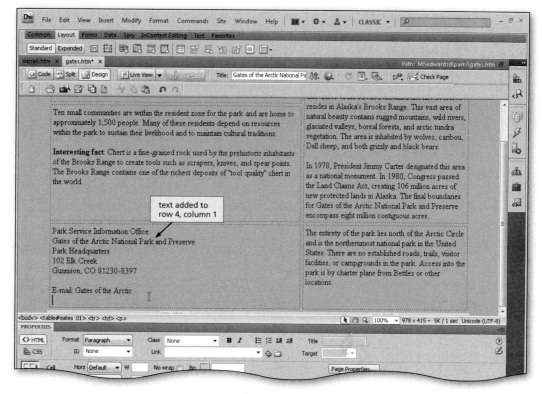

Figure 3–62

Adding Images and Image Borders

The purpose of most tables in a Web page is to provide a structure for the positioning of text and images. When a table is created within Dreamweaver, therefore, the default border is 0 (zero), or no visible border. You added a border to the table earlier in this chapter when you created the table. When the table is selected, the table border option also is available through the Property inspector.

You also can add borders to images. The **Border** command specifies the width, in pixels, of the line that frames the image. Adding a border to an image transforms the image into a graphical element itself. Depending on the content, a border can become a visual cue for the reader by separating content. The alignment options for images are listed in Table 3–6.

Table 3–6 Image Alignment Options

Alignment Option	Description
Default	Specifies a baseline alignment; default may vary depending on the user's browser
Baseline	Aligns the cell content at the bottom of the cell (same as Bottom)
Top	Aligns the cell content at the top of the cell
Bottom	Aligns the cell content at the bottom of the cell
TextTop	Aligns the top of the image with the top of the tallest character in the text line
Absolute Middle	Aligns the middle of the image with the middle of the text in the current line
Absolute Bottom	Aligns the bottom of the image with the bottom of the line of text
Left	Places the selected image on the left margin, wrapping text around it to the right; if left-aligned text precedes the object on the line, it generally forces left-aligned objects to wrap to a new line
Middle	Aligns the middle of the image with the baseline of the current line
Right	Places the image on the right margin, wrapping text around the object to the left; if right-aligned text precedes the object on the line, it generally forces right-aligned objects to wrap to a new line

To Add Images, Image Borders, and a Table Border

The next task is to add images to the Web page. In the following steps, you insert, resize, align, and add a border to the images.

1

- Click the panel groups expander arrow to display the panel groups. If necessary, click the Assets tab to display the Assets panel.

- Click row 2, column 1 to select the first cell in row 2, and then drag the gates_plane image to the insertion point in row 2, column 1.

- Click the ID text box in the Property inspector and then type `gates_plane` as the image ID.

- Change the width in the W box to 335 and the height in the H box to 245 to resize the image.

- Click the H Space box and then type `50` to set the horizontal spacing.

- Click the Alt box, type `Floating plane` as the Alt text, and then press ENTER.

- Click the Border text box and then type 2 to set the border thickness.

- Click the Align button arrow and then click Absolute Middle to align the image in the middle of row 2, column 1 (Figure 3–63).

Q&A

What if the column is wider than that shown in Figure 3–63?

Click outside the cell containing the image to restore the column to its appropriate width, and then click the image again to select it.

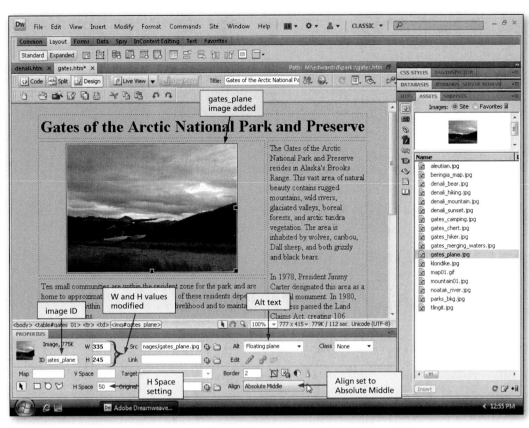

Figure 3–63

- Click <table#gates_01> in the tag selector to select the table, and then enter 5 in the Border text box to add a border to the table.

- If necessary, scroll down and click at the end of the first paragraph in row 3, column 1 and then press ENTER to prepare for inserting the next image (Figure 3–64).

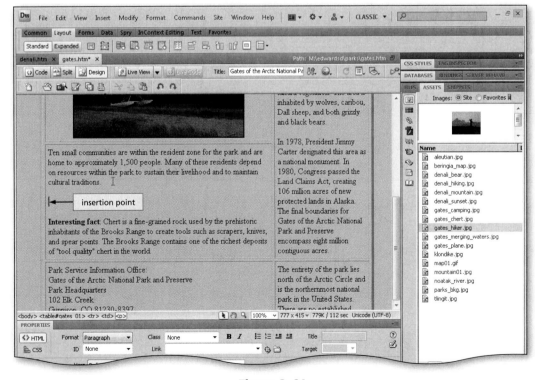

Figure 3–64

3

- Drag the gates_hiker image to the insertion point.

- Collapse the Assets panel to better view the image.

- Click the ID text box and then type `hiker01` as the image ID.

- Change the W value to 320 and the H value to 225 to resize the image.

- Click the V Space box and then type `25` to set the vertical spacing.

- Click the H Space box and then type `50` to set the horizontal spacing.

- Click the Align button arrow and then select Middle to align the image in the middle of the cell.

- Click the Border text box and then type `5` to set the border thickness.

- Click the Alt text box and then type `Hiking in the Gates National Park` as the Alt text (Figure 3–65).

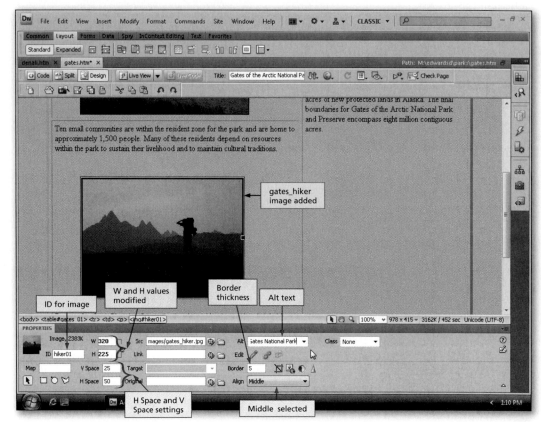

Figure 3–65

4

- Select the text in row 4, column 1, click the Horz button arrow, and then select Right to right-align the text (Figure 3–66).

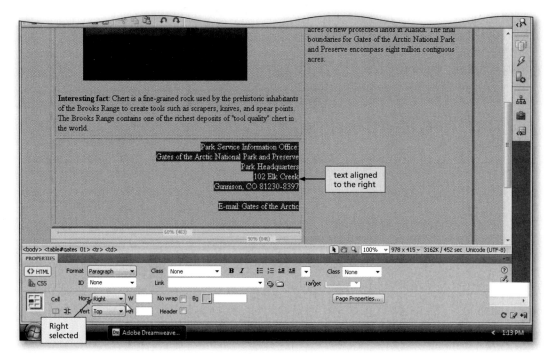

Figure 3–66

5

- Display the Assets panel again to prepare for inserting the next image.

- Click to the left of the first line, and then drag the gates_chert image to the insertion point to insert the image in the cell.

- Click the ID text box and then type chert as the image ID.

- Click the Align button arrow and then click Left to left-align the image.

- Type Chert as the Alt text and then press ENTER (Figure 3–67).

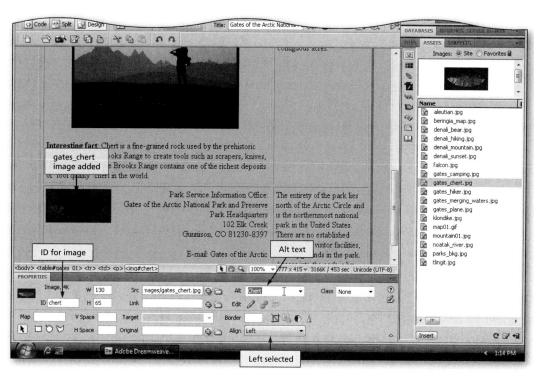

Figure 3–67

6

- Select the cells in rows 2 and 3, column 2, and then click the Merge Cells button to merge the cells.

- Click below the first paragraph in row 3, column 2, and then drag the gates_ camping image to the insertion point to insert the image in the cell.

- Change the W value to 190 and the H value to 250.

- Click the H Space box, type 75, and then press ENTER to set the horizontal spacing.

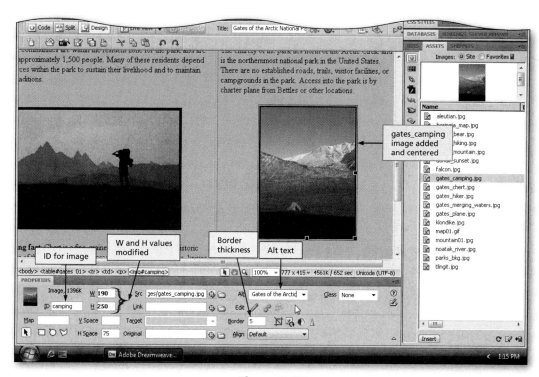

Figure 3–68

- Click Format on the Application bar, point to Align, and then click Center to center the image.

- Click the ID box in the Property inspector, and then type camping as the image ID.

- Click the Border box, type 5, and then press ENTER to set the border thickness.

- Click the Alt text box and then type Camping in the Gates of the Arctic to specify the Alt text (Figure 3–68).

- Click to the right of the gates_camping image, press ENTER twice, and then drag the gates_merging_waters image to the insertion point to insert the image in the cell.

- Click the ID text box and then type gates_merging_waters as the image ID.

- Press the TAB key and type 310 in the W box to set the width of the image.

- Press the TAB key and type 210 in the H box to set the height of the image.

- Click the H Space box and type 30 to specify the horizontal spacing.

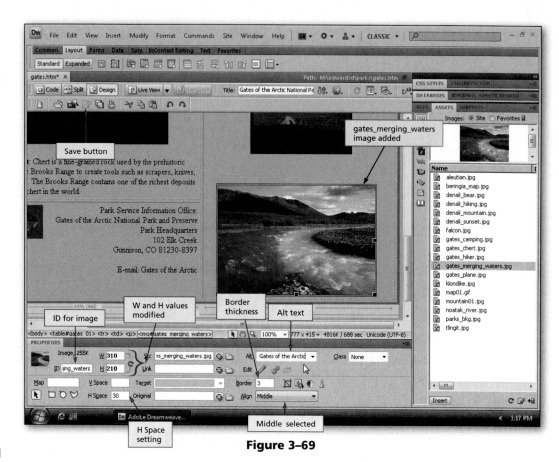

Figure 3–69

- Click the Align button arrow and then click Middle to align the image in the middle of the cell.

- Click the Border box, type 3, and then press ENTER to set the border thickness.

- Click the Alt text box and then type Merging waters in Gates of the Arctic to specify the Alt text.

- Click the Save button to save your work (Figure 3–69).

To Add Links to and Spell Check the Gates of the Arctic National Park and Preserve Web Page

The following steps illustrate how to add the absolute, relative, and e-mail links to the Gates of the Arctic National Park and Preserve page, copy the Links table from the Denali National Park and Preserve page and paste it as a footer in the Gates of the Arctic National Park and Preserve page. You then spell check the Web page, save it, and view it in a browser.

- Collapse the Assets panel to create more work space in the document window.

- If necessary, scroll down and select the text Gates of the Arctic National Park and Preserve in the address in row 4, column 1. Type http://www.nps.gov/gaar/ in the Link box and then press ENTER to create an absolute link.

- Select the text Gates of the Arctic, click Insert on the Application bar, and then click Email Link to display the Email Link dialog box.

- Type gaar@parks. gov in the E-mail text box, and then click the OK button to create an e-mail link.

- If necessary, open the Denali National Park and Preserve page, scroll down, and then click in the Links table to set the focus on the Links table.

- Click <table#alaska_ parks_links> in the Tag selector, and then press CTRL+C to copy the Links table.

- Click the gates. htm document tab to return to the Gates of the Arctic National Park and Preserve page.

- Click to the right of the table, press ENTER to move the insertion point to the next line, and then press CTRL+V to paste the Links table.

- If necessary, select the Links table, and then click the Align button arrow and select Center to center the table. Click anywhere in the document to deselect the Links table.

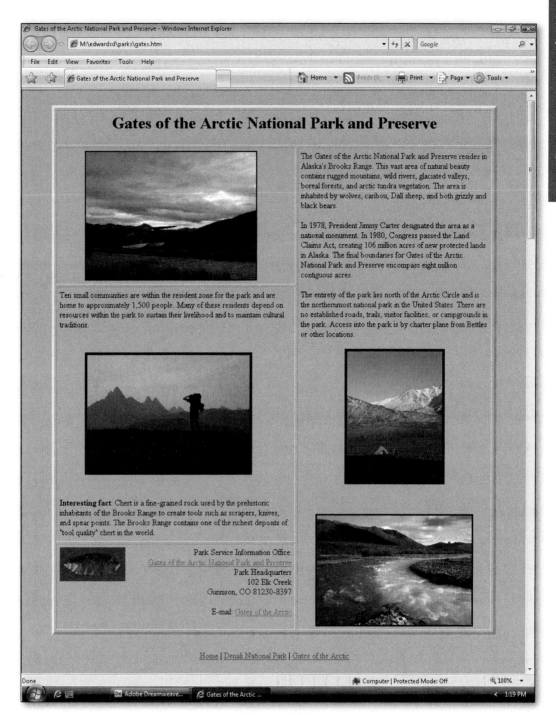

Figure 3–70

- Click Commands on the Application bar, and then click Check Spelling to begin spell checking the page.

- Check the spelling and make any necessary corrections.

- Click the Save button on the Standard toolbar to save your work.

- Press the F12 key to view the Web page in your browser (Figure 3–70).

- Close the browser.

Using Meta Tags
Meta tags are information inserted into the head content area of Web pages. The meta description tag allows you to influence the description of a page in the search engines that support the tag.

Head Content

HTML files consist of two main sections: the head section and the body section. The head section is one of the more important sections of a Web page. A standard HTML page contains a <head> tag and a <body> tag. Contained within the head section is site and page information. With the exception of the title, the information contained in the head is not displayed in the browser. Some of the information contained in the head is accessed by the browser, and other information is accessed by other programs such as search engines and server software.

Head Content Elements

Dreamweaver makes it easy to add content to the head section through the Insert menu. To access these commands, point to HTML, and then point to the submenu of the command you want to select.

Meta   A <meta> tag contains information about the current document. This information is used by servers, browsers, and search engines. HTML documents can have as many <meta> tags as needed. Each item uses a different set of tags.

Keywords   Keywords are a list of words that someone would type into a search engine search field.

Description   The description contains a sentence or two that can be used in a search engine's results page.

Refresh   The <refresh> tag is processed by the browser to reload the page or load a new page after a specified amount of time has elapsed.

Base   The base tag sets the base URL to provide an absolute link and/or a link target that the browser can use to resolve link conflicts.

Link   The link element defines a relationship between the current document and another file. This is not the same as a link in the Document window.

Keywords, descriptions, and refresh settings are special-use cases of the meta tag.

Plan Ahead

Preparing Head Content

Browsers and Web search tools refer to information contained in the head section of a Web page. Although this section is not displayed in the browser window, you can set the properties of the head elements to control how your pages are identified. At a minimum, you should set properties for the following head elements:

- **Keywords:** Enter keywords you anticipate users and search engines might use to find your page. Because some search engines limit the number of keywords or characters they track, enter only a few accurate, descriptive keywords.

- **Description:** Many search engines also read the contents of the Description text. Some search engines display the Description text in the search results, so be sure to enter a meaningful Description.

To Add Keywords and a Description to the Index Page

The following steps show how to add keywords and a description to the index.htm page.

1

- Open the index.htm file.

- Click Insert on the Application bar, point to HTML, point to Head Tags on the HTML submenu, and then point to Keywords on the Head Tags submenu (Figure 3–71).

Q&A What is a keyword?

A keyword is a word or phrase that someone might type into a search engine search field.

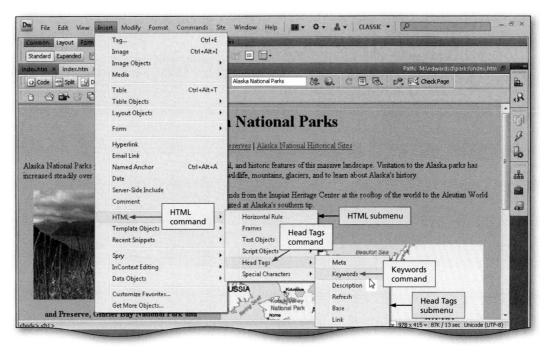

Figure 3–71

2

- Click the Keywords command to display the Keywords dialog box.

- Type parks, Alaska, national parks, national preserves in the Keywords text box to add the keywords to the Keywords dialog box (Figure 3–72).

Q&A What does a search engine typically do with the keywords?

When a search engine begins a search for any of the keywords, the Web site address will be displayed in the search results.

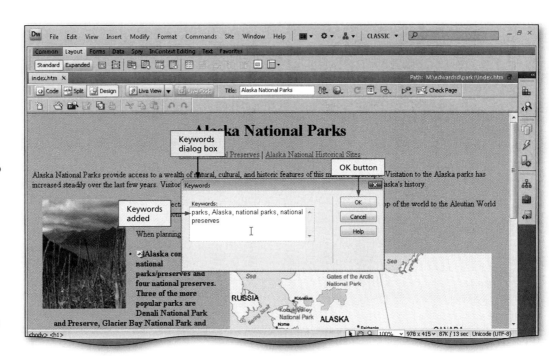

Figure 3–72

- Click the OK button to close the Keywords dialog box.

- Click Insert on the Application bar, point to HTML, point to Head Tags on the HTML submenu, and then click Description on the Head Tags submenu to open the Description dialog box.

- Type A Web site featuring Alaska National Parks

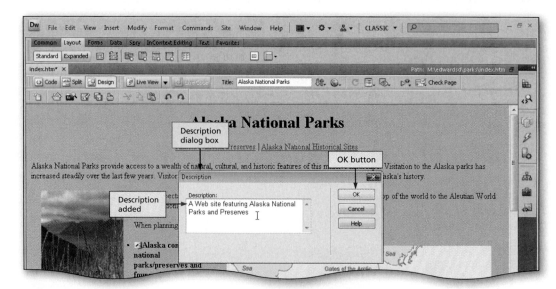

Figure 3–73

and Preserves in the Description text box to specify the description of the Web page (Figure 3–73).

Q&A

What is the purpose of the description?

The description contains a sentence or two that can be used in a search engine's results page.

- Click the OK button to close the Description dialog box.

- Click the Code button on the Document toolbar to display the page in Code view (Figure 3–74).

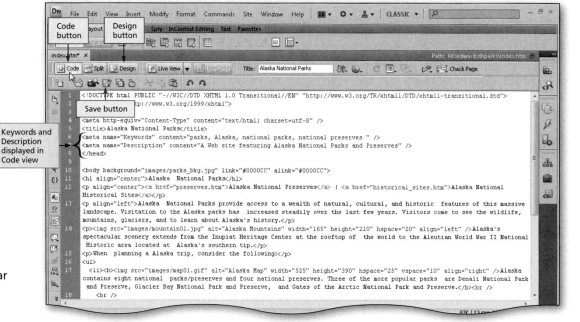

- Click the Design button on the Document toolbar to return to Design view.

- Click the Save button on the Standard toolbar to save your work.

Figure 3–74

Other Ways

1. Click Code button on Document toolbar, type keywords code in code window

2. Click Insert on the Application bar, point to HTML, point to Head Tags, and then click Description or Keywords

To Add Links to the Index Page

The Web site has expanded to include two additional pages. To integrate the pages within the Web site, you need to modify the index.htm page by adding a footer table at the bottom of the page. The following steps show how to delete the existing links and add a Links table.

1

- Click the gates.htm document tab to display that Web page.

- Scroll to the bottom of the page, select the Links table, right-click the selection to display the context menu, and then click Copy to copy the table.

- If necessary, open the index.htm page.

- Scroll to the bottom of the page, click to the right of the last sentence, and then press ENTER to move the insertion point to the next line.

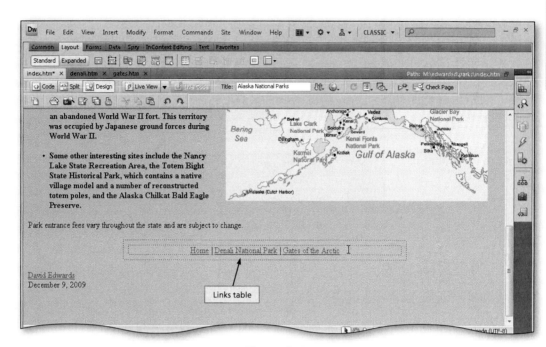

Figure 3–75

- Right-click near the insertion point to display the context menu and then click Paste to paste the Links table into the index page (Figure 3–75).

2

- Click to the right of the Gates of the Arctic text in the Links table, press SHIFT + | (vertical bar) and then press the SPACEBAR.

- Scroll to the top of the index.htm page, select the links, right-click the links to display the context menu, and then click Cut to remove the links from the top of the page.

- Scroll to the bottom of the page, right-click to the right of the last vertical bar to display the context menu, and then click Paste to paste the links into the Links table (Figure 3–76).

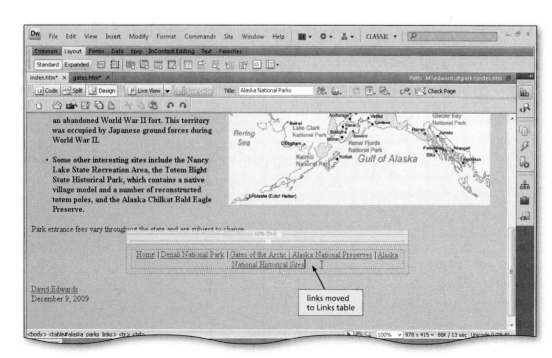

Figure 3–76

3

- Click the table and drag the middle-right selection handle to the right to widen the table and accommodate the links on one line (Figure 3–77).

4

- Click the page to deselect the table.

- Test each of the links to verify that they work.

- Click the Save button to save your changes.

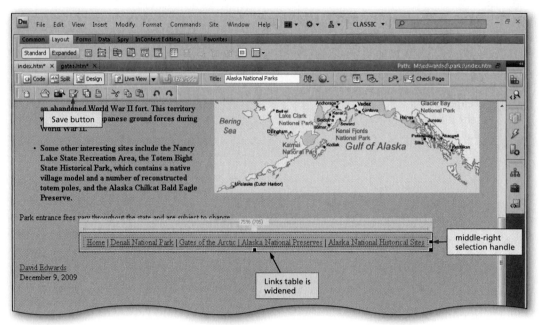

Figure 3–77

Publishing a Web Site

In Chapter 1 you defined a local site, and in Chapters 1, 2, and 3 you added Web pages to the local site. This local site resides on your computer's hard disk, a network drive, or possibly a USB drive. You can view the organization of all files and folders in your site through the Files panel.

To prepare a Web site and make it available for others to view requires that you publish your site by putting it on a Web server for public access. A Web server is an Internet- or intranet-connected computer that delivers, or *serves up*, Web pages. You upload files to a folder on a server and download files to a folder in the Files panel on your computer. Generally, when Web site designers publish to a folder on a Web site, they do so by using a file transfer (FTP) program such as WS_FTP, Cute FTP, or Windows Web Folders. Dreamweaver, however, includes built-in support that enables you to connect and transfer your local site to a Web server without using an additional program. To publish to a Web server requires that you have access to a Web server.

Publishing and maintaining your site using Dreamweaver involves the following steps:

1. Using the Site Definition Wizard to enter the FTP information
2. Specifying the Web server to which you want to publish your Web site
3. Connecting to the Web server and uploading the files
4. Synchronizing the local and remote sites

Your school or company may have a server that you can use to upload your Web site. Free Web hosting services such as those provided by Angelfire, Tripod, or GeoCities are other options. These services, as well as many other hosting services, also offer low-cost Web hosting from approximately $3.95 to $9.95 a month. The FreeSite.com Web site contains a list of free and inexpensive hosting services, and FreeWebspace.net provides a PowerSearch form for free and low-cost hosting.

Table 3–7 contains a list of Web hosting services. Appendix C contains step-by-step instructions on publishing a Web site to a remote folder.

Table 3–7 Web Site Hosting Services		
Name	**Web Site**	**Cost**
Angelfire	angelfire.lycos.com	Free (ad-supported); starting at $4.95 monthly ad-free
Yahoo! GeoCities	yahoo.com	Free (ad-supported); starting at $4.95 monthly ad-free
Tripod	tripod.lycos.com	Free (ad-supported); starting at $4.95 monthly ad-free
The FreeSite.com	thefreesite.com/Free_Web_Space	A list of free and inexpensive hosting sites
FreeWebspace.net	freewebspace.net	A searchable guide for free Web space

If required by your instructor, publish the Alaska Parks Web site to a remote server by following the steps in Appendix C.

Quitting Dreamweaver

After you add pages to your Web site and add the head content, Chapter 3 is complete, so you can quit Dreamweaver.

To Close the Web Site and Quit Dreamweaver

The following step illustrates how to close the Web site, quit Dreamweaver CS4, and return to Windows.

- Click the Close button on the right corner of the Dreamweaver title bar. If prompted, click the Yes button to save any changes.

Chapter Summary

Chapter 3 introduced you to tables and to Web page design using tables. You created two Web pages. You added a border to one of the Web pages. You merged and split cells and learned how to add text and images to the tables and how to create links to other pages. Finally, you added head content to one of the Web pages. The items listed below include all the new skills you have learned in this chapter.

1. Insert a table (DW 189)
2. Select and center a table (DW 197)
3. Change vertical alignment from Middle to Top (DW 199)
4. Specify column width (DW 201)
5. Add a table ID to the Denali National Park and Preserve table (DW 202)
6. Add text to the Denali National Park and Preserve Web page (DW 203)
7. Add a second table to the Denali National Park and Preserve Web page (DW 205)
8. Adjust the table width, center the text, and add the table ID (DW 208)
9. Add links to the Denali National Park and Preserve Web page (DW 209)
10. Merge two cells in a table (DW 212)
11. Disable the Image Tag Accessibility Attributes dialog box (DW 213)
12. Add images to a table (DW 214)
13. Add images, image borders, and a table border (DW 228)
14. Add keywords and a description to the index page (DW 235)

Learn It Online

Test your knowledge of chapter content and key terms.

Instructions: To complete the Learn It Online exercises, start your browser, click the Address bar, and then enter the Web address scsite.com/dsCS4/learn. When the Dreamweaver CS4 Learn It Online page is displayed, click the link for the exercise you want to complete and then read the instructions.

Chapter Reinforcement TF, MC, and SA
A series of true/false, multiple choice, and short answer questions that test your knowledge of the chapter content.

Flash Cards
An interactive learning environment where you identify chapter key terms associated with displayed definitions.

Practice Test
A series of multiple choice questions that test your knowledge of chapter content and key terms.

Who Wants to Be a Computer Genius?
An interactive game that challenges your knowledge of chapter content in the style of the television quiz show.

Wheel of Terms
An interactive game that challenges your knowledge of chapter key terms in the style of the television show *Wheel of Fortune*.

Crossword Puzzle Challenge
A crossword puzzle that challenges your knowledge of key terms presented in the chapter.

Apply Your Knowledge

Reinforce the skills and apply the concepts you learned in this chapter.

Adding a Table to a Web Page

Instructions: In this activity, you modify a Web page by adding a table and then inserting images in the table. Figure 3–78 shows the completed Web page. Make sure you have downloaded the data files for this chapter. See the inside back cover of this book for instructions for downloading the Data Files for Students, or contact your instructor for information about accessing the required files for this book.

Figure 3–78

Continued >

Apply Your Knowledge *continued*

Perform the following tasks:

1. Start Dreamweaver.

2. Copy apply_ch03.htm from the Chapter03\apply data file folder into the apply folder and the other files into the apply\images folder for your Apply Exercises local Web site.

3. Open the Apply Exercises site, and open the apply_ch03.htm page. Add the apply_bkg background image to the page.

4. Click to the right of the "Enjoying the View" heading and then press ENTER.

5. Insert a one-row, two-column table with a table width of 75 percent, cell padding and cell spacing of 10, and a border of 3.

6. Click the Summary box and then type Enjoying the View.

7. Center the table.

8. Insert the dog01 image into row 1, column 1.

9. Use red_dog1 as the image ID. Use the following text as the Alt text: Red dog viewed from right.

10. Change the W to 320 and the H to 240.

11. Insert the dog02 image into row 1, column 2.

12. Use red_dog2 as the image ID. Use the following text as the Alt text: Red dog viewed from left.

13. Change the W to 320 and the H to 240.

14. Apply a border of 2 to each of the images.

15. Save your document and then view it in your browser. Submit the Web page in the format specified by your instructor.

Extend Your Knowledge

Extend the skills you learned in this chapter and experiment with new skills. You may need to use Help to complete the assignment.

Adding, Aligning, and Resizing an Image on a Web Page

Instructions: In this activity, you create a Web page, insert text, add a table, insert images, and then align and resize the images. Figure 3–79 shows the completed Web page. Make sure you have downloaded the data files for this chapter. See the inside back cover of this book for instructions for downloading the Data Files for Students, or contact your instructor for information about accessing the required files for this book.

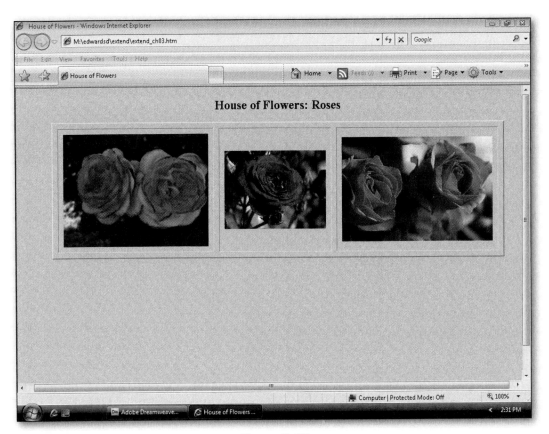

Figure 3–79

Perform the following tasks:

1. Start Dreamweaver.
2. Copy the files from the Chapter03\extend data file folder into the extend\images folder for your Extend Exercises local Web site.
3. Open the Extend Exercises site, open a new document window, and then save the page as extend_ch03.htm. Apply the extend_bkg background image to the page.
4. Enter the following heading at the top of the page: House of Flowers: Roses. Apply the Heading 2 format to the heading and then center the heading.
5. Click to the right of the heading and then press ENTER.

Continued >

Extend Your Knowledge *continued*

6. Insert a one-row, three-column table with a table width of 75 percent, cell padding and cell spacing of 10, and a border of 2.

7. Use Roses as the Summary text.

8. Center the table.

9. Drag the roses01 image to cell 1. Modify the following properties of the image: ID – light_pink_roses; W – 288; H – 216; Alt text – Light pink roses.

10. Drag the roses02 image to cell 2. Modify the following properties of the image: ID – red_rose; W – 200; H – 150; Alt text – Red rose.

11. Drag the roses03 image to cell 3. Modify the following properties of the image: ID – bright_pink_roses; W – 300; H – 200; Alt text – Bright pink roses.

12. Align each image in the middle of the cell.

13. Use the following text as the page title: House of Flowers.

14. Save your document and then view it in your browser. Submit the Web page in the format specified by your instructor.

Make It Right

Analyze a Web page and correct all errors and/or improve the design.

Adding an Image and E-mail Address to a Web Page

Instructions: In this activity, you modify an existing Web page to add a heading and a table with images. Figure 3–80 shows the completed Web page. Table 3–8 lists the properties you should use for the table and images. Make sure you have downloaded the data files for Chapter03\right. See the inside back cover of this book for instructions for downloading the Data Files for Students, or contact your instructor for information about accessing the required files for this book.

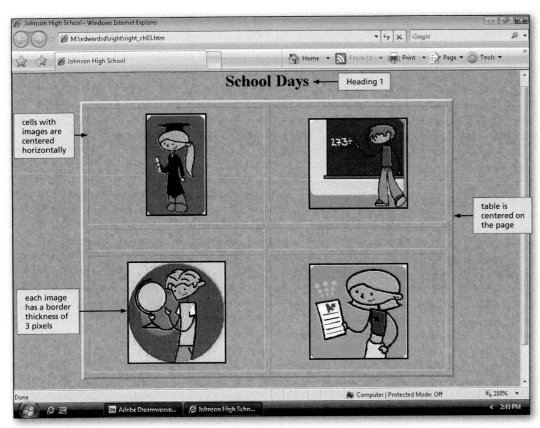

Figure 3–80

Table 3–8 Properties for Table and Images

Table Section	Properties or Image
Entire table	Width: 75 percent Border: 4 Alignment: Center Cell padding: 10 Cell spacing: 10
Column 1, row 1	Image: school01
Column 2, row 1	Image: school02
Column 1, row 2	blank
Column 2, row 2	blank
Column 1, row 3	Image: school03
Column 2, row 3	Image: school04

Perform the following tasks:

1. Start Dreamweaver.
2. Copy right_ch03.htm from the Chapter03\right data file folder into the right folder and the other files into the right\images folder for your Right Exercises local Web site.
3. Open the Right Exercises site, and then open the right_ch03.htm page. Apply the right_bkg background image to the page.

Continued >

Make It Right *continued*

4. If necessary, expand the Local Files panel and the Property inspector. Verify that HTML is selected.

5. The Web page you need to create is shown in Figure 3–80 on the previous page. Refer to Table 3–8 for details about the properties to apply to the table and the images to insert in the cells. In addition, note that each cell should be centered horizontally and each image should have a border thickness of 3 pixels. Do not change the width or height of the images. The page heading should be formatting as Heading 1 and centered on the page. The table should also be centered on the page.

6. Save your document and then view it in your browser.

7. Submit your Web page in the format specified by your instructor.

In the Lab

Create a document using the guidelines, concepts, and skills presented in this chapter. Labs are listed in order of increasing difficulty.

Lab 1: Modifying the Mobile Pet Services Web Site

Problem: Now that Bryan has a basic Web site for his Mobile Pet Services Web site, he wants to make the site more appealing to visitors. The Bryan's Mobile Pet Services Web site currently contains three pages. Bryan asks you to add a fourth page with a seven-row, three-column centered table that includes a list of services, information about how often the services are scheduled, and the price of each service. In the table, you should merge one of the rows, add and center an image in the row, and then apply a border to the entire table. You also add keywords and a description to the table. You then add a link to the home page and save the page (Figure 3–81).

Software and hardware settings determine how a Web page is displayed in a browser. Your Web page may appear different from the one shown in Figure 3–81. Appendix C contains instructions for uploading your local site to a remote site.

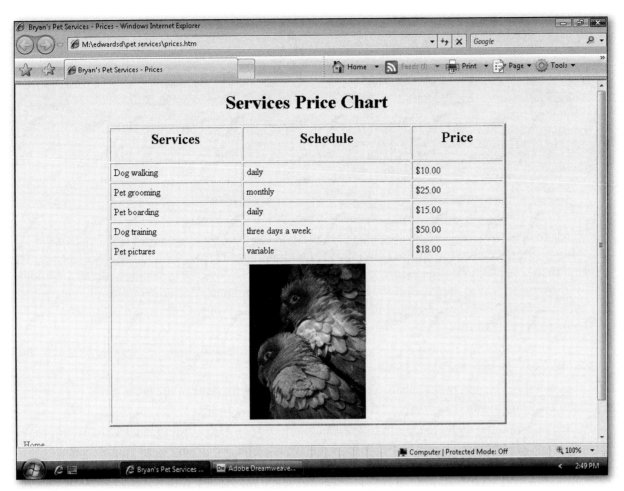

Figure 3–81

Perform the following tasks:

1. In Dreamweaver, copy the bird02 image from the Chapter03\pets data file folder to the pets\ images folder for your Pet Services local Web site.

2. Select Pet Services from the Files pop-up menu in the Files panel. Click File on the menu bar and then click New. If necessary, click Blank Page, accept the other defaults, and then click the Create button. Save the new page as prices.htm.

3. Use the Page Properties dialog box to apply the pets_bkg background image to the new page.

4. In the upper-left corner of the Document window, add a title with the text Services Price Chart (as shown in Figure 3–81). Apply Heading 1 to the title and then center it. Deselect the title, press the ENTER key after the title, and then click the Layout tab on the Insert bar. Click the Table button on the Layout tab. Enter the following values in the Table dialog box: 7 for Rows, 3 for Columns, 70 for Table width, 3 for Border thickness, 5 for Cell padding, and 2 for Cell spacing. If necessary, select percent using the button to the right of the Table width text box. In the Summary text box, enter Pricing chart for pet services. Click the OK button.

5. In the first six rows of the table, enter the text as shown in Table 3–9. Apply the Heading 2 format to the column title cells and center-align them. Press the TAB key to move from cell to cell.

Continued >

STUDENT ASSIGNMENTS

In the Lab continued

Table 3–9 Text for Table on Prices Page

Column 1	Column 2	Column 3
Services	Schedule	Price
Dog walking	daily	$10.00
Pet grooming	monthly	$25.00
Pet boarding	daily	$15.00
Dog training	three days a week	$50.00
Pet pictures	variable	$18.00

6. Click anywhere in row 7 and then click the <tr> tag in the tag selector to select row 7. Click the Merge selected cells using spans button. Click the Horz button arrow in the Property inspector, and then select Center. If necessary, display the Assets panel. With the insertion point in the middle of the merged row 7, drag the bird02 image to the insertion point. With the image still selected, type parrots in the ID text box and then type Parrots as the Alt text. Change the W value to 200 and the H value to 260.

7. Click the <table> tag in the tag selector, click the Align button, and then click Center to center the table. Click the Table text box and then type services as the ID.

8. Position the insertion point outside the table by clicking to the right of the table. Press the ENTER key. Type Home and then create a relative link to the index.htm file.

9. Click Insert on the menu bar, point to HTML, point to Head Tags, and then click the Keywords command. When the Keywords dialog box is displayed, type the following text in the Keywords text box: pet service, price schedule, your name. Click the OK button. Click Insert on the menu bar, point to HTML, point to Head Tags, and then click the Description command. When the Description dialog box is displayed, type the following text in the Description text box: Bryan's Pet Service price schedule. Click the OK button.

10. Title the page Bryan's Pet Services – Prices. Check the spelling, and then save the prices.htm Web page.

11. Open the index.htm page and then scroll to the end of the page. Click at the end of the sentence that reads, "Our mission is to be the premier…" and then press the ENTER key. Type Check our prices!. Center the new line, if necessary. Create a link from the words Check our prices! to the prices.htm page. Save the index.htm Web page.

12. View the pages in your browser. Verify that your links work. The index page should look similar to Figure 3–82 on the next page.

13. Submit your Web pages in the format specified by your instructor.

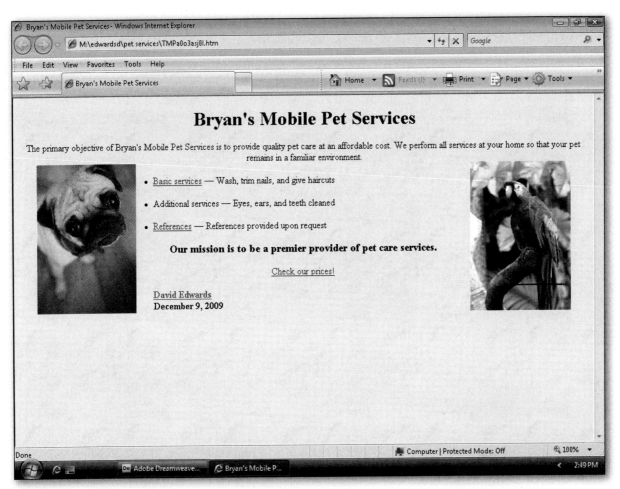

Figure 3–82

In the Lab

Lab 2: Adding a Page with a Table to the Jewelry by Eve Web Site

Problem: Publicity from the Jewelry by Eve Web site has generated several requests for examples of Eve Perry's jewelry. Eve has asked you to add a page to the site that shows some of her creations and the price of each piece. The new Web page will be named products and should include a link to the home page. The new page is shown in Figure 3–83 on the next page.

Software and hardware settings determine how a Web page is displayed in a browser. Your Web page may appear different from the one shown in Figure 3–83. Appendix C contains instructions for uploading your local site to a remote site.

Continued >

In the Lab continued

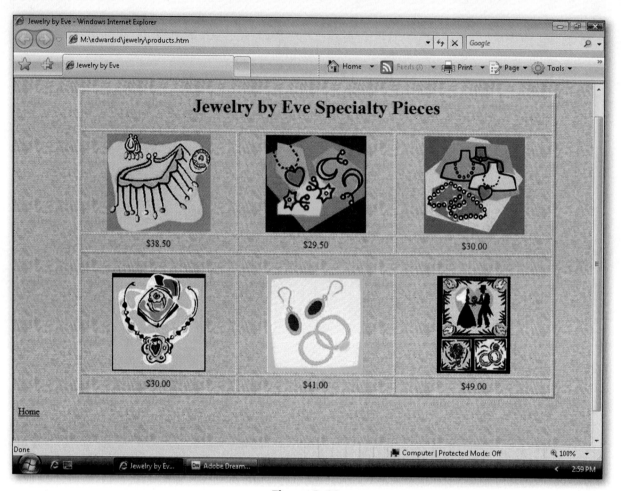

Figure 3–83

Perform the following tasks:

1. In Dreamweaver, copy the six images (jewelry1 through jewelry6) from the Chapter03\jewelry folder to the jewelry\images folder for your Jewelry Business local Web site. Select Jewelry Business from the Files pop-up menu in the Files panel. Add a new blank page named products.htm to this Web site.

2. Use the Page Properties dialog box to apply the jewelry_bkg background image to the Web page. Title the page Jewelry by Eve.

3. Click the upper-left corner of the page and then press the ENTER key to insert a blank line.

4. Insert a table with the following properties:

Rows	6
Columns	3
Table width	80 percent
Border thickness	3
Cell padding	3
Cell spacing	3
ID	jewelry
Summary	Jewelry examples

5. Merge the three cells in row 1 into one cell. Center row 1 horizontally. Type the following heading for the table in row 1: Jewelry by Eve Specialty Pieces. Apply Heading 1 to the table heading and then center it.

6. Center rows 2 through 6 horizontally and apply a Middle vertical alignment. Set the width of each column to 33%.

7. Using the Assets panel, drag the jewelry1 image to row 2, column 1. Repeat this step, dragging the jewelry2 image to row 2, column 2, and the jewelry3 image to row 2, column 3.

8. Type the following information in row 3:

Column 1 $38.50

Column 2 $29.50

Column 3 $30.00

9. Merge the three cells in row 4.

10. Add the following images in row 5:

Column 1   jewelry4

Column 2   jewelry5

Column 3   jewelry6

11. Type the following information in row 6:

Column 1 $30.00

Column 2 $41.00

Column 3 $49.00

12. Select the table by clicking <table#jewelry> in the tag inspector. Use the Property inspector to center-align the table.

13. Insert a blank line after the table. On a new line, type Home and then use this text to create a link from the products.htm page to the index.htm page. Save the products.htm page.

14. Open the index.htm page and click to the right of the Company History link. Press ENTER. Type Products and then use this text to create a link to the products.htm page. Save the index.htm page.

15. View the pages in your browser. Verify that your links work.

16. Submit your Web pages in the format specified by your instructor.

In the Lab

Lab 3: Adding a Page with a Table to the Credit Web Site

Problem: The Credit Protection Web site has become very popular. Linda Reyes receives numerous e-mail messages requesting that the Web site be expanded. Several messages have included a request to provide some hints and tips about how to save money. Linda asks you to create a new page for the Web site so she can share some of this information. Figure 3–84 shows the completed Web page.

Software and hardware settings determine how a Web page is displayed in a browser. Your Web page may appear different from the one shown in Figure 3–84. Appendix C contains instructions for uploading your local site to a remote site.

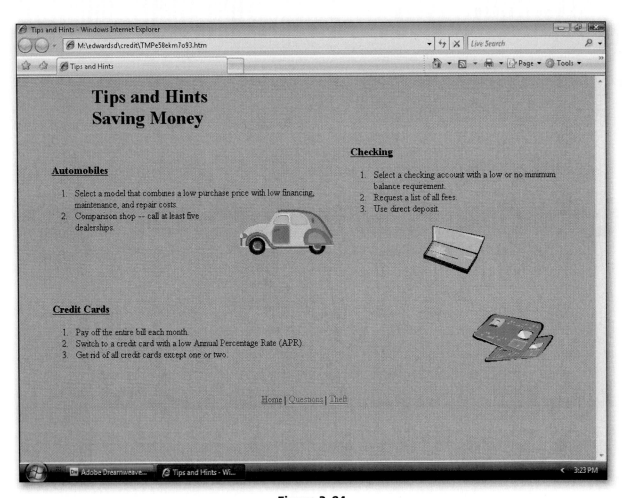

Figure 3–84

Perform the following tasks:

1. In Dreamweaver, copy the three images (car, check, and credit_card) from the Chapter03\credit folder to the credit\images folder for your Credit Protection Web site. Select Credit Protection from the Site pop-up menu in the Files panel. Add a new blank Web page named saving.htm to this Web site.

2. Apply the credit_bkg background image to the new page. Title the page Tips and Hints.

3. Create a table with a width of 90%, four rows, two columns, cell padding of 5, and cell spacing of 5. Add the following summary text: Tips and hints for saving money. Set the width of each column to 50%.

4. Use Figure 3–84 on the previous page as a guide to add content to the table. Use the information in Table 3–10 for the specific properties.

Table 3–10 Credit Protection Table Guide

Cells	Merge	Cell Text	Image Name	Image Location	Image Alignment	Alt Text
Row 1, columns 1 and 2	Merge cells in columns 1 and 2	Tips and Hints<ENTER> Saving Money	None	None	None	None
Row 2, column 1	None	Automobiles<ENTER> 1. Select a model that combines a low purchase price with low financing, maintenance, and repair costs. 2. Comparison shop — call at least five dealerships.	car.gif	At the end of Step 1, after "repair costs"	Right	Car
Row 2, column 2	None	Checking<ENTER> 1. Select a checking account with a low or no minimum balance requirement. 2. Request a list of all fees. 3. Use direct deposit. <ENTER>	check.gif	Below Step 3, "Use direct deposit."	Center	Checking Account
Row 3, columns 1 and 2	Merge cells in columns 1 and 2	Credit Cards<ENTER> 1. Pay off the entire bill each month. 2. Switch to a credit card with a low Annual Percentage Rate (APR). 3. Get rid of all credit cards except one or two.	credit_card.gif	At the end of the "Credit Cards" heading	Right	Credit Cards
Row 4, columns 1 and 2	Merge cells in columns 1 and 2	Home	Questions	Theft	None	None	None	None

5. Use Table 3–10 as a reference and type the text into each of the cells. Apply Heading 1 to the text in the first cell. Apply Heading 3 to the "Automobiles," "Checking, and "Credit Cards" headings and then underline the headings.

6. Insert the images into the cells in the locations specified in Table 3–10. Format the images as shown in Table 3–10.

7. Center the text in the last row. Add the appropriate relative links to this text, using Table 3–11 as a guide.

Continued >

In the Lab *continued*

Table 3–11 Links for Last Row	
Text	**Link**
Home	index.htm
Questions	questions.htm
Theft	theft.htm

8. Select the table, and then center the table.

9. Add the following keywords to the Head section: credit, money, tips, checking, saving, your name. Add the following description: Tips and hints on how to save money. Save the Web page.

10. Open the index.htm page and click to the right of the last bulleted item. Press the ENTER key twice. Type Tips and Hints on Saving and create a link from this text to the saving.htm page. Save the index.htm page.

11. View the pages in your browser. Verify that your links work.

12. Submit your Web pages in the format specified by your instructor.

Cases and Places

Apply your creative thinking and problem solving skills to design and implement a solution.

• Easier   ••More Difficult

• 1: Add a Web Page to the Favorite Sports Web Site

The sports Web site has become very popular. Several of your friends have suggested that you add a statistics page. You agree that this is a good idea. Create the new page. Using the Internet or other resources, find statistics about your selected sport. Add a background image to the page and use Standard mode to insert a table that contains your statistical information. Add an appropriate heading to the table and an appropriate title for the page. Create a link to the home page. Save the page in your sports Web site. For a selection of images and backgrounds, visit the Dreamweaver CS4 Media Web page (scsite.com/dwcs4/media) and then click Media below Chapter 3.

• 2: Expand the Hobby Web Site

Modify your hobby Web site. Add a new page that includes a table created in Standard mode. The table should contain a minimum of three rows and three columns, and a border. Include information in the table about your hobby. Include a minimum of two images in the table. Merge one of the rows or one of the columns and change the default border thickness. Add a background image to the page and give your page a title. Create a link to the home page. Save the page in your hobby Web site. For a selection of images and backgrounds, visit the Dreamweaver CS4 Media Web page (scsite.com/dwcs4/media) and then click Media below Chapter 3.

•• 3: Add a Web Page to the Politics Web Site

Your campaign for office is going well. You want to add a new page to the Web site to include pictures and text listing some of your outstanding achievements. Apply a background image to the page. Insert a table with a minimum of four cells. Include your picture in one of the cells. Add an appropriate title, keywords, and a description to the page. Center the table. Save the page in the folder for the politics site and then view the page in your browser. Appendix C contains instructions for uploading your local site to a remote site. For a selection of images and backgrounds, visit the Dreamweaver CS4 Media Web page (scsite.com/dwcs4/media) and then click Media below Chapter 3.

•• 4: Modify the Favorite Music Web Site

Make It Personal

Modify your favorite music Web site by adding a new page. The new page should contain a table with four rows and three columns. Merge one of the rows and add a background color to the row. Add at least two images to your table. Center the images in the cell. View your Web pages in your browser. Give your page a title and save the page in the folder for the music site. Appendix C contains instructions for uploading your local site to a remote site. For a selection of images and backgrounds, visit the Dreamweaver CS4 Media Web page (scsite.com/dwcs4/media) and then click Media below Chapter 3.

Continued >

Cases and Places *continued*

•• 5: Upgrade the Student Trips Web Site

Working Together

The students at your school are requesting more information about the student trips. To accommodate the request, the members of your team decide to add another page to the Web site. Each team member is responsible for researching possible destinations and developing content for the selected destination. Add a heading to the new page and format it appropriately. Insert a table with a minimum of six cells. Each member adds at least one image and text content to a cell. One member formats the page — including the text and images. Add a title, keywords, and a description. Save the page and view it in your browser. Appendix C contains instructions for uploading your local site to a remote site. For a selection of images and backgrounds, visit the Dreamweaver CS4 Media Web page (scsite.com/dwcs4/media) and then click Media below Chapter 3.

4 | Forms

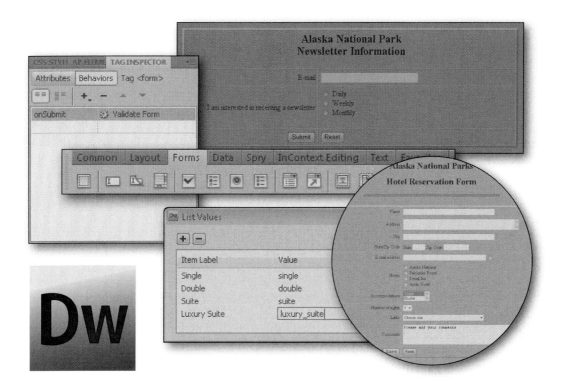

Objectives

You will have mastered the material in this chapter when you can:

- Discuss form processing
- Describe the difference between client-side and server-side form processing
- Add a horizontal rule to a Web page
- Create a form
- Insert a table into a form
- Describe form objects
- Describe and add text fields and text areas to a form

- Describe and add check boxes and radio buttons to a form
- Describe and add lists and menus to a form
- Describe and add form buttons to a form
- Describe form accessibility options
- Apply behaviors to a form
- View and test a form

4 | Forms

Introduction

Chapter 4 introduces the use of tables for page layout and the addition of head content elements. Page layout is an important part of Web design because it determines the way your page will be displayed in the browser. This is one of the major challenges for any Web designer.

Dreamweaver's table feature is a great tool for designing a Web page. The table feature is very similar to the table feature in word processing programs such as Microsoft Word. A table allows you to add vertical and horizontal structure to a Web page. Using a table, you can put just about anything on your page and have it be displayed in a specific location. Using the many table features, you can create columns of text or navigation bars, and lay out tabular data. You can delete, split, and merge rows and columns; modify table, row, or cell properties to add color and adjust alignment; and copy, paste, and delete cells in the table structure. Tables also enable the Web site designer to use this format to layout and create forms.

Project — Adding Forms to a Web Site

In this chapter, you learn to use tables to create forms and to add form fields to the forms. You add forms to two Web pages — a general information page and a hotel reservations form page. The Hotel Reservation Form, shown in Figure 4–1a, also contains a relative link to the Alaska National Parks index page. The hotel reservations form page contains a request for a hotel reservation at one of four Alaska hotels and provides a jump menu with an absolute link to a National Park Service Web page. The general information page, sponsored by the Alaska National Parks Volunteer Association, is shown in Figure 4–1b. This Web page contains a small form that provides the viewer with an opportunity to subscribe to a free newsletter. This page also contains a link to the Alaska National Parks index page. Both forms contain the same background used for the previous pages in the parks Web site and contain a horizontal rule separating the heading and the form.

Forms enable the Web page designer to provide visitors with dynamic information and to obtain and process information and feedback from the people viewing the Web page. Web forms are a highly versatile tool that can be used for surveys, guest books, order forms, tests, automated responses, user questions, and reservations. As you complete the activities in this chapter, you will find that forms are one of the more important sources of interactivity on the Web and are one of the standard tools for the Web page designer.

BTW

Form Design
When designing a form, keep the form simple and to the point. Before you create the form, sketch it on paper. The layout should be clear and uncomplicated.

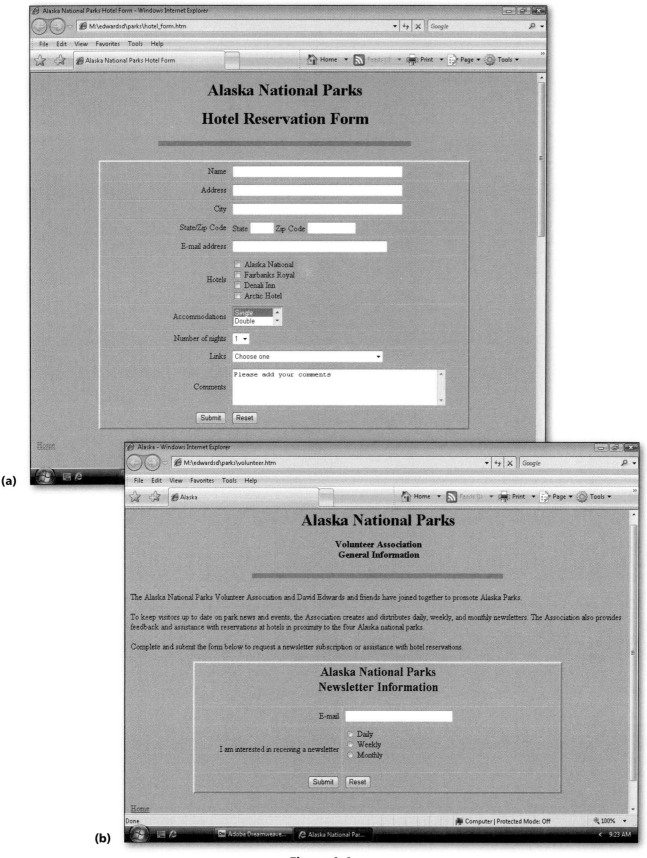

(a)

(b)

Figure 4–1

Overview

As you read this chapter, you will learn how to add to your Web site the pages shown in Figure 4–1a and Figure 4–1b on the previous page by performing these general tasks:

- Insert and center a heading
- Insert a table into a Dreamweaver Web page
- Insert a form and set the form properties
- Specify column width and merge cells
- Add form objects
- Add accessibility attributes
- Add text and images to the table
- Add links
- Add borders to tables and images

Plan Ahead

General Project Guidelines

When adding pages to a Web site, you must consider the appearance and characteristics of the completed page. As you create and add the two Web pages to the Alaska Parks Web site shown in Figure 4–1a and Figure 4–1b, you should follow these general guidelines.

1. **Plan the format of the form pages**. Determine the purpose of the form. Consider how the form pages will best fit into the Web site. Where will the data be stored?

2. **Organize your content**. Create and organize the content for the two new pages.

3. **Consider the data you will collect**. Use the data to determine rows and columns that will be included as part of the form. Decide if column headings will be named and if so, what names will be given to the columns. Consider the audience that will use the form and what is the best way to collect the data.

4. **Margins**. Establish the minimum margin width that is to be allowed on all sides of the form. Determine whether there is a limit to the length of the form.

5. **Images**. Decide if you will add images to your form, and if so, where you will place them. Consider the vertical and horizontal space that will need to be designated to place the image better. Determine if the image will need to be resized, and if so, how much resizing will need to be done.

6. **Determine the types of controls you will add to the form**. The controls you add will determine and affect the type of data you can collect.

7. **Consider Web content accessibility factors**. When an object is inserted into an HTML form, you can make the form object accessible.

8. **Link the new content**. Consider the content of each new page and how it will link to and from the other pages in the Web site.

9. **Create, test, and validate the form**. After creating the form, it should be tested to verify that all controls work as intended, including the Submit and Reset buttons. The Validate Form behavior checks the contents of specified text fields to ensure that the user has entered the correct type of data.

When necessary, more specific details concerning the above guidelines are presented at appropriate points in the chapter. The chapter also will identify the actions performed and decisions made regarding these guidelines during the creation of the Web pages shown in Figures 4–1a and 4–1b.

Starting Dreamweaver and Opening a Web Site

Each time you start Dreamweaver, it opens to the last site displayed when you closed the program. It therefore may be necessary for you to open the parks Web site. Clicking the **Files pop-up menu** in the Files panel lists the sites you have defined. When you open the site, a list of pages and subfolders within the site is displayed.

To Start Dreamweaver and Create a New Page on the Alaska Parks Web Site

With a good understanding of the requirements and an understanding of the necessary decisions and planning process, the next step is to start Dreamweaver and open the Alaska Parks Web site.

1

- Click the Start button on the Windows taskbar.

- Click Adobe Dreamweaver CS4 on the Start menu or point to All Programs on the Start menu, and then click Adobe Dreamweaver CS4 on the All Programs list to start Dreamweaver.

- If necessary, display the panel groups.

- If the Alaska Parks hierarchy is not displayed, click the Files panel button and then click Alaska Parks on the Files pop-up menu to display the Alaska Parks Web site hierarchy in the Files panel (Figure 4–2).

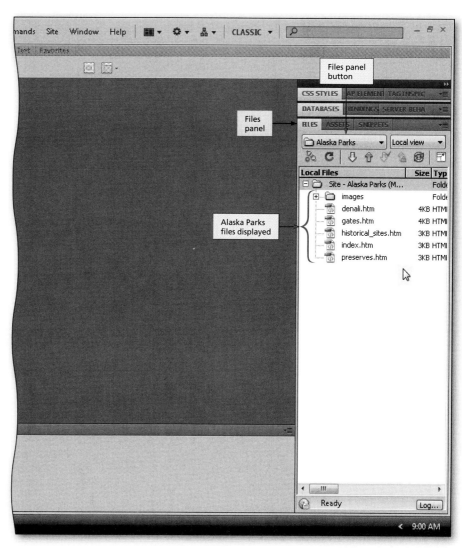

Figure 4–2

Copying Data Files to the Local Web Site

In the following steps, the data files for this chapter are stored on drive M:. The location on your computer may be different. If necessary, verify the location of the data files with your instructor.

To Copy Data Files to the Parks Web Site

In the following steps, you copy the data file for the Chapter 4 project from the Chapter04 folder to the parks folder stored in the *your name* folder.

- Click the Files panel button, and then click the name of the drive containing your data files, such as Removable Disk (M:).

- If necessary, click the plus sign (+) next to the folder containing your data files to expand that folder, and then click the plus sign (+) next to the Chapter04 folder to expand it.

- Expand the parks folder to display the data file.

- Click the volunteer.htm file to select it.

- Press CTRL+C to copy the file.

- If necessary, click the Files panel button, and then click the Alaska Parks Web site. Expand the *your name* folder and then the parks folder to select it.

- Press CTRL+V to paste the volunteer file in the parks folder.

Q&A | Is there another method for copying a data file into the Web site folder?
Yes, you can copy the file using the Windows Computer tool.

To Open a New Document Window

The following step illustrates how to open a new document window and save the page as hotel_form.htm.

1

- Click File on the Application bar and then click New to open the New Document dialog box. If necessary, click Blank Page, click HTML in the Page Type list, click <none> in the Layout list, and then click the Create button to create a Web page.

- Click the Save button on the Standard toolbar to open the Save As dialog box.

- Type hotel_form as the file name. If necessary, select the parks folder, and then click the Save button to save the hotel_form.htm page in the Alaska Parks local folder. The path and file name appear on the document tab (Figure 4–3).

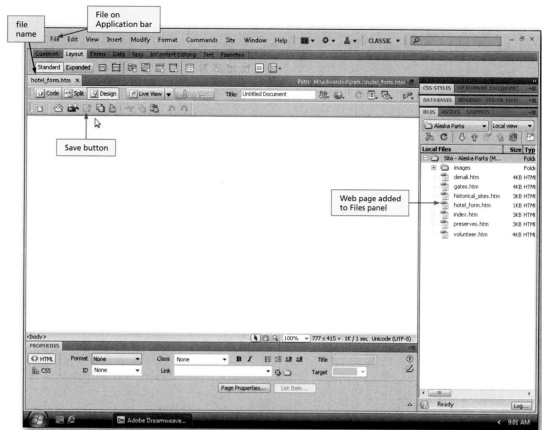

Figure 4–3

Creating the Hotel Reservation Form Web Page

You start creating the Hotel Reservation Form page by applying a background image. This is the same background image you used for the Alaska Parks Web site pages in previous chapters.

To Add a Background Image to the Hotel_form Page

To provide additional space in the document window and to create a better overview of the layout, you start by collapsing the panel groups. You expand the Property inspector to display the additional table options. Then you apply the background image to the hotel_form page.

- If necessary, click the panel groups Collapse to Icons arrow to collapse the panel groups.

- If necessary, click the Property inspector expander arrow to display both the upper and lower sections.

- Click the Page Properties button in the Property inspector to open the Page Properties dialog box.

- If necessary, click Appearance (HTML) in the Category column to display the HTML options.

- Click the Browse button to the right of the Background image box to open the Select Image Source dialog box.

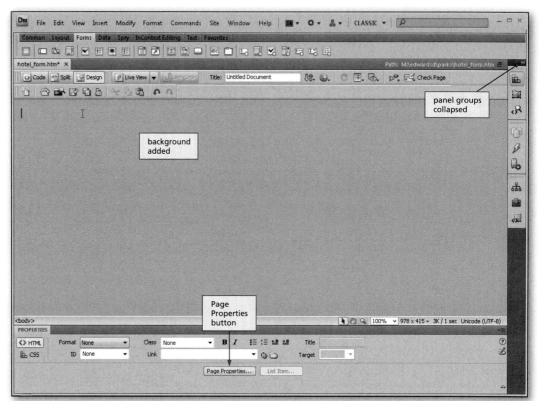

Figure 4–4

- If necessary, navigate to the parks\images folder.

- Click parks_bkg.jpg and then click the OK button in the Select Image Source dialog box to select the image.

- Click the OK button in the Page Properties dialog box. If necessary, click the document window to display the hotel_form Web page with the background applied and the insertion point aligned at the left (Figure 4–4).

To Insert and Format the Page Title

Next, you insert and format the page title. You apply the same heading format you applied to the heading in the index page. The following steps show how to add the title and apply Heading 1.

- If necessary, click the document window, and then type `Alaska National Parks` as the heading.

- Press ENTER and then type `Hotel Reservation Form` as the second heading.

- Select both heading lines.

- Click Format on the Application bar, point to Align, and then click Center to center the headings.

- Apply Heading 1 to both lines to format the headings.

- Click anywhere on the page to deselect the headings.

❸

- Title the page Alaska National Parks Hotel Form and then press ENTER.

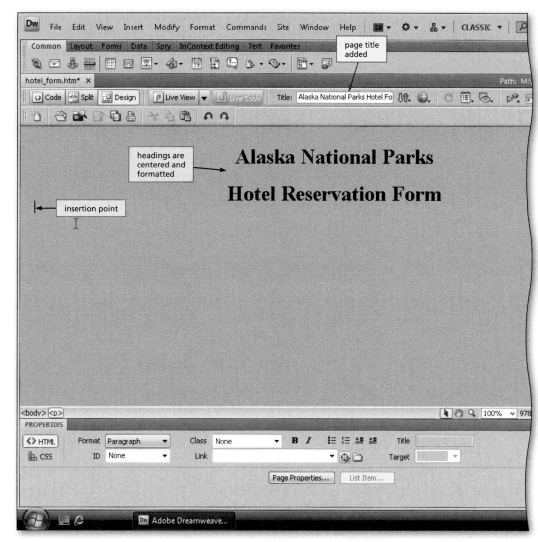

Figure 4–5

- Click the Save button on the Standard toolbar to save the page with the centered and formatted heading.

- Press the ENTER key to move the insertion point below the second heading (Figure 4–5).

Understanding How Forms Work

Forms are interactive elements that provide a way for the Web site visitor to interact with the site. A form provides a method for a user to give feedback, submit an order for merchandise or services, request information, and so on. Forms are created using HTML tags. Each form must have a beginning <form> tag and an ending </form> tag. You cannot nest forms. Each HTML document, however, may contain multiple forms.

Form Processing

A form provides a popular way to collect data from a Web site visitor. Forms, however, do not process data. Forms require a script in order for the form input data to be processed. Such a script generally is a text file that is executed within an application and usually is written in Perl, VBScript, JavaScript, Java, or C++. These scripts reside on a server. Therefore, they are called **server-side scripts**. Other server-side technologies include Adobe ColdFusion, ASP, ASP.NET, PHP, and JavaServer Pages (JSP). Some type of database application typically supports these technologies.

A common way to process form data is through a **Common Gateway Interface (CGI)** script. When a browser collects data, the data is sent to a Hypertext Transfer Protocol (HTTP) server (a gateway) specified in the HTML form. The server then starts a program (which also is specified in the HTML form) that can process the collected data. The gateway can process the input however you choose. It may return customized HTML based on the user's input, log the input to a file, or e-mail the input to someone.

The **<form> tag** includes parameters that allow you to specify a path to the server-side script or application that processes the form data and indicate which HTTP method to use when transmitting data from the browser to the server. The two HTTP methods are GET and POST, and both of these methods are attributes of the <form> tag. The **GET method** sends the data with a URL. This method is not widely used because it places a limitation on the amount and format of the data that is transmitted to the application. Another limitation of the GET method is that the information being sent is visible in the browser's Address bar. The **POST method** is more efficient because it sends the data to the application as standard input with no limits. The POST method can send much more information than the typical GET method. With POST, the information is not sent with the URL, so the data is invisible to the site visitor.

As an example of form data processing, when a user enters information into a form and clicks the Submit button, the information is sent to the server, where the server-side script or application processes it. The server then responds by sending the requested information back to the user, or performing some other action based on the content of the form.

The specifics of setting up scripts and database applications are beyond the scope of this book. Another option for form data processing exists, however, in which a form can be set up to send data to an e-mail address. The e-mail action is not 100 percent reliable and may not work if your Internet connection has extensive security parameters. In some instances, submitting a mailto form results in just a blank mail message being displayed. Nothing is harmed when this happens, but no data is attached to and sent with the message. Additionally, some browsers display a warning message whenever a form button using mailto is processed. This book uses the e-mail action, however, because this is the action more widely available for most students and users. On the other hand, your instructor may have server-side scripting available. Verify with your instructor the action you are to use.

Between the <form> and </form> tags are the tags that create the body of the form and collect the data. These tags are <input>, <select>, and <textarea>. The most widely used is the **<input> tag**, which collects data from check boxes, option buttons (called radio buttons in Dreamweaver), single-line text fields, form/image buttons, and passwords. The **<select> tag** is used with list and pop-up menu boxes. The **<textarea> tag** collects the data from multi-line text fields.

If you are using Internet Explorer with Windows Vista or with Windows XP Service Pack 2 (SP2), in many instances, Internet Explorer automatically blocks content such as form elements. Thus, for all instances in this chapter where pages containing forms are displayed in Internet Explorer, you may have to choose to "allow blocked content" by right-clicking the Information Bar and selecting the Allow Blocked Content command from the context menu, or modify the Internet Explorer security settings to allow form elements to display.

Horizontal Rules

A horizontal rule (or line) is useful for organizing information and visually separating text and objects. You can specify the width and height of the rule in pixels or as a percentage of the page size. The rule can be aligned to the left, center, or right, and you can add shading or draw the line in a solid color. These attributes are available through the Property inspector. The HTML tag for a horizontal rule is <hr>.

To Insert a Horizontal Rule

In the following steps, you insert a horizontal rule between the document heading and the form on the Hotel Reservation Form Web page. You also change the width and the height of the rule, and select no shading.

1

- Click Insert on the Application bar, point to HTML, and then point to Horizontal Rule to highlight the Horizontal Rule command (Figure 4–6).

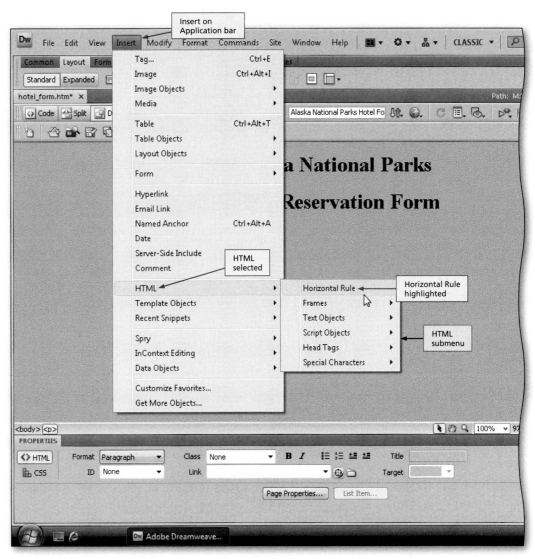

Figure 4–6

2

- Click Horizontal Rule to insert the horizontal rule below the heading and to display the Horizontal rule Property inspector (Figure 4–7).

3

- Click the Horizontal rule text box in the Property inspector and type horz_rule as the ID for the horizontal rule.

- Click the W (Width) text box and type 500 to decrease the line width. Press the TAB key two times to move the insertion point to the H box.

- Type 10 in the H (Height) text box to increase the line height.

- If necessary, click the Shading check box to deselect it (Figure 4–8).

4

- Click below the horizontal rule, and then click the Save button to save the hotel reservations form page.

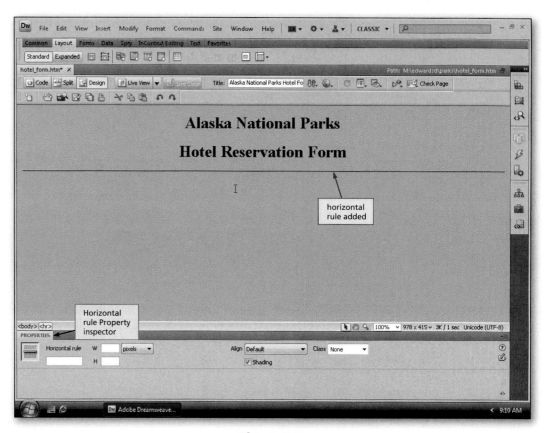

Figure 4–7

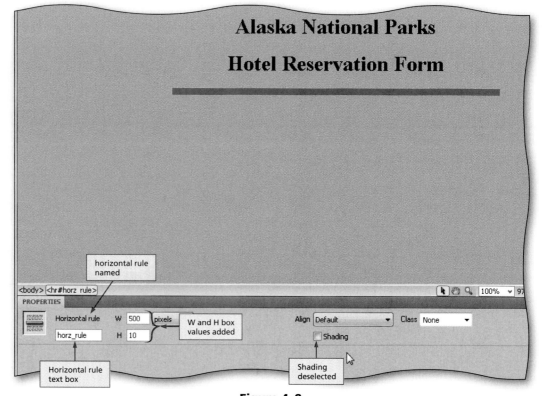

Figure 4–8

Forms and Web Pages

Web page designers create forms consisting of a collection of input fields so users can obtain useful information and enter data. When a user clicks the form's Send or Submit button, the data is processed with a server-side script or is sent to a specified e-mail address. A typical form, such as the one created in this chapter, is composed of form objects. A **form object** can be a text box, check box, radio button, list, menu, or other buttons. Form objects are discussed in more detail later in this chapter.

Inserting a Form

You insert a form in the same manner as you would a table or any other object in Dreamweaver. Simply position the insertion point where you want the form to start and then click the Form button on the Forms tab on the Insert bar. Dreamweaver inserts the <form> and </form> tags into the source code and then displays a dotted red outline to represent the form in Design view. You cannot resize a form by dragging the borders. Rather, the form expands as objects are inserted into the form. When viewed in a browser, the form outline is not displayed; therefore, no visible border exists to turn on or off.

To Insert a Form

The following steps illustrate how to insert a form into the hotel_form.htm page.

1
- Click the Forms tab on the Insert bar to display the Form buttons (Figure 4–9).

Figure 4–9

2

- Verify that Invisible Elements is selected by clicking View on the Application bar, and then pointing to Visual Aids. If necessary, click Invisible Elements on the Visual Aids submenu to select it (Figure 4–10).

Q&A

Should I have the same items checked on the Visual Aids submenu as in Figure 4–10?

The checked items on your Visual Aids submenu might be different. To make sure your screens match the figures in this chapter, your checked items should match those in Figure 4–10.

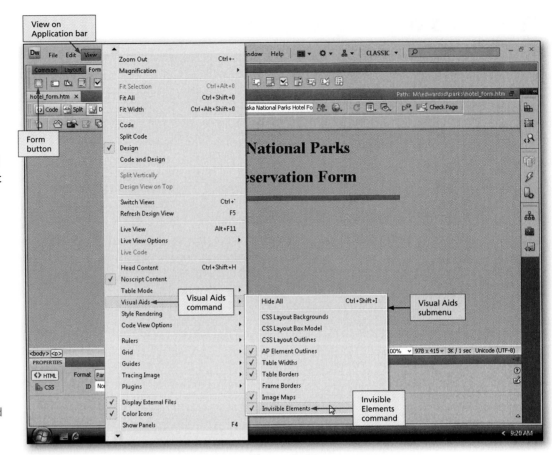

Figure 4–10

- Click the Form button on the Forms tab to insert a form into the document window and to display the Form Property inspector.

Form Property Inspector

As you have seen, the Property inspector options change depending on the selected object. The following section describes the form-related features of the Property inspector shown in Figure 4–11.

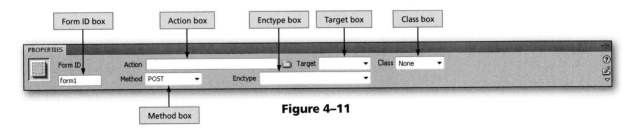

Figure 4–11

Form ID   Naming a form makes it possible to reference or control the form with a scripting language, such as JavaScript or VBScript.

Action   Contains the mailto address or specifies the URL to the dynamic page or script that will process the form.

Target   Specifies the window or frame in which to display the data after processing if a script specifies that a new page should be displayed. The four targets are _blank, _parent, _self, and _top. The _blank target opens the referenced link (or processed data) in a new browser window, leaving the current window untouched. The **_blank** target is the one most often used with a jump menu, which is discussed later in this chapter. The **_self** target opens the destination document in the same window as the one in which the form was submitted. The two other targets mostly are used with frames and are discussed in Chapter 7.

Method   Indicates the method by which the form data is transferred to the server. The three options are POST, which embeds the form data in the HTTP request; GET, which appends the form data to the URL requesting the page; and **Default**, which uses the browser's default setting to send the form data to the server. Generally, the default is the GET method. The POST and GET methods were discussed earlier in this chapter.

Enctype   Specifies a **MIME (Multipurpose Internet Mail Extensions)** type for the data being submitted to the server so the server software will know how to interpret the data. The default is application/x-www-form-urlencode and typically is used in conjunction with the POST method. This default automatically encodes the form response with non-alphanumeric characters in hexadecimal format. The multipart/form-data MIME type is used with a form object that enables the user to upload a file. You can select one of these two values from the Enctype list box or manually enter a value in the Enctype list box. The text/plain value is useful for e-mail replies, but is not an option in the Enctype list box and must be entered manually. This value enables the data to be transmitted in a readable format instead of as one long string of data.

Class   Sets style sheet attributes and/or attaches a style sheet to the current document.

Setting Form Properties

When naming the form and the form elements (discussed later in this chapter), use names that identify the form or form element. Be consistent with your naming conventions and do not use spaces or other special characters, except the underscore. This chapter uses lowercase letters to name the form and form elements. If you are using server-side scripting, be aware of and avoid reserved words in the scripting language.

BTW

The GET Method
Do not use the GET method to send long forms. URLs are limited to 8,192 characters. If the amount of data sent is too large, data will be truncated, leading to unexpected or failed processing results.

BTW

Dreamweaver and Forms
Dreamweaver makes it easy to add forms to your Web pages. The Forms tab on the Insert bar contains all of the traditional form objects. When the object is entered into the form, Dreamweaver creates the JavaScript necessary for processing the form.

To Set the Form Properties

The following steps illustrate how to name the form and to set the other form properties, including using the mailto action. Verify with your instructor that this is the correct action and that the form data is not to be processed with a server-side script.

- Double-click the Form ID text box in the Property inspector to select the default form name. Type hotel_form and then press the TAB key to name the form (Figure 4–12).

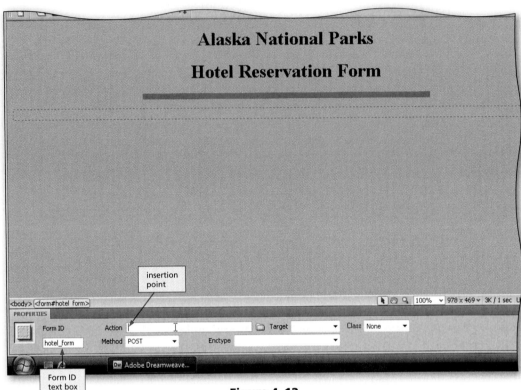

Figure 4–12

- Type mailto:dedwards@parks. com (use your own e-mail address) in the Action text box (Figure 4–13).

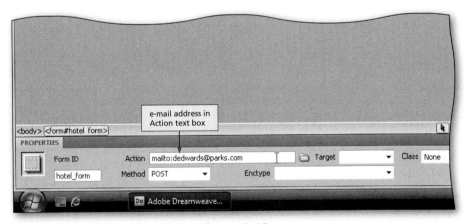

Figure 4–13

- Click the Target box arrow, select _self, and then press the TAB key to move the insertion point to the Enctype box (Figure 4–14).

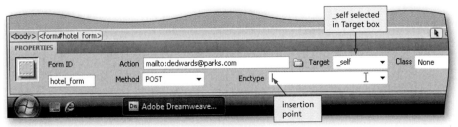

Figure 4–14

- Type text/plain and press the ENTER key to display text/plain in the Enctype box (Figure 4–15).

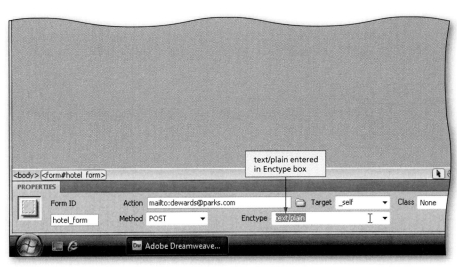

Figure 4–15

Inserting a Table into a Form

Adding and lining up labels within a form sometimes can be a problem. The text field width for labels is measured in **monospace**, meaning that each character has the same width. Most regular fonts, however, are not monospaced; they are proportional. To align labels properly using preformatted text requires the insertion of extra spaces. Two options to solve this problem are preformatted text and tables. Using tables and text alignment, therefore, is a faster and easier method to use when creating a form.

To Insert a Table into a Form

The following steps show how to add an 11-row, 2-column table to the form.

- Click inside the form (the dotted red outline).

- Click Insert on the Application bar to display the Insert menu, and then point to Table (Figure 4–16).

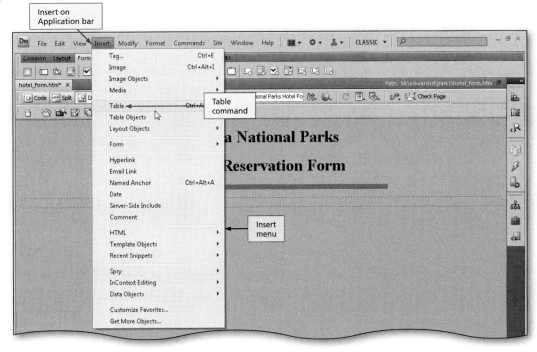

Figure 4–16

2

• Click Table to display the Table dialog box.

• Type the following values in the Table dialog box:

Rows: 11

Columns: 2

Table width: 75 percent

Border thickness: 4

Cell padding: 5

Cell spacing: 0

• Summary text: Hotel reservation form for Alaska National Parks (Figure 4–17).

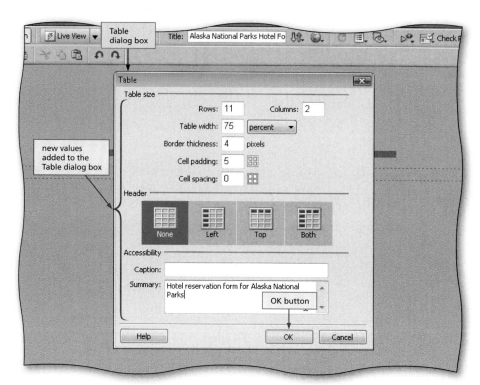

Figure 4–17

3

• Click the OK button to insert the table into the form.

• Verify that the table is selected. Click the Align button in the Property inspector, and then select Center to center the table in the form outline and to display the table properties in the Property inspector (Figure 4–18).

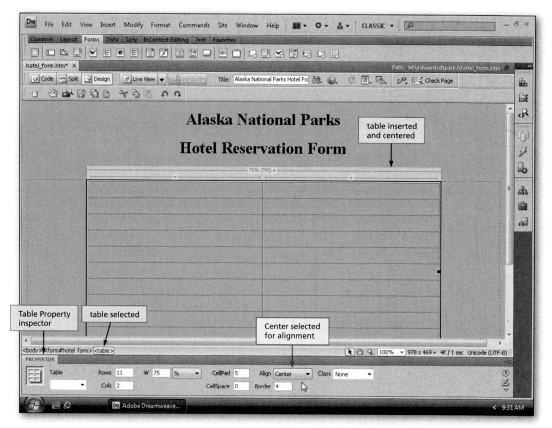

Figure 4–18

Formatting the Table Within the Form

Adding formatting to a form creates a more attractive page. In this instance, formatting includes changing the column width, and aligning the text for the labels in column 1 to the right. Based on the settings within Dreamweaver, when alignment is set to right or justified in a table cell, a dotted line may be displayed within the cell.

To Format the Form

The following steps show how to format the form.

1

- If necessary, select the table. In the Property inspector, click the Table box, type reservations as the ID, and then press the ENTER key to name the table (Figure 4–19).

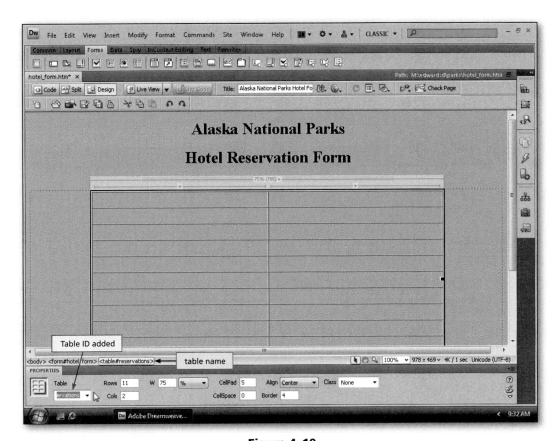

Figure 4–19

2

• If necessary, scroll up, click row 1, column 1, and then drag to select all of column 1. Click the W text box, type 35%, and then press the ENTER key to set the column width to 35 percent (Figure 4–20).

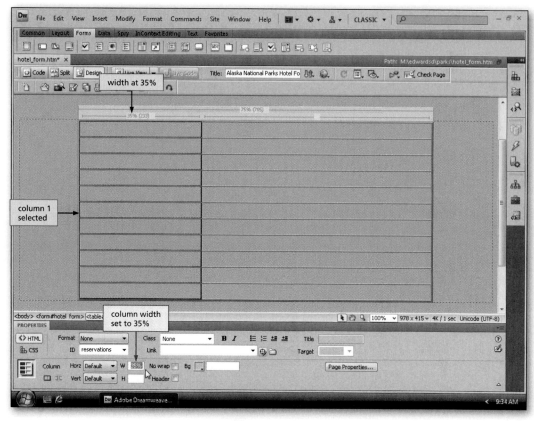

Figure 4–20

3

• The column still should be selected. Click Format on the Application bar, point to Align, and then click Right to right-align any text entered into column 1.

• Click the Save button on the Standard toolbar to save the table (Figure 4–21).

 Why doesn't the appearance of column 1 change after right-aligning it?

The right-alignment applies to the text the column will contain. When you enter text in column 1, it will be right-aligned.

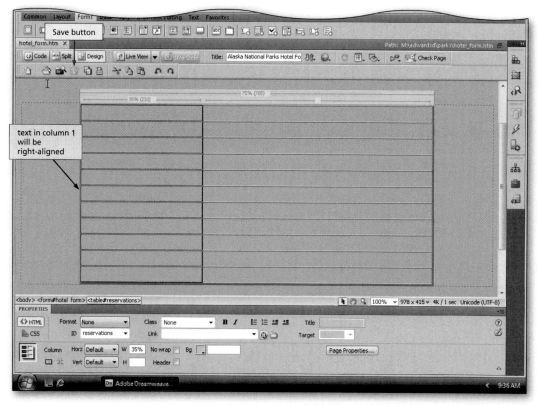

Figure 4–21

Form Objects

In Dreamweaver, data is entered through form input types called form objects. After you add a form to your Web page, you begin creating the form by adding form objects such as text fields, check boxes, and radio buttons. Each form object should have a unique name — except radio buttons within the same group, which should share the same name. To insert a form field in a Web page, (1) add the form field and any descriptive labels, and (2) modify the properties of the form object. All Dreamweaver form objects are available on the Forms tab on the Insert bar (Figure 4–22). Table 4–1 lists the button names and descriptions.

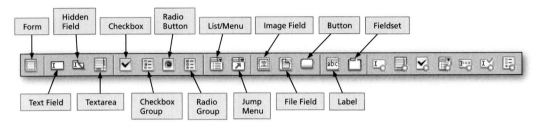

Figure 4–22

Button Name	Description
Form	Inserts a form into the Document window
Text Field	Accepts any type of alphanumeric text entry
Hidden Field	Stores information entered by a user and then uses that data within the site database
Textarea	Provides a multiline text entry field
Checkbox	Represents a selection
Checkbox Group	Allows multiple responses in a single group of options, letting the user select as many options as apply
Radio Button	Represents an exclusive choice; only one item in a group of buttons can be selected
Radio Group	Represents a group of radio buttons
List/Menu	List displays option values within a scrolling list that allows users to select multiple options; Menu displays the option values in a pop-up menu that allows users to select only a single item
Jump Menu	Special form of a pop-up menu that lets the viewer link to another document or file
Image Field	Creates a custom, graphical button
File Field	Allows users to browse to a file on their computers and upload the file as form data
Button	Performs actions when clicked; Submit and Reset buttons send data to the server and clear the form fields
Label	Provides a way to associate the text label for a field with the field structurally
Fieldset	Inserts a container tag for a logical group of form elements

Table 4–1 Buttons on the Insert Bar Forms Tab

Adding objects to a form.

After creating a form and inserting a table to align the form contents, you add objects to the form that users select to enter information into the form. Select objects depending on the type of information you want to collect: TextFields and Textareas for text entries such as addresses, Checkboxes, RadioButtons, and List/Menus for options users select, and Buttons for submitting and resetting the form.

Plan
Ahead

Text Fields

A **text field** is a form object in which users enter a response. Forms support three types of text fields: single-line, multiple-line, and password. Input into a text field can consist of alphanumeric and punctuation characters. When you insert a text field into a form, the TextField Property inspector is displayed (Figure 4–23).

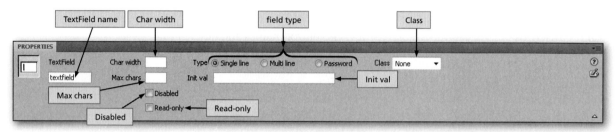

Figure 4–23

The following section describes the text field attributes for a single-line and password form. The multiple-line attributes are described later in this chapter.

TextField   Assigns a unique name to the form object.

Char Width   Specifies the maximum number of characters that can be displayed in the field.

Max Chars   Specifies the maximum number of characters that can be entered into the field.

Type   Designates the field as a single-line, multiple-line, or password field.

Init Val   Assigns the value that is displayed in the field when the form first loads.

Class   Establishes an attribute used with Cascading Style Sheets.

Disabled   Disables the text area.

Read Only   Makes the text area a read-only text area.

Typically, a **single-line text field** provides for a single word or short phrase response. A **password text field** is a single-line text box that contains special characters. When a user types in a password field, asterisks or bullets replace the text as a security precaution. Note, however, that passwords sent to a server using a password field are not encrypted and can be intercepted and read as alphanumeric text. For this reason, you always should provide encryption for data you want to keep secure. A **multiple-line text field** provides a larger text area in which to enter a response.

Inserting Text in a Form

You will notice as you insert form objects in a Web page that typically they contain no text label. **Labels** identify the type of data to be entered into the Text Field form object. Adding a descriptive label to the form that indicates the type of information requested provides a visual cue to the Web site visitors about the type of data they should type into the text box. Inserting text in a form is as simple as positioning the insertion point and then typing.

Single-Line Text Fields

Use single-line text fields for short, concise answers such as a word or phrase. Set the following properties in the TextField Property inspector after entering single-line text fields:

- *TextField*: Enter a unique name for each text field in the form. Server-side scripts use this name to process the data. If you use the mailto option, the name is contained within the data in the e-mail that is sent to your e-mail address. Form object names are case sensitive and cannot contain spaces or special characters other than an underscore.
- *Char width*: The default setting is 20 characters. You can change the default, however, by typing in another number. If the Char width is left as the 20-character default and a user enters 50 characters, the text scrolls to the right and only the last 20 of those characters are displayed in the text field. Even though the characters are not displayed, they are recognized by the form field object and will be sent to the server for processing or contained within the data if mailto is used.
- *Max chars*: Entering a value into the Max chars field defines the size limit of the text field and is used to validate the form. If a user tries to exceed the limit, an alert is sounded. If the Max chars field is left blank, users can enter any amount of text.
- *Init val*: To display a default text value in a field, type the default text in the Init val text box. When the form is displayed in the browser, this text is displayed.

To Add Descriptive Labels and Single-Line Text Fields to the Hotel Reservation Form

The following steps show how to add name, address, and e-mail single-line text boxes to the hotel reservation form.

1

- If necessary, scroll up and then click row 1, column 1 to place the insertion point in the cell (Figure 4–24).

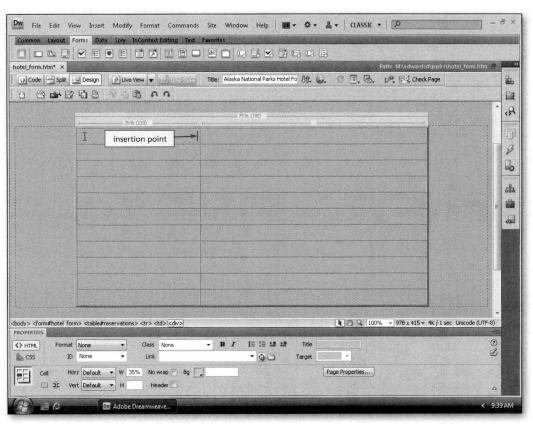

Figure 4–24

2

• Type Name as the descriptive label and then press the TAB key to place the insertion point in row 1, column 2 (Figure 4–25).

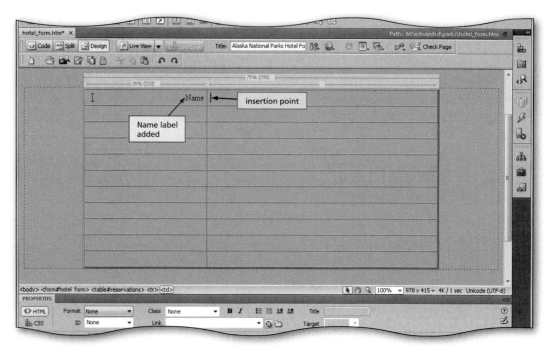

Figure 4–25

3

• Click the Text Field button on the Forms tab to insert a Text Field form object (Figure 4–26).

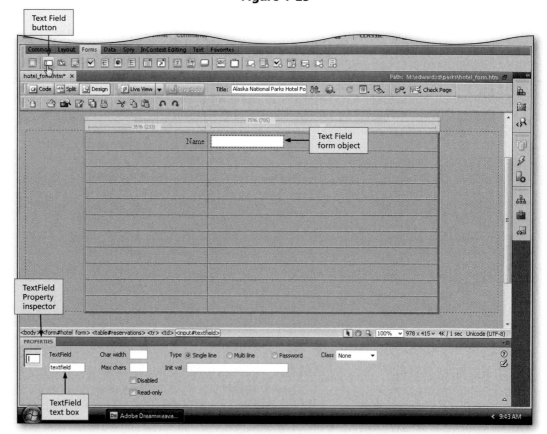

Figure 4–26

④

- Double-click the TextField text box in the Property inspector to select the default name, type name to rename the TextField, and then press the TAB key.

- Type 50 in the Char width text box and then press the TAB key. If necessary, click Single line as the Type (Figure 4–27).

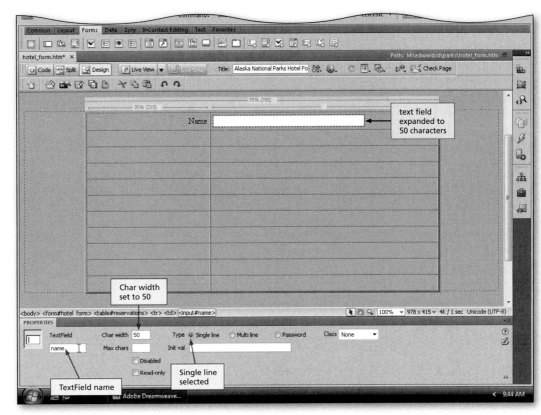

Figure 4–27

⑤

- Click row 2, column 1, type Address, and then press the TAB key.

- Click the Text Field button on the Forms tab to insert the Text Field form object (Figure 4–28).

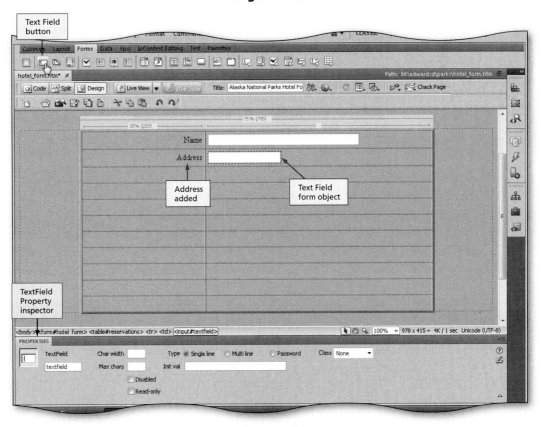

Figure 4–28

6

- Double-click the TextField text box in the Property inspector, type address, and then press the TAB key.

- Type 50 in the Char width text box and then press the TAB key to expand the text field width. If necessary, click Single line as the Type (Figure 4–29).

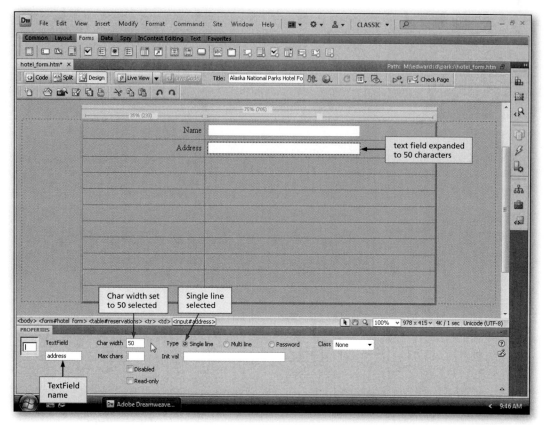

Figure 4–29

7

- Click row 3, column 1, and then type City. Press the TAB key to move the insertion point to column 2.

- Click the Text Field button on the Forms tab to insert a text field.

- Type city as the TextField name.

- Type 50 in the Char width text box and then press the TAB key to expand the field. Ensure that Single line is selected (Figure 4–30).

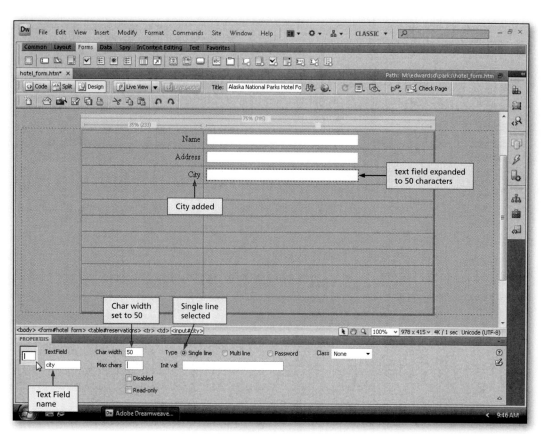

Figure 4–30

- Click row 4, column 1. Type `State/Zip Code` as the label and then press the TAB key to move the insertion point to row 4, column 2 (Figure 4–31).

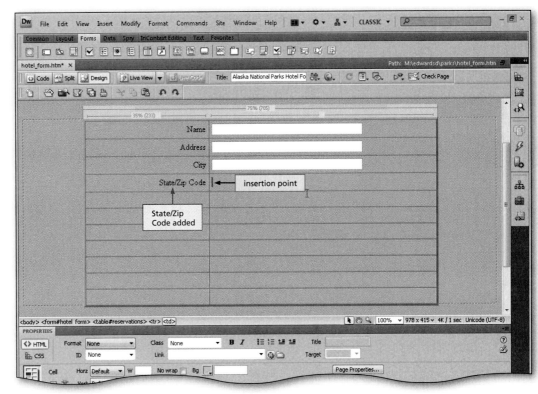

Figure 4–31

- Type `State` and then press the SPACEBAR to add the State descriptive label (Figure 4–32).

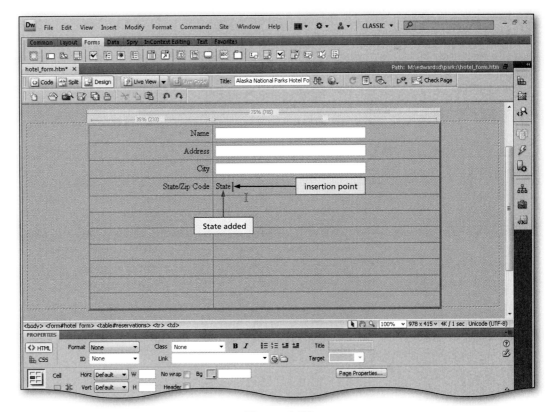

Figure 4–32

10

• Click the Text Field button to insert a text field for State. Type state as the TextField name in the Property inspector.

• Type 2 for the Char width and Max chars values. Press the TAB key to resize the text field. Ensure that Single line is selected (Figure 4–33).

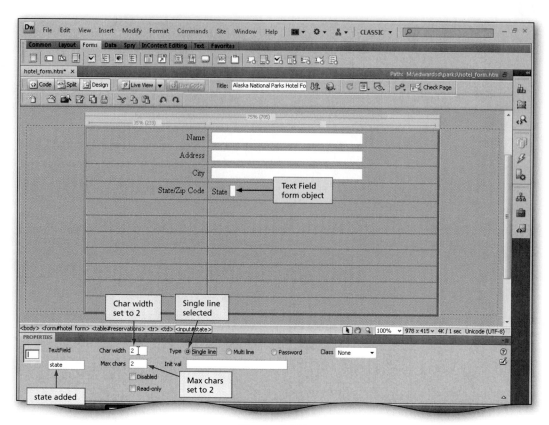

Figure 4–33

11

• Click to the right of the State Text Field form object and then press the SPACEBAR. Type Zip Code and then press the SPACEBAR to add Zip Code as the descriptive label.

• Click the Text Field button on the Forms tab to insert a text field for Zip Code.

• Type zip as the TextField name.

• Type 10 for the Char width and Max chars values and then press the TAB key to set the values to 10.

• Ensure that Single line is selected (Figure 4–34).

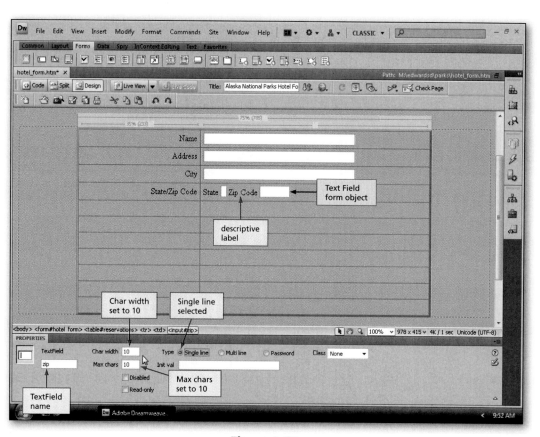

Figure 4–34

- If necessary, scroll down. Click row 5, column 1, and then type E-mail address for the descriptive label.

- Press the TAB key and then click the Text Field button to insert a text field for E-mail address (Figure 4–35).

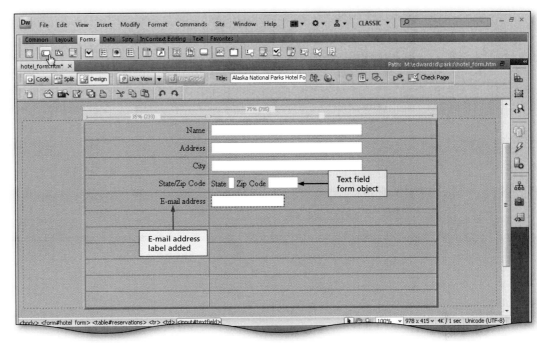

Figure 4–35

- Type email as the TextField name to name the text field.

- Type 45 for the Char width value and then press the ENTER key to adjust the size. Ensure that Single line is selected (Figure 4–36).

- Press CTRL+S to save the page.

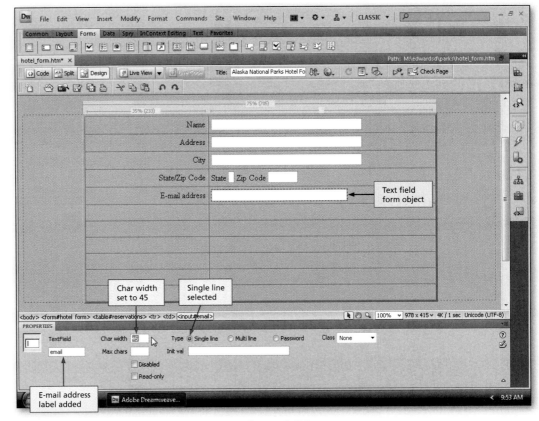

Figure 4–36

Other Ways
1. On Insert menu, point to Form, click Text Field

Check Boxes

Check boxes allow the Web visitor to click a box to toggle a value to either yes or no. They frequently are used to enable the visitor to select as many of the listed options as desired. Figure 4–37 displays the Property inspector for a check box. Just like a text field, each check box should have a unique name. The Checked value text box contains the information you want to send to the script or include in the mailto information to identify the data. For the Initial state, the default is Unchecked. Click Checked if you want an option to appear selected when the form first loads in the browser.

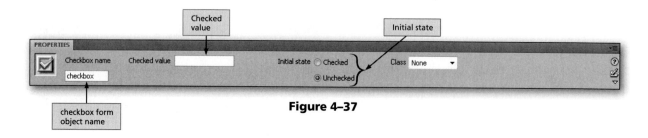

Figure 4–37

To Add Check Boxes

The following steps illustrate how to add four check boxes to the hotel reservations form.

1

- Click row 6, column 1, type Hotels as the descriptive label, and then press the TAB key.

- Click the Checkbox button on the Forms tab to add the check box to the form (Figure 4–38).

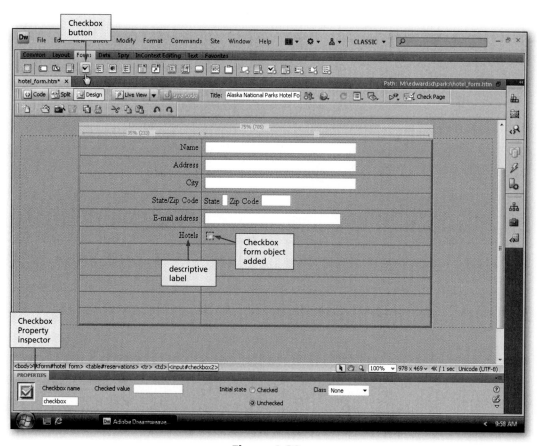

Figure 4–38

2

- Type `hotel1` as the Checkbox name.

- Press the TAB key and then type `alaska_national` in the Checked value text box. Press the ENTER key to display the properties for the first check box (Figure 4–39).

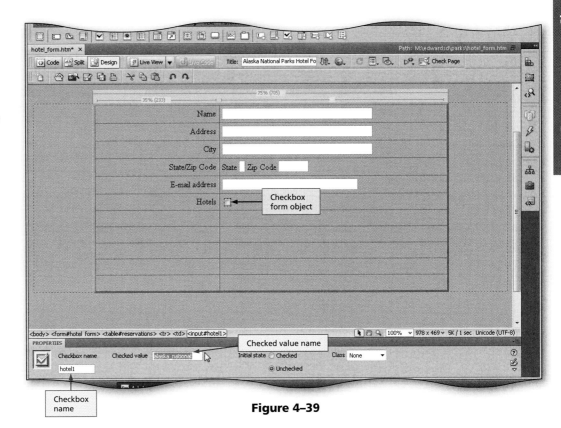

Figure 4–39

3

- Click to the right of the Checkbox form object and then press SHIFT+ENTER to add a line break and to position the insertion point below the first check box (Figure 4–40).

  My insertion point is very small. Is that correct?

Yes. The insertion point is always small after a line break.

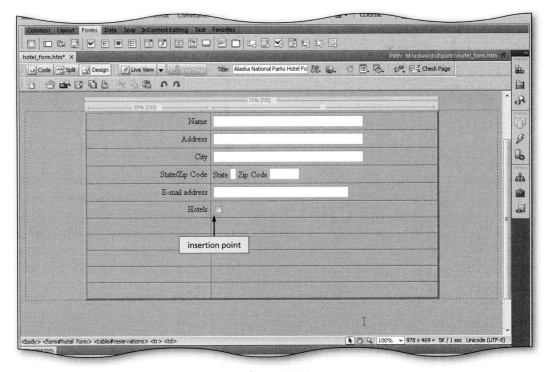

Figure 4–40

4
- Click the Checkbox button on the Forms tab to insert a second check box.

- Type `hotel2` as the Checkbox name. Press the TAB key and then type `fairbanks_royal` in the Checked value text box to add the second check box. Press the ENTER key (Figure 4–41).

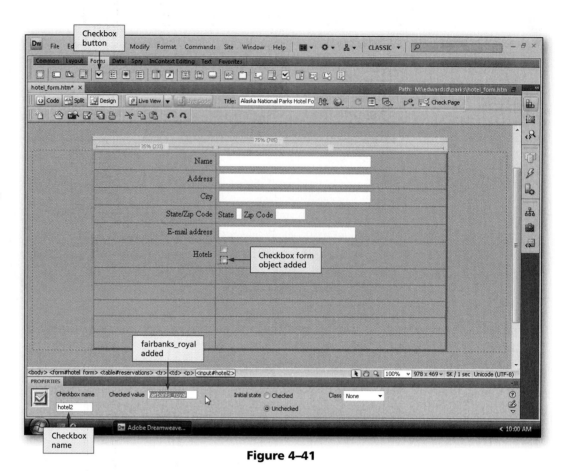

Figure 4–41

5
- Click to the right of the second check box, press SHIFT+ENTER to add a line break, and then click the Checkbox button on the Forms tab to insert a third check box.

- Type `hotel3` as the Checkbox name.

- Press the TAB key and then type `denali_inn` in the Checked value text box. Press the ENTER key to add the third check box (Figure 4–42).

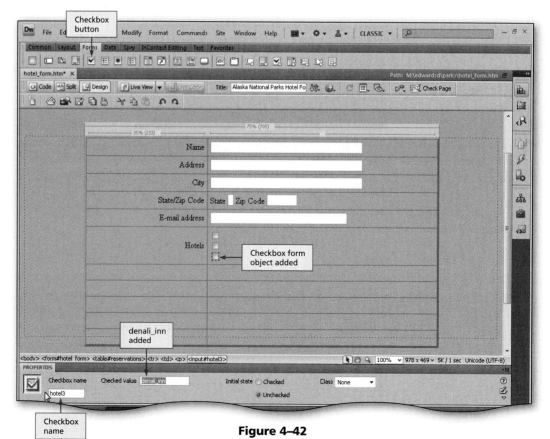

Figure 4–42

6

- Click to the right of the third check box, press SHIFT+ENTER to add a line break, and then click the Checkbox button on the Forms tab to insert a fourth check box.

- Type `hotel4` as the Checkbox name.

- Press the TAB key and then type `arctic_hotel` in the Checked value text box. Press the ENTER key to add the properties for the fourth check box (Figure 4–43).

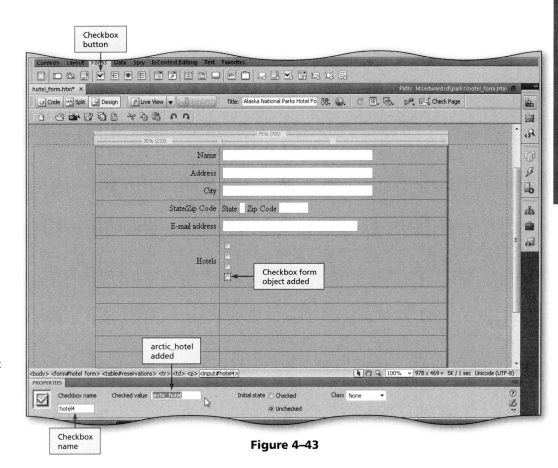

Figure 4–43

7

- Click to the right of the first check box.

- Type `Alaska National` as the descriptive label for the first check box, and then press the DOWN ARROW key.

- Type `Fairbanks Royal` as the descriptive label for the second check box, press the DOWN ARROW key, and then type `Denali Inn` as the label for the third check box.

- Press the DOWN ARROW key, and then type `Arctic Hotel` as the label for the fourth check box to add the descriptive labels for all four check boxes (Figure 4–44).

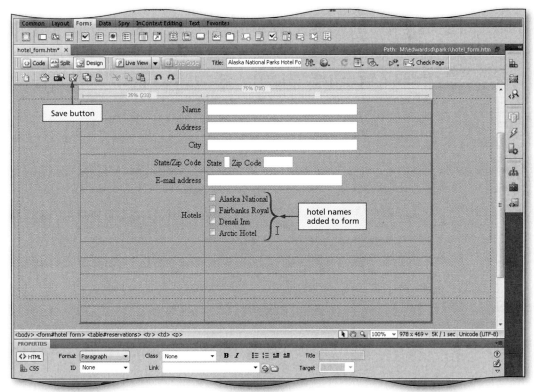

Figure 4–44

8

• Click the Save button on the Standard toolbar to save your work.

List/Menu

Another way to provide form field options for your Web site visitor is with lists and menus. These options provide many choices within a limited space. A **list** provides a scroll bar with up and down arrows that lets a user scroll the list, whereas a menu contains a pop-up list. Multiple selections can be made from a list, while users can select only one item from a menu. The menu option is discussed later in this chapter. Figure 4–45 illustrates the Property inspector for a list.

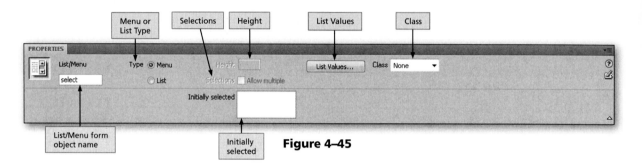

Figure 4–45

List/Menu Assigns a name to the list or menu.

Type Designates if the form object is a pop-up menu or a scrolling list.

Height Specifies the number of lines that display in the form; the default is 1.

Selections Designates if the user can select more than one option; not available with the menu option.

List Values Opens the List Values dialog box.

Initially Selected Contains a list of available items from which the user can select.

Class An attribute used with Cascading Style Sheets.

As with all other form objects, the list should be named. You control the height of the list by specifying a number in the Height box. You can elect to show one item at a time or show the entire list. If you display the entire list, the scroll bar is not displayed. Selecting the Selections check box allows the user to make multiple selections. Clicking the List Values button opens the List Values dialog box so you can add items to a list or pop-up menu or remove them. These added items are displayed in the Initially selected box. Each item in the list has a label and a value. The label represents the text that appears in the list, and the value is sent to the processing application if the item is selected. If no value is specified, the label is sent to the processing application instead.

To Create a Scrolling List

The following steps show how to add a scrolling list to the hotel reservations form.

1
- Click row 7, column 1. Type Accommodations to add the label and then press the TAB key. Click the List/ Menu button on the Forms tab (Figure 4–46).

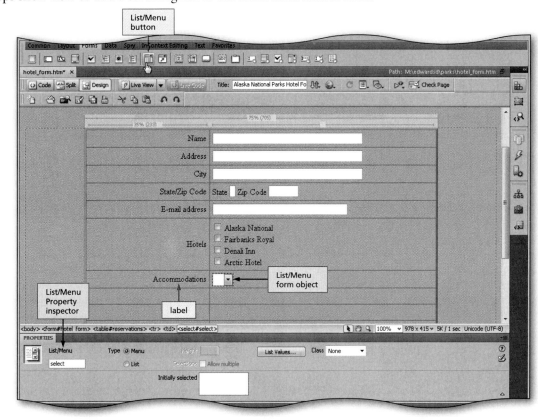

Figure 4–46

2
- Type accommodations as the List/Menu name to name the list.

- Click List in the Type options.

- Select the value in the Height box, and then type 2 to set the height to 2.

- Click the Selections check box to allow multiple selections (Figure 4–47).

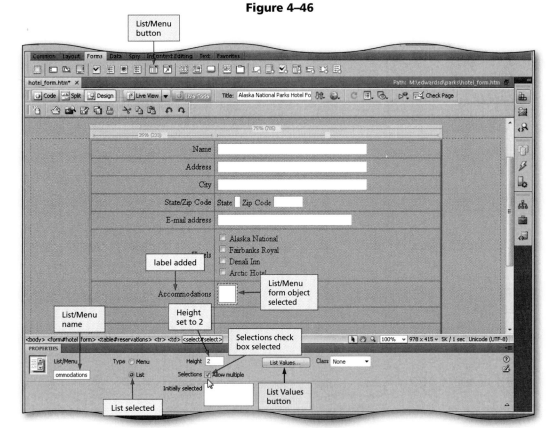

Figure 4–47

- Click the List Values
  button in the
  Property inspector
  to display the List
  Values dialog box
  (Figure 4–48).

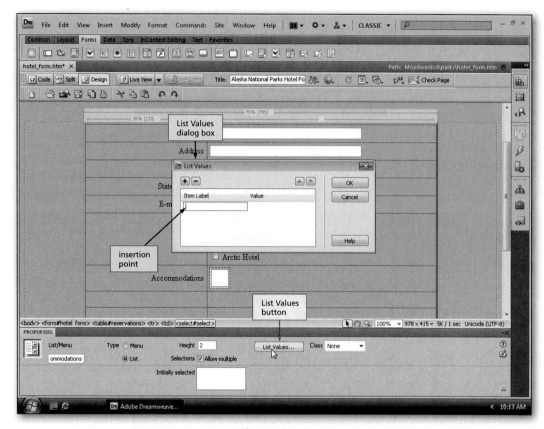

Figure 4–48

- Type Single as the
  first Item Label, press
  the TAB key, and
  then type single
  as the Value to add
  a second line to the
  Item Label list.

- Press the TAB key
  (Figure 4–49).

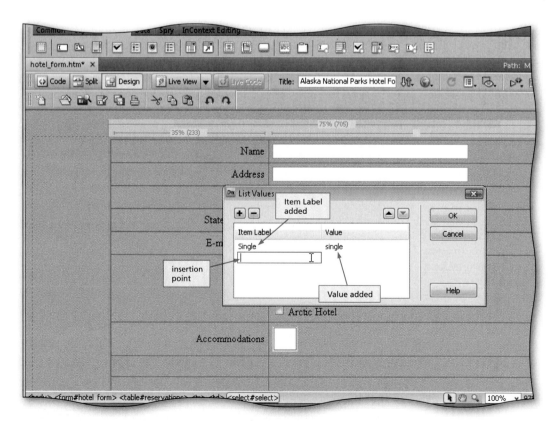

Figure 4–49

5

- Type Double as the second Item Label, and then press the TAB key.

- Type double as the Value and then press the TAB key.

- Type Suite as the third Item Label, and then press the TAB key.

- Type suite as the Value and then press the TAB key.

- Type Luxury Suite as the fourth Item Label, and then press the TAB key.

- Type luxury_suite as the Value to complete the items list (Figure 4–50).

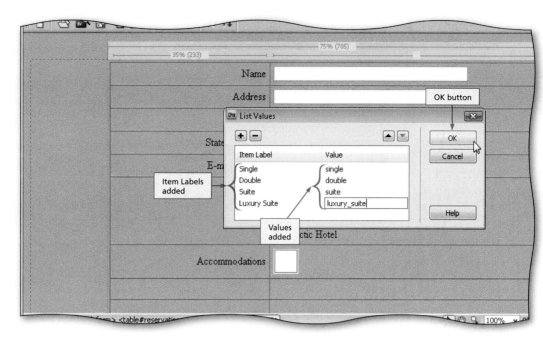

Figure 4–50

6

- Click the OK button to display the list (Figure 4–51).

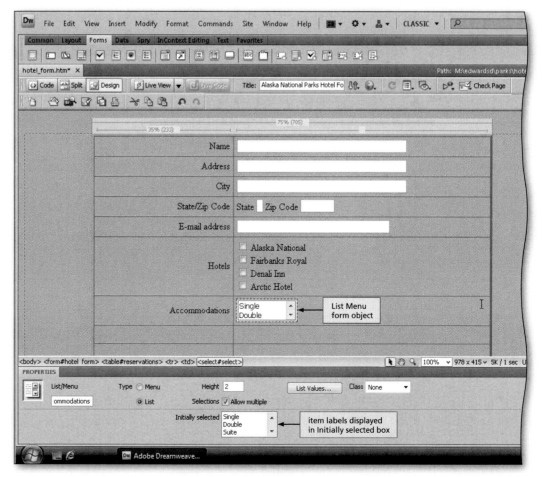

Figure 4–51

● Click Single in the Initially selected box in the Property inspector to designate it as the default item in the list (Figure 4–52).

● Click the Save button on the Standard toolbar to save your work.

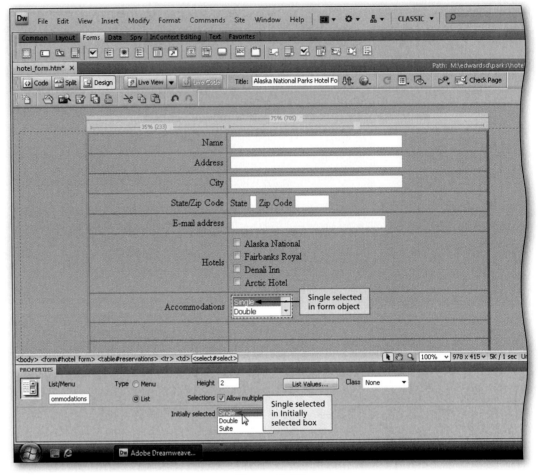

Figure 4–52

Pop-Up Menus

You can offer your Web site visitors a range of choices by using a pop-up menu. This type of menu (also called a drop-down menu) lets a user select a single item from a list of many options. A **pop-up menu** is useful when you have a limited amount of space because it occupies only a single line of vertical space in the form. Only one option choice is visible when the menu form object displays in the browser. Clicking a down arrow displays the entire list. The user then clicks one of the menu items to make a choice.

To Create a Pop-Up Menu

The following steps illustrate how to create a pop-up menu.

1

- If necessary, scroll down and then click row 8, column 1.

- Type Number of nights and then press the TAB key.

- Click the List/Menu button on the Forms tab to display the List/Menu form object (Figure 4–53).

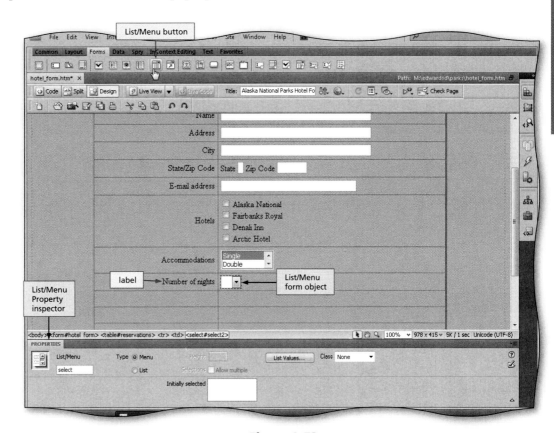

Figure 4–53

2

- Type nights in the List/Menu text box to name the pop-up menu, and make sure Menu is selected as the Type (Figure 4–54).

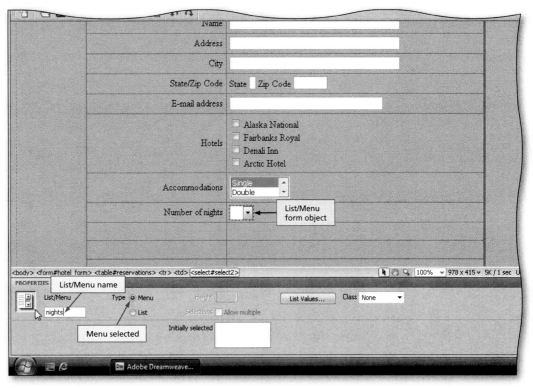

Figure 4–54

3

- Click the List Values button in the Property inspector to display the List Values dialog box. Type 1 as the Item Label, press the TAB key, and then type 1 for the Value (Figure 4–55).

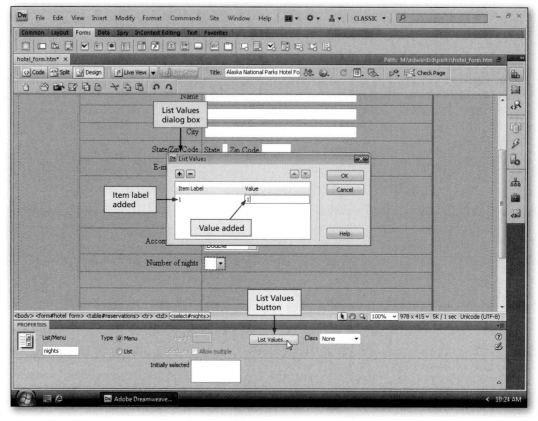

Figure 4–55

4

- Press the TAB key. Repeat Step 3, incrementing the number each time by 1 in the Item Label and Value fields, until the number 7 is added to the Item Label field and the Value field (Figure 4–56).

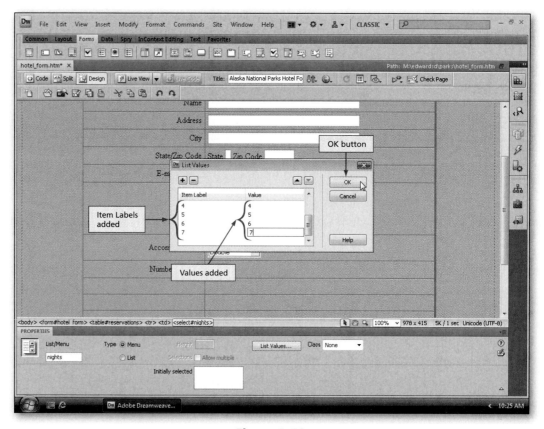

Figure 4–56

❺
• Click the OK button to display the numbers in the Initially selected box (Figure 4–57).

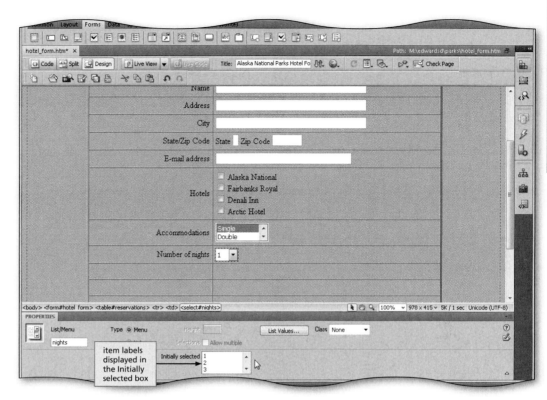

item labels displayed in the Initially selected box

Figure 4–57

❻
• Click the number 1 in the Initially selected box in the Property inspector to create the default value (Figure 4–58).

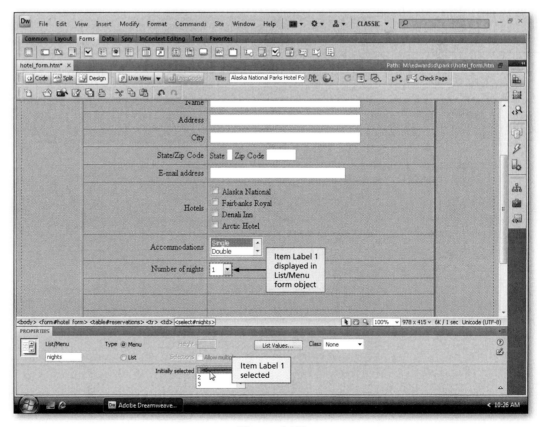

Item Label 1 displayed in List/Menu form object

Item Label 1 selected

Figure 4–58

Jump Menus

A **jump menu** is a special type of pop-up menu that provides options that link to documents or files. You can create links to documents on your Web site, links to documents on other Web sites, e-mail links, links to graphics, or links to any other file type that can be opened in a browser. A jump menu can contain three basic components:

- An optional menu selection prompt: This could be a category description for the menu items or instructions, such as Choose one.
- A required list of linked menu items: When the user chooses an option, a linked document or file is opened.
- An optional Go button: With a Go button, the user makes a selection from the menu, and the new page loads when the Go button is clicked. Without a Go button, the new page loads as soon as the user makes a selection from the menu.

To Insert a Jump Menu

The following steps illustrate how to add a jump menu with a link to a Web site to four national parks. The menu will contain a "Choose one" selection prompt, and the linked Web site will open in the main window.

- Click row 9, column 1, type Links, and then press the TAB key (Figure 4–59).

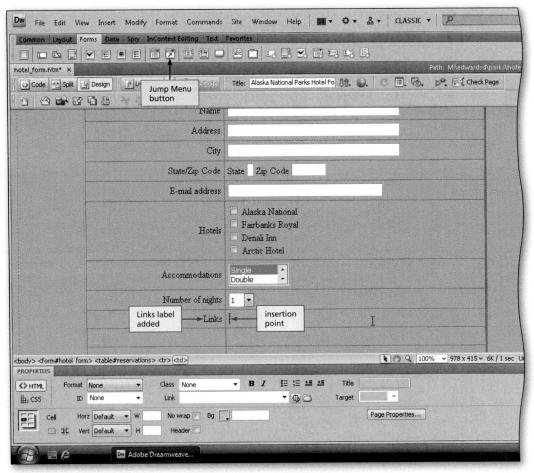

Figure 4–59

2

- Click the Jump Menu button on the Forms tab to display the Insert Jump Menu dialog box.

- If necessary, double-click the Text text box to select it, type Choose one, and then click the Plus (+) button to add "Choose one" as a menu item (Figure 4–60).

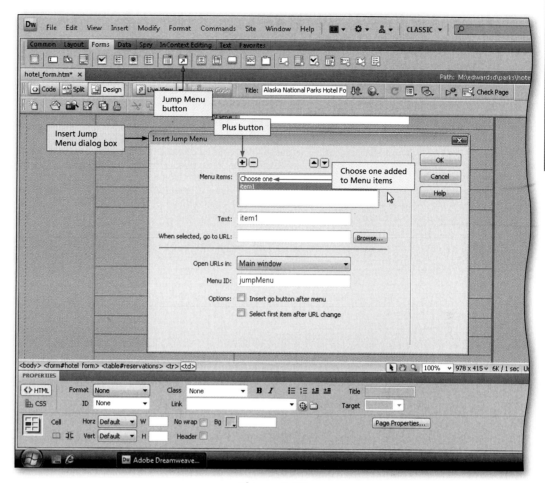

Figure 4–60

3

- Double-click the Text text box.

- Type Denali National Park and Preserve as the text for the second menu item and then press the TAB key to move to the When selected, go to URL: text box (Figure 4–61).

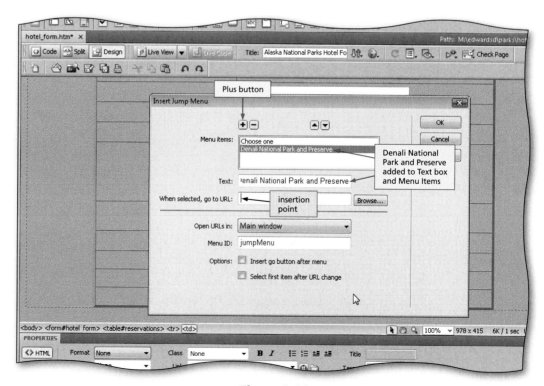

Figure 4–61

4

- Type http://www.
  nps.gov/dena
  and then point to
  the Plus button
  (Figure 4–62).

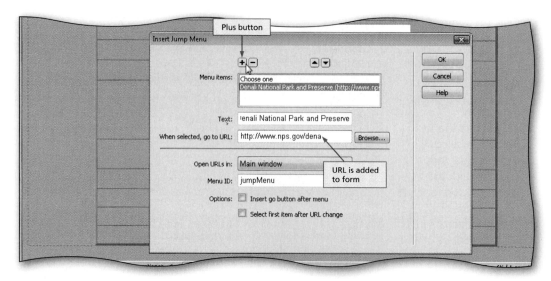

Figure 4–62

5

- Click the Plus button,
  double-click the Text
  text box, type Gates
  of the Arctic
  National Park
  and Preserve as
  the entry, and then
  press the TAB key.

- Type http://www.
  nps.gov/gaar
  to add Gates of
  the Arctic as the
  next menu item
  (Figure 4–63).

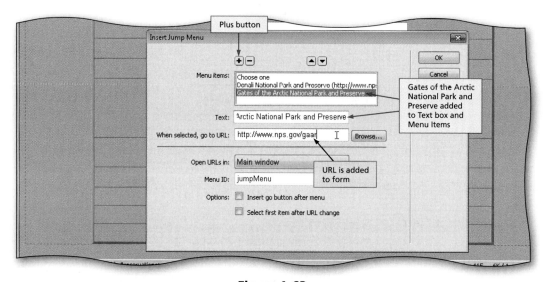

Figure 4–63

6

- Click the Plus button,
  double-click the Text
  text box, type Noatak
  National Preserve
  as the entry, and then
  press the TAB key.

- Type http://www.
  nps.gov/noat to
  add Noatak National
  Preserve as the
  fourth menu item
  (Figure 4–64).

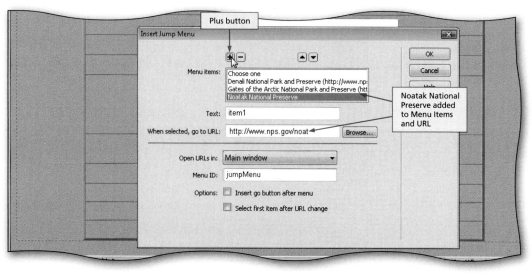

Figure 4–64

• Click the Plus
button, double-click
the Text text box, type
`Sitka National
Historical Park`
as the entry, and then
press the TAB key.

• Type `http://www.
nps.gov/sitk`
for the link to add
Sitka National
Historical Park as
the fifth menu item
and to add the URL
to the Insert Jump
menu dialog box
(Figure 4–65).

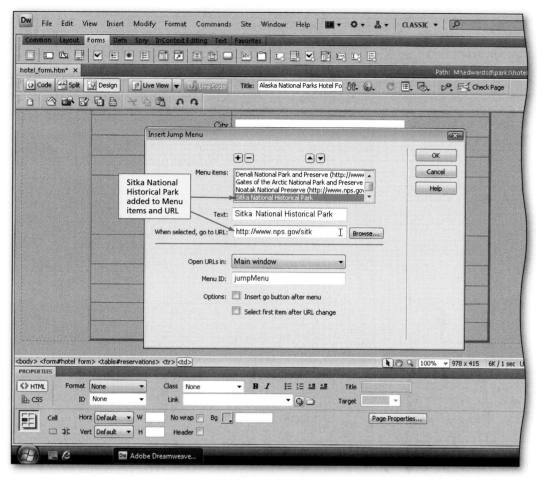

Figure 4–65

8

• Double-click in the
Menu ID text box
and type `park_web_
sites` to name
the menu.

• Click the Select
first item after
URL change check
box to select
the option
(Figure 4–66).

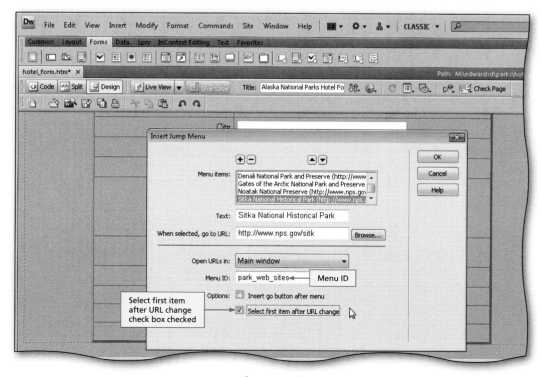

Figure 4–66

9

- Click the OK button to add the jump menu to the form.

- Click Choose one in the Initially selected box in the Property inspector.

- Click the Save button on the Standard tool-bar (Figure 4–67).

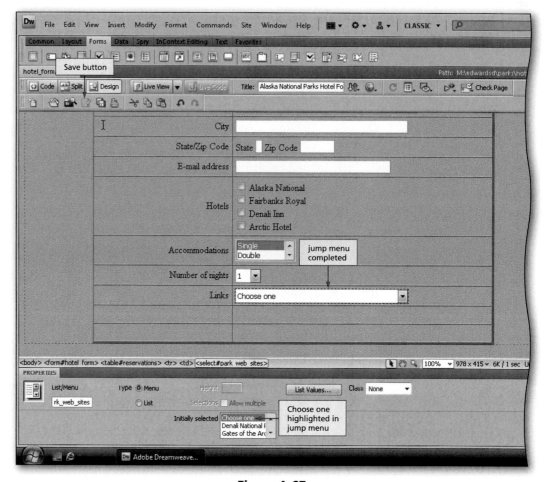

Figure 4–67

Other Ways

1. On Insert menu, point to Form, click Jump Menu

Textarea Text Fields

Earlier in this chapter, you added several single-line Text Field form objects to the hotel reservations form. A second type of text field is the textarea form object, which supports multiline objects. The Property inspector settings for the textarea text field are similar to those for single-line text fields, except you can specify the maximum number of lines the user can enter and specify the wrap attributes. The Property inspector for a textarea text field is shown in Figure 4–68.

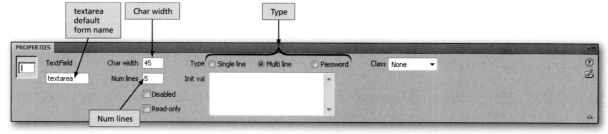

Figure 4–68

The Wrap pop-up menu in the Property inspector enables the Web page designer to select one of four options: Off, Default, Virtual, or Physical. Selecting **Off** or **Default** prevents the text from wrapping to the next line and requires the user to press the ENTER key to move the insertion point to the next line. **Virtual** limits word wrap to the text area. If the user's input exceeds the right boundary of the text area, the text wraps to the next line. When data is submitted for processing, however, it is submitted as one string of data. **Physical** sets word wrap in the text area and applies it to the data when it is submitted for processing.

An initial value can be added to the Init val box. When the user clicks the textarea text field, this initial value is highlighted and then deleted when the user begins to enter text.

To Add a Textarea Text Field

The following steps illustrate how to add a multiline text field to create a comments text area in your hotel reservations form.

1

- If necessary, scroll down. Click row 10, column 1.

- Type Comments and then press the TAB key to insert the label.

- Click the Textarea button on the Forms tab to add the Textarea form object to the form (Figure 4–69).

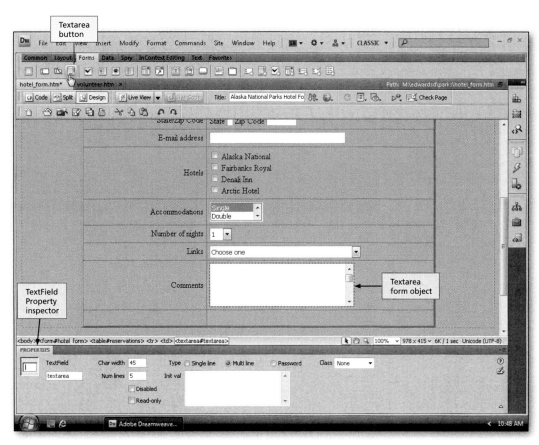

Figure 4–69

- In the Property inspector, type comments as the name for the TextField.

- Press the TAB key and type 50 for the Char width value. Press the TAB key and type 4 for the Num lines value.

- Click the Init val box, type Please add your comments as the entry.

- Verify that Multi line is selected.

- Click the textarea in the form to display the initial value.

- Click the Save button on the Standard toolbar to save the form (Figure 4–70).

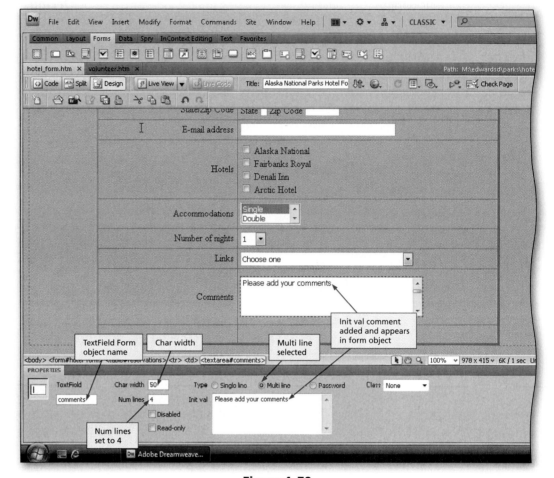

Figure 4–70

Other Ways

1. On Insert menu, point to Form, click Textarea

Form Buttons

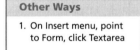

Form buttons control form operations. HTML provides three basic types of form buttons: Submit, Reset, and Command. Submit and Reset buttons are standard features of almost every form. When the user presses the Submit button, the data entered into a form is sent to a server for processing or forwarded to an e-mail address. In some instances, the data is edited by JavaScript or other code prior to processing. The Reset button clears all the fields in the form. You also can assign to a Command button other processing tasks that you have defined in a script. For example, a Command button might calculate the total cost of a hotel room for a week. Command buttons require that additional code be added using Code view. The Button name Property inspector is displayed in Figure 4–71.

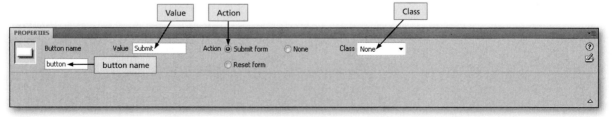

Figure 4–71

Button Name   Assigns a name to the button. Submit and Reset are reserved names.

Submit Button   Tells the form to submit the form data to the processing application or script or to send the data to an e-mail address.

Reset Button   Tells the form to reset all the form fields to their original values.

Value   Determines the text that appears on the button.

Action   Determines what happens when the button is clicked and how the data is to be processed. Form processing was discussed earlier in this chapter. The three processing options are to submit the contents of the form, to clear the contents of the form, or to do nothing.

Class   An attribute used with Cascading Style Sheets.

To Add the Submit and Reset Buttons

The following steps illustrate how to add the Submit and Reset buttons to the hotel reservation form.

1
- If necessary, scroll down and then click row 11, column 1 (Figure 4–72).

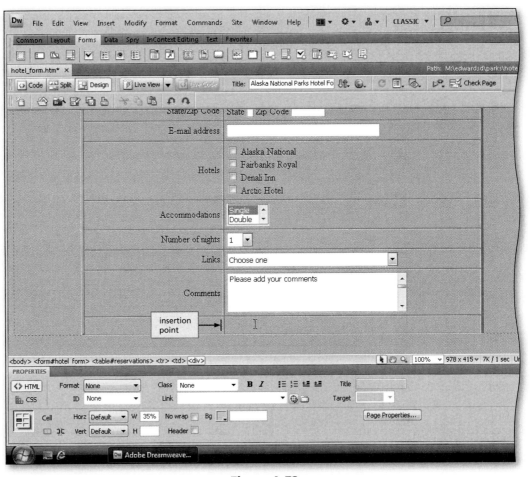

Figure 4–72

2

- Click the Button button on the Forms tab to add the Submit button to the form.

- Type submit in the Button name text box and then press the TAB key.

- Make sure Submit appears in the Value text box and that Submit form is selected as the Action (Figure 4–73).

Q&A

The Input Tag Accessibility Attributes dialog box is displayed after I add the Submit button. What should I do?

If the Input Tag Accessibility Attributes dialog box is displayed, click the Cancel button.

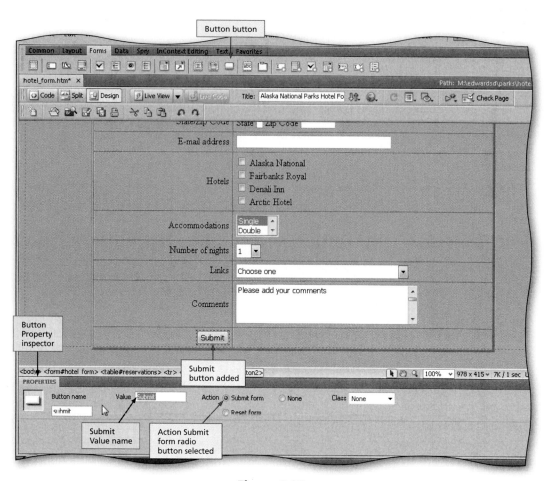

Figure 4–73

3

- Click row 11, column 2, and then click the Button button on the Forms tab to add the Submit button form object (Figure 4–74).

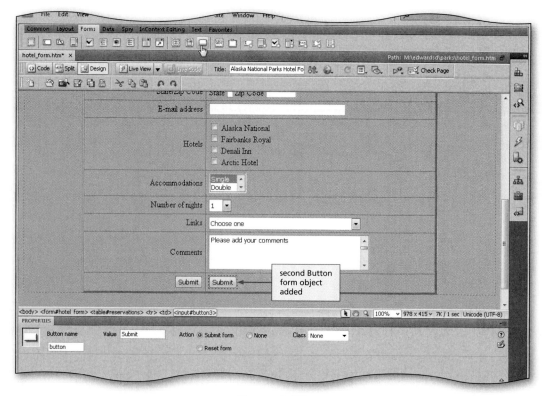

Figure 4–74

④
- Type reset in the Button name text box and then press the TAB key.

- Type Reset in the Value text box to rename the button and then click the Reset form option button in the Action area (Figure 4–75).

- Click the Save button on the Standard toolbar.

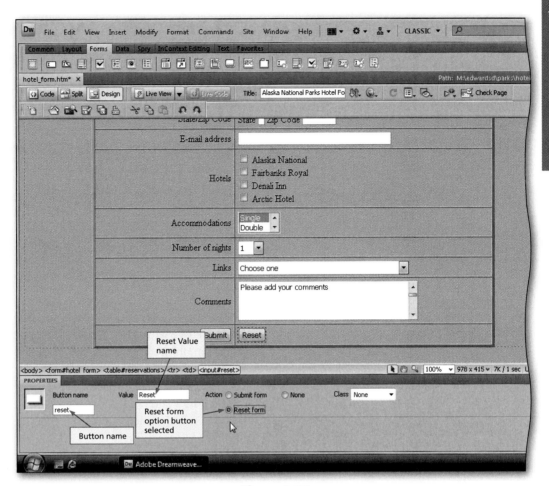

Figure 4–75

Other Ways

1. On Insert menu, point to Form, click Button

Radio Buttons and Radio Button Groups

Radio buttons provide a set of options from which the user can select only one button. Clicking a second button automatically deselects the first choice. Each button in a form consists of a radio button and a corresponding descriptive label. In Dreamweaver, you can insert radio buttons one at a time or insert a radio button group. When you insert an individual radio button, the Property inspector shown in Figure 4–76 is displayed. In the Property inspector's Radio Button text box, type a descriptive name. If you are inserting individual radio buttons to create a group, you must label each button. In the Checked value text box, enter the value you want sent to the server-side script or application when a user selects this radio button. For the Initial state, click Checked if you want an option to appear selected when the form first loads in the browser.

Figure 4–76

A radio button group is a commonly used option. If you are adding multiple radio buttons to a form, each set of radio buttons must have a unique name. When you click the Radio Group button on the Forms tab, the Radio Group dialog box is displayed. Radio button groups are discussed later in this chapter.

Form Objects, the Label Button, and Accessibility

So far, when you added a form object to a page, you also added a descriptive label to identify the object. Traditionally, this is the way most Web page authors label form objects. The current HTML specifications, however, provide the <label> tag. This tag adds functionality to the form object by associating the descriptive label for the form object directly with that object. This is particularly helpful for the users of speech-based browsers.

The Insert bar Forms tab contains a Label button. To add a label, select the specific form object to which you want to associate the label, and then click the Label button. When you click a radio button, for instance, and then click the Label button, Code view is displayed. You then manually type the descriptive text between the <label> and </label> tags. Similarly, Dreamweaver does not provide a Property inspector for labels, so any editing of labels is done in Code view.

Manual editing of the <label> tag can be time-consuming and error-prone, but Dreamweaver provides an alternative with the Accessibility options for form objects. When the Accessibility options for form objects are enabled, Dreamweaver displays the Input Tag Accessibility Attributes dialog box (Figure 4–77). Table 4–2 contains a description of the options in this dialog box. Recall that Accessibility options are turned on by clicking Edit on the menu bar and then selecting Preferences. In the Preferences dialog box, click the Accessibility category and then click the check box for Form objects. Appendix B contains an expanded discussion of accessibility options.

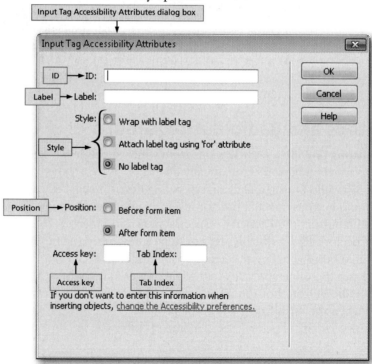

Figure 4–77

Table 4–2 Input Tag Accessibility Attributes

Attribute Name	Description
ID	Assigns an ID value that can be used to refer to a field from JavaScript and also used as an attribute value.
Label	The descriptive text that identifies the form object.
Style	Provides three options for the <label> tag: *Wrap with label tag* wraps a label tag around the form item. *Attach label tag using 'for' attribute* allows the user to associate a label with a form element, even if the two are in different table cells. *No label tag* turns off the Accessibility option.
Position	Determines the placement of the label text in relation to the form object — before or after the form object.
Access key	Selects the form object in the browser using a keyboard shortcut (one letter). This key is used in combination with the CTRL key (Windows) to access the object.
Tab Index	Specifies the order in which the form objects are selected when pressing the TAB key. The tab order goes from the lowest to highest numbers.

To Open the Volunteer.htm Web Page

The next step is to add a form and radio button group form field to the volunteer.htm Web page. Informational text already has been added and the background image applied to this data file. You open the file and then add a form containing an e-mail form object and a radio button group. The following steps illustrate how to open the volunteer.htm Web page, and then add a form and table to the page.

- If necessary, click the Expand Panels button to display the panel groups.

- Double-click volunteer.htm in the Files panel.

- Click the Collapse to Icons button to collapse the panel groups.

- Click below the text (Figure 4–78).

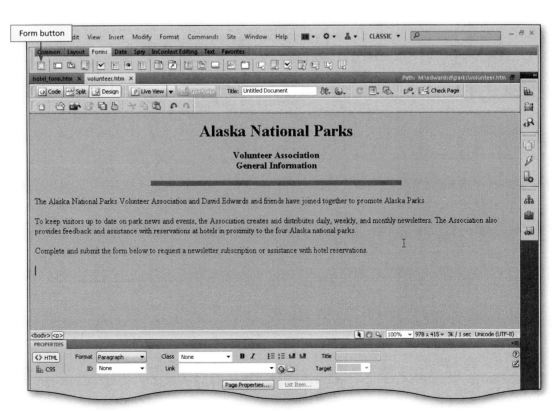

Figure 4–78

- If necessary, scroll down and then position the insertion point at the end of the last line of text. Press the ENTER key.

- Click the Form button on the Forms tab to insert a form.

- In the Property inspector, type newsletter as the Form ID.

- Use the mailto: format and type your e-mail address in the Action text box.

- Select _self on the Target pop-up menu.

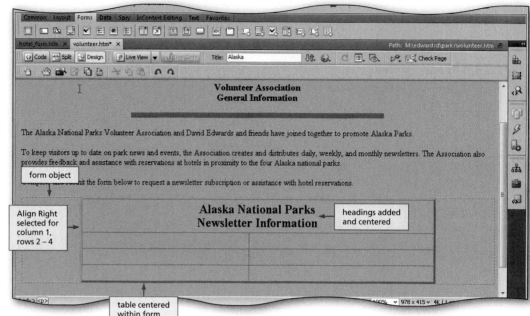

Figure 4–79

- Type text/plain in the Enctype box, and then press the ENTER key.

- Click inside the form in the document window. Click Insert on the Application bar and then click the Table command to display the Table dialog box.

- Create a four-row, two-column table, with a width of 75%, a border thickness of 4, and a cell padding of 5. Type Alaska National Parks newsletter in the Summary text box.

- Click the OK button to insert the table in the form.

- Scroll up and down as necessary to display the entire table.

- If necessary, select the table, click Format on the Application bar, point to Align, and then select Center to center the table.

- Click the Table text box and type newsletter_form as the ID.

- Select row 1, columns 1 and 2, and then merge the cells.

- Click in row 1, type Alaska National Parks as the entry, and then press SHIFT+ENTER to insert a line break.

Q&A

My insertion point is not visible. What should I do?

The insertion point is very small, but should be located on the line below the first entry.

- Type Newsletter Information and then select the two lines of text.

- Apply Heading 2 and center the headings.

- Select rows 2 through 4, column 1, click Format on the Application bar, point to Align, and then click Right to right-align the text.

- Select rows 2 through 4, column 2, click the Horz button in the Property inspector, and then click Left to left-align the cells. Click outside of the table to deselect the cells.

- Click the Save button on the Standard toolbar to add the form and table (Figure 4–79).

To Add the E-mail Address

Next, you adjust the column width and add descriptive text for the e-mail address and a single-line text field for user input to row 2. The following steps illustrate how to adjust the column width and how to add the e-mail address and a single-line text form object.

1
- Select rows 2 through 4, column 1, and then set the column width to 40%.

2
- Click row 2, column 1. Type E-mail as the entry and then press the TAB key.

3
- Click the Text Field button on the Forms tab to insert a text field.

4
- Double-click the TextField text box in the Property inspector. Type email and then press the TAB key.

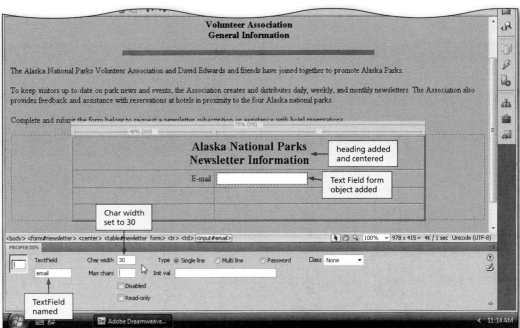

Figure 4–80

5
- Type 30 as the Char width and then press the TAB key to add the descriptive text and the text form object (Figure 4–80).

Radio Groups

When you are adding multiple radio buttons to a form, the **Radio Group** form object is the fastest and easiest method to use. At times, the table may extend outside the form boundaries. If this happens, ignore it.

To Add a Radio Group

The following steps show how to add descriptive text and a radio group to the Newsletter Information form.

1

- Click row 3, column 1. Type I am interested in receiving a newsletter and then press the TAB key (Figure 4–81).

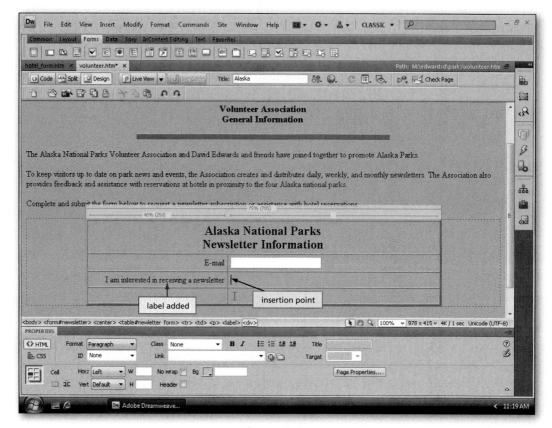

Figure 4–81

2

- Click the Radio Group button on the Forms tab to display the Radio Group dialog box (Figure 4–82).

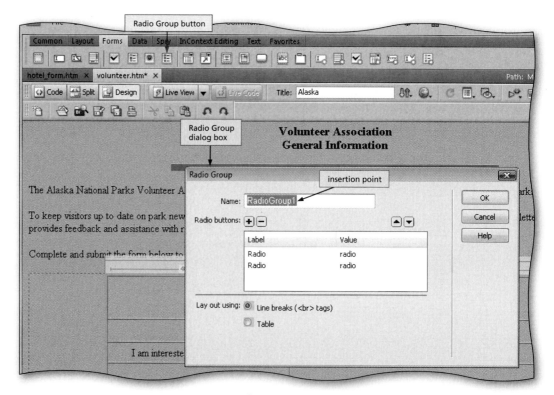

Figure 4–82

- Type newsletter in the Name text box, and then click to select the first instance of Radio in the Label field (Figure 4–83).

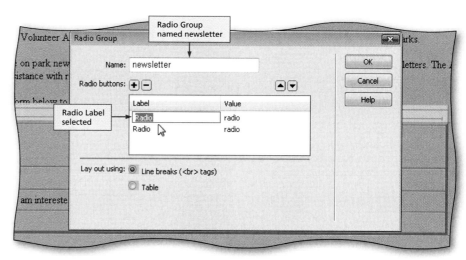

Figure 4–83

- Type Daily as the Label and then press the TAB key to enter the label.

- Type daily as the Value (Figure 4–84).

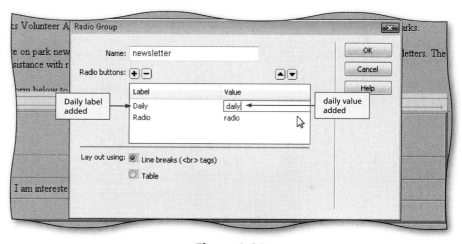

Figure 4–84

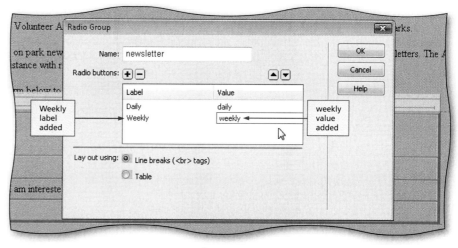

- Press the TAB key, type Weekly in the Label field to enter the label, and then press the TAB key.

- Type weekly as the Value entry (Figure 4–85).

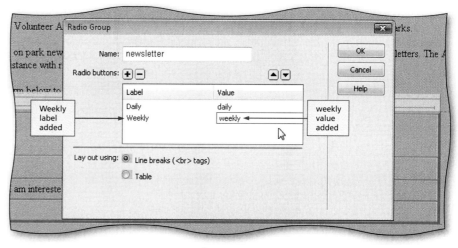

Figure 4–85

● Press the TAB key, and then type
Monthly in the Label field. Press
the TAB key.

● Type monthly as the Value entry
(Figure 4–86).

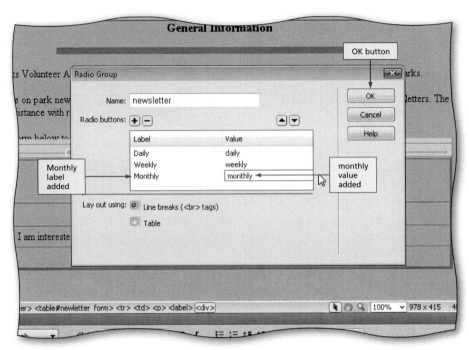

Figure 4–86

● Click the OK button
to insert the radio
group and labels
(Figure 4–87).

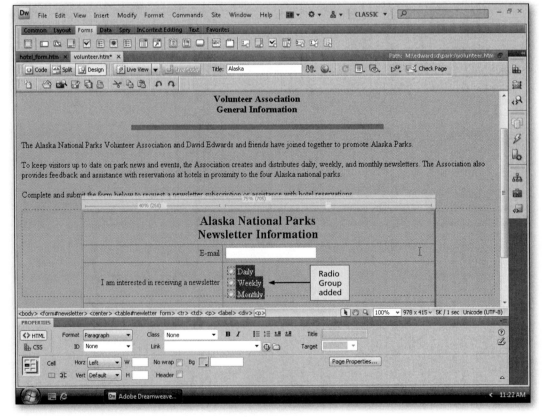

Figure 4–87

To Add the Submit and Reset Buttons to the Volunteer.htm Form

The final step is to add the Submit and Reset buttons to the form. The following step shows how to add these two buttons.

1

- If necessary, scroll down. Click row 4, column 1, and then click the Button button on the Forms tab to insert the Submit button.

- In the Property inspector, enter submit as the Button name.

- Click row 4, column 2 in the table, and then click the Button button on the Forms tab.

- Type reset as the Button name and then press the TAB key to name the Reset button.

- Type Reset in the Value text box and then click Reset form in the Action area.

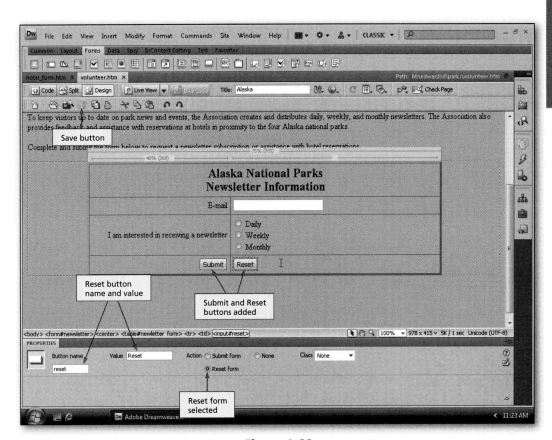

Figure 4–88

- Click the Save button on the Standard toolbar (Figure 4–88).

Other Ways

1. On Insert menu, point to Form, click Radio Group

To Add Links to and from the Volunteer.htm, Hotel_form.htm, and Index.htm Web Pages

Chapter 2 discussed the different types of links, including relative links, absolute links, named anchors, and e-mail links. The following steps illustrate how to add links to the volunteer.htm and hotel_form.htm Web pages, and how to add links from the index.htm Web page to the volunteer.htm and hotel_form.htm Web pages.

- Display the panel groups and open the index.htm Web page.

- Scroll to the end of the Web page and then add a line break after your name.

- Type Alaska National Parks Volunteer Association.

- Add a line break, and then type Alaska National Parks Hotel Reservations as the entry.

- Select the text Alaska National Parks Volunteer Association and create a link to the volunteer.htm Web page.

- Select the text Alaska National Parks Hotel Reservations and create a link to the hotel_form.htm Web page.

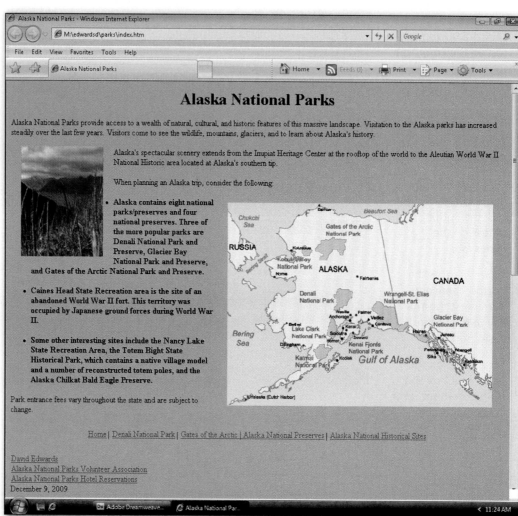

Figure 4–89

- Save the index.htm Web page and then press the F12 key to display the page in your browser (Figure 4–89).

- Verify that the links work and close the browser. Close the index.htm Web page.

2

- If necessary, click the volunteer.htm tab and then scroll to the bottom of the page. Click below the table and then type Home.

- Select the Home text and then create a link to the index.htm Web page.

- Save the volunteer. htm Web page.

- Press the F12 key to display the Web page in your browser and then verify that the links work (Figure 4–90).

- Close the browser.

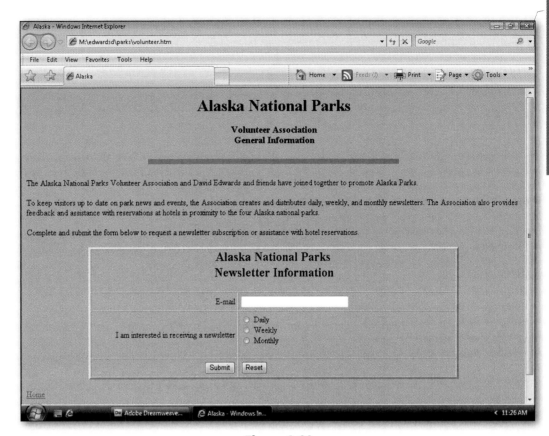

Figure 4–90

- Click the hotel_form.htm tab and then, if necessary, scroll to the bottom of the page.

- Click under the table and then type Home.

- Select the Home text and then create a link to the index.htm Web page.

- Save the hotel_form.htm Web page.

- Press the F12 key to display the Web page in your browser and then verify that the link works (Figure 4–91).

- Close the browser.

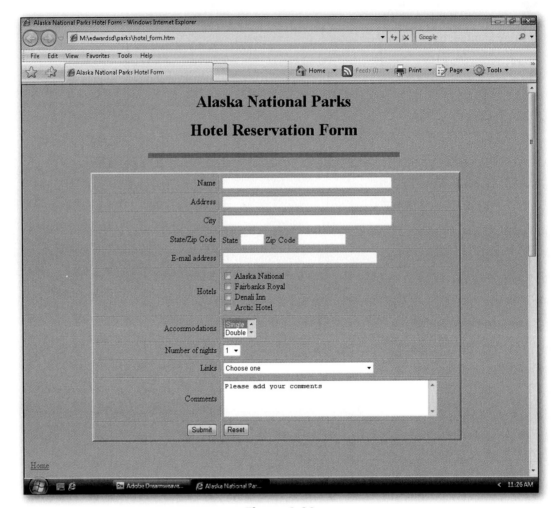

Figure 4–91

Behaviors

A **behavior** is a combination of an event and an action. Behaviors are attached to a specific element on the Web page. The element can be a table, an image, a link, a form, a form object, and so on. When a behavior is initiated, Dreamweaver uses JavaScript to write the code. **JavaScript** is a scripting language written as a text file. After a behavior is attached to a page element, and when the event specified occurs for that element, the browser calls the action (the JavaScript code) that is associated with that event. A scripting language, such as JavaScript, provides flexibility, interaction, and power to any Web site.

To create this type of user interaction with almost any other software program requires that you write the JavaScript. When you attach a behavior in Dreamweaver, however, the JavaScript is produced and inserted into the code for you.

Using behaviors with forms.

Dreamweaver provides two form-related behaviors: Validate Form and Set Text of Text Field. These behaviors are available only if a text field has been inserted into the form:

- **Validate Form**: This behavior verifies that the user has entered data into each designated field. The form is checked when the user clicks the Submit button. If omissions or other errors occur, a Microsoft Internet Explorer (or other browser) dialog box is displayed. The errors then must be corrected before the form can be submitted successfully.

- **Set Text of Text Field**: This action replaces the content of a form's text field with the content you specify when creating the behavior. For example, you could use this behavior to insert the current date.

Plan
Ahead

The Behaviors panel is displayed in Figure 4–92.

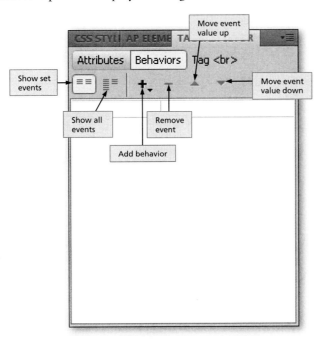

Figure 4–92

To Add the Validate Form Behavior

The following steps show how to add the Validate Form behavior to the hotel reservations form.

1
- Display the panel groups and collapse the Property inspector.

- If necessary, click the hotel_form.htm tab.

- Click Window on the Application bar to display the Window menu and then point to Behaviors (Figure 4–93).

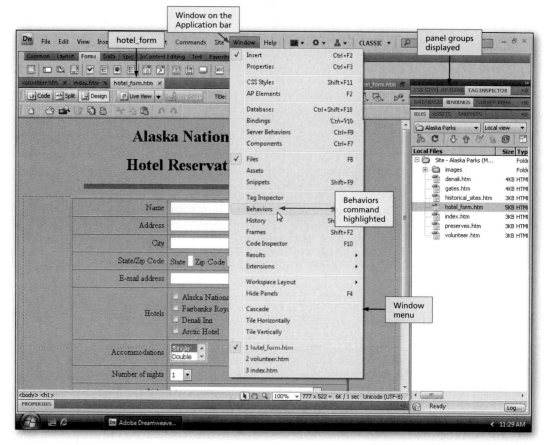

Figure 4–93

2
- Click Behaviors to display the Behaviors panel (Figure 4–94).

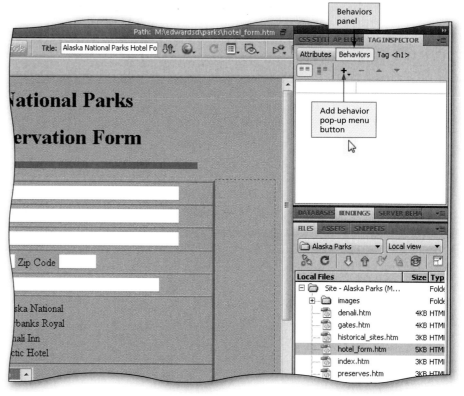

Figure 4–94

3

- If necessary, click anywhere inside the form. Click <form#hotel_form> in the tag selector to select the form.

- Click the Add behavior button in the Behaviors panel and then point to Validate Form on the pop-up menu to highlight the command (Figure 4–95).

Q&A
What should I do if form#hotel_form is not displayed in the tag selector?

Verify that the insertion point is in the form.

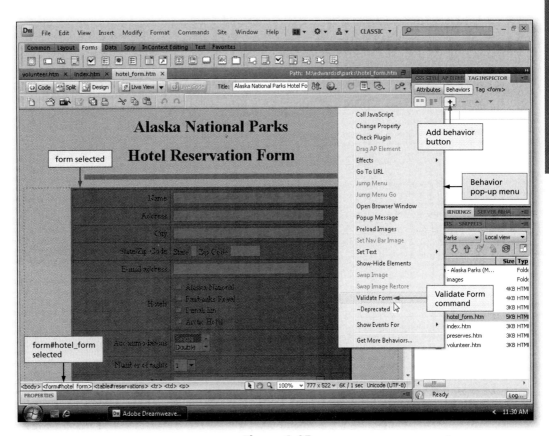

Figure 4–95

4

- Click Validate Form to display the Validate Form dialog box (Figure 4–96).

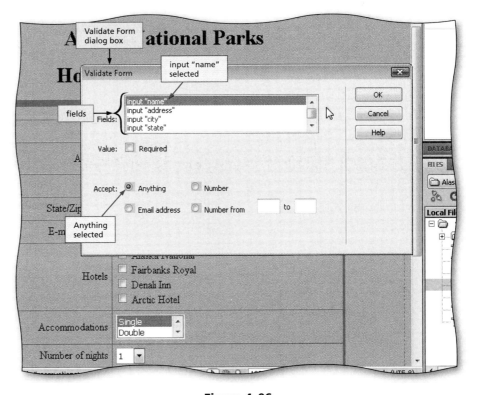

Figure 4–96

5

- Click the Value Required check box to insert an (R) to the right of the name field name.

- Click the text input "address", and then click the Value Required check box to insert an (R) to the right of the address field name.

- Click the text input "city" and then click the Value Required check box to insert an (R) to the right of the city field name.

- Click the text input "state" and then click the Value Required check box to insert an (R) to the right of the state field name (Figure 4–97).

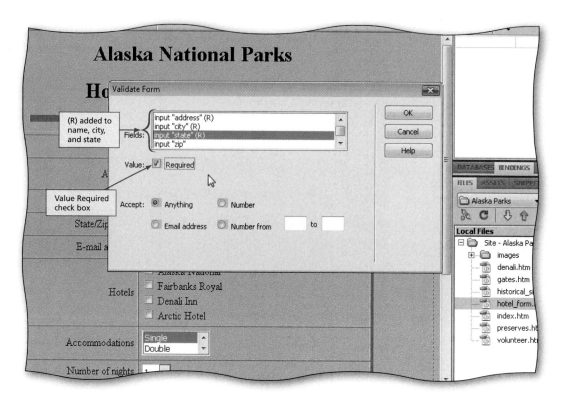

Figure 4–97

6

- Scroll down if necessary. Click the text input "zip", and then click the Value Required box and the Number button in the Accept section to insert (RisNum) to the right of the zip field name.

- Click the text input "email", and then click the Value Required check box and the Email address option button to insert (RisNum) to the right of the email field name (Figure 4–98).

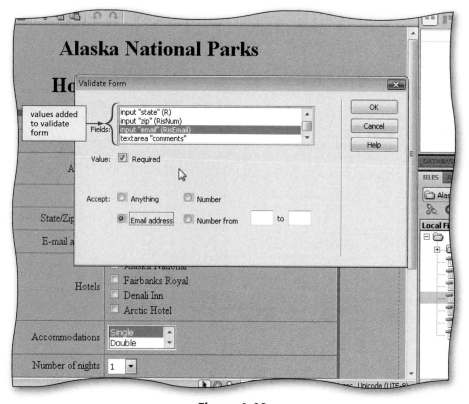

Figure 4–98

- Click the OK button.

- Click in the form outside the table to deselect the form and display the Event and Action in the Behaviors panel.

- Click the Save button on the Standard toolbar (Figure 4–99).

Q&A I clicked Save, but nothing happens. Is that correct?

Yes. At this point, no visible changes are evident in the document window.

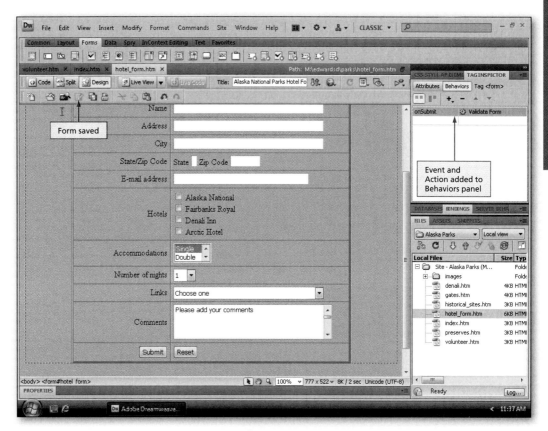

Figure 4–99

Viewing and Testing the Forms

To ensure that the form objects work correctly, they are viewed through the browser and each of the form objects is tested. The steps on the next page illustrate how to add behaviors to and how to view and test the hotel_form.htm form.

To View and Test the Hotel_Form.htm Form

To ensure that the form objects work correctly, they are viewed through the browser and each of the form objects is tested. The following steps illustrate how to view and test the hotel_form.htm.

1

• Press the F12 key to display the hotel_form page in the browser (Figure 4–100).

Q&A
An information bar appears in the browser window. What should I do?

If an information bar is displayed, click the bar to allow the content, and then click the Yes button in the Security Warning dialog box.

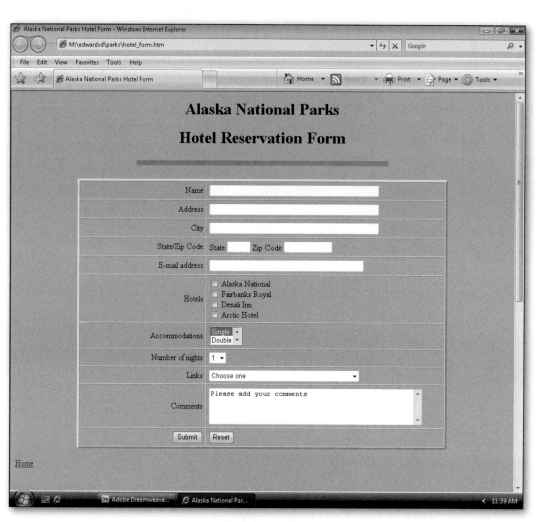

Figure 4–100

2

• Complete the form, typing data in each field, but skipping the Links jump menu, and then click the Submit button to display a Windows Internet Explorer dialog box (Figure 4–101).

3

• Read the information in the dialog box, and then click the OK button to process the form and to have the data automatically e-mailed to you.

4

• Check your e-mail to verify that the data is e-mailed to you. In some instances, your e-mail message may not include the data attachment. This is determined by the e-mail program server and the security set up on your computer.

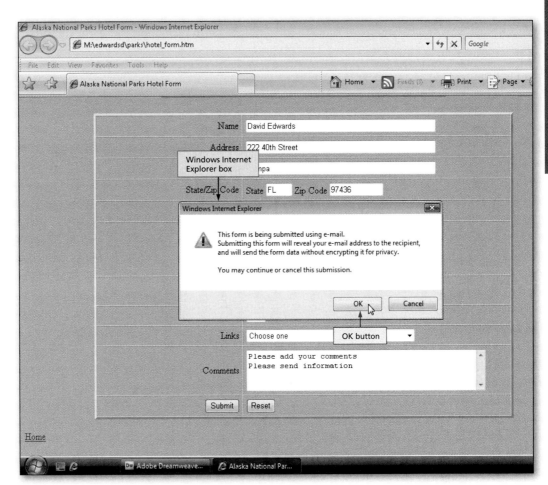

Figure 4–101

Q&A What should I do if I receive an error message when I try to process the form?

Most likely, you need to publish the Web site before you can process the form.

• Close the browser and return to Dreamweaver.

Q&A When you are using form validation, what is the difference between the onBlur event and the onSubmit event?

Use the onBlur event to validate the fields as the user is filling out the form, and use the onSubmit event to validate several text fields at once when the user clicks the Submit button.

To Add Behaviors, View, and Test the Volunteer.htm Form

Next, you add behaviors to validate the volunteer.htm form, and then you view and test the form.

- Click the volunteer.htm tab. Click inside the form and then click <form#newsletter> in the tag selector. Verify that form#newsletter is selected in the tag selector.

- Click the Add behavior button on the Behaviors panel and then click Validate Form on the pop-up menu.

- Click the Value Required check box and the Email address radio button and then click the OK button.

- Save the form.

- Press the F12 key to display the form in your browser (Figure 4–102).

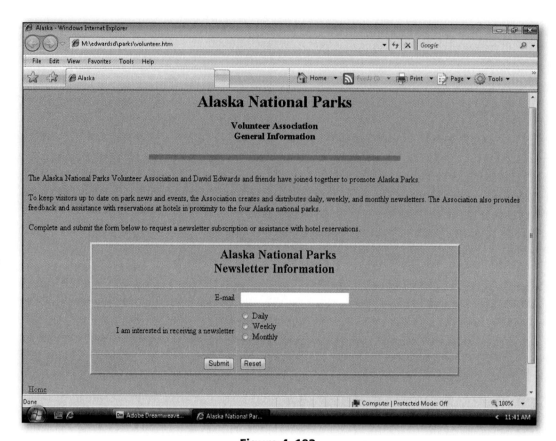

Figure 4–102

Q&A An information bar appears in the browser window. What should I do?

If an information bar is displayed, click the bar to allow the content, and then click the Yes button in the Security Warning dialog box.

- Click the E-mail form object and then type your e-mail address.

- Click the Weekly radio button and then click the Submit button.

- Click the OK button in the Windows Internet Explorer dialog box to e-mail the data.

- Check your e-mail to verify that the data is e-mailed to you.

Q&A What if the message I receive does not include the data attachment?

In some instances, your e-mail message may not include the data attachment. This is determined by the e-mail program, server, and security set up on your computer.

- Close the browser and return to Dreamweaver.

3
- If instructed to do so, upload your Web site to a remote server.

Q&A How do I upload my Web site to a remote server?

Appendix C contains information on uploading to a remote server. A remote folder is required before you can upload to a remote server. Generally, the remote folder is defined by the Web server administrator or your instructor.

Quitting Dreamweaver

After you have created your forms, tested and verified that the forms work, and uploaded the Web site to a remote server, Chapter 4 is complete.

To Close the Web Site and Quit Dreamweaver

The following step shows how to close the Web site, quit Dreamweaver CS4, and return control to Windows.

1
- Click the Close button on the upper-right corner of the Dreamweaver title bar to close the Dreamweaver window, the Document windows, and the parks Web site. If you have unsaved changes, click the Yes button in the Dreamweaver dialog box to save the page.

Chapter Summary

In this chapter, you have learned how to create forms on Web pages. You created two forms and added a table to each of the forms to format them. In the hotel reservations form, you added the following form objects: text fields, check boxes, a list and pop-up menu, a jump menu, a text area, and Submit and Reset buttons. You added a text field, radio group buttons, and Submit and Reset buttons to the Newsletter Information form. You then used the Behaviors panel to attach the Validate Form behavior to both forms. Finally, you viewed and tested the forms in your browser. The items listed below include all the new skills you have learned in this chapter.

1. Insert a horizontal rule (DW 267)
2. Insert a form (DW 269)
3. Set the form properties (DW 272)
4. Insert a table into a form (DW 273)
5. Format the form (DW 275)
6. Add descriptive labels and single-line text fields to the hotel reservation form (DW 279)
7. Add check boxes (DW 286)
8. Create a scrolling list (DW 291)
9. Create a pop-up menu (DW 295)
10. Insert a jump menu (DW 298)
11. Add a textarea text field (DW 303)
12. Add the Submit and Reset buttons (DW 305)
13. Add the e-mail address (DW 311)
14. Add a radio group (DW 312)
15. Add the validate form behavior (DW 320)
16. Add behaviors, view, and test the volunteer.htm form (DW 326)

Learn It Online

Test your knowledge of chapter content and key terms.

Instructions: To complete the Learn It Online exercises, start your browser, click the Address bar, and then enter the Web address scsite.com/dwCS4/learn. When the Dreamweaver CS4 Learn It Online page is displayed, click the link for the exercise you want to complete and then read the instructions.

Chapter Reinforcement TF, MC, and SA
A series of true/false, multiple choice, and short answer questions that test your knowledge of the chapter content.

Flash Cards
An interactive learning environment where you identify chapter key terms associated with displayed definitions.

Practice Test
A series of multiple choice questions that test your knowledge of chapter content and key terms.

Who Wants To Be a Computer Genius?
An interactive game that challenges your knowledge of chapter content in the style of a television quiz show.

Wheel of Terms
An interactive game that challenges your knowledge of chapter key terms in the style of the television show *Wheel of Fortune*.

Crossword Puzzle Challenge
A crossword puzzle that challenges your knowledge of key terms presented in the chapter.

Apply Your Knowledge

Reinforce the skills and apply the concepts you learned in this chapter.

Adding a Form to a Web Page
Instructions: In this activity, you create a new Web page, add a background, and then add a general information form to the page (Figure 4–103). Data files are not required for this exercise.

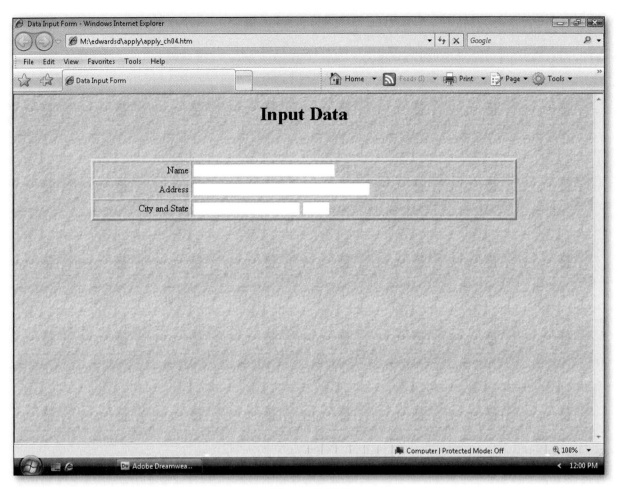

Figure 4–103

Perform the following tasks:

1. Start Dreamweaver and open the Apply Exercises Web site.

2. Create a new document and save it as apply_ch04.htm in the apply folder.

3. Add the apply_bkg.jpg image to the background.

4. Type Input Data for the heading, apply Heading 1, and then center the title.

5. Click to the right of the heading and then press ENTER twice.

6. Click the Form button to insert a form.

7. In the new form, insert a three-row, two column table with a table width of 75 percent, cell padding and cell spacing of 2, and a border of 3 pixels.

8. Click the Summary box and then type Data Input.

9. Center the table in the form, and then left-align the contents of column 2.

10. Select column 1, click the Horz button in the Property inspector and select Right.

11. With column 1 still selected, click the Vert button and select Middle.

12. Click column 1, row 1 and type Name.

13. Click column 1, row 2 and type Address.

14. Click column 1, row 3 and type City and State.

15. Click column 2, row 1.

Continued >

Apply Your Knowledge *continued*

16. Insert a text field and name the text field username.

17. Set the Char width and Max chars to 35. Verify that Single line is selected.

18. Click column 2, row 2.

19. Insert a text field and name it address.

20. Set the Char width and Max chars to 45. Verify that Single line is selected.

21. Click column 2, row 3.

22. Insert a text field and name it city.

23. Set the Char width and Max chars to 25. Verify that Single line is selected.

24. Click to the right of the city text field, press the SPACEBAR, and insert a text field. Name the text field state.

25. Set the Char width and Max chars to 2 and verify that Single line is selected.

26. Title your page Data Input Form and then save the apply_ch04.htm Web page.

27. View the form in your browser. Verify that you can input data in the form.

28. Submit the form in the format specified by your instructor.

Extend Your Knowledge

Extend the skills you learned in this chapter and experiment with new skills. You may need to use Help to complete the assignment.

Adding a Form to a Web Page

Instructions: In this activity, you modify a Web page by adding a form and then adding a table with images and form objects to the form (Figure 4–104). Data files are not required for this exercise.

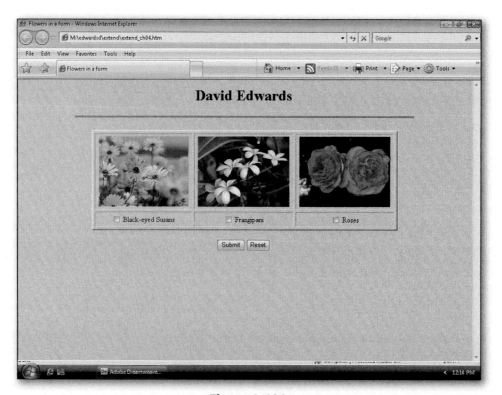

Figure 4–104

Perform the following tasks:

1. Start Dreamweaver and open the Extend Exercises Web site.

2. Create a new page, save it as extend_ch04, and then apply the extend_bkg to the page.

3. Add and then center your name at the top of the page.

4. Apply Heading 1 to your name and then press the ENTER key.

5. Insert a horizontal rule and name it rule, set the Width at 750 and the Height at 4. Shading should be deselected.

6. Click at the end of the horizontal rule line and press the ENTER key.

7. Insert a form below the horizontal rule and name the form images.

8. If necessary, click inside the form and insert a three-column, two-row table with a table width of 75 percent, a Border thickness of 3 pixels, and cell padding and cell spacing of 5 pixels. Center the table and name the table flowers.

9. In row 1, column 1 of the table, insert the flowers01.jpg file. In row 1, column 2, insert flowers02.jpg. In row 1, column 3, insert roses01.jpg. Resize all images to a width of 200 and a height of 150.

10. In row 2, add check boxes with the properties shown in Table 4–3.

11. Click to the right of the table, and then press ENTER to insert a blank line at the bottom of the form. Add Submit and Reset buttons centered at the bottom of the form. Name the Submit button submit, and the Reset button reset. Set the value of the Reset button to Reset. Assign appropriate actions to the buttons.

12. Title your document Flowers in a form.

13. Save your document and then view it in your browser. Submit it in the format specified by your instructor.

Table 4–3 Properties for the Checkboxes

Property	Checkbox 1	Checkbox 2	Checkbox 3
Location	Row 2, column 1	Row 2, column 2	Row 2, column 3
Descriptive text	Black-eyed Susans	Frangipani	Roses
Check box name	flower1	flower2	flower3
Checked value	blackeyed_susans	frangipani	roses
Initial state	unchecked	unchecked	unchecked

Make It Right

Analyze a Web page with a form and correct all errors and/or improve the design.

Modifying a Web Page Form
Instructions: In this activity, you modify an existing Web page by correcting errors within a form (Figure 4–105 on the next page).

Continued >

Make It Right *continued*

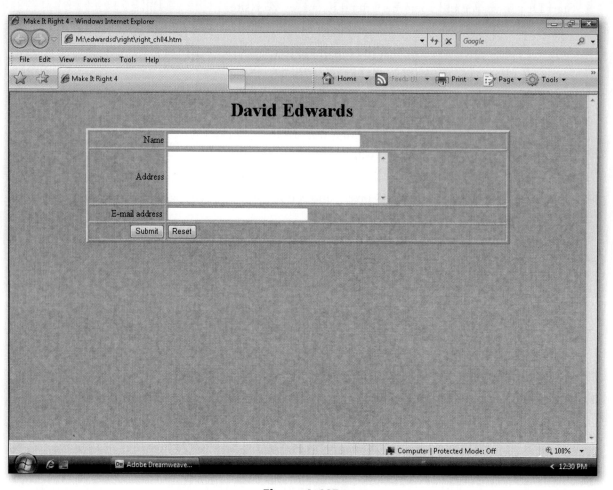

Figure 4–105

Perform the following tasks:

1. If necessary, start Dreamweaver and then open the Right Exercises Web site. Copy the right_ch04 file from the Chapter04\right folder provided with your data files to your Right Exercises site.

2. The Web page is a modified version of what you see in Figure 4–105. Substitute your name for David Edwards.

3. Make the other necessary changes so that the page looks similar to Figure 4–105. Use a character width of 50 for the name field, 45 characters and five lines for the textarea, and 35 characters for the e-mail address. Provide an appropriate name for each of these elements.

4. Add the Submit and Reset buttons.

5. Save your document and then view it in your browser.

6. Submit your Web page in the format specified by your instructor.

In the Lab

Create a document using the guidelines, concepts, and skills presented in this chapter. Labs are listed in order of increasing difficulty.

Lab 1: Creating a Web Form for Bryan's Mobile Pet Services Web Site

Problem: Bryan's Mobile Pet Services is growing, and he needs a way for clients to request services on his Web site. The Web site currently contains five pages. You will add a sixth page with a form containing a table. You add to this page a heading and a form with single-line text fields and textarea fields, a list, Submit and Reset buttons, and links to and from the Bryan's Mobile Pet Services page. Clients can use this to submit service requests. The new page added to the Web site is shown in Figure 4–106.

Software and hardware settings determine how a Web page is displayed in a browser. Your Web page may display differently than the one shown in Figure 4–106. Appendix C contains instructions for uploading your local site to a remote server.

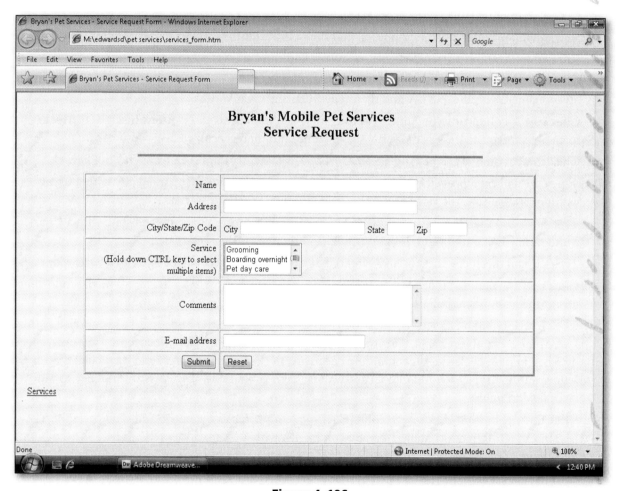

Figure 4–106

Perform the following tasks:

1. In Dreamweaver, open the Pet Services Web site, and then open a new HTML document. Save the page as services_form.htm.

2. Apply the pets_bkg.jpg background image, which can be found in the images folder.

3. If necessary, display the Insert bar and then click the Forms tab.

Continued >

In the Lab continued

6. In the upper-left corner of the document window, type Bryan's Mobile Pet Services and then press the SHIFT+ENTER keys. Type Service Request and then press the ENTER key.

7. Select both lines. Apply Heading 2 and then center the two lines of text.

8. Click below the headings. Click Insert on the menu bar, point to HTML, and then click Horizontal Rule. Specify a width of 600 pixels, a height of 4, center alignment, and no shading.

9. Click below the horizontal rule. Click the Form button on the Forms tab. Double-click the Form ID text box in the Property inspector and then type services as the form name. Click the Action text box and then type mailto:bryan@hometown.com (substitute your name and e-mail address). Click the Target box arrow and then select _self. Click the Enctype box and then type text/plain as the entry.

8. Click inside the form. Click Insert on the menu bar and then click Table. Insert a seven-row, two-column table with a width of 80%, a border thickness of 3, a cell padding of 5, and a cell spacing of 0.

9. If necessary, select the table. Click the Align button arrow in the Property inspector and then click Center. Name the table service_request.

10. Select column 1, click the Horz button, and then click Right. Set the column W (width) to 30%.

11. Click row 1, column 1; type Name as the entry; and then press the TAB key.

12. Click the Text Field button on the Forms tab. In the Property inspector, type name as the form object name. Press the TAB key and then type 50 as the Char width.

13. Click row 2, column 1; type Address as the entry; and then press the TAB key. Insert a TextField form object, type address as the form object name, and then specify a Char width of 50.

14. Click row 3, column 1; type City/State/Zip Code as the entry; and then press the TAB key.

15. Type City and then press the SPACEBAR. Insert a TextField form object named city with a Char width of 30. Click to the right of the text field and then press the SPACEBAR.

16. Type State and then press the SPACEBAR. Insert a TextField form object named state with a Char width of 2. Click to the right of the text field and then press the SPACEBAR.

17. Type Zip and then press the SPACEBAR. Insert a TextField form object named zip with a Char width of 5.

18. Click row 4, column 1; type Service as the entry; and then press SHIFT+ENTER. Type the following text as the entry, including the parentheses: (Hold down CTRL key to select multiple items).

19. Click row 4, column 2, and then click the List/Menu button on the Forms tab. Type service as the List/Menu form object name, click the List radio button in the Property inspector Type area, specify a height of 3, click the Allow multiple check box in the Selections area, and then click the List Values button. Type each Item Label and Value as shown in Table 4–4. Press the TAB key to move from field to field.

20. Click the OK button; click row 5, column 1; type Comments as the entry; and then press the TAB key. Insert a Textarea form object named comments, with a Char width of 40. Type 4 for the Num lines value.

21. Click row 6, column 1; type E-mail address as the entry; and then press the TAB key. Insert a Text Field form object named email, with a Char width of 35.

22. Click row 7, column 1, and then insert a Submit button. Click row 7, column 2, and then insert a button. Type Reset in the Value text box, and then click the Reset form radio button in the Action area.

23. If necessary, display the Behaviors panel. Click form#services in the tag selector and then click the Add behavior button in the Behaviors panel. Click Validate Form on the Add behavior menu.

24. In the Validate Form dialog box, click the Required check box for all fields except the Comments text area. In the Accept area, make sure the Anything radio button is selected for all fields except the email field. For the e-mail field, click Email address. Click the OK button in the Validate Form dialog box.

25. Click below the form. Type Services, select the text, and then create a link to the services.htm Web page. Title the page Bryan's Pet Services - Service Request, and then click the Save button on the Standard toolbar.

26. Open the services.htm Web page and then scroll down to the bottom of the page. Click below the Home link. Type Service Request Form and then create a link to the services_form.htm Web page. Save the Web page.

27. Press F12 to display the services.htm Web page in your browser. Click the Service Request Form link to display the services_form.htm Web page. Input data into the form and then click the Submit button to test the form. Then test the link to the services.htm Web page. Close the browser.

28. Submit your assignment in the format specified by your instructor. Close Dreamweaver.

Table 4–4 Pet Services List Values

Item Label	Value
Grooming	groom
Boarding overnight	boarding
Pet day care	day care
Nail trimming	nail trimming
Spa baths	baths
Obedience training	obedience

In the Lab

Lab 2: Creating a Web Form for the Jewelry by Eve Web Site

Problem: Eve has decided she would like to conduct a survey to determine which jewelry items her Web site visitors like best. She wants to include a comments section and provide a copy of the results to those visitors who are interested. To create the survey, she has requested that you add a form to the Jewelry by Eve site. The completed form is shown in Figure 4–107 on the next page. Appendix C contains instructions for uploading your local site to a remote server.

Continued >

In the Lab *continued*

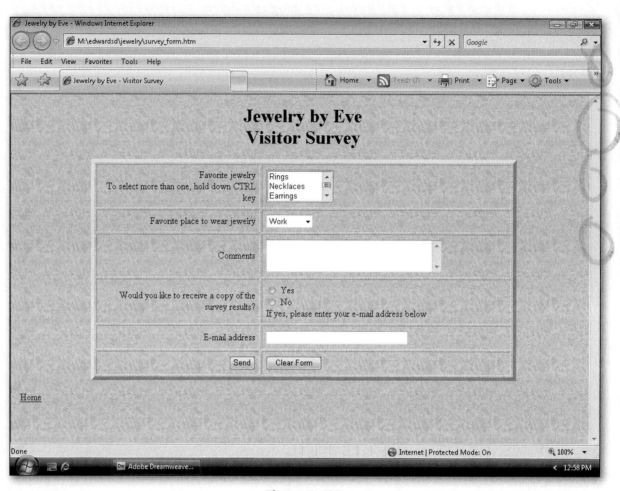

Figure 4–107

Perform the following tasks:

1. In Dreamweaver, open the Jewelry Business Web site, and then open a new HTML document. Save the page as survey_form.htm.

2. Apply the jewelry_bkg.jpg background image, which can be found in the images folder.

3. Use "Jewelry by Eve - Visitor Survey" as the title for the Web page.

4. Click the upper-left corner of the Document window. Add and center the two-line heading, Jewelry by Eve Visitor Survey, as shown in Figure 4–107. Apply Heading 1 to both lines.

5. Press the ENTER key after the second heading. If necessary, click the Forms tab on the Insert bar and then click the Form button. Type survey_form as the Form ID. Type mailto:eve@hometown. com (substitute your e-mail address) as the action. Select _self in the Target box. Click the Enctype box and then type text/plain as the entry.

6. Click inside the form and then insert a table with the following attributes: 6 rows, 2 columns, width of 75%, border thickness of 6, cell padding of 7, and cell spacing of 3. Center the table in the form and then specify a width of 40%, right-alignment for column 1, and left-alignment for column 2.

7. Click row 1, column 1; type Favorite jewelry as the entry; and then enter a line break. Type the following text and then press the TAB key: To select more than one, hold down CTRL key. Press the TAB key.

8. Click the List/Menu button on the Forms tab. Type favorite as the List/Menu name, click List in the Type area, type 3 in the Height box, and then click the Allow multiple check box.

9. Click the List Values button. Type each Item Label and Value as shown in Table 4–5. Press the TAB key to move from field to field. Click the OK button when you are finished entering the list values.

Table 4–5 Jewelry by Eve

Item Label	Value
Rings	rings
Necklaces	necklaces
Earrings	earrings
Pendants	pendants
Hair ornaments	hair ornaments

10. Click row 2, column 1. Type Favorite place to wear jewelry and then press the TAB key. Click the List/Menu button on the Forms tab. Type wear as the menu name. If necessary, click Menu in the Type area, and then click the List Values button. Type each Item Label and Value as shown in Table 4–6. Press the TAB key to move from field to field. Select Work in the Initially selected list box.

Table 4–6 Jewelry Items Menu Values

Item Label	Value
Work	work
Dinner	dinner
Meetings	meetings
Movies	movies

11. Click row 3, column 1; type Comments as the entry; and then press the TAB key. Insert a Textarea form object named comments, with a Char width of 35 and Num lines of 3.

12. Click row 4, column 1. Type the following text and then press the TAB key: Would you like to receive a copy of the survey results?.

13. Insert a Radio Group form object named group results. Click the first instance of Radio below Label, type Yes as the Label, and then press the TAB key. Type yes for the Value and then press the TAB key. Type No for the second Label field, press the TAB key, and then type no for the second Value. Click the OK button.

14. Position the insertion point to the right of No and then insert a line break. Type the following text and then press the TAB key: If yes, please enter your e-mail address below.

15. Click in row 5, column 1. Type the following text and then press the TAB key: E-mail address. Insert a TextField form object named email and then set a Char width of 35.

16. Click row 6, column 1, and then insert a Button form object named send. Type Send in the Value text box.

17. Click row 6, column 2, and then insert a Button form object named clear. Type Clear Form in the Value text box, and then click Reset form in the Action area.

18. Below the form, type Home, insert a line break, left-align the text, and then add a link to the index.htm Web page. Click the Save button on the Standard toolbar. Press the F12 key to view the Web page in your browser. Input data into the form and then click the Send button to test the form.

Continued >

In the Lab *continued*

19. Open the index.htm Web page and then scroll down to the bottom of the page. Click at the end of the Products link and press the ENTER key. Type Survey and create a link to the survey_form.htm Web page.

20. Save the Web page and then test the link in your browser. Submit your assignment in the format specified by your instructor.

In the Lab

Lab 3: Creating a Form Web Page for the Credit Protection Web Site

Problem: Linda Reyes recently received several e-mails asking for suggestions on how to spend money wisely. She has created three informational articles and would like to provide these articles to her Web site visitors. Linda asks you to create a form so she can provide this information. The form is shown in Figure 4–108. Appendix C contains instructions for uploading your local site to a remote server.

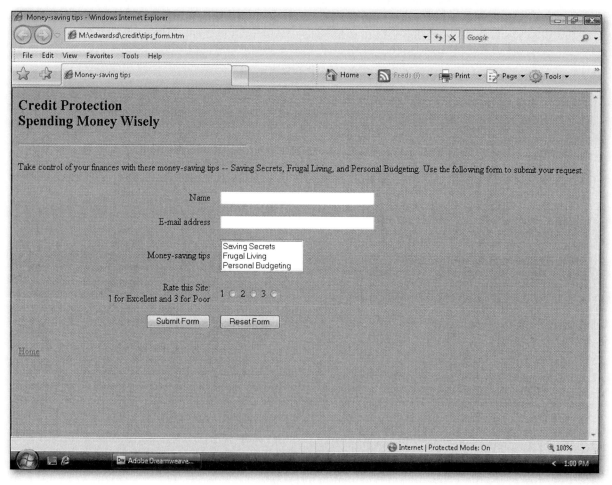

Figure 4–108

1. In Dreamweaver, copy the tips_form.htm file from the Chapter04\credit folder provided with your data files to your credit folder.

2. Open the Credit Protection Web site.

3. Double-click tips_form.htm to open the Web page.

4. Click to the right of the last sentence and then press the ENTER key. If necessary, click the Forms tab on the Insert bar and then click the Form button. Name the form guest_comments. Type mailto:linda@credit.com (substitute your e-mail address) as the action. Select _self in the Target box. Click the Enctype box and then type text/plain as the entry.

5. Click inside the form and then insert a table with the following attributes: 5 rows, 2 columns, width of 75%, border thickness of 0, cell padding of 7, and a cell spacing of 3. Center the table in the form and specify a width of 30% for column 1.

6. Select column 1 and then click Format on the Application bar, point to Align, and then click Right.

7. Click row 1, column 1; type Name as the entry; and then press the TAB key. Add a single-line text field named name, with a Char width of 40.

8. Click row 2, column 1; type E-mail address as the entry; and then press the TAB key. Add a single-line text field named email, with a Char width of 40.

9. Click row 3, column 1; type the following text and then press the TAB key: Money-saving tips. Insert a List/Menu form object named saving, with a Type of List and a Height of 3. Click the Allow multiple check box.

10. In the List Values dialog box, type each Item Label and Value as shown in Table 4–7. Press the TAB key to move from field to field.

11. Click row 4, column 1. Type the following text: Rate this Site: and then insert a line break. Type 1 for Excellent and 3 for Poor. Insert a Radio Button object named excellent. Type excellent in the Checked value text box. Click to the left of the radio button, type 1 and press the SPACEBAR. Insert a space to the right of the radio button, type 2 and press the SPACEBAR. Insert a Radio Button object named average. Type average in the Checked value text box. Insert a space to the right of the radio button, type 3 and then press the SPACEBAR. Insert a Radio Button object named poor. Type poor in the Checked value text box.

12. Click row 5, column 1. Insert the Submit button and change the Value to Submit Form. Click row 5, column 2. Insert another button, type Reset Form as the Value, and then click Reset form in the Action area.

13. At the bottom of the page, type Home, and then make the text a link to the index.htm Web page.

14. If necessary, press SHIFT+F4 to display the Behaviors panel. Select the form. Click the Add behavior button and then select the Validate Form command to open the Validate Form dialog box. Require a value in the name field, and accept only e-mail addresses in the e-mail field.

15. Insert a left-aligned horizontal rule under the second line in the heading. The horizontal rule should have a width of 400 pixels, a height of 3, and shading applied.

16. Save the form.

17. Open the index.htm Web page, scroll down to the bottom of the page, click to the right of Theft, and then add a line break. Type Information Request as the entry, select the text, and then create a link to the tips_form.htm Web page.

18. View the Web pages in your browser. Input data into the form and then click the Submit Form button to test the form. Close the browser. Submit your assignment in the format specified by your instructor.

Table 4–7 Credit Protection List Values	
Item Label	**Value**
Saving Secrets	saving
Frugal Living	frugal
Personal Budgeting	budget

Cases and Places

Apply your creative thinking and problem solving skills to design and implement a solution.

● EASIER ●● MORE DIFFICULT

● 1: Add a Form to the Favorite Sports Web Site

Your sports Web site is receiving more hits each day. You have received many e-mails asking for statistics and other information. You decide to start a weekly newsletter and want to add a form so your visitors can subscribe to the newsletter. Add a background image to the page and add a title to the page. Insert a form and name the form appropriately. Add a horizontal rule below the heading on your page. Next, add a table to your form. Include text fields for name and e-mail address and a text area for comments. Add descriptive text asking if the visitor would like to subscribe to the newsletter and then include a radio group with Yes and No options. Add Submit and Reset buttons. Create links to and from the home page. Save the page in your sports Web site. Open the pages in your browser and then check your links and forms.

● 2: Add a Survey to the Hobby Web Site

You would like to add some interactivity to your hobby Web site. You decide to do this by adding a survey. First, add a background image to the page and then add an appropriate title. Add a horizontal rule below the heading on your page. Insert a form and then add a table to your form. Add a four-pixel border to the form. Add a list form object that contains a list of hobbies. Ask your viewers to select their favorite hobbies. Create an e-mail text field for those visitors who would like a copy of your survey results. Add Submit and Reset buttons. Create links to and from the home page. Save your Web pages, open the pages in your browser, and then check your links and forms. Upload the page to a remote site, if instructed to do so.

●● 3: Create a Companion Web Site for the Politics Web Site

Your campaign for political office is progressing well. Create a new Web site and name it office_form. Add two pages with forms to the new site. The first page should contain a form asking for opinions and comments about your political views. The second form should contain form objects requesting donations and campaign volunteers. Add a horizontal rule below the headings on each of your two pages. Create links to and from the home page. Save your pages, open your pages in your browser, and then check your links and forms. Upload the office_form Web site to a remote server.

●● 4: Add a Form to the Favorite Music Web Site

Make It Personal

Add an informational form to your music hobby Web site and then add a background to the page. Add a horizontal rule below the heading on your page. Insert a form and a table. Include form objects for name, address, telephone number, and e-mail address. Include a menu with at least five choices and then add the Submit and Reset buttons. Rename the buttons. Fill in all relevant attributes in the Property inspector for each object. Create links to and from the home page. Save your Web pages, open the pages in your browser, and then check your links and forms. Upload the page to a remote site.

•• 5: Add a Form to the Student Trips Web Site

Working Together

Last week, the student government officers selected three possible vacation sites to visit. Now they would like to have a form page for students to provide feedback about each of the three sites. Each student in your group creates a page with introductory text and a form listing each of the three student trip locations. Provide form objects so the Web site visitors can vote on which trip they would like to take and offer feedback regarding the number of days, minimum and maximum costs, and other related information. Integrate the three pages into one. Add a horizontal rule below the heading on your page. Create links to and from the home page. Save your Web pages, open the pages in your browser, and then check your links and forms.

5 | Templates and Style Sheets

Objectives

You will have mastered the material in this chapter when you can:

- Describe a template
- Create a template
- Describe different types of style sheets
- Create a Cascading Style Sheet
- Apply Cascading Style Sheet attributes to a template
- Create a Web page from a template

5 | Templates and Style Sheets

Introduction

Designing a Web site is a complex process that requires you to make decisions about the structure of the site and the appearance and content of each Web page within the site. As you develop a Web site, you can use a template to provide a basic framework for the structured organization of the entire Web site. For example, an educational institution could have a template for student home pages. The student supplies the content for the Web page. The template then takes care of the rest of the job and displays the page in a format that promotes consistency between student Web pages. Another example is the content within an e-commerce catalog page. Using a template, the content developer easily can add and delete new products, change prices, and make other modifications.

Project — Adding a Template and Applying Styles

In this chapter, you continue adding pages to the Alaska Parks Web site. You learn how to create a Dreamweaver template. Using the template, you then create a Web page highlighting one of Alaska's national monuments.

First, you create a single page that has all the elements you want to include in your Web page, and then you save the page as a template. After creating the template, you create the style sheet and then apply the style sheet attributes to the template. Next, you use the template, containing the style sheet attributes, to create a Web page featuring one of Alaska's monuments — Aniakchak National Monument — shown in Figure 5–1. This Web page contains a logo and four designated regions that can be edited. The editable regions are as follows: a heading, a short description, and two tables. You use styles to apply font and color attributes to the heading and the description and to apply fonts, font color attributes, a background, and a border to the two tables. The first table contains template cells for monument images. You also will add a short description of each image. The second table contains cells for links. You also add a relative link to your home page and an absolute link to the Aniakchak National Monument Web site.

Figure 5–1

DW 345

Overview

As you read this chapter, you will learn how to add to your Web site the pages shown in Figure 5–1 on the previous page by performing these general tasks:

- Create and save a template document
- Add a background image and title
- Add a logo image
- Add editable regions
- Add tables
- Create editable regions
- Add styles
- Add images
- Add links

<table>
<tr><td>Plan
Ahead</td><td>

General Project Guidelines

When adding pages to a Web site, consider the appearance and characteristics of the completed site. As you create the Web page shown in Figure 5–1, you should follow these general guidelines:

1. **Plan the Web page.** Determine how the page will fit into the Web site.

2. **Organize your content.** Create and organize the content for the new page. The images should be copied and pasted into the images folder.

3. **Create a template.** Determine what elements will be contained in the template.

4. **Identify editable and noneditable regions.** Consider which part of the template will be editable and which areas will be non-editable.

5. **Organize and place images.** Organize your images within the Assets panel. Consider how you will place the images within the table. Determine the vertical and horizontal space that you need to better place the image. Determine which images need to be resized and how much resizing needs to be done.

6. **Select text to identify images.** Determine what text you will use to identify each of the images.

When necessary, more specific details concerning the above guidelines are presented at appropriate points in the chapter. The chapter also will identify the actions performed and decisions made regarding these guidelines during the creation of the Web pages shown in Figure 5–1.

</td></tr>
</table>

Starting Dreamweaver and Opening a Web Site

Each time you start Dreamweaver, it opens to the last site displayed when you closed the program. It therefore may be necessary for you to open the Alaska Parks Web site. Clicking the Files pop-up menu in the Files panel lists the sites you have defined. When you open the site, a list of pages and subfolders within the site is displayed.

To Start Dreamweaver and Open the Alaska Parks Web Site

With a good understanding of the requirements, and an understanding of the necessary decisions and planning process, the next step is to start Dreamweaver and open the Alaska Parks Web site.

1

- Click the Start button on the Windows taskbar.

- Point to Adobe Dreamweaver CS4 on the Start menu or point to All Programs on the Start menu, and then point to Adobe Dreamweaver CS4 on the All Programs list.

- Click Adobe Dreamweaver CS4 to start Dreamweaver.

- If necessary, display the panel groups.

- If the Alaska Parks Web site hierarchy is not displayed, click the Files panel arrow and then click Alaska Parks on the Files pop-up menu to display the Alaska Parks Web site hierarchy in the Files panel (Figure 5–2).

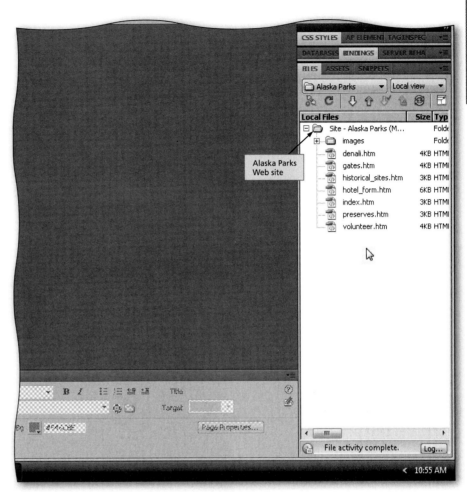

Figure 5–2

To Copy Data Files to the Parks Web Site

Before you start enhancing and adding to your Web site, you need to copy the data files into the site's folder hierarchy. In the steps on the next page, you copy the data files for the Chapter 5 project from the Chapter05 folder on a USB drive to the parks\images folder stored in the *your name* folder on the same USB drive. In the following steps, the data files for this chapter are stored on drive M:. The location on your computer may be different. If necessary, verify the location of the data files with your instructor.

- Click the Files panel button, and then click the name of the drive containing your data files, such as Removable Disk (M:).

- If necessary, click the plus sign (+) next to the folder containing your data files to expand that folder, and then click the plus sign (+) next to the Chapter05 folder to expand it.

- Expand the parks folder to display the data files.

- Click the aniak01.jpg image file or the first file in the list to select it.

- Hold down the SHIFT key and then click the logo.jpg image file, or the last file in the list.

- Press CTRL+C to copy the files.

- If necessary, click the Files panel button, and then click the drive containing the Alaska Parks Web site. Expand the *your name* folder and the parks folder. Click the images folder to select it.

2

- Press CTRL+V to paste the image files in the images folder (Figure 5–3).

Q&A

Is there another method for copying data files into the Web site folder?

Yes, you can copy the files using the Windows Computer tool.

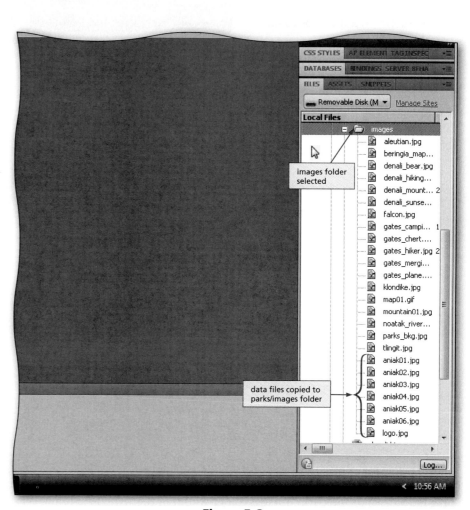

Figure 5–3

You copied the images necessary to begin creating your template and the new Web page to the Alaska Parks local root folder in the Files panel. You will create the template and then add Cascading Style Sheet attributes to the template. Next, you use the template to create a Web page focusing on one of Alaska's remote and least visited national monuments — the Aniakchak National Monument and Preserve.

Understanding Templates

Templates exist in many forms. A stencil, for instance, is a type of template. Or you may have used a template in Microsoft Office or other software applications to create documents with a repeated design. In Web site development with Dreamweaver, a **template** is a predesigned Web page that defines the appearance of the page, including items such as the default font, font size, logos and images, and backgrounds. A template provides an alternative to separately creating many similar pages on your Web site. Instead, you create a basic layout and navigation system and use it as the basis for each similar page. A template page functions as a pattern for other pages. Using a template can save time and can help create a consistent and standardized design.

Planning is an important element in creating a template. Organizing the information and deciding how to structure the template will make it user-friendly and a more effective site-design tool. The first step is to determine the look of the page, including backgrounds, fonts, and logos. Other elements to consider are heading styles, links, tables, graphics, and other media.

Creating a Template

Dreamweaver provides three methods to create a template: (1) create a template from an existing file, (2) create a template from a new document Basic page, or (3) use the File menu New command and select HTML template in the New Document dialog box. To create a template from an existing file, you open the file, use the Save as Template command on the File menu, and then define the editable regions. To create a template from a new document Basic page, use the Save as Template command on the File menu. In this chapter, you use the third method — selecting the HTML Template category in the New Document dialog box.

To Create a New Template Document

The following steps show how to create a new template document.

1

● Click the Files panel arrow in the Files panel, and then click Alaska Parks, if necessary, to open the Alaska Parks Web site.

● Click File on the Application bar, and then click New to display the New Document dialog box (Figure 5–4).

File on Application bar

New Document dialog box

Figure 5–4

2

● Click Blank Template and then click HTML template in the Template Type list (Figure 5–5).

● In the Files panel, click the minus symbol (-) next to the images folder to collapse the folder.

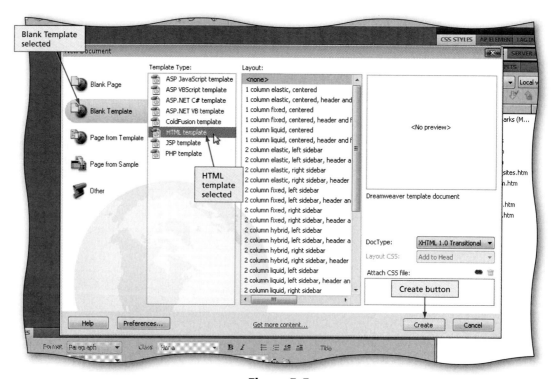

Blank Template selected

HTML template selected

Create button

Figure 5–5

3

- Click the Create button to create the template document.

- If the Insert bar is not displayed, click Window on the Application bar and then click Insert.

- If the Common category is not selected, click the Common tab on the Insert bar (Figure 5–6).

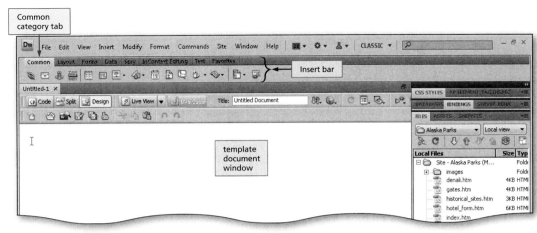

Figure 5–6

Saving a Template

When the first template for a Web site is saved, Dreamweaver automatically creates a Templates folder in the Web site local root folder and then saves the template with a **.dwt extension** within that folder. Any additional templates added to the Web site are saved in the Templates folder automatically.

To Save the Web Page as a Template

The following steps illustrate how to save the Web page as a template and to have Dreamweaver create the Templates folder.

1

- Click File on the Application bar and then click Save to display the Save As Template dialog box (Figure 5–7).

Q&A

After clicking File on the menu bar and then clicking Save, a Dreamweaver Warning box appears, not the Save As Template dialog box. What should I do?

If a Dreamweaver Warning box is displayed, click OK.

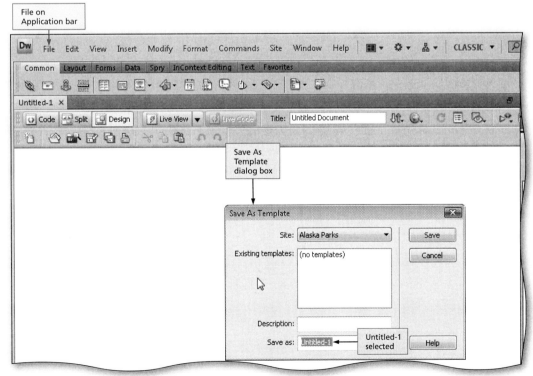

Figure 5–7

2

- Type spotlight_monuments in the Save as text box to name the template (Figure 5–8).

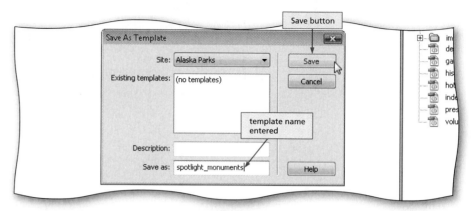

Figure 5–8

3

- Click the Save button to save the template in the Templates folder (Figure 5–9).

Q&A The Templates folder does not appear in my Files panel. What should I do?

Click the Refresh button in the Files panel or press the F5 key to refresh the display of the Files panel.

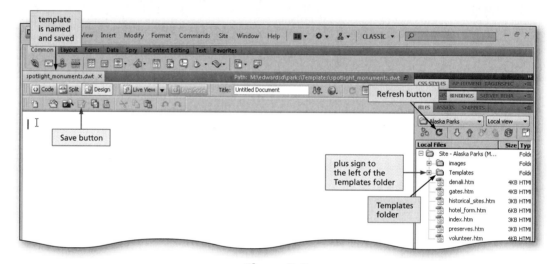

Figure 5–9

Q&A How did the Templates folder get created?

Dreamweaver created the Templates folder automatically.

4

- Click the plus sign to the left of the Templates folder to expand the folder and view the template file name with the .dwt extension (Figure 5–10).

Q&A What does the extension .dwt indicate?

The .dwt extension indicates it is a template file.

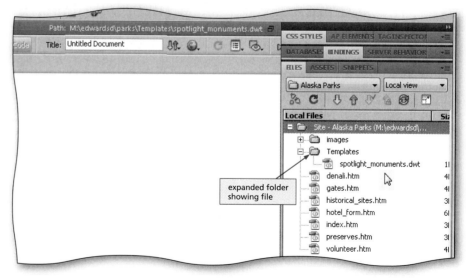

Figure 5–10

Using the Dreamweaver Template

A **Dreamweaver template** is a special type of HTML document. When you create a template, Dreamweaver inserts special code into the template. A **template instance**, which is a Web page based on a template, looks identical to the template. The difference, however, is that you can make changes only to designated parts of the template instance. The designated parts of the page to which you can make changes are called editable regions. An editable region can be any part of a page: a heading, a paragraph, a table, a table cell, and so on. You designate the editable regions when you design the template. Once the designation is complete, other parts of the page are locked so that others cannot change them.

One of the more powerful benefits that templates provide is the ability to update multiple pages at once. After a new document is created from a template, the document remains attached to the original template unless it specifically is separated. Therefore, you can modify a template and immediately update the design in all of the documents based on it.

To Add a Background Image and Title to the Template Page

The purpose of the template created in this chapter is to use it as a foundation to spotlight a different monument each month. The next step shows how to begin creating the spotlight template page.

- Click Modify on the Application bar and then click Page Properties to open the Page Properties dialog box.

- Click Appearance (HTML) in the Category list, if necessary, and then click the Browse button to the right of the Background image box to open the Select Image Source dialog box.

- If necessary, navigate to the images folder. Click parks_bkg.jpg and then click the OK button to select the background image.

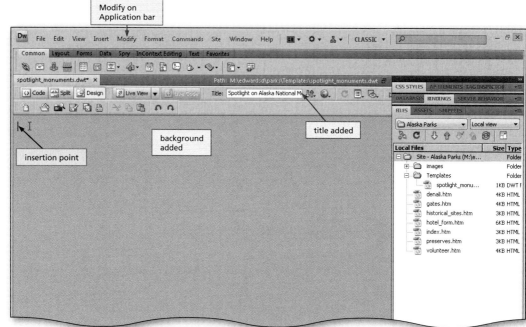

Figure 5–11

- Click the OK button in the Page Properties dialog box to add the background image to the template page.

- Click the Title text box on the Document toolbar, delete Untitled Document, and type Spotlight on Alaska National Monuments as the entry.

- Press the ENTER key. If necessary, click the document window (Figure 5–11).

Specifying Editable and Noneditable Regions

When you first create a template, Dreamweaver automatically locks most parts of the template document. The title, however, is not locked. As the template author, you define which regions of a template-based document are editable by inserting editable regions or editable parameters in the template. Dreamweaver supports four different types of regions in a template: editable regions, repeating regions, optional regions, and editable tag attributes.

Editable Region   An **editable region** is the basic building block of a template and is an unlocked region. You can define any area of a template as editable. Thus, this is a section a content developer can edit; it can be a heading, a paragraph, a table, or another type of section. A template can and usually does contain multiple editable regions. For a template to be functional, it should contain at least one editable region; otherwise, pages based on the template cannot be changed.

Repeating Region   A **repeating region** is a section in a document that is set to repeat. You can use repeating regions to control the layout of regions that are repeated on a page. The two types of repeating template objects are repeating table and repeating region. For instance, a list of catalog products may include a name, description, price, and picture in a single row. You can repeat the table row to allow the content developer to create an expanding list, while keeping the design under your control. A repeating region is a section of a template that can be duplicated as often as desired in a template-based page. By default, the repeating region does not include an editable region, but you can insert an editable region into the repeating region. A repeating region generally is used with a table, but also can be defined for other page elements.

Optional Region   An **optional region** lets the content developer show or hide content on a page-by-page basis. For example, you may want to include an optional region that would contain special promotional products.

Editable Tag Attribute   An **editable tag** attribute lets the content developer unlock a tag attribute in a template and edit the tag in a template-based page. For instance, you could unlock the table border attribute, but keep locked other table attributes such as padding, spacing, and alignment.

To Add the Logo Image to the Template

The following steps show how to add a logo image to the template. This logo, once added, becomes part of the template and is a noneditable item. When a content developer uses this template, the logo image will remain as is and cannot be deleted or aligned to another position.

- Click the Assets tab in the panel groups. If necessary, click the Images icon. Scroll down, if necessary, and click the logo.jpg file to select it (Figure 5–12).

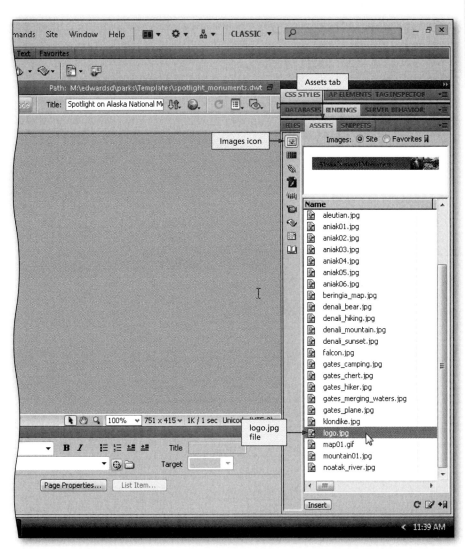

Figure 5–12

2

• Drag the logo.jpg image to the upper-left corner of the document window to insert the logo image at the top of the page.

• In the Property inspector, click the Alt text box, type `Alaska National Monuments logo` as the entry, and then press the ENTER key.

• Click anywhere on the page to deselect the image and then press the ENTER key (Figure 5–13).

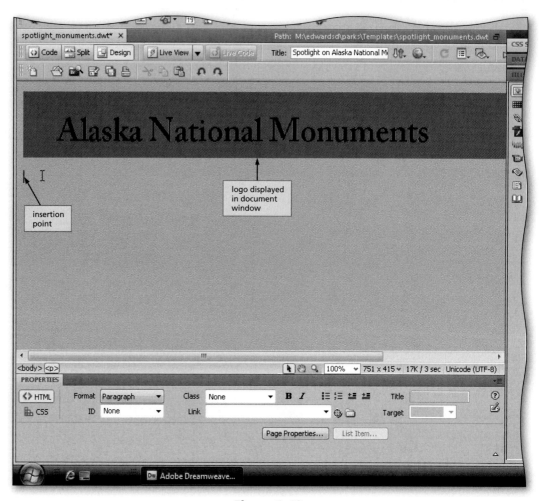

Figure 5–13

BTW

Template Editing
Using the Assets panel, you can edit, rename, or delete a template. Select the template name and then right-click it to display the context menu. Choose Edit and then select the Rename or Delete command.

Designing the Template

When you are creating a template, one of the best methods is to finalize a single page that includes all the elements you want in the template. Then, save the document as a template and mark all of the editable regions. Consider the following when designing your template page:

• Include as much content as possible. Structure and design will enable the content developer to produce a Web page based on the template more quickly.

• Use prompts in the editable regions to inform the content developer as to the type of content to be added to a particular region.

• Give your editable regions meaningful names.

• Use placeholders if possible, particularly for images.

To Add the Monument Name and Monument Description Prompts for the First Two Editable Regions

The following steps show how to add prompts for two editable regions in the template page. The prompt for the first editable region is the heading and includes instructions to add the monument name; the prompt for the second editable region is the instruction to add a short description of the monument.

- Collapse the panel groups, but leave the Property inspector open and expanded.

- Type Spotlight on [name of national monument] as the heading prompt below the logo image (Figure 5–14).

Figure 5–14

- Click the Format button arrow in the Property inspector and apply Heading 2 to the spotlight prompt (Figure 5–15).

Figure 5–15

- Press the ENTER key to move the insertion point below the prompt (Figure 5–16).

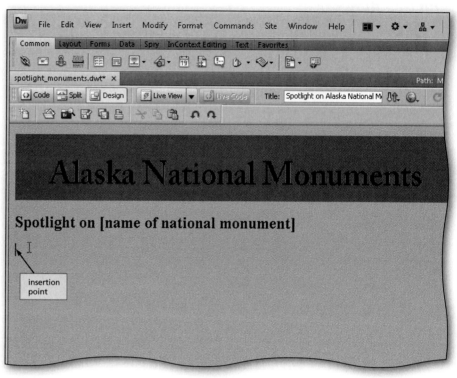

Figure 5–16

- Type Add short description of monument as the prompt for the second editable region.

- Bold the text, click at the end of the text to deselect it, and then press the ENTER key to move the insertion point below the description prompt (Figure 5–17).

Figure 5–17

Adding Tables for Images and Links

The third editable region will consist of a one-row, two-column centered table that will contain centered images and a short description immediately below each image. The table is editable, so depending on the monument to be spotlighted and the number of available images, the content developer can add rows and columns to the table as needed. Instructions for the table are contained in row 1, column 1, and an image placeholder is contained in row 1, column 2. A placeholder provides the Web page developer with a guide as to what is to be placed in the cell and the required format, such as right, left, or centered.

A second table will become the fourth editable region. This one-row, two-column centered table will contain cells for a relative link to the Alaska National Monuments index page and an absolute link to the Aniakchak National Monument Web page. This second table also is editable, which will permit the content developer to modify or add additional links as needed.

BTW

Editable Tables
You can define an individual cell or an entire table as an editable region. You cannot, however, select several nonadjacent cells and define them as one editable region.

To Add and Center a Table as the Third Editable Region

The following steps show how to add the first table as the third editable region.

1

• Click Insert on the Application bar and then click Table.

• Enter the following data in the Table dialog box: 1 for Rows, 2 for Columns, 70 percent for Table width, 0 for Border thickness, 5 for Cell padding, and 5 for Cell spacing. Type `Spotlight on Alaska national monuments` as the Summary text (Figure 5–18).

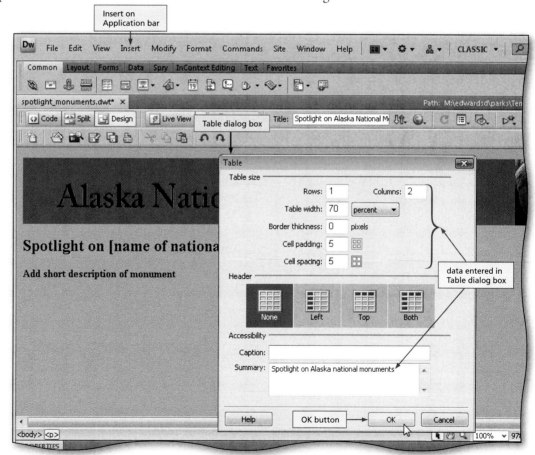

Figure 5–18

- Click the OK button to add the table to the template.

- Click the Align button arrow in the Property inspector, and then click Center to center the table in the document window (Figure 5–19).

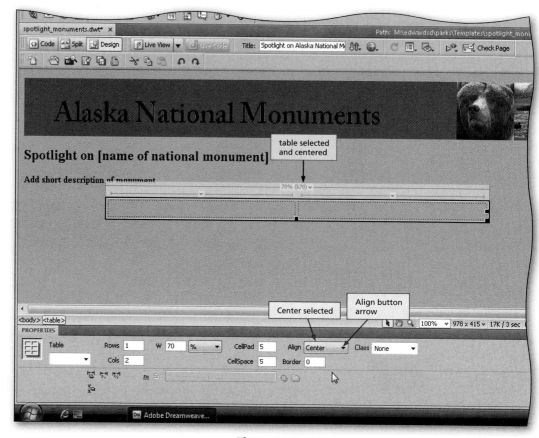

Figure 5–19

- Click the left cell in the table and then drag to select both cells in the table (Figure 5–20).

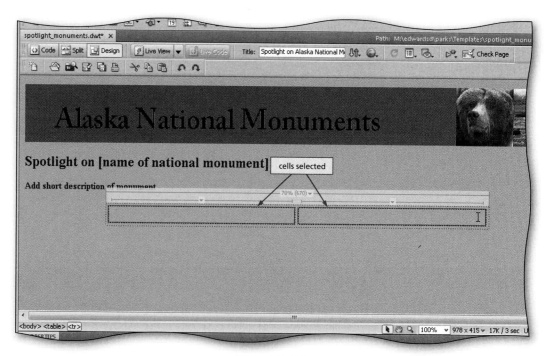

Figure 5–20

4

- Click the Horz button arrow in the Property inspector and then click Center.

- Click the Vert button arrow and then click Middle to apply the specified attributes to the table cells.

- Click the left cell in the table and then type Add additional columns and rows as necessary. Add images and short descriptions of image to each cell in the table. as the prompt, and then click the right cell (Figure 5–21).

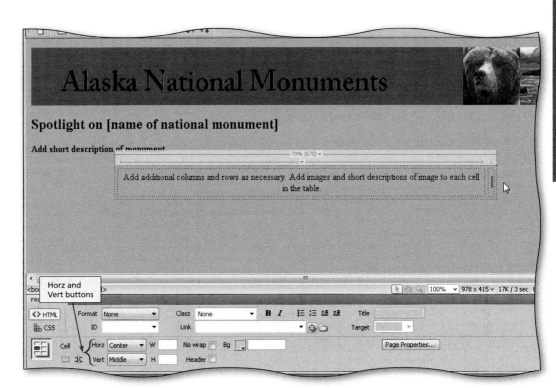

Figure 5–21

Q&A

Why does the left cell expand to take up most of the table?

The cell expands to accommodate the placeholder text. When you add content to the right cell, the table will adjust accordingly.

5

- Click Insert on the Application bar, point to Image Objects, and then point to Image Placeholder (Figure 5–22).

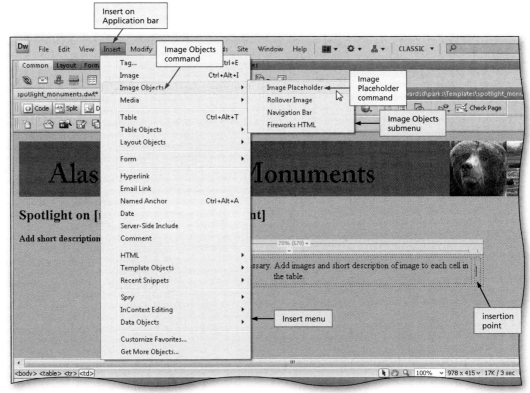

Figure 5–22

6

- Click Image Placeholder to display the Image Placeholder dialog box.

- Type add_image in the Name text box as the prompt.

- Press the TAB key.

- Type 64 for the Width.

- Press the TAB key. If necessary, type 32 for the Height (Figure 5–23).

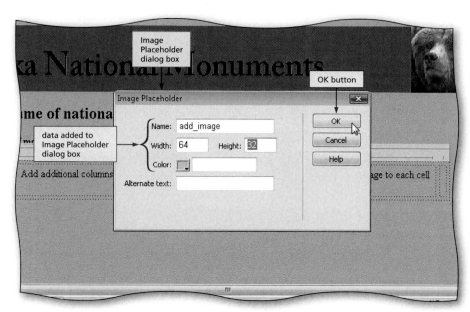

Figure 5–23

7

- Click the OK button to add the place-holder to the table (Figure 5–24).

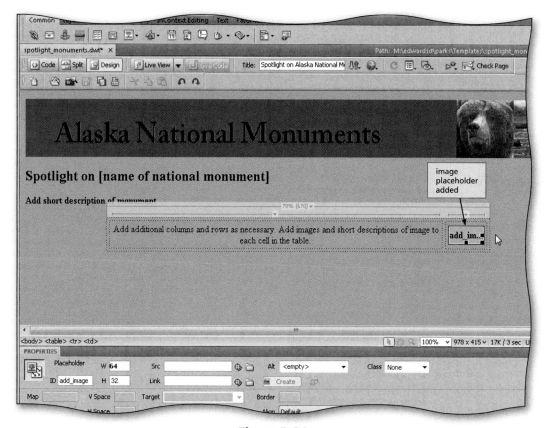

Figure 5–24

8
- Click <table> in the tag selector to select the table, and then type spotlight in the Table box to name the table.
- Press the ENTER key (Figure 5–25).

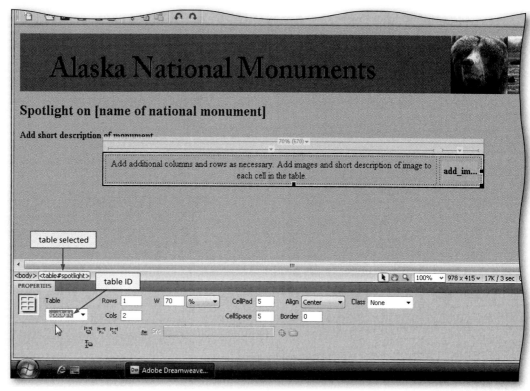

table selected

table ID

Figure 5–25

9
- Click to the right of the table and then press the ENTER key two times to insert a blank line after the table (Figure 5–26).

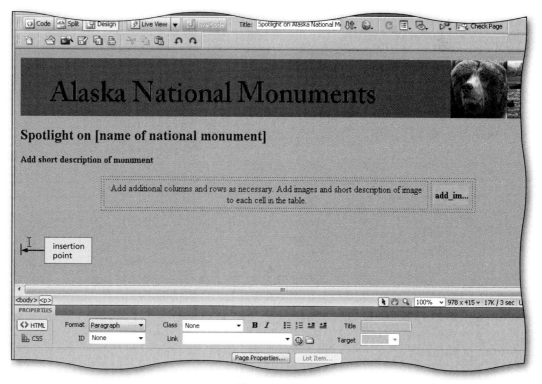

insertion point

Figure 5–26

To Add and Center a Table as the Fourth Editable Region

The second table will serve as a table for links. The following step shows how to add the link table as the fourth editable region.

- Click Insert on the Application bar and then click Table to display the Table dialog box.

- Enter the following data in the Insert Table dialog box: 1 for Rows, 2 for Columns, 50 percent for Table width, 0 for Border thickness, 5 for Cell padding, and 0 for Cell spacing. Type Web site links as the Summary text. Click the OK button.

- Click the Align button arrow in the Property inspector, and then center the table.

- Click the left cell and then drag to select both cells in the table.

- Click the Horz button arrow in the Property inspector and then click Center. Click the Vert button arrow and then click Middle.

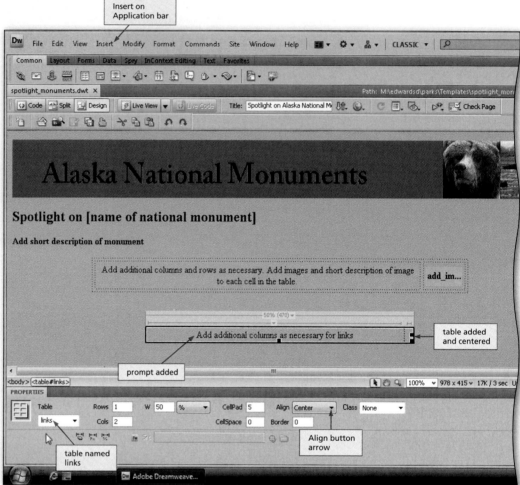

Figure 5–27

- Click the left cell and then type Add additional columns as necessary for links as the prompt.

- Select the table and name it links. Press the ENTER key.

- Press CTRL+S to save the file. If a Dreamweaver warning box is displayed, click the OK button (Figure 5–27).

Adding Editable Regions

As previously discussed on pages DW 354, Dreamweaver supports four different regions in a template: editable regions, repeating regions, optional regions, and editable tag attributes. All Dreamweaver region objects, along with other template-related objects, are available through the Templates pop-up menu on the Common category tab of the Insert bar. Figure 5–28 shows the Templates pop-up menu.

Figure 5–28

Table 5–1 lists the commands and descriptions on the Templates pop-up menu.

Table 5–1 Commands on the Templates Pop-Up Menu	
Command Name	**Description**
Make Template	Displays the Save As Template dialog box; features in the dialog box include selecting a Web site in which to save the template, a list of existing templates, and a Save As box to name the template
Make Nested Template	Creates a template whose design and editable regions are based on another template; useful for sites in which all pages share certain elements and subsections of those pages share a subset of page elements
Editable Region	Creates an unlocked region; the basic building block of a template
Optional Region	Designates a region that can be used to show or hide content on a page-by-page basis; use an optional region to set conditions for displaying content in a document
Repeating Region	Creates a section of a template that can be duplicated as often as desired in a template-based page
Editable Optional Region	Designates a region that can be used to show or hide content on a page-by-page basis
Repeating Table	Defines a table and then defines the location of editable regions in each cell in the table

Marking Existing Content as an Editable Region

As discussed previously, an editable region is one that the content developer can change. Editable template regions control which areas of a template-based page can be edited. Each editable region must have a unique name. Dreamweaver uses the name to identify the editable region when new content is entered or the template is applied.

To Create the First Editable Region

The following steps show how to make the heading an editable region.

1
- If necessary, click the Common tab on the Insert bar.
- Click the Property inspector title bar to collapse the Property inspector.
- Click to the left of the heading prompt (Figure 5–29).

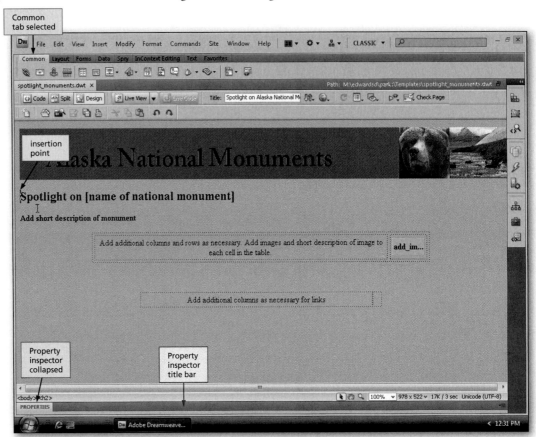

Figure 5–29

2

- Click the <h2> tag in the Tag selector to select the prompt for the title (Figure 5–30).

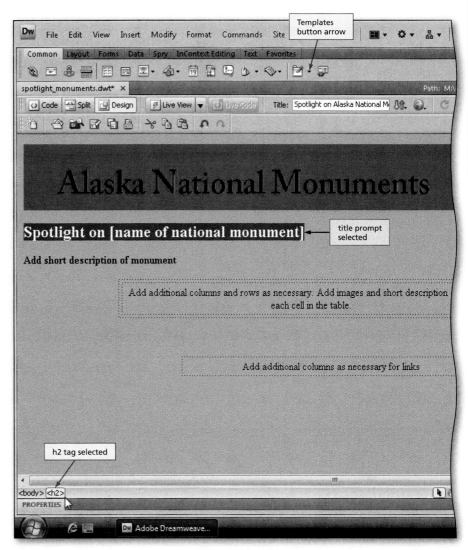

Figure 5–30

3

- On the Common tab, click the Templates button arrow to open the Templates pop-up menu, and then point to Editable Region (Figure 5–31).

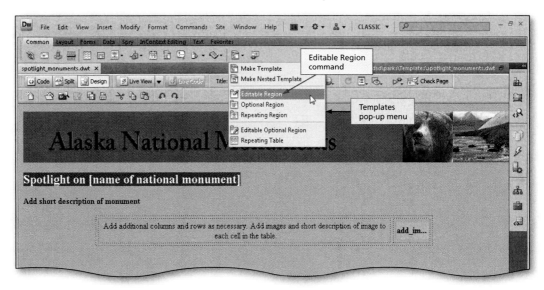

Figure 5–31

4

- Click Editable Region to display the New Editable Region dialog box.

- Type monument_name in the Name text box to provide a name for the new editable region (Figure 5–32).

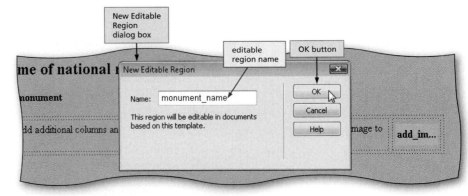

Figure 5–32

- Click the OK button to designate the selected text as an editable region (Figure 5–33).

Figure 5–33

Other Ways

1. Click Insert on the Application bar, point to Template Objects, click Editable Region on Template Objects submenu

2. Right-click selected content, point to Templates, click New Editable Region on the Templates submenu

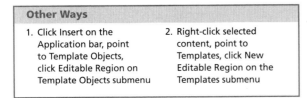

To Create the Second Editable Region

The second editable region that needs to be identified and given a name is the text area that will provide a short description of the featured monument. The following steps illustrate how to make the monument description section an editable region.

1

- Click to the left of the prompt, Add short description of monument, in the document window (Figure 5–34).

Figure 5–34

- Click the <p> tag in the tag selector to select the line.

- Click the Templates button arrow and then click Editable Region to display the New Editable Region dialog box (Figure 5–35).

The name in my New Editable Region dialog box has a different number at the end. Why is that?

Dreamweaver numbers the name of the editable region according to how many editable regions you've already created. You rename the editable region in the next step.

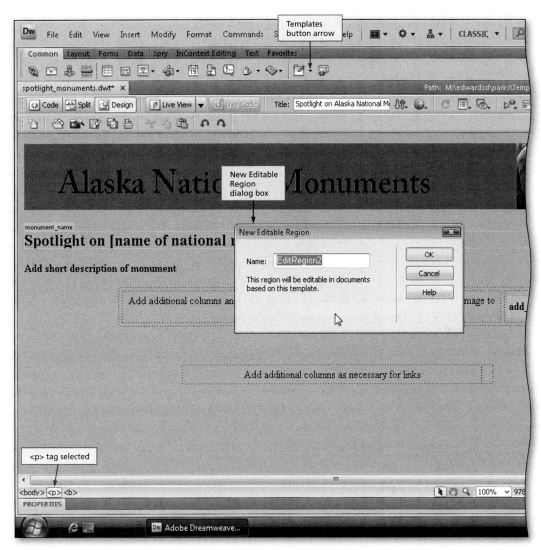

Figure 5–35

2

- Type monument_description in the Name text box and then click the OK button to name the selected editable region (Figure 5–36).

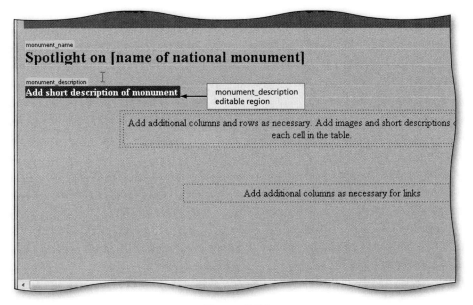

Figure 5–36

To Create the Third and Fourth Editable Regions

The third and fourth editable regions are the two tables that were added to the template. The following steps show how to make both tables editable regions.

1

- Click in the left cell of the first table and then click the <table#spotlight> tag in the tag selector to select the table (Figure 5–37).

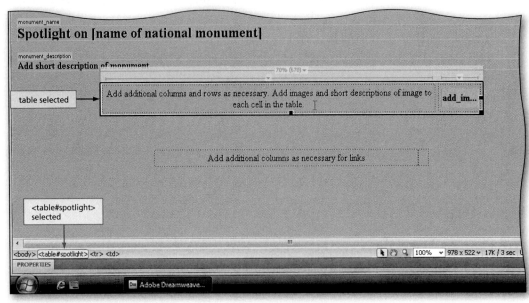

Figure 5–37

2

- Click the Templates button arrow, and then click the Editable Region command.

- Type monument_ images in the Name text box, and then click the OK button to add the editable region name (Figure 5–38).

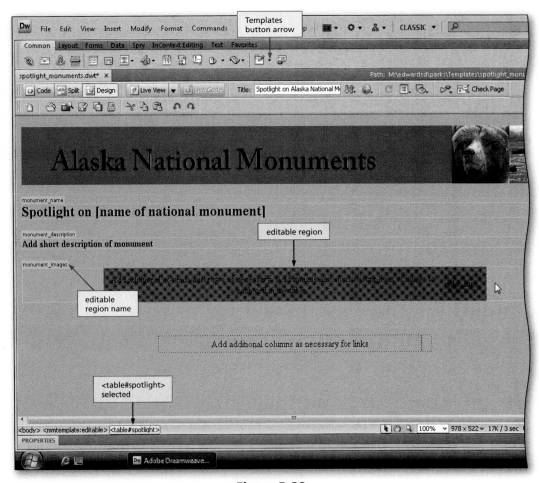

Figure 5–38

3

- Click in the left cell of the second table, click the <table#links> tag in the tag selector, and then click the Editable Region command on the Templates pop-up menu to display the New Editable Region dialog box (Figure 5–39).

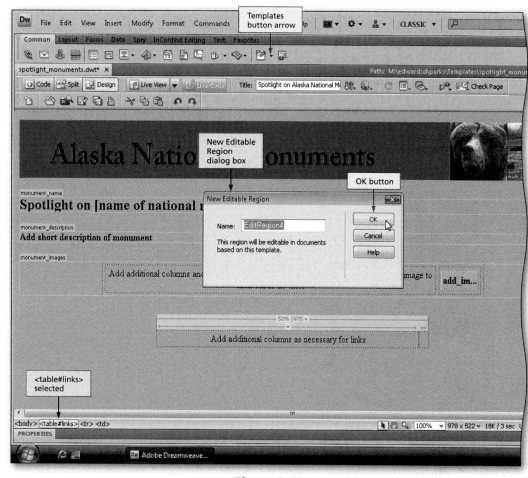

Figure 5–39

4

- Type links in the Name text box and then click the OK button to add links as the editable region name (Figure 5–40).

Q&A What should I do if a warning dialog box appears?

If a warning dialog box is displayed, indicating you have placed an editable region inside a <p> tag, click Cancel, and then repeat Steps 3 and 4.

5

- If necessary, display the Standard toolbar and then click the Save button.

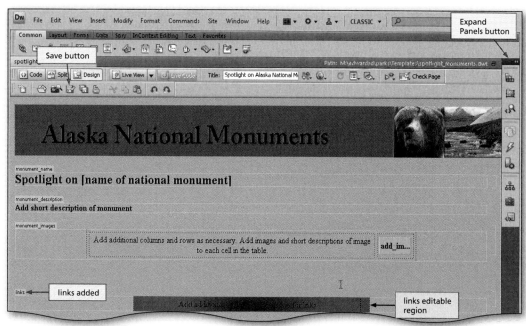

Figure 5–40

BTW

Detaching a Page from a Template
To detach a page from a template, click Modify on the Application bar, point to Templates, and then click Detach from Template on the Templates submenu. The page becomes a regular document, and the locked regions become editable.

You have completed adding the editable regions to the template. Next, you create a style sheet and apply the style attributes to the text and tables contained within the template.

Introduction to Style Sheets

If you have used styles in a word processing program such as Microsoft Word, then the concept of styles within HTML and Dreamweaver will be familiar. A **style** is a rule describing how a specific object is formatted. A style sheet (discussed later in this section) is a file that contains a collection of these rules or styles. One style sheet, for example, can control the typography, color, and other layout elements for an entire Web site.

Dreamweaver supports two types of styles: HTML styles and Cascading Style Sheets (CSS).

HTML Styles

BTW

HTML Styles
Use the HTML Styles panel to record the HTML styles you use in your Web site. Then you can share the styles with other users, local sites, or remote sites.

Thus far, when you have formatted text, you have selected the text in the document window and then applied font attributes using the Property inspector. You selected and then formatted each text element individually: the heading, character, word, paragraph, and so on. **HTML styles**, however, are a Dreamweaver feature that a Web page developer can use to apply formatting options quickly and easily to text in a Web page. HTML styles use HTML tags such as the <h1> and <b> tags to apply the formatting. Once you have created and saved an HTML style, you can apply it to any document in the Web site.

One advantage of HTML styles is that they consist only of font tags, and therefore are displayed in just about all browsers, including Internet Explorer 7.0 and earlier versions. One of the main disadvantages of HTML styles, however, is that changes made to an HTML style are not updated automatically in the document. If a style is applied and then the style is modified, the style must be reapplied to the text to update the formatting. To use HTML styles, you must deselect the Use CSS instead of HTML Tags option in the General category of the Preferences dialog box.

The HTML 4.0 specification released by the World Wide Web Consortium (W3C) in early 1998 discourages the use of HTML formatting tags in favor of Cascading Style Sheets (CSS). This chapter, therefore, focuses on Cascading Style Sheets.

Cascading Style Sheets

BTW

External Style Sheets
External style sheets are separate files and are independent of any HTML pages within the Web site. Any Web page in a Web site can access a common set of properties by linking to the same external style sheet.

Cascading Style Sheets, also called **CSS** and **style sheets**, are a collection of formatting rules that control the appearance of content in a Web page. Cascading Style Sheets are the cornerstone of Dynamic HTML (DHTML). **DHTML** is an extension to HTML that enables a Web page to respond to user input without sending a request to the Web server. Compared with HTML styles, style sheets provide the Web site developer with more precision and control over many aspects of page design.

Dreamweaver contains three different selectors: Class, Tag, and Advanced. Selectors are types of rules that Dreamweaver uses to define a style. A CSS style rule contains two parts: the **selector**, which is the name of the style, and the **declaration**, which defines the style elements. An example of a selector is h2 (defining the HTML h2 tag) and an example of a declaration is 24 pt Courier, defining the font size and type to apply to the h2 tag.

- *Class*: Also considered a custom style, class is the most flexible way to define a style. In a **custom style**, you specify all the attributes you want the style to include. The name of a custom style always begins with a period. This type of style can be applied to any text within the document.

- *Tag*: The tag style provides the option to make global changes to existing Web pages by modifying the properties or attributes of an HTML tag. When this option is selected in the New CSS Rule dialog box, the Tag pop-up menu provides a selection of over 90 HTML tags listed in alphabetical order.

- *Advanced*: Also known as pseudo-class, this type of style commonly is applied to hyperlinks to create a rollover effect. For example, when the mouse pointer moves over or hovers over a link, the link changes color. Dreamweaver provides the a:active, a:hover, a:link, and a:visited link options through the pop-up menu. You are not limited to these four options. You can enter one or more of any HTML tag in the Selector text box and apply a single attribute or a combination of attributes to that tag.

After creating a style, you can apply it instantly to text, margins, images, and other Web page elements. Some of the advantages of style sheets include the following:

- Precise layout control
- Smaller, faster downloading pages
- Browser-friendly — browsers not supporting CSS simply ignore the code
- All attached Web pages can be updated at one time

The capability of updating every element with a designated style simultaneously is one of the main benefits of style sheets. For example, suppose you create a custom text style defined as 24-point Times New Roman bold. Later, you decide to change the text color to red. All elements formatted with that style instantly are changed and are displayed in red.

Conflicting Styles

The term **cascading** refers to the capability of applying multiple style sheets to the same Web page. When more than one style is applied to the same Web page, an order of preference is involved. Styles are used as described and applied in the following preference order:

- An **external style sheet** is a single style sheet that is used to create uniform formatting and contains no HTML code. An external style sheet can be linked to any page within the Web site or imported into a Web site. Using the Import command creates an @import tag in the HTML code and references the URL where the published style sheet is located. This method does not work with Netscape Navigator.

- An **internal style sheet**, or **embedded style sheet**, contains styles that apply to a specific page. The styles that apply to the page are embedded in the <head> portion of the Web page.

- A specified element within a page can have its own style.

In some instances, two styles will be applied to the same element. When this occurs, the browser displays all attributes of both styles unless an attribute conflict exists. For example, one style may specify Arial as the font and the other style may specify Times New Roman. When this happens, the browser displays the attribute of the style closest to the text within the HTML code.

The CSS Styles Panel

To develop a style sheet, you start with the **CSS Styles panel** (Figure 5–41 on the next page). Styles are created and controlled through the CSS Styles panel. A **custom style** is a style you can create and name, in which you specify all the attributes you want the style to include.

The name of a custom style always begins with a period.

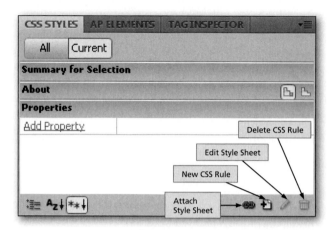

Figure 5–41

In the lower-right corner of the CSS Styles panel are four buttons. These buttons are used for the following tasks:

- The **Attach Style Sheet** button opens the Link External Style Sheet dialog box. Select an external style sheet to link to or import into your current document.

- The **New CSS Rule** button opens the New CSS Rule dialog box. Use the New CSS Rule dialog box to define a type of style.

- The **Edit Style Sheet** button opens the CSS Style Definition dialog box. Edit any of the styles in the current document or in an external style sheet.

- The **Delete CSS Rule** button removes the selected style from the CSS Styles panel, and removes the formatting from any element to which it was applied.

To Display the CSS Styles Panel

The following steps show how to display the CSS Styles panel.

- Click the Expand Panels button to expand the panel groups, and then click the Files tab, if necessary, to display the Alaska Parks Web site (Figure 5–42).

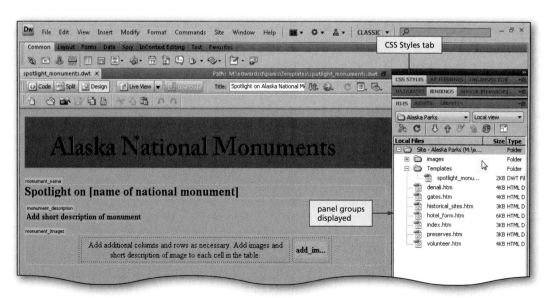

Figure 5–42

②

- If necessary, click Window on the Application bar and then click CSS Styles to display the panel group containing the CSS Styles tab.

- If necessary, click the CSS Styles tab to display the CSS Styles panel.

- If necessary, click the Current button, and then click the Show information about selected property button on the About bar.

- If necessary, drag the Properties bar in the CSS Styles panel up to display the Properties section (Figure 5–43).

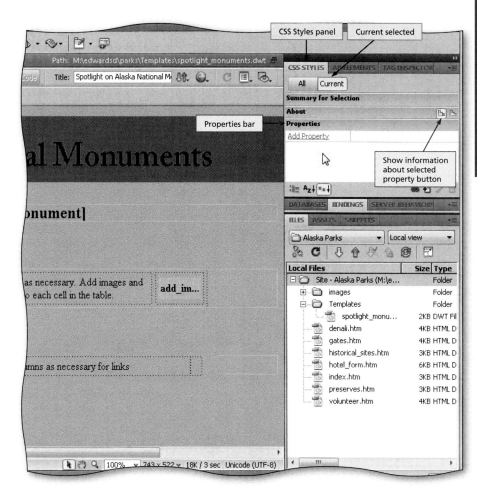

Figure 5–43

Other Ways

1. Press SHIFT+F11

Defining Style Attributes

Dreamweaver makes it easy to add style attributes to the style sheet. This is done through the CSS Rule Definition dialog box (Figure 5–44 on the next page). The CSS Rule Definition dialog box contains eight categories with more than 70 different CSS attributes. As you are defining a style, select a category to access the attributes for that category. Styles from more than one category can be applied to the same element. Tables 5–4 through 5–11 on pages DW 405–407 describe each attribute in each of the eight categories.

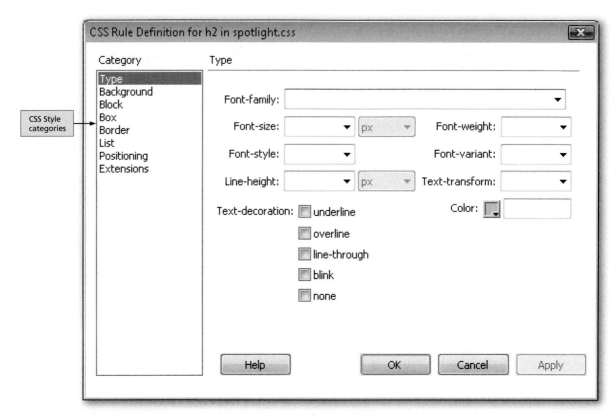

Figure 5–44

Adding a Style and Saving the Style Sheet

Recall that styles and style sheets are applied in a variety of formats: an external style sheet can be linked or imported to any number of Web pages, an embedded style sheet is contained within one Web page, or you can apply a style to a specific element within a Web page. The spotlight style sheet you create in the following steps is an external style sheet that is linked to the spotlight template page. When you apply the first style, a document window with a .css extension opens behind the original document window. This window contains the code for the applied styles; it is not displayed in Design view. When you complete adding styles, you also save and close the .css window.

In this chapter, the original document window contains a template. The document window, however, does not have to show a template. It can be a basic page or a frame to which you can apply styles.

To Add a Style and Save the Style Sheet

The following steps show how to create the heading style and then save the style sheet.

1

- Click to the left of the text, Spotlight on [name of national monument], in the monument_name editable region, and then click the <h2> tag in the tag selector to select the heading prompt (Figure 5–45).

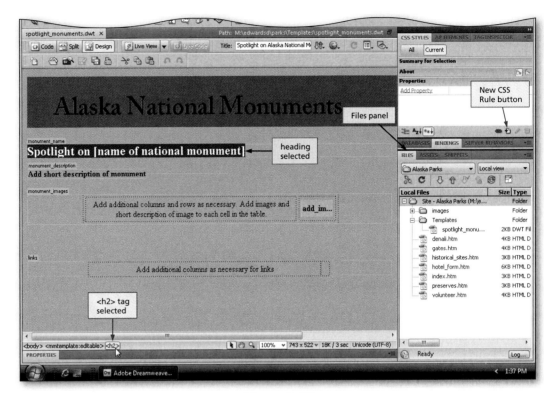

Figure 5–45

2

- Click the New CSS Rule button in the CSS Styles panel to display the New CSS Rule dialog box.

- Click the Selector Type arrow and then point to Tag (redefines an HTML element) (Figure 5–46).

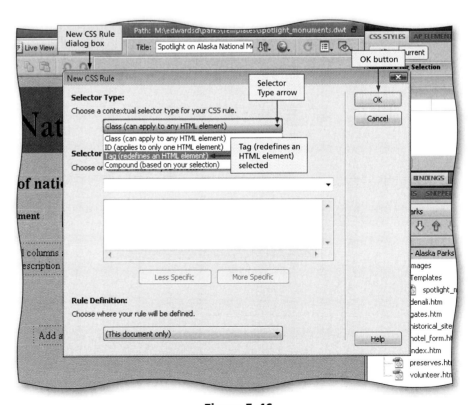

Figure 5–46

3

- Click Tag (redefines an HTML element) to select that selector type.

- Click the Selector Name text box and type h2 as the selector name, if necessary.

- Click the Rule Definition arrow, and then click (New Style Sheet File) to specify that you want to create an external style sheet (Figure 5–47).

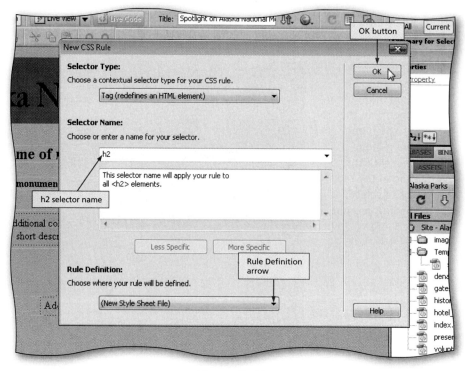

Figure 5–47

4

- Click the OK button to display the Save Style Sheet File As dialog box.

- If necessary, click the Save in box arrow and then click the parks folder.

- Click the File name text box and then type spotlight in the File name text box.

- Click the Save as type arrow and select Style Sheet Files (*.css), if necessary (Figure 5–48).

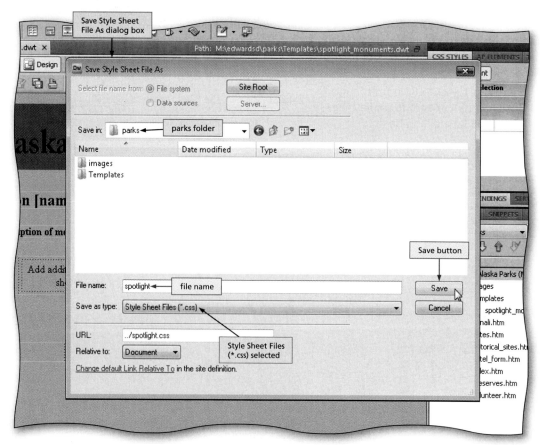

Figure 5–48

5

- Click the Save button to display the CSS Rule Definition for h2 in spotlight.css dialog box.

- Click Type in the Category list, if necessary (Figure 5–49).

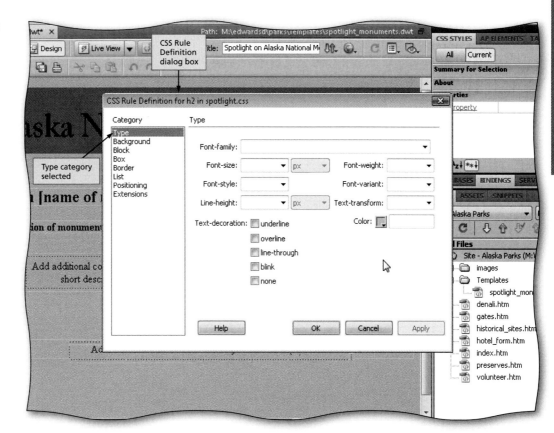

Figure 5–49

6

- Click the Font-family box arrow, and then click Arial, Helvetica, sans-serif in the Font-family list.

- Click the Font-size box arrow, and then click 24 in the Size list.

- Click the Font-weight box arrow, and then click bolder.

- Click the Color text box, type #000 for black text, and then press the TAB key to enter the style definitions (Figure 5–50).

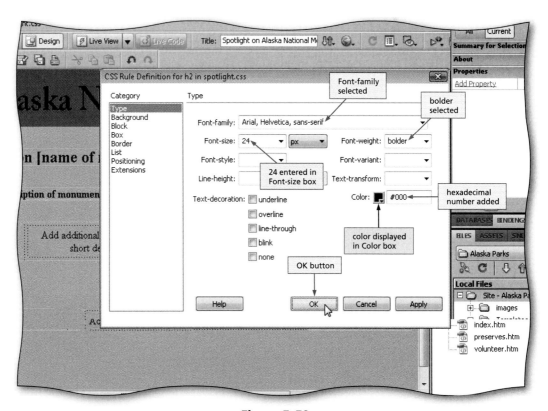

Figure 5–50

7

• Click the OK button and then click anywhere in the monument_name editable region to deselect the heading prompt, which displays the new style (Figure 5–51).

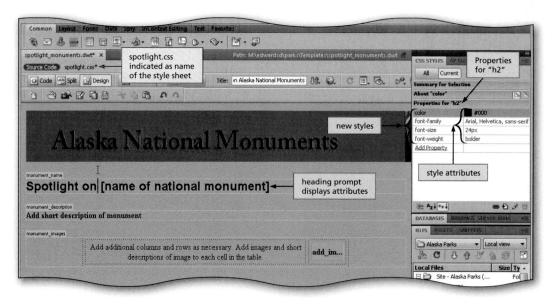

Figure 5–51

To Create a Style for the Paragraph Text

Next, you create a style for the paragraph text. The following steps illustrate how to redefine the HTML paragraph tag for the monument_description editable region.

1

• Click to the left of the prompt, Add short description of monument, and then click the <p> tag in the tag selector to select the prompt (Figure 5–52).

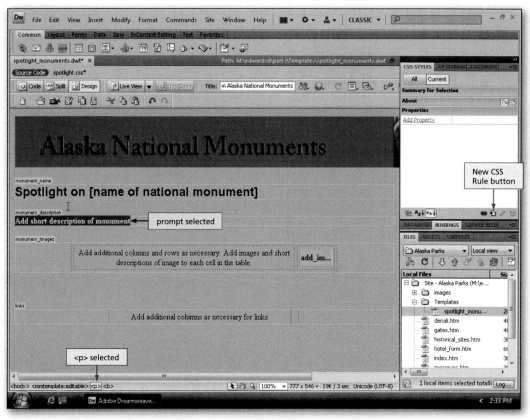

Figure 5–52

- Click the New CSS Rule button in the CSS Styles panel to display the New CSS Rule dialog box.

- Click the Selector Type arrow and then select Tag (redefines an HTML element).

- Verify that the p tag is displayed in the Selector Name text box.

- Click the Rule Definition arrow, and then click (This document only) (Figure 5–53).

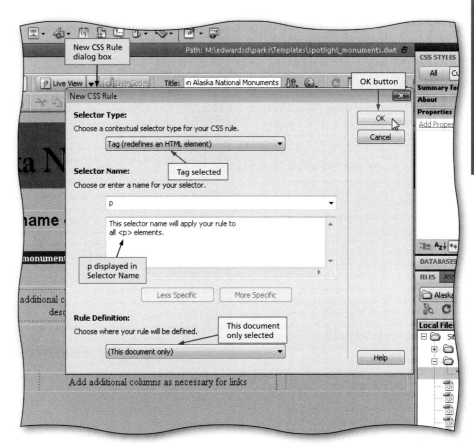

Figure 5–53

- Click the OK button to display the CSS Rule definition for p dialog box.

- Verify that the Type category is selected (Figure 5–54).

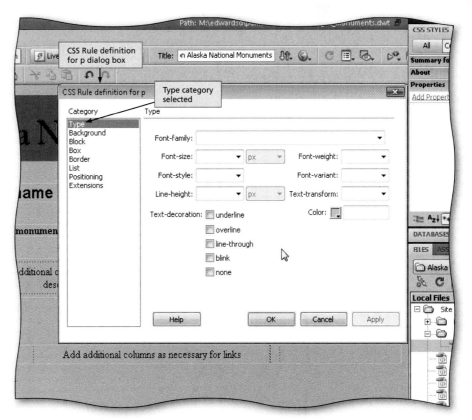

Figure 5–54

4

- Click the Font-family box arrow and then click Arial, Helvetica, sans-serif.

- Click the Font-size box arrow and then click 12.

- Click the Font-weight box arrow and then click bold.

- Click the Color text box and then type #000 for the color. Press the TAB key to add the CSS Rule Definition Type attributes (Figure 5–55).

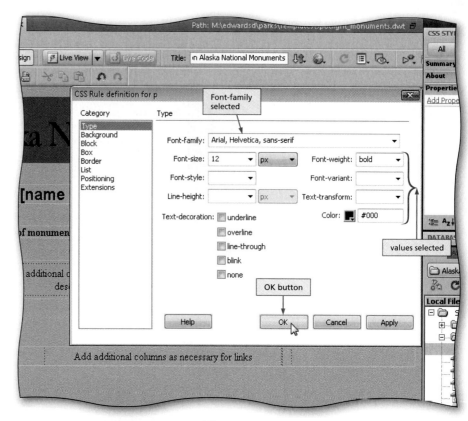

Figure 5–55

5

- Click the OK button to apply the styles to the current paragraph.

- Click to the right of the paragraph and observe the new attributes (Figure 5–56).

- Click the Save button on the Standard toolbar.

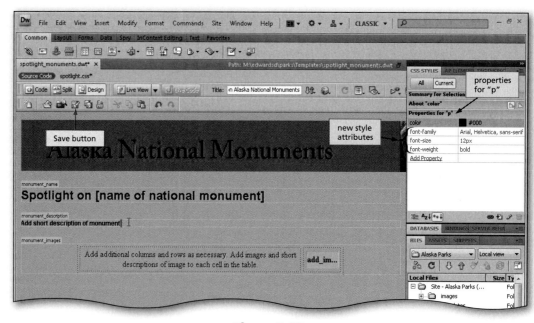

Figure 5–56

Other Ways

1. Select content, right-click selected content, point to CSS Styles on context menu, click New on CSS Styles submenu

To Add a Background, Border, and Text Color to a Table

Adding a background, border, and text color to the tables is your next goal. To accomplish this, you use the Type, Background, and Border categories in the CSS Style Definition dialog box. The following steps show how to select a font, a background color of maroon, and a shade of tan for the border.

1

- Click in the first cell of the monument_ images table.

- To select the table, click the <table#spotlight> tag in the tag selector.

- Click the New CSS Rule button in the CSS Styles panel to open the New CSS Rule dialog box.

- Click the Selector Type arrow, and then click Tag (redefines an HTML element).

- If necessary, type table in the Selector name text box (Figure 5–57).

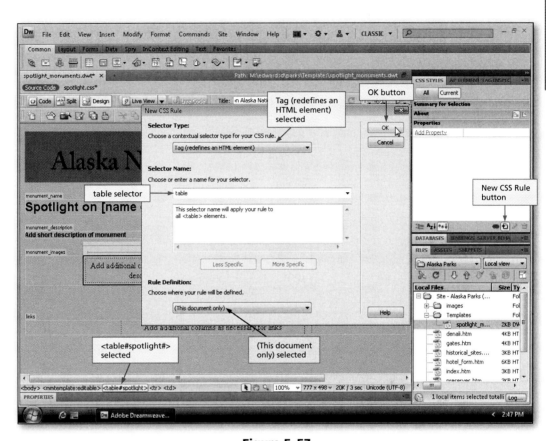

Figure 5–57

2

- Click the OK button to display the CSS Rule dialog box.

- Verify that the Type category is selected (Figure 5–58).

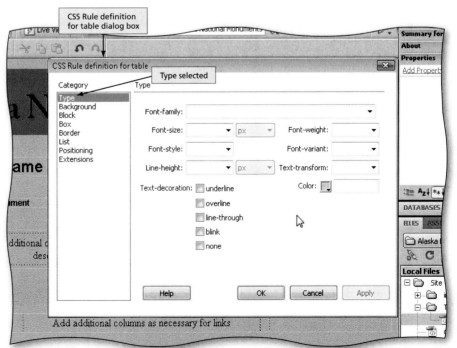

Figure 5–58

3

- Click the Font-family box arrow and then click Arial, Helvetica, sans-serif.

- Click the Color text box, type #000, and then press the TAB key to display the font and selected color (Figure 5–59).

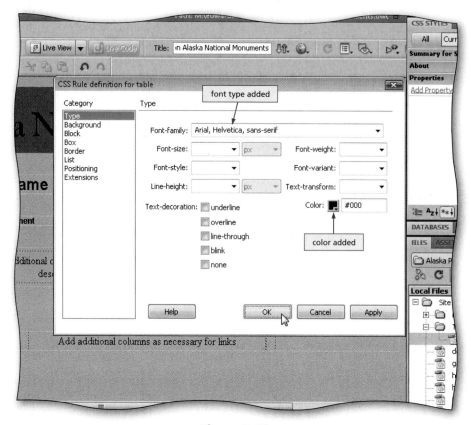

Figure 5–59

4

- Click Background in the Category list to display the Background properties.

- Click the Background-color text box, type #546C8E as the color, and then press the TAB key to display the background color in the Background color box. Click the Apply button (Figure 5–60).

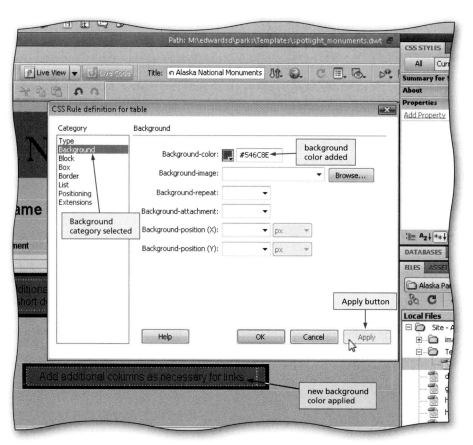

Figure 5–60

⑤

- Click Border in the Category list to display the Border properties.

- Verify that the Same for all check boxes are selected for Style, Width, and Color.

- Click the Top box arrow and then click groove.

- Click the first Width box arrow and then click thick.

- Click the first text box in the Color area and then type #000 for the border color.

- Press the TAB key to define the attributes (Figure 5–61).

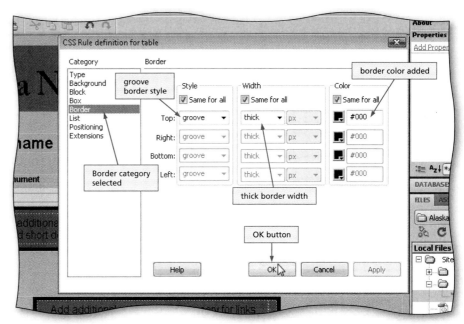

Figure 5–61

⑥

- Click the OK button and then click in the first table.

- Click <table#spotlight> in the tag selector to select the spotlight table.

- If necessary, drag the panels below the CSS Styles panel to display the Summary for Selection, the About "border" section, and the Properties for "table" section (Figure 5–62).

⑦

- Click the Save button on the Standard toolbar.

Q&A How do I access a full view of the attributes in the CSS Styles panel second column?

Expand the panel groups. Move the pointer over the vertical bar until it turns into a two-headed arrow and then drag to the left.

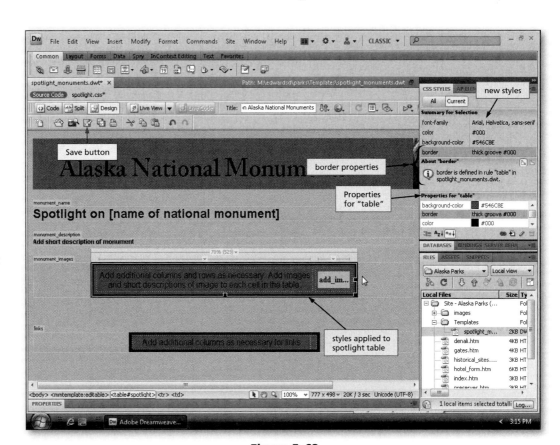

Figure 5–62

Style Sheets and Links

When you selected the <table> tag for the monument_images table and applied the attributes, you added the attributes to all tables in the template. Now you will add two links to the links table — a relative link to the Alaska National Monuments index Web page and an absolute link to the Aniakchak National Monument page.

<table>
<tr><td>Plan
Ahead</td><td>

Using Style Sheets to Display Links

Style sheets provide new ways to display links, which enable the content developer to match the style of the links with that of the rest of the Web page. When you are defining the style for links, you can apply the following four attributes:

- **Link color** defines the style of an unvisited link.
- **Visited links** defines the style of a link to a Web site that you have visited.
- **Rollover links** defines the style of a link when the mouse pointer moves over the link.
- **Active links** defines the style of a clicked link.

</td></tr>
</table>

BTW

Browsers and Style Sheets
In some cases, Internet Explorer and Mosaic Firefox interpret some style sheet commands differently. Be sure to view your Web pages in these two browsers and as many other browsers as possible.

Using the Page Properties dialog box, you can specify that the links will use white for the text color and will not contain an underline when displayed in the browser. The Underline style within the Page Properties dialog box provides options to Always underline, Never underline, Show underline only on rollover, and Hide underline on rollover. The default setting for regular text is none. The default setting for links is Always underline. You also can specify that when the mouse pointer rolls over a link, the underline is displayed. This indicates to the Web page visitor that the link is available.

To Modify the A:Link Attribute

The following steps show how to add the attributes for formatting the links as the browser will display them.

1
- Collapse the panel groups to icons.

- Click the title bar of the Property inspector to display it, click outside the spotlight table, and then click the CSS button in the Property inspector to display the CSS properties.

- Scroll down, and then click anywhere in the links table (Figure 5–63).

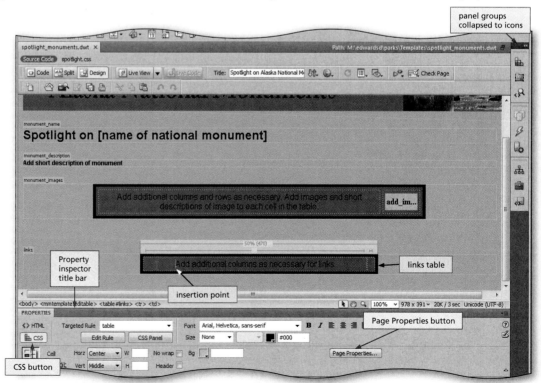

Figure 5–63

2

- Click the Page Properties button to open the Page Properties dialog box, and then click the Links (CSS) category (Figure 5–64).

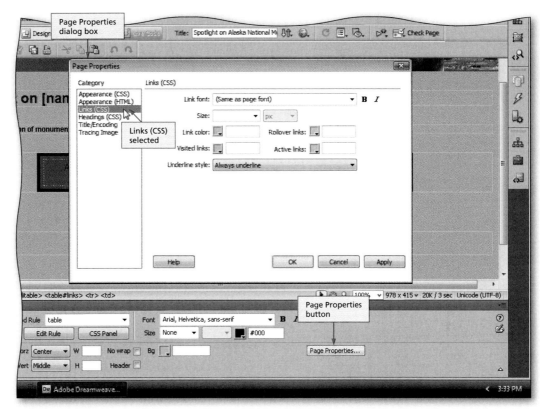

Figure 5–64

3

- Click the Link color box and then point to white (#FFF) (Figure 5–65).

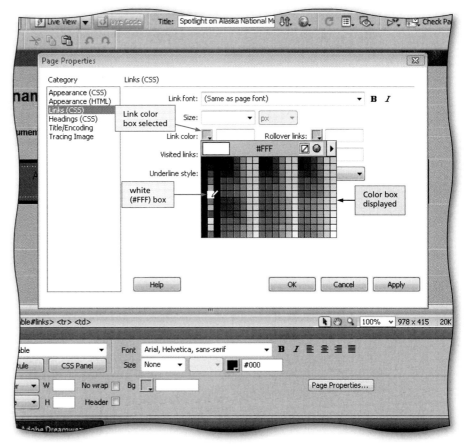

Figure 5–65

- Click white to add the color (Figure 5–66).

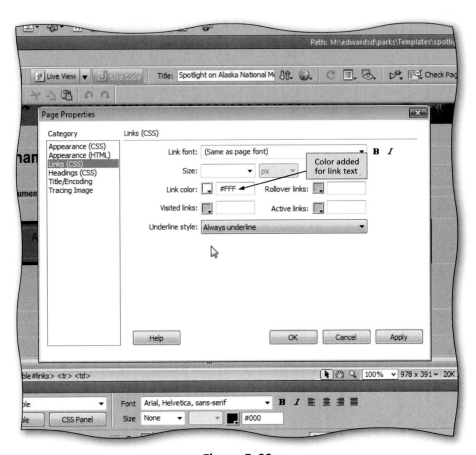

Figure 5–66

- Click the Rollover links color box and then click yellow (#FF0).

- Click the Visited links color box and then click red (#F00).

- Click the Active links color box and then click white (#FFF).

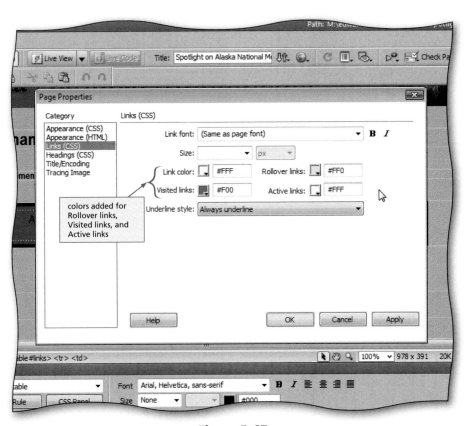

Figure 5–67

6

- Click the Underline style arrow and select Hide underline on rollover (Figure 5–68).

How can I remove a style?

To remove a style from an element on a Web page, select the element and then click the Delete CSS Rule button in the CSS Styles panel.

7

- Click the OK button to add the link attribute to the template.

- Click the Save button on the Standard toolbar to save your changes.

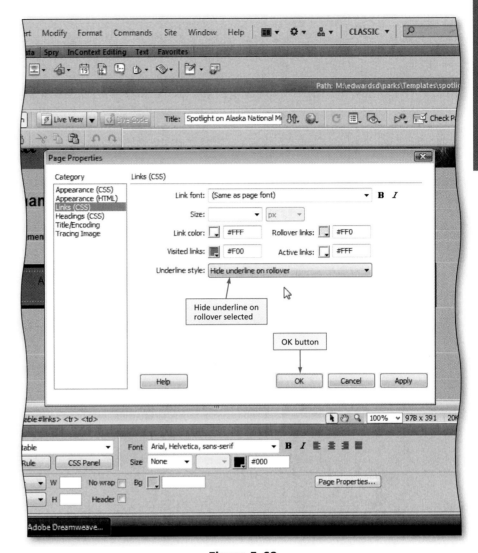

Figure 5–68

Plan
Ahead

Maintaining Style Sheets

After a style is created, you can edit, delete, or duplicate it. You apply these commands using buttons at the bottom of the CSS Styles panel.

- **Current button**: When the Current button is selected, you can view the CSS rules that relate to the currently selected element.

- **All button**: When the All button is selected, the panel displays CSS rules that relate to the full document. Figure 5–69 shows an expanded view of the CSS panel with the All button selected. In Figure 5–69, for example, the properties you applied to the table are displayed. Note that Current mode contains three panes — Summary for Selection, Rules, and Properties.

  You can change any of these properties either in All view or Current view. Select the property and then click the Edit Rule button to display the CSS Rule Definition dialog box. Make your changes and then click the OK button.

  Below the Properties pane are three buttons that you can use to change the view in the Properties pane:

- **Show Category View button**: Clicking the Show Category View button divides the CSS properties into categories. Double-clicking the property opens a box to the right of the selected text. Clicking the arrow in the box provides a list of properties that can be applied to the selected property.

- **Show List View button**: The Show List View button displays all Dreamweaver CSS properties in alphabetical order.

- **Set Properties View button**: Set Properties View (default view) displays only set properties.

Figure 5–69

Creating a Web Page from a Template

After you create and save a template, you can use it to create a Web page. All the pages created from a template contain the same content as appears in the noneditable regions of the template. Content developers and others can change the content in the editable regions.

To Create the Aniakchak National Monument Spotlight Web Page

Now that you have created the template, and added styles to it, you are ready to use the template to create the Aniakchak National Monument Spotlight Web page.

1

- Close the spotlight_ monuments.dwt file. Expand the panel groups.

Q&A

What should I do if a Dreamweaver dialog box appears and asks whether to save changes to spotlight.css?

Click Yes to save any changes.

- Click File on the Application bar and then click New.

- Click Blank Page in the New Document dialog box, verify that HTML is selected in the Page Type column, and then click the Create button.

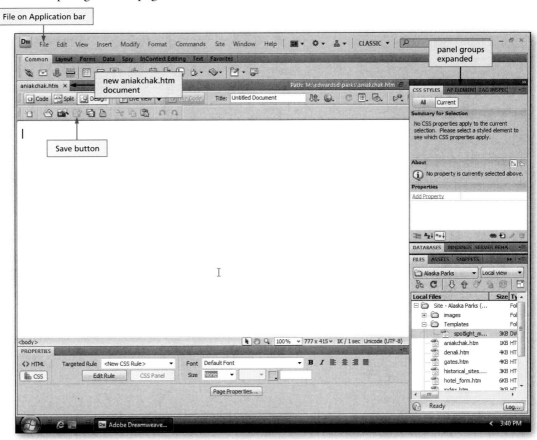

Figure 5–70

- Click the Save button on the Standard toolbar and then save the page in the parks folder. Use aniakchak.htm as the file name (Figure 5–70).

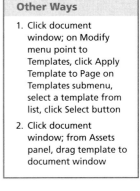

Other Ways

1. Click document window; on Modify menu point to Templates, click Apply Template to Page on Templates submenu, select a template from list, click Select button

2. Click document window; from Assets panel, drag template to document window

To Apply a Template to the Aniakchak National Monument Web Page

To apply a template to a document, you use the Assets panel. The following steps illustrate how to display the Assets panel and apply the template to the Aniakchak National Monument Web page.

- Double-click the CSS Styles tab to collapse the panel.

- Click the Assets panel tab in the Files group panel.

- Click the Templates icon in the Assets panel.

- Click spotlight_monuments to select the template (Figure 5–71).

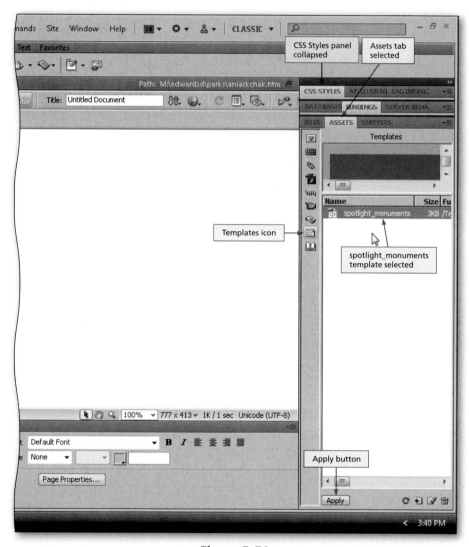

Figure 5–71

- Click the Apply button to apply the template.

- Collapse the panel groups (Figure 5-72).

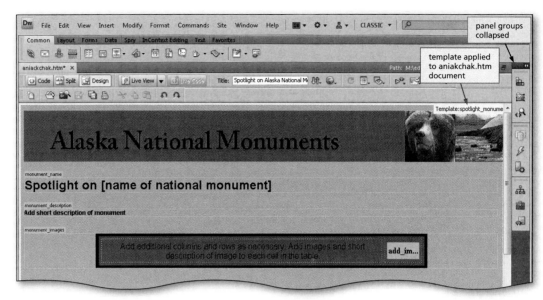

Figure 5-72

To Add the Monument Name and Monument Description to the Aniakchak National Monument Web Page

Now you use the template to create the Aniakchak National Monument Web page. You first add the name of the monument and then add a short description of the monument. The following steps show how to add the monument name and monument description.

1

- If necessary, click anywhere on the document. Move the mouse pointer over the page and note that in the noneditable sections, such as the logo image, the pointer changes to a circle with a line through the middle.

- Select the text and brackets, [name of national monument], in the monument_name editable region (Figure 5-73).

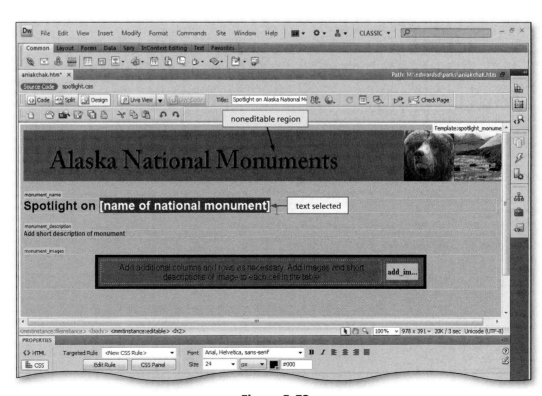

Figure 5-73

• Type Aniakchak
National
Monument as the
monument name
(Figure 5–74).

Figure 5–74

• Select the prompt,
Add short descrip-
tion of monument,
in the monument_
description editable
region.

• Type the following
text: Aniakchak
Caldera is six
miles across and
3,000 feet deep.
The area
originally was a
7,000 foot
mountain. The
caldera was
created by a
volcanic eruption
approximately
3,500 years ago,
which caused the
mountain to
collapse.
(Figure 5–75).

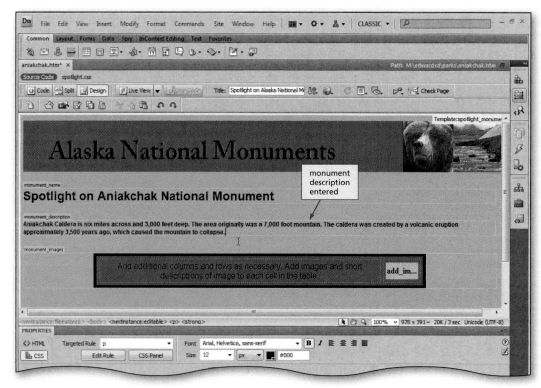

Figure 5–75

The Aniakchak National Monument Web page table will contain six images in three rows and two columns. The monument_images editable table currently contains only one row and two columns.

To Add Rows to the Monument_images Table

The following steps show how to add two additional rows.

1

- Click in the left cell of the monument_images table.

- Click Modify on the Application bar, point to Table, and then point to Insert Rows or Columns to highlight the command (Figure 5–76).

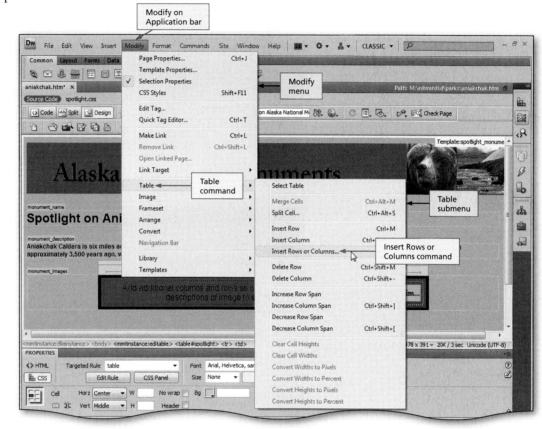

Figure 5–76

2

- Click Insert Rows or Columns to display the Insert Rows or Columns dialog box (Figure 5–77).

Q&A

The settings in my dialog box are different from those in Figure 5–77. Is that a problem?

No. The number of rows displayed may be different on your screen.

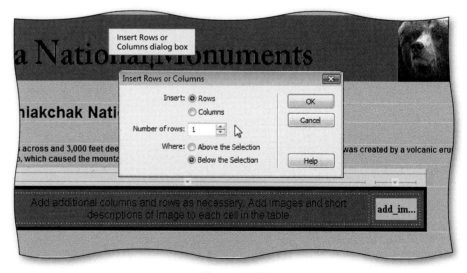

Figure 5–77

• Double-click the Number of rows text box and then type 2 for the number of rows (Figure 5–78).

• Click the OK button to add the two rows to the monument_images table.

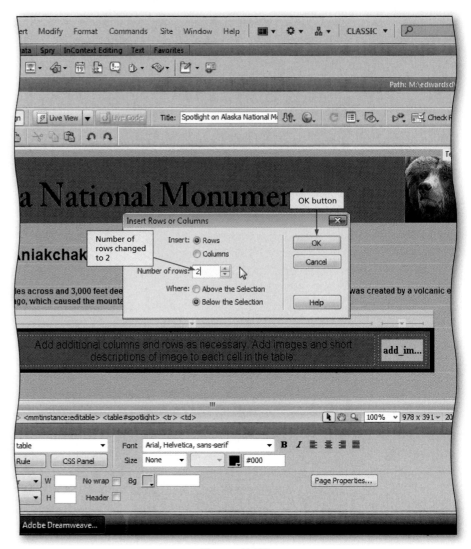

Figure 5–78

Expanded Tables Mode

Inserting an image into a table cell and then clicking to the right or left of the image is somewhat awkward in Dreamweaver. Recall that you used Expanded Tables mode in Chapter 3 to add cell padding and spacing temporarily to all tables in a document and increase the tables' borders to make editing easier. Expanded Tables mode enables you to select items in tables or precisely place the insertion point. You return to Standard mode when you finish adding images and text to the table.

To Add Images to the Monument_images Table

To add an image, you drag the image from the Assets panel to a table cell. You use Expanded Tables mode to assist with insertion point placement. You add a <br> tag by holding down the SHIFT key and pressing the ENTER key. Then you type the image description.

The following steps illustrate how to add the six images and a short description of each image.

1

- Click the title bar on the Property inspector to collapse it.

- Expand the panel groups to display the Assets tab.

- Select the text in row 1, column 1 of the monument_ images table and then press the DELETE key to delete the placeholder text.

- Click the Layout tab on the Insert bar, and then click the Expanded button to switch to Expanded Tables mode (Figure 5–79).

Q&A

What should I do if a Getting Started in Expanded Tables Mode dialog box is displayed?

Read the information and then click the OK button.

- Click the Images icon in the Assets panel.

- Drag the aniak01.jpg file to row 1, column 1 of the monument_images table.

- Click to the right of the image (Figure 5–80).

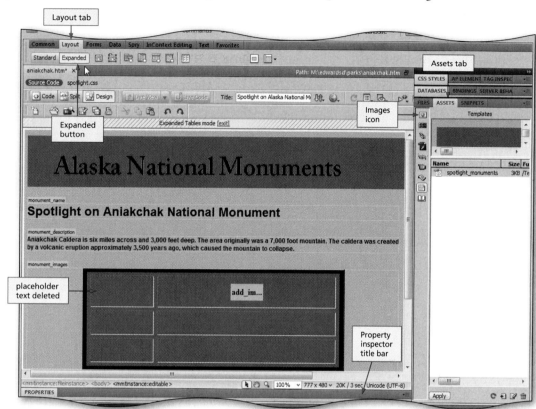

Figure 5–79

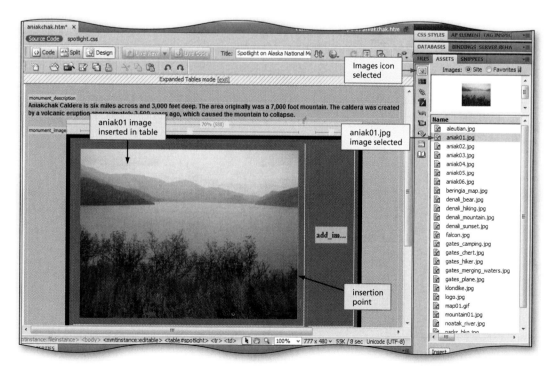

Figure 5–80

2

- Hold down the SHIFT key and then press the ENTER key to insert a line break.

- Type Smoky morning as the description (Figure 5–81).

Q&A Where is the insertion point?

You may not see the insertion point until you begin typing.

Figure 5–81

- Press the TAB key to move the insertion point to row 1, column 2 to select the image placeholder (Figure 5–82).

Figure 5–82

3

- Press the DELETE key to delete the image placeholder and then drag the aniak02.jpg file to the cell.

- Click to the right of the image.

- Hold down the SHIFT key and then press the ENTER key to insert a line break.

- Type Riverside as the description (Figure 5–83).

Figure 5–83

4

- Add the four other images and descriptions to the monument_images table as indicated in Table 5–2 on the next page (Figure 5–84).

 Q&A

How should I add the four other images and descriptions?

Scrolling as necessary, drag each image to the appropriate table cell, click to the right of the image, hold down SHIFT and press the ENTER key, and then type the description. Press the TAB key to move from cell to cell.

Figure 5–84

• Collapse the panel groups, and then click the title bar of the Property inspector to expand it.

• Click each image and add the Alt text for each image as listed in Table 5–3 (Figure 5–85).

Figure 5–85

Table 5–2 Aniakchak Monument Image File Names and Descriptions		
Cell	**Image**	**Image Description**
Row 1, Column 1	aniak01.jpg	Smoky morning
Row 1, Column 2	aniak02.jpg	Riverside
Row 2, Column 1	aniak03.jpg	Salmon fishing
Row 2, Column 2	aniak04.jpg	River cabin
Row 3, Column 1	aniak05.jpg	Brown bear
Row 3, Column 2	aniak06.jpg	Caldera

Table 5–3 Aniakchak Monument	
Image	**Alt Text**
aniak01.jpg	Aniakchak smoky morning
aniak02.jpg	Aniakchak riverside
aniak03.jpg	Aniakchak salmon
aniak04.jpg	Aniakchak river cabin
aniak05.jpg	Aniakchak brown bear
aniak06.jpg	Aniakchak caldera

To complete the Aniakchak National Monument Web page, you add two links in the links table. The first link is a relative link to the Alaska National Parks index page. The second link is an absolute link to the Aniakchak National Monument Web page.

Thus far, when creating links, you used the default and did not specify a target. The target for your links, therefore, has been to open the linked document in the same browser window.

When you create the link to the Aniakchak National Monument Web page, however, the page opens in a new browser window. Recall from Chapter 2 that the Target option in the Property inspector specifies the frame or window in which the linked page is displayed. When the _blank target is specified, the linked document opens in a new browser window. The other three choices in the Target option are _parent, _self, and _top. These options are discussed in detail in Chapter 7, when you create a framed Web site.

To Add Links to the Links Table and to Add Image Borders

The following steps show how to add the two links to the links table and how to add borders to the images.

1
- If necessary, scroll down to display the links table. Select the text in the left cell of the links table and then press the DELETE key to delete all of the text from the cell (Figure 5–86).

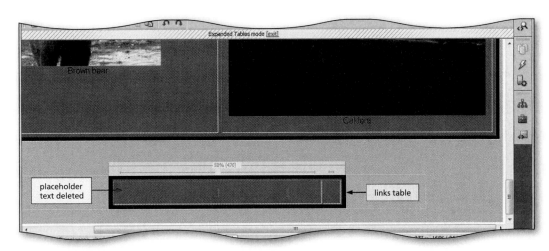

Figure 5–86

2
- Type Home as the text link in the left cell and then select the text.

- In the Property inspector, click the HTML button and then click the Link text box.

- Type index.htm as the link, and then press the TAB key to add the link to the home page and center it in the cell.

- Click anywhere in the Home link to deselect the text (Figure 5–87).

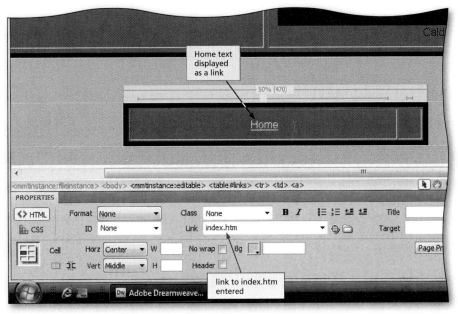

Figure 5–87

3

- Click the right cell in the links table. Type Aniakchak National Monument as the text for the link and then select the text.

- Click the Link text box in the Property inspector and then type http://www.nps.gov/ania/index.htm as the entry.

- Click the Target box arrow and select _blank.

- Click anywhere in the links table to deselect the text (Figure 5–88).

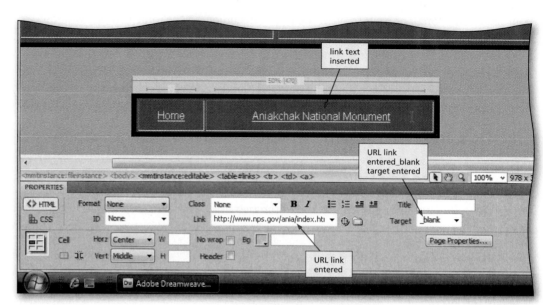

Figure 5–88

Q&A What will happen when a user clicks the Aniakchak National Monument link?

The linked page will open in a new window when the link is clicked.

4

- Exit the Expanded Tables mode.

- Scroll to the top of the page and select the Smoky morning image.

- Click the Border box in the Property inspector and type 4 to add a border.

- Press the TAB key to apply the border, and then click anywhere in the monument images table to deselect the Smoky morning image (Figure 5–89).

Figure 5–89

- Select each of the other images and apply a 4 pixel border, and then resize each image so it has a Width of 375 pixels and a Height of 285 pixels.

- Click the Save button and then view the page in your browser (Figure 5–90).

6

- Close the browser window.

Figure 5–90

To Add a Link from the Index Page to the Aniakchak National Monument Page

The following steps illustrate how to complete the update of the Alaska Parks Web site by adding a link from the index page to the Aniakchak National Monument page.

1

- Expand the panel groups and then click the Files tab.

- Open the index.htm page.

- Scroll down, and then click to the right of the Alaska National Historical Sites link in the links table, press the SPACEBAR, and then insert a vertical line.

- Select the space and line you just typed, and then delete the historical_sites.htm text in the Link box if necessary, to make sure the previous link does not continue to the new one.

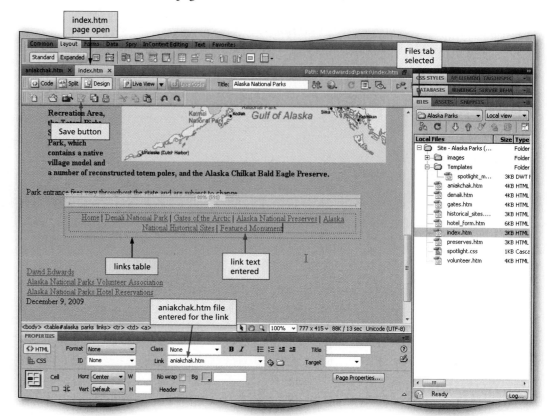

Figure 5–91

- Insert a space after the vertical line, and then type Featured Monument as the link text.

- Select the text and then drag aniakchak.htm from the Files panel to the Property inspector Link text box.

- Click the Save button on the Standard toolbar, and then press the right arrow key to deselect the text (Figure 5–91).

2

- Press the F12 key to preview the index.htm page in your browser.

- Scroll down and then click the Featured Monument link to view the Aniakchak National Monument Web page.

- Verify that the Aniakchak National Monument Web page links work.

- If instructed to do so, print a copy of the Aniakchak National Monument Web page and submit it to your instructor.

- If instructed to do so, upload your Web site to a remote server.

Q&A

How do I upload the Web site to a remote server?

Appendix C contains information on uploading to a remote server. A remote folder is required before you can upload to a remote server. Generally, the remote folder is defined by the Web server administrator or your instructor.

- Close the browser.

Quitting Dreamweaver

After you have created your Web page based on a template with applied styles, and tested and verified that the links work, Chapter 5 is complete.

To Close the Web Site and Quit Dreamweaver

The following step shows how to close the Web site, quit Dreamweaver CS4, and return control to Windows.

- Click the Close button on the upper-right corner of the Dreamweaver title bar to close the Dreamweaver window, the document window, and the Alaska National Parks Web site.

- If you have unsaved changes, click the Yes button in response to the Dreamweaver prompt.

CSS Style Definition Category Descriptions

The following tables list the attributes and descriptions of the eight categories available through the CSS Rule Definition dialog box. Not all browsers support all properties; browser support is indicated in the Description column. The phrase "both browsers" refers to Microsoft Internet Explorer and Netscape Navigator.

Table 5–4 CSS Style Type Properties	
Attributes	**Description**
Font-family	Sets the font family for the style. Supported by both browsers.
Font-size	Defines the size of the text. Enter or select a number and then select a unit of measurement. Selecting pixels prevents Web site visitors from adjusting the text size in their Web browsers. Supported by both browsers.
Font-weight	Defines the thickness of the font. Thirteen different choices are available; normal and bold are the most common and work in all browsers that support CSS.
Font-style	Specifies normal, italic, or oblique as the font style. Supported by both browsers.
Font-variant	Specifies small-caps or normal. Dreamweaver does not display this attribute in the Document window. Not supported by Netscape Navigator.
Line-height	Refers to the amount of space between lines of text; also called leading. Normal allows the line height for the font size to be calculated automatically. Supported by both browsers.
Text-transform	Capitalizes the first letter of each word in the selection or sets the text to all uppercase or lowercase. Supported by both browsers.
Text-decoration	Adds an underline, overline, or line-through to the text, or makes the text blink. Supported by both browsers.
Color	Sets the text color. Supported by both browsers.

Table 5–5 CSS Style Background Properties

Attributes	Description
Background-color	Sets the background color for an element — a character, a word, a paragraph, or even the Web page itself. Supported by both browsers.
Background-image	Adds a background image to either a Web page or a table. Supported by both browsers.
Background-repeat	Repeats the background image. Supported by both browsers.
Background-attachment	Determines whether the background image is fixed at its original position or scrolls along with the content. Not supported by Netscape Navigator.
Background-position (X)	Specifies a position for selected text or other Web page elements. Can be used to align a background.
Background-position (Y)	image to the center of the page, both vertically and horizontally, or to align the element relative to the Document window. Not supported by Netscape Navigator.

Table 5–6 CSS Style Block Properties

Attributes	Description
Word-spacing	Sets the spacing between words; not displayed in the document window. The bigger the number, the more space between the words. Supported by both browsers.
Letter-spacing	Sets the spacing between letters or characters. Supported by both browsers.
Vertical-align	Specifies the vertical alignment of the element to which it is applied. Is displayed in the document window only when applied to an image. Supported by both browsers.
Text-align	Sets the text alignment within the element. Supported by both browsers.
Text-indent	Specifies the amount of space the first line of text is indented. Supported by both browsers.
White-space	Determines how the browser displays extra white space. Supported by Netscape Navigator and Internet Explorer 5.5 and higher.
Display	Specifies whether an element is displayed, and, if so, how it is displayed. Supported by both browsers.

Table 5–7 CSS Style Box Properties

Attributes	Description
Width and Height	Sets the width and height of an element. Supported by both browsers.
Float	Sets which side other elements, such as text, layers, and tables, will float around an element. Supported by both browsers.
Clear	Prevents an element from wrapping around an object with a right or left float. Supported by both browsers.
Padding	Specifies the amount of space between the content of an element and its border (or margin if there is no border). Supported by both browsers.
Margin	Specifies the amount of space between the border of an element (or the padding if there is no border) and another element. Supported by both browsers.
Same for All	Sets the same padding or margin attributes to the Top, Right, Bottom, and Left of the Padding and element to which it is applied. Supported by both browsers.

Table 5–8 CSS Style Border Properties

Attributes	Description
Style	Sets the style appearance of the border. Appearance may be rendered differently in different browsers. Supported by both browsers.
Width	Sets the thickness of the element. Supported by both browsers.
Color	Sets the color of the border. Supported by both browsers.
Same For All	Applies the same style, thickness, or color to the Top, Bottom, Right, and Left of the element to which it is applied. Supported by both browsers.

Table 5–9 CSS Style List Properties

Attributes	Description
List-style-type	Sets the appearance of bullets or numbers. Supported by both browsers.
List-style-image	Specifies a custom image for the bullet. Supported by both browsers.
List-style-Position	Sets whether list item text wraps and indents (outside) or whether the text wraps to the left margin (inside). Supported by both browsers.

Table 5–10 CSS Style Positioning Properties (Used with AP Elements)

Attributes	Description
Type	Determines how the browser should position the element (absolute, relative, fixed, or static). Supported by both browsers.
Visibility	Determines the initial display condition of the layer. Supported by both browsers.
Width	Sets the width of the layer. Supported by both browsers.
Z-Index	Determines the stacking order of the layer. Supported by both browsers.
Height	Sets the height of the layer. Supported by both browsers.
Overflow	Determines what happens if the content of a layer exceeds its size. CSS layers only.
Placement	Specifies the location and size of the layer (Left, Top, Right, or Bottom). Supported by both browsers.
Clip	Defines the part of the layer that is visible (Left, Top, Right, or Bottom). Supported by both browsers.

Table 5–11 CSS Style Extension Properties

Attributes	Description
Page break (before and after)	Creates a page break during printing either before or after the object controlled by the style. Supported by both browsers.
Visual effect (Cursor and Filter)	Cursor changes the pointer image when the pointer is over the object controlled by style. Supported by both browsers. Filter applies special effects to the object controlled by the style. Supported by both browsers.

Chapter Summary

In this chapter, you learned about templates and style sheets. You created a template document, and then defined editable and noneditable regions on the page. You designed the template by adding a logo, text, and table for images and links. You also created a style sheet and added a style to it. You created a new Web page based on the template, added images and links to the tables, and then tested the links on the new page. The items listed below include all the new skills you have learned in this chapter.

1. Create a New Template Document (DW 350)
2. Save the Web Page as a Template (DW 351)
3. Add the Monument Name and Monument Description Prompts for the First Two Editable Regions (DW 357)
4. Add and Center a Table as the Third Editable Region (DW 359)
5. Add and Center a Table as the Fourth Editable Region (DW 364)
6. Create the First Editable Region (DW 366)
7. Create the Second Editable Region (DW 368)
8. Create the Third and Fourth Editable Regions (DW 370)
9. Display the CSS Styles Panel (DW 374)
10. Add a Style and Save the Style Sheet (DW 377)
11. Create a Style for the Paragraph Text (DW 380)
12. Modify the A:Link Attribute (DW 386)
13. Apply a Template to the Aniakchak National Monument Web Page (DW 392)

Learn It Online

Test your knowledge of chapter content and key terms.

Instructions: To complete the Learn It Online exercises, start your browser, click the Address bar, and then enter the Web address scsite.com/dwCS4/learn. When the Dreamweaver CS4 Learn It Online page is displayed, click the link for the exercise you want to complete and then read the instructions.

Chapter Reinforcement TF, MC, and SA
A series of true/false, multiple choice, and short answer questions that test your knowledge of the chapter content.

Flash Cards
An interactive learning environment where you identify chapter key terms associated with displayed definitions.

Practice Test
A series of multiple choice questions that test your knowledge of chapter content and key terms.

Who Wants To Be a Computer Genius?
An interactive game that challenges your knowledge of chapter content in the style of a television quiz show.

Wheel of Terms
An interactive game that challenges your knowledge of chapter key terms in the style of the television show *Wheel of Fortune*.

Crossword Puzzle Challenge
A crossword puzzle that challenges your knowledge of key terms presented in the chapter.

Apply Your Knowledge

Reinforce the skills and apply the concepts you learned in this chapter.

Create a Template and Apply It to a Web Page

Instructions: In this activity, you add a background color and some text to a template and then apply the template to a Web page (Figure 5–92 and Figure 5–93 on the next page).

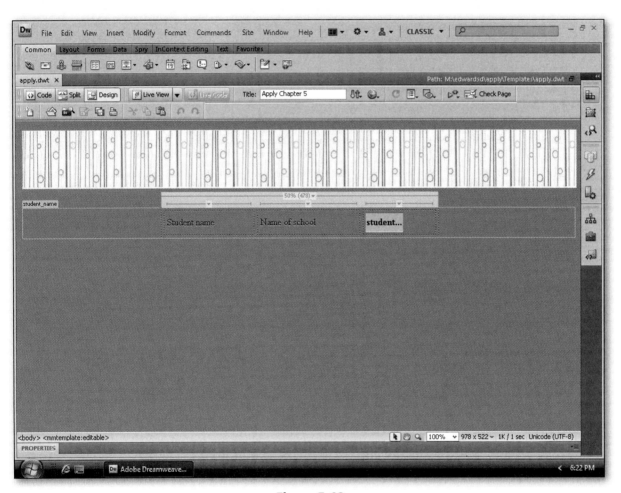

Figure 5–92

Continued >

Apply Your Knowledge *continued*

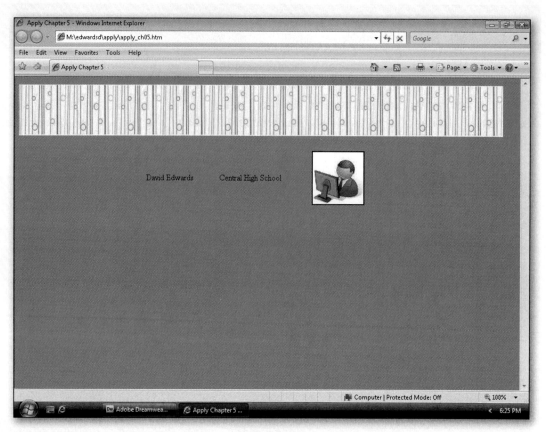

Figure 5–93

Perform the following tasks:

1. Start Dreamweaver and open the Apply Exercises Web site. Copy the apply data files to the images folder for your Apply Exercises Web site.

2. Create a blank HTML template, and then save it as a template named apply.dwt.

3. Modify page properties by applying #09F as the background color.

4. Insert the banner.jpg image at the top of the template page.

5. Insert a one-row, three-column table with a width of 50 percent, cell padding of 5, and cell spacing of 5.

6. Center the table.

7. Type Student name in the first cell and Name of school in the second cell.

8. Add an image placeholder named student to the third cell. Resize the placeholder to 64 (W) by 32 (H) pixels.

9. Select the table, click Insert on the Application bar, point to Template Objects, and then click Editable Region.

10. Name the editable region student_name.

11. Title the template document Apply Chapter 5, and then save the template (Figure 5–92 on the previous page).

12. Create a new blank document and save it as apply_ch05.htm.

13. Apply the template to the new page.

14. Type your name in the Student name column and the name of your school in the Name of school column.

15. Insert the student_female.jpg or student_male.jpg image in the third column. Resize the image to 100 (W) by 100 (H) pixels, and add a 2-pixel border to the image.

16. Save the document and then view it in your browser (Figure 5–93).

Extend Your Knowledge

Extend the skills you learned in this chapter and experiment with new skills. You may need to use Help to complete the assignment.

Creating a Template

Instructions: In this activity, you create a template with a background, a table, and text, and then apply styles to a Web page (Figure 5–94). Make sure you have downloaded the data files provided for this exercise.

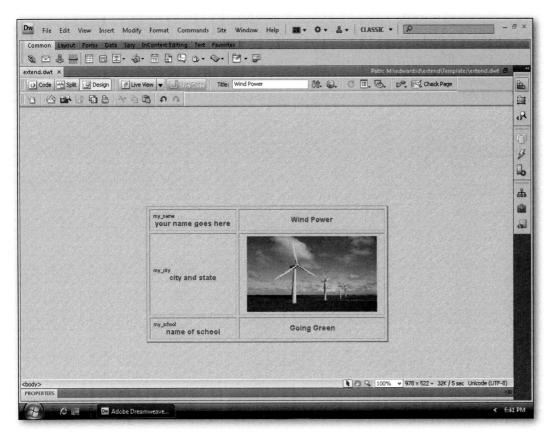

Figure 5–94

Perform the following tasks:

1. If necessary, start Dreamweaver and then open the Extend Exercises Web site. Copy the extend data files to the images folder for your Extend Exercises Web site.

2. Create a blank HTML template page and save it as a template named extend.dwt.

3. Add the extend_bkg image as the background image for the template.

4. Press ENTER five times and then insert a three-row, two-column table with a width of 50 percent, 5 for cell padding and cell spacing, and a border of 2 pixels.

5. Center the table.

6. Click row 1, column 1, and then type the following text: your name goes here.

7. Click row 2, column 1, and then type the following text: city and state.

8. Click row 3, column 1, and then type the following text: name of school.

9. Click row 1, column 2 and then type the following text: Wind Power.

Continued >

Extend Your Knowledge *continued*

10. Drag the wind.jpg image to the row 2, column 2. Center the image. Change the W value for the image to 258, and change the H value to 145.

11. Click row 3, column 2, and then type the following text: Going Green.

12. Select row 1, column 1, and make it an editable region named my_name.

13. Select row 2, column 1, and make it an editable region named my_city.

14. Select row 3, column 1, and make it an editable region named my_school.

15. Select the table. Click Modify on the Application bar, and then select Page Properties.

16. In the Appearance (CSS) category, select Arial, Helvetica, sans-serif for the Page font and 14 for the Size. Enter #060 for the text color, and then apply the settings to the template.

17. Bold all the text in the table, and then center the text.

18. Title the template document Wind Power.

19. Save the template, and then submit it in the format specified by your instructor.

Make It Right

Analyze a Web page template and correct all errors and/or improve the design.

Modifying a Template

Instructions: In this activity, you modify a template and add your name and the name of a raffle item to a Web page (Figure 5–95). Make sure you have downloaded the data files provided for this exercise.

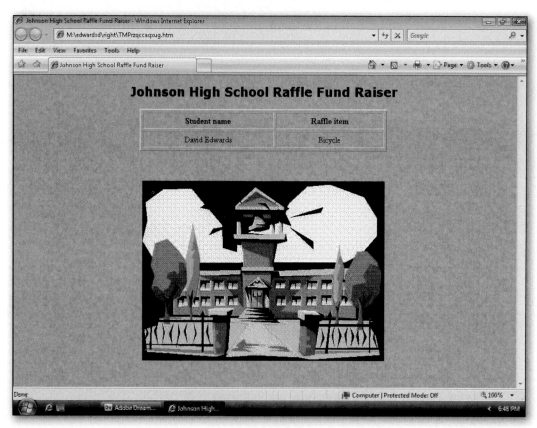

Figure 5–95

Perform the following tasks:

1. If necessary, start Dreamweaver and then open the Right Exercises Web site.

2. In the Right Exercises Web site, create a new folder and name it Templates. Copy the right.dwt file into the Templates folder.

3. Open the right.dwt template.

4. Center the table. Change the width to 50 percent and the cell padding and cell spacing to 5. Apply a 2 px border. Name the table student_name.

5. In row 2, column 1, type [Enter your first and last name]. Make that text an editable region named student.

6. In row 2, column 2, type [Enter your raffle item]. Make that text an editable region named raffle_item.

7. Center the text in the table.

8. Insert the school.gif image from your images folder two lines below the table. Center the image on the page.

9. Save the template.

10. Create a new HTML page named right_ch05.htm, and then apply the template to the new page.

11. Select the placeholder text in the first column in the table and then type your name.

12. Select the placeholder text in the second column in the table and then type Bicycle.

13. Save your document and then view it in your browser.

14. Submit your Web page in the format specified by your instructor.

In the Lab

Create a document using the guidelines, concepts, and skills presented in this chapter. Labs are listed in order of increasing difficulty.

Lab 1: Creating a Template and Style Sheet for Bryan's Mobile Pet Services Web Site

Problem: The proprietors of Bryan's Mobile Pet Services would like to add a page to their Web site that features different breeds of dogs. They want something that can be modified easily, so they plan to use a template used. To create this template and then add styles, you copy five images from the pets folder provided with your data files to the Pet Services Web site images folder. You begin the process by creating a template, and then you define styles. When this is completed, you apply this template to a new blank page and create a page for breeds of dogs. Finally, you add a link to and from the Bryan's Pet Mobile Pet Services home page.

The template is shown in Figure 5–96 on the next page; the Web page is shown in Figure 5–97 on the next page. Software and hardware settings determine how a Web page is displayed in a browser. Your Web pages may display differently than the ones shown in Figures 5–96 and 5–97. Appendix C contains instructions for uploading your local site to a remote server.

Continued >

STUDENT ASSIGNMENTS

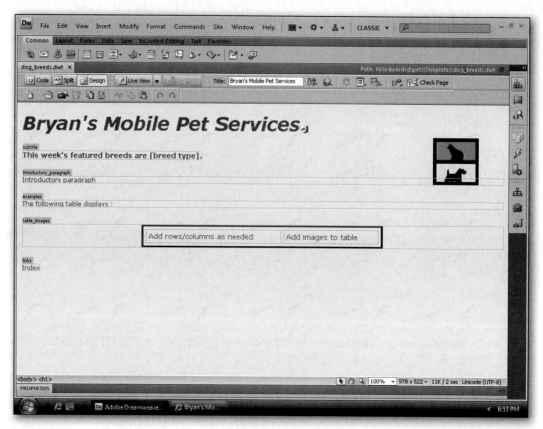

Figure 5–96

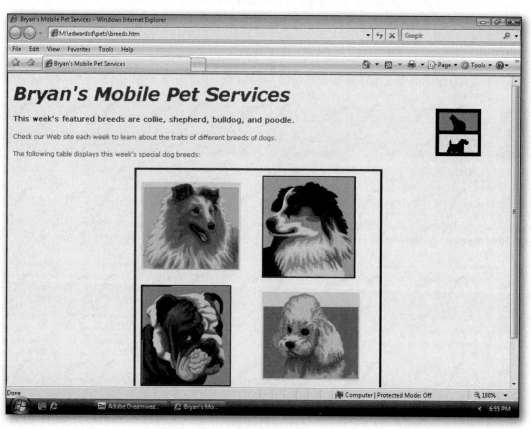

Figure 5–97

Perform the following tasks:

1. If necessary, start Dreamweaver and then open the Pet Services Web site. Copy the pets data files to the images folder for your Pet Services Web site.

2. Create a blank HTML template. Save it as a template named dog_breeds.dwt.

3. Apply the pets_bkg.jpg image, which can be found in the images folder, to the background of the page.

4. Click the upper-left corner of the document window. Type Bryan's Mobile Pet Services as the heading, and then press ENTER.

5. Select the heading and apply Heading 1.

6. Below the heading, type the following text: This week's featured breeds are [breed type]. Apply Heading 3 and then press the ENTER key.

7. Type Introductory paragraph and then press the ENTER key.

8. Type The following table displays: and then press the ENTER key.

9. Insert a one-row, two-column table with a width of 50 percent, border of 0, cell padding of 5, and cell spacing of 5. In cell 1, type Add rows/columns as needed and type Add images to table in cell 2. Center-align the table.

10. Click to the right of the table in the document window, press the ENTER key, and then type Index.

11. Drag the logo.jpg image to the right of the "Bryan's Mobile Pet Services" heading. If necessary, select the image. Set a V Space of 4 and H Space of 50. Type pet services logo as the Alt text. Right-align the logo.jpg image.

12. Using the Editable Region command on the Templates pop-up menu, create the five editable regions indicated in Table 5–12 on the next page.

13. Click the CSS Styles button in the Property inspector, if necessary, to display the CSS properties. Double-click the CSS Styles tab in the panel group, if necessary, to display the CSS Styles panel.

14. Click anywhere in the heading, Bryan's Mobile Pet Services, and then click the <h1> tag in the tag selector. Click the New CSS Rule button in the CSS Styles panel. In the New CSS Rule dialog box, select Tag (redefines an HTML element), h1, and (This document only) as necessary, and then click the OK button. In the CSS Rule definition for h1 dialog box, set the following values in the Type category: Verdana, Geneva, sans-serif for the Font-family; 36 pixels for the Font-size; bolder for the Font-weight; oblique for the Font-style; and #336633 (a dark green) for the Color. Click the OK button.

15. Click anywhere in the subtitle prompt, This week's featured breeds are [breed type], and then click the <h3> tag in the tag selector. Click the New CSS Rule button in the CSS Styles panel. In the New CSS Rule dialog box, select Tag (redefines an HTML element), h3, and (This document only) as necessary, and then click the OK button. Set the following values in the Type category: Verdana, Geneva, sans-serif for the Font-family; 14 pixels for the Font-size; 600 for the Font-weight; and #336633 for the Color. Click the OK button.

16. Click anywhere in the introductory_paragraph prompt, and then click the <p> tag in the tag selector. Click the New CSS Rule button in the CSS Styles panel. In the New CSS Rule dialog box, select Tag (redefines an HTML element), p, and (This document only) as necessary, and then click the OK button. Set the following values in the Type category: Verdana, Geneva, sans-serif for the Font-family; 12 pixels for the Font-size; and #336633 for the Color. Click the OK button. Verify that the style is applied to the examples text.

Continued >

In the Lab *continued*

17. Click anywhere in the table and then click the <table> tag in the tag selector. Click the New CSS Rule button in the CSS Styles panel. In the New CSS Rule dialog box, select Tag (redefines an HTML element), table, and (This document only) as necessary, and then click the OK button. Set the following values in the Type category: Verdana, Geneva, sans-serif for the Font-family; 14 pixels for the Font-size; and #336633 for the Color. Set the following values in the Border category: outset for the Style and #336633 for the Color. Make sure the Same for all boxes are checked. Click the OK button.

18. Select the text, Index, and then click the Page Properties button in the Property inspector. In the Category list, click Links (CSS). Enter #336633 as the Link color. Click the Rollover links text box and type #0F0 for the color, #F00 for Visited links, and #336633 for Active links. Click the Underline style arrow and then select Show underline only on rollover. Click the Apply button and then click the OK button.

19. Title the template Bryan's Mobile Pet Services, and then save the document. (Click OK if any Dreamweaver dialog boxes appear.)

20. Open a new blank HTML page, and save it as breeds.htm in the pets folder.

21. Click the Assets tab in the Files panel group and then click the Templates button. Click the Apply button to apply the dog_breeds template to the breeds.htm page.

22. Use Table 5–13 as a guide to add content to each of the editable regions.

23. Save the document. Open the services.htm file. Scroll to the bottom of the page and then click to the right of the Home link. Press the END key, insert a line break, and then type Dog Breeds as the link text. Add a link to the breeds.htm page. Save the services.htm page.

24. Press the F12 key to view the page in your browser. Click the Dog Breeds link. Submit your assignment in the format specified by your instructor.

Table 5–12 Bryan's Mobile Pet Services Editable Regions

Region Text	Region Name
This week's featured breeds are [breed type].	subtitle
Introductory paragraph	introductory_paragraph
The following table displays :	examples
The table	table_images
Index	links

Table 5–13 Bryan's Mobile Pet Services Page Content

Region Text	Region Name
This week's featured breeds are collie, shepherd, bulldog, and poodle.	subtitle
Check our Web site each week to learn about the traits of different breeds of dogs.	introductory_paragraph
The following table displays this week's special dog breeds:	examples
(Note: Press TAB to move from cell to cell):	table_images
Row 1, column 1	collie.jpg
Row 1, column 2	shepherd.jpg
Row 2, column 1	bulldog.jpg
Row 2, column 2	poodle.jpg

In the Lab

Lab 2: Creating a Template for the Jewelry by Eve Web Site

Problem: The Jewelry by Eve Web site is receiving a large number of hits every day, and Eve is receiving increasingly more orders each day. She foresees a time when she will need to expand the Web site and is considering a standard design for her pages. Eve is not sure exactly how a template works within a Web site and has requested that you put together an example. You know that she has been considering a promotional page for her business, so you decide to create the page using this topic. The template is shown in Figure 5–98 and the Web page is shown in Figure 5–99 on the next page. The template contains five tables — one non-editable table and four editable tables. Your Web pages may be displayed differently than the ones shown in Figures 5–98 and 5–99. Appendix C contains instructions for uploading your local site to a remote server.

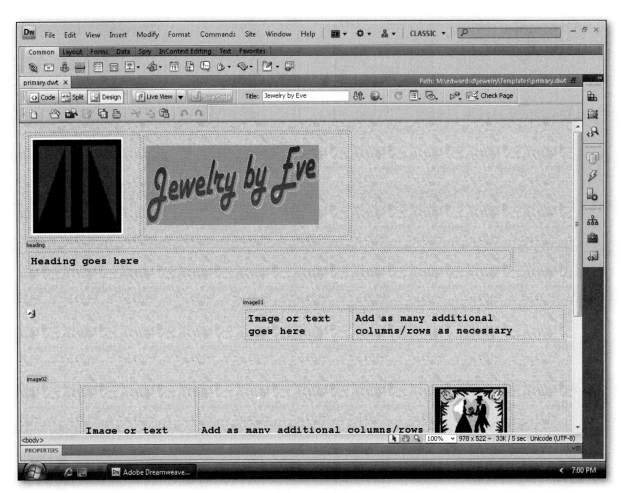

Figure 5–98

Continued >

In the Lab *continued*

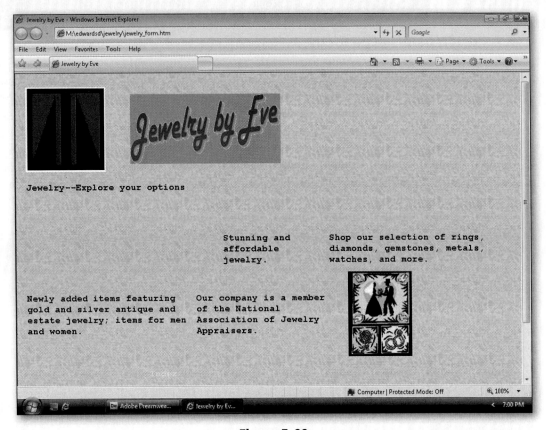

Figure 5–99

Perform the following tasks:

1. In Dreamweaver, open the Jewelry Business Web site. Copy the jewelry data files to the images folder for your Jewelry Business Web site.

2. Create a blank HTML template and then save it as a template named primary.dwt.

3. Use the Page Properties button in the Property inspector to add the jewelry_bkg.jpg background image to the page.

4. Create a one-row, two-column table with a table width of 60 percent, border of 0, cell padding of 5, and cell spacing of 5. Type Jewelry by Eve logo table as the Summary text. Select the table cells and set Vert to Middle. Drag the logo01.jpg image to the first cell and then type Logo Image 1 as the Alt text.

5. Drag the logo02.jpg image to the second cell and then type Logo Image 2 as the Alt text.

6. Click to the right of the table and then press the ENTER key. Add a one-row, one-column table with a width of 90 percent, border of 0, cell padding of 5, and cell spacing of 5. Click in the table and type Heading goes here as the prompt. Select the text and then click the New CSS Rule button in the CSS Styles panel. In the New CSS Rule dialog box, select Tag (redefines an HTML element), td, and (This document only) as necessary, and then click the OK button. In the CSS Rule definition for td dialog box, select the Type category, if necessary, select Courier New, Courier, monospace in the Font-family text box, select 18 for the Font-size, and bolder for the Font-weight. Click the OK button.

7. Click below the table and then press ENTER. Add a one-row, two-column table with a width of 60 percent, border thickness of 0, cell padding of 5, and cell spacing of 5. Align the table to the right. Select the table cells and set Vert to Middle. In the first cell, type Image or text goes here as the text prompt, and in the second cell, type Add as many additional columns/rows as necessary as the text prompt. Click to the right of the table and then press the ENTER key two times.

8. Add a third editable table with one row and three columns. Use a width of 80 percent, border thickness of 0, cell padding of 5, and cell spacing of 5. Center the table. In the first cell, type Image or text goes here as the prompt, and in the second cell, type Add as many additional columns/rows as necessary as the prompt. Drag the jewelry6.jpg image to the third cell. Click to the right of the table and then press the ENTER key.

9. Insert a fourth editable table — a one-row, two-column table with a width of 50 percent, border thickness of 0, cell padding of 5, and cell spacing of 5. Align to the center. Type Links go here in the first table cell.

10. With the insertion point still in the first table cell, click the New CSS Rule button in the CSS Styles panel. For Selector Type, choose Tag (redefines an HTML element). In the Selector Name text box, type link. If necessary, select (This document only). Click OK. Click Cancel to close the CSS Rule definition for link dialog box.

11. Select the links table, click Modify on the Application bar, and then click Page Properties. In the Page Properties dialog box, select Links (CSS). Click the Link color box and type #000; type #C0F in the Rollover links box, #FF0 in the Visited links text box, and #000 for Active links. Select Show underline only on rollover as the Underline style. Click OK.

12. Use the Insert menu and select Template Objects to create three editable regions in the template — the first with the entire heading table and then the three tables below it. Name the first editable region heading, name the second region image01, the third region image02, and the fourth region links.

13. Enter Jewelry by Eve as the title of the template, and then save the document.

14. Open a new blank HTML page and save it as jewelry_form.htm. Click the Assets tab in the Files panel group. Apply the template to the jewelry_form document.

15. Select the Heading goes here text and then type Jewelry — Explore your options in the heading editable region.

16. Select the text in the left column of the image01 editable region and type the following text: Stunning and affordable jewelry. Select the text in the right column, and then type Shop our selection of rings, diamonds, gemstones, metals, watches, and more.

17. Select the text in the left cell of the text_image02 editable region and then type Newly added items featuring gold and silver antique and estate jewelry; items for men and women. Select the text in the center cell of the second table and then type Our company is a member of the National Association of Jewelry Appraisers.

18. Delete the text in the links table. Drag index.htm from the Files panel to the links table as the entry. Edit the text so it appears as Index. Save the page.

19. Open the index.htm file. Scroll to the bottom of the page, click to the right of the Survey link and then press the END key. Insert a line break and then type Jewelry Form as the link text. Create a link to the jewelry_form.htm page. Save the index page.

20. Press the F12 key to view the page in your browser. Click the Jewelry Form link. Submit your assignment in the format specified by your instructor.

In the Lab

Lab 3: Creating a Template and Applying a Style Sheet for the Credit Protection Web Site

Problem: Linda Reyes has decided to add additional Web pages emphasizing the ABCs of Credit. She would like to have a uniform format for these pages and has asked you to create a template. She has provided you with content for the first page. The template is shown in Figure 5–100 and the Web page is shown in Figure 5–101. Appendix C contains instructions for uploading your local site to a remote server.

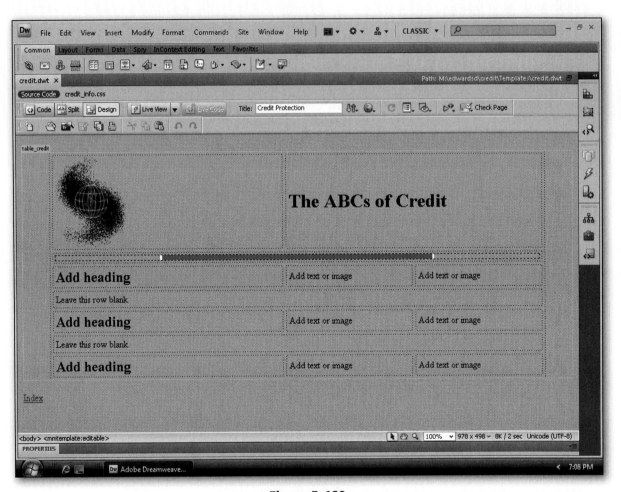

Figure 5–100

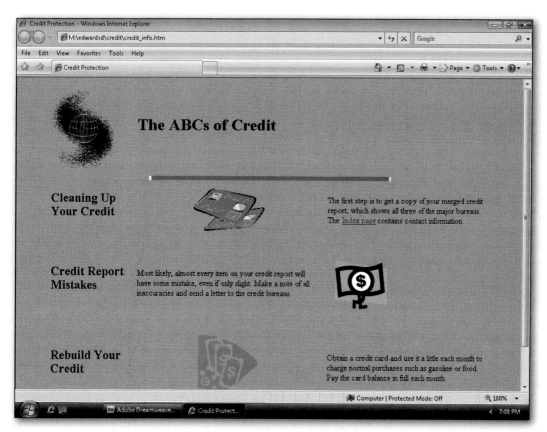

Figure 5–101

Perform the following tasks:

1. In Dreamweaver, open the Credit Protection Web site, and then copy the credit data files to the images folder for your Credit Protection Web site.

2. Create a blank HTML template and save it as a template named credit.dwt. Apply the credit_bkg.jpg background image to the page.

3. Insert a seven-row, three-column table with a width of 90 percent, border thickness of 0, cell padding of 5, cell spacing of 5, and Summary text of ABCs of Credit. Center the table. Drag the logo.gif image to the first cell in the first row. Merge the last two cells in row 1. Type The ABCs of Credit in the merged cells and apply the Heading 1 format.

4. Merge all three cells in row 2. Drag the line.gif image to the merged row, and then center the line in the cell.

5. Merge all three cells in row 4 and then type Leave this row blank in the cell. Repeat this step for row 6.

6. Click row 3, column 1, type Add heading as the entry, and then apply Heading 2 to this text. Repeat this instruction in column 1 of rows 5 and 7.

7. Click row 3, column 2; type Add text or image as the entry; and then copy this text. Paste the text into row 3, column 3; row 5, columns 2 and 3; and row 7, columns 2 and 3.

8. Click to the right of the table, press the ENTER key, and then type Index as the entry. Create a link from this text to the index.htm page.

9. Click anywhere in the table and then click the <table> tag in the Tag selector. Use the Editable Regions menu item on the Templates pop-up menu to name the editable region table_credit.

Continued >

In the Lab *continued*

10. Open the CSS Styles panel and then click the New CSS Rule button. In the New CSS Rule dialog box, select Tag (redefines an HTML element), table, and (New Style Sheet File) as necessary, and then click the OK button. Name the style sheet credit_info.css and save it in your credit folder. Apply the following attributes in the Type category: Georgia, Times New Roman, Times, serif for the Font-family; 16 for the Font-size; and bold for the Font-weight. Click the OK button and close the template. Save and close the credit_info.css style sheet.

11. Open a new blank HTML page and save it as credit_info.htm. Click the Assets panel tab and then click the Apply button. Delete the text, Leave this row blank, from all cells.

12. Select the "Add heading" text in row 3, column 1; type Cleaning Up Your Credit as the entry; and then select the text in row 3, column 3. Type The first step is to get a copy of your merged credit report, which shows all three of the major bureaus. The Index page contains contact information. Select the text "Index page" and add a link to the index.htm page. Delete the text in row 3, column 2, and drag the credit_card.gif image to the cell, and then center the image.

13. Select the "Add heading" text in row 5, column 1, type Credit Report Mistakes as the entry, and then select the text in row 5, column 2. Type Most likely, almost every item on your credit report will have some mistake, even if only slight. Make a note of all inaccuracies and send a letter to the credit bureaus. Delete the text in row 5, column 3 and then drag the money2.gif image to the cell.

14. Select the text in row 7, column 1; type Rebuild Your Credit as the entry; and then select the text in row 7, column 3. Type Obtain a credit card and use it a little each month to charge normal purchases such as gasoline or food. Pay the card balance in full each month. Delete the text in row 7, column 2, drag the rebuild.gif image to the cell, and then center the image.

15. Save the document and the credit_info.css page. Open the index.htm file. Scroll to the bottom of the page, click to the right of the Information Request link, and then press the END key. Insert a line break and then type Credit Information as the link text. Create a link to the credit_info.htm page. Press the ENTER key and save the page.

16. Press the F12 key to view the page in your browser. Click the Credit Information link. Submit your assignment in the format specified by your instructor.

Cases and Places

Apply your creative thinking and problem solving skills to design and implement a solution.

• Easier   ••More Difficult

• 1: Create a Template for the Favorite Sports Web Site

Your sports Web site has become very popular. You have received many e-mails asking for statistics and other information. You decide to add a Web page that will contain statistics and will be updated on a weekly basis. Add a background image to the page and add a title to the page. Create a template using tables. Add descriptive prompts and then create editable regions. Add styles to the headings and text. Then create a page, apply the template, and save the page in your sports Web site. Create links to and from the home page.

• 2: Create a Template and New Web Page for the Hobby Web Site

You have decided to add a do-it-yourself section to your hobby Web site and want to use a consistent format and look for the page. You decide to use a template to create this new section. Create the template using a logo, tables, and links. Add descriptive prompts to the editable regions and apply styles to enhance the text and text size. Create the first do-it-yourself Web page and apply the template. Create links to and from the home page. Upload the pages to a remote server, if instructed to do so.

•• 3: Create a Template and Style Sheet for the Politics Web Site

Your campaign for political office is progressing well, and you are one of the top two candidates. You have decided to add a new section to your Web site featuring your campaign supporters. To provide consistency and control, you use a template for this site. After completing the template, attach styles. Next, create two new pages for the site and then apply the template. Create links to and from the home page. Upload the new pages to a remote server, if instructed to do so.

•• 4: Create a Template for the Favorite Music Web Site

Make It Personal

Create a template for your music hobby Web site and then add a background to the page. Insert logos, tables, and other appropriate elements. Add a background image to a table. Apply a border to the table. Use the CSS Styles panel and apply styles to the elements on the page. Create a new Web page featuring a new topic for your Web site and apply the template. Create links to and from the home page. Upload the page to a remote server, if instructed to do so.

•• 5: Create a Template and New Web Page for the Student Trips Web Site

Working Together

Each member of the group decides to create a template for the three vacation sites previously selected. Include on the templates headings, tables, links, and graphics. Present the three templates to the group and determine which one best meets the needs of the Web site. Next, add appropriate styles, including styles from the Type, Background, and Border categories. Include at least two images and a logo on the template. Create the three vacation site Web pages and apply the template. Then create links to and from the home page. Upload the new pages to a remote server, if instructed to do so.

6 | Absolute Positioning, Image Maps, and Navigation Bars

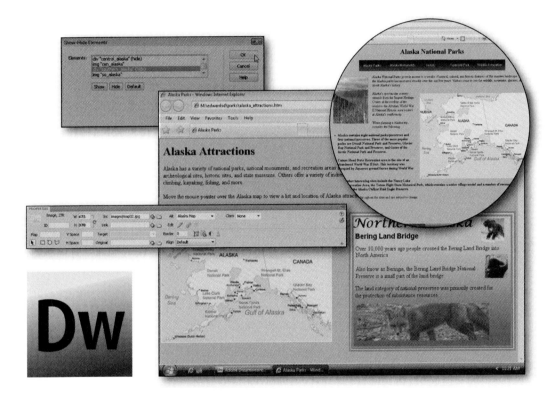

Objectives

You will have mastered the material in this chapter when you can:

- Explain the concept of AP elements
- Insert, select, resize, and move an AP element
- Name an AP element
- Align AP elements
- Describe an image map

- Create an image map
- Add and edit behaviors
- Describe a navigation bar
- Create a navigation bar
- Insert a Date object

6 | Absolute Positioning, Image Maps, and Navigation Bars

Introduction

Chapter 6 introduces three unique Dreamweaver features: absolute positioning, image maps, and navigation bars. Web developers have long dreamed of being able to position graphics, text, and other HTML objects at specific pixel coordinates. Tables provide some placement control, but not absolute precision. Dreamweaver's AP elements, however, can be positioned anywhere on the page. They remain in the same position relative to the top and left margins of the window regardless of how a user resizes the browser window.

An image map is the second feature discussed in this chapter. An image map is a picture that is divided into regions, called hotspots. When a user clicks a hotspot, an assigned action occurs. You can create multiple hotspots in an image, and you can have more than one image map on a single Web page.

The third feature introduced in this chapter is the navigation bar. Navigation bars often provide an easy way to move among the pages and files on a site. The linking elements within a navigation bar can consist of text, images, and/or a combination of text and images. To complement the Alaska Parks Web site with these new elements, you modify the index page by adding an interactive navigation bar. As you complete the activities in this chapter, you will find that adding these features to a Web page offers greater interactivity and excitement for the user.

Project — Using AP Elements and Image Maps, and Creating a Navigation Bar

In this chapter, you continue adding pages to the Alaska Parks Web site. You learn how to use and apply three favorite Dreamweaver tools to the Alaska Parks Web site. You begin the chapter by adding a new page to the Web site, containing an image map and AP elements, also previously known as layers (Figure 6–1a). Four separate elements are added to the page, and images then are embedded in each element. One element contains an Alaska map, which serves as the image map. Within the image map, moving the mouse pointer over different spots will display a list of the parks and other attractions in northern, central, and southern Alaska. Next, you revise the index page by deleting the existing links and adding a navigation bar (Figure 6–1b). The navigation bar adds a more professional look by bringing all of the links together in one location at the top of the Web page. When the mouse pointer moves over an image link within the navigation bar, the image changes color to indicate that this is an active link. Each image also has alternate text to address accessibility issues.

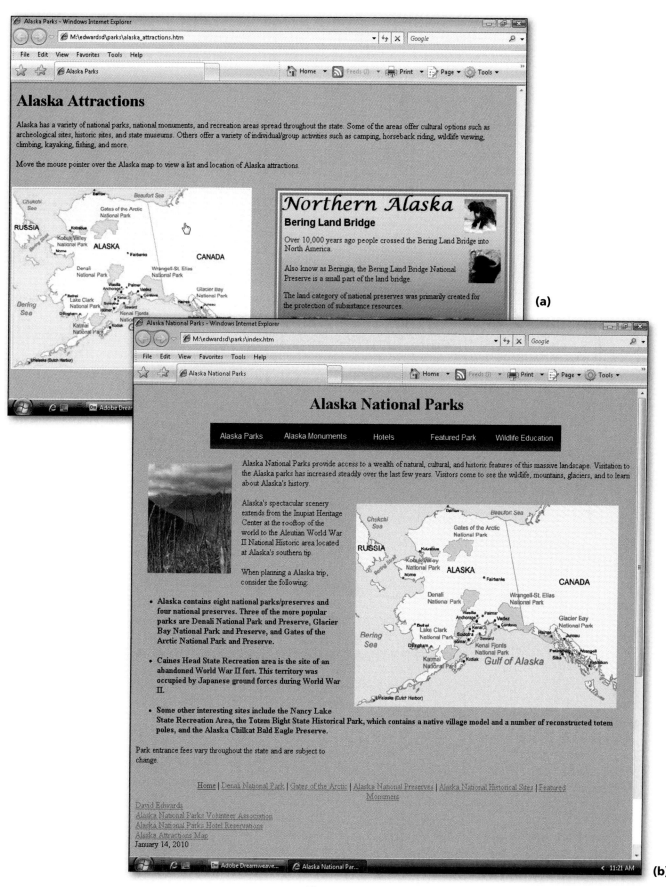

Figure 6–1

Overview

As you read this chapter, you will learn how to add to your Web site the pages shown in Figure 6–1 on the previous page by performing these general tasks:

- Create and save an image map.
- Insert, select, resize, and align an AP element.
- Add editable regions.
- Add and edit behaviors.
- Create and describe a navigation bar.
- Insert a date object.
- Add links.

Plan Ahead

General Project Guidelines

When adding pages to a Web site, consider the appearance and characteristics of the completed site. As you create the Web pages shown in Figure 6–1, you should follow these general guidelines:

1. **Plan the Web page.** Determine how the page will fit into the Web site.

2. **Organize your content.** Create and organize the content for the new page. The images should be copied and pasted into the images folder.

3. **Using AP elements.** Determine where and how the elements will be used on the page.

4. **Using an Image Map.** Consider where the image map will be displayed on the page and how the sections will be divided.

5. **Organize images and place images.** Organize your images within the Assets panel. Consider how the images will display on the image map. Determine which images need to be resized and how much resizing needs to be done.

6. **Navigation bar.** Determine which images you will use in the navigation bar and the position in which the images will be placed.

When necessary, more specific details concerning the above guidelines are presented at appropriate points in the chapter. The chapter also will identify the actions performed and decisions made regarding these guidelines during the creation of the Web pages shown in Figure 6–1.

Starting Dreamweaver and Opening a Web Site

Each time you start Dreamweaver, it opens to the last site displayed when you closed the program. It therefore may be necessary for you to open the parks Web site. Clicking the Files pop-up menu in the Files panel lists the sites you have defined. When you open the site, a list of pages and subfolders within the site is displayed.

To Start Dreamweaver and Open the Alaska Parks Web Site

With a good understanding of the requirements, and an understanding of the necessary decisions and planning process, the first step is to start Dreamweaver and open the Alaska Parks Web site.

- Click the Start button on the Windows taskbar.

- Click Adobe Dreamweaver CS4 on the Start menu, or point to All Programs on the Start menu, and then click Adobe Dreamweaver CS4 to start Dreamweaver.

- If necessary, display the panel groups.

- If the Alaska Parks Web site hierarchy is not displayed, click the Files panel arrow and then click Alaska Parks on the Files pop-up menu to display the Alaska Parks Web site hierarchy in the Files panel.

To Copy Data Files to the Parks Web Site

Before you start enhancing and adding to your Web site, you need to copy the data files into the site's folder hierarchy. In the following steps, you copy the data files for the Chapter 6 project from the Chapter06 folder on a USB drive to the parks and the parks\images folder stored in the *your name* folder on the same USB drive. In the following steps, the data files for this chapter are stored on drive M:. The location on your computer may be different. If necessary, verify the location of the data files with your instructor.

- Click the Files panel button, and then click the name of the drive containing your data files, such as Removable Disk (M:).

- If necessary, click the plus sign (+) next to the folder containing your data files to expand that folder, and then click the plus sign (+) next to the Chapter06 folder to expand it.

- Expand the parks folder to display the data files.

- Click the alaska_attractions document to select it and then copy it to the parks folder.

- Double-click the images folder. Click the button01a.jpg file or the first file in the list. Hold down the SHIFT key and then click the southern_alaska.jpg image file, or the last file in the list.

- Press CTRL+C to copy the files.

- If necessary, click the Files panel button, and then click the drive containing the Alaska Parks Web site. Expand the *your name* folder and the parks folder. Click the images folder to select it.

• Press CTRL+V to paste the image
files in the images folder
(Figure 6–2).

Q&A

How can I alphabetize the files in
the Local Files list?

Click the Refresh button in the
Files panel to refresh the list.

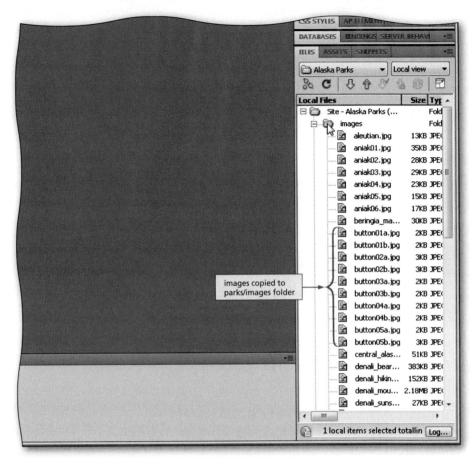

images copied to
parks/images folder

Figure 6–2

You copied the files necessary to begin creating your new Web page to the Alaska
Parks local root folder in the Files panel. You begin the chapter by adding a new page to
the Web site, containing an image map and AP elements, also previously known as layers. Four separate elements are added to the page, and images then are embedded in each
element. One element contains an Alaska map, which serves as the image map. With the
image map, moving the mouse pointer over different spots will display a list of the parks
and other attractions in northern, central, and southern Alaska. Next, you revise the index
page by deleting the existing links and adding a navigation bar. The navigation bar adds a
more professional look by bringing all of the links together in one location at the top of
the Web page. When the mouse pointer moves over an image link within the navigation
bar, the image changes color to indicate that this is an active link. Each image also has
alternate text to address accessibility issues.

Understanding AP Elements

An **AP element** is similar to a table — it is a container that holds other types of content,
such as images, text, form objects, and even other AP elements (nested elements). Anything
you can put in an HTML document, you also can put into an AP element. The AP elements can be stacked on top of one another, placed side by side, or overlapped. They easily
can be moved, dragged, or resized. Web site developers use AP elements for page layout

much as they use tables. An AP element, however, provides more flexibility than a table because it can be placed in an exact spot anywhere on the page with pixel-perfect precision. It remains in this position (relative to the top and left margins of the page) regardless of how the Web page visitor resizes the browser window or views the text size. This is called **absolute positioning** and is possible because AP elements are positioned using a standard x-, y-, and z-coordinate system, similar to what you would use to create a graph on graph paper. Instead of having the point of origin be in the lower-left corner, however, the x- and y-coordinates correspond to the AP element's top and left positions within the page. The z-coordinate, also called the **z-index**, determines an AP element's stacking order when more than one element are added to a page.

Netscape does not fully support absolute positioning. If you are designing for Netscape, it is best to convert the AP elements to tables. To convert the elements to tables, click the Modify menu, point to Convert, and then select the AP Divs to Table command.

AP Divs and DHTML

Absolute Positioning (AP) is a component of dynamic HTML (DHTML) — an extension of HTML that gives Web page developers the capability of precisely positioning objects on the Web page. DHTML combines AP Divs, Cascading Style Sheets (CSS), and JavaScript coding, enabling the creation of dynamic page elements. Additionally, because an AP Div uses both DHTML and CSS, it offers a wide range of flexibility and control. Some possible effects you can accomplish using DHTML are as follows:

- Add images that are hidden from view initially and then display when a user clicks a button or hotspot
- Create pop-up menus
- Position objects side by side
- Drag and drop objects
- Create animations
- Provide feedback to right and wrong answers

A disadvantage of using AP elements is that older browsers do not support them. Internet Explorer 4.0 and Netscape Navigator 4.0 (and later) support AP Divs under the original W3C Cascading Style Sheets-Positioning (CSS-P) specifications. Browsers older than version 4.0, however, ignore the AP Div code and display the content in the normal flow of the page (no absolute positioning). Also, even though current browsers support AP elements, Internet Explorer and Netscape Navigator implement DHTML differently, and, therefore, some discrepancy in the display of AP elements exists. Navigator 4.0 in particular has a difficult time with AP elements and often displays them incorrectly. Dreamweaver, however, contains a Netscape 4 Resize Fix option, which is available through the AP Elements category in the Preferences dialog box.

Dreamweaver provides two options for creating AP elements: the Draw AP Div button located on the Layout tab on the Insert bar, and the Layout Objects submenu available through the Insert menu. In this chapter, you use the Draw AP Div button on the Layout tab on the Insert bar, modify attributes through the CSS-P Elements Property inspector, and control visibility through the AP Elements panel. Displaying Dreamweaver's layout tools, such as the rulers or the grid, helps with precise positioning. In this chapter, you use the rulers.

To Open the Alaska Attractions Page and Display the Rulers

The following steps show how to open the alaska_attractions.htm page and to display the rulers.

- Collapse the image folder, if necessary, in the Files panel, and then double-click the alaska_attractions.htm file to open the file and to display the insertion point at the top of the window (Figure 6–3).

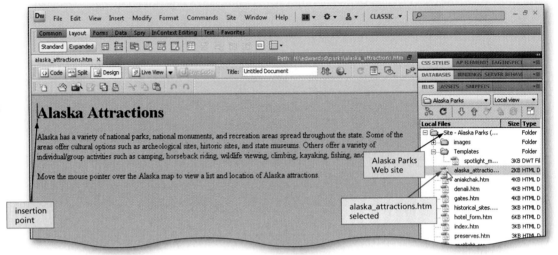

Figure 6–3

- Click the Property inspector title bar to collapse the Property inspector.

- Click View on the Application bar, point to Rulers, and then point to Show to highlight the Show command on the Rulers submenu (Figure 6–4).

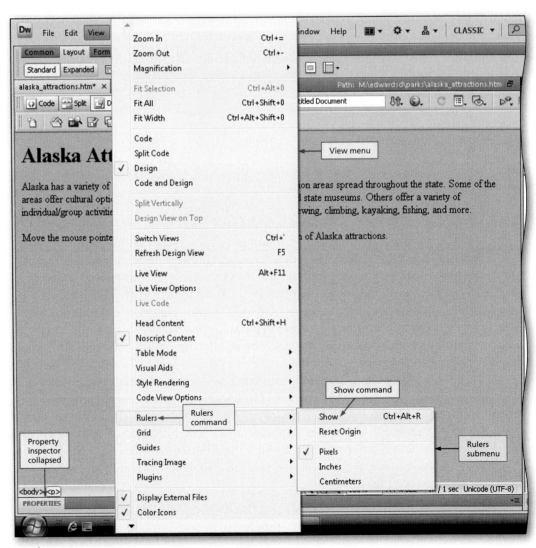

Figure 6–4

2

- If necessary, click Show to display the rulers in the document window and to display the ruler-origin icon in the upper-left corner (Figure 6–5).

Q&A What should I do if my ruler shows inches?

Right-click the ruler and then click Pixels.

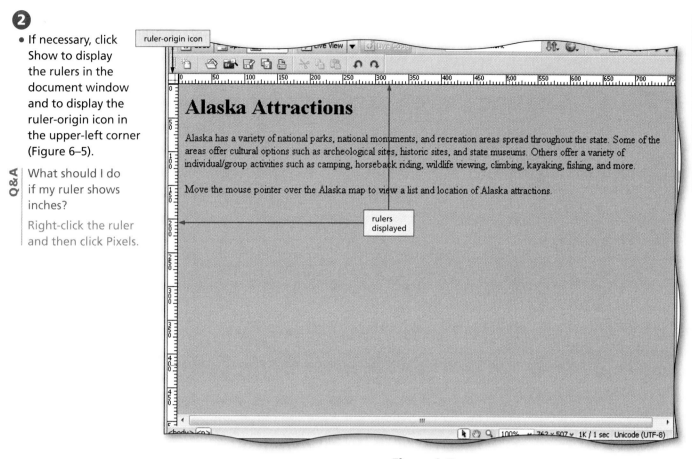

Figure 6–5

AP Div Property Inspector

When you insert an AP element into a Web page and the element is selected, Dreamweaver displays the AP Div Property inspector (Figure 6–6). The following section describes the properties that are available through the Property inspector.

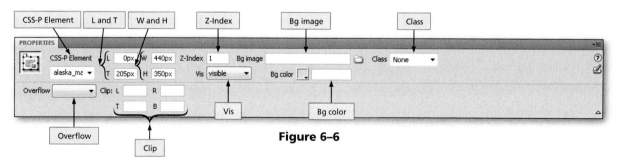

Figure 6–6

CSS-P Element ID Assigns a unique name to identify the element in the AP Elements panel and in JavaScript code. Element names must start with a letter and can contain only standard alphanumeric characters.

L and T Specifies the position of the element's top-left corner relative to the top-left corner of the page, or the top-left corner of the parent element if the element is nested. A nested element, or child element, is an element whose code is contained in another element.

Nesting often is used to group elements together. A nested element moves with its parent element and can be set to inherit visibility from its parent. Parent and child elements are discussed in more detail in the section on nesting, overlapping, and stacking elements, later in this chapter.

W and H Specifies the width and height of the element in Design view. In Design view, if the content of the element exceeds the specified size, the bottom edge of the element stretches to accommodate the content. When the element appears in a browser, however, the bottom edge does not stretch unless the Overflow property is set to visible. The default unit for position and size is pixels (px). Other units include pc (picas), pt (points), in (inches), mm (millimeters), cm (centimeters), and % (percentage of the parent element's corresponding value). The abbreviations must follow the value without a space: for example, 3mm indicates 3 millimeters.

Z-Index Determines the stacking order of the element. In a browser, higher-numbered elements appear in front of lower-numbered ones. The z-index values can be positive or negative. The stacking order can be changed through the AP Elements panel.

Vis Specifies whether the element is visible initially or not. The following options are available:

- **default** does not specify a visibility property. When no visibility is specified, most browsers default to inherit.
- **inherit** uses the visibility property of the element's parent.
- **visible** displays the element contents, regardless of the parent's value.
- **hidden** hides the element contents, regardless of the parent's value. Note that hidden elements created with ilayer (a tag unique to Netscape Navigator) still take up the same space as if they were visible.

Bg Image Specifies a background image for the element.

Bg Color Specifies a background color for the element. Leave this option blank to specify a transparent background.

Class Lets you apply CSS rules to the selected object.

BTW

<div> versus <span> Tags
The difference between the <div> and <span> tags is that browsers that do not support AP elements place extra line breaks before and after the <div> tag. In most cases, it is better for AP element content to appear in a paragraph of its own in browsers that do not support elements. Therefore, in most cases, it is better to use <div> than <span>.

Overflow Works only with the <div> and <span> tags and controls how elements appear in a browser when the content exceeds the element's specified size. The following options are available:

- **visible** indicates that the extra content appears in the element.
- **hidden** specifies that the extra content is not displayed in the browser.
- **scroll** specifies that the browser should add scroll bars to the element whether or not they are needed.
- **auto** causes the browser to display scroll bars for the element only when the element's contents exceed its boundaries.

Clip Defines the visible area of a element. Specify left, top, right, and bottom coordinates to define a rectangle in the coordinate space of the element (counting from the top-left corner of the element). The element is clipped so that only the specified rectangle is visible.

Using the Rulers as a Visual Guide

You use the rulers as a visual guide to create an AP element that will be a container for the Alaska map image. When you draw the AP element in the document window, a rectangular image appears, representing the element. (If the AP element borders do not display in the document window, they can be turned on by selecting AP Element outlines through the Visual Aids submenu accessed through the View menu.) This rectangular box, however, is not displayed when the page is viewed in a browser. Instead, only the content of what is contained within the AP element is displayed in the browser.

The default rulers appear on the left and top borders of the document window, marked in pixels. The **ruler origin** is the 0 point, or the location on the page where the horizontal and vertical lines meet and read 0. The 0 point is represented by the **ruler-origin icon**, which is located in the document window when the page is displayed in Design view and the rulers are displayed (see Figure 6–6 on page DW 433). Generally, this location is the upper-left corner of the document window.

Using the rulers as a drawing guideline can be somewhat difficult to manage if done from the default 0 point. To make measuring easier, however, you can move the 0 point anywhere within the document window. To move the 0 point, move the mouse pointer to the upper-left corner where the vertical and horizontal lines meet, and then click and drag the crosshairs to the desired location. When you move the 0 point, the crosshairs are displayed in the document window and follow the mouse pointer. The mouse pointer position is indicated with a dotted line on both the vertical and horizontal ruler lines.

Relocating the 0 point does not affect the page content. You can relocate the 0 point as many times as necessary. You also can reset the ruler origin by right-clicking anywhere on the rulers and then selecting Reset Origin on the context menu.

BTW

Rulers
You can change the ruler unit of measurement from the default pixels to inches or centimeters by right-clicking anywhere on the rulers and then selecting a different unit of measurement on the context menu.

The AP Element Marker

When you insert an AP element, a **code marker** appears in the document window. This small yellow square indicates that an AP element is on the page. For the code marker to display, the Anchor points for AP elements check box must be selected through the Invisible Elements category in the Preferences dialog box. When the Invisible Elements option is turned on, the markers may cause the elements on the page in the document window to appear to shift position. These markers, however, are not displayed in the browser. When you view the page in your browser, the AP elements and other objects are displayed in the correct positions.

The code marker is similar in appearance to the invisible element marker that displayed when you inserted images into a Web page in Chapter 2. In Chapter 2, dragging the image marker to another position in the document window also moved the image to another position. Normally, the position of HTML objects in the document window and in the browser is determined by their order in the HTML source code. They are displayed in a top-to-bottom sequence that mirrors their order in the source code.

Dragging or moving the AP element marker, however, generally does not reposition the element and has no effect on the way a Web page displays the AP element in a browser. When you move an AP element marker, you are not moving the element; instead, you are repositioning the element's code in the HTML of the page. Moving an element marker, therefore, can affect how the code is interpreted and the order in which the element content is loaded. It is possible to have an element's content displayed at the top of the Web page while the source code is at the end of the page.

If your Web page contains tables, do not drag the element marker into a table cell. This can cause display problems in some browsers. You can drag an AP element, however, to overlap a table or make a label display so it appears to be inside the table cell, as long as the code marker itself is not in the table cell. When you use the AP Div button to create the AP element, Dreamweaver will not put the code into a table cell.

To Create and Select an AP Element for the Alaska Map Image

The following steps illustrate how to create and select an AP element.

1

● If necessary, display the Insert bar and then select the Layout tab. Expand the Property inspector by clicking its title bar.

● Click at the end of the last line of text in the document window, and then press ENTER.

● Click the ruler-origin icon and drag it to the insertion point, making sure that the insertion point is blinking below the last line of text in the document window and the vertical ruler 0 point is to the left of the insertion point (Figure 6–7).

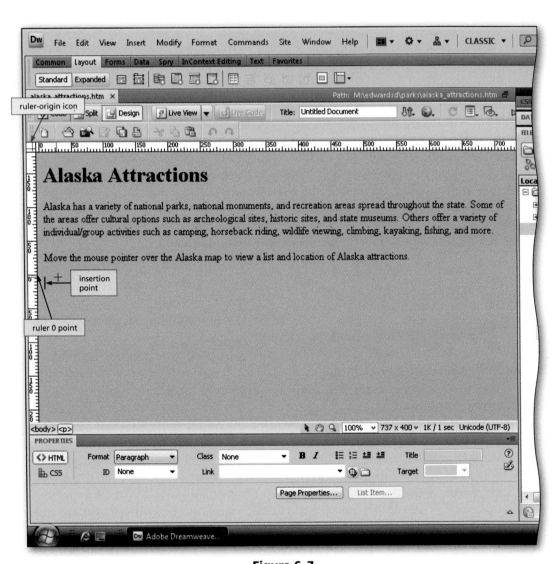

Figure 6–7

2

- Click the Draw AP Div button on the Layout tab and then move the pointer to the insertion point so that the AP element pointer is displayed in the document window (Figure 6–8).

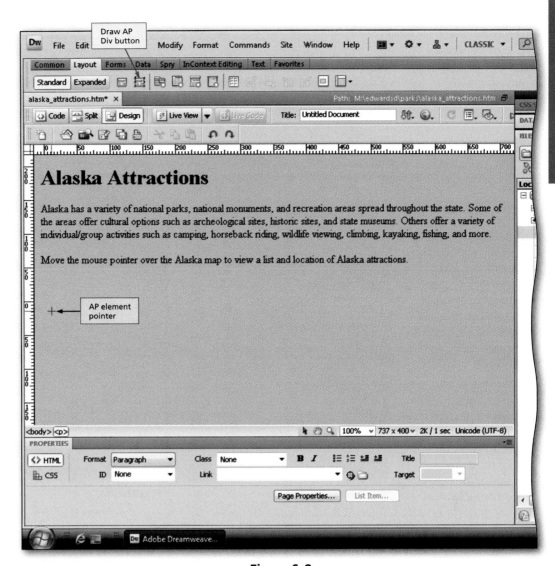

Figure 6–8

3

- Using the rulers as a guide, draw an AP element approximately 470 pixels wide and 375 pixels high.

Q&A What should I do if I have trouble drawing the AP element beyond the bottom of the document window?

Draw as much as you can. You set the exact dimensions next.

Q&A What should I do if the element outline does not appear in the document window?

If the element outline does not appear in the document window, click View on the Application bar, point to Visual Aids, and then click Add Element Outlines on the Visual Aids submenu.

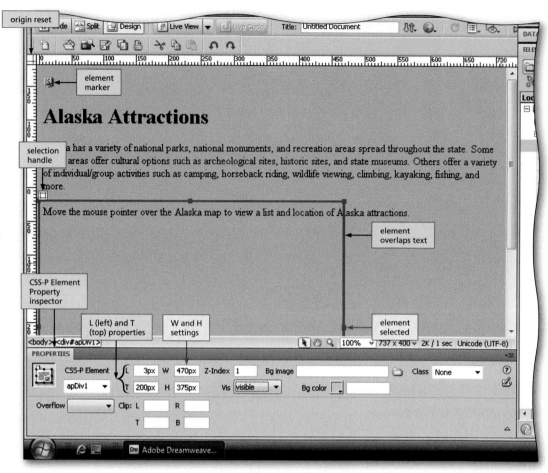

Figure 6–9

- Click the AP element to select it, and then, if necessary, make the following changes in the CSS-P Element Property inspector: L – 3px, T – 200px, W – 470px, and H – 375px.

- Scroll to the top of the document window.

- Right-click anywhere on the rulers and click Reset Origin on the context menu (Figure 6–9).

Q&A What should I do if the element marker is not displayed?

If the element marker is not displayed, click Edit on the Application bar, select Preferences, and then click the Invisible Elements tab. Click the Anchor points for AP elements check box and then click the OK button.

Other Ways

1. On Insert menu, click Layout Objects, click AP Div

At this point, the element should be displayed and selected. The ruler's vertical 0 point is returned to its original position. In some instances, the element will overlap some of the text (as it does in Figure 6–9). This depends on the location of the element starting point and on your computer settings. If this occurs, it will be corrected later in this chapter when the element's coordinates are added. The AP element marker is displayed at the top of the page, and the CSS-P Element Property inspector is displayed.

The AP Elements Panel

The **AP Elements panel**, part of the CSS panel group, is helpful in managing the elements in your document. Use the AP Elements panel to prevent overlaps, to change the visibility of elements, to nest or stack elements, and to select one or more elements. All of the AP elements on a Web page are listed in the panel. The AP Elements panel contains three columns: Visibility, Name, and Z-Index. The Visibility column uses eye icons. A **closed-eye icon** indicates that an element is hidden; an **open-eye icon** indicates that the element is visible. The absence of an eye icon indicates that the element is in its default state — that it is showing, but not defined as showing in the HTML code. The middle column displays the names of the elements. Clicking an element name in the AP Elements panel is another way to select an element. In the Z-Index column, elements are displayed in order of their z-index values. The first element created appears at the bottom of the list, and the most recently created element at the top of the list. Nested elements are displayed as indented names connected to parent elements (as discussed later in this chapter). The Prevent overlaps check box, when clicked, prevents elements from overlapping. When the Prevent overlaps option is on, an element cannot be created in front of, moved or resized over, or nested within an existing element.

To Display the AP Elements Panel

The following step illustrates how to display the AP Elements panel.

1

- Click Window on the Application bar and then click AP Elements to display the AP Elements panel. If necessary to view the AP Elements panel, move the mouse pointer over the bottom of the AP Elements panel until the pointer changes to a two-headed arrow. Drag the border of the AP Elements panel down about two inches so that it is not covering the text (Figure 6–10).

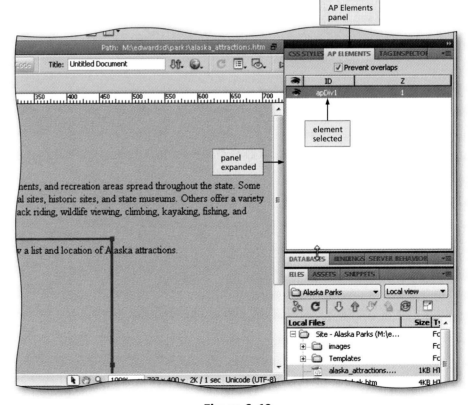

Figure 6–10

Other Ways
1. Press the F2 key

To Name the AP Element and Adjust the AP Element Properties

The default name for AP elements is apDiv1, apDiv2, and so on. The next step is to use the Property inspector to rename the element and to adjust the element width and height properties.

- Click the CSS-P Element text box in the Property inspector and then type alaska_map as the element name. Press the ENTER key to make the change in the Property inspector (Figure 6–11).

Q&A

I noticed that the L and T values changed and that Vis was changed to visible in the Property inspector. What should I do?

Leave those settings as they are for now. You will change them later.

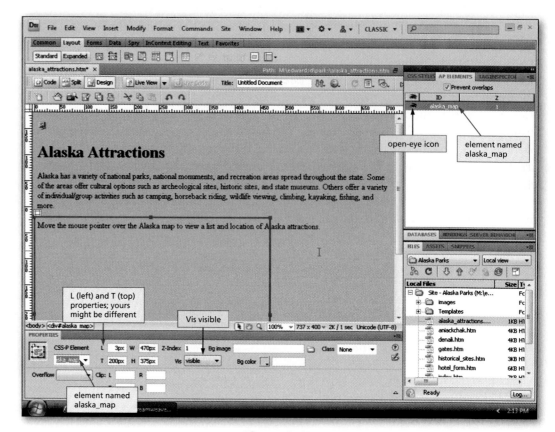

Figure 6–11

Other Ways

1. Double-click element name in AP Elements panel

Adding Objects to AP Elements

As indicated previously, an AP element is a container that can hold objects. The objects can be anything that can be added to an HTML page and include such items as images, text, form objects, and even other elements (nested elements). Objects, including images, can be inserted onto elements through the Insert menu. Images also can be dragged from the Files or Assets panels onto the element. The following steps show how to add the Alaska map image to the alaska_map AP element.

To Add an Image to the alaska_map AP Element

1

- In the Files panel, click the plus sign next to the images folder to expand the folder.

- Scroll to locate and click the map02.jpg image.

2

- Drag the map02.jpg image onto the element. Scroll down if necessary to display the entire map.

- Click the image ID box in the Property inspector and type `map` as the entry. Click the Alt text box and type `Alaska Map` as the entry. Press the TAB key.

- Change the W to 470 and the H to 375 to resize the map image.

- Type `Alaska Parks` in the Title text box on the Document toolbar to title the page.

- Click the Save button on the Standard toolbar to save your work (Figure 6–12).

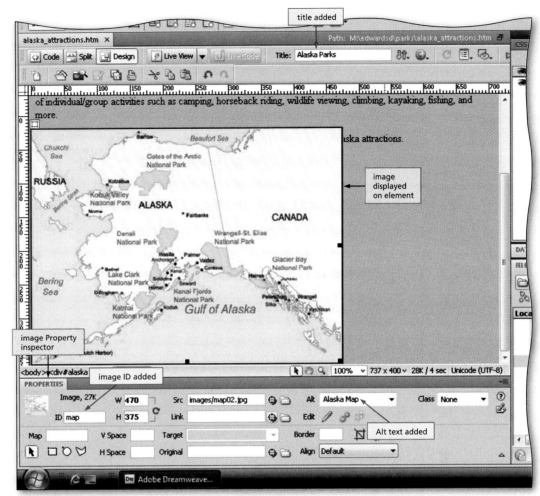

Figure 6–12

3

- Press F12 and view the Web page in your browser.

- Close the browser.

Other Ways

1. On Insert menu, click Image, select file name in the Select Image Source dialog box, click OK button

Nesting, Overlapping, and Stacking Elements

Several methods are available to manage and manipulate elements. As noted previously, elements can be nested, overlapped, or stacked one on top of another.

Nesting is used to group elements. This process also is referred to as creating a parent-child relation. A nested element, also called a **child element**, is similar in concept to a nested table or a nested frame. Having a nested element, however, does not neces-sarily mean that one element resides within another element. Rather, it means that the HTML code for one element is written inside the code for another element. The nested element can be displayed anywhere on the page. It does not even have to touch the **parent element**, which is the element containing the code for the other elements. The primary advantage of nested elements is that the parent element controls the behavior of its child elements. If the parent element is moved on the screen, the nested elements move with it. Additionally, if you hide the parent element, you also hide any nested elements. In the AP Elements panel, nested elements are indented below the parent element.

To create a nested element, draw the element inside an existing element while holding down the CTRL key. To unnest a nested element, drag the element marker to a different location in the document window, or, in the AP Elements panel, drag the nested element to an empty spot.

Elements also can overlap and/or be stacked one on top of another. Elements that float on top of each other have a **stacking order**. In the HTML source code, the stacking order, or z-index, of the elements is determined by the order in which they are created. The first element you draw is 1, the second is 2, and so on. The element with the highest number appears on top or in front of elements with lower numbers. Stacking elements provides opportunities for techniques such as hiding and displaying elements and/or parts of elements, creating draggable elements, and creating animation.

Two different methods are available through the AP Elements panel to change the z-index for an element and set which element appears in front of or behind another ele-ment. First, you can click the element name and then drag it up or down in the list. A line appears, indicating where the element will be placed. The second method is to click the number of the element you want to change in the Z column, and then type a higher num-ber to move the element up or a lower number to move the element down in the stacking order. After you change the z-index, Dreamweaver automatically rearranges the elements from highest to lowest, with the highest number on top. You also can turn off the overlap-ping feature in the AP Elements panel. When the Prevent overlaps check box is selected, elements cannot be overlapped or stacked.

To Create Stacked Elements

The following steps illustrate how to draw three stacked elements, one on top of the other. The placement of the elements in Figures 6–13 through 6–22 on pages DW 443–DW 450 is approximate. Later in this chapter, you align and position the elements.

1

- Click the ruler-origin icon and drag it about 50 pixels to the right of the alaska_map element to prepare for adding the stacked elements.

- Collapse the Panel groups so you have more room to work.

- Click the Draw AP Div button on the Layout tab, and then use the rulers as a visual guide to draw an AP element measuring approximately 400px in width and 350px in height to the right of the alaska_map element.

- Move the mouse pointer over any border of the AP element outline and then click the border to select the element.

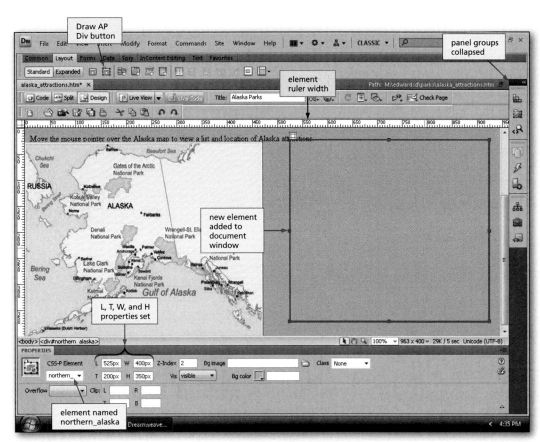

Figure 6–13

- Click the CSS-P Element text box and then type `northern_alaska` as the CSS-P Element. Enter the following properties: W – 400px, H – 350px, and Vis – hidden. If necessary, change L to 525px and T to 200px.

- Press the TAB key when you are finished entering the properties for the northern_alaska AP element (Figure 6–13).

- Right-click anywhere on the rulers and then click Reset Origin on the context menu.

- Scroll as necessary to display all of the northern_alaska element.

- Click the Draw AP Div button on the Layout tab and then draw a second AP element directly on top of the northern_alaska element.

- If necessary, select the AP element. Add and modify the following properties in the Property inspector: CSS-P Element – central_alaska, W – 400px, H – 350px, and Vis – hidden. If necessary, change L to 525px and T to 200px.

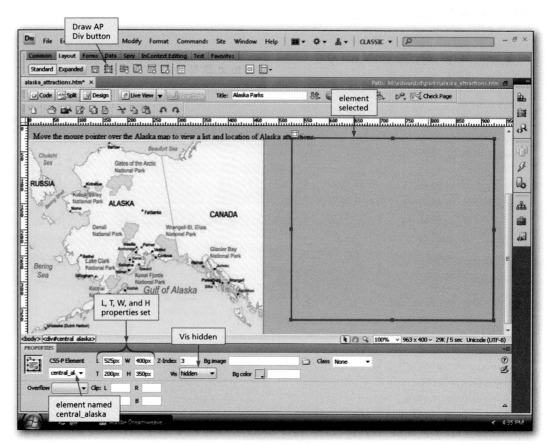

Figure 6–14

- Press the TAB key to add the modified properties for the central_alaska element (Figure 6–14).

- With the central_ alaska AP element still selected, click the Draw AP Div button on the Layout tab and then draw a third element on top of the central_alaska element.

- If necessary, select the AP element. Add and modify the following attributes in the Property inspector: CSS-P Element ID – southern_alaska, W – 400px, H – 350px, L – 525px, T – 200px, and Vis – hidden.

- Press the TAB key to add the properties for the southern_ alaska element (Figure 6–15).

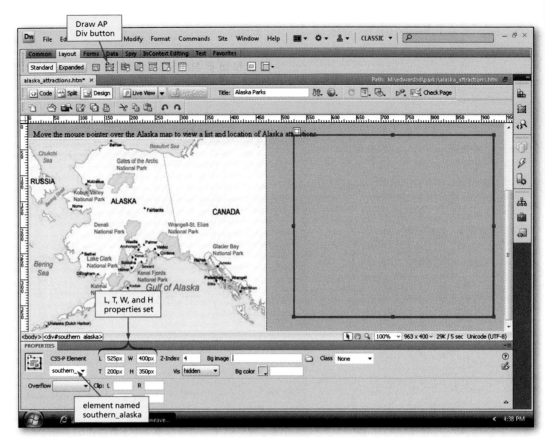

Figure 6–15

Selecting Stacked AP Elements

The next step is to add images to each of the AP elements, but before you add the images, you first must select the correct element. Dreamweaver provides the following options for selecting AP elements:

- Click the name of the desired element in the AP elements panel.
- Click an element's selection handle. If the selection handle is not visible, click anywhere inside the element to make the handle visible.
- Click an element's border.
- Press CTRL+SHIFT+click. If multiple elements are selected, this deselects all other elements and selects only the one that you clicked.
- Click the AP element marker (in Design view) that represents the element's location in the HTML code.

To Select AP Elements and Add Images

When elements are stacked, the easiest way to select an element is to click the name in the AP Elements panel. The next steps illustrate how to select AP elements and add images to each element.

- Expand the Panel groups.

- In the AP Elements panel, click the eye icons so that closed-eye icons are displayed to the left of the central_alaska and northern_alaska elements. If necessary, click to display an open-eye icon appears next to the southern_alaska element. Then click the southern_alaska element to select it (Figure 6–16).

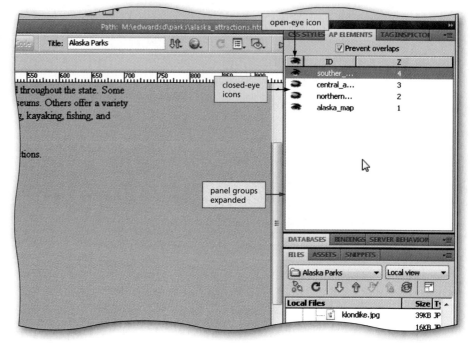

Figure 6–16

- If necessary, scroll to the right in the document window so that the entire AP element is displayed.

- Locate the southern_alaska.jpg file in the Files panel and drag the southern_alaska.jpg image onto the southern_alaska AP element.

- Click the image ID box and type so_alaska as the image ID.

- Click the Alt text box and type Southern Alaska Features as the entry. If necessary, press the TAB key so that the southern_alaska.jpg image is displayed in the southern_alaska element (Figure 6–17).

Figure 6–17

3

- In the AP Elements panel, click the eye icon to the left of southern_alaska twice to close the eye.

- Click the eye icon next to central_ alaska to display an open eye, and then click central_alaska to select it.

- If necessary, scroll up in the Files panel and locate the central_alaska. jpg file. Drag the central_alaska.jpg image onto the central_alaska AP element.

- Click the image ID box and type cen_ alaska as the image ID. Click the Alt text box and type Central Alaska Features as the entry, and then press the TAB key (Figure 6–18).

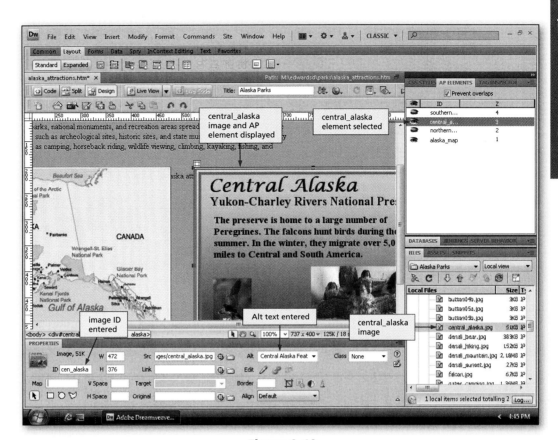

Figure 6–18

4

- In the AP Elements panel, click the eye icon to the left twice of central_alaska to close the eye.

- Click the eye icon to the left of northern_alaska to open the eye, and then click northern_alaska to select the element.

- Locate the northern_alaska.jpg image in the Files panel and drag the image onto the northern_alaska AP element.

- Click the image ID box and type nor_alaska as the entry.

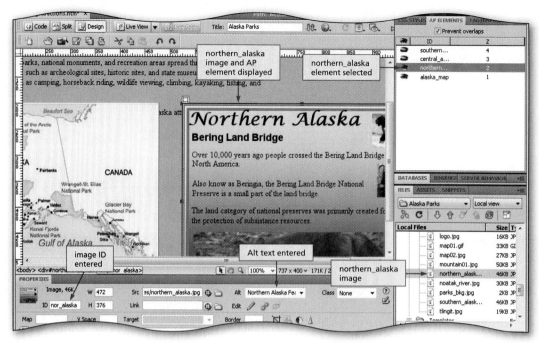

Figure 6–19

- Click the Alt text box and type Northern Alaska Features as the entry, and then press the TAB key (Figure 6–19).

Q&A
What should I do if the AP elements change position?

After adding the images to the AP elements, select each element in the AP Elements panel, and then set L to 525 and T to 200, except for the alaska_map element. For alaska_map, set L to 3 and T to 200.

- Save the alaska_attractions page.

BTW

Image Maps
Image maps are images with hotspots that are clickable. When the Web site visitor clicks a hotspot, the visitor is transferred to other Web pages or activates a behavior.

Image Maps

Image maps are an exciting and interesting way to liven up your Web site. An **image map** is an image that has one or more hotspots placed on top of it. A **hotspot** is a designated area on an image map that the user clicks to cause an action to occur. You can create a hotspot on an image map to link to different parts of the same Web page, to link to other Web pages within the Web site or outside the Web site, or to display content within a hidden AP element.

Two types of image maps exist: server-side and client-side. The way in which **map data** is stored and interpreted depends on the type of map. Map data is the description in the HTML code of the mapped regions or hotspots within the image. A Web server interprets the code or map data for **server-side maps**. When a visitor to a Web page clicks a hotspot in a server-side image map, the browser transfers data to a program running on a Web server for processing. The code for **client-side maps** is stored as part of the Web page HTML code. The Web browser, therefore, interprets the code for client-side maps. When a visitor to a Web page clicks a hotspot in a client-side image map, the browser processes the HTML code without interacting with the Web server. The code for client-side maps is processed faster because it does not have to be sent to a server.

You can add both client-side image maps and server-side image maps to the same document in Dreamweaver. Browsers that support both types of image maps give priority to client-side image maps. When you create an image map in the document window, Dreamweaver automatically creates the code for client-side image maps. To include a server-side image map in a document, you must write the appropriate HTML code in Code view. In this chapter, you create a client-side image map.

Creating a Client-Side Image Map

The first step in creating the image map is to place the image on the Web page. In this chapter, the image is an Alaska map. Earlier in this chapter, you placed the image on the alaska_map element. It is not necessary to place an image on an element to create an image map. You can insert the image anywhere on the page, just as you previously have inserted images in earlier chapters. Placing the image on an element, however, provides absolute positioning. Using this method, you can be assured that the image map will display properly in all browsers supporting CSS-P.

When you create an image map and add a hotspot, you are creating an area that is clickable on the image. To define a hotspot, use one of three shapes: a rectangle, a circle (or oval), or a polygon. Select the tool you want to use and then drag the pointer over the image to create the hotspot. Use the **Rectangular Hotspot Tool** to create a rectangular-shaped hotspot. Use the **Oval Hotspot Tool** to define an oval or circular hotspot area. Use the **Polygon Hotspot Tool** to define an irregularly shaped hotspot. Click the **Pointer Hotspot Tool** (arrow) to close the polygon shape.

When an image is selected, the Property inspector for images is displayed. The Map name text box and hotspot tools are available in the lower portion of the Property inspector (Figure 6–20a).

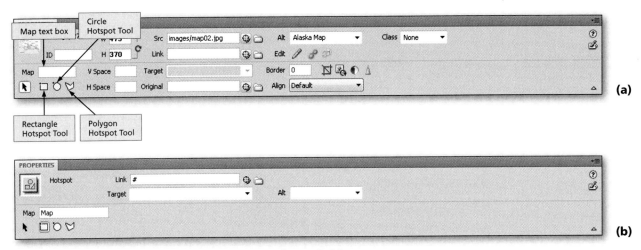

Figure 6–20

The **Map name** and the **hotspot tools** allow you to label and create a client-side image map. The other properties in the Image Property inspector are described in Chapter 2 on pages DW 127 – DW 128.

After you create a hotspot, Dreamweaver displays the Property inspector for a hotspot (Figure 6–20b). If you are linking to other locations within the same Web page or to Web pages outside of your existing Web site, the link or URL is inserted into the Link text box. On the Target pop-up menu, choose the window in which the file should open in the Target field. If the Web site contains frames, a list of the frame names is contained on the pop-up menu. You also can select from the reserved target names: _blank, _parent, _self, and _top. See Chapter 7 for a discussion about these target names. The target option is not available unless the selected hotspot contains a link.

In this image map, you will not link to another Web site or Web page. Instead, you add behaviors to the hotspots to link to and to display hidden AP elements. Behaviors are discussed later in this chapter. Clicking the top third of the Alaska map displays an image listing some of the more popular features in northern Alaska. Clicking the middle portion of the map displays an image listing some of the more popular features in central Alaska. Clicking the lower third of the map displays an image listing some of the more popular features in southern Alaska.

If Windows Vista or Windows XP SP2 is installed on your computer, the Internet Explorer security settings can prevent the display of active content such as the AP elements associated with the hotspots. To display the content, right-click the information bar at the top of the Internet Explorer window, and choose to allow blocked content.

Earlier in this chapter, you used the View menu to select Visual Aids, and then verified that AP Element Outlines was selected. This same menu also contains an Image Maps command. To see a visual of the hotspot on the image, the Image Maps command must be active.

To Create Hotspots on the Alaska Map Image

The following steps illustrate how to verify that the Image Maps command is selected and how to create three rectangular hotspots on the Alaska map image.

1

- Collapse the panel groups.

- If necessary, scroll to display the upper-left corner of the alaska_map AP element. Click the map image in the alaska_map element to select it (Figure 6–21).

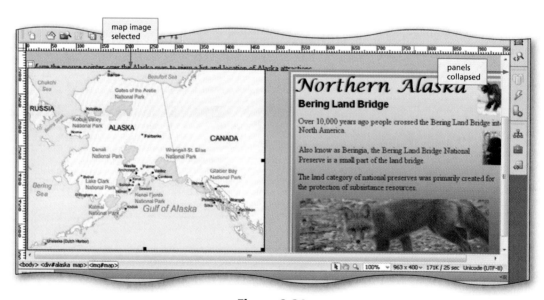

Figure 6–21

2

- Click the Rectangle Hotspot tool in the Property inspector, and then move the crosshair pointer to the upper-left corner of the map02.jpg image (Figure 6–22).

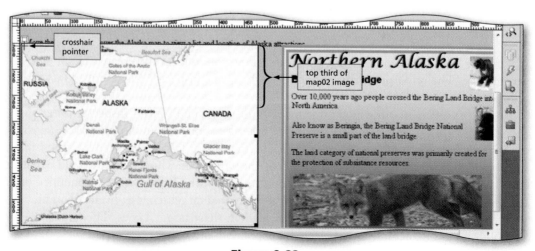

Figure 6–22

3

- Drag to draw a rectangle encompassing approximately the top third of the map02.jpg image. (Figure 6–23).

Q&A

What should I do if the rectangular hotspot does not appear?

If the rectangular hotspot does not appear, click View on the Application bar, point to Visual Aids, and then click Image Maps on the Visual Aids submenu to display the rectangular hotspot.

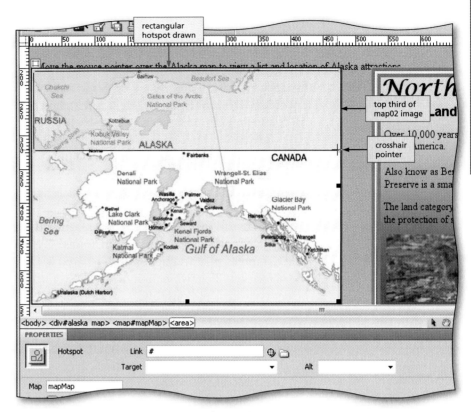

Figure 6–23

4

- Draw two more hotspots on the map02.jpg image by dragging the crosshair pointer over the middle third of the image and then over the lower third of the image.

- Click anywhere in the window to cancel the crosshair pointer, and then, if necessary, scroll down to display the entire map02 image (Figure 6–24).

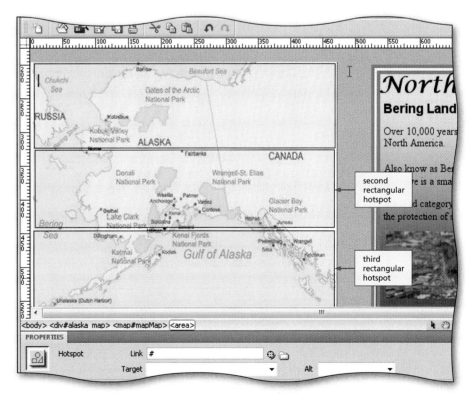

Figure 6–24

BTW

Behaviors
Use Dreamweaver behaviors to allow visitors to interact with a Web page. Simply specify the action and the event that triggers that action.

Behaviors

In Chapter 4, you learned about the Behaviors panel and about using behaviors with forms. Recall that a behavior is a combination of an event and an action. Behaviors are attached to a specific element on a Web page. The element can be a table, an image, a link, a form, a form object, and even a hotspot on an image map. Some of the actions you can attach to hotspots (or other elements) include Show Pop-Up Menu, Play Sound, Drag AP Element, Swap Image, and Show-Hide AP Elements.

Dreamweaver contains two standard events designed expressly for working with AP Elements: Drag AP Element and Show-Hide Elements. **Drag AP Element** is used to set up an interactive process in which the user can drag or rearrange elements of the design. **Show-Hide Elements** is used to make visible or to hide an element and the element's content.

Actions to invoke these events are **onMouseOut**, which initiates whatever action is associated with the event when the mouse is moved out of an object; **onMouseOver**, which initiates whatever action is associated with the event when the mouse is moved over the object; **onClick**, which initiates whatever action is associated with the event when the object is clicked; and **onDblClick**, which initiates whatever action is associated with the event when the object is double-clicked. These actions are selected through the Behaviors panel. The default is onMouseOver. To change the action for an event, click the existing event in the Behaviors panel. An arrow then is displayed to the right of the event, listing the four actions. Click the arrow to display a pop-up menu and to select another action: onClick, onDblClick, onMouseOut, or onMouseOver. Note that the arrow for the pop-up menu does not display until the existing event is clicked.

Adding Behaviors

Selecting a hotspot and then clicking the Add behavior (+) pop-up menu in the Behaviors panel displays a menu of actions that can be attached to the hotspot. When you choose an action on this menu, Dreamweaver displays a dialog box in which you can specify the parameters for the action. In this chapter, you use the Show-Hide Elements action.

To Add the Show-Hide Elements Action to the Image Map Hotspots

The following steps show how to attach the Show-Hide Elements action to each of the three image map hotspots.

1

- Display the panel groups and collapse the Property inspector (Figure 6–25).

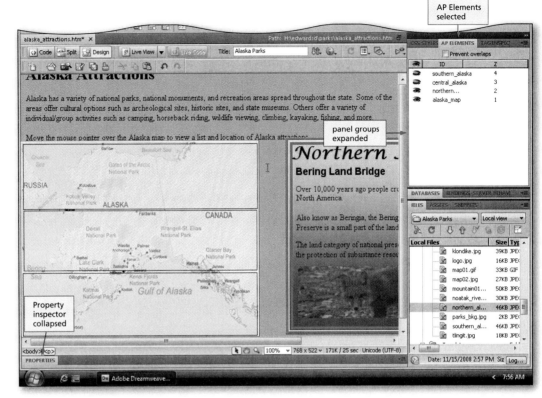

Figure 6–25

2

- Click the top rectangular hotspot on the map02.jpg image to select it (Figure 6–26).

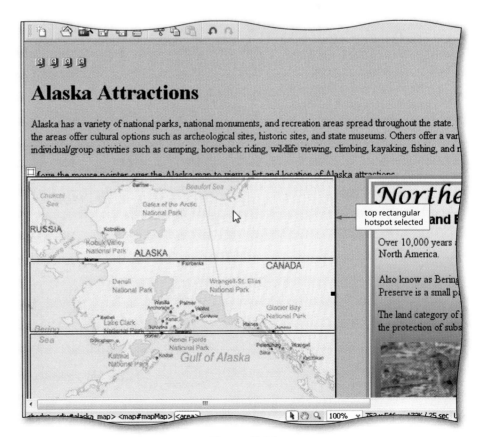

Figure 6–26

3

- Click Window on the Application bar, and then click Behaviors to display the Behaviors panel.

- Click the Add behavior button to display the Actions pop-up menu in the Behaviors panel.

- Point to Show-Hide Elements (Figure 6–27).

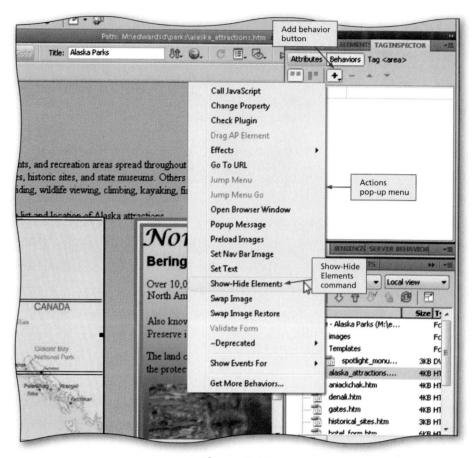

Figure 6–27

4

- Click Show-Hide Elements to open the Show-Hide Elements dialog box. If necessary, click div "alaska_map" in the Elements list to select it (Figure 6–28).

 The order of the elements is different in my dialog box. Is that a problem?

No. The order of the elements in your dialog box may be different.

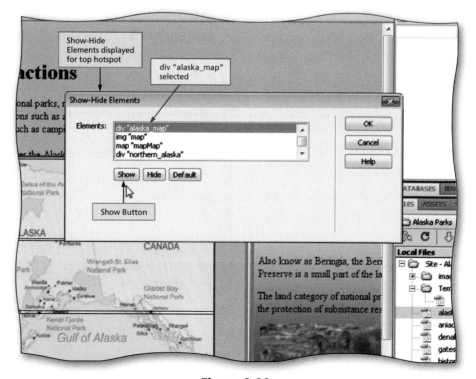

Figure 6–28

- Click the Show button to set the alaska_map element to display this element when the pointer is over the top rectangular hotspot.

- Click div "northern_alaska" and then click the Show button to display this element when the pointer is over the top rectangular hotspot.

- Click div "central_alaska" and then click the Hide button to hide the element when the pointer is over the top rectangular hotspot.

- Click div "southern_alaska" and then click the Hide button to complete adding the Show-Hide Elements behaviors (Figure 6–29).

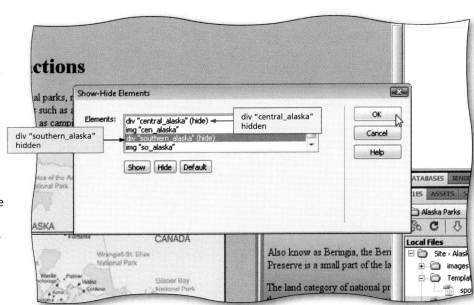

Figure 6–29

- Click the OK button.

- Click the middle hotspot on the map02.jpg image, click the Add behavior button in the Behaviors panel, and then click Show-Hide Elements on the Actions pop-up menu to display the Show-Hide Elements dialog box (Figure 6–30).

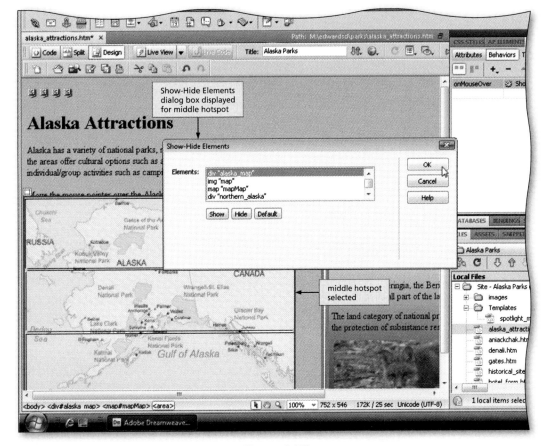

Figure 6–30

- If necessary, click div "alaska_map" and then click the Show button. Click div "northern_alaska" and then click the Hide button to hide the element when the pointer is over the middle rectangular hotspot. Click div "central_alaska" and then click the Show button to show the element when the pointer is over the middle rectangular hotspot. Click div "southern_alaska" and then click the Hide button to hide the element when the pointer is over the middle rectangular hotspot (Figure 6–31).

- Click the OK button.

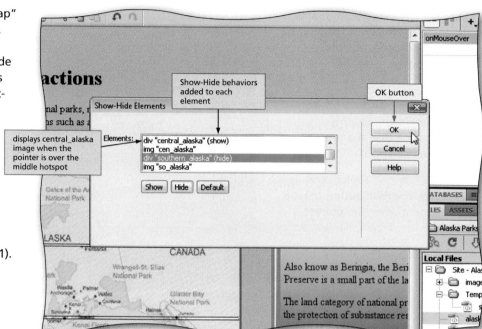

Figure 6–31

- If necessary, scroll down in the document window and then click the third hotspot on the map02.jpg image.

- Click the Add behavior button in the Behaviors panel, and then click Show-Hide Elements on the Actions pop-up menu to open the Show-Hide Elements dialog box (Figure 6–32).

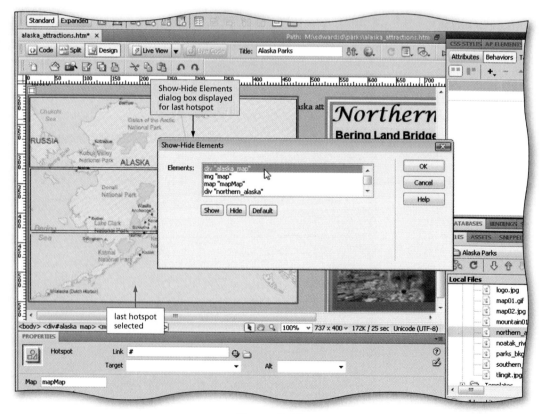

Figure 6–32

- With div "alaska_map" selected, click the Show button. Click div "northern_alaska" and then click the Hide button. Click div "central_alaska" and then click the Hide button. Click div "southern_alaska" and then click the Show button to show the element when the pointer is over the bottom rectangular hotspot (Figure 6–33).

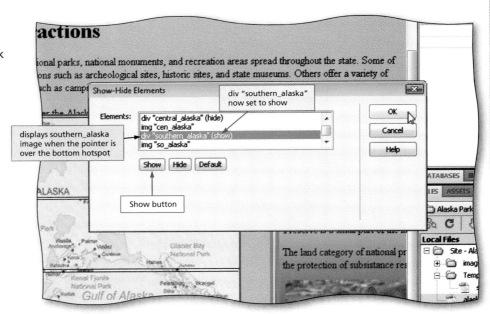

Figure 6–33

- Click the OK button.

- Click the Save button on the Standard toolbar and then press the F12 key to display the Web page in your browser.

- If necessary, maximize the browser window. (Allow blocked content, if necessary.)

- Move the mouse pointer over the hotspots on the map02.jpg image to display each of the hidden elements (Figure 6–34 and Figures 6–35 and 6–36 on the next page).

⑪

- Close the browser window and return to Dreamweaver.

Figure 6–34

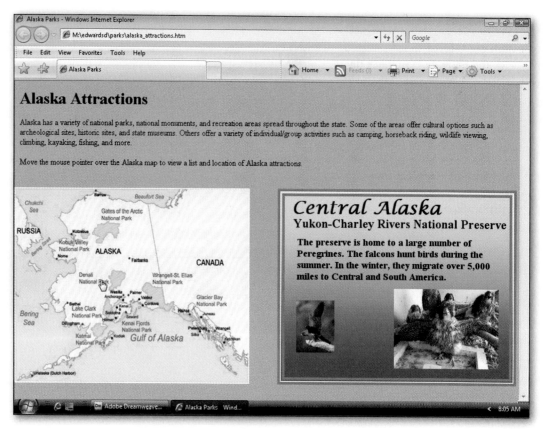

Figure 6–35

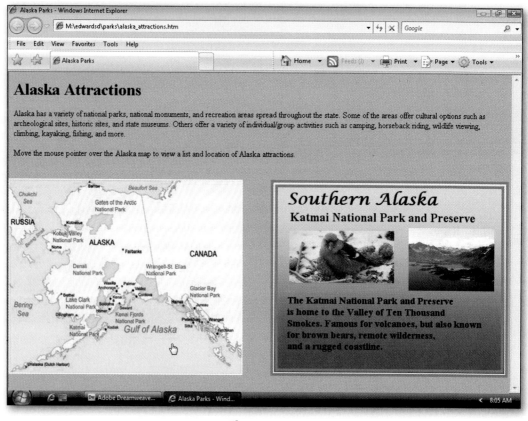

Figure 6–36

Positioning AP Elements

When you displayed the Alaska map image and the images in the browser, you may have noticed that the spacing between the images and between the text was not quite right. One advantage of using AP elements is that they can be positioned on the page. In some instances, to eliminate extra space, it is necessary to drag the image over existing text. Even though the text is covered in the document window, it is displayed correctly in the browser.

This sometimes can be a trial-and-error process. You can select and drag the element by the selection handle or you can move the element pixel by pixel by selecting the image, holding down the SHIFT key, and then pressing one of the arrow keys.

To Adjust AP Element Placement

In some instances, the map and the AP element may overlap the text. If this happens, the following steps show how to adjust the position of the alaska_map element. If the elements do not overlap, you do not need to complete these steps.

- Display the Property inspector and the AP Elements panel. Click alaska_map in the AP Elements panel and then, if necessary, scroll up in the document window to display the top of the alaska_map element.

- If necessary, double-click the T text box in the Property inspector and type 205px as the T value.

- Press the TAB key and then click anywhere in the document window.

Q&A | What should I do if some of the text overlaps?

Leave it as is. The overlapped text will not be displayed as overlapped when viewed in the browser.

- Click the Save button on the Standard toolbar to save any changes.

Selecting, Aligning, and Resizing Multiple AP Elements

Dreamweaver contains yet another command that you can use to lay out your Web page: the **Arrange command**. This command, which is accessed through the Modify menu, lets you align elements to their left, right, top, or bottom edges. The Arrange command also provides an option to make the width and/or height of selected elements the same. When you are using the Arrange command, the element you select last controls the alignment selection. For instance, if you first select northern_alaska, then central_alaska, and finally southern_alaska, the alignment placement is determined by southern_alaska. Likewise, if you select the option to make the width and/or height of selected elements the same, the last element selected is the one whose values are used as the values for the other elements.

To align two or more elements, you first must select the elements. To select multiple elements in the AP Elements panel, you select one element, hold down the SHIFT key, and then click the other elements you want to align. A second method for selecting multiple elements is to click the border of one element, hold down the SHIFT key, and then click the border of any other elements. When multiple elements are selected, the handles of the last selected element are highlighted in black. The resize handles of the other elements are highlighted in white.

BTW | **Positioning AP Elements**
Control the absolute positioning of AP elements on a Web page by setting five attributes: Left, Top, Width, Height, and Z-Index.

BTW

Resizing AP Elements
To resize an element one pixel at a time, hold down the CTRL key while pressing an arrow key.

AP elements do not have to be stacked or overlapped to be aligned. The three elements you aligned, however, are stacked one on top of the other. Thus, the best method for selecting the three elements is through the AP Elements panel.

The final steps for this Web page are to use the Align command to align the tops of the three hidden elements with the alaska_map element, make the three hidden elements the same height and width if necessary, and then align the three elements to the left. Finally, you add a link from the natl_parks.htm Web page to this new alaska_attractions.htm page.

To Select and Align Multiple AP Elements

The next steps illustrate how to complete the alignment options and add the link.

1

- Select the southern_alaska element in the AP Elements panel. Hold down the SHIFT key and then select the central_alaska, northern_alaska, and alaska_map elements so that all four elements are selected (Figure 6–37).

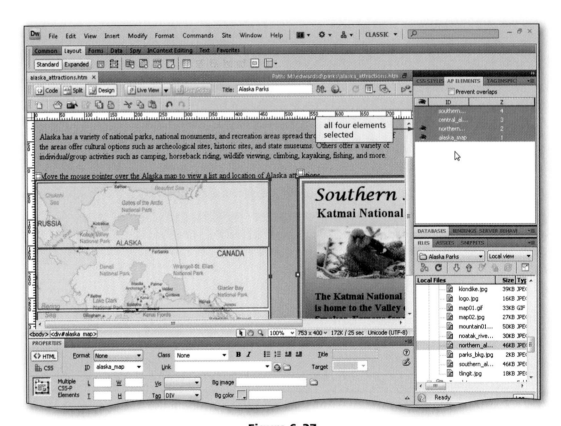

Figure 6–37

• Click Modify on the Application bar, point to Arrange, and then point to Align Top on the Arrange sub-menu to display the Modify menu and Arrange submenu (Figure 6–38).

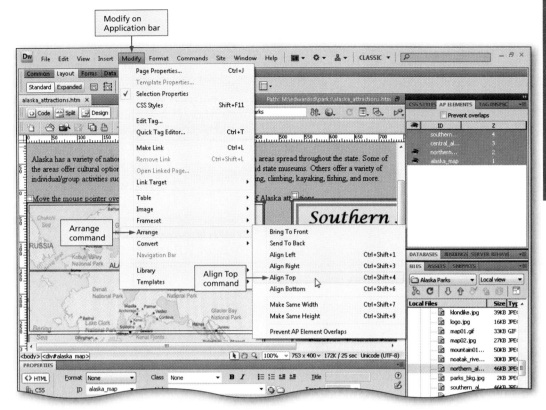

Figure 6–38

• Click Align Top to align all four elements at the top. If necessary, scroll down in the document window (Figure 6–39).

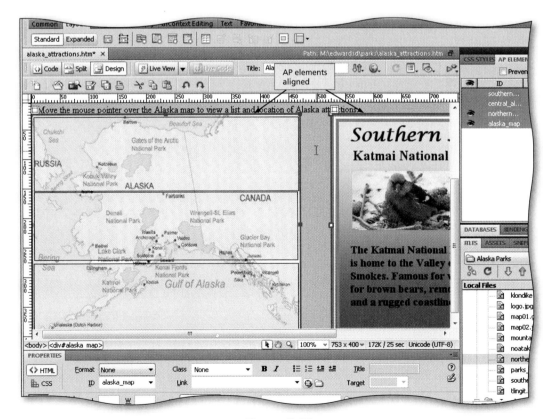

Figure 6–39

4

- Hold down the SHIFT key and then click alaska_map in the AP Elements panel to deselect it (Figure 6–40).

Figure 6–40

5

- Click Modify on the Application bar, point to Arrange, and then click Align Left on the Arrange submenu to align all elements to the left.

- Click Modify on the Application bar, point to Arrange, and then click Make Same Width on the Arrange submenu to make all elements the same width.

- Click Modify on the Application bar, point to Arrange, and then click Make Same Height on the Arrange submenu to make all elements the same height.

- Click View on the Application bar, point to Rulers, and then click Show on the Rulers submenu to hide the rulers.

Figure 6–41

- Click the Save button on the Standard toolbar to save your work.

- Press the F12 key to view the Web page in your browser. Allow blocked content, if necessary. Move the mouse pointer over the Alaska map to verify that the images are displayed and that they are aligned properly (Figure 6–41).

- Close the browser and return to Dreamweaver. Close the alaska_attractions page.

- Press F2 to collapse the AP Elements panel group and then press SHIFT+F4 twice to collapse the Tag Inspector panel group.

- In the Files panel, open the index.htm file and scroll to the bottom of the page. Click to the right of the Alaska National Parks Hotel Reservations link and press SHIFT+ENTER. Type

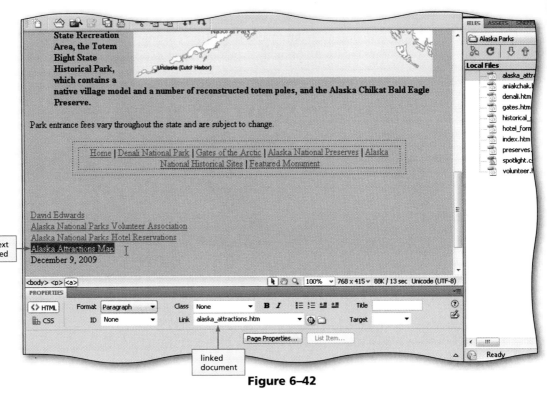

Figure 6–42

Alaska Attractions Map as the entry, create a link to the alaska_attractions.htm page, and then save the index.htm file (Figure 6–42).

- Press F12 to view the Web page and test the link. Close the browser to return to Dreamweaver.

The Navigation Bar and Date Object

In earlier chapters, you used text to add links to your Web pages. Dreamweaver provides another quick-and-easy method to provide navigation: a navigation bar. A **navigation bar** (or **nav bar**) is a set of interactive buttons that the Web site visitor uses as links to other Web pages, Web sites, or frames. The Insert Navigation Bar dialog box provides an option to insert the navigation bar horizontally or vertically. Many Web site developers consider a navigation bar to be a convenient, customized alternative to a browser's Back and Forward buttons.

Dreamweaver also provides the **Date object**, which inserts the current date in a format of your preference and provides the option of updating the date (with or without the time) whenever you save the file.

BTW

Navigation Bar
Dreamweaver's navigation bar feature provides a visually interesting option that allows visitors to navigate the Web site easily. A navigation bar often extends along the top or side of a Web page and can include text, images, or animations that link to other sections or pages in the site.

Preparing the Index Page and Adding the Date Object

You add these two objects (Date object and navigation bar) to the index page. You open the index.htm page, delete the existing links, and then insert a navigation bar to replace these links. Additionally, you delete the static date and replace it with the Date object.

To Prepare the Index Page by Inserting the Date Object and Deleting Existing Links

The first step in modifying the index page is to remove the static date placed at the bottom of the page and replace it with a new format using the Dreamweaver Date object. The second step is to delete the two links at the top of the page. The following steps show how to insert the Date object and delete the existing links.

- If necessary, collapse the Property inspector and the panel groups.

- At the bottom of the index.htm page, select the date and then press the DELETE key to delete the date.

- Click Insert on the Application bar to display the Insert menu and then point to Date (Figure 6–43).

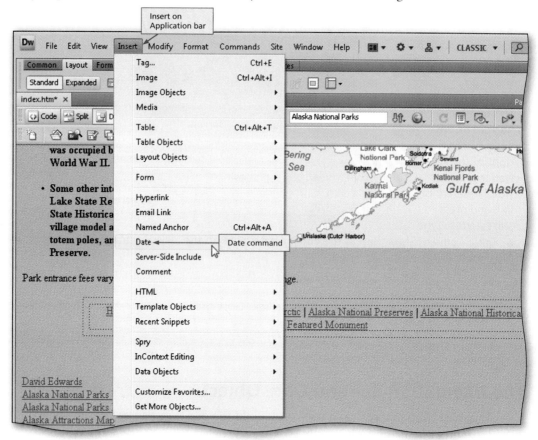

Figure 6–43

- Click Date to display the Insert Date dialog box and to display the dates and times available formats.

- Click the Update automatically on save check box to apply the default date format (Figure 6–44).

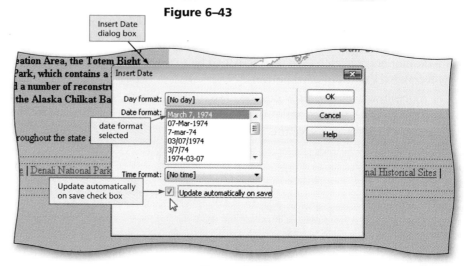

Figure 6–44

4

- Click the OK button to display the current date on the index page and then click anywhere on the page to deselect the date.

- Click the Save button on the Standard toolbar to save your work (Figure 6–45).

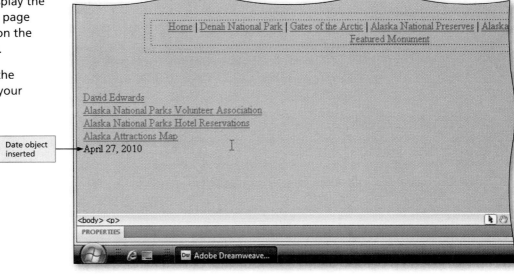

Date object inserted

Home | Denali National Park | Gates of the Arctic | Alaska National Preserves | Alaska Featured Monument

David Edwards
Alaska National Parks Volunteer Association
Alaska National Parks Hotel Reservations
Alaska Attractions Map
April 27, 2010

<body> <p>

PROPERTIES

Adobe Dreamweave...

Figure 6–45

Other Ways

1. Click Common tab on Insert bar, click the Date button on Common tab, select Date format in Insert Date dialog box, click OK button

Creating a Navigation Bar

You create a navigation bar using icon or button elements. Each element is a slightly different shape or a different color. An element in a navigation bar is called a **rollover** if animation takes place when you move the mouse pointer over the element or click the element. The original image is swapped out for a different one, thus creating a simple animation.

Each element in a Dreamweaver navigation bar can have up to four different states. It is not necessary, however, to include images for all four states. The four possible images and states are as follows:

- **Up**: the image that is displayed when the visitor has not clicked or interacted with the element.

- **Over**: the image that appears when the mouse pointer is moved over the Up image.

- **Down**: the image that appears after the element is clicked.

- **Over While Down**: the image that appears when the pointer is rolled over the Down image after the element is clicked.

Dreamweaver also provides several features that contribute to the versatility of the navigation bar. Some of these features are:

- The navigation bar can be placed within a table or directly integrated into the HTML code.

- An Alternate text text box is available for use with nongraphical browsers and as an accessibility option.

- You can copy the navigation bar to other Web pages.

- A Preload images check box is available; select Preload images to download the images when the page loads.

- Check the Show "Down image" check box to display the selected element initially in its Down state when the page is displayed, instead of in its default Up state.

Modifying a navigation bar is easy. After you create the navigation bar, you can add or remove images by using the Navigation Bar command on the Modify menu. You can use this command to change an image or set of images, to change which file opens when an element is clicked, to select a different window or frame in which to open a file, and to reorder the images.

The Alaska Parks navigation bar contains five links. You specify three different states for each link — Up, Over, and Down. The same image is used for the Over and Down states.

To Create the Navigation Bar

The following steps illustrate how to create the navigation bar.

1

• Display the Property inspector.

• Scroll up to the top of the index. htm page in the document window and then insert a blank line below the heading. If necessary, click the Center button. Click Insert on the Application bar, point to Image Objects, and then point to Navigation Bar on the Image Objects submenu (Figure 6–46).

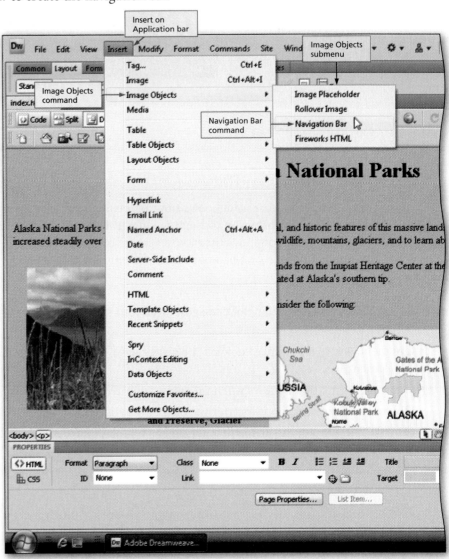

Figure 6–46

2

- Click Navigation Bar to display the Insert Navigation Bar dialog box (Figure 6–47).

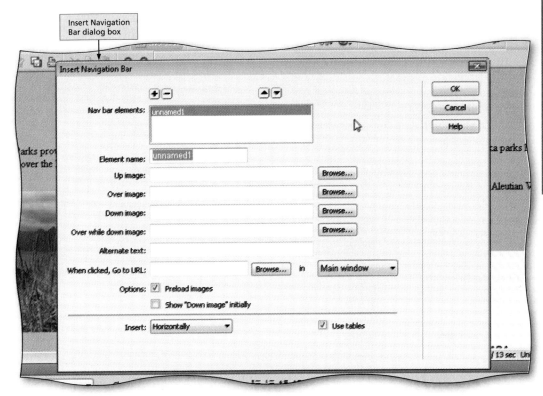

Figure 6–47

3

- Type alaska_parks in the Element name text box and then press the TAB key. If necessary, click the Use tables check box to select it and verify that Horizontally is selected in the Insert pop-up menu. Point to the Browse button for the Up image text box (Figure 6–48).

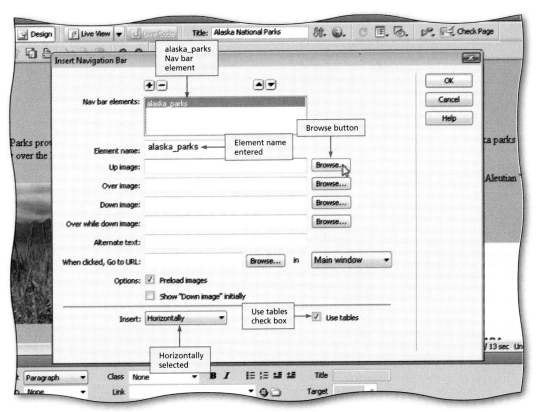

Figure 6–48

- Click the Browse button to the right of the Up image text box. If necessary, double-click the images folder in the Select image source dialog box. If necessary, click the View Menu button and select List. Verify that the Preview Images check box is selected.

- Click the button01a image (Figure 6–49).

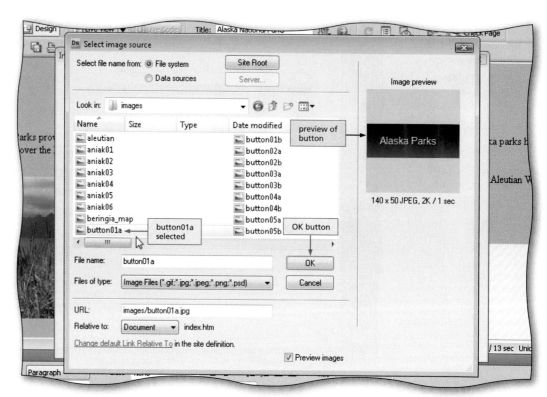

Figure 6–49

- Click the OK button in the Select image source dialog box and then point to the Browse button to the right of the Over image text box (Figure 6–50).

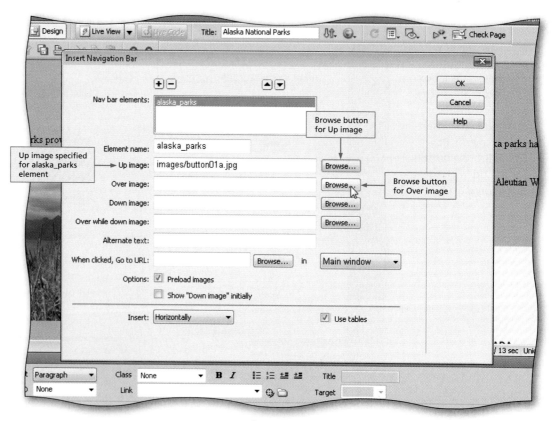

Figure 6–50

6

- Click the Browse button to the right of the Over image text box, click button01b to select the button, and then click OK.

- Click the Alternate text text box and then type Alaska Parks as the alternate text.

- Click the When clicked, Go to URL: text box. Click the Browse button and then click denali.htm (Figure 6–51).

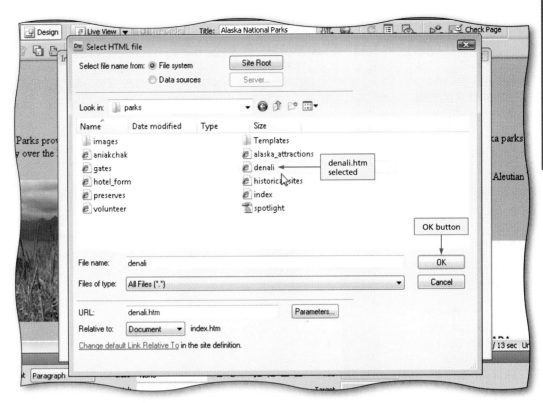

Figure 6–51

7

- Click OK to select the denali.htm file.

- Click the Plus button above the Nav bar elements box (Figure 6–52).

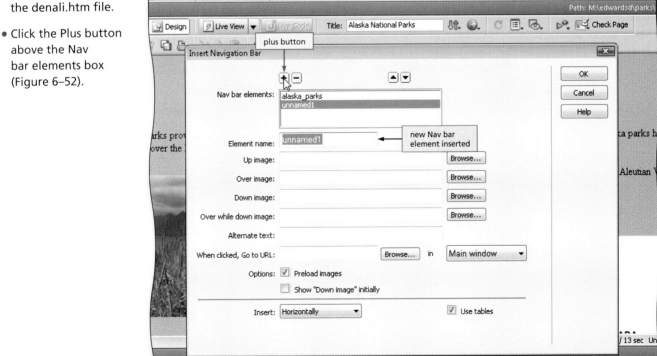

Figure 6–52

- In the Element name text box, type `alaska_monuments`.

- Click the Browse button to the right of the Up image text box.

- Click button02a and then click OK.

- Click the Browse button to the right of the Over image text box.

- Click button02b and then click OK.

- Click the Alternate text text box and then type `Alaska Monuments` as the alternate text.

- Click the Browse button for the When clicked, Go to URL: text box, select aniakchak. htm, and then click OK (Figure 6–53).

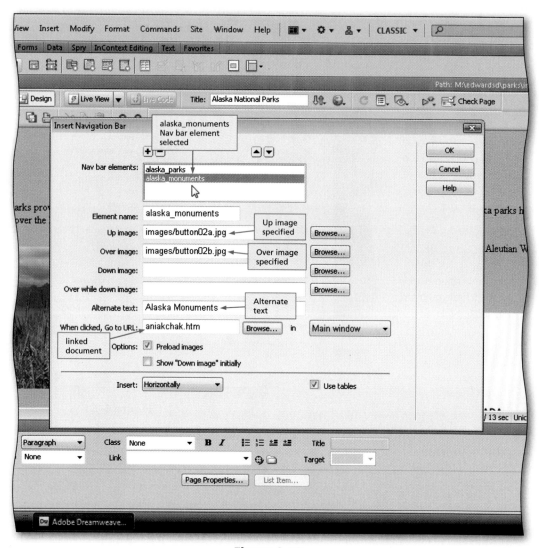

Figure 6–53

9

- Click the Plus button above the Nav bar elements box.

- In the Element name text box, type `Hotels`, and then press the TAB key.

- Click the Browse button to the right of the Up image text box, click button03a, and then click OK.

- Click the Browse button to the right of the Over image text box, click button03b, and then click OK.

- Click the Alternate text text box and then type `Hotels` as the alternate text.

- Click the Browse button next to the When clicked, Go to URL: text box, click hotel_form.htm, and then click OK. (Figure 6–54).

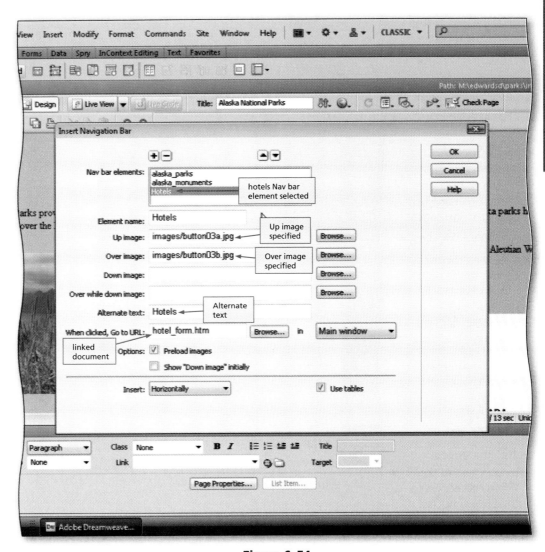

Figure 6–54

- Click the Plus button above the Nav bar elements box.

- In the Element name text box, type featured_park, and then press the TAB key.

- Click the Browse button to the right of the Up image text box, click button04a, and then click OK.

- Click the Browse button to the right of the Over image text box, click button04b, and then click OK.

- Click the Alternate text text box and then type Featured Park as the alternate text.

- Click the Browse button next to the When clicked, Go to URL: text box, click alaska_attractions, and then click OK (Figure 6–55).

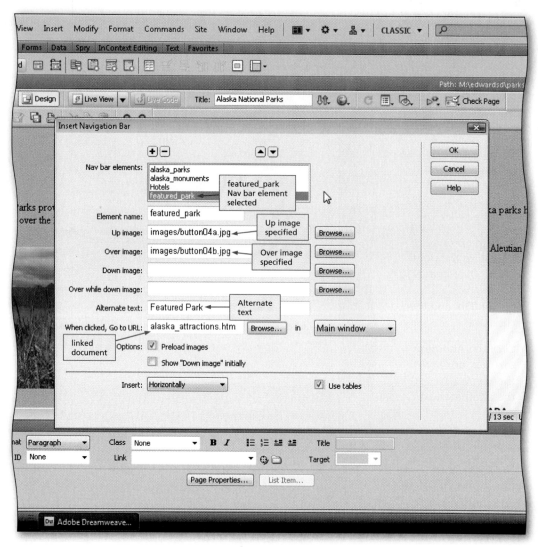

Figure 6–55

- Click the Plus button above the Nav bar elements box.

- In the Element name text box, type wildlife_ education, and then press the TAB key.

- Click the Browse button to the right of the Up image text box, click button05a, and then click OK.

- Click the Browse button to the right of the Over image text box, click button05b, and then click OK.

- Click the Alternate text text box, and then type Wildlife Education as the alternate text.

- Click the When clicked, Go to URL: text box, and then type http://www. nature.nps.gov (Figure 6–56).

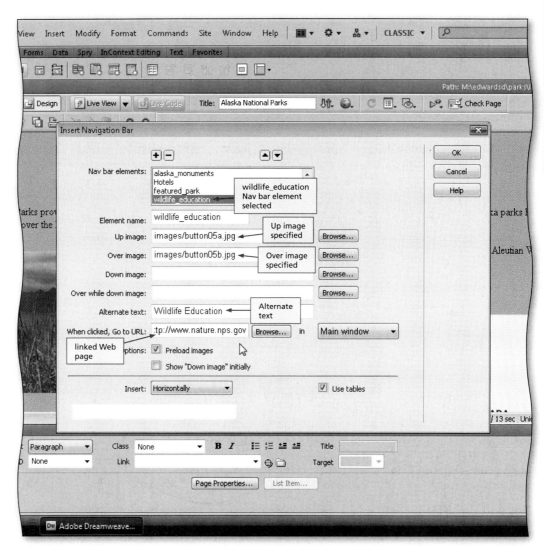

Figure 6–56

- Click the OK button to insert the navigation bar.

- If necessary, select the table, click the Align button in the Property inspector, and then click Center (Figure 6–57).

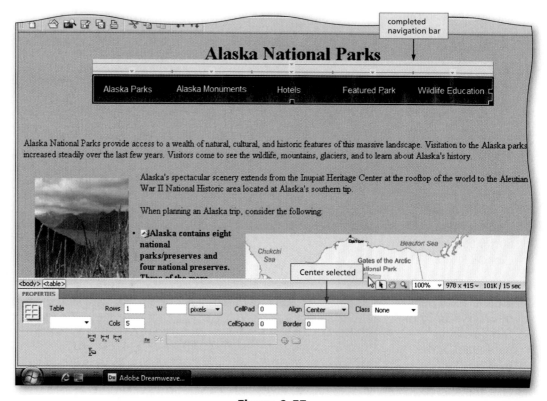

Figure 6–57

- Click the OK button and then click the Save button on the Standard toolbar to save your work.

- Press the F12 key to view the navigation bar in your browser, allow blocked content, and test each of the links (Figure 6–58).

- Close the browser.

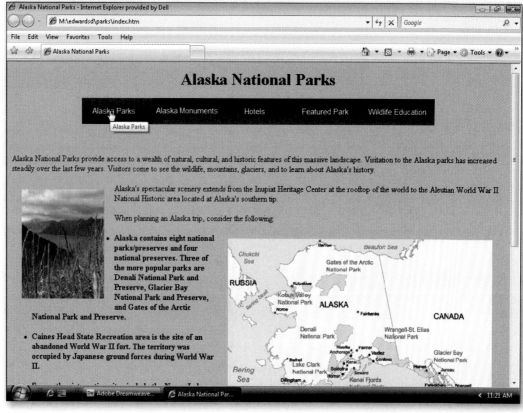

Figure 6–58

To Close the Web Site and Quit Dreamweaver

After you have created your Web page based on a template with applied styles, and tested and verified that the links work, Chapter 6 is complete. The following step closes the Web site and quits Dreamweaver.

- Click the Close button in the upper-right corner of the Dreamweaver title bar to close the Dreamweaver window, the document window, and the Alaska Parks Web site.

Chapter Summary

Chapter 6 introduced you to AP elements, image maps, navigation bars, and the Date object. You added single AP elements and stacked elements. You selected and aligned several elements. Next, you created an image map and then added hotspots that displayed hidden AP elements. Then, you modified the existing index page by deleting links and replacing those links with a navigation bar. You also inserted a Date object on the index page. The items listed below include all the new skills you have learned in this chapter.

1. Open the Alaska Attractions page and Display the Rulers (DW 432)
2. Create and Select an AP Element for the Alaska Map Image (DW 436)
3. Display the AP Elements Panel (DW 439)
4. Name the Element and Adjust the AP Element Properties (DW 440)
5. Add an Image to the alaska_map Element (DW 441)
6. Create Stacked Elements (DW 443)
7. Select AP Elements and Add Images (DW 446)
8. Create Hotspots on the Alaska Map Image (DW 450)
9. Add the Show-Hide Elements Action to the Image Map Hotspots (DW 453)
10. Adjust AP Element Placement (DW 459)
11. Select and Align Multiple Elements (DW 460)
12. Insert the Date Object and Delete Existing Links (DW 464)
13. Create the Navigation Bar (DW 466)

Learn It Online

Test your knowledge of chapter content and key terms.

Instructions: To complete the Learn It Online exercises, start your browser, click the Address bar, and then enter the Web address scsite.com/dwCS4/learn. When the Dreamweaver CS4 Learn It Online page is displayed, click the link for the exercise you want to complete and then read the instructions.

Chapter Reinforcement TF, MC, and SA
A series of true/false, multiple choice, and short answer questions that test your knowledge of the chapter content.

Flash Cards
An interactive learning environment where you identify chapter key terms associated with displayed definitions.

Practice Test
A series of multiple choice questions that test your knowledge of chapter content and key terms.

Who Wants To Be a Computer Genius?
An interactive game that challenges your knowledge of chapter content in the style of a television quiz show.

Wheel of Terms
An interactive game that challenges your knowledge of chapter key terms in the style of the television show *Wheel of Fortune*.

Crossword Puzzle Challenge
A crossword puzzle that challenges your knowledge of key terms presented in the chapter.

Apply Your Knowledge

Reinforce the skills and apply the concepts you learned in this chapter.

Inserting a Date Object

Instructions: In this activity, you insert a Date object on a Web page (Figure 6–59). Data files are not required for this exercise.

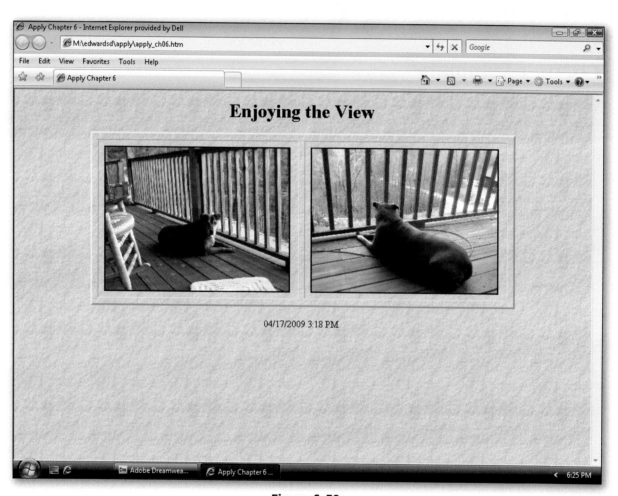

Figure 6–59

Perform the following tasks:

1. Start Dreamweaver and open the Apply Exercises Web site. Open the apply_ch03.htm document, which you created in Chapter 3.

2. Save the document as apply_ch06, and then change the title to Apply Chapter 6.

3. Click to the right of the table containing the pictures of the dog and then press the ENTER key.

4. Click Insert on the Application bar and then click Date.

5. In the Insert Date dialog box, select a date format that you prefer.

6. Click the Time Format arrow and select a format that you prefer.

7. Click the Update automatically on Save check box and then click the OK button to insert the date and time. Save the document, display it in a browser, and then submit it to your instructor as requested.

Extend Your Knowledge

Extend the skills you learned in this chapter and experiment with new skills. You may need to use Help to complete the assignment.

Creating a Navigation Menu

Instructions: In this activity, you add a navigation menu to an existing Web page (Figure 6–60). Make sure you have downloaded the data files provided for this exercise.

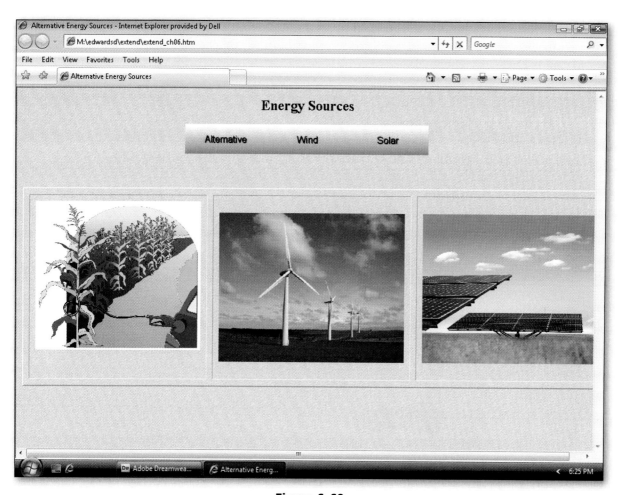

Figure 6–60

Perform the following tasks:

1. If necessary, start Dreamweaver and then open the Extend Exercises Web site. Copy the extend data files to the extend and images folders for your Extend Exercises Web site.
2. Open the extend_ch06.htm page.
3. Click to the right of the title and then press ENTER.
4. Click Insert on the Application bar, point to Image Objects, and then select Navigation Bar.
5. Use to Table 6–1 on the next page to create the navigation bar.

Continued >

Extend Your Knowledge *continued*

Table 6–1 Navigation Bar Properties

Element Name	Up Image	Over Image	Down Image	Alternate Text	URL
Alternative	extend01a	extend01b	extend01b	Alternative power	http://wikipedia.org/wiki/Energy_sources
Wind	extend02a	extend02b	extend02b	Wind power	http://wikipedia.org/wiki/Wind_power
Solar	extend03a	extend03b	extend03b	Solar power	http://wikipedia.org/wiki/Solar_power

6. Center the navigation bar.

7. Save the document, display it in your browser, allow blocked content, and then submit the document to your instructor as requested.

Make It Right

Analyze a Web page template and correct all errors and/or improve the design.

Creating Links with Buttons

Instructions: In this activity, you modify a Web page by adding a background image and correcting button images and links (Figure 6–61). Make sure you have downloaded the data files provided for this exercise.

Figure 6–61

Perform the following tasks:

1. If necessary, start Dreamweaver and then open the Right Exercises Web site. Copy the right_ch06. htm file to the Right Exercises folder. Copy the images from the right\images data files to the Right Exercises images folder.

2. Open the right_ch06.htm file.

3. Below the heading, draw an AP element 160 px wide and 50 px high. Set the L for the AP element to 280 px and the T to 110 px. Name the element jar_candles.

4. Draw another AP element on top of the jar_candles element. Make it the same size and position it in the same location. Name this second AP element taper_candles.

5. Draw a third AP element on top of the first two. Make it the same size and position it in the same location. Name the third AP element pillar_candles.

6. Open the AP Elements panel. Select the jar_candles element, and then drag the candle01.jpg image to the element. Select the taper_candles element, and then drag the candle02.jpg image to the element. Select the pillar_candles AP element, and then drag the candle03.jpg image to the element.

7. In the fundraiser AP element, draw three rectangular hotspots, one for each type of candle.

8. Open the Behaviors panel.

9. Click the first hotspot, click the Add behavior button, and then show the jar_candles div element. Hide the taper_candles and pillar_candles elements.

10. Click the second hotspot, and then show the taper_candles element. Hide the jar_candles and pillar_candles elements.

11. Click the third hotspot, and then show the pillar_candles element. Hide the jar_candles and taper_candles elements.

12. Save the page and then open the page in your browser. Allow blocked content, and then test the hotspots.

13. Close the browser, and then submit the document to your instructor as requested.

In the Lab

Create a document using the guidelines, concepts, and skills presented in this chapter. Labs are listed in order of increasing difficulty.

Lab 1: Adding AP Elements to the Bryan's Mobile Pet Services Web Site

Problem: The proprietors of Bryan's Mobile Pet Services would like to make some additions to their Web site. First, they would like to add a navigation bar to the main page. Second, they would like to have an additional informational page that provides grooming tips for pets. You begin the process by adding a navigation bar to the index.htm page. Next, you open a data file and add AP elements to show some illustrations. The modified index.htm page and the new grooming_tips page are shown in Figures 6–62 and 6–63.

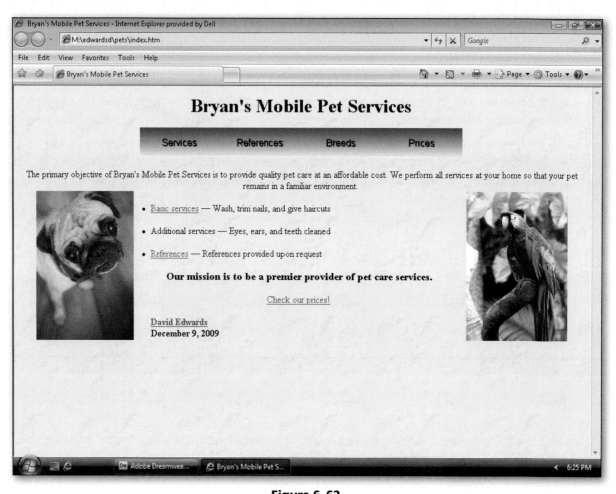

Figure 6–62

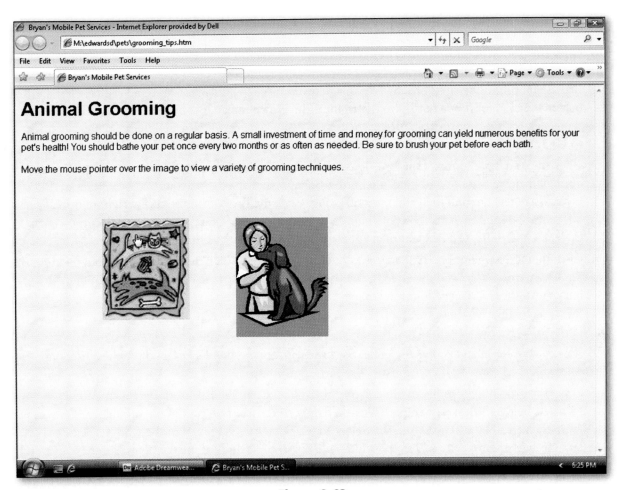

Figure 6–63

Perform the following tasks:

1. If necessary, start Dreamweaver and then open the Pet Services Web site.

2. Copy the grooming_tips.htm data file from the Chapter06 folder to the pets folder for your Pet Services Web site, and copy the image files to your pets/images folder.

3. Open the index.htm page. Click to the right of the Bryan's Mobile Pet Services heading and press the ENTER key. Click Format on the Application bar, point to Align, and then click Center.

4. Click Insert on the Application bar, point to Image Objects, and then click Navigation Bar on the Image Objects submenu. Verify that Horizontally is selected, and that the Use tables check box is selected in the Insert Navigation Bar dialog box.

5. Type Services as the Element name. Click the Browse button to the right of the Up image text box. Navigate to the yourname/pets/images folder, click button01a.jpg, and then click the OK button. Click the Browse button to the right of the Over image text box. Click button01b.jpg, and then click the OK button. Click the Browse button to the right of the Down image text box, click button01b.jpg, and then click the OK button. Click the Alternate text box and then type Pet Services. Click the When clicked, Go to URL text box and then select services.htm as the linked text.

Continued >

In the Lab *continued*

6. Click the Add item button. Type References as the Element name. Click the Browse button to the right of the Up image text box, click button02a.jpg, and then click the OK button. Click the Browse button to the right of the Over image text box, click button02b.jpg, and then click the OK button. Click the Browse button to the right of the Down image text box, click button02b.jpg, and then click the OK button. Type References in the Alternate text box. Click the When clicked, Go to URL text box and then enter references.htm.

7. Click the Add item button. Type Breeds as the Element name. Click the Browse button to the right of the Up image text box and then add button03a.jpg. Click the Browse button to the right of the Over image text box and then add button03b.jpg. Click the Browse button to the right of the Down image text box and then add button03b.jpg. Type Breeds in the Alternate text box. Click the When clicked, Go to URL text box and then enter breeds.htm. Click the OK button.

8. Click the Add item button. Type Prices as the Element name. Click the Browse button to the right of the Up image text box and then add button04a.jpg. Click the Browse button to the right of the Over image text box and then add button04b.jpg. Click the Browse button to the right of the Down image text box and then add button04b.gif. Type Prices in the Alternate text box. Click the When clicked, Go to URL text box and then enter prices.htm. Click the OK button.

9. If necessary, select and center the table. Save the page, press the F12 key, and then test each link. Allow blocked content, if necessary. Close the index.htm page.

10. Open the grooming_tips.htm page. Display the rulers. Click the ruler-origin icon and drag it about 25 pixels below the last paragraph. Click the Draw AP Div button on the Layout tab, and draw an AP element 150 by 170 pixels in size. Select the AP element, type map in the CSS-P Element ID text box, and then specify 150 as the width and 170 as the height of the element. Enter 150px in the L text box and 220px in the T text box. Drag the grooming.jpg image onto the AP element. Select the element. Click the Overflow button arrow and then click hidden, if necessary.

11. Add three more AP elements to the right of the map element. Use the rulers to approximate the L and T positions on the page, as indicated in Table 6–2. Name the elements and drag the corresponding images onto each element, using the data as indicated in the table. Before you drag an image to the element, make sure an insertion point appears in the element. Set the Overflow property after you drag the images onto each element. Make any other necessary adjustments in the Property inspector.

Table 6–2 AP Element Properties

AP Element ID Properties	L and T Properties	W and H Properties	Vis Property	Overflow	Image
groom01	380px, 220px	160px, 200px	hidden	hidden	grooming01.jpg
groom02	380px, 220px	160px, 200px	hidden	hidden	grooming02.jpg
groom03	380px, 220px	160px, 200px	hidden	hidden	grooming03.jpg

12. Resize the grooming02 and grooming03 images to 160 W and 200 H. Readjust the settings as shown in Table 6–2 as needed.

13. Add three rectangular hotspots to the grooming.jpg image. Each hotspot should cover about one-third of the image (the first hotspot should cover the top third of the image, the second hotspot should cover the middle third of the image, and the third hotspot should cover the bottom third of the image). Display the Behaviors panel. Select the top hotspot, click the Add behavior button in the Behaviors panel, and then click Show-Hide Elements on the Add behavior pop-up menu. In the Show-Hide Elements dialog box, show element "map" and element "groom01." Hide element "groom02" and element "groom03." Click the OK button. Click the middle hotspot and then click the Add behavior button in the Behaviors panel. Click Show-Hide Elements on the Add behavior pop-up menu. Show element "map" and element "groom02." Hide element "groom01" and element "groom03." Click the OK button. Click the bottom hotspot, click the Add behavior button in the Behaviors panel, and then click Show-Hide Elements on the Add behavior pop-up menu. Show element "map" and element "groom03." Hide element "groom01" and element "groom02." Click the OK button to close the Show-Hide Elements dialog box.

14. Click the Save button and then press the F12 key to view the Web page in your browser. Allow blocked content, if necessary. Test all the hotspots and links.

15. Submit your files in the format provided by your instructor.

In the Lab

Lab 2: Jewelry by Eve Web Site

Problem: The Jewelry by Eve Web site has become very popular. Eve would like to redesign the index page and give it a more professional look. She has requested that you help her with this project by adding a navigation bar, rearranging some of the text by using AP elements, adding an automatic Date object so the current date is displayed on the page, and aligning existing AP elements. You agree to help her. The revised Web page is shown in Figure 6–64 on the next page. Appendix C contains instructions for uploading your local site to a remote server.

Continued >

In the Lab *continued*

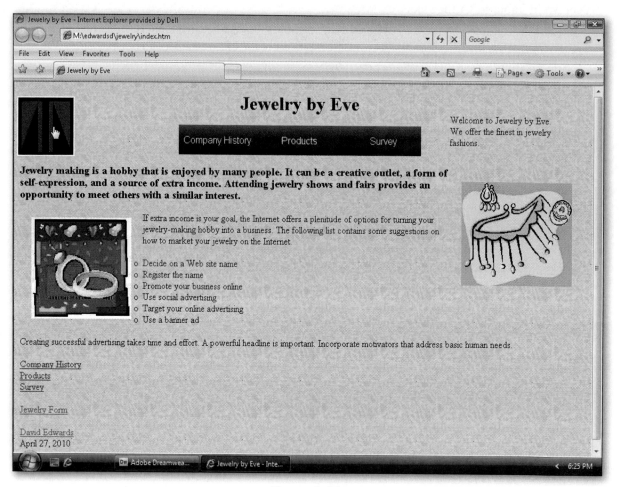

Figure 6–64

Perform the following tasks:

1. If necessary, start Dreamweaver and then open the Jewelry Business Web site.

2. Copy the data file images from the Chapter06 folder to your jewelry/images folder.

3. Open the index.htm file.

4. The first task is to add a navigation bar with three links. Click at the end of the Jewelry by Eve heading, before the image marker, and then press ENTER. With the insertion point on the new blank line, click Insert on the Application bar, point to Image Objects, then click Navigation Bar on the Image Objects submenu. Verify that Use tables and Horizontally are selected.

5. Use the data in Table 6–3 to complete the Insert Navigation Bar dialog box.

Table 6–3 Navigation Bar Data

Element	Up Image	Over Image	Down Image	Alternate Text	When Clicked, Go to Url Name
History	jewelry01a.jpg	jewelry01b.jpg	jewelry01b.jpg	Company history	history.htm
Products	jewelry02a.jpg	jewelry02b.jpg	jewelry02b.jpg	Products	products.htm
Survey	jewelry03a.jpg	jewelry03b.jpg	jewelry03b.jpg	Survey	survey_form.htm

6. After all the data is entered, click the OK button to insert the navigation bar. Select the table and then center it.

7. Next, you add an AP element for the logo. Click the Draw AP Div button on the Layout tab and then draw an element in the upper-left corner of the page with an approximate width of 75px and height of 75px. Change the L to 5px and the T to 25px. Name the element, logo. Click the Vis box arrow and then click visible. Drag the logo01 image onto the AP element.

8. Next, you add an AP element to the right of the Jewelry by Eve heading. Draw an AP element about 100 pixels to the right of the heading. Set the following properties for the elements: ID – heading, L – 800px, T – 50px, W – 190px, H – 65px, Vis – hidden.

9. Click in the heading AP element to move the insertion point to the element. Type the following text: Welcome to Jewelry by Eve. We offer the finest in jewelry fashions.

10. Draw a rectangular hotspot of the entire logo01 image on the left side of the page.

11. Select the hotspot, open the Behaviors panel, click the Add behavior button, and then click Show-Hide Elements on the pop-up menu. Show the logo and the heading elements when the pointer is over the hotspot.

12. Delete the date at the end of the page, and then insert a date that is automatically updated on save. Select the format that matches March 4, 1974.

13. Save your work, and then press the F12 key to view the page in your browser. Allow blocked content, if necessary. Click each of the links in the navigation bar to verify that they work. Point to the logo to display the text. Submit your files in the format provided by your instructor.

In the Lab

Lab 3: Modifying the Questions Web Page for the Credit Protection Web Site

Problem: Linda would like to add more interaction to the Credit Protection Web site and has asked you for ideas. You suggest that the questions.htm page could be revised so that when a question is pointed to, the answer to the question is displayed. Tracy likes your suggestion, and you agree to revise the page. The revised page is shown in Figure 6–65 on the next page; it displays the answer to a question that is pointed to. Appendix C contains instructions for uploading your local site to a remote server.

Continued >

STUDENT ASSIGNMENTS

In the Lab *continued*

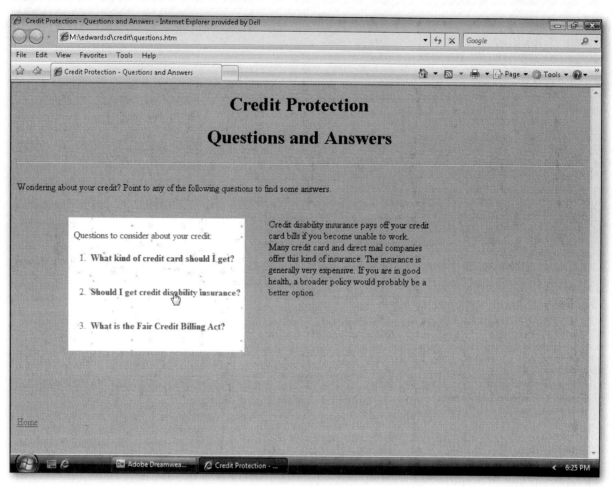

Figure 6–65

Perform the following tasks:

1. In Dreamweaver, open the Credit Protection Web site, and then copy the credit data files to the credit folder and the images folder for your Credit Protection Web site. The data files contain a questions.htm file, which will replace the existing questions.htm file. If necessary, click the Copy and Replace button in response to the Copy File dialog box.

2. If necessary, display the panel groups and the Layout tab.

3. Open the questions.htm file. Display the rulers. Position the insertion point below the horizontal line and type Wondering about your credit? Point to any of the following questions to find some answers. Press the ENTER key two times.

4. Click the Draw AP Div button on the Layout tab and use the rulers as a guide to draw an AP element with the following properties: CSS-P Element ID – questions, L – 100px, T – 225px, W – 305px, H – 220px, Vis – visible. Drag the questions.gif image from the Files panel onto the questions element.

5. Draw three more AP elements to the right of the questions element. Use the rulers as a guide to draw the elements. Use Table 6–4 to enter the properties for each element. After you create each element, type the text as listed in the Text column.

6. Select the questions element and then draw a rectangular hotspot over the first question. With the hotspot selected, click the Add behavior button in the Behaviors panel and then click Show–Hide Elements on the Add behavior pop-up menu. Show element "questions" and element "quest01." Hide elements "quest02" and "quest03."

7. Draw a second rectangular hotspot over the second question. With the hotspot selected, click the Add behavior button in the Behaviors panel and then click Show-Hide Elements on the Add behavior pop-up menu. Show element "questions" and element "quest02." Hide elements "quest01" and "quest03."

8. Draw a third rectangular hotspot over the third question. With the hotspot selected, click the Add behavior button in the Behaviors panel and then click Show-Hide Elements on the Add behavior pop-up menu. Show element "questions" and element "quest03." Hide elements "quest01" and "quest02."

9. Press CTRL+S to save the questions.htm Web page.

10. Press the F12 key to view the page in your browser. Allow blocked content, if necessary. Roll over each of the hotspots to verify that they work correctly. Submit your files in the format provided by your instructor.

Table 6–4 AP Elements Properties

AP Element ID	L and T (px)	W and H (px)	Vis	Text
quest01	450/225	280/205	hidden	Consider how you will use the card. Do you pay the entire balance at the end of every month? Or, do you make minimum payments? For those individuals who pay the entire balance each month, interest rate is not a priority. Most likely, you will not have to pay finance charges. Instead, look for a company that does not charge an annual fee. If you tend to carry an outstanding balance, search for a card issuer that charges very low interest rates.
quest02	450/225	275/145	hidden	Credit disability insurance pays off your credit card bills if you become unable to work. Many credit card and direct mail companies offer this type of insurance. The insurance is generally very expensive. If you are in good health, a broader policy would probably be a better option.
quest03	450/225	285/160	hidden	The Fair Credit Billing Act is a federal law that determines how billing errors and disputes involving credit and charge cards are handled. If you check the back of your monthly statement, generally you will find information about this process. If the company violates any provision of the law, you can sue to recover any damages.

Cases and Places

Apply your creative thinking and problem solving skills to design and implement a solution.

• Easier   ••More Difficult

• 1: Add a Navigation Bar for the Favorite Sports Web Site

You would like to add some interactivity to your sports Web site. You have looked at some other Web sites and are impressed with navigation bars. You decide to modify the index page and add a navigation bar to your sports Web site. You also decide to add the Date object so the date will be updated automatically when you save the page. Create a navigation bar for your sports site. Determine if a vertical or horizontal bar will best fit your needs. Then insert the Date object at the end of the page.

• 2: Add a Navigation Bar for the Hobby Web Site

Your hobby Web page has become very popular and you want to give it a more professional look. One object you can add is a navigation bar. Determine if a vertical or horizontal bar will best suit your particular Web page. Next, use AP elements to create a new layout for one of your pages. Determine which page in your Web site you will revise and then add at least four elements to the page. Name each element and place it appropriately on the page. Add images and/or text to the elements. Upload the page to a remote site if instructed to do so.

•• 3: Add a Navigation Bar and an Image Map to the Politics Web Site

You are receiving a lot of e-mail about what a great Web site you have for your political office campaign. You decide to make it more interactive by adding a navigation bar on the index page, adding an element with an image map, and then adding two additional elements. Create the navigation bar and then create the three elements — the first one with the image map and the other two displaying images related to your music site. Add hotspots to your image map to show and hide the two images. Upload the revised pages to a remote site.

•• 4: Add a Navigation Bar and an Image Map for the Favorite Music Web Site

Make It Personal

You are receiving a lot of e-mail about what a great Web site you have for your music hobby. You decide to make it more interactive by adding a navigation bar on the index page, adding an element with an image map, and then adding two additional elements. Create the navigation bar and then create the three elements — the first one with the image map and the other two displaying images related to your music site. Add hotspots to your image map to show and hide the two images. Upload the revised pages to a remote site.

•• 5: Add a Navigation Bar and an Image Map for the Student Trips Web Site

Working Together

The student trips Web site still is receiving numerous hits, and the debate about which location to pick for the trip is continuing. Add a new page to the Web site. Include a navigation bar that will link to various Web sites which provide information about three different possible vacation spots. Then, add at least four elements to the Web site. The first element will contain a map of the United States. The other three elements will contain pictures of possible trip locations. Add hotspots to the image map on the individual states and then add the Show-Hide Layers action. Upload the new pages to a remote server.

Adobe Dreamweaver CS4

Appendix A
Adobe Dreamweaver CS4 Help

Getting Help with Dreamweaver CS4

This appendix shows you how to use Dreamweaver Help. The Help system is a complete reference manual at your fingertips. You can access and use the Help system through the Help menu in Dreamweaver CS4, which connects you to up-to-date Help information online at the Adobe Web site. Or, if you prefer, you can download the Help topics to your computer in a single PDF file, which you can open and read with Adobe Reader. The Help system contains comprehensive information about all Dreamweaver features, including the following:

- A table of contents in which the information is organized by subject.
- A resource link to Community Help, which includes a variety of examples, instructional tutorials, support articles, videos, and other instructional links.
- A search tool, which is used to locate specific topics.

Additional tutorials and online movies are available on the Adobe Dreamweaver resources Web site at http://help.adobe.com.

The Dreamweaver Help Menu

One of the more commonly used methods to access Dreamweaver's Help features is through the Help menu and function keys. Dreamweaver's Help menu provides an easy system to access the available Help options (see Figure A–1 on the next page). Most of these commands start your default browser and display the appropriate up-to-date Help information on the Adobe Web site. Table A–1 on the next page summarizes the commands available through the Help menu.

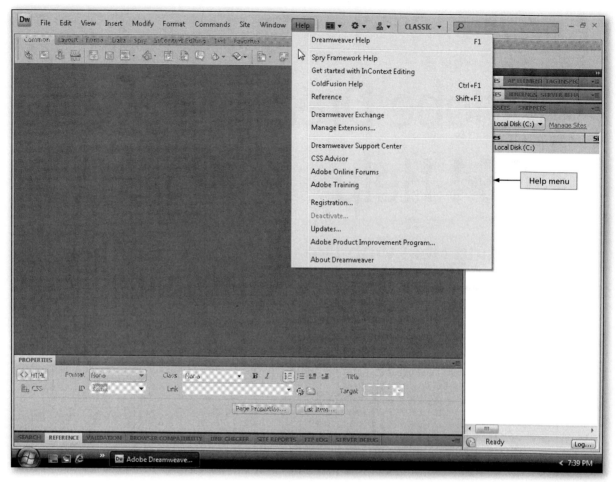

Figure A–1

Table A–1 Summary of Commands on the Help Menu

Command on Help menu	Description
Dreamweaver Help	Starts your default Web browser and displays the Dreamweaver CS4 online help system at the Adobe Web site.
Spry Framework Help	Displays a complete Help document for the Spry framework for Ajax, a JavaScript library that provides the Web site developer with an option to incorporate XML data and other kinds of effects.
Get started with InContext Editing	Provides information on how to make Web pages editable through any common browser so that content editors can revise Web page text while designers focus on design.
ColdFusion Help	Displays the complete Help document for ColdFusion, a Web application server that lets you create applications that interact with databases.
Reference	Opens the Reference panel group, which is displayed below the Document window. The Reference panel group contains the complete text from several reference manuals, including references on HTML, Cascading Style Sheets, JavaScript, and other Web-related features.
Dreamweaver Exchange	Links to the Adobe Exchange Web site, where you can download for free and/or purchase a variety of Dreamweaver add-on features.
Manage Extensions	Displays the Adobe Extension Manager window where you can install, enable, and disable extensions. An extension is an add-on piece of software or a plug-in that enhances Dreamweaver's capabilities. Extensions provide the Dreamweaver developer with the capability to customize how Dreamweaver looks and works.

Table A–1 Summary of Commands on the Help Menu (*continued*)

Command on Help menu	Description
Dreamweaver Support Center	Provides access to the online Adobe Dreamweaver support center.
CSS Advisor	Connects to the online Adobe CSS Advisor Web site, which provides solutions to CSS and browser compatibility issues, and encourages you to share tips, hints, and best practices for working with CSS.
Adobe Online Forums	Accesses the Adobe Online Forums Web page. The forums provide a place for developers of all experience levels to share ideas and techniques.
Adobe Training	Provides online information and links related to training and certification.
Registration	Displays your registration information and provides a print option.
Deactivate	Deactivates the installation of Dreamweaver CS4. If you have a single-user retail license, you can activate two computers. If you want to install Dreamweaver CS4 on a third computer, you need to deactivate it first on another computer.
Updates	Lets you check for updates to Adobe software online and then install the updates as necessary.
Adobe Product Improvement Program	Displays a dialog box that explains the Adobe Product Improvement Program and allows you to participate in the program.
About Dreamweaver	Opens a window that provides copyright information and the product license number.

Exploring the Dreamweaver CS4 Help System

The Dreamweaver Help command accesses Dreamweaver's primary Help system at the Adobe Web site and provides comprehensive information about all Dreamweaver features. Three options are available, as shown in Figure A–2 on the next page: Dreamweaver CS4 Resources, Using Dreamweaver CS4, and Download Help PDF.

BTW

Navigating to the Adobe Dreamweaver CS4 Page
If the Dreamweaver Help and Support page opens instead of the Using Adobe Dreamweaver CS4 page shown in Figure A–2 when you click Help on the Application bar and then click Dreamweaver Help (or press F1), click the Dreamweaver help (web) link on the Dreamweaver Help and Support page to navigate to the Using Adobe Dreamweaver CS4 page.

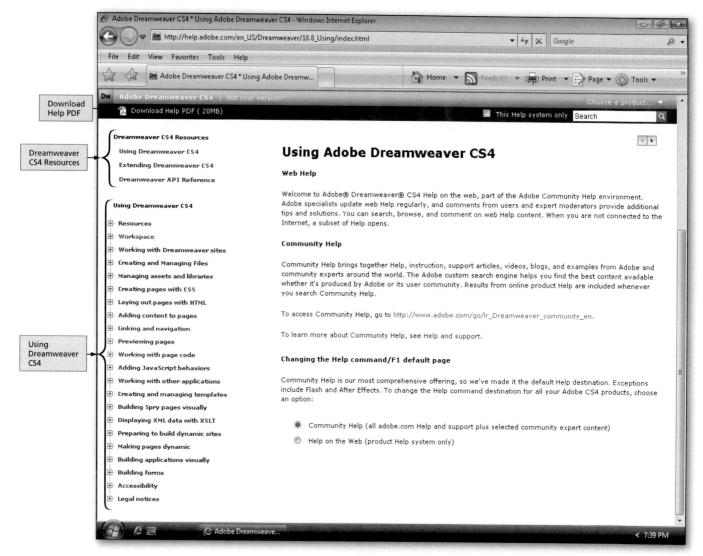

Figure A–2

Dreamweaver CS4 Resources This section provides access to three extensive Help documents: Using Dreamweaver CS4 online help, Extending Dreamweaver CS4, and the Dreamweaver API Reference. Select Extending Dreamweaver CS4 to open the Extending Dreamweaver CS4 online Help Web page, which provides resources for developers creating Web applications. Select Dreamweaver API Reference to open the Dreamweaver API Reference online Help Web page, which also provides resources for Web developers.

Download Help PDF Click this link to download a Portable Document Format (PDF) file that contains Dreamweaver CS4 Help information. You then can open the PDF file using Adobe Acrobat and use Acrobat features to read, search, and print Help information.

Using Dreamweaver CS4 This section provides extensive Help information for using Dreamweaver CS4. Like the other Help documents, Using Dreamweaver CS4 is organized into a contents panel on the left and a panel displaying the Help information on the right.

Using the Contents Panel

The **contents** panel is useful for displaying Help when you know the general category of the topic in question, but not the specifics.

To Find Help Using the Contents Panel

To find help using the contents panel, you click a plus icon to expand a Help category and display a list of specific topics. You then can click a topic to open a page related to that topic. The following steps show how to use the contents panel to find information on displaying toolbars.

- In Dreamweaver, click Help on the Application bar, and then click Dreamweaver Help to display the main online Help page (Figure A–3).

Figure A–3

- Click the plus sign to the left of Workspace to expand that topic if necessary, and then click the Workspace link to display information about the Dreamweaver workspace (Figure A–4).

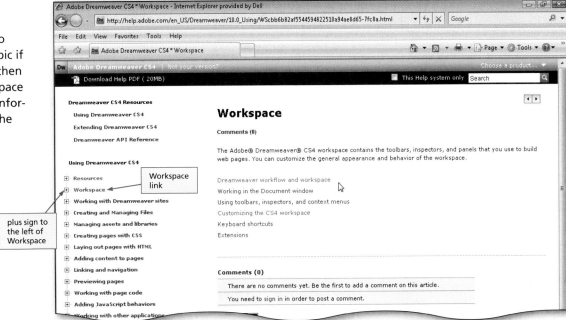

Figure A–4

- Click Using toolbars, inspectors, and context menus to display that Help page, and then click the Display toolbars link to display steps for showing or hiding toolbars (Figure A–5).

Q&A

What is the purpose of the links listed at the bottom of the Help topic?

You can click a link to navigate directly to a Help page about that topic.

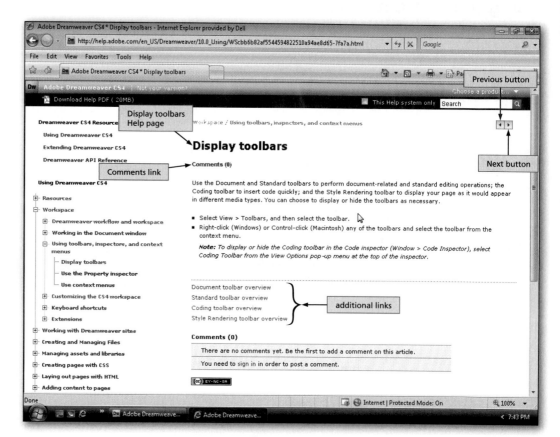

Figure A–5

When the information on the subtopic is displayed, you can read it, click a link contained within the subtopic, or click the Previous or Next button to open the previous or next Help page in sequence. To view comments other users or experts have made about this topic, click the Comments link. You also can use the browser's tools to print or save the page.

Using the Search Feature

Using the Search feature allows you to find any character string, anywhere in the text of the Help system.

To Use the Search Feature

The next steps show how to use the Search feature to obtain help about cropping images.

1
- On a Using Dreamweaver CS4 Help page, click the Search text box, and then type `cropping` to indicate you want to search for Help on cropping.

- Click the This Help system only check box to indicate you want to search the Dreamweaver CS4 Help pages only, not all of the Adobe Web site (Figure A–6).

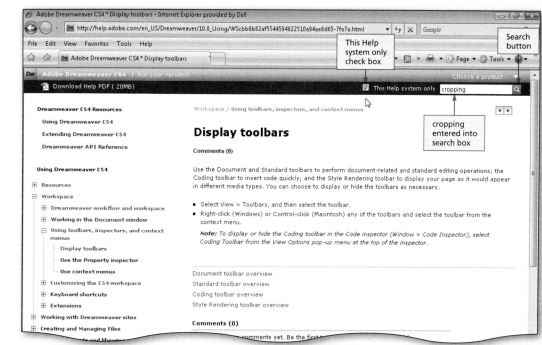

Figure A–6

- Click the Search button to display the results, and then point to the Adobe Dreamweaver CS4 * Edit images in Dreamweaver link (Figure A–7).

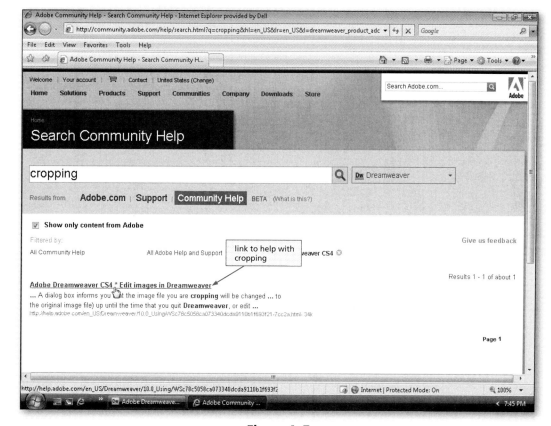

Figure A–7

2

- Click the Adobe Dreamweaver CS4 * Edit images in Dreamweaver link to display the Edit images in Dreamweaver Help page (Figure A–8).

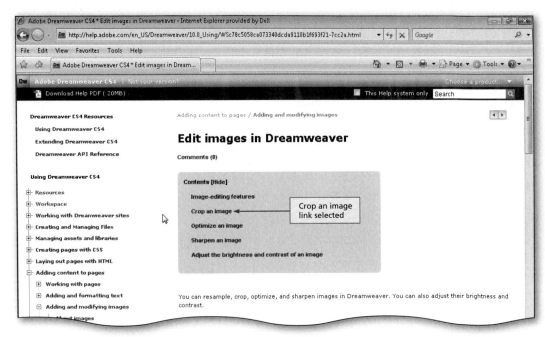

Figure A–8

3

- In the Contents box, click the Crop an image link to display the instructions on how to crop an image (Figure A–9).

4

- Close the browser window.

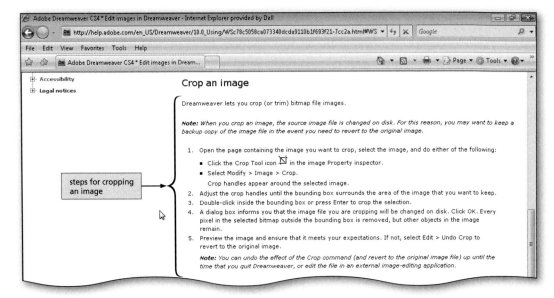

Figure A–9

Context-Sensitive Help

Using **context-sensitive help**, you can open a relevant Help topic in panels, inspectors, and most dialog boxes. To view these Help features, you click a Help button in a dialog box, choose Help on the Options pop-up menu in a panel group, or click the question mark icon in a panel or inspector.

To Display Context-Sensitive Help on Text Using the Question Mark

Many of the panels and inspectors within Dreamweaver contain a question mark icon. Clicking this icon displays context-sensitive help. The following steps show how to use the question mark icon to view context-sensitive help through the Property inspector. In this example, the default Property inspector for text is displayed.

- Open a new document in Dreamweaver, right-click the panel groups title bar and then click Close Tab Group to hide the panel groups, if necessary.

- Display the Property inspector, if necessary, to gain access to the question mark icon.

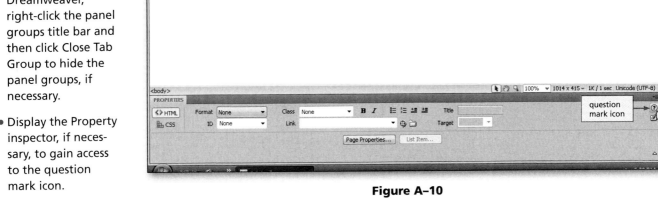

Figure A–10

- Point to the question mark icon in the Property inspector (Figure A–10).

- Click the question mark icon to display an online Help page on setting text properties in the Property inspector (Figure A–11).

- Close the browser window.

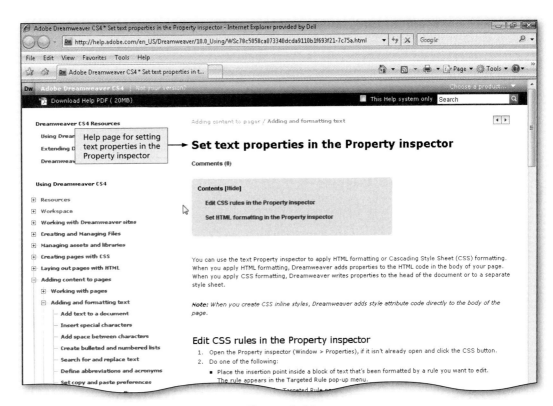

Figure A–11

To Use the Options Menu to Display Context-Sensitive Help for the Files Panel

Panels and dialog boxes also contain context-sensitive help. The following steps show how to display context-sensitive help for the Files panel. In this example, the Files panel is open and displayed within the Dreamweaver window.

- Click Window on the Application bar, and then, if necessary, click Files to display the Files panel.

- Click the Options button on the Files panel, and then point to Help (Figure A–12).

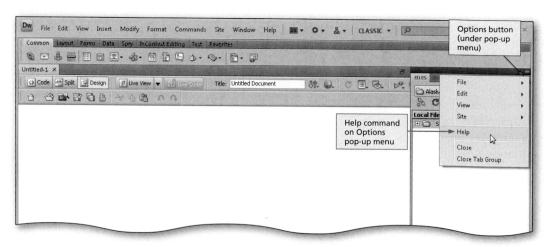

Figure A–12

- Click the Help command to display an online Help page about using the Files panel (Figure A–13).

- Close the browser window.

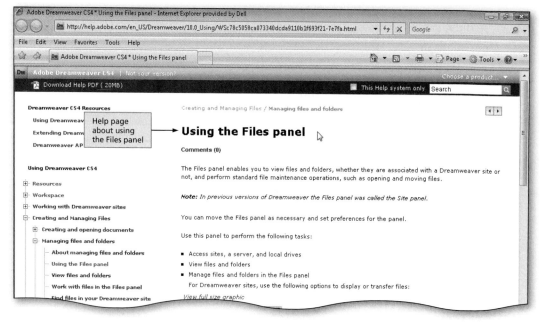

Figure A–13

Using the Reference Panel

The Reference panel is another valuable Dreamweaver resource. This panel provides you with a quick reference tool for HTML tags, JavaScript objects, Cascading Style Sheets, and other Dreamweaver features.

To Use the Reference Panel

The following steps show how to access the Reference panel, review the various options, and select and display information on the <body> tag.

- Click Help on the Application bar, and then point to Reference (Figure A–14).

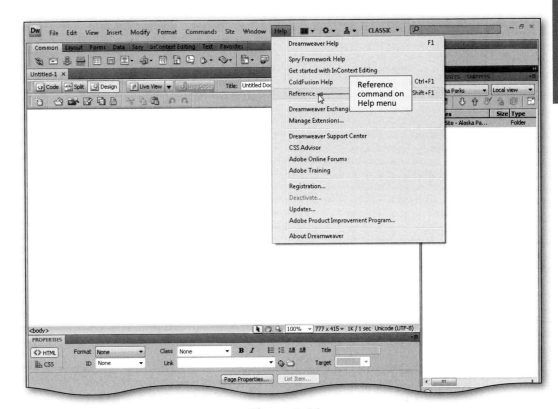

Figure A–14

- Click Reference to open the Reference panel.

- If necessary, click O'REILLY HTML Reference in the Book pop-up menu to display information about HTML tags (Figure A–15).

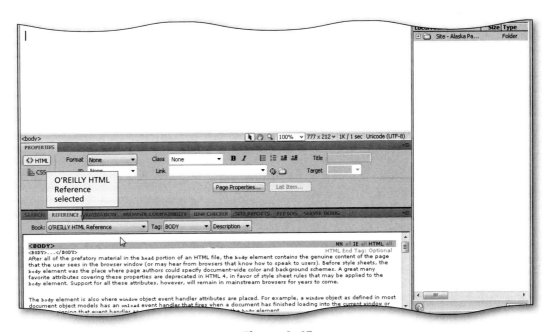

Figure A–15

- Click the Tag button arrow and then point to H1 in the tag list (Figure A–16).

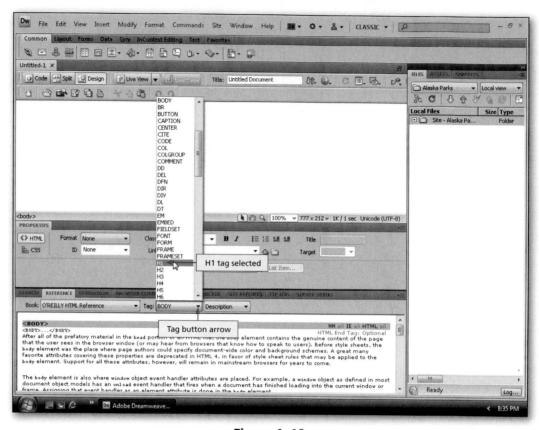

Figure A–16

- Click H1 to display information on the <H1> tag (Figure A–17).

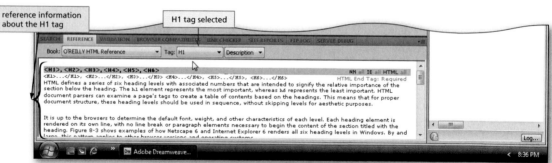

Figure A–17

- Click the Book button arrow and review the list of available reference books (Figure A–18).

6

- Click the Book button arrow, and then right-click the horizontal bar on the Reference panel and then click Close Tab Group to close the panel.

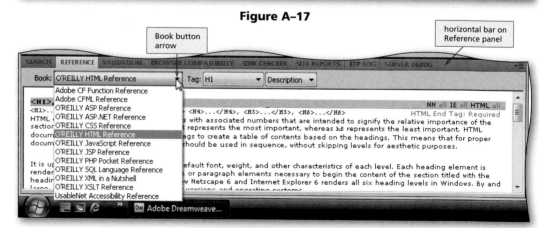

Figure A–18

Apply Your Knowledge

Reinforce the skills and apply the concepts you learned in this appendix.

Viewing the Dreamweaver Help Resources

Instructions: Start Dreamweaver. Perform the following tasks using the Dreamweaver Help command.

1. Click Help on the Application bar and then click Dreamweaver Help.

2. Click the plus sign to the left of Working with Dreamweaver sites, click the plus sign to the left of Setting up a Dreamweaver site, and then click the About Dreamweaver sites link.

3. Read the Help page, and then use a word processing program to write a short overview of what you learned.

4. Submit your assignment in the format specified by your instructor.

Using the Search Box

Instructions: Start Dreamweaver. Perform the following tasks using the Search box in the Dreamweaver CS4 online Help system.

1. Press the F1 key to display the Using Dreamweaver CS4 Help page.

2. Click the This Help system only check box.

3. Click in the Search box, type Adding Sound, and then click the Search button.

4. Click an appropriate link in the search results to open a Help page, click a link on the Help page about embedding a sound file, and then read the Help topic.

5. Use a word processing program to write a short overview of what you learned.

6. Submit your assignment in the format specified by your instructor.

Using Community Help

Instructions: Start Dreamweaver. Perform the following tasks using the online Community Web page.

1. Click Help on the Application bar, and then click Dreamweaver Support Center.

2. Click the Get started with Dreamweaver link.

3. View the Getting started with Dreamweaver videos and tutorials list and then select the Designing for web publishing link.

4. Review the Designing for web publishing article.

5. Use your word processing program to prepare a report on three new concepts.

6. Submit your assignment in the format specified by your instructor.

Appendix B

Dreamweaver and Accessibility

Web Accessibility

Tim Berners-Lee, World Wide Web Consortium (W3C) founder and inventor of the World Wide Web, indicates that the power of the Web is in its universality. He says that access by everyone, regardless of disability, is an essential aspect of the Web. In 1997, the W3C launched the **Web Accessibility Initiative** and made a commitment to lead the Web to its full potential. The initiative includes promoting a high degree of usability for people with disabilities. The United States government established a second initiative addressing accessibility and the Web through Section 508 of the Federal Rehabilitation Act.

Dreamweaver includes features that assist you in creating accessible content. Designing accessible content requires that you understand accessibility requirements and make subjective decisions as you create a Web site. Dreamweaver supports three accessibility options: screen readers, keyboard navigation, and operating system accessibility features.

Using Screen Readers with Dreamweaver

Screen readers assist the blind and vision-impaired by reciting text that is displayed on the screen through a speaker or headphones. The screen reader starts at the upper-left corner of the page and reads the page content. If the Web site developer uses accessibility tags or attributes during the creation of the Web site, the screen reader also recites this information and reads nontextual information such as button labels and image descriptions. Dreamweaver makes it easy to add text equivalents for graphical elements and to add HTML elements to tables and forms through the accessibility dialog boxes. Dreamweaver supports two screen readers: JAWS and Window Eyes.

Activating the Accessibility Dialog Boxes

To create accessible pages in Dreamweaver, you associate information, such as labels and descriptions, with your page objects. After you have created this association, the screen reader can recite the label and description information.

You create the association by activating the accessibility dialog boxes that request accessibility information such as labels and descriptions when you insert an object for which you have activated the corresponding Accessibility dialog box. You activate the Accessibility dialog boxes through the Preferences dialog box. You can activate Accessibility dialog boxes for form objects, frames, images, and media. Accessibility for tables is accomplished by adding Summary text to the Table dialog box and adding image IDs and Alt text through the Property inspector.

To Activate the Image Tag Accessibility Attributes Dialog Box

The following steps use the Alaska Parks index page as an example to show how to display the Preferences dialog box and activate the Image Tag Accessibility Attributes dialog box.

- Start Dreamweaver and, if necessary, open the Alaska Parks site.

- Double-click index.htm in the Files panel to open the index.htm page, and then collapse the panels to icons to provide additional workspace.

- Click Edit on the Application bar and then point to Preferences (Figure B–1).

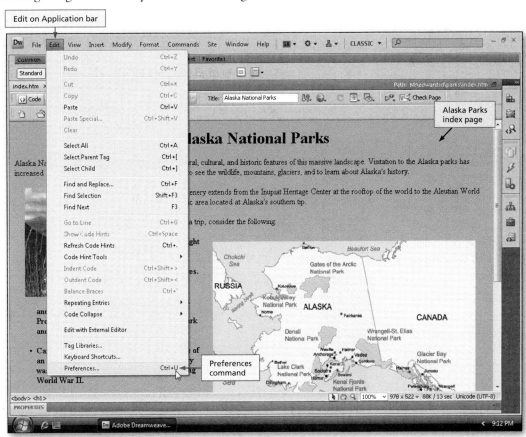

Figure B–1

- Click Preferences to display the Preferences dialog box (Figure B–2).

Q&A When I open the Preferences dialog box, it displays different options. What should I do?

The Preferences dialog box displays the last category of options selected. Continue to Step 3.

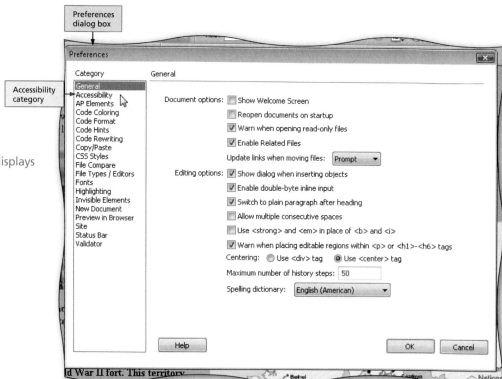

Figure B–2

- Click Accessibility in the Category list to display the accessibility options, and then click the Images check box in the Accessibility area to select it, if necessary.

- Deselect the other check boxes, if necessary, and then point to the OK button (Figure B–3).

- Click the OK button to activate the Image Tag Accessibility Attributes dialog box for images and to close the Preferences dialog box. No change is apparent in the Document window.

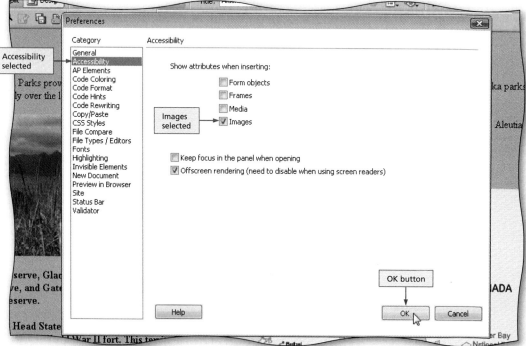

Figure B–3

Inserting Accessible Images

Selecting Images in the Accessibility category activates the Image Tag Accessibility Attributes dialog box. Thus, any time you insert an image into a Web page, this dialog box will be displayed. This dialog box contains two text boxes: Alternate text and Long description. The screen reader reads the information you enter in both text boxes. You should limit your Alternate text entry to about 50 characters. For longer descriptions, provide a link in the Long description text box to a file that gives more information about the image. It is not required that you enter data into both text boxes.

To Insert Accessible Images

The following steps show how to use the Image Tag Accessibility Attributes dialog box when inserting an image.

1

• Expand the panels, if necessary.

• Position the insertion point where you want to insert the image.

• Click Insert on the Application bar and then point to Image (Figure B–4).

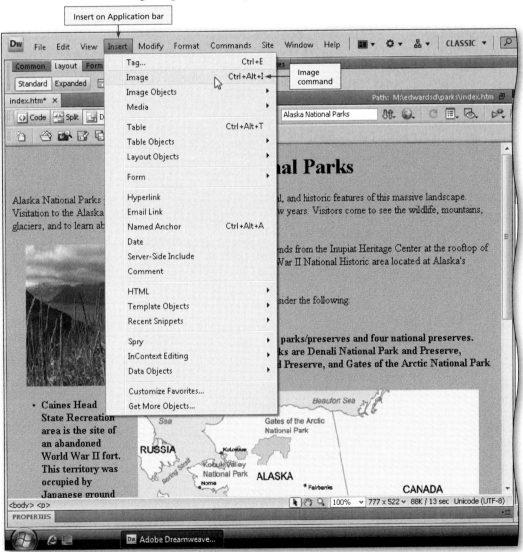

Figure B–4

- Click Image to display the Select Image Source dialog box.

- If necessary, open the images folder and then click a file name of your choice.

- Point to the OK button (Figure B–5).

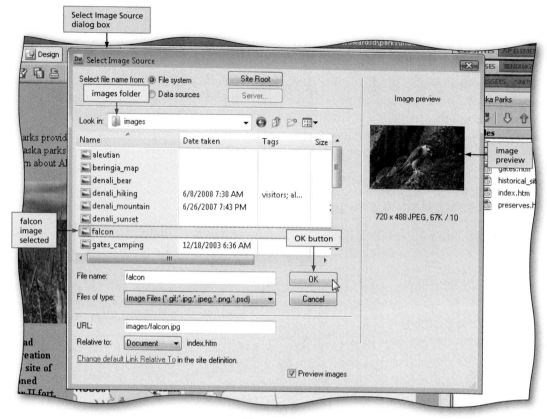

Figure B–5

- Click the OK button to display the Image Tag Accessibility Attributes dialog box (Figure B–6).

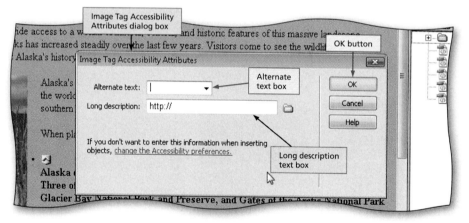

Figure B–6

- Type a brief description of the image in the Alternate text text box.

- Type a longer description in the Long description text box (Figure B–7).

Q&A

How do I indicate that the screen reader should access a file instead of reading text in the Long description text box?

Click the Browse icon next to the Long description text box, and then use the Select File dialog box to select an .htm file that contains a long description of the image.

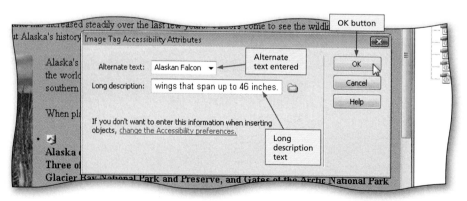

Figure B–7

⑤

• Click the OK button to close the Image Tag Accessibility Attributes dialog box.

Q&A What is the effect of providing alternate text and a long description?

Although no changes are displayed in the Document window, when the page is displayed in the browser, the screen reader recites the information you entered in the Image Tag Accessibility Attributes Alternate text text box. If you included a link to a file with additional information in the Long description text box, the screen reader accesses the file and recites the text contained within the file. If you typed additional information in the Long description text box, the screen reader accesses and recites the text.

Navigating Dreamweaver with the Keyboard

Keyboard navigation is a core aspect of accessibility. This feature also is of particular importance to users who have repetitive strain injuries (RSIs) or other disabilities, and to those users who would prefer to use the keyboard instead of a mouse. You can use the keyboard to navigate the following elements in Dreamweaver: panels, inspectors, dialog boxes, frames, and tables.

Using the Keyboard to Navigate Panels

When you are working in Dreamweaver, several panels may be open at one time. A dotted outline around the panel title bar indicates that the panel is selected. Press CTRL+F6 to move from panel to panel. If necessary, expand the selected panel by pressing the SPACEBAR. Pressing the SPACEBAR again collapses the panel. Use the arrow keys to scroll the panel. Press the SPACEBAR to make a selection. Placing focus on the panel title bar and then pressing the SPACEBAR collapses and expands the panels. Press the TAB key to move within a panel.

To Use the Keyboard to Hide and Display the Property Inspector

The following steps use the Alaska Parks index page to show how to use the keyboard to hide and display the Property inspector and then change a setting.

• Start Dreamweaver and, if necessary, open the Alaska Parks site. Double-click index.htm in the Files panel to open the index.htm file, and then click the first line (the "Alaska National Parks" heading). Press CTRL+F3 to hide the Property inspector and then CTRL+F3 to redisplay the Property inspector (Figure B–8).

Figure B–8

- Press the TAB key four times to move to the Format button and the selected Heading 1 format.

- Press the UP ARROW key to select the Paragraph format (Figure B–9).

- Press the DOWN ARROW key to select the Heading 1 format again.

- Close Dreamweaver. Do not save any of the changes.

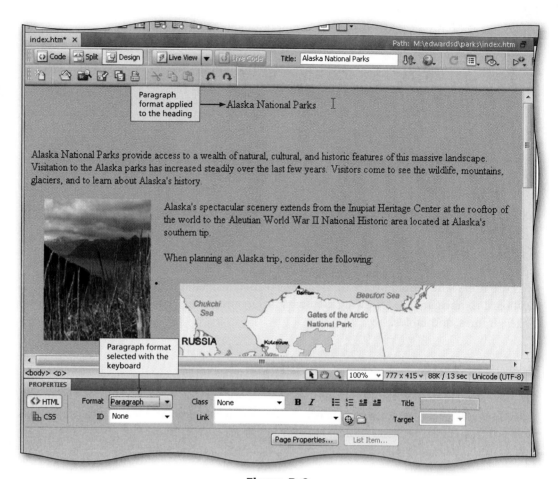

Figure B–9

Operating System Accessibility Features

The third method of accessibility support in Dreamweaver is through the Windows operating system's high contrast settings. **High contrast** changes the desktop color schemes for individuals who have vision impairment. The color schemes make the screen easier to view by heightening screen contrast with alternative color combinations. Some of the high contrast schemes also change font sizes.

You activate this option through the Windows Control Panel. The high contrast setting affects Dreamweaver in two ways:

- The dialog boxes and panels use system color settings.
- Code view syntax color is turned off.

Design view, however, continues to use the background and text colors you set in the Page Properties dialog box. The pages you design, therefore, continue to render colors as they will display in a browser.

To Turn On High Contrast

The following steps show how to turn on high contrast and how to change the current high contrast settings in Windows Vista.

- In Windows Vista, click the Start button on the taskbar and then click Control Panel on the Start menu to open the Control Panel (Figure B–10).

Figure B–10

- In the Appearance and Personalization category, click Change the color scheme to display the Appearance Settings dialog box (Figure B–11).

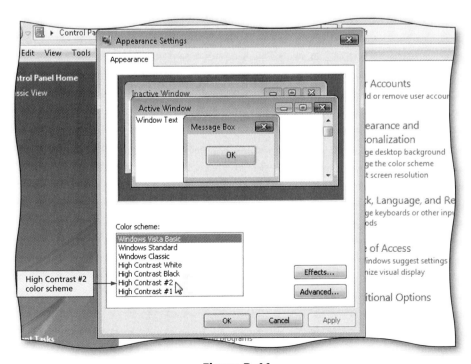

Figure B–11

• Click High Contrast #2 to display a preview of High Contrast #2 (Figure B–12).

• Click the Cancel button to close the Appearance Settings dialog box and return the settings to their original values.

Q&A

What should I do if I want to retain the High Contrast #2 color scheme?

To retain these settings on your computer, you would click the OK button.

• Close the Control Panel to redisplay the Windows Vista desktop.

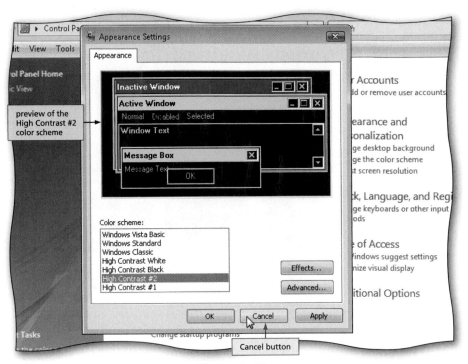

Figure B–12

Other Ways

1. Right-click desktop, click Personalize, click Window Color and Appearance

Publishing to a Web Server

Publishing to a Remote Site

With Dreamweaver, Web designers usually define a local site and then do the majority of their designing using the local site. You defined a local site in Chapter 1. In creating the projects in this book, you have added Web pages to the local site, which resides on your computer's hard drive, a network drive, a USB drive, or possibly a CD-RW.

To prepare a Web site and make it available for others to view requires that you publish your site by uploading it to a Web server for public access. A Web server is an Internet- or intranet-connected computer that delivers the Web pages to online visitors. Dreamweaver includes built-in support that enables you to connect and transfer your local site to a Web server. Publishing to a Web server requires that you have access to a Web server. Your instructor will provide you with the location, user name, and password information for the Web server on which you will publish your site.

After you establish access to a Web server, you will need a remote site folder. The remote folder will reside on the Web server and will contain your Web site files. Generally, the remote folder is defined by the Web server administrator or your instructor. The name of the local root folder in this example is the author's first and last name. Most likely, the name of your remote folder also will be your last name and first initial or your first and last name. You upload your local site to the remote folder on the Web server. The remote site connection information must be defined in Dreamweaver through the Site Definition Wizard. You display the Site Definition Wizard and then enter the remote site information. Dreamweaver provides five different protocols for connecting to a remote site. These methods are as follows:

- **FTP (File Transfer Protocol)**: This protocol is used on the Internet for sending and receiving files. It is the most widely used method for uploading and downloading pages to and from a Web server.

- **Local/Network**: This option is used when the Web server is located on a local area network (LAN) or a company, school, or other organization intranet. Files on LANs generally are available for internal viewing only.

- **SourceSafe Database, RDS (Remote Development Services), and WebDAV**: These three protocols are systems that permit users to edit and manage files collaboratively on remote Web servers.

Most likely you will use the FTP option to upload your Web site to a remote server.

Defining a Remote Site

You define the remote site by changing some of the settings in the Site Definition dialog box. To allow you to create a remote site using FTP, your instructor will supply you with the following information:

- **FTP host**: The Web address for the remote host of your Web server
- **Host directory**: The directory name and path on the server where your remote site will be located
- **Login**: Your user name
- **Password**: The FTP password to authenticate and access your account

To Define a Remote Site

Assume for the following steps that you are defining a remote site for the Alaska Parks Web site.

- If necessary, open Dreamweaver, select the Alaska Parks site, and then open the index.htm page.

- Click Site on the Application bar and then click Manage Sites to open the Manage Sites dialog box.

- Click Alaska Parks to select the Alaska Parks Web site (Figure C–1).

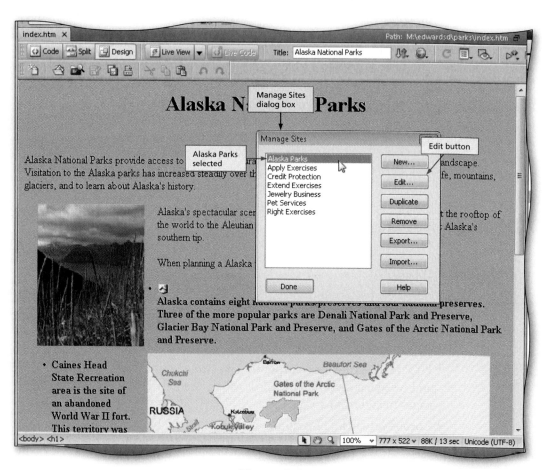

Figure C–1

2

• Click the Edit button to open the Site Definition for Alaska Parks dialog box, and then click the Advanced tab to display the Advanced options (Figure C–2).

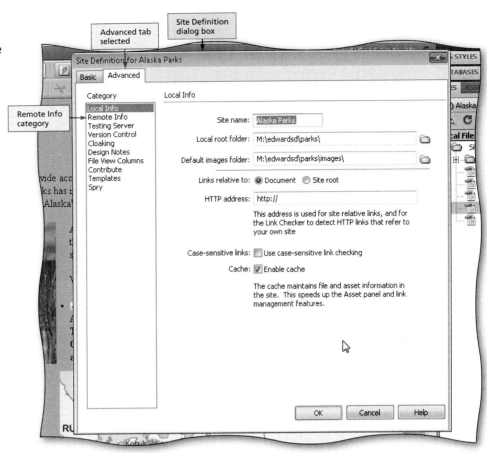

Figure C–2

3

• Click the Remote Info category to display the Remote Info options.

• Click the Access button in the Remote Info pane, and then point to FTP in the pop-up menu (Figure C–3).

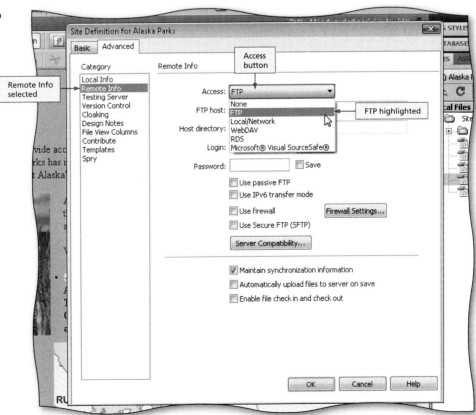

Figure C–3

- Click FTP to select FTP as the protocol for connecting to a remote site.

- Click each of the following boxes in the Site Definition for Alaska Parks dialog box, and fill in the information as provided by your instructor: FTP host, Host directory (if necessary), Login, and Password (Figure C–4).

Q&A What if I am required to enter different information?

Your information will most likely differ from that in Figure C–4.

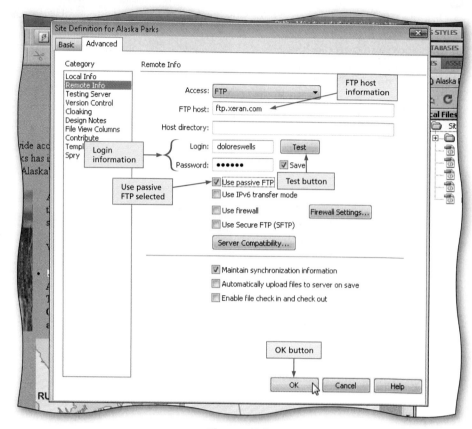

Figure C–4

- Click the Test button to test the connection and to display the Dreamweaver dialog box with the message "Dreamweaver connected to your Web server successfully" (Figure C–5).

Q&A What should I do if a security dialog box is displayed?

If a Windows Security Alert dialog box is displayed, click the Unblock button.

Q&A What should I do if my connection is not successful?

If your connection is not successful, review your text box entries and make any necessary corrections. If all entries are correct, check with your instructor. Your screen should look similar to Figure C–5.

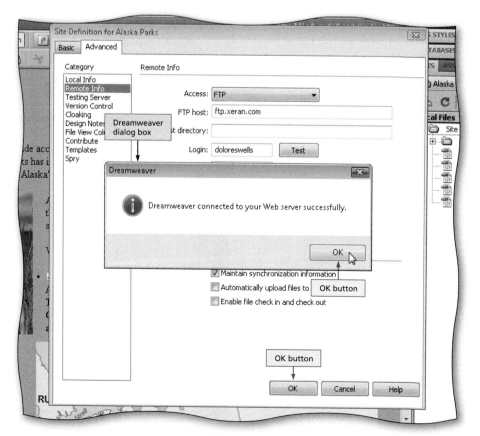

Figure C–5

6

- Click the OK button to close the Dreamweaver dialog box, and then click the OK button to close the Site Definition for Alaska Parks dialog box.

Q&A
What should I do if another Dreamweaver dialog box is displayed?

If another Dreamweaver dialog box is displayed, click the OK button.

- Click the Done button to close the Manage Sites dialog box.

Connecting to a Remote Site

Now that you have completed the remote site information and tested your connection, you can interact with the remote server. The remote site folder on the Web server for your Web site must be established before a connection can be made. This folder, called the **remote site root**, generally is created automatically by the Web server administrator of the hosting company or by your instructor. The naming convention generally is determined by the hosting company.

This book uses the last and first name of the author for the login to the remote site folder. Naming conventions other than your last and first name may be used on the Web server to which you are connecting. Your instructor will supply you with this information. If all information is correct, connecting to the remote site is accomplished easily through the Files panel.

To Connect to a Remote Site

The following steps illustrate how to connect to the remote server and display your remote site folder.

1

- Point to the Expand to show local and remote sites button on the Files panel toolbar (Figure C–6).

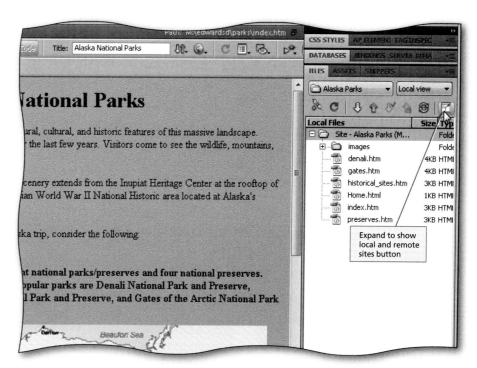

Figure C–6

- Click the Expand to show local and remote sites button to expand the Site pane and show both a right (Local Files) and left (Remote Site) pane (Figure C–7).

Q&A

What do the right and left expanded panes display?

The right pane contains the local site, and the left pane contains information for viewing your remote files by clicking the Connects to remote host button.

Q&A

What happens after I click the Connects to remote host button?

The Connects to remote host/Disconnects from remote host button changes to indicate that the connection has been made, and a default Home.html folder is created automatically.

- Verify that the root folder is selected in the Local Files pane.

- Click the Connects to remote host button to make the connection (Figure C–8).

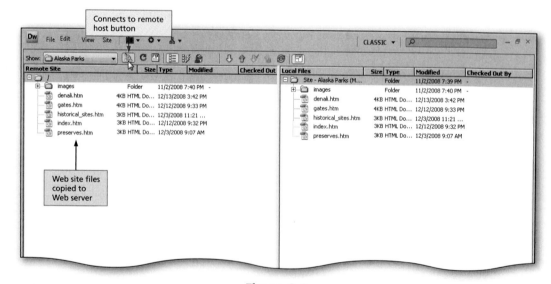

Figure C–7

Figure C–8

Uploading Files to a Remote Server

Uploading is the process of transferring your files from your computer to the remote server. **Downloading** is the process of transferring files from the remote server to your computer. Dreamweaver uses the term **put** for uploading and **get** for downloading.

To Upload Files to a Remote Server

The following steps illustrate how to upload your files to the remote server.

- If necessary, click the Alaska Parks root folder to select it.

- Click the Put File(s) button, and then point to the OK button in the Dreamweaver dialog box (Figure C–9).

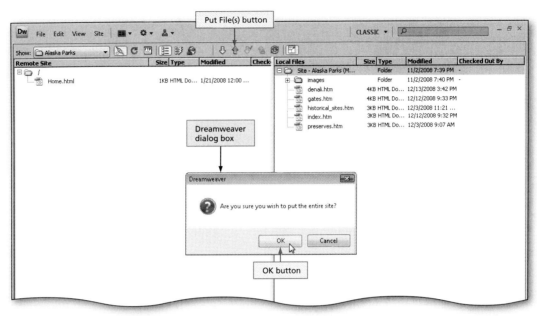

Figure C–9

- Click the OK button to begin uploading the files and to display a dialog box that shows progress information (Figure C–10).

Q&A My files are uploaded, but they appear in a different order. Is that okay?

The files that are uploaded to the server may be displayed in a different order from that on the local site based on the server settings.

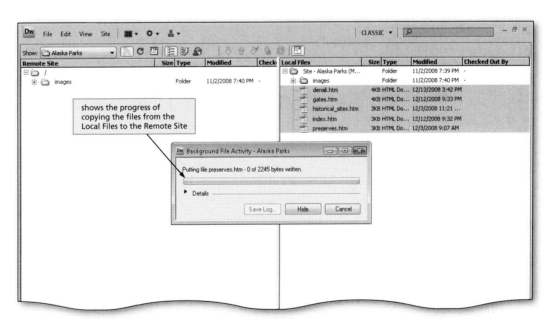

Figure C–10

- Close Dreamweaver.

Remote Site Maintenance and Site Synchronization

Now that your Web site is on a Web server, you will want to continue to maintain the site. When you are connected to the remote site, you can apply many of the same commands to a folder or file on the remote site as you do to a folder or file on the local site. You can create and delete folders; cut, copy, delete, duplicate, paste, and rename files; and so on. These commands are available through the context menu.

To mirror the local site on the remote site, Dreamweaver provides a synchronization feature. Synchronizing is the process of transferring files between the local and remote sites so both sites have an identical set of the most recent files. You can select to synchronize the entire Web site or select only specific files. You also can specify Direction. Within Direction, you have three options: upload the newer files from the local site to the remote site (put); download newer files from the remote site to the local site (get); or upload and download files to and from the remote and local sites. Once you specify a direction, Dreamweaver automatically synchronizes files. If the files are already in sync, Dreamweaver lets you know that no synchronization is necessary. To access the Synchronize command, you first connect to the remote server and then select Synchronize on the Site menu (Figure C–11).

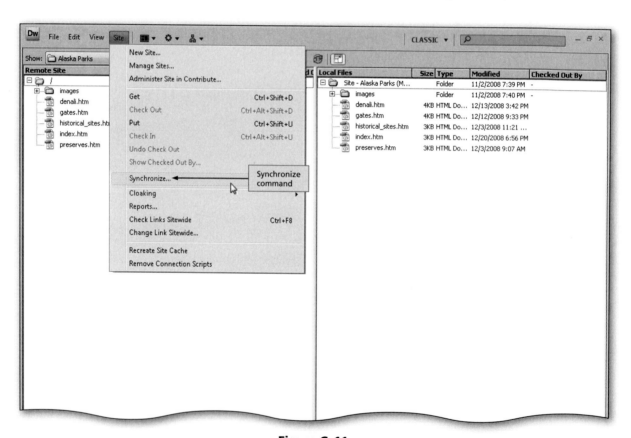

Figure C–11

To save the verification information to a local file, click the Save Log button at the completion of the synchronization process. Another feature within Dreamweaver allows you to verify which files are newer on the local site or the remote site; choose the Remote view by selecting Select Newer Local or Select Newer Remote commands. These options are available through the Files panel Edit menu when the Remote site panel is displayed.

Apply Your Knowledge

Reinforce the skills and apply the concepts you learned in this appendix.

Defining and Uploading the Bryan's Mobile Pet Services Web Site to a Remote Server

Instructions: Perform the following tasks to define and upload the Bryan's Mobile Pet Services Web site to a remote server.

1. If necessary, start Dreamweaver. Click Site on the Application bar, click Manage Sites, and then click Pet Services. Click the Edit button to display the Site Definition dialog box. Click the Advanced tab and then click Remote Info. Fill in the information as provided by your instructor, and then test the connection. Click the OK button to close the Site Definition dialog box, and then click the Done button to close the Manage Sites dialog box.

2. Click the Expand to show local and remote sites button on the Files panel toolbar and then click the Connects to remote host button. Click the local file root folder and then click the Put File(s) button on the Site panel toolbar to upload your Web site. Click the OK button in response to the "Are you sure you wish to put the entire site?" dialog box. Review your files to verify that they were uploaded. The files on the remote server may be displayed in a different order from those on the local site.

3. Click the Disconnects from remote host button on the Files panel toolbar. Click the Collapse to show only local or remote site button on the Files panel toolbar to display the local site and the Document window.

Defining and Uploading the Jewelry by Eve Web Site to a Remote Server

Instructions: Perform the following tasks to define and upload the Jewelry by Eve Web site to a remote server.

1. If necessary, start Dreamweaver. Click Site on the Application bar, click Manage Sites, and then click Jewelry Business. Click the Edit button to display the Site Definition dialog box. Click the Advanced tab and then click Remote Info. Fill in the information as provided by your instructor, and then test the connection. Click the OK button to close the Site Definition dialog box, and then click the Done button to close the Manage Sites dialog box.

2. Click the Expand to show local and remote sites button on the Files panel toolbar and then click the Connects to remote host button. Click the local file root folder and then click the Put File(s) button on the Files panel toolbar to upload your Web site. Click the OK button in response to the "Are you sure you wish to put the entire site?" dialog box. Review your files to verify that they were uploaded. The files on the remote server may display in a different order from those on the local site.

3. Click the Disconnects from remote host button. Click the Collapse to show only local or remote site button on the Files panel toolbar to display the local site and the Document window.

Defining and Uploading the Credit Protection Web Site to a Remote Server

Instructions: Perform the following tasks to define and upload the Credit Protection Web site to a remote server.

1. If necessary, start Dreamweaver. Click Site on the Application bar, click Manage Sites, and then click Credit Protection. Click the Edit button. Click the Advanced tab and then click Remote Info. Fill in the information as provided by your instructor, and then test the connection. Click the OK button to close the Site Definition dialog box, and then click the Done button to close the Manage Sites dialog box.

2. Click the Expand to show local and remote sites button on the Files panel toolbar and then click the Connects to remote host button. Click the local file root folder and then click the Put File(s) button on the Files panel toolbar to upload your Web site. Click the OK button in response to the "Are you sure you wish to put the entire site?" dialog box. Upload your files to the remote site. Review your files to verify that they were uploaded. The files on the remote server may display in a different order from those on the local site.

3. Disconnect from the site. Click the Collapse to show only local or remote site button on the Files panel toolbar to display the local site and the Document window.

Appendix D

Customizing Adobe Dreamweaver CS4

This appendix explains how to change the screen resolution in Windows Vista to the resolution used in this book.

Changing Screen Resolution

Screen resolution indicates the number of pixels (dots) that the computer uses to display the letters, numbers, graphics, and background you see on the screen. When you increase the screen resolution, Windows displays more information on the screen, but the information decreases in size. The reverse also is true: as you decrease the screen resolution, Windows displays less information on the screen, but the information increases in size.

The screen resolution usually is stated as the product of two numbers, such as 1024 × 768 (pronounced "ten twenty-four by seven sixty-eight"). A 1024 × 768 screen resolution results in a display of 1,024 distinct pixels on each of 768 lines, or about 786,432 pixels. The figures in this book were created using a screen resolution of 1024 × 768.

The screen resolutions most commonly used today are 800 × 600 and 1024 × 768, although some Web designers set their computers at a much higher screen resolution, such as 2048 × 1536.

To Change the Screen Resolution

The following steps change the screen resolution to 1024 × 768 to match the figures in this book.

1

• If necessary, minimize all programs so that the Windows Vista desktop appears.

• Right-click the Windows Vista desktop to display the Windows Vista desktop shortcut menu (Figure D–1).

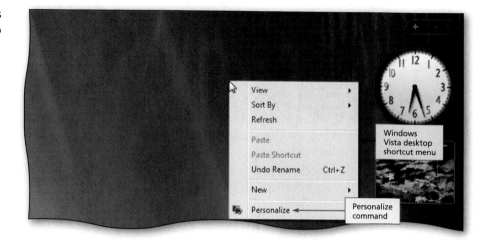

Figure D–1

2

• Click Personalize on the shortcut menu to open the Personalization window.

• Click Display Settings in the Personalization window to display the Display Settings dialog box (Figure D–2).

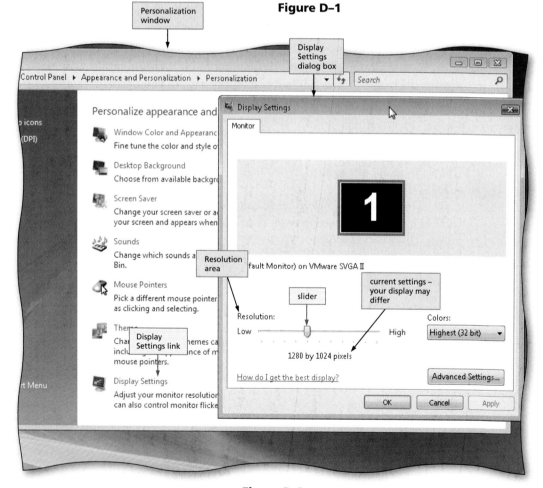

Figure D–2

• If necessary, drag the slider in the Resolution area so that the screen resolution is set to 1024 × 768 (Figure D–3).

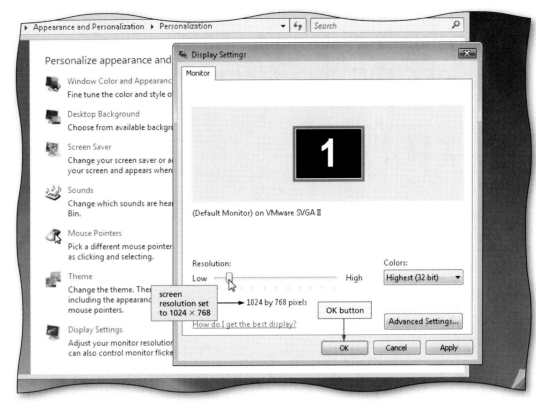

Figure D–3

4

• Click the OK button to set the screen resolution to 1024 × 768 (Figure D–4).

• Click the Yes button in the Display Settings dialog box to accept the new screen resolution.

• Click the Close button to close the Personalization Window.

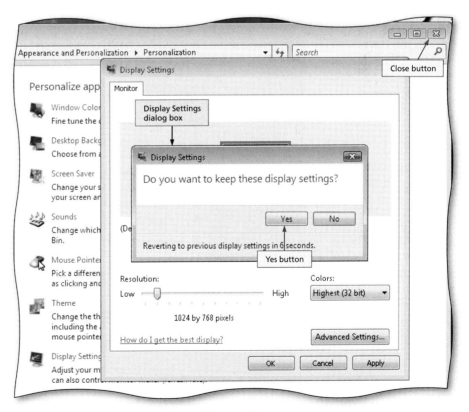

Figure D–4

Appendix E

Steps for the Windows XP User

For the XP User of this Book

For most tasks, no differences exist between using Adobe Dreamweaver CS4 under the Windows Vista operating system or the Windows XP operating system. With some tasks, however, you will see some differences, or need to complete the tasks using different steps. This appendix shows how to start Dreamweaver, save a Web page, and copy data files to the local Web site while using Dreamweaver with Windows XP.

To Start Dreamweaver

The following steps, which assume Windows is running, start Dreamweaver based on a typical installation. You may need to ask your instructor how to start Dreamweaver for your computer.

- Click the Start button on the Windows taskbar to display the Start menu.

- Point to All Programs on the Start menu to display the All Programs submenu.

- Point to Adobe Dreamweaver CS4 on the All Programs submenu to display the Adobe Dreamweaver CS4 submenu (Figure E–1).

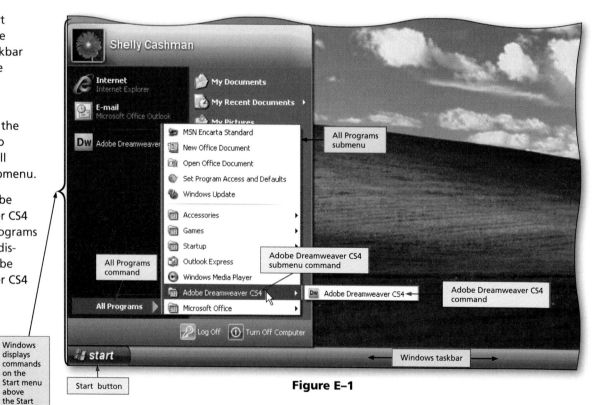

Figure E–1

- Click Adobe Dreamweaver CS4 to start Dreamweaver and display the Welcome screen (Figure E–2).

- If the Dreamweaver window is not maximized, click the Maximize button to maximize the window.

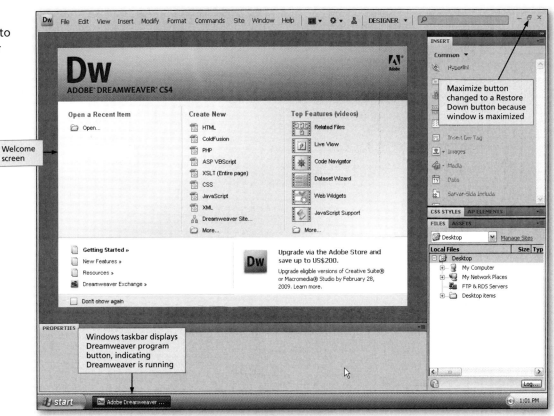

Figure E–2

Other Ways	
1. Double-click Dreamweaver icon on desktop, if one is present	2. Click Adobe Dreamweaver CS4 on Start menu

To Save a Web Page

After adding a page to a Web site, you should save the page. The following steps save a new document in the local root folder on a USB flash drive using the file name index.htm.

1

- With a USB flash drive connected to one of the computer's USB ports, click the Save button on the Standard toolbar to display the Save As dialog box (Figure E–3).

Q&A Do I have to save to a USB flash drive?

No. You can save to any device or folder that contains your local root folder.

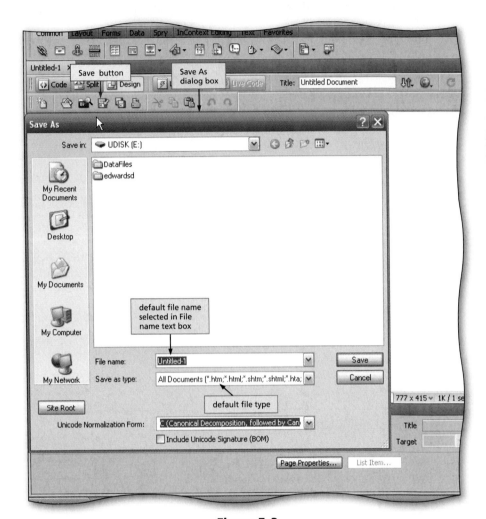

Figure E–3

• Type the name of your file (index. htm in this example) in the File name text box to change the file name. Do not press the ENTER key after typing the file name (Figure E–4).

Q&A Do I need to specify the path or folder for the Web page?

No. Dreamweaver assumes you want to save the new Web page in the local root folder.

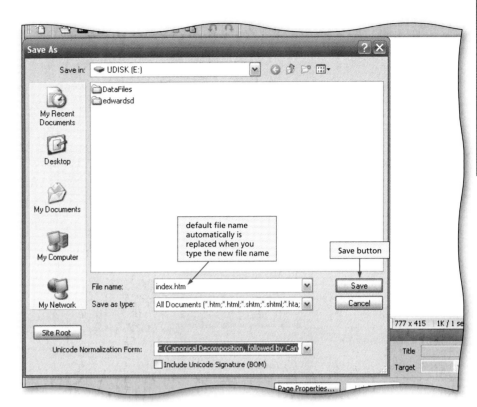

Figure E–4

• Click the Save button to save the page in the local root folder (Figure E–5).

Q&A What if my USB flash drive has a different name or letter?

It is very likely that your USB flash drive will have a different name and drive letter and be connected to a different port. Verify that the device in your Save in list is correct.

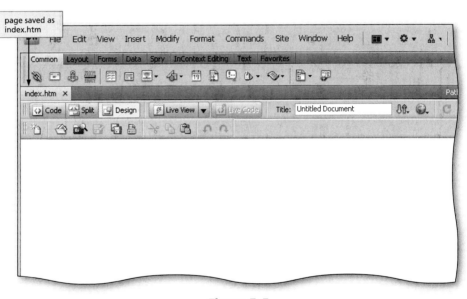

Figure E–5

Other Ways

1. On File menu, click Save, type file name, click Save button
2. Press CTRL+S, type file name, click Save button

To Copy Data Files to the Local Web Site

The following steps illustrate how to copy data files to the local Web site using Windows XP. The steps assume you have downloaded your data files and stored them on a USB drive. The steps also assume you are copying the Chapter01 data files for the parks Web site and that the parks Web site is stored on the USB drive in the *your name* folder. In other words, your data files are stored in a folder such as E:\DataFiles\Chapter01 and your Web site is stored in a folder such as E:\edwardsd\parks.

1

- Click the Start button on the Windows taskbar and then click My Computer to display the My Computer window.

- Navigate to the location of the data files for this book (Figure E–6).

Q&A

What if my data files are located on a different drive?

In Figure E–6, the location is UDISK (E:), a USB drive. Most likely your data files are stored in a different location.

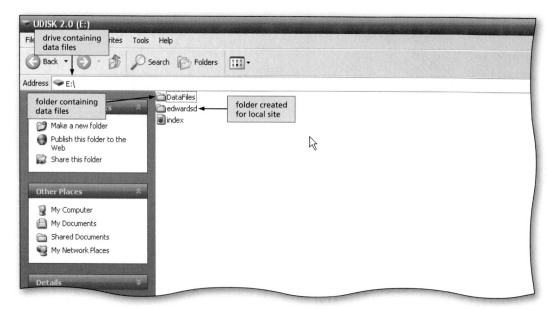

Figure E–6

2

- Double-click the folder containing your data files, and then double-click the appropriate Chapter*xx* folder, such as Chapter01, to open it.

- Double-click the parks folder to open it and display the data file (Figure E–7).

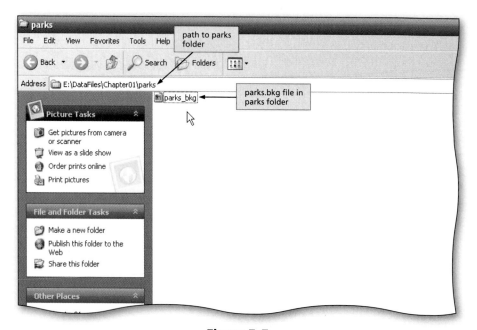

Figure E–7

Dreamweaver Appendix E

3

- Select the data file, right-click the selected file to display a context menu, and then point to the Copy command on the context menu to highlight the command (Figure E–8).

Q&A What if I need to copy more than one file?

Select all the files first. Click the first file in the list, hold down the SHIFT key, and then click the last file in the list to select all of the files. Right-click the selected files to display the context menu.

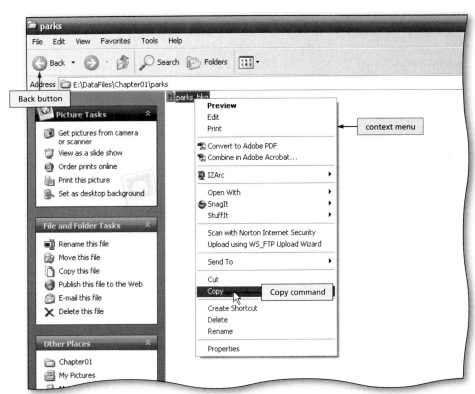

Figure E–8

4

- Click the Copy command and then click the My Computer Back button the number of times necessary to navigate to the root directory for the drive.

Q&A What should I do if my Web site is stored on a different drive?

Click the My Computer Back button the number of times necessary to return to the My Computer window, double-click the drive containing your Web site, and then continue the steps.

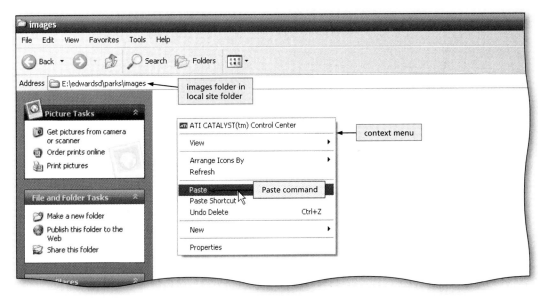

Figure E–9

- Navigate to the *your name* folder, double-click the *your name* folder, double-click the parks folder, and then double-click the images folder to open it.

- Right-click anywhere in the open window to display the context menu, and then point to the Paste command to highlight it (Figure E–9).

5

- Click the Paste command to paste the image(s) into the Alaska Parks Web site images folder (Figure E–10).

 6

- Click the images window's Close button to close the images window.

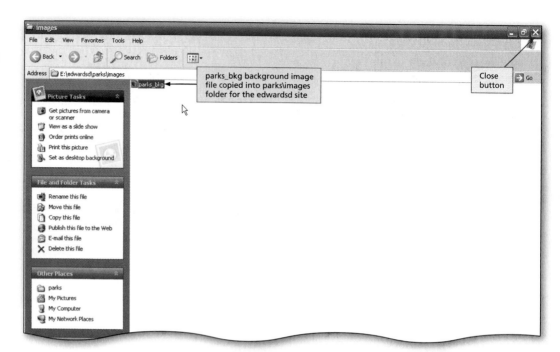

Figure E–10

FILE MENU

Action	Shortcut
New	Ctrl+N
Open	Ctrl+O
Browse in Bridge	Ctrl+Alt+O
Open in Frame	Ctrl+Shift+O
Close	Ctrl+W
Close All	Ctrl+Shift+W
Save	Ctrl+S
Save As	Ctrl+Shift+S
Print Code	Ctrl+P
Preview in Browser Submenu	
Firefox	Ctrl+F12
IExplore	F12
Device Central	Ctrl+Alt+F12
Check Page Submenu	
Links	Shift+F8
Validate Submenu	
Markup	Shift+F6
Exit	Ctrl+Q

EDIT MENU

Action	Shortcut
Undo	Ctrl+Z or Alt+BkSp
Redo	Ctrl+Y or Ctrl+Shift+Z
Cut	Ctrl+X or Shift+Del
Copy	Ctrl+C or Ctrl+Ins
Paste	Ctrl+V
Paste Special	Ctrl+Shift+V
Select All	Ctrl+A
Select Parent Tag	Ctrl+[
Select Child	Ctrl+]
Find and Replace	Ctrl+F
Find Selection	Shift+F3
Find Next	F3
Go to Line	Ctrl+G
Show Code Hints	Ctrl+Space
Refresh Code Hints	Ctrl+.
Indent Code	Ctrl+Shift+>
Outdent Code	Ctrl+Shift+<
Balance Braces	Ctrl+'
Code Collapse Submenu	
Collapse Selection	Ctrl+Shift+C
Collapse Outside Selection	Ctrl+Alt+C

Action	Shortcut
Expand Selection	Ctrl+Shift+E
Collapse Full Tag	Ctrl+Shift+J
Collapse Outside Full Tag	Ctrl+Alt+J
Expand All	Ctrl+Alt+E
Preferences	Ctrl+U

VIEW MENU

Action	Shortcut
Zoom In	Ctrl+=
Zoom Out	Ctrl+-
Magnification Submenu	
50%	Ctrl+Alt+5
100%	Ctrl+Alt+1
200%	Ctrl+Alt+2
300%	Ctrl+Alt+3
400%	Ctrl+Alt+4
800%	Ctrl+Alt+8
1600%	Ctrl+Alt+6
Fit Selection	Ctrl+Alt+0
Fit All	Ctrl+Shift+0
Fit Width	Ctrl+Alt+Shift+0
Switch Views	Ctrl+`
Refresh Design View	F5
Live View	Alt+F11
Live View Options Submenu	
Freeze JavaScript	F6
Head Content	Ctrl+Shift+H
Table Mode Submenu	
Expanded Tables Mode	F6
Visual Aids Submenu	
Hide All	Ctrl+Shift+I
Rulers Submenu	
Show/Hide	Ctrl+Alt+R
Grid Submenu	
Show/Hide Grid	Ctrl+Alt+G
Snap To Grid	Ctrl+Alt+Shift+G
Guides Submenu	
Show/Hide Guides	Ctrl+;
Lock Guides	Ctrl+Alt+;
Snap To Guides	Ctrl+Shift+;
Guides Snap To Elements	Ctrl+Shift+/
Plugins Submenu	
Play	Ctrl+Alt+P
Stop	Ctrl+Alt+X

Action	Shortcut
Play All	Ctrl+Alt+Shift+P
Stop All	Ctrl+Alt+Shift+X
Show/Hide Panels	F4

INSERT MENU

Action	Shortcut
Tag	Ctrl+E
Image	Ctrl+Alt+I
Media Submenu	
SWF	Ctrl+Alt+F
Table	Ctrl+Alt+T
Named Anchor	Ctrl+Alt+A
HTML Submenu	
Special Characters Submenu	
Line Break	Shift+Enter
Nonbreaking Space	Ctrl+Shift+Space
Template Objects Submenu	
Editable Region	Ctrl+Alt+V

MODIFY MENU

Action	Shortcut
Page Properties	Ctrl+J
CSS Styles	Shift+F11
Quick Tag Editor	Ctrl+T
Make Link	Ctrl+L
Remove Link	Ctrl+Shift+L
Table Submenu	
Select Table	Ctrl+A
Merge Cells	Ctrl+Alt+M
Split Cell	Ctrl+Alt+S
Insert Row	Ctrl+M
Insert Column	Ctrl+Shift+A
Delete Row	Ctrl+Shift+M
Delete Column	Ctrl+Shift+-
Increase Column Span	Ctrl+Shift+]
Decrease Column Span	Ctrl+Shift+[
Arrange Submenu	
Align Left	Ctrl+Shift+1
Align Right	Ctrl+Shift+3
Align Top	Ctrl+Shift+4
Align Bottom	Ctrl+Shift+6
Make Same Width	Ctrl+Shift+7
Make Same Height	Ctrl+Shift+9

FORMAT MENU

Action	Shortcut
Indent	Ctrl+Alt+]
Outdent	Ctrl+Alt+[
Paragraph Format Submenu	
None	Ctrl+0
Paragraph	Ctrl+Shift+P
Heading 1	Ctrl+1
Heading 2	Ctrl+2
Heading 3	Ctrl+3
Heading 4	Ctrl+4
Heading 5	Ctrl+5
Heading 6	Ctrl+6
Align Submenu	
Left	Ctrl+Alt+Shift+L
Center	Ctrl+Alt+Shift+C
Right	Ctrl+Alt+Shift+R
Justify	Ctrl+Alt+Shift+J
Style Submenu	
Bold	Ctrl+B
Italic	Ctrl+I

COMMANDS MENU

Action	Shortcut
Start Recording	Ctrl+Shift+X
Check Spelling	Shift+F7

SITE MENU

Action	Shortcut
Get	Ctrl+Shift+D
Check Out	Ctrl+Alt+Shift+D
Put	Ctrl+Shift+U
Check In	Ctrl+Alt+Shift+U
Check Links Sitewide	Ctrl+F8

WINDOW MENU

Action	Shortcut
Insert	Ctrl+F2
Properties	Ctrl+F3
CSS Styles	Shift+F11
AP Elements	F2
Databases	Ctrl+Shift+F10
Bindings	Ctrl+F10
Server Behaviors	Ctrl+F9
Components	Ctrl+F7
Files	F8
Snippets	Shift+F9
Tag Inspector	F9
Behaviors	Shift+F4
History	Shift+F10
Frames	Shift+F2
Results Submenu	
Search	F7
Show/Hide Panels	F4

HELP MENU

Action	Shortcut
Dreamweaver Help	F1
ColdFusion Help	Ctrl+F1
Reference	Shift+F1

PAGE VIEWS

To toggle the display of	Shortcut
Expanded Tables mode	F6
Live Data mode	Ctrl+R
Live Data	Ctrl+Shift+R
Switch between Design and Code views	Ctrl+`
Head content	Ctrl+Shift+H
Server debug	Ctrl+Shift+G
Refresh Design view	F5
Switch to next document	Ctrl+Tab
Switch to previous document	Ctrl+Shift+Tab
Close window	Ctrl+F4

VIEWING PAGE ELEMENTS

To toggle the display of	Shortcut
Visual aids	Ctrl+Shift+I
Rulers	Ctrl+Alt+R
Guides	Ctrl+;
Lock guides	Ctrl+Alt+;
Snap to guides	Ctrl+Shift+;
Guides snap to elements	Ctrl+Shift+/
Grid	Ctrl+Alt+G
Snap to grid	Ctrl+Alt+Shift+G
Page properties	Ctrl+J

EDITING TEXT

Action	Shortcut
Create a new paragraph	Enter
Insert a line break 	Shift+Enter
Insert a nonbreaking space	Ctrl+Shift+ Spacebar
Move text or object to another place in the page	Drag selected item to new location
Copy text or object to another place in the page	Ctrl-drag selected item to new location
Select a word	Double-click
Go to next word	Ctrl+Right
Go to previous word	Ctrl+Left
Go to previous paragraph	Ctrl+Up
Go to next paragraph	Ctrl+Down
Select until next word	Ctrl+Shift+Right
Select from previous word	Ctrl+Shift+Left
Select until next paragraph	Ctrl+Shift+Down
Select from previous paragraph	Ctrl+Shift+Up
Open and close the Property inspector	Ctrl+F3
Check spelling	Shift+F7

FORMATTING TEXT

Action	Shortcut
Indent	Ctrl+Alt+]
Outdent	Ctrl+Alt+[
Format > None	Ctrl+0 (zero)
Paragraph Format	Ctrl+Shift+P
Apply Headings 1 through 6 to a paragraph	Ctrl+1 through 6
Align > Left	Ctrl+Alt+Shift+L
Align > Center	Ctrl+Alt+Shift+C
Align > Right	Ctrl+Alt+Shift+R
Align > Justify	Ctrl+Alt+Shift+J
Make selected text bold	Ctrl+B
Make selected text italic	Ctrl+I

Note: Some text formatting shortcuts have no effect when working in the code editors.

FINDING AND REPLACING TEXT

Action	Shortcut
Find	Ctrl+F
Find next/Find again	F3
Find selection	Shift+F3

CODE EDITING

Action	Shortcut
Switch to Design view	Ctrl+`
Print code	Ctrl+P
Validate markup	Shift+F6
Edit tag	Shift+F5
Open Quick Tag Editor	Ctrl+T
Open Snippets panel	Shift+F9
Show code hints	Ctrl+ Spacebar
Insert tag	Ctrl+E
Surround with #	Ctrl+Shift+3
Select parent tag	Ctrl+[
Balance braces	Ctrl+'
Select all	Ctrl+A
Bold	Ctrl+B
Italic	Ctrl+I
Copy	Ctrl+C
Find and replace	Ctrl+F
Find selection	Shift+F3
Find next	F3
Paste	Ctrl+V
Paste Special	n/a
Cut	Ctrl+X
Redo	Ctrl+Y
Undo	Ctrl+Z
Delete word left	Ctrl+ Backspace
Delete word right	Ctrl+Delete
Go to line	Ctrl+G
Select line up	Shift+Up
Select line down	Shift+Down
Character select left	Shift+Left
Character select right	Shift+Right
Move to page up	Page Up
Move to page down	Page Down
Select to page up	Shift+Page Up
Select to page down	Shift+Page Down
Move word left	Ctrl+Left
Move word right	Ctrl+Right
Select word left	Ctrl+ Shift+Left

Action	Shortcut
Select word right	Ctrl+ Shift+Right
Move to start of line	Home
Move to end of line	End
Select to start of line	Shift+Home
Select to end of line	Shift+End
Move to top of code	Ctrl+Home
Move to end of code	Ctrl+End
Select to top of code	Ctrl+ Shift+Home
Select to end of code	Ctrl+ Shift+End
Collapse selection	Ctrl+ Shift+C
Collapse outside selection	Ctrl+Alt+C
Expand selection	Ctrl+Shift+E
Collapse full tag	Ctrl+Shift+J
Collapse outside full tag	Ctrl+Alt+J
Expand All	Ctrl+Alt+E

WORKING IN TABLES

Action	Shortcut
Select table (with insertion point inside the table)	Ctrl+A (+A, +A)
Move to the next cell	Tab
Move to the previous cell	Shift+Tab
Insert a row (before current)	Ctrl+M
Add a row at end of table	Tab in the last cell
Delete the current row	Ctrl+ Shift+M
Insert a column	Ctrl+ Shift+A
Delete a column	Ctrl+ Shift+ - (hyphen)
Merge selected table cells	Ctrl+Alt+M
Split table cell	Ctrl+Alt+S
Increase column span	Ctrl+Shift+]
Decrease column span	Ctrl+Shift+[

WORKING IN FRAMES

Action	Shortcut
Select a frame	Alt-click in frame
Select next frame or frameset	Alt+Right Arrow
Select previous frame or frameset	Alt+Left Arrow

Action	Shortcut
Select parent frameset	Alt+Up Arrow
Select first child frame or frameset	Alt+Down Arrow
Add a new frame to frameset	Alt-drag frame border
Add a new frame to frameset	Alt+Ctrl-drag frame border using push method

WORKING WITH TEMPLATES

Action	Shortcut
Create new editable region	Ctrl+Alt+V

WORKING WITH AP ELEMENTS

Action	Shortcut
Select an element	Ctrl+ Shift-click
Select and move element	Shift+ Ctrl-drag
Add or remove element from selection	Shift-click element border
Move selected element by pixels	Arrow keys
Move selected element by snapping increment	Shift+arrow keys
Resize selected element by pixels	Ctrl+arrow keys
Resize selected element by snapping increment	Ctrl+Shift+ arrow keys
Align element left	Ctrl+Shift+1
Align element right	Ctrl+Shift+3
Align element top	Ctrl+Shift+4
Align element bottom	Ctrl+Shift+6
Make same width	Ctrl+Shift+7
Make same height	Ctrl+Shift+9

WORKING WITH IMAGES

Action	Shortcut
Change image source attribute	Double-click image
Edit image in external editor	Ctrl-double-click image

ZOOMING

Action	Shortcut
Zoom in	Ctrl+=
Zoom out	Ctrl+-
Magnify 50%	Ctrl+Alt+5
Magnify 100%	Ctrl+Alt+1
Magnify 200%	Ctrl+Alt+2
Fit selection	Ctrl+Alt+0
Fit all	Ctrl+Shift+0
Fit width	Ctrl+Shift+Alt+0
Switch to Zoom mode from Regular mode	Shift+Ctrl+Alt+Z
Switch to Regular mode from Zoom mode	V+0
Switch to Hand mode from Regular mode	Shift+Ctrl+Alt+H
Switch to Hand mode from Zoom mode	H+Spacebar

MANAGING HYPERLINKS

Action	Shortcut
Check links	Shift+F8
Create hyperlink (select text)	Ctrl+L
Remove hyperlink	Ctrl+Shift+L
Drag and drop to create a hyperlink from a document to a file in the Files panel	Select the text, image, or object, then Shift-drag the selection
Drag and drop to create a hyperlink using the Property inspector	Select the text, image, or object, then drag the point-to-file icon in Property inspector to a file in the Files panel
Open the linked-to document in Dreamweaver	Ctrl-double-click link
Check links in the entire site	Ctrl+F8

TARGETING AND PREVIEWING IN BROWSERS

Action	Shortcut
Preview in primary browser	F12
Preview in secondary browser	Shift+F12 or Ctrl+F12

DEBUGGING IN BROWSERS

Action	Shortcut
Debug in primary browser	Alt+F12
Debug in secondary browser	Ctrl+Alt+F12

SITE MANAGEMENT AND FTP

Action	Shortcut
Refresh	F5
Create new file	Ctrl+Shift+N
Create new folder	Ctrl+Alt+Shift+N
Delete file	Delete
Copy file	Ctrl+C
Cut file	Ctrl+X
Paste file	Ctrl+V
Duplicate file	Ctrl+D
Rename file	F2
Get selected files or folders from remote FTP site	Ctrl+Shift+D or drag files from Remote to Local pane in Files panel
Put selected files or folders to remote FTP site	Ctrl+Shift+U or drag files from Local to Remote pane in Files panel
Check out	Ctrl+Alt+Shift+D
Check in	Ctrl+Alt+Shift+U
View site map	Alt+F8
Cancel FTP	Escape

SITE MAP

Action	Shortcut
View site files	F8
View as root	Ctrl+Shift+R
Link to existing file	Ctrl+Shift+K
Change link	Ctrl+L
Remove link	Ctrl+Shift+L
Show/Hide link	Ctrl+Shift+Y
Show page titles	Ctrl+Shift+T

PLAYING PLUGINS

Action	Shortcut
Play plugin	Ctrl+Alt+P
Stop plugin	Ctrl+Alt+X
Play all plugins	Ctrl+Alt+Shift+P
Stop all plugins	Ctrl+Alt+Shift+X

INSERTING OBJECTS

Action	Shortcut
Any object (such as an image or Shockwave movie)	Drag file from the Explorer or Files panel to the Document window
Image	Ctrl+Alt+I
Table	Ctrl+Alt+T
Flash	Ctrl+Alt+F
Shockwave	Ctrl+Alt+D
Named anchor	Ctrl+Alt+A

OPENING AND CLOSING PANELS

Action	Shortcut
Insert bar	Ctrl+F2
Properties	Ctrl+F3
CSS Styles	Shift+F11
Behaviors	Shift+F4
Tag Inspector	F9
Snippets	Shift+F9
Reference	Shift+F1
Databases	Ctrl+Shift+F10
Bindings	Ctrl+F10
Server Behaviors	Ctrl+F9
Components	Ctrl+F7
Files	F8
Assets	F11
Results	F7
Code inspector	F10
Frames	Shift+F2
History	Shift+F10
AP Elements	F2
Timeline	Alt+F9
Show/Hide panels	F4

FILES PANEL OPTIONS MENU

Action	Shortcut
New File	Ctrl+Shift+N
New Folder	Ctrl+Alt+Shift+N
Rename	F2
Delete	Del
Preview in Browser Menu	
Check Links	Shift+F8
Edit Menu	
Cut	Ctrl+X
Copy	Ctrl+C
Paste	Ctrl+V
Duplicate	Ctrl+D
Select All	Ctrl+A
View Menu	
Refresh	F5
Site Map Options Menu	
Show/Hide Link	Ctrl+Shift+Y
View as Root	Ctrl+Shift+R
Show Page Titles	Ctrl+Shift+T
Site Map	Alt+F8
Site Menu	
Get	Ctrl+Shift+D
Check Out	Ctrl+Alt+Shift+D
Put	Ctrl+Shift+U
Check In	Ctrl+Alt+Shift+U
Cloaking Menu	
Check Links Sitewide	Ctrl+F8
Link to New File...	Ctrl+Shift+N
Link to Existing File...	Ctrl+Shift+K
Change Link...	Ctrl+L
Remove Link	Ctrl+Shift+L

Index